Proceedings

DCC '94

Data Compression Conference

Data Compression Conference (4th : 1994 : Snowbird, Utah)

Proceedings

DCC '94

Data Compression Conference

March 29-31, 1994 Snowbird, Utah

Edited by
James A. Storer
Martin Cohn

Sponsored by
IEEE Computer Society Technical Committee
on Computer Communications

In cooperation with
NASA/CESDIS

IEEE Computer Society Press
Los Alamitos, California

Washington • Brussels • Tokyo

The papers in this book comprise the proceedings of the meeting mentioned on the cover and title page. They reflect the authors' opinions and, in the interests of timely dissemination, are published as presented and without change. Their inclusion in this publication does not necessarily constitute endorsement by the editors, the IEEE Computer Society Press, or the Institute of Electrical and Electronics Engineers, Inc.

Published by the
IEEE Computer Society Press
10662 Los Vaqueros Circle
P.O. Box 3014
Los Alamitos, CA 90720-1264

IEEE Catalog Number 94TH0626-2
ISBN 0-8186-5637-9 (softbound)
ISBN 0-8186-5636-0 (microfiche)
ISSN: 1068-0314
IEEE Computer Soc. Press No. 5637-02

IEEE Computer Society Press
Customer Service Center
10662 Los Vaqueros Circle
P.O. Box 3014
Los Alamitos, CA 90720-1264
Tel: (714) 821-8380
Fax: (714) 821-4641
Email: cs.books@computer.org

IEEE Service Center
445 Hoes Lane
P.O. Box 1331
Piscataway, NJ 08855-1331
Tel: (908) 981-1393
Fax: (908) 981-9667

IEEE Computer Society
13, avenue de l'Aquilon
B-1200 Brussels
BELGIUM
Tel: +32-2-770-2198
Fax: +32-2-770-8505

IEEE Computer Society
Ooshima Building
2-19-1 Minami-Aoyama
Minato-ku, Tokyo 107
JAPAN
Tel: +81-3-3408-3118
Fax: +81-3-3408-3553

Production Editor: Lisa O'Conner
Printed in the United States of America by BookCrafters

The Institute of Electrical and Electronics Engineers, Inc.

DCC 1994

This book contains the presentations from the fourth Data Compression Conference held March 29-31, 1994 in Snowbird, Utah. This conference was sponsored by the IEEE Computer Society Technical Committee on Computer Communications (TCCC) in cooperation with NASA/CESDIS.

GENERAL CHAIR: James A. Storer, *Brandeis U.*
PROGRAM CHAIR: Martin Cohn, *Brandeis U.*
PUBLICITY CHAIR: Terrence Pratt, *NASA/CESDIS*

PROGRAM COMMITTEE:

Julia Abrahams, *ONR*
Alberto Apostolico, *Purdue/Padova*
Ronald B. Arps, *IBM*
Richard Baker, *PictureTel Inc.*
Abraham Bookstein, *U. Chicago*
Martin Cohn, *Brandeis U.*
Robert Gray, *Stanford U.*
Daniel Hirschberg, *UC Irvine*
Glen Langdon, *UC Santa Cruz*
Abraham Lempel, *Technion*
Bradley J. Lucier, *Purdue U.*
John H. Reif, *Duke U.*
Robert Renner, *TRW*
Eve A. Riskin, *U. Washington*
Ken Rose, *UCSB*
Dafna Sheinwald, *IBM*
James A. Storer, *Brandeis U.*
James Tilton, *NASA*
Martin Vetterli, *UC Berkeley*
Jeffrey Vitter, *Duke U.*
Ian H. Witten, *U. Waikato*
Xiaolin Wu, *U. W. Ontario*
Jacob Ziv, *Technion*

ACKNOWLEDGEMENTS

The Program Committee gratefully acknowledge the support of NASA/CESDIS and the Computer Science Department of Brandeis University. In particular, we thank Nancy Campbell, Georgia Flanagan, and Anne Marie Murphy of NASA/CESDIS, Myrna Fox and Cathy Rossi of Brandeis University, and Lisa O'Conner of the IEEE Computer Society Press for their efforts in the administration of the conference and the production of these proceedings.

CONTENTS

Technical Sessions

Session 1

Session 2

Session 3

Session 4

Session 5

Session 6

Session 7

Session 8

Session 9

Session 10

Poster Session

TECHNICAL SESSIONS

Variable Dimension Weighted Universal Vector Quantization and Noiseless Coding *

M. Effros,* P. A. Chou,† and R. M. Gray‡

* *Information Systems Laboratory, Stanford, CA 94305-4055, phone: (415) 723-2675, fax: (415) 723-8473, email: effros@isl.stanford.edu*

† *Xerox Palo Alto Research Center, 3333 Coyote Road, Palo Alto, CA 94304 phone: (415) 812-4496, fax: (415) 812-4241, email: chou@parc.xerox.com*

‡ *Information Systems Laboratory, Stanford, CA 94305-4055, phone: (415) 723-4001, fax: (415) 723-8473, email: gray@isl.stanford.edu*

Abstract

A new algorithm for variable dimension weighted universal coding is introduced. Combining the multi-codebook system of weighted universal vector quantization (WUVQ), the partitioning technique of variable dimension vector quantization, and the optimal design strategy common to both, variable dimension WUVQ allows mixture sources to be effectively carved into their component subsources, each of which can then be encoded with the codebook best matched to that source. Application of variable dimension WUVQ to a sequence of medical images provides up to 4.8 dB improvement in signal to quantization noise ratio over WUVQ and up to 11 dB improvement over a standard full-search vector quantizer followed by an entropy code. The optimal partitioning technique can likewise be applied with a collection of noiseless codes, as found in weighted universal noiseless coding (WUNC). The resulting algorithm for variable dimension WUNC is also described.

1 Introduction

Weighted universal vector quantizers and weighted universal noiseless codes [1, 2, 3] are two-stage codes. In each, an incoming data string is broken into supervectors, which are blocks of vectors. All of the vectors in a particular supervector are encoded with a single code. Given some collection of codes, the encoder chooses the code that

*This material is based upon work partially supported by an AT&T Bell Laboratories Ph.D. Scholarship and by a grant from the Center for Telecommunications at Stanford. The authors would also like to thank Professor Eve Riskin for the use of an HP 720 donated by Hewlett Packard Laboratories.

most closely matches the statistics of the vectors in the supervector at hand. The first stage of a two-stage code describes the chosen quantizer or noiseless code, and the second stage describes the data using that code. By keeping a variety of codes and allowing the code in use to change from supervector to supervector, WUVQs and WUNCs can roughly track local variation in source statistics. The expense of tracking this information is the side information necessary to describe the code used on each supervector.

While WUVQ and WUNC use fixed supervector lengths, variable dimension WUVQ (VDWUVQ) and variable dimension WUNC (VDWUNC) employ the optimal partitioning algorithm of variable dimension VQ (VDVQ) [4, 5] to break the image into variable sized supervectors in an optimal fashion. The basic algorithm proceeds as follows. An incoming data stream is partitioned into variable length supervectors. The encoder then describes these supervectors, one by one, to the decoder. To describe a supervector, the encoder first sends the length of the supervector, then describes the index of the code with which that supervector's component vectors will be encoded, and finally describes the component vectors using the chosen code. The optimal partition is the partition that minimizes the overall distortion subject to a constraint on the rate, which now includes the rate associated with describing the length of each supervector. The employment of optimally chosen supervectors of variable sizes allows the VDWUVQ to better carve the data into its component subsources, each of which is then encoded separately by an encoder matched to that source.

Section 2 reviews the basic WUVQ and WUNC algorithms. The VDWUVQ and VDWUNC algorithms are then described in section 3. The final section presents results achieved by applying the VDWUVQ algorithm to a set of medical images. While both fixed- and variable-rate versions of VDWUVQ and VDWUNC are possible, this paper focuses on the variable-rate case.

2 The WUVQ and WUNC Algorithms

Given a class, Λ, of process measures and a distribution over that class, a weighted universal code is a sequence of block codes for which the expected performance over all $\theta \in \Lambda$ approaches, with increasing block size, the theoretically optimal expected performance. To be more exact, let $\{X_i\}$ be a random process with alphabet $\mathcal{X}$ and process measure P_θ, $\theta \in \Lambda$, and let $\beta^n \circ \alpha^n$ be a length-n block code with encoder $\alpha^n : \mathcal{X}^n \to \mathcal{S}$ and decoder $\beta^n : \mathcal{S} \to \hat{\mathcal{X}}^n$, where $\mathcal{S} \subset \{0,1\}^*$ is a binary prefix code, $|\alpha^n(x^n)|$ is the length of the code for x^n, and $\hat{\mathcal{X}}$ is the reproduction alphabet. In weighted universal quantization, $\hat{\mathcal{X}}$ is not required to equal $\mathcal{X}$, $\mathcal{X}$ may be uncountably infinite, and $\beta^n(\alpha^n(x^n)) = \hat{x}^n$ with distortion $d_n(x^n, \hat{x}^n) = \sum_i d_1(x_i, \hat{x}_i)$, where, $d_1(x_i, \hat{x}_i)$ is an additive fidelity criterion. In noiseless coding, $\hat{\mathcal{X}} = \mathcal{X}$, $\mathcal{X}$ is finite or countably infinite, and $\beta^n(\alpha^n(x^n)) = x^n$ for all $x^n \in \mathcal{X}$. A weighted universal source code is a sequence of block codes $\{(\alpha^n, \beta^n)\}$ such that for each $\theta \in \Lambda$ there exists a corresponding sequence of points $\{(R_{n,\theta}, D_{n,\theta})\}$ on the graph of the nth order

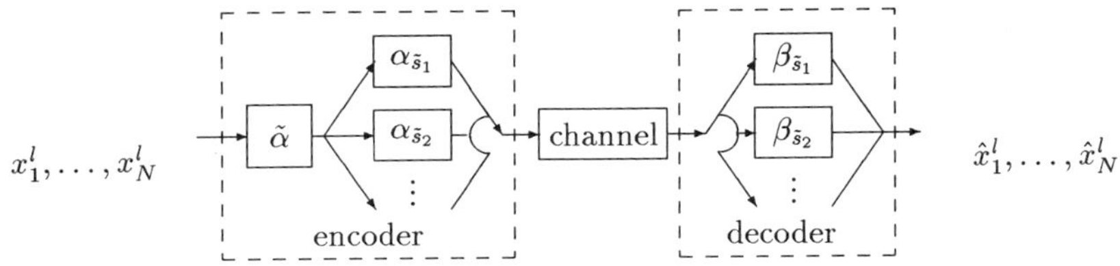

Figure 1: Weighted Universal VQ

operational distortion-rate function for P_θ for which the per letter "rate" redundancy

$$\frac{1}{n} E_\theta |\alpha^n(X^n)| - R_{n,\theta}$$

and the per-letter "distortion" redundancy

$$\frac{1}{n} E_\theta d_n(X^n, \beta^n(\alpha^n(X^n))) - D_{n,\theta}$$

each go to zero in expectation with respect to a probability measure (weighting) on θ. Notice that the distortion redundancy requirement is trivially satisfied for all noiseless codes.

In [6], Neuhoff, Gray, and Davisson show that a weighted universal source code can be constructed from a sequence of multi-codebook vector quantizers; in [1], Chou develops an algorithm for the design of weighted universal vector quantizers, which are locally optimal multi-codebook vector quantizers for weighted universal source coding; and in [7], Chou and Effros provide bounds on the rates at which the expected rate and distortion redundancies go to zero for WUVQ. Two-stage universal noiseless codes were earlier developed in [8] and [9]. In this section we describe WUVQs and WUNCs and the algorithm by which they can be optimally designed.

The WUVQ and WUNC algorithms [1, 2, 3] treat the optimal design of two-stage weighted universal vector quantizers and noiseless coders. In both cases, the first stage of the system is a "quantizer" which maps the input space of possible data vectors to the output space of possible block codes; the chosen second-stage block code then maps the data vector to the output space of possible reproductions. In universal variable-rate quantization the block codes are variable-rate quantizers, while in universal noiseless coding, these block codes are block noiseless codes.

Figure 1 shows a two-stage coder. The vector sequence $x_1^l, \ldots, x_N^l \in \mathbb{R}^l$ is partitioned evenly into supervectors $y_1, \ldots, y_K \in \mathbb{R}^{ln}$, where each supervector contains n l-vectors. For simplicity it is assumed that n evenly divides N, so that $K = N/n$ is an integer. The first-stage quantizer contains an encoder $\tilde{\alpha} : \mathcal{X}^{ln} \rightarrow \tilde{\mathcal{S}}$ which maps the input space of possible supervectors to the output space of code descriptors. The first-stage description of the supervector y_i, $\tilde{s} = \tilde{\alpha}(y_i) \in \tilde{\mathcal{S}}$, indexes the chosen length-l block code used to code the l-vectors of y_i. We use $|\tilde{s}|$ to denote the first-stage description length. The second-stage block code contains an encoder and a decoder. Let $\{\alpha_{\tilde{s}} : \tilde{s} \in \tilde{\mathcal{S}}\}$ and $\{\beta_{\tilde{s}} : \tilde{s} \in \tilde{\mathcal{S}}\}$ be the collections of block encoders and decoders respectively. For any $\tilde{s} \in \tilde{\mathcal{S}}$, $\alpha_{\tilde{s}} : \mathcal{X}^l \to \mathcal{S}_{\tilde{s}}$ and $\beta_{\tilde{s}} : \mathcal{S}_{\tilde{s}} \to \hat{\mathcal{X}}^l$. Denote the component vectors of supervector y_i by $y_{i,1}, \ldots, y_{i,n}$. If $\tilde{s}$ is the first-stage description of y_i, then $s_{\tilde{s}} = \alpha_{\tilde{s}}(y_{i,j}) \in \mathcal{S}_{\tilde{s}}$ is the second-stage description of component vector $y_{i,j}$, $|s_{\tilde{s}}|$ is the length of the second-stage description of $y_{i,j}$, and $d_l(y_{i,j}, \beta_{\tilde{s}}(\alpha_{\tilde{s}}(y_{i,j})))$ is the distortion incurred by using the block code indexed by $\tilde{s}$ on $y_{i,j}$. The distortion is always zero in noiseless coding. The total distortion and rate associated with encoding supervector y_i (a block of n l-vectors) with codebook $\tilde{s}$ are

$$d(y_i, \tilde{s}) = \sum_{j=1}^{n} d_l(y_{i,j}, \beta_{\tilde{s}}(\alpha_{\tilde{s}}(y_{i,j})))$$

and

$$r(y_i, \tilde{s}) = |\tilde{s}| + \sum_{j=1}^{n} |\alpha_{\tilde{s}}(y_{i,j})|.$$

For two-stage noiseless codes and two-stage variable-rate quantizers, $\tilde{\mathcal{S}}$ and $\mathcal{S}_{\tilde{s}}$ are Huffman codes matched to the probabilities of the block codes and codewords, respectively.

Two-stage source codes are designed using an extension of the generalized Lloyd algorithm to minimize

$$\sum_{i=1}^{K} \sum_{\tilde{s} \in \tilde{\mathcal{S}}} J_\lambda(y_i, \tilde{s}) 1(\tilde{\alpha}(y_i) = \tilde{s})$$

on a training sequence, where $1(A)$ is 1 if statement A is true and 0 otherwise, the Lagrangian functional J_λ is defined as

$$J_\lambda(y_i, \tilde{s}) = d(y_i, \tilde{s}) + \lambda r(y_i, \tilde{s}),$$

and λ is the Lagrange multiplier. In noiseless coding, where the distortion is always equal to zero, λ is chosen to equal one, so that J_λ equals the total rate. In variable-rate vector quantization, nonnegative λ values are chosen based on the desired final rate of the system. The optimization process consists of a nested descent algorithm in which the Lloyd algorithm's nearest neighbor and centroid conditions are employed on both stages of the system. In the first-stage quantizer, satisfying the nearest neighbor condition means mapping each supervector to the codebook that will best encode that supervector's component vectors. In the second stage, satisfying the nearest neighbor condition means mapping each vector to the best codeword. In both cases, "best" is measured by the functional J_λ. By satisfying the centroid condition, we optimize the decoder for a given encoder. The first-stage quantizer meets this condition by redesigning each codebook in its collection of codebooks to match the statistics of the data mapped to that codebook. Each second-stage decoder likewise meets this condition by redesigning each of its codewords to match the data mapped to it.

3 The VDWUVQ and VDWUNC Algorithms

VDWUVQ and VDWUNC are two-stage coding systems where the length of the supervectors is allowed to vary. An incoming data sequence, $x_1^l, \ldots, x_N^l$, is broken into supervectors of varying length, say $y_1, \ldots, y_K$, of lengths $|y_1|, \ldots, |y_K|$ vectors. The number of supervectors and their lengths are subject only to the constraint that the sum of the lengths must equal the initial data length ($\sum_i |y_i| = N$). Using x_1^{lN} to denote the sequence $x_1^l, \ldots x_N^l$, let $\{y_i\} \prec x_1^{lN}$ mean that $\{y_i\}$ partitions x_1^{lN} and satisfies the above constraint. Since the supervector length is allowed to vary, it must be described to the decoder along with the first- and second-stage code information. The encoder thus uses an entropy code γ to describe that length to the decoder, where $|\gamma(n)|$ is the rate associated with describing a supervector length of n. Notice that if $|\gamma(\cdot)|$ is zero for length n and infinity otherwise, VDWUVQ and VDWUNC will behave exactly like WUVQ and WUNC. Thus VDWUVQ and VDWUNC can only exceed their predecessors in performance, but they do so at the expense of the additional complexity necessary for obtaining the optimal partition.

The optimal design algorithm for VDWUVQs and VDWUNCs is again a variation on the generalized Lloyd algorithm, which iteratively achieves descent on the weighted sum of the total distortion and rate

$$\sum_{i=1}^{K} \sum_{\tilde{s} \in \tilde{\mathcal{S}}} J_\lambda(y_i, \tilde{s}) 1(\tilde{\alpha}(y_i) = \tilde{s}),$$

where the Lagrangian is now

$$J_\lambda(y_i, \tilde{s}) = d(y_i, \tilde{s}) + \lambda(r(y_i, \tilde{s}) + |\gamma(|y_i|)|).$$

Let $|\{y_i\}|$ denote the number of elements in the partition, then the training algorithm proceeds as follows:

1. Optimally parse the data for fixed γ, $\tilde{\alpha}$, $\tilde{\mathcal{S}}$, and $\{(\alpha_{\tilde{s}}, \beta_{\tilde{s}}, \mathcal{S}_{\tilde{s}})\}$ and then update γ to match the new partition. The optimal partition satisfies

   $$\{y_i\} = \arg \min_{\{z_i\} \prec x_1^{lN}} \sum_i \sum_{\tilde{s} \in \tilde{\mathcal{S}}} J_\lambda(z_i, \tilde{s}) 1(\tilde{\alpha}(z_i) = \tilde{s}).$$

   Thus update γ to satisfy $|\gamma(n)| = \lceil -\log_2 [\sum_i 1(|y_i| = n) / |\{y_i\}|] \rceil$.

2. Optimize the first-stage encoder $\tilde{\alpha}$ for fixed $\{y_i\}$, γ, $\tilde{\mathcal{S}}$, and $\{(\alpha_{\tilde{s}}, \beta_{\tilde{s}}, \mathcal{S}_{\tilde{s}})\}$ and then redesign the prefix code. The resulting encoder is

   $$\tilde{\alpha}(y_i) = \arg \min_{\tilde{s} \in \tilde{\mathcal{S}}} [d(y_i, \tilde{s}) + \lambda r(y_i, \tilde{s})],$$

   and for each $\tilde{s} \in \tilde{\mathcal{S}}$ its new prefix code satisfies $|\tilde{s}| = \lceil -\log_2 [\sum_i 1(\tilde{\alpha}(y_i) = \tilde{s}) / |\{y_i\}|] \rceil$.

3. Optimize each block code for fixed $\{y_i\}$, γ, $\tilde{\alpha}$, and $\tilde{\mathcal{S}}$. This is accomplished for each $\tilde{s} \in \tilde{\mathcal{S}}$ by iteratively optimizing $\alpha_{\tilde{s}}, \beta_{\tilde{s}}$, and $\mathcal{S}_{\tilde{s}}$ until convergence, where the optimal encoder, decoder, and prefix code respectively satisfy the following three conditions. (Note that the change to the decoder has no effect in the case of noiseless coding.)

   $$\alpha_{\tilde{s}}(y_{i,j}) = \arg \min_{s_{\tilde{s}} \in \mathcal{S}_{\tilde{s}}} [d_l(y_{i,j}, \beta_{\tilde{s}}(s_{\tilde{s}})) + \lambda |s_{\tilde{s}}|] \qquad \forall y_{i,j} \text{ s.t. } \tilde{\alpha}(y_i) = \tilde{s}.$$

$$\beta_{\tilde{s}}(s_{\tilde{s}}) = \arg\min_{\hat{x}^l \in \hat{\mathcal{X}}^l} \sum_i \sum_j d_l(y_{i,j}, \hat{x}^l) 1(\alpha_{\tilde{s}}(y_{i,j}) = s_{\tilde{s}}) 1(\tilde{\alpha}(y_i) = \tilde{s}) \qquad \forall s_{\tilde{s}} \in \mathcal{S}_{\tilde{s}}$$

$$|s_{\tilde{s}}| = \left\lceil -\log_2 \left[\sum_i \sum_j 1(\alpha_{\tilde{s}}(y_{i,j}) = s_{\tilde{s}}) 1(\tilde{\alpha}(y_i) = \tilde{s}) / \sum_i \sum_j 1(\tilde{\alpha}(y_i) = \tilde{s}) \right] \right\rceil \qquad \forall s_{\tilde{s}} \in \mathcal{S}_{\tilde{s}}$$

4. Iterate steps 1-3 until convergence.

The optimal partition in step 1 of the above described algorithm is accomplished using the dynamic programming argument of VDVQ [5]. The argument proceeds as follows. Let $J_n = \min_{\{y_i\} \prec x_1^{ln}} \sum_i J_\lambda(y_i, \tilde{\alpha}(y_i))$ be the score of the best partitioning of the partial data sequence $x_1^l, \ldots, x_n^l$. If B is the maximum allowed supervector length, then for $1 \leq n \leq N$,

$$J_n = \min_{b \in \{1,\ldots,B\}} \left\{ J_{n-b} + \min_{\tilde{s} \in \tilde{\mathcal{S}}} J_\lambda(x_{n-b+1}^{lb}, \tilde{s}) \right\},$$

where $J_0 = 0$ and $J_n = \infty$ for $n < 0$. Now let b_n be the last supervector in the optimal partition of x_1^n, that is the supervector of length $\arg\min_{1 \leq b \leq B} \left\{ J_{n-b} + \min_{\tilde{s} \in \tilde{\mathcal{S}}} J_\lambda(x_{n-b+1}^{lb}, \tilde{s}) \right\}$ ending with the nth vector. Then the optimal partition of x_1^{lN} can be found by back-tracking:

$$\{y_i\} = \{\ldots b_{N-|b_N|-|b_{N-|b_N|}|}, b_{N-|b_N|}, b_N\}.$$

While partitioning and encoding have been described as separate processes, they can be accomplished simultaneously (at the expense of greater storage requirements) by tracking not only the optimal performance and last supervector length at each time n but also the encoding information for that supervector.

4 Experimental Results

We here compare the performance of VDWUVQ with that of WUVQ and standard full-search VQ. The data sequence considered contains 25 magnetic resonance (MR) brain scans at an original 9 bpp. The first 20 images are used for training and the final 5 are used for testing. All of the vector quantizers use vectors of dimension 2×2 and the vectors are ordered according to a Peano scan (e.g., [10]). The supervectors in VDWUVQ are allowed to contain up to 16 vectors while the WUVQ has a constant supervector size of 4. All multi-codebook systems consisted of at most 256 codebooks, each with no more than 4 codewords.

Figure 2 shows the performance of variable-rate VDWUVQ and WUVQ with varying values of λ and the performance of standard full-search VQ. All rates are reported in terms of entropy. Signal to quantization noise ratio (SQNR) is calculated as $-10\log(D/D_0)$, where D is the current distortion, D_0 is the zero rate distortion of a standard full-search VQ, and all distortion is measured by the squared error fidelity criterion. VDWUVQ shows its greatest improvement over WUVQ at very low rates, below .1 bpp, with an SQNR up to 4.8 dB higher. Both VDWUVQ and WUVQ achieve their greatest gains over standard full-search VQ at slightly higher rates.

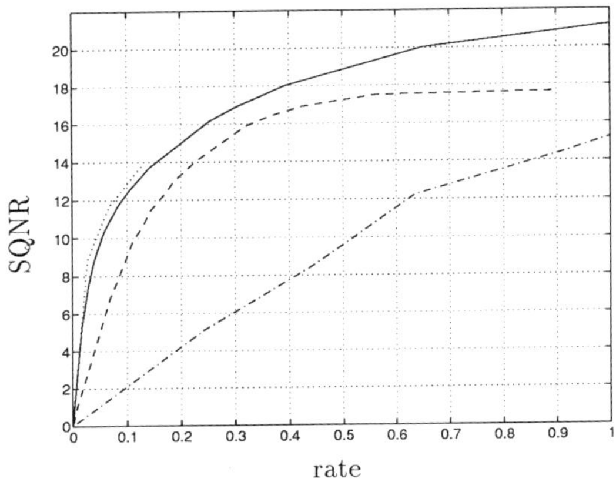

Figure 2: VDWUVQ, WUVQ, and standard full-search VQ on medical test sequence.
... variable-rate VDWUVQ with maximum supervector size 256,
— variable-rate VDWUVQ with maximum supervector size 16,
- - variable-rate WUVQ, -.- standard full-search VQ followed by an entropy code

VDWUVQ shows up to 11 dB improvement over standard VQ. Allowing supervector lengths up to 256 vectors improves performance by about another dB at the expense of increased computation.

Figure 3 compares the images resulting from quantizing the data at around .2 bpp, while figure 4 demonstrates the sizes and shapes of the supervectors used by the VDWUVQ algorithm in the previous figure.

References

[1] P. A. Chou. Code clustering for weighted universal VQ and other applications. In *Proceedings of the IEEE International Symposium on Information Theory*, page 253, Budapest, Hungary, June 1991.

[2] B. D. Andrews, M. Effros, P. A. Chou, and R. M. Gray. A mean-removed variation of weighted universal vector quantization for image coding. In *Proceedings of the Data Compression Conference*, pages 302–309, Snow Bird, UT, April 1993. IEEE Computer Society.

[3] P.A. Chou, M. Effros, and R.M. Gray. A vector quantization approach to universal noiseless coding and quantization. *IEEE Transactions on Information Theory*. In preparation.

[4] P. A. Chou and T. Lookabaugh. Locally optimal variable-to-variable length source source coding with respect to a fidelity criterion. In *Proceedings of the IEEE International Symposium on Information Theory*, page 238, Budapest, Hungary, June 1991.

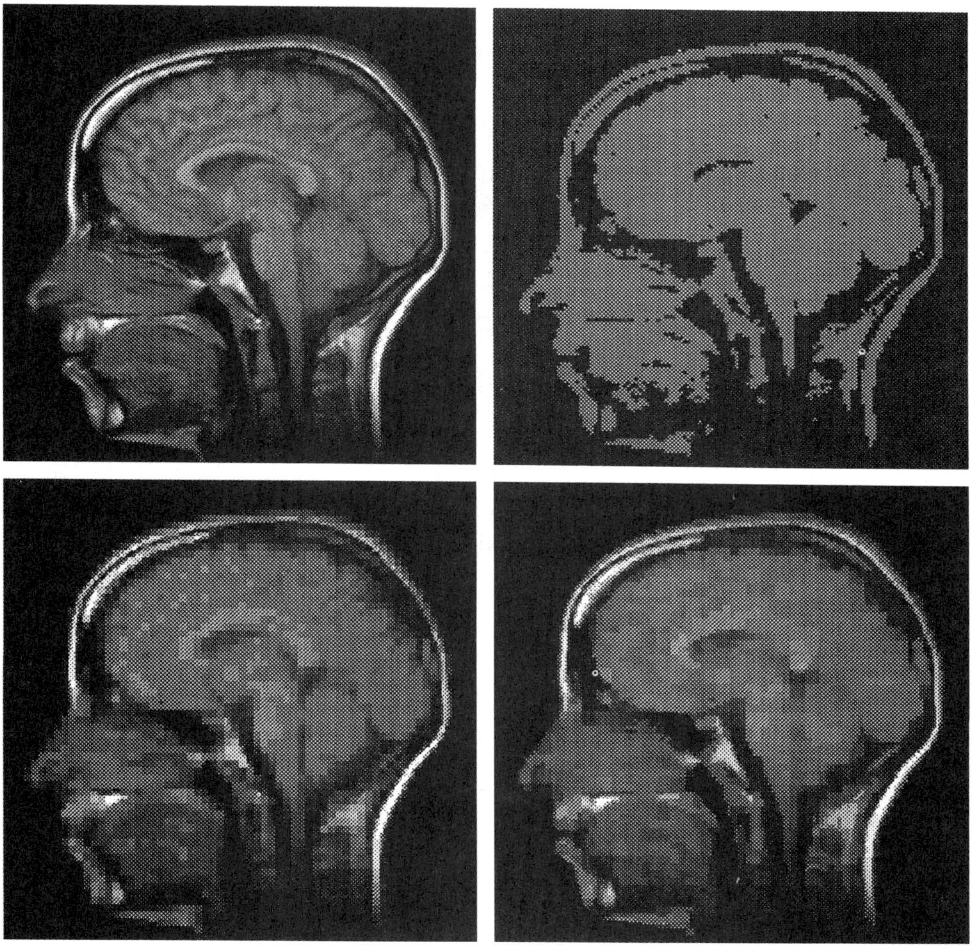

Figure 3: From top left to bottom right: The original 9 bpp image, standard VQ at .25 bpp and SQNR = 6.75 dB, WUVQ at .184 bpp and SQNR = 11.6 dB, and VDWUVQ at .166 bpp and SQNR = 13.2 dB.

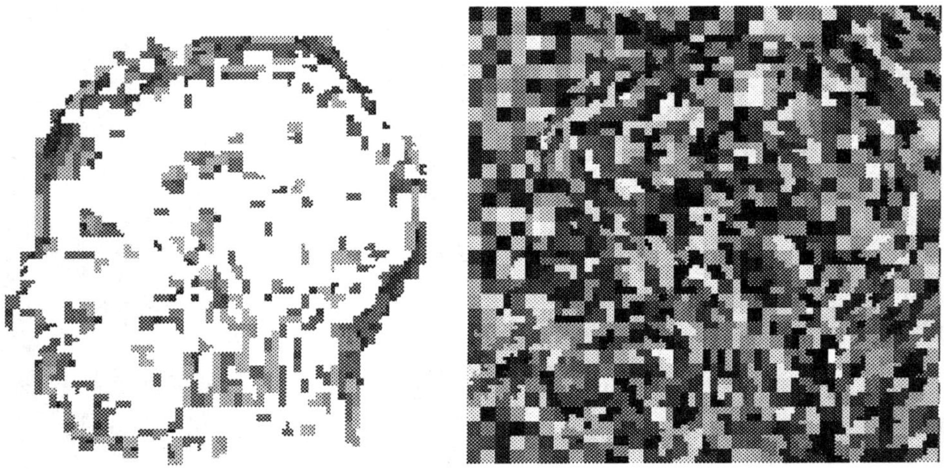

Figure 4: Supervector sizes and shapes for the .166 bpp image. The picture on the left shows the size of the supervector in which each pixel was coded, with supervector sizes from 1 to 16 vectors denoted in shades from black to white. The picture on the right gives a random shade to each supervector in order to demonstrate supervector shapes.

[5] P.A. Chou and T. Lookabaugh. Variable dimension vector quantization of linear predictive coefficients of speech. In *Proceedings of the IEEE International Conference on Acoustics, Speech, and Signal Processing*, Adelaide, Australia, April 1994.

[6] D. L. Neuhoff, R. M. Gray, and L. D. Davisson. Fixed rate universal block source coding with a fidelity criterion. *IEEE Transactions on Information Theory*, 21(5):511–523, September 1975.

[7] P. A. Chou and M. Effros. Rate and distortion redundancies for source coding with respect to a fidelity criterion. In *IEEE International Symposium on Information Theory*, page 53, San Antonio, Texas, January 1993.

[8] R. F. Rice and J. R. Plaunt. Adaptive variable-length coding for efficient compression of spacecraft television data. *IEEE Transactions on Communications*, 19(12):889–897, December 1971.

[9] L. D. Davisson. Universal noiseless coding. *IEEE Transactions on Information Theory*, 19(6):783–795, November 1973.

[10] R. J. Stevens, A. F. Lehar, and F. H. Preston. Manipulation and presentation of multidimensional image data using the peano scan. *IEEE Transactions on Pattern Analysis and Machine Intelligence*, PAMI-5(5):520–533, September 1983.

ENTROPY-CONSTRAINED TREE-STRUCTURED VECTOR QUANTIZER DESIGN BY THE MINIMUM CROSS ENTROPY PRINCIPLE*

Kenneth Rose, David Miller, and Allen Gersho
Department of Electrical and Computer Engineering
University of California
Santa Barbara, CA 93106
email: rose@ece.ucsb.edu

Abstract

We address the variable rate tree-structured vector quantizer design problem, wherein the rate is measured by the quantizer's entropy. For this problem, tree pruning via the Generalized Breiman-Friedman-Olshen-Stone algorithm obtains solutions which are optimal over the restricted solution space consisting of all pruned trees derivable from an initial tree. However, the restrictions imposed on such solutions have several implications. In addition to depending on the tree initialization, growing and pruning solutions result in tree-structured vector quantizers which use a sub-optimal encoding rule. To remedy the latter problem, we consider a "tree-constrained" version of entropy-constrained vector quantizer design. This leads to an optimal tree-structured encoding rule for the leaves. In practice, though, improvements obtained in this fashion are limited by the tree initialization, as well as by the sub-optimal encoding performed at non-leaf nodes. To address these problems, we develop a joint optimization method which is inspired by the deterministic annealing algorithm for data clustering, and which extends our previous work on tree-structured vector quantization. The method is based on the principle of minimum cross entropy, using informative priors to approximate the unstructured solution while imposing the structural constraint. As in the original deterministic annealing method, the number of distinct codevectors (and hence the tree) grows by a sequence of bifurcations in the process, which occur as solutions of a free energy minimization. Our method obtains performance gains over growing and pruning methods for variable rate quantization of Gauss-Markov and Gaussian mixture sources.

1 Introduction

Vector Quantization (VQ) [1] involves the representation of a data set by a smaller number of reproductions or prototypes, also known as a codebook. Originally, VQ was a theoretical construct which allowed the asymptotic achievement of the rate/distortion

*This work was supported in part by the UC Micro program, Rockwell International Corporation, Hughes Aircraft Company, Echo Speech Corporation, Signal Technology, Inc., Qualcomm, Inc., and Lockheed Missiles and Space Company.

bound, by increasing the vector dimension. However, recently, VQ has found important applications in compressing speech and images, as well as other information sources. Correspondingly, a variety of VQ structures and design methods have been proposed for diverse applications. One of the more fundamental extensions of the basic VQ problem was the proposal to incorporate an entropy constraint within the design, so as to produce quantizers optimized for subsequent entropy coding [2, 3, 4]. In [4], entropy-constrained vector quantizers were shown to outperform a number of other variable rate quantization schemes. However, a practical limitation of the approach is the encoding search complexity, which grows linearly with the codebook size and hence exponentially with the vector dimension and with the rate. Thus, in practice, vector quantizers of reduced encoding search complexity (as well as possibly of reduced memory storage) may need to be considered.

Tree-structured vector quantizers (TSVQs) [5] replace the unstructured partition (which may require an exhaustive encoding search) with a lower complexity tree-structured partition, allowing a drastic reduction in encoding search. Typically, the structural constraint also implies some inherent loss in performance. Another source of performance degradation is the design approach for TSVQ. The conventional, standard design methods for TSVQ are greedy, growing trees one node at a time to minimize a local, heuristic cost function, e.g. [5, 6, 7]. These methods do not ensure convergence to a local optimum even for a simple instance of the problem – e.g., given a binary tree of fixed size (for example, three layers), find an optimal location for the test vectors and decoder codevectors. Moreover, for TSVQ, there are no iterative methods akin to the Generalized Lloyd Algorithm (GLA) [8] for descending in the tree-structured VQ distortion. One approach to improve the performance of TSVQs is to grow a large tree and then prune it back to find the best (i.e., minimum distortion) pruned tree satisfying a given cost constraint. A method for optimally pruning trees for classification was first proposed in [9] and is known as the Breiman-Friedman-Olshen-Stone (BFOS) algorithm. In [10], the BFOS approach was extended to incorporate a more general class of costs defined on trees, and the resulting method was called the Generalized BFOS (GBFOS) algorithm. While GBFOS can be used to search for the minimum distortion TSVQ which satisfies an entropy constraint, there are some inherent difficulties with such an approach, which result in suboptimality of the solution.

In the first part of the paper we discuss greedy growing and pruning procedures for variable rate TSVQ design, wherein the rate is assumed to be measured by the quantizer's entropy. We identify the problems associated with these methods and suggest an approach to improve their solutions, by re-optimizing the partition and the decoder at the leaves. This modification is presented to illustrate the suboptimality of known methods. In practice, only small improvements will be obtained by such a local approach. In order to improve the tree-structured solution in a significant and fundamental way, we then develop a more global approach, which considers a joint optimization over the entire tree. Our method for entropy-constrained TSVQ design is an extension of the tree-structured approach we have previously developed [11, 12], which was itself inspired by the deterministic annealing algorithm for data clustering [13]. This new approach is shown to obtain performance gains over greedy growing and optimal pruning when the cost is entropy of the codeword indices. Finally, we discuss phase transitions (which consist of codevector splitting) and codevector merging – these are the two mechanisms for changing the effective codebook size in our method. Analytical conditions governing these phenomena may provide insights into the "right" codebook size for the entropy-constrained problem.

2 Pruning With An Entropy Constraint

The conventional approach for designing variable rate TSVQs is a two-phase procedure which involves growing an initial tree and then pruning the tree back so as to achieve the best possible rate/distortion tradeoff. Although the growing "phase" of the design is greedy and sub-optimal, tree pruning via the GBFOS algorithm [10] allows one to determine in an efficient manner a sequence of tree solutions which are optimal in a well-defined sense. In particular, if we consider the set of rate/distortion operating points corresponding to the pruned trees derivable from the given initial tree, then the solutions found by GBFOS are the extreme points on the set's convex hull. Thus, the GBFOS approach does have both practical and theoretical significance for TSVQ design.

However, the GBFOS framework also imposes substantial constraints on the solution space over which the search for the optimal TSVQ is conducted. First, we note that the solutions obtained by GBFOS depend on the initial tree, which is typically generated in a greedy fashion, either by the splitting algorithm [5] or by greedy growing [7]. In previous work, we have shown for the fixed rate case that splitting and greedy growing of unbalanced trees are sub-optimal procedures and that performance gains can be achieved over these methods [11]. Thus, dependence on the initial tree is a limitation.

A second problem relates to the fact that GBFOS only finds a finite set of TSVQ solutions (and, hence, a convex hull uniquely specified by these extreme points). If one is interested in obtaining a rate between two extreme points, then it is possible to "time-share" between the two pruned tree solutions so as to achieve a point on the convex hull with the given rate. However, since the actual rate/distortion curve is almost always strictly convex, it is likely that there is a better tree-structured solution (albeit, not obtainable by pruning of the initial tree) below the convex hull point at the prescribed rate. If instead of time-sharing between the solutions before and after a pruning operation, we obtain intermediate solutions by gradual "merging" or "vanishing" of the branches to be pruned (to be explained below), then the resulting curve may lie below the straight connecting line assumed by GBFOS.

A final, and perhaps most fundamental, shortcoming is the encoding rule employed by GBFOS solutions, which connects directly to the aforementioned branch "merging" or "vanishing". We observe that GBFOS (and pruning in general) generally trades rate for distortion, but does not explicitly incorporate an entropy constraint within the TSVQ design. The result is that the entropy (rate) does not affect the encoding rule in the way it is optimally modified in the (non-tree-structured) entropy-constrained VQ (ECVQ) case. In ECVQ [4] the rate constraint causes the following modification of the nearest neighbor encoding rule:

$$x \in C_j \ \text{ only if } \ d(x, y_j) - \lambda \log p_j \leq d(x, y_k) - \lambda \log p_k, \qquad \forall k.$$

Here, the usual nearest neighbor rule (for partition region C_j) between a data point x and codevector y_j is modified to include an entropy cost, based on the mass p_j. In this expression λ is a Lagrange multiplier which determines the value of the entropy. This modified encoding rule *which varies with the rate* must be satisfied by an optimal entropy-constrained solution. This suggests that one may be able to improve the rate/distortion performance of the set of solutions obtained by GBFOS through the explicit incorporation of such a rate constraint. To do so, we have to associate masses and positions (codevectors) with the leaves of the tree. By optimizing over these variables we can obviously make leaves gradually "vanish" by decreasing their mass to zero, or by "merging" their codevectors.

Consider a TSVQ solution Q which is an extreme point on the convex hull of the operational rate/distortion curve, with rate $R(Q)$. We now explicitly incorporate the entropy constraint within the quantizer design at the leaves. Regarding Q as an initialization, fix the tree-structured partition through the parent layer of the leaves and pose the optimization problem

$$\min_{Y=\{y_j\},P=\{p_j\}} D + \lambda R. \tag{1}$$

subject to

$$\sum_j p_j = 1. \tag{2}$$

Here, D is the distortion cost over the data set. This is a "tree-constrained" version of the entropy-constrained VQ problem, which optimizes over sibling pairs of codevectors $\{y_j\}$ and masses $\{p_j\}$ at the leaf layer. The solution for $\lambda = 0$ is just the initial quantizer $Q = Q(0)$. By varying λ over the positive real line and solving the "tree-constrained" ECVQ problem, we generate a sequence of solutions $\{Q(\lambda)\}$ which use the optimal entropy-constrained nearest neighbor rule at the leaves [4]. Now, note that all the GBFOS solutions implicitly set $\lambda = 0$. For any finite rate, the encoding rule associated with these solutions cannot be optimal except for the very special case in which all codevectors are equiprobable. (This statement of suboptimal encoding is true for the entropy cost as well as other costs which, when explicitly enforced, lead to solutions with a modified optimal encoding rule.) Starting with a GBFOS solution, we can generate a set of solutions $\{Q(\lambda)\}$, i.e., new rate/distortion points. One cannot in general state that these new points will all lie below the operational rate/distortion curve of GBFOS. First, the cost function is non-convex and thus there may be local optima to trap the optimization. Second, by fixing the tree except for the leaves, we effectively limit the rate/distortion performance achievable starting from an initial tree $Q(0)$. It is possible that better performance for a particular rate will be achieved by "running" our method with a different convex hull extreme point as initialization. However, it is clear that GBFOS is suboptimal and it is very likely that this simple improvement method will find at least some solution points (perhaps corresponding to an interval in λ) below GBFOS's convex hull for *each* extreme point on the convex hull.

While such a procedure does illustrate a way to improve upon GBFOS solutions, the improvements attainable by this method are limited by the tree initialization as well as by the sub-optimal encoding performed at non-leaf nodes. In the next section, we develop a joint optimization method inspired by the deterministic annealing algorithm, in order to address these problems.

3 An Entropy-constrained TSVQ Method

As suggested in the previous section, the performance of variable rate TSVQs can be improved by introducing an entropy constraint directly within the VQ design. In this section, we develop such a method, which also addresses the important problems of tree initialization and optimization of the tree-structured encoder. Our approach will be to extend a method previously proposed for fixed rate TSVQ design [11, 12], which was itself inspired by the deterministic annealing algorithm (DA) for data clustering.

The DA method [13] is derived within a probabilistic framework, using principles from information theory. In particular, the principle of maximum entropy [14] is applied to induce a probability distribution over the set of all deterministic quantizers. Maximizing this distribution over the exhaustive set of quantizers is an intractable problem. However, maximizing the marginal distribution over the codebook leads to a practical algorithm which can be interpreted as a deterministic approximation to simulated annealing [15]. A fundamental implication of the probabilistic framework is that, unlike conventional methods which optimize over the hard partition, the DA method considers data points to be associated *in probability* with partition regions. In the sequel, we initiate development of our entropy-constrained tree-structured method by considering the optimization problem at the leaf layer and, in particular, how to obtain association probabilities between a data set and the leaf partition regions.

3.1 Optimization of the Leaf Layer

For the unstructured VQ problem, no prior knowledge existed other than that embodied in the clustering distortion constraint. Accordingly, the basic DA method invoked the principle of maximum entropy, subject to a constraint on clustering distortion, to obtain association probabilities between partition regions and data. By contrast, in the tree-structured case, there is a significant structural constraint (in addition to the entropy constraint) imposed on the solution. One way of introducing this constraint is to suppose that it can be expressed as a prior probability distribution which influences the leaf/data association probabilities. Define this prior as the probability of association $P_H[x \in S_j]$ where S_j is the set of all points classified to node j in the layer of the tree directly above (i.e., the parent layer of) the leaves. Let us suppose that the leaf codebook $\{y_{jk}\}$ and the masses $\{p_{jk}\}$ are fixed and seek the probabilities of association between the leaf partition region C_{jk} and the data samples. Here, index k refers to a sibling node at the leaves with parent node j. The leaf associations must "agree" with the prior distribution, and at the same time must reflect the cost associated with encoding a data sample. Since there is a prior, it is natural to invoke *the principle of minimum cross entropy*, which is a generalization of the maximum entropy principle and which has been shown to be *the* consistent principle of inference when including prior knowledge [16]. Accordingly, we pose the problem

$$\min_{P_L} \sum_j \sum_k P_L[x \in C_{jk}] \log \frac{P_L[x \in C_{jk}]}{(P_H[x \in S_j]/K)} \tag{3}$$

subject to

$$< D_x >= \sum_j \sum_k P_L[x \in C_{jk}]\{d(x, y_{jk} - \lambda \log p_{jk}\}). \tag{4}$$

Note that the prior at the parent node is equally split between all K of its descendants at the leaves (assuming K-ary splits). The solution is the so-called "tilted" distribution which appears, for example, in rate distortion function computation, i.e.

$$P_L[x \in C_{jk}] = \frac{P_H[x \in S_j] e^{-\beta\{d(x,y_{jk}) - \lambda \log p_{jk}\}}}{\sum_{lm} P_H[x \in S_l] e^{-\beta\{d(x,y_{lm}) - \lambda \log p_{lm}\}}}. \tag{5}$$

The Lagrange multiplier β determines the average level of clustering distortion $< D_x >$. It also has the interpretation of an inverse "temperature" influencing the degree of fuzziness of the distribution. For $\{P_H[x \in S_j]\}$ uniform and $\beta = 0$, the association probabilities are uniform over all partition regions C_{jk}. At the other extreme, if $\{P_H[x \in S_j]\}$ specifies a hard classifier with a tree structure then, as $\beta \to \infty$, $\{P_L[\cdot]\}$ specifies a tree-structured partition associated with a "tree-constrained" ECVQ solution. The partition function associated with a single datum is the denominator of (5). Assuming the data are independently encoded, the total partition function is then the product

$$Z = \prod_x Z_x = \prod_x \sum_l P_H[x \in S_l] \sum_m e^{-\beta\{d(x,y_{lm}) - \lambda \log p_{lm}\}} \tag{6}$$

Correspondingly, the free energy is

$$F \equiv -\frac{1}{\beta} \log Z = -\frac{1}{\beta} \sum_x \log \sum_l P_H[x \in S_l] \sum_m e^{-\beta\{d(x,y_{lm}) - \lambda \log p_{lm}\}}. \tag{7}$$

Note that the free energy is the quantity "stochastically" minimized in isothermal equilibrium by simulated annealing. This makes the connection between our approach and statistical mechanics, and hence simulated annealing, clear. Rather than "stochastically" minimize the free energy, we perform a "deterministic" minimization of this cost. If $\{P_H[\cdot]\}$ specifies a hard tree-structured partition, then for $\beta \to \infty$ the free energy is equivalent to the distortion associated with a variable rate TSVQ. As in the basic DA method, minimization of the quantizer distortion is accomplished by an annealing approach, minimizing F starting from high temperature (small β) and tracking the solution while gradually lowering the temperature. At low temperature, this approach minimizes the variable rate TSVQ cost. In this variable rate case, the minimization must be performed subject to the constraint that the masses $\{p_{jk}\}$ sum to unity. Necessary conditions for optimizing the free energy at any temperature, subject to the constraint are

$$\sum_x P_L[x \in C_{jk}] \frac{\partial}{\partial y_{jk}} d(x, y_{jk}) = 0, \qquad \forall j, k \tag{8}$$

and

$$\sum_x P_L[x \in C_{jk}] - \alpha p_{jk} = 0, \qquad \forall j, k. \tag{9}$$

For the squared distances measure, this allows us to write the following "centroid" and "mass" rules:

$$y_{jk} = \frac{\sum_x x P_L[x \in C_{jk}]}{\sum_x P_L[x \in C_{jk}]} \tag{10}$$

and

$$p_{jk} = \frac{1}{N} \sum_x P_L[x \in C_{jk}], \tag{11}$$

which must be iterated until a fixed point is reached. Note that the mass rule is satisfied independent of the distance measure chosen.

3.2 Optimization of the Hierarchy

In the previous sub-section, we considered "random coding" equivalents of the centroid and mass rules for variable rate TSVQ design, but we have not yet addressed optimization of the tree-structured encoder partition. To simplify notation, we will derive our approach for the simple case of a two layer binary tree. Note that the derivation in the sequel is extendible to a general class of TSVQs of any depth [11]. Also note that this derivation parallels the one presented in [12]. In optimizing the leaves, we assumed the existence of a prior distribution $P_H[x \in S_j]$ to the parent layer of the leaves. Now, correspondingly, we will optimize the hierarchy (and hence $P_H[\cdot]$) under the assumption that the leaves are fixed and determine a suitable prior distribution. A significant constraint on the distribution $P_H[\cdot]$ is that, according to some limiting behavior, it must determine a tree-structured partitioning of the data space. For the two layer binary tree, if squared distance is used at the non-leaf layer, the non-leaf layer partition boundary is a hyperplane. Then, an appropriate choice of parametrization justified by the principle of maximum entropy is the Gibbs distribution

$$P_H[x \in S_j] = \frac{e^{-\gamma d(x,s_j)}}{e^{-\gamma d(x,s_j)} + e^{-\gamma d(x,s_j^c)}}. \tag{12}$$

This distribution depends on the scale parameter γ and on the vectors s_j and its sibling s_j^c. When $\gamma \to \infty$, the test vectors determine a hyperplane decision boundary whereas for γ finite, we have a probabilistic encoder.

Now, we observe that a well-motivated paradigm for optimization of the hierarchy is *to choose a partition which, given fixed leaves, agrees as closely as possible with the ideal entropy-constrained partition, while maintaining the structural constraint.* Within the annealing framework, *given the temperature of the system*, the probabilistic analogue of the ideal partition is (by the principle of maximum entropy) the Gibbs distribution

$$P_I[x \in C_{jk}] = \frac{e^{-\beta\{d(x,y_{jk}) - \lambda \log p_{jk}\}}}{\sum_{l,m} e^{-\beta\{d(x,y_{lm}) - \lambda \log p_{lm}\}}}. \tag{13}$$

For each parent node, we obtain

$$P_I[x \in S_j] = \sum_k P_I[x \in C_{jk}], \tag{14}$$

where k sums over the descendents at the leaves. A common measure of statistical risk between probability distributions is the cross entropy (also known as the Kullback-Leibler distance or the asymmetric divergence). Accordingly, to optimize the hierarchy, we pose the problem

$$\min_{\gamma,\{s\}} J(\gamma,\{s\}) = \min_{\gamma,\{s\}} \sum_x \sum_j P_I[x \in S_j] \log \frac{P_I[x \in S_j]}{P_H[x \in S_j]}. \tag{15}$$

If $d(\cdot,\cdot)$ is the squared distance, then taking the gradient with respect to a test vector leads to

$$\nabla_{s_j} J \propto -\sum_x (x - s_j)\{P_I[x \in S_j](1 - P_H[x \in S_j]) - (1 - P_I[x \in S_j])P_H[x \in S_j]\}. \tag{16}$$

Initialize the location parameters to the global centroid of the data set.
Initialize the masses to a uniform distribution.
Initialize β and the scale parameters to small values.
do {
  do {
    Minimize the free energy F of (7) to obtain new leaves.
    Minimize the cross entropy of (15) to obtain a new hierarchy.
  } while not converged
  Increase β.
} while $\beta < \beta_{max}$

Table 1: A summary of the basic tree-structured DA method.

As was noted in [12], the gradient rule of (16) can be given the interpretation of a probabilistic, batch generalization of the Perceptron learning rule. We can now summarize our annealing approach for tree-structured VQ. It is listed in pseudo-code in Table 1.

4 Splitting and Merging Phase Transitions

In the basic DA method, the number of codevectors grows by a sequence of bifurcations (phase transitions in the physical analogy) in the process, which occur at well-defined, computable critical temperatures [13]. Bifurcations ("splits") also occur in the tree-structured DA approach [11] and relate to growth in the size and structure of the tree. For $\beta = 0$, the free energy is uniquely minimized at the global centroid of the data set. Thus, initially, regardless of the tree size "thrown into" the method, there is effectively one natural codevector, corresponding to a zero layer tree. As β is increased, the number of natural codevectors (and hence the tree) grows by a sequence of bifurcations in the process. We can state the result (proved in [11] for the fixed rate tree method and the squared distance measure) that bifurcations in the process occur when, for any codevector y_{jk}, we have that $\beta_c = \frac{1}{2\lambda_{max}}$. Here, λ_{max} is the principal eigenvalue of the covariance matrix Σ_{jk} associated with the cell partition C_{jk}, i.e.

$$\Sigma_{jk} = \frac{\sum_{x}(x - y_{jk})(x - y_{jk})^T P_L[x \in C_{jk}]}{\sum_{x} P_L[x \in C_{jk}]}. \tag{17}$$

In addition to codevector "splits", there are also codevector "merges" in our process. Merges occur when two codevectors coincide and one codevector loses its mass to the other, thus reducing the effective codebook size. Unlike the case of splitting, we have not yet developed a rigorous analysis of merging phase transitions. However, we can show that if two codevectors are coincident but both have non-zero mass, then a merge will occur if $\beta\lambda > 1$. It is expected that a complete analysis of phase transitions in the process will provide insights relating to the "correct" codebook size for entropy-constrained quantization. In particular, such analysis may help to answer the question of whether or not the optimal codebook size is finite for a given rate.

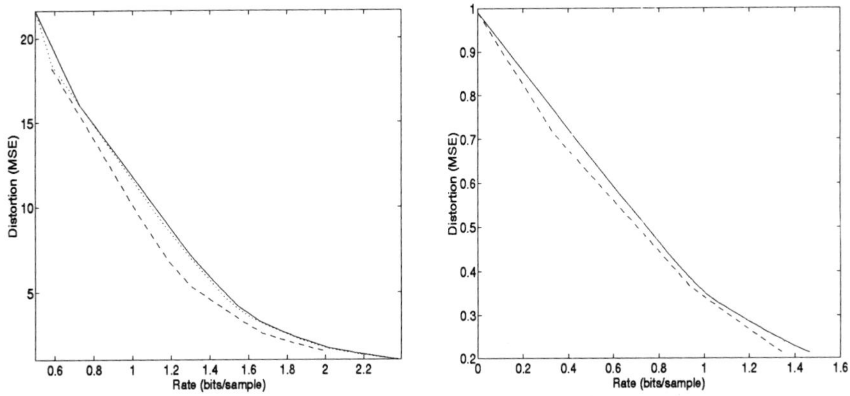

Figure 1: Rate/Distortion performance for a four dimensional sixteen component Gaussian mixture source (left figure) and for a four dimensional Gaussian source (right figure). The solid curve is the GBFOS result, the dotted curve (left) is obtained by re-optimizing GBFOS solutions at the leaves, and the dashed curve is generated by the entropy-constrained, tree-structured DA method.

5 Results

We have tested our approach in comparison with greedy growing and optimal pruning, wherein the rate used in the growing design is measured by the entropy of the reproduction indices, and pruning is performed to minimize distortion, subject to an entropy constraint. Figure 1 displays rate/distortion performance on a vector Gaussian mixture source (left) and on a vector Gaussian source (right). The vector dimension was chosen to be four. The results are for low rate quantization (the maximum tree depth is six). The DA curve is based on a set of quantizer solutions at target values of λ. The graphs demonstrate that fairly significant performance gains are achieved by our method. As an example, for a Gaussian source at a rate of 1.34 bits/sample, our approach achieved 0.53 dB gain over tree growing and pruning. For the mixture source, we also tested the heuristic for improving GBFOS solutions which involves simply re-optimizing the leaf codevectors to reflect the entropy constraint. As seen from the figure, only very small improvement is achieved by this constrained approach.

Since our DA method explicitly optimizes the encoder to reflect the entropy constraint, it may utilize a much larger set of leaves than a tree solution derived from greedy growing, while achieving the same rate. For example, a two-layer tree with three leaves derived from greedy growing achieved a rate of 0.37 bits/sample for the vector Gaussian source (Note that this solution is not on the GBFOS convex hull). By comparison, the entropy-constrained tree-structured DA method produced a tree with twenty-six leaves and a lower rate (0.33 bits/sample), as well as a lower distortion (a gain of 0.23 dB). This result suggests that, in addition to outperforming greedy methods at prescribed rates, our approach may also be useful for *directly* obtaining low rates with a single quantizer which can only otherwise be achieved by time-sharing greedily grown quantizers.

6 Conclusion

In this paper, the problem of entropy-constrained TSVQ design has been addressed. It was observed that greedy tree growing and associated pruning solutions use a sub-optimal encoding rule at the leaf layer. This prompted the development of a new design method which directly incorporates the entropy constraint. The approach uses an optimal encoding rule at the leaves and optimizes the TSVQ to approximate an (unstructured) entropy-constrained vector quantizer solution. The method was shown to obtain performance gains over growing and pruning approaches for low rate TSVQ design.

References

[1] A. Gersho and R. Gray, *Vector quantization and signal compression.* Boston, Ma.: Kluwer Academic Publishers, 1992.

[2] T. Berger, "Minimum entropy quantizers and permutation codes," *IEEE Transactions on Information Theory*, vol. IT-28, pp. 149–157, 1982.

[3] N. Farvardin and J. Modestino, "Optimum quantizer performance for a class of non-gaussian memoryless sources," *IEEE Transactions on Information Theory*, vol. IT-30, pp. 485–497, 1984.

[4] P. A. Chou, T. Lookabaugh, and R. M. Gray, "Entropy-constrained vector quantization," *IEEE Transactions on Acoustics, Speech, and Signal Processing*, vol. ASSP-37, pp. 31–42, 1989.

[5] A. Buzo, A. G. Jr., R. Gray, and J. Markel, "Speech coding based on vector quantization," *IEEE Transactions on Acoustics, Speech, and Signal Processing*, vol. 28, pp. 562–574, 1980.

[6] J. Makhoul, S. Roucos, and H. Gish, "Vector quantization in speech coding," *Proceedings of the IEEE*, vol. 73, pp. 1551–1588, 1985.

[7] E. Riskin and R. Gray, "A greedy growing algorithm for the design of variable rate vector quantizers," *IEEE Transactions on Signal Processing*, vol. 39, pp. 2500–2507, 1991.

[8] Y. Linde, A. Buzo, and R. M. Gray, "An algorithm for vector quantizer design," *IEEE Transactions on Communications*, vol. COM-28, pp. 84–95, 1980.

[9] L. Breiman, J. Friedman, R. Olshen, and C. Stone, *Classification and regression trees.* Belmont,CA.: The Wadsworth Statistics/Probability Series, 1980.

[10] P. Chou, T. Lookabaugh, and R. Gray, "Optimal pruning with applications to tree-structured source coding and modeling," *IEEE Transactions on Information Theory*, vol. 35, pp. 299–315, 1989.

[11] D. Miller and K. Rose, "Structured vector quantization by deterministic annealing with minimum cross entropy inference." (Submitted to IEEE Transactions on Information Theory.), 1993.

[12] D. Miller and K. Rose, "An improved sequential search multistage vector quantizer," in *Proceedings of the Data Compression Conference*, pp. 8–14, 1993.

[13] K. Rose, E. Gurewitz, and G. C. Fox, "Vector quantization by deterministic annealing," *IEEE Transactions on Information Theory*, vol. 38, pp. 1249–1258, 1992.

[14] E. T. Jaynes, "Information theory and statistical mechanics," in *Papers on probability, statistics and statistical physics* (R. D. Rosenkrantz, ed.), Dordrecht, The Netherlands: Kluwer Academic Publishers, 1989. (Reprint of the original 1957 papers in *Physical Review*).

[15] S. Kirkpatrick, C. D. Gelatt, and M. P. Vecchi, "Optimization by simulated annealing," *Science*, vol. 220, pp. 671–680, 1983.

[16] J. E. Shore and R. W. Johnson, "Axiomatic derivation of the principle of maximum entropy and the principle of minimum cross-entropy," *IEEE Transactions on Information Theory*, vol. IT-26, pp. 26–37, 1980.

A Subjective Distortion Measure for Vector Quantization

Xiaolin Wu and Kaizhong Zhang *
Department of Computer Science
University of Western Ontario
London, Ontario, Canada N6A 5B7.

1 Introduction

The ultimate goal of lossy signal compression is to reproduce (approximate) the original signal, at the lowest possible bit rate, within a tolerance of degradation in signal fidelity that is judged by human users. For maximum performance of a lossy coder, we need to remove both statistical and subjective redundancies in the input signal. The subjective redundancy refers to the characteristics of the signal that can be removed or altered for compression gains without perceived degradation in signal quality. Needless to say, a subjectively meaningful distortion measure for signal quantization is crucial for end-user-perceived quantizer performance. Unfortunately, for vector quantization, there seems to be a lack of research on subjective distortion measure. This has probably prevented the full realization of the potential of VQ in signal compression applications. Despite the well-known fact that VQ is superior to transform coding in the sense of rate-distortion optimality, the subjective quality of VQ coders does not, in many cases, surpass that of transform or subband coders. A large part of this disappointment is due to the absence of a better distortion measure that reflects human perception more accurately than the ubiquitous mean-squares criterion currently used in VQ practice. On the other hand, transform coders can readily exploit the well-documented characteristics of human perception of signals in frequency domain by making the quantization resolutions of transform coefficients

*Both authors are supported by the Natural Sciences and Engineering Research Council of Canada.

proportional to sensitivity of human perception in different frequency ranges.

This extended abstract contains some preliminary results of our ongoing study on subjective VQ distortion measure in time/spatial domain. We first propose a context-based distortion measure between two vectors. The new measure is intuitively appealing, and we present some empirical evidence for its subjective significance. Although the measure is formulated as a matrix norm, it is computationally no more difficult than mean-squares error. This measure quantifies the quantization distortion in the context (shape) of signal waveform, but it is amplitude-invariant. So we combine the context distortion measure with a weighted mean distortion measure to obtain a unified subjective distortion measure $D(\cdot,\cdot)$. We show that $D(\cdot,\cdot)$ is a distance measure and can be easily computed. Moreover, the process of computing the centroid of a set of training vectors and designing the VQ codebook under the new subjective distortion measure $D(\cdot,\cdot)$ is as simple as the conventional VQ. Specifically, the LBG algorithm can be applied to design the subjective VQ codebook after a simple linear transformation of the vector space in which signal samples are originally taken. Also interestingly, we can analytically relate our subjective distortion measure to the ubiquitous mean-squares measure, and demonstrate that the latter is only a special case of the former. In this research, we also observe that the mean-removed VQ [1] in a sense clusters training vectors under the proposed context distortion measure. This observation can explain the good subjective performance of mean-removed and gain-shape VQ techniques.

2 Context-Based Distortion Measure

Consider two d-vectors $\mathbf{x} = (x_1, x_2, \cdots, x_d)$ and $\mathbf{y} = (y_1, y_2, \cdots, y_d)$ which correspond to two blocks of signal samples in time/spatial domain. For human perception, an isolated signal sample without any reference or context hardly makes any sense. Instead, the relation between neighboring samples in time/spatial domain forms patterns that convey signal semantics to our visual/audio systems. In order to measure how different two groups (vectors) of neighboring samples $\mathbf{x}$ and $\mathbf{y}$ appear to our sensory systems, we need to quantify how different the relations between individual samples (vector elements) are from $\mathbf{x}$ to $\mathbf{y}$. For this purpose, we define an error term

$$e_{ij}(\mathbf{x}, \mathbf{y}) \equiv (x_i - x_j) - (y_i - y_j), \tag{1}$$

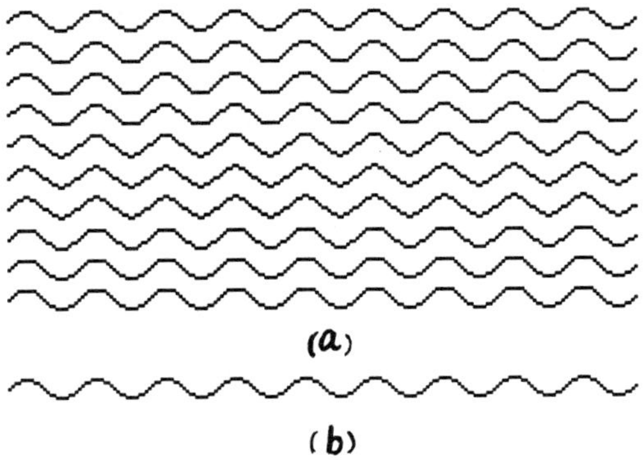

Figure 1: An empirical evidence for the subjective validity of the context distortion measure $\|E(\mathbf{x},\mathbf{y})\|$. The signal before quantization is $f(t) = \frac{10}{\pi}\sin(\frac{\pi}{11}t) + h$, where $h \in \{0.0, 0.1, 0.2, \cdots, 0.9\}$. (a) The waveforms generated by conventional VQ under the mean-squares distortion measure. (b) The waveform generated by VQ encoding under the new context distortion measure. The new measure is translation-invariant.

which measures the difference between the displacements of signal amplitudes with respect to two given time/spatial positions i and j. Let $\mathbf{y}$ be the reproduction of $\mathbf{x}$ by quantizer Q, i.e., $\mathbf{y} = Q(\mathbf{x})$. We call $e_{ij}(\mathbf{x},\mathbf{y})$ the context error with respect to time moments (or spatial positions) i and j, because it measures the distortion of signal context between samples x_i and x_j caused by quantization. Note that $e_{ij}(\mathbf{x},\mathbf{y})$ is only a local measure involving a pair of samples. In order to measure the global subjective quality of the reproduction vector $\mathbf{y}$ as an approximation of the input vector $\mathbf{x}$, we need to account for the context quantization errors between all pairs of samples. Thus we form the $k \times k$ matrix

$$E(\mathbf{x},\mathbf{y}) = \{e_{ij}(\mathbf{x},\mathbf{y})\}, \quad 1 \le i,j \le k, \tag{2}$$

of all pairwise context quantization errors, and define a matrix norm $\|E(\mathbf{x},\mathbf{y})\|$ to be a context-based quantization distortion measure. Then by this definition, the new quantization distortion measure $\|E(\mathbf{x},\mathbf{y})\|$ is a distance measure.

The fundamental difference between the Euclidean distance $\|\mathbf{x},\mathbf{y}\|$ and the matrix-based distance $\|E(\mathbf{x},\mathbf{y})\|$, while both being used as distortion measure in vector quantization, is in that the former does not but the latter does account for the context of signal samples in a block. If we think $\mathbf{x}$, $\mathbf{y}$ as two segments of digital waveforms, the

Euclidean distance separately considers the differences of corresponding samples $e_i = x_i - y_i$, whereas the matrix norm $\|E(\mathbf{x}, \mathbf{y})\|$ measures how the two waveforms differ in dynamic context, or their dynamic waveforms. To visualize this important distinction between the two measures, we present in Figure 1 the different results of encoding the time-variant signal $f(t) = \frac{10}{\pi}\sin(\frac{\pi}{11}t) + h$ using a same uniform lattice VQ codebook C but under two criteria: one is the nearest neighbor match as in conventional VQ coding, while the other is to map an input vector $\mathbf{x}$ to the reproduction codeword $\mathbf{c}^*$ such that

$$\|E(\mathbf{x}, \mathbf{c}^*)\| = \min_{\mathbf{c} \in C} \|E(\mathbf{x}, \mathbf{c})\|. \tag{3}$$

It is evident in Figure 1 that the digital waveform quantized under the new distortion measure preserves the dynamics or overall shape of sinusoidal function much better than the one quantized under the Euclidean metric. It has been widely accepted that the mean-squares error is not a suitable distortion measure for removing subjective redundancy in signal compression. The proposed context-based quantization distortion measure should be and appears to be subjectively more meaningful than the mean-squares error measure, reflecting the fact that human perceptual and cognitive process is highly sensitive to the context or dynamics of the input signals.

Besides its subjective validity, a quantization distortion measure must be algorithmically tractable to be useful in practice. In order to develop efficient algorithm to compute the norm of context error matrix, we next seek for special properties of the matrix.

3 Properties of Context Error Matrix

We consider three common matrix norms, $\|E\|_1$, $\|E\|_\infty$ and $\|E\|_2$ to be the variants of our context-based quantization distortion measure. Since the matrix E is antisymmetric, i.e., $e_{ij} = -e_{ji}$, we have $\|E\|_1 = \|E\|_\infty$. So we only need to investigate two different matrix norms. For a pair of d-vectors $\mathbf{x}$ and $\mathbf{y}$, let $e_i = x_i - y_i$, and then $e_{ij} = e_i - e_j$. The entire matrix E is determined by $\mathbf{e} = (e_1, e_2, \cdots, e_d)$, $1 \le i \le d$. Note that the order of elements in $\mathbf{e}$ is immaterial because exchanging e_i and e_j means exchanging rows i and j, and then exchanging columns i and j of matrix E. This does not affect the value of $\|E\|$.

PROPERTY 1 *Let* $e_1 \le e_2 \le \cdots \le e_d$ *and* $s_k = \sum_{i=1}^{d} \mid e_i - e_k \mid$ *for* $1 \le k \le d$, *then*

$$s_1 \ge s_2 \ge \cdots \ge s_{\lfloor (d+1)/2 \rfloor} \le \cdots \le s_{d-1} \le s_d.$$

Proof: Since $s_k = \sum_{i=1}^{k}(e_k - e_i) + \sum_{i=k+1}^{d}(e_i - e_k)$ and $s_{k+1} = \sum_{i=1}^{k}(e_{k+1} - e_i) + \sum_{i=k+1}^{d}(e_i - e_{k+1})$, it follows that $s_{k+1} = s_k + (2k-d)(e_{k+1} - e_k)$ for $1 \le k \le d-1$, Hence $s_1 \ge s_2 \ge \cdots \ge s_{\lfloor (d+1)/2 \rfloor} \le \cdots \le s_{d-1} \le s_d$. □

For easy denotation, let $\bar{e} = \sum_{i=1}^{d} e_i/d$, and define the radius of $\mathbf{e}$ to be

$$r(\mathbf{e}) = \max\{\bar{e} - \min_i e_i \ , \ \max_i e_i - \bar{e}\} \ . \tag{4}$$

LEMMA 1 $\|E\|_1 = d \cdot r(\mathbf{e})$.

Proof: Let $s_k = \sum_{i=1}^{d} \mid e_i - e_k \mid$ for $1 \le k \le d$. Let m and M be integers such that $1 \le m, M \le d$, $e_m = \min_i e_i$, and $e_M = \max_i e_i$. By the definition of matrix 1-norm $\|E\|_1 = max_j\{s_j\}$. By Property 1 $\max_j\{s_j\} = \max\{s_m, s_M\}$. Therefore

$$\begin{aligned} \|E\|_1 &= \max\{s_m, s_M\} \\ &= \max\{\textstyle\sum_{i=1}^{d}(e_i - e_m), \sum_{i=1}^{d}(e_M - e_i)\} \\ &= \max\{d \cdot (\bar{e} - e_m), d \cdot (e_M - \bar{e})\} \\ &= d \cdot \max\{\bar{e} - e_m, e_M - \bar{e}\} \\ &= d \cdot r(e_1, e_2, \ldots, e_d). \end{aligned}$$

□

LEMMA 2 $\|E\|_2 = \sqrt{d \sum_{i=1}^{d}(e_i - \bar{e})^2}$.

Proof: Notice that

$$\begin{aligned} E = \{e_{ij}\} = \{e_i - e_j\} &= \{e_i - \bar{e}) - (e_j - \bar{e})\} \\ &= \begin{pmatrix} e_1 - \bar{e} \\ e_2 - \bar{e} \\ \vdots \\ e_d - \bar{e} \end{pmatrix} (1, 1, \ldots, 1) - \begin{pmatrix} 1 \\ 1 \\ \vdots \\ 1 \end{pmatrix} (e_1 - \bar{e}, e_2 - \bar{e}, \ldots, e_d - \bar{e}). \end{aligned}$$

Let $\mathbf{f} = \begin{pmatrix} 1 \\ 1 \\ \vdots \\ 1 \end{pmatrix}$ and $\mathbf{g} = \begin{pmatrix} e_1 - \bar{e} \\ e_2 - \bar{e} \\ \vdots \\ e_d - \bar{e} \end{pmatrix}$.

Since $\mathbf{f}^t \cdot \mathbf{g} = \mathbf{g}^t \cdot \mathbf{f} = 0$, we have that $E\mathbf{g} = -\sum_{i=1}^{d}(e_i - \bar{e})^2 \cdot \mathbf{f}$ and $E\mathbf{f} = d \cdot \mathbf{g}$. Consequently, $E^tE\mathbf{f} = d\sum_{i=1}^{d}(e_i - \bar{e})^2 \cdot \mathbf{f}$ and $E^tE\mathbf{g} = d\sum_{i=1}^{d}(e_i - \bar{e})^2 \cdot \mathbf{g}$. On the other hand, $E\mathbf{x} = 0$ if vector $\mathbf{x}$ satisfies $\mathbf{x} \perp \mathbf{f}$ and $\mathbf{x} \perp \mathbf{g}$. Hence the largest eigenvalue of $E^t E$ is $d \cdot \sum_{i=1}^{d} (e_i - \bar{e})^2$. □

It follows from Eq(1) that

$$e_{ij}(\mathbf{x}, \mathbf{y}) = e_{ij}(\mathbf{x} + a\mathbf{1}, \mathbf{y} + b\mathbf{1}). \tag{5}$$

This means that the context error matrix $E = \{e_{ij}\}$ is invariant to the means of vectors $\mathbf{x}$ and $\mathbf{y}$. More interestingly, by Lemma 2, we have

$$\begin{aligned} \|E(\mathbf{x}, \mathbf{y})\|_2 &= \sqrt{d \sum_{i=1}^{d} (e_i - \bar{e})^2} \\ &= \sqrt{d \sum_{i=1}^{d} [(x_i - \bar{x}) - (y_i - \bar{y})]^2} \end{aligned} \tag{6}$$

where $\bar{x} = \sum_{1 \le k \le d} x_k / d$ and $\bar{y} = \sum_{1 \le k \le d} y_k / d$. Let $\mathbf{x}' = \mathbf{x} - \bar{x} \cdot \mathbf{1}$ and $\mathbf{y}' = \mathbf{y} - \bar{y} \cdot \mathbf{1}$, then the above leads to

$$\|E(\mathbf{x}, \mathbf{y})\|_2 = \|E(\mathbf{x}', \mathbf{y}')\|_2 = \sqrt{d \sum_{i=1}^{d} (x_i' - y_i')^2}. \tag{7}$$

Therefore, we can simplify the computation of $\|E(\mathbf{x}, \mathbf{y})\|_2$ by removing the means of $\mathbf{x}$ and $\mathbf{y}$ and then summing up the squared distances between corresponding components of the mean-removed vectors $\mathbf{x}'$ and $\mathbf{y}'$.

By now the reader may have also realized that the mean-removed VQ [1, 3] is in fact a VQ scheme using the context-based subjective quantization distortion measure of matrix 2-norm $\|E(\cdot, \cdot)\|_2$. Indeed, Eq(7) reveals that the context-based distance $\|E(\mathbf{x}, \mathbf{y})\|_2$ is $\sqrt{d}$ times the Euclidean distance $\|\mathbf{x}', \mathbf{y}'\|$ between the corresponding mean-removed vectors. Since $\|E(\mathbf{x}, \mathbf{y})\|_2$ is a subjective quantization distortion measure as we argued before, the above analysis offers a rationale to use the mean-removed VQ to preserve the shape of input signal waveform, thus retain good subjective quality of the compressed signal. In practice, the advantage of mean-removed VQ over ordinary VQ in subjective quality was observed by the authors of [3]. The relation $\|E(\mathbf{x}, \mathbf{y})\|_2 = \sqrt{d} \|\mathbf{x}', \mathbf{y}'\|$ offers computational advantages to subjective VQ coding. We simply remove the means of the training vectors $\mathbf{x}$, and design a locally optimal context (shape) codebook by clustering $\mathbf{x}' = \mathbf{x} - \mathbf{1}\bar{x}$ using the LBG algorithm. A separate optimal scalar quantizer can be designed for the means of the training vectors. As a result, a product VQ coder is formulated. The encoder can be made optimal with respect to the product context-mean codebook in the nearest neighbor sense by mapping an input vector to its nearest context codeword and its nearest mean codeword separately. See section 12.9 of the text [2] for the details of mean-removed VQ.

4 Unified Context-Mean Distortion Measure

We have seen in Eq(7) that the proposed context-based quantization distortion measure $\|E(\mathbf{x},\mathbf{y})\|_2$ is mean-invariant. But the signal amplitude also contributes to signal semantics. A distortion measure concerning only sample context (shape of waveform) does not suffice. Information about the vector means must be present. The problem is how to combine the context quantization error and the mean quantization error together to form a unified subjective distortion measure.

Let us resort to a mathematical expediency, and assume that our perceptual sensitivities to signal amplitude and to signal context are independent of each other. Thus we can formulate a new subjective distortion measure D to be a linear combination of the context quantization error and the mean quantization error

$$D(\mathbf{x},\mathbf{y}) \quad = \quad \sqrt{\|E(\mathbf{x},\mathbf{y})\|_2^2 + \lambda\|\bar{x},\bar{y}\|^2}. \tag{8}$$

LEMMA 3 $D(\mathbf{x},\mathbf{y})$ *is a distance measure.*
Proof: It is easy to see that $D(\mathbf{x},\mathbf{y}) = D(\mathbf{y},\mathbf{x})$, and $D(\mathbf{x},\mathbf{y}) \geq 0$ with the equality being valid if and only if $\mathbf{x} = \mathbf{y}$. We show that given two distance measures $U(\cdot,\cdot)$ and $V(\cdot,\cdot)$, $\sqrt{U^2(\cdot,\cdot) + \lambda V^2(\cdot,\cdot)}$ is also a distance measure.

$$\begin{aligned}
& U^2(\mathbf{x},\mathbf{z}) + \lambda V^2(\mathbf{x},\mathbf{z}) \\
< \; & U^2(\mathbf{x},\mathbf{y}) + U^2(\mathbf{y},\mathbf{z}) + \lambda[V^2(\mathbf{x},\mathbf{y}) + V^2(\mathbf{y},\mathbf{z})] + 2U(\mathbf{x},\mathbf{y})U(\mathbf{y},\mathbf{z}) + 2\lambda V(\mathbf{x},\mathbf{y})V(\mathbf{y},\mathbf{z}) \\
= \; & U^2(\mathbf{x},\mathbf{y}) + U^2(\mathbf{y},\mathbf{z}) + \lambda[V^2(\mathbf{x},\mathbf{y}) + V^2(\mathbf{y},\mathbf{z})] + \\
& 2\sqrt{U^2(\mathbf{x},\mathbf{y})U^2(\mathbf{y},\mathbf{z}) + \lambda^2 V^2(\mathbf{x},\mathbf{y})V^2(\mathbf{y},\mathbf{z}) + 2\lambda U(\mathbf{x},\mathbf{y})U(\mathbf{y},\mathbf{z})V(\mathbf{x},\mathbf{y})V(\mathbf{y},\mathbf{z})} \\
< \; & U^2(\mathbf{x},\mathbf{y}) + U^2(\mathbf{y},\mathbf{z}) + \lambda[V^2(\mathbf{x},\mathbf{y}) + V^2(\mathbf{y},\mathbf{z})] + \\
& 2\sqrt{U^2(\mathbf{x},\mathbf{y})U^2(\mathbf{y},\mathbf{z}) + \lambda^2 V^2(\mathbf{x},\mathbf{y})V^2(\mathbf{y},\mathbf{z}) + \lambda[V^2(\mathbf{x},\mathbf{y})U^2(\mathbf{y},\mathbf{z}) + U^2(\mathbf{x},\mathbf{y})V^2(\mathbf{y},\mathbf{z})]} \\
= \; & \left[\sqrt{U^2(\mathbf{x},\mathbf{y}) + \lambda V^2(\mathbf{x},\mathbf{y})} + \sqrt{U^2(\mathbf{y},\mathbf{z}) + \lambda V^2(\mathbf{y},\mathbf{z})}\right]^2.
\end{aligned}$$

$\square$.

In order to use the distortion measure $D(\mathbf{x},\mathbf{y})$ for VQ codebook design, we need to find the centroid $\mathbf{c}$ of a given set of training vectors $S = \{\mathbf{x}_1, \mathbf{x}_2, \cdots, \mathbf{x}_N\}$ under the new measure. The centroid $\mathbf{c}$ is defined to be the point (codeword) such that

$$D(\mathbf{x},\mathbf{c}) = \min_{\mathbf{y}\in\Re^d} \sum_{\mathbf{x}\in S} D(\mathbf{x},\mathbf{y}). \tag{9}$$

Since the minimum of $\sum_{\mathbf{x}\in S} D(\mathbf{x},\mathbf{y})$ is the same as that of $F(\mathbf{y}) = \sum_{\mathbf{x}\in S} D^2(\mathbf{x},\mathbf{y})$, we set the partial derivatives of $F(\mathbf{y})$ to zero to find $\mathbf{c}$. From Eq(6), we have

$$\begin{aligned} F(\mathbf{y}) = \sum_{1\le n\le N} D^2(\mathbf{x}_n,\mathbf{y}) &= \sum_{1\le n\le N} \left\{ d\sum_{i=1}^{d}[(x_{ni}-\bar{x}_n)-(y_i-\bar{y})]^2 + \lambda(\bar{x}_n-\bar{y})^2 \right\} \\ &= \sum_{1\le n\le N} \left\{ d\sum_{i=1}^{d}(x_{ni}-y_i)^2 + (\lambda-d^2)(\bar{x}_n-\bar{y})^2 \right\}, \end{aligned} \tag{10}$$

and let

$$\frac{\partial F}{\partial y_i} = -2\sum_{1\le n\le N}\left[d(x_{ni}-y_i) + \frac{(\lambda-d^2)}{d}(\bar{x}_n-\bar{y})\right] = 0, \quad 1\le i\le d. \tag{11}$$

Solving the above equation yields

$$c_i = \frac{\sum_{1\le n\le N} x_{ni}}{N} + \frac{\lambda-d^2}{d^2}\left[\frac{\sum_{1\le n\le N}\bar{x}_n}{N} - \bar{\mathbf{c}}\right], \quad 1\le i\le d. \tag{12}$$

Averaging all c_i at the left side of Eq(12), one can show

$$\bar{\mathbf{c}} = \frac{\sum_{1\le i\le d} c_i}{d} = \frac{\sum_{1\le i\le d}\sum_{1\le n\le N} x_{ni}}{dN}. \tag{13}$$

Substituting Eq(13) into Eq(12), finally we have

$$c_i = \frac{\sum_{1\le n\le N} x_{ni}}{N}, \quad 1\le i\le d. \tag{14}$$

It seems surprising that the centroid of S under the new distortion measure D is exactly the same as under the mean-squared error measure. But on a second reflection, we can explain this. By the definitions of Eq(1) and Eq(2), the context error matrix $E(\mathbf{x},\mathbf{y}) = \{e_{ij}(\mathbf{x},\mathbf{y})\}$ is translation invariant, i.e., $E(\mathbf{x},\mathbf{y}) = E(\mathbf{x}+a\cdot\mathbf{1},\mathbf{y}+b\cdot\mathbf{1})$ for any constants a and b. Thus we can first project all training vectors $\mathbf{x}\in S$ onto the $(d-1)$-dimensional hyperplane $x_1+x_2+\cdots+x_d=0$, and let $\mathbf{c}_0$ be the centroid of the N projected points to minimize the term $\|E(\mathbf{x},\mathbf{y})\|_2^2$ of D. Note that $\bar{\mathbf{c}_0}=0$ since the projected points lie on the hyperplane passing the origin. Next we let $\mathbf{c}=\mathbf{c}_0+\bar{x}\cdot\mathbf{1}$ to minimize the other term $\|\bar{x},\bar{y}\|^2$ of D. But $\mathbf{c}$ also minimizes $\|E(\mathbf{x},\mathbf{y})\|_2^2$ due to the translation-invariant property. Therefore, $\mathbf{c}$ is the centroid of S under both the new distortion measure and the mean-squares measure.

However, the above observation does not imply that the two measures are equivalent for VQ codebook design. Using Eq(7), we have

$$\begin{aligned} D^2(\mathbf{x},\mathbf{y}) &= d\|(\mathbf{x}-\bar{x}\cdot\mathbf{1})-(\mathbf{y}-\bar{y}\cdot\mathbf{1})\|^2+\lambda(\bar{x}-\bar{y})^2 \\ &= d\left[\|(\mathbf{x}-\bar{x}\cdot\mathbf{1})-(\mathbf{y}-\bar{y}\cdot\mathbf{1})\|^2+d\left(\sqrt{\lambda/d^2}\bar{x}-\sqrt{\lambda/d^2}\bar{y}\right)^2\right]. \end{aligned} \quad (15)$$

By the relation

$$\|\mathbf{x}-\mathbf{y}\|^2=\|(\mathbf{x}-\bar{x}\cdot\mathbf{1})-(\mathbf{y}-\bar{y}\cdot\mathbf{1})\|^2+d(\bar{x}-\bar{y})^2, \quad (16)$$

Eq(15) becomes

$$D^2(\mathbf{x},\mathbf{y})=d\left\|\left(\mathbf{x}+(\sqrt{\lambda/d^2}-1)\bar{x}\cdot\mathbf{1}\right)-\left(\mathbf{y}+(\sqrt{\lambda/d^2}-1)\bar{y}\cdot\mathbf{1}\right)\right\|^2 \quad (17)$$

Immediately from the above equation, we see that the ubiquitous mean-squares error measure $\|\mathbf{x},\mathbf{y}\|^2$ is only a special case of $D^2(\mathbf{x},\mathbf{y})$. If $\lambda = d^2$, then the distance D becomes $\sqrt{d}$ times the Euclidean distance. For other λ values, clustering training vectors by minimizing the new distortion measure will in general generate different quantizer cells from clustering under mean-squares distortion measure.

Geometrically, we may consider that the new distortion measure $D(\cdot,\cdot)$ has the effect of scaling a bounded vector space $\Omega \subset \Re^d$ that contains all training vectors in the diagonal direction $(1,1,\cdots,1)$. The scaling factor is $\sqrt{\lambda/d^2}$. By increasing or decreasing λ, the new measure stretches or compacts the bounded sample space Ω in the diagonal direction, to the effect of emphasizing or deemphasizing the mean. When $\lambda = d^2$, Ω is neither compacted or stretched. At the time of this writing, investigation is under way to associate the value of λ in $D(\cdot,\cdot)$ with the perceptual importance of the average signal amplitude in a block of signal samples. Our ultimate goal, a challenging one, is to transform Ω into another space $\mho$ that is perceptually uniform. The perceptual uniformity of the space $\mho$ means that points (blocks of signal samples) of equal Euclidean distance in $\mho$ are perceived as equally distant, after the sample vectors taken in Ω are transformed into $\mho$. A model for this type of research is the 1976 CIE *Luv* uniform color space. In this extended abstract, we only point out the mathematical provision by the new VQ distortion measure to incorporate human perception factors.

Suppose that a satisfactory constant λ can be found to achieve a proper weighting of context and mean distortions toward the removal of subjective redundancy. Then the transform from Ω to $\mho$ is a linear one $T : \Omega \to \mho$. Namely, $T(x) = \mathbf{x} + (\sqrt{\lambda/d^2} - 1)\bar{x} \cdot \mathbf{1}$. But probably, a non-linear transform is required here, since the weighting factor λ is likely a function of input vector $\mathbf{x}$. For instance, for image coding, $\lambda(\mathbf{x})$ needs to reflect the Weber-Fechner logarithmic sensitivity.

It is computationally advantageous to transform the training vectors into a perceptually uniform space prior to VQ codebook design. In this way, we can still employ the LBG VQ design algorithm or its variants to classify the transformed training vectors in $\mho$ into codewords. A similar approach was adopted by Xie and Stockham [4]. But they transform the pixel values instead of vectors of pixel values into a so-called visual space and design VQ codebook in that space. Their transform destroys the original context of VQ blocks, while our method does not because $\|E(\mathbf{x}_1, \mathbf{x}_2)\| = \|E(T(\mathbf{x}_1), T(\mathbf{x}_2))\|$.

Unlike mean-residual or gain-shape VQ approaches, the proposed subjective VQ technique is not a product code VQ. Thus it does not suffer performance loss inherent to product code structure. Its rate-distortion performance is only limited by the optimality of the VQ design algorithm. The product code structure is no longer necessary here because we integrate the context distortion and mean distortion into a unified subjective distortion measure.

References

[1] R. L. Baker, "Vector quantization of digital images," Ph.D. dissertation, Stanford Univ., Stanford, CA., June 1984.

[2] A. Gersho and R. M. Gray, *Vector Quantization and Signal Compression*, Kluwer Academic Publishers, Boston, 1992.

[3] R. L. Baker and R. M. Gray, "Differential vector quantization of achromatic imagery," *Proc. of the Intel. Picture Coding Symposium*, March, 1983.

[4] Z. Xie and T. G. Stockham Jr., "Previsualized image vector quantization with optimized pre- and postprocessors," *IEEE Trans. on Comm.*, vol. 39, no. 11, p. 1662-1670, Nov., 1991.

Multidimensional Rotations for Quantization

Andy C. Hung and Teresa H.-Y. Meng
Information Systems Laboratory
Stanford University, Stanford, CA 94305

Abstract

Laplacian and generalized Gaussian data arise in image and speech coding. Simple rotations of independent, identically distributed Laplacian and generalized Gaussian data in multiple dimensions can improve the granular and overload characteristics for quantization. In this paper, we describe the practical properties of multidimensional rotations for both scalar and lattice quantization and then apply them to image compression over noisy channels.

1 Introduction

Laplacian and similarly peaked generalized Gaussian distributions arise in both speech and image coding. They are difficult to quantize because their probability extends far from the origin, causing overloading and granular distortion for scalar and lattice quantization. In this paper, we introduce a method of rotations which solves these problems effectively and then show how rotations can be applied to image compression.

To reduce the overloading for scalar quantization of speech with transient peaks, all-pass filters can be used to smear out the energy over time [1]. Recently, this method has been extended to fixed-rate scalar quantization [2], noting that the all-pass filters changed the source characteristics to look more like a Gaussian distribution, which is easier to scalar quantize than a Laplacian-like distribution. This procedure involved pre-filtering the source with an all-pass filter (about 30 taps), and then quantizing with a Gaussian Lloyd-Max quantizer. At the decoder, the quantized values are passed through the pseudo-inverse all-pass post-filter to obtain the reconstructed output. Rotations achieve a similar effect to all-pass filtering, but with less computation, as shown in this paper.

Lattice quantizer overloading can be alleviated using a spherical support-set [3] rather than a cubic support-set, partitioning the lattice points into concentric spherical shells around the origin. For the specific case of Laplacian-like variables, the pyramid encoding technique developed by Fisher [4] has been employed [5][6][7] to define the support-set of lattice points in the volume of a multidimensional pyramid, thereby containing the set of the most probable points for a Laplacian distribution. This paper describes how the pyramid structure of the Laplacian density can be exploited through rotations.

This research has been sponsored by ARPA.

 1068-0314/94 $3.00 © 1994 IEEE

Our approach is to use rotations to align the multidimensional Laplacian pyramid to the smallest bounding cube. The rotation is accomplished using a Walsh-Hadamard Transform (WHT), requiring only a few additions and subtractions per pel. The reduction of the bounding cube is important to improving quantization performance.

The paper is divided into four parts: the first part describes the geometry of Laplacian-like random variables; the second part shows the advantages of rotations on fixed-rate scalar quantization; the third part describes rotations for efficient lattice quantization; and the final part applies rotated scalar quantization to image compression over noisy channels.

2 The Geometry of Pyramids

In this section, we will examine the geometric nature of independent, identically distributed Laplacian random variables. In n dimensions, the Laplacian random variable is given by the following equation for a vector $\boldsymbol{x} = [x_1, x_2, \ldots x_n]$,

$$f(\boldsymbol{x}) = (\lambda/2)^n e^{-\lambda\Sigma|x_i|}. \tag{1}$$

The surface of equal probability is a multidimensional pyramid for some parameter k,

$$\sum_{i=1}^{n} |x_i| = k. \tag{2}$$

Figure 1 shows the effects of rotations on the Laplacian random variable. In two dimensions, the geometric probability density of a Laplacian random variable is a diamond. A simple 45 degree rotation of the diamond yields equal probability distributions in the shape of a square. The rotation has aligned the probability contours with the axes, reducing the bounding box.

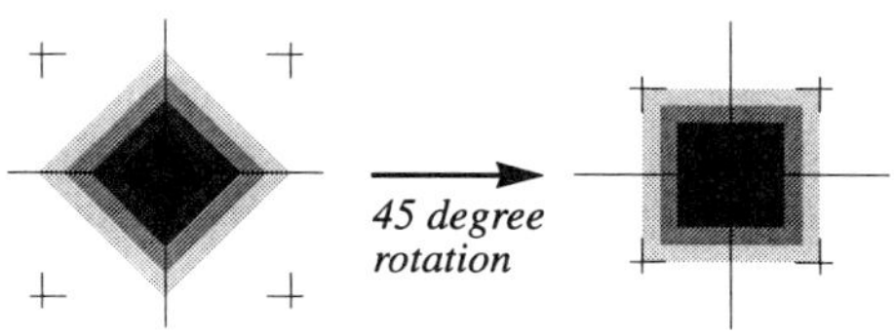

Figure 1. The equiprobable contours of a 2D Laplacian pyramid before and after rotation.

In higher dimensions, these 45 degree rotations are related to the class of unitary matrices known as the Walsh-Hadamard Transform (WHT). The WHT can be thought of as a reflection which reverses the order of the input vector elements, followed by a series of 45 degree rotations; the reflection causes the WHT transform to become its own inverse. Since the reflection is just a permutation of the input vector elements, we will refer to the WHT as simply a rotation. In two dimensions, the WHT transform matrix is expressed as

$$W_2 = (1/\sqrt{2})\begin{bmatrix} 1 & 1 \\ 1 & -1 \end{bmatrix}. \tag{3}$$

The WHT is recursively defined for powers of 2 as

$$W_{2^N} = \frac{1}{\sqrt{2}}\begin{bmatrix} W_{2^{N-1}} & W_{2^{N-1}} \\ W_{2^{N-1}} & -W_{2^{N-1}} \end{bmatrix}, \tag{4}$$

which can be implemented by a butterfly operation [8], taking only N additions per pel for a WHT of dimension 2^N, ignoring an overall scale on each vector element which can be incorporated into quantizer codebooks.

In general, an n dimensional pyramid has $2n$ corners, but an n dimensional cube has 2^n corners. Clearly, for dimensions greater than 2, the pyramid does not completely fill the bounding cube's volume even if the pyramid can be aligned properly. The following theorem shows that the Laplacian pyramid corners can be aligned to the cube corners through a WHT.

Theorem 1. *If n is a power of two, all of the corners of an n dimensional pyramid can be aligned to the corners of a n dimensional cube through a WHT.*

Proof: The multidimensional pyramid corner can be expressed as vectors of $[0, 0, \ldots, \pm 1, \ldots 0]$. The n dimensional WHT applied to this corner yields exactly one basis vector. Since each WHT basis vector is in the set of cube corners $(1/\sqrt{n})\ [\pm 1, \pm 1, \ldots, \pm 1]$, the WHT transform of the pyramid aligns each pyramidal corner with one of the points of cube, with sides of length $2/\sqrt{n}$. ∎

After the WHT rotation, all the pyramid corners are aligned to cube corners and vectors within the pyramid correspond to vectors whose elements have magnitude less than $1/\sqrt{n}$. This volumetric reduction of the bounding cube by the WHT rotation of the pyramid shape results in both better scalar quantization and smaller lattice support regions. These WHT advantages can be realized with simple hardware and techniques, whereas directly exploiting the pyramid structure requires enumerative codes. We will investigate the use of WHT rotations of the input data in the next three sections.

3 Rotations for Scalar Quantization

The WHT rotation on symmetric i.i.d. variables results in identically distributed variables which are *not*, in general, independent. For a Laplacian variable, the distribution of the rotated variables can be expressed in the form

$$f_X(x) = e^{-\lambda|x|}\sum_{i=0}^{n-1} c_i|x|^i, \tag{5}$$

where n is the dimension of the rotation. This form can be symbolically integrated to find the 0th moment, the 1st moment and the 2nd moment, and thus the optimal Lloyd-Max quantization points.

For very large n, *almost any* independent, identically distributed source converges in distribution to a Gaussian by the Central Limit Theorem. Therefore, the maximum gain from rotation is the difference in distortion between scalar quantizing the original probabilistic source and scalar quantizing a Gaussian source with equal variance. The generalized Gaussian random variable is parameterized by γ, and is expressed as

$$f_X(x) = a(\gamma)\, e^{-|b(\gamma)x|^{\gamma}}, \tag{6}$$

where $a(\gamma) = (\gamma b(\gamma))/(2\Gamma(1/\gamma))$, $b(\gamma) = \sqrt{\Gamma(3/\gamma)/(\sigma^2\Gamma(1/\gamma))}$, and $\Gamma(x)$ is the gamma function. The generalized Gaussian distribution is identical to the Laplacian distribution for $\gamma = 1$ and identical to the Gaussian distribution for $\gamma = 2$. For the generalized Gaussian distribution, the quantization distortion is again a parameter of γ, and can be calculated from high-resolutional distortion theory as

$$D(\gamma) = \frac{\sigma^2}{12m^2}\frac{3^{3/\gamma}}{(a(\gamma))^2}. \tag{7}$$

The high-rate/dimension gain in dB of WHT rotating a generalized Gaussian random variable can be expressed by the log ratio of the quantization distortion of the original source versus that of a Gaussian.

$$G(\gamma) = 10\log_{10}\left(\frac{D(\gamma)}{D(2)}\right) = 10\log_{10}\left(\frac{3^{3((1/\gamma)-(1/2))}}{2\pi(a(\gamma))^2}\right). \tag{8}$$

The high-rate/dimension gain by WHT rotation for scalar quantization is approximately 2.19 dB for Laplacian distributed data ($\gamma = 1$). The gains for varying γ are shown in the left graph of Figure 2, where the generalized Gaussian region between $0.5 \le \gamma \le 1.0$, which seems to fit the distribution of transform and subband coefficients, is shaded [9]. In order to ascertain the performance of the WHT rotation for different dimensions and bit rates for a Laplacian data source, we symbolically calculated equation (5) for an exact distribution formula, and applied Lloyd-Max techniques to derive the quantization codebook. The performance of rotations on Laplacian data for different dimensions and quantizer bit rates is shown in the right graph of Figure 2.

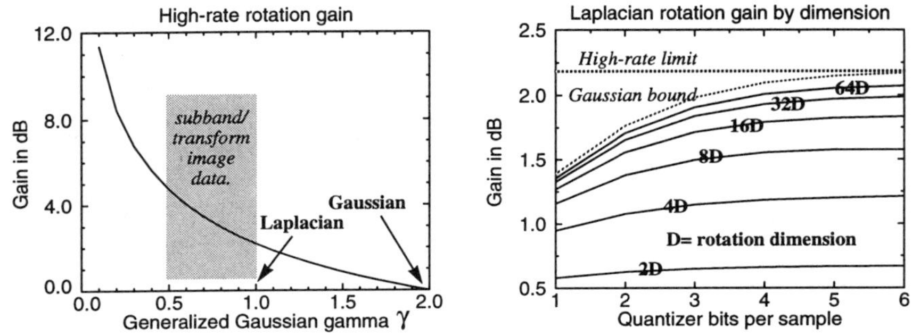

Figure 2. The WHT rotation gain for fixed-rate scalar quantization.

Figure 2 shows that just one addition per pel (a 2D WHT rotation) achieves over 0.5 dB gain over normal scalar quantization for the Laplacian distribution. Only two additions per pel (a 4D WHT rotation) achieves over 1 dB gain. These gains increase by the quantizer bit rate and by the dimension of the rotation. Since the gain properties are due to the Central Limit Theorem, the quantization codebooks for very high dimensional rotations are approximately Gaussian, independent of the source input distribution.

4 Rotations for Lattice Vector Quantization

Lattice vector quantization can be used in conjunction with entropy coding to achieve compression very close to the rate-distortion bound [10][11][12]. Lattice vector quantization of a vector x involves finding the nearest lattice point to x and then (optionally) entropy coding the index to the point. Since the number of lattice points in multidimensional space is infinite, practical lattice VQ systems often restrict the possible points or support-set for the lattice to a cube, sphere, or pyramid in space. The quantization of a vector lying *outside* the support-set results in *overload error*, which is the difference between the vector and the nearest centroid in the support-set. The quantization of a vector lying *within* the support-set results in *granular error*, which is the difference between a vector within a lattice cell in the support-set and the centroid of that lattice cell. These types of error are shown in Figure 3.

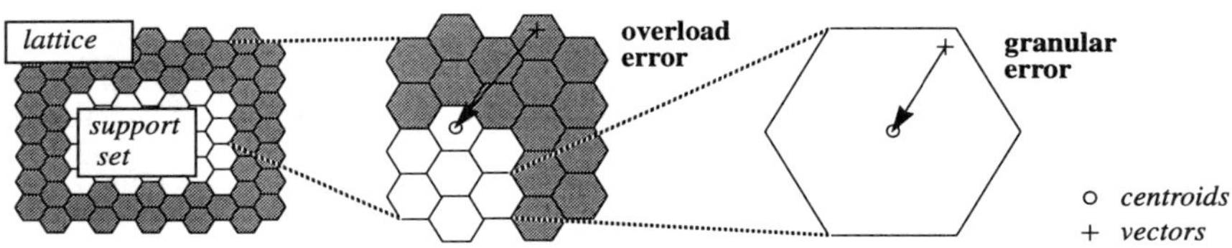

Figure 3. Overload and granular error for a hexagonal 2D lattice vector quantizer.

Granular error is a characteristic of the lattice cell whereas overload error is a property of the support-set shape. Since the granular error is fixed per lattice, the idea is to choose the support-set shape to minimize the overload error given a fixed volume. The cubic restriction is the simplest, but usually performs poorly. The spherical and pyramidal support-set require complicated enumerating schemes. A simple and effective alternative for a cubic support-set lattice quantizer is to perform a like-dimensional WHT rotation on the data before lattice quantization. The dimension of the WHT rotation is identical to the lattice to avoid changing the underlying probability structure.

4.1 Lattice simulation

The lattice overload is characterized by two principal values: 1) *overload error*, expressed in dB SNR quality, due to projecting vectors outside the support-set to the support-set; and 2) *overload probability*, the likelihood that a source vector is outside the support-set. In our simulations, we use one million vectors and examine the overload error and probability for a *unit* support-set volume, given a Laplacian source with varying λ. The four support-set shapes are as follows: the pyramid *(Pyramid)*, WHT rotation/cube *(WHT Rotated)*, the sphere *(Sphere)*, and the (unrotated data) cube *(Cube)*.

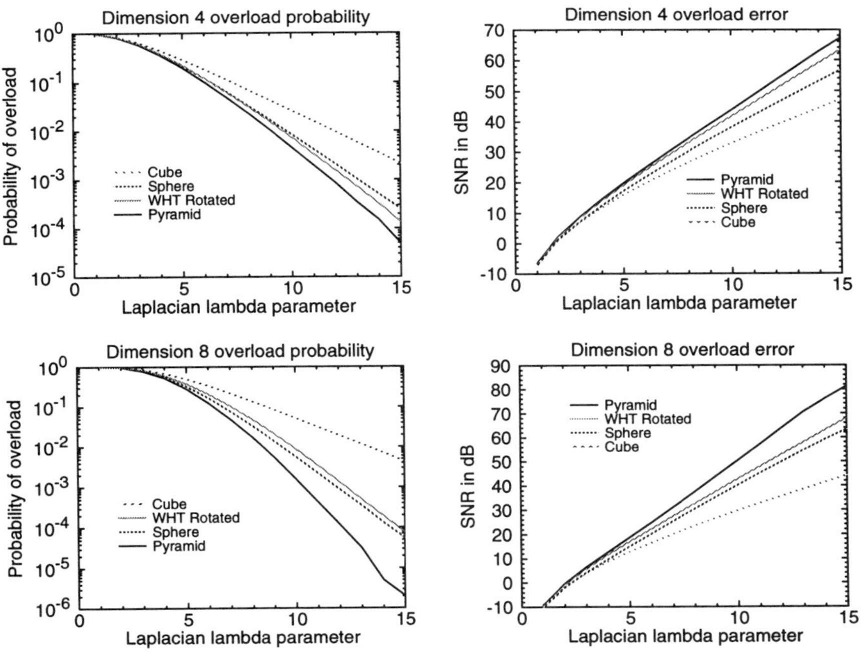

Figure 4. The overload in four and eight dimensions.

In two dimensions the pyramid support-set and the WHT rotated data/cubic support-set are identical (and are not shown). In four dimensions, the WHT rotated data/cubic support-set has a smaller overload error and probability over the spherical support-set and a substantial reduction over the unrotated data/cube support-set. In eight dimensions, the WHT rotated data/cubic support-set has about the same performance as a spherical support-set. The pyramidal support-set performs the best, as expected for the Laplacian random variable. However, the significant complexity of indexing the pyramidal or spherical support-set for complicated lattices, makes the simple cubic support-set with rotated input data an excellent choice for practical lattice quantization with (or without) entropy coding.

5 Rotations for Image Compression

In section 3, we showed how rotations achieve better compression with fixed-rate scalar quantization. In this section we will look at the performance of fixed-rate scalar quantization through rotations for transmitting images over noisy channels.

A subband decomposition is recursively applied to the lowest frequency band of the image for four levels, with a 9 tap QMF filter (0.5645751 0.2927051 -0.05224239 -0.04270508 0.01995484) [15]. The lowest band is quantized with a Gaussian Lloyd-Max scalar quantizer. The upper bands are first scrambled into a random order to break up any correlation and then rotated through a WHT of the same length as the subband. The subband is then scalar quantized with a Gaussian Lloyd-Max scalar quantizer. The quantizer bit allocation is determined through integer bit allocation techniques. Two other coders are used for comparison. The first coder applies scalar compression without rotation, using a Gaussian quantizer on the lowest band and a generalized Gaussian $\gamma = 0.6$ Lloyd-Max quantizer on the upper bands. The second coder applies the JPEG algorithm [17] using custom generated Huffman tables and the suggested JPEG quantization matrix, scaled for different rates. Figure 5 shows the results for two USC database images.

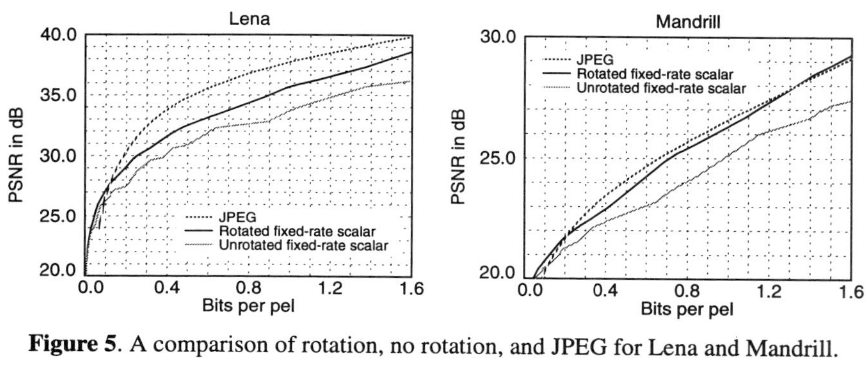

Figure 5. A comparison of rotation, no rotation, and JPEG for Lena and Mandrill.

The difference between the predicted error via the integer bit allocation techniques and the actual error, for bit-rates between 0.1 to 1.6 bits per pel, is within approximately 0.05 dB, typically much less, because the rotations have almost completely converted the subband data to a Gaussian distribution. The performance between the JPEG and the rotated fixed-rate scalar quantization is close even though the JPEG method uses variable length entropy coding whereas the fixed-rate techniques do not. In fact, for Mandrill, the rotated fixed-rate scalar quantizer technique exceeds the performance of JPEG at some rates. The advantages of rotated data over unrotated data for fixed-rate scalar quantization at coding rates greater than 0.2 bits per pel is between 1 to 2 dB. The gain from rotations increase with rate, which indirectly increases quantizer resolution and number of coded bands.

5.1 Channel robustness

In our mobile communications model, the encoder always transmits the same compressed image regardless of the actual channel because it does not know the current noise characteristics of communication to each receiver. The experiments with channel robustness focus on the Lena image at a source coding bit-rate of 0.496 bits per pel (bpp). The PSNR under noiseless conditions is 32.5 dB. Six images are shown at the end of this paper, (going left to right, top to bottom): 1) unrotated quantization at 0.01 bit error rate (ber); 2) rotated quantization at 0.01 bit error rate; 3) unrotated quantization at 0.01 bit error rate, channel protection; 4) rotated quantization at 0.01 bit error rate, channel protection; 5) unrotated quantization at 0.1 bit error rate, channel protection; 6) rotated quantization at 0.1 bit error rate, channel protection. The channel protection involves an additional 0.14 bpp of channel coding, along with adaptive decoder optimization techniques [16]. The only difference between the images on the left and the right is just that the upper frequency bands are rotated before quantization and that a Gaussian Lloyd Max quantizer is used, rather than using a generalized Gaussian $\gamma = 0.6$ quantizer directly on the upper frequency bands.

At 0.1 bit error rate, some artifacts begin to appear in the rotated channel protected image, though it is superior to the corresponding unrotated image. This is because the rotations naturally distribute the error throughout the image, preserving image detail even in the presence of bit-errors and fades. The rotated, channel protected image is reasonably robust, maintaining semblance of the image at up to 0.3 bit error rate.

6 Conclusion

Rotating i.i.d. Laplacian-like variables in multiple dimensions through a Walsh Hadamard Transform reduces the bounding multidimensional cube required for a surface of constant probability. This geometric advantage results in the simulated and theoretical benefits for quantization. Rotations can be applied to fixed-rate scalar quantization to improve compression by over 2 dB, and to lattice quantization for use with simple cubic support-sets. Furthermore, its application requires only a few additions and subtractions per pel because of fast implementations of the WHT. Rotations are also a promising solution to image compression over noisy channels, where it can both improve quantizer performance and distribute the effects of bit-errors and fades randomly throughout the image.

References

[1] H. W. Strube, "How to make an all-pass filter with a desired impulse response," *IEEE Transactions on Acoustics, Speech and Signal Processing*, vol. ASSP-30, No. 3, April 1982, pp. 336-337.

[2] K. Popat and K. Zeger, "Robust quantization of memoryless sources using dispersive FIR filters," *IEEE Transactions on Communications*, vol. 40, no. 11, November 1992, pp. 1670-1674.

[3] K. Sayood, J. D. Gibson, and M. C. Rost, "An algorithm for uniform vector quantizer design," *IEEE Transactions on Information Theory*, vol. IT-30, No. 6, November 1984, pp. 805-814.

[4] T. R. Fischer, "A pyramid vector quantizer," *IEEE Transactions on Information Theory*, vol. IT-32, no. 4, July 1986, pp. 568-583.

[5] M. Barlaud, P. Sole, M. Antonini, P. Mathieu, T. Gaidon, "Pyramidal lattice vector quantization for multiscale image coding," *Universite de Nice, Sophia Antipolis*, Report 91-26.

[6] P. F. Swaszek, "A vector quantizer for the Laplace source," *IEEE Transactions on Information Theory*, vol. IT-37, No. 5, Sept. 1991, pp. 1355-1365.

[7] D. G. Jeong and J. D. Gibson, "Uniform and piecewise uniform lattice vector quantization for memoryless Gaussian and Laplacian sources," *IEEE Transactions on Information Theory*, vol. IT-39, no. 3, pp. 786-804.

[8] A. K Jain, *Fundamentals of Digital Image Processing*, Prentice Hall, Englewood Cliffs, 1989.

[9] N. Tanabe and N. Farvardin, "Subband image coding using entropy-coded quantization over noisy channels," *IEEE Journal on Selected Areas in Communications*, vol. 10, no. 5, June 1992, pp. 926-943.

[10] A. Gersho, "Asymptotically optimal block quantization," *IEEE Transactions on Information Theory*, vol. IT-25, no. 4, July 1979, pp. 373-380.

[11] J. Ziv, "On universal quantization," *IEEE Transactions on Information Theory*, vol. IT-31, no. 3, May 1985, pp. 344-347.

[12] A. Gersho and R. M. Gray, *Vector Quantization*, Kluwer Academic Publishers, Boston, 1992.

[13] T. R. Fischer, "Geometric source coding and vector quantization," *IEEE Transactions on Information Theory,* January 1989, pp.137-145.

[14] M. Antonini, M. Barlaud, P. Mathieu, "Image coding using lattice vector quantization of wavelet coefficients," *IEEE ICASSP-92*, pp. IV-401-404.

[15] T. Senoo and B. Girod, "Vector quantization for entropy coding of image subbands," *IEEE Transactions on Image Processing*, vol. 1, no. 4, October 1992, pp. 526-532.

[16] A. C. Hung and T. H.-Y. Meng, "Adaptive channel optimization of vector quantized data," *Data Compression Conference*, April 1993, pp. 282-291.

[17] W. B. Pennebaker and J. L. Mitchell, *JPEG still image data compression standard*, van Nostrand Reinhold, 1993.

1) 0.01 ber, unrotated
2) 0.01 ber, rotated
3) 0.01 ber, unrotated, channel protected
4) 0.01 ber, rotated, channel protected
5) 0.1 ber, unrotated, channel protected
6) 0.1 ber, rotated, channel protected

A New Multiple Path Search Technique for Residual Vector Quantizers

Christopher F. Barnes

Georgia Tech Research Institute

Abstract

Multiple path searching can provide varying degrees of joint search optimization of residual vector quantizer encoder stages. A short coming of the conventional multiple path M-search algorithm, however, is that joint search optimization of encoder stages is limited to consecutive stages. A new *iterated multipath (IM)-search* algorithm is introduced that is not subject to any particular ordering of the residual quantizer stages. The IM-search algorithm may be combined with the sequential M-search algorithm to provide additional enhancement of residual vector quantization encoder performance. Furthermore, additional details of design methods for residual quantizers with separate, and, in general, different encoder and decoder codebooks are given. Separate encoder and decoder codebooks facilitate the use and design of various suboptimal, but computationally efficient encoder structures, while maintaining the use of decoder stage codebooks which satisfy necessary conditions for the joint optimality of direct sum codebooks.

1 RVQ Encoder and Decoder Codebook Structures

Multiple stage residual vector quantizers (RVQs) are subject to two structural constraints: a sequential search encoder constraint, and a direct sum codebook constraint. The purpose of the sequential search constraint is to reduce computation requirements. The purpose of the direct sum constraint is to reduce memory requirements.

The performance of RVQ decoders can be improved by using stage codebooks which satisfy necessary conditions for joint optimality [1]. However, direct sum codebooks do not necessarily give good RVQ encoder performance when they are sequentially searched, especially if the RVQ has a high output rate, or many stages. Poor sequential search performance can be attributed to entanglement of the direct sum codebook structure [2]. The optimal partitioning structure associated with entangled direct sum codebooks is not compatible with the simple partitioning structure required by efficient sequential search encoders [3]. Hence, the use of separate, and, in general, different direct sum codebooks at the RVQ encoder and decoder is advantageous [4]. Direct sum encoder codebooks should be designed to give good sequential search performance. Direct sum decoder codebooks should be designed to satisfy conditions necessary for joint optimality. A design method for RVQ is required that is capable of providing separate encoder and decoder codebooks, but where the two sets of codebooks work together to provide good overall RVQ performance.

2 Separate Encoder/Decoder Codebook Design Methods

A commonly used source code design method is to iteratively optimize the encoder and decoder while the other is held fixed, thus lowering the distortion at each design step [5]. Since RVQ encoders have a sequential search structural constraint not required at the decoder, and since methods for optimizing sequential search encoders are either unknown or difficult to apply, direct application of the Generalized Lloyd Algorithm (GLA) [6] to RVQ presents some problems. Fortunately, RVQs with good performance, and encoder and decoder codebooks well matched to their respective structural constraints, can be generated by modifying the GLA design procedure.

Assume the design process has reached the point where the decoder has just been optimized for a fixed encoder. The next design step is to find an optimal encoder partition while holding the decoder codebooks fixed. The main problem with designing RVQs with the GLA is that if the GLA paradigm is strictly adhered to, then optimization of the encoder partition for a fixed set of direct sum decoder codebooks can violate the desired structural simplicity of the sequential search encoder constraint. Optimal sequential search partitioning for a fixed set of direct sum codebooks often requires stage decision regions that are not connected or convex, while efficient sequential search encoders generally require well behaved stage partition cells. Failure to account for the inherent complexity of optimal direct sum stage partition structures can lead to a performance decrease in blind application of sequential nearest neighbor search encoders to direct sum codebooks during the GLA procedure.

To correct this lack of monotonicity in the RVQ GLA design process, the following approach can be used. Instead of seeking a new encoder that is *optimal* for the *new decoder* (as required by the GLA), when designing RVQs with sequential search encoders, it is easier to find a new encoder that is only *improved* relative to the *old encoder*. This design goal is more easily obtained if the encoder and decoder codebooks are permitted to be different. More specifically, given fixed direct sum encoder codebooks, new direct sum decoder codebooks are selected to be jointly optimal for the fixed direct sum partition induced by the imposed sequential search structure. Given a fixed set of direct sum decoder codebooks, and a fixed set of old direct sum encoder codebooks, a combination of some subset of the old encoder stage codebooks and some subset of the new decoder stages codebooks is selected to produce a new sequential search encoder with improved performance. The trick to this design method is finding efficient rules for choosing different stages from the different systems. An understanding of the effect of entanglement on sequential search performance can provide reasonable heuristic guidelines for either accepting or rejecting various subsets of optimized decoder stage codebooks as new encoder stage codebooks.

Experiments have shown that there usually exist combinations of old encoder and new decoder stage codebooks that form a new set of RVQ encoder codebooks that give improved performance relative to the previous set of old encoder codebooks. However, if no such combination exists, the set of old encoder codebooks can be retained to guarantee that the performance of the sequential search encoder does not decrease as the design process is continued.

This modified design method has several benefits. First, it solves the monotonicity problem sometimes encountered with descent algorithms for RVQs. Second, it improves the successive approximation quantization properties of RVQs. Third, it is well suited to the design of residual quantizers subject to various encoder structures, e.g., lattice encoders [4], M-search encoders [7], trellis-search encoders [8], entropy-constrained encoders [9], etc., and to a new form of nonsequential multipath searching introduced later in this paper.

3 Successive Approximation with Residual Quantizers

Although optimal nonuniform *pointwise or deterministic* successive refinement of information is not always possible for all sources [10], RVQs designed with the monotonically convergent iterative RVQ design procedure described above provide a type of *probabilistic or stochastic* successive approximation during both the design process and application of the codebooks. Each iteration of the modified design procedure gives nondecreasing RVQ performance, and each stage of the encoder provides encoding decisions where the expected distortion (relative to the encoder codebooks) is smaller than the expected distortion at the output of the prior encoder stage. This is in contrast to results obtained by designing jointly optimal RVQs with sequential search encoders and identical encoder and decoder codebooks, where monotonicity is not guaranteed, and occasionally, catastrophically poor performance results may be obtained, especially if the RVQ has a high output rate or many stages.

The performance of stochastic successive RVQ refinement is generally not optimal in a rate-distortion sense at each stage of refinement. In fact, even though the expected distortion decreases with each RVQ stage, there may exist a subset of the inputs of a RVQ stage where the representation for each point in the subset degrades with the additional stage. We also note that although RVQs designed with sequential application of the GLA [11] give monotonically increasing performance during both the design process and with increasing numbers of stages, the extremely poor performance [12] of such RVQs with many stages or high output rates make them unworthy of further consideration here.

To guarantee the best possible successive refinement direct sum decoder representation with the use of sequential search encoding and different encoder and decoder codebooks, multiple sets of jointly optimized direct sum decoder codebooks with different numbers of stages may be required at the receiver (the joint optimization process depends on the number of stages used at each point of successive refinement). Each set of direct sum decoder codebooks is designed to be jointly optimal for a given number of stages.

In addition to improving design behavior and successive refinement properties, the use of separate encoder and decoder direct sum codebooks facilitates the use of various encoder structures, and in particular, facilitates a new nonsequential multiple path search technique introduced in the next section. The structure of this multiple path encoder is related only to the direct sum codebook structural constraint, and hence is not subject to the imposed codebook ordering resulting from the sequential search encoder constraint. The new method can be combined with other multipath search techniques, such as the M-search algorithm [13]. Such RVQs employ two encoding steps: 1) a sequential multiple path search, and 2) a related nonsequential multiple path search. The second search provides a method of examining paths in the direct sum codebook structure that are related to the path identified by the first search, but where the second search is not restricted by any particular ordering of the stage codebooks. (Although this extended abstract emphasizes the application of the new search algorithm to RVQs with separate encoder and decoder codebooks, this search method can also be used on RVQs where the codebooks are identical.)

4 A New Multipath Search Method

Given fixed direct sum stage codebooks, necessary conditions for the optimality of sequential search stage partitions are known [2]. However, the implementation complexity required to satisfy these conditions for arbitrary codebooks may be very large. These necessary conditions do suggest, however, a method of multiple path searching. To present these concepts, let us establish notation. The pth stage of an RVQ is a k-dimensional vector quantizer defined by the mapping $\boldsymbol{Q}_p : \mathbf{R}^k \mapsto \boldsymbol{C}_p$, where

- $\mathbf{R}^k$ is the k-dimensional quantizer input space,
- $p \in \{1, 2, \ldots, P\}$ is the *stage index,*
- $\boldsymbol{C}_p = \{\boldsymbol{y}_p(0), \boldsymbol{y}_p(1), \ldots, \boldsymbol{y}_p(N_p - 1)\}$ is the pth stage *codebook,*
- $\boldsymbol{y}_p(i_p) \in \mathbf{R}^k$ are pth stage *code vectors,* and
- i_p is an *index* in the pth stage *index set* $\boldsymbol{I}_p = \{0, 1, \ldots, N_p - 1\}$.

Residual quantizer stage mappings are collectively equivalent to a single stage mapping $\mathbf{Q} : \mathbf{R}^k \mapsto \mathbf{C}$, where

- $\mathbf{C}$ is the *direct sum codebook* $\{\mathbf{y}(\mathbf{i}) : \mathbf{i} \in \mathbf{I}\}$,
- $\mathbf{y}(\mathbf{i})$ is a *direct sum code vector* $\mathbf{y}(\mathbf{i}) = \boldsymbol{y}_1(i_1) + \boldsymbol{y}_2(i_2) + \cdots + \boldsymbol{y}_P(i_P)$, and
- $\mathbf{i} = (i_1 i_2 \cdots i_P)$ is a *P-tuple index* contained in $\mathbf{I} = \boldsymbol{I}_1 \times \boldsymbol{I}_2 \times \cdots \times \boldsymbol{I}_P$.

The direct sum codebook is the direct sum of the stage codebooks, $\mathbf{C} = \boldsymbol{C}_1 + \boldsymbol{C}_2 + \cdots + \boldsymbol{C}_P$. If the direct sum codebook is fixed, then the optimal direct sum mapping and corresponding direct sum partition are defined by a nearest neighbor encoding rule,

$$\mathbf{Q}(\boldsymbol{x}_1) = \mathbf{y}(\mathbf{i}) \quad \Leftrightarrow \quad d(\boldsymbol{x}_1, \mathbf{y}(\mathbf{i})) \leq d(\boldsymbol{x}_1, \mathbf{C}), \tag{1}$$

where the distance $d(\cdot, \cdot)$ between the source output $\boldsymbol{x}_1$ and the set $\mathbf{C}$ is defined in the usual way. As always, any arbitrary rule may be used in the event of a tie between two or more code vectors. For the sake of discussions that follow, $d(\cdot, \cdot)$ is assumed to be translation invariant).

A sequential search encoder that induces a direct sum partition which satisfies (1) is said to be optimal, and can be described by the following sequence of stage encoding rules:

$$\boldsymbol{Q}_p(\boldsymbol{x}_p) = \boldsymbol{y}_p(i_p) \quad \Leftrightarrow \quad d(\boldsymbol{x}_p, \boldsymbol{y}_p(i_p) + \boldsymbol{C}_{p+1} + \cdots + \boldsymbol{C}_P) \leq d(\boldsymbol{x}_p, \boldsymbol{C}_p + \boldsymbol{C}_{p+1} + \cdots + \boldsymbol{C}_P) \tag{2}$$

for $p = 1, 2, \ldots, P$, and where $\boldsymbol{x}_p = \boldsymbol{x}_1 - \sum_{j=1}^{p-1} \boldsymbol{Q}_j(\boldsymbol{x}_j)$ is the pth stage *causal residual.* Using the language of group theory [14, 15, 16], the pth stage encoding rule (2) requires that all $\boldsymbol{x}_p$ that are mapped to $\boldsymbol{y}_p(i_p)$ be at least as close to a point in the *coset* $\boldsymbol{y}_p(i_p) + \boldsymbol{C}_{p+1} + \cdots + \boldsymbol{C}_P$ as to any point in the cosets $\boldsymbol{y}_p(k_p) + \boldsymbol{C}_{p+1} + \cdots + \boldsymbol{C}_P$ with $k_p = 0, 1, \ldots, N_p - 1$ and $k_p \neq i_p$. Using the language of trees [2], the optimal (sequential search) pth stage decision region corresponding to $\boldsymbol{y}_p(i_p)$ is a Voronoi region with respect to the leaf nodes of the *subtree* $\boldsymbol{y}_p(i_p) + \boldsymbol{C}_{p+1} + \cdots + \boldsymbol{C}_P$ of the *tree* $\mathbf{0} + \boldsymbol{C}_p + \boldsymbol{C}_{p+1} + \cdots + \boldsymbol{C}_P$, where $\mathbf{0}$ is the origin of $\mathbf{R}^k$.

Application of the stage encoding rules expressed by (2) is done in sequence. Consider, for example, the first and last stage encoding rules:

$$d(\boldsymbol{x}_1, \boldsymbol{y}_1(i_1) + \boldsymbol{C}_2 + \cdots + \boldsymbol{C}_P) \leq d(\boldsymbol{x}_1, \boldsymbol{C}_1 + \boldsymbol{C}_2 + \cdots + \boldsymbol{C}_P), \tag{3}$$

$$\vdots$$

$$d(\boldsymbol{x}_P, \boldsymbol{y}_P(i_P)) \leq d(\boldsymbol{x}_P, \boldsymbol{C}_P). \tag{4}$$

These stage encoding rules may be very expensive to implement. (This is not true in all cases. There exist direct sum codebook structures, for example, corresponding to *reflected residual quantizers* [3, 17], where the search complexity of an optimal sequential search encoder is proportional to the stage codebook size.) However, note that the last stage encoding rule (4) is relatively easy to implement. Given encoding decisions by all previous stages, the optimal last stage encoder is simply a nearest neighbor mapping of the last stage input $\boldsymbol{x}_P$ onto the last stage codebook $\boldsymbol{C}_P$. The new multipath search technique is based, in part, on this fact and on the following observation. The local optimality of the last stage encoder is not dependent upon the correctness of the encoding decisions of prior stages. Here, the word "correct" describes a stage encoding decision that is consistent with (1), otherwise a stage encoding decision is termed "incorrect". Given either correct or incorrect encoding decisions from all previous stages, the locally optimal last stage encoding rule is a simple nearest neighbor search of the last stage codebook.

The new nonsequential multiple path search technique is obtained by removing the codebook ordering imposed by the sequential search encoder constraint, and by applying the optimal last stage encoding rule described above to all RVQ stages. More specifically, given any $p \in \{1, 2, \ldots, P\}$, and given either correct or incorrect encoding decisions from all other stages, the new multipath search encoder forms a residual at the pth stage from the given encoding decisions of all other stages and makes the best possible local decision by a nearest neighbor search of the pth stage codebook.

To see that execution of this multiple path search technique reduces the distortion at each stage, note that if an arbitrary set, $\{k_1, \ldots, k_{p-1}, k_{p+1}, \ldots, k_P\}$, of encoding decisions are given for all stages but the pth stage, then a $\boldsymbol{y}_p(i_p)$ that satisfies

$$d(\boldsymbol{x}_1, \boldsymbol{y}_1(k_1)+\cdots+\boldsymbol{y}_p(i_p)+\cdots+\boldsymbol{y}_P(k_P)) \leq d(\boldsymbol{x}_1, \boldsymbol{y}_1(k_1)+\cdots+\boldsymbol{C}_p+\cdots+\boldsymbol{y}_P(k_P)) \quad (5)$$

is clearly the optimal local encoding decision. In terms of a residual vector, (5) can be written,

$$d(\boldsymbol{x}_1 - [\boldsymbol{y}_1(k_1) + \cdots + \boldsymbol{y}_P(k_P)], \boldsymbol{y}_p(i_p)) \leq d(\boldsymbol{x}_1 - [\boldsymbol{y}_1(k_1) + \cdots + \boldsymbol{y}_P(k_P)], \boldsymbol{C}_p), \quad (6)$$

which reveals more explicitly the required nearest neighbor search of the pth stage codebook with the residual $\boldsymbol{x}_1 - [\boldsymbol{y}_1(k_1) + \cdots + \boldsymbol{y}_P(k_P)]$.

To be more precise in our description of the new search algorithm, the introduction of additional notation and nomenclature is useful:

- $\check{\mathbf{i}}_p = (i_1 i_2 \cdots i_{p-1} i_{p+1} \cdots i_P)$ is a *one-stage punctured index* obtained by removing i_p from $\mathbf{i}$,
- $\check{\mathbf{y}}_p(\check{\mathbf{i}}_p) = \mathbf{y}(\mathbf{i}) - \boldsymbol{y}_p(i_p)$ is a *one-stage punctured direct sum code vector,* and
- $\check{\boldsymbol{x}}_p(\check{\mathbf{i}}_p) = \boldsymbol{x}_1 - \check{\mathbf{y}}_p(\check{\mathbf{i}}_p)$ is a *one-stage punctured residual vector.*

Using the nomenclature given above, the following describes the new multipath search algorithm:

1. Using some initial search technique, encode all training set vectors $\{\boldsymbol{x}_{1,l} : l = 1, 2, \ldots, L\}$ to obtain corresponding candidate P-tuple indices $\{\boldsymbol{i}_l\}$.
2. Clear a counter for encoding decision changes.
3. Do for $p = 1, 2, \ldots, P$:
   (a) Do for each training set vector $\boldsymbol{x}_{1,l}$:
      i. Form the one-stage punctured residual $\check{\boldsymbol{x}}_{p,l}(\check{\mathbf{i}}_{p,l})$.
      ii. Perform a nearest neighbor mapping of $\check{\boldsymbol{x}}_{p,l}(\check{\mathbf{i}}_{p,l})$ into the pth stage codebook C_p.
      iii. If the resulting nearest neighbor encoding decision k_p is different from the i_p obtain by puncturing $\boldsymbol{i}_l$, replace i_p with k_p and increment the counter for encoding decision changes.
4. If the counter for encoding decision changes is nonzero, repeat from step 2, otherwise stop.

Similar to the joint optimization process for RVQ decoders [2], this multipath search technique is applied in repeated round robin fashion to all stages. Hence, the name, *iterated multiple path search.* The new multiple path search technique must be iterated because a change made at one stage, may, at a later iteration at the same stage, require another change due to an intermediate modification made at some other stage. Since any encoding decision change can only decrease the positive distortion measure, the algorithm converges.

The iterated multipath search technique is not limited to single stage punctured residuals, multiple stage punctured residuals can also be used. However, instead of nearest neighbor searches over a single stage codebook, if Q stages are punctured, then a nearest neighbor search over a Q-stage direct sum codebook is required. There are $P!/Q!(P-Q)!$ different ways to choose Q of P stage codebooks. So, similar to single stage puncturing where the algorithm is iterated over all stages, with multiple stage puncturing, the algorithm is iterated over all combinations of Q of P stages. However, to control the computational complexity of the algorithm, iterations can be performed only over some preselected subset of the possible Q-element stage combinations.

To be more explicit in our description of the iterated multipath search technique with multiple stage puncturing, let $\boldsymbol{p}_Q = (p_1 p_2 \cdots p_Q)$ be a Q-tuple that indicates which stages have been selected for puncturing for one iteration of the multipath search algorithm. Let $\boldsymbol{\Pi}(P,Q)$ be the set of all such $\boldsymbol{p}_Q$. Hence, we have the following generalizations:

- $\check{\mathbf{i}}_{\boldsymbol{p}_Q}$ is a *Q-stage punctured index* obtained by removing $\{i_{p_1}, i_{p_2}, \ldots, i_{p_Q}\}$ from $\mathbf{i}$,
- $\check{\mathbf{y}}_{\boldsymbol{p}_Q}(\check{\mathbf{i}}_{\boldsymbol{p}_Q}) = \mathbf{y}(\mathbf{i}) - [\boldsymbol{y}_{p_1}(i_{p_1}) + \boldsymbol{y}_{p_2}(i_{p_2}) + \cdots + \boldsymbol{y}_{p_Q}(i_{p_Q})]$ is a *Q-stage punctured direct sum code vector,* and
- $\check{\boldsymbol{x}}_{\boldsymbol{p}_Q}(\check{\mathbf{i}}_{\boldsymbol{p}_Q}) = \boldsymbol{x}_1 - \check{\mathbf{y}}_{\boldsymbol{p}_Q}(\check{\mathbf{i}}_{\boldsymbol{p}_Q})$ is a *Q-stage punctured residual vector.*

The following describes the iterated multipath search algorithm for *multiple stage puncturing:*

1. Using some initial search technique, encode all training set vectors $\{\boldsymbol{x}_{1,l} : l = 1, 2, \ldots, L\}$ to obtain corresponding candidate P-tuple indices $\{\boldsymbol{i}_l\}$.
2. Clear a counter for encoding decision changes.
3. Do either for all, or some predetermined subset of the $\boldsymbol{p}_Q \in \boldsymbol{\Pi}(P,Q)$:
   (a) Do for each training set vector $\boldsymbol{x}_{1,l}$:
      i. Form the Q-stage punctured residual $\check{\boldsymbol{x}}_{\boldsymbol{p}_Q,l}(\check{\mathbf{i}}_{\boldsymbol{p}_Q,l})$.
      ii. Perform a nearest neighbor mapping of $\check{\boldsymbol{x}}_{\boldsymbol{p}_Q,l}(\check{\mathbf{i}}_{\boldsymbol{p}_Q,l})$ into the Q-stage direct sum codebook $\mathbf{C}_{\boldsymbol{p}_Q} = \boldsymbol{C}_{p_1} + \boldsymbol{C}_{p_2} + \cdots + \boldsymbol{C}_{p_Q}$.
      iii. If the resulting nearest neighbor encoding decision k_{p_j} is different from the i_{p_j} obtain by puncturing $\boldsymbol{i}_l$ for any $j \in \{1, 2, \ldots, Q\}$, replace i_{p_j} with k_{p_j} and increment the counter for each such encoding decision change.
4. If the counter for encoding decision changes is nonzero, repeat from step 2, otherwise stop.

IM-Search Experimental Results						
Search Method	Rate (bpp)	0.063	0.127	0.190	0.254	0.317
	Number of Stages	8	16	24	32	40
	Stage Codebook Size	4	4	4	4	4
$M = 1$	PSNR (dB)	26.80	28.40	29.66	30.56	31.50
$M = 1$ & $IM = 1$	PSNR (dB)	26.84	28.50	29.75	30.66	31.57
$M = 4$	PSNR (dB)	27.12	28.87	30.04	31.04	31.88
$M = 4$ & $IM = 1$	PSNR (dB)	27.15	28.88	30.07	31.09	31.92
	Number of Stages	4	8	12	16	20
	Stage Codebook Size	16	16	16	16	16
$M = 1$	PSNR (dB)	27.34	28.95	29.99	30.92	31.71
$M = 1$ & $IM = 1$	PSNR (dB)	27.37	29.03	30.13	31.03	31.87
$M = 4$	PSNR (dB)	27.65	29.40	30.55	31.49	32.32
$M = 4$ & $IM = 1$	PSNR (dB)	27.67	29.41	30.57	31.52	32.38

Table 1: Performance of RVQs with 4 and 16 vectors per stage on green band of LANDSAT imagery.

Note the nonsequential nature of this multipath search technique. Conventional M-search algorithms require multipath searches over sequential combinations of stages (the size of M determines exactly how many consecutive stages), whereas the stage combinations selected for puncturing in the new method are arbitrary. For example, the first and last stages may be simultaneously punctured to improve the degree of joint encoder optimality between these two stages.

5 Experiments

The following experiments were conducted as a preliminary evaluation of the effectiveness of the new *iterated multipath* (IM)-search algorithm. First, RVQs with both sequential and M-search encoder codebooks where designed using the modified general iterative design procedure. The encoder codebooks were IM-searched, and one final joint optimization procedure was then applied to the decoder codebooks to insure decoder optimality with respect to the encoding decisions made by the combined M-search/IM-search encoder structure. (Note that if the encoder and decoder codebooks were identical, then this last joint decoder optimization procedure could not be performed without possibly corrupting the sequential search performance of the encoder.) Performance was then measured and compared to systems without the IM-search encoding step.

The test imagery was multispectral LANDSAT imagery. LANDSAT data consists of seven spectral bands. The RVQ code vectors were of size $252 = 6 \times 6 \times 7$ (6×6 spatial pixels across 7 spectral bands). Performance was measured as the peak signal-to-noise ratio (PSNR) for only the "green" spectral band (the peak signal value was assumed to be 255). As shown in Table , the performance gain obtained in these experiments ranged from 0.01 to 0.16 dB for RVQs with output rates from 0.063 to 0.317 bits per pixel (bpp). Generally, the higher the RVQ output rate, the larger the performance gain.

6 Some Observations

Greater performance gains are expected if the value of IM is increased by using multiple stage puncturing instead of single stage puncturing, and if similar to the M-search method, the IM-search algorithm is embedded into the design process. Research on methods of utilizing computationally efficient variations of the IM-search algorithm throughout the RVQ design process are on going. Since IM-search techniques satisfy necessary conditions for local joint optimality of RVQ encoder stages, additional work should lead to the development of computationally efficient RVQ encoders that can tolerate a high degree of direct sum codebook entanglement. Such an advance would be important because direct sum codebook entanglement permits a form of variable code vector density with direct sum codebooks, and hence, increased fidelity for sources with nonuniform distributions.

References

[1] C. F. Barnes and R. L. Frost. Necessary conditions for the optimality of residual vector quantizers. In *Abstracts of the IEEE International Symposium on Information Theory*, page 34, San Diego, CA, January 14–19, 1990.

[2] C. F. Barnes and R. L. Frost. Vector quantizers with direct sum codebooks. *IEEE Transactions on Information Theory*, 39(2):565–580, March 1993.

[3] C. F. Barnes and R. L. Frost. *Image Mathematics and Image Processing*, volume 84 of *Advances in Electronics and Electron Physics*, chapter Residual Vector Quantizers with Jointly Optimized Code Books, pages 1–59. Academic Press, 1992. Editited by P. W. Hawkes.

[4] C. F. Barnes and E. J. Holder. Successive approximation quantization with generalized decoding for wavelet transform image coding. In *Proceedings of the Twenty-Seventh Asilomar Conference on Signals, Systems, and Computers*, Pacific Grove, CA, November 1–3, 1993.

[5] T. Fine. Properties of an optimum digital system and applications. *IEEE Transactions on Information Theory*, pages 287–296, 1964.

[6] S. P. Lloyd. Least squares quantization in PCM. *Bell Laboratories Technical Note*, 1957. Published in the March 1982 Special Issue on Quantization: *IEEE Transactions on Information Theory, Part 1*, IT-28:129–137.

[7] F. Kossentini, M. J. T. Smith, and C. F. Barnes. Large block RVQ with multipath searching. In *Proceedings of the IEEE International Symposium on Circuts and Systems*, volume 5, pages 2276–2279, San Diego, CA, May 10–13, 1992.

[8] R. L. Frost and F. Xu. Trellis coded vector quantizers with direct sum codebooks. *to appear in IEEE Transactions on Communications*, 1994.

[9] F. Kossentini, M. J. T. Smith, and C. F. Barnes. Entropy-constrained residual vector quantization. In *Proceedings of the IEEE International Conference on Acoustics, Speech, and Signal Processing*, volume V, pages 598–601, 1993.

[10] H. R. Equitz and T. M. Cover. Successive refinement of information. *IEEE Transactions on Information Theory*, IT-37(2):269–275, March 1991.

[11] B. H. Juang and A. H. Gray. Multiple stage vector quantization for speech coding. In *Proceedings of the IEEE International Conference on Acoustics, Speech, and Signal Processing*, volume 1, pages 597–600, April 1982.

[12] C. F. Barnes and E. J. Holder. Classified variable rate residual vector quantization applied to image subband coding. In *Proceedings of the Data Compression Conference*, pages 272–281, Snowbird, UT, March 30–April 2, 1993.

[13] F. Jelinek and J. B. Anderson. Instrumentable tree encoding of information sources. *IEEE Transactions on Information Theory*, IT-17:118–119, January 1971.

[14] C. F. Barnes. Two-dimensional signal constellations for non-linear coset codes based on multistage codes. In *Proceedings of the Conference on Information Sciences and Systems*, page 405, The Johns Hopkins University, March 20–22, 1991.

[15] C. F. Barnes. Direct sum signal constellations for coded modulation. In *Proceedings of the Conference on Information Sciences and Systems*, volume I, pages 300–306, Princeton University, March 18–22, 1992.

[16] C. F. Barnes. *Coding and Quantization*, volume 14 of *DIMACS Series in Discrete Mathematics and Theoretical Computer Science*, chapter Tree Structured Signal Space Codes, pages 33–53. American Mathematical Society, DIMACS/IEEE Workshop, Rutgers University, October 19–22, 1992. Editited by R. Calderbank, G. D. Forney, Jr, and N. Moayeri.

[17] J. Salillas and N. Farvardin. Adaptive multi-stage vector quantization of images. In *Proceedings, EUSIPCO*, pages 1239–1242, Brussels, Belgium, August 1992.

The Minimax Redundancy is a Lower Bound for Most Sources *

Neri Merhav† Meir Feder‡

Abstract

The capacity of the channel induced by a given class of sources is well known to be an attainable lower bound on the redundancy of universal codes w.r.t this class, both in the minimax sense and in the Bayesian (maximin) sense. Our main contribution is a relatively simple proof that the capacity is essentially a lower bound also in a stronger sense, that is, for "most" sources in the class. This result extends Rissanen's lower bound for parametric families. Finally, we demonstrate the applicability of this result in several examples.

I. Introduction

In the traditional probabilistic setting of the problem of universal lossless source coding w.r.t a given class of information sources, the objective is to design a single data compression scheme that performs well, in some sense, for every source in the class. The sources in this class are usually assumed to be indexed by some variable $\theta \in \Lambda$. The performance of a given code, with a length function $L(\cdot)$, is judged on the basis of redundancy function $R_n(L, \theta)$, which is defined as the difference between the expected code length of $L(\cdot)$ w.r.t a given source in the class P_θ and the nth order entropy of P_θ normalized by the length n of the input vector to be encoded.

There are several notions of universality that were first defined by Davisson [2]. The main ones are the *maximin* universality and the *minimax* universality. In the former, there is a Bayesian approach: the universal encoder treats the index θ as a random variable whose probability distribution is assumed worst in the sense of maximizing the minimum *expected* redundancy, i.e., the maximin redundancy. In the latter, the variable θ is considered deterministic and the goal is to find a code that

*This research was supported by the Wolfson Research Awards administrated by the Israel Academy of Science and Humanities.

†N. Merhav is with the Department of Electrical Engineering, Technion-Israel Institute of Technology, Haifa 32000, Israel.

‡M. Feder is with the Department of Electrical Engineering - Systems, Tel Aviv University, Tel Aviv 69978, Israel. Part of this research was done while he visited Sonderforschungsbereich 343, "Diskrete Strukturen in der Mathematik", Universität Bielefeld, Germany.

minimizes the worst case redundancy $\sup_\theta R_n(L, \theta)$, namely, to achieve the minimax redundancy.

Several years after Davisson's paper [2] it was established, first by Gallager [5], and then independently by Davisson and Leon-Garcia [3], Ryabko [7] and others, that the minimax redundancy and the maximin redundancy are equivalent and that they are both equal to the capacity of the channel defined by the set of conditional probability measures $P_\theta(x^n)$, of the data $x^n = (x_1, \ldots, x_n)$ given θ. In particular, for parametric families of sources, that is, for the case where θ is a k-dimensional parameter vector, the minimax redundancy, and hence also the maximin redundancy and the capacity of the corresponding channel, was shown to be given by $0.5k \log n/n$ plus higher order terms, under certain regularity conditions

Rissanen [6] has strengthened the notion of universality w.r.t parametric families by showing that $0.5k \log n/n$ is not only an achievable lower bound in the minimax sense or the Bayesian sense, but also a lower bound for "most" sources in the class. Here by "most" sources we mean *every* point θ except for a subset of points whose volume (Lebesgue measure) vanishes as n grows. Rissanen's proof, however, relies heavily on the structure of the parametric family and essentially the main insight that can be gained from his work is that the redundancy is strongly related to the richness of the class, which in the parametric case is proportional to the dimension k of the parameter vector.

Our first main result is an extension of Rissanen's stronger notion of universality to the general case. Specifically, we show in Section II that the Shannon capacity of the induced channel is a lower bound on the redundancy that holds simultaneously for all sources in the class except for a subset of points whose probability, under the capacity-achieving probability measure, is vanishing as n tends to infinity. This means that the minimax redundancy and the lower bound essentially coincide for most choices of θ. Weighting the index θ by the capacity-achieving prior makes sense for reasons that will be explained in Section II. Moreover, if the capacity-achieving probability density happens to be bounded away from zero, as is normally the case in parametric families, the above result holds also for most sources in the Lebesgue measure sense and therefore Rissanen's result for parametric families can be obtained as a special case.

The proof of the bound in Section II is completely different and considerably simpler than Rissanen's proof [6]. However, it does not allow a free choice of any prior, other than the capacity-achieving prior, that might be reasonable as well for weighting the set of points that violate the bound. In Section III, we provide another variant of our result which enables any prior on the index set, but then the *random coding* capacity of the induced channel rather than its Shannon capacity is obtained as a lower bound. Here the random coding capacity refers to the normalized logarithm of the maximum number M of randomly chosen points $\theta_1, \ldots, \theta_M$ (corresponding to a random channel code), which form, with high probability, a set of distinguishable sources $P_{\theta_1}, \ldots, P_{\theta_M}$. Strictly speaking, this result is slightly weaker than the former because the random coding capacity might be smaller than the Shannon capacity in some cases (e.g., nonergodic channels). However, for most cases of practical interest in the context of universal coding (as we demonstrate in Section IV), the Shannon capacity and the random coding capacity are equivalent and hence the resulting bound is virtually as tight. We believe that another advantage of this random coding capacity result is that it may add some new insight about the relation between redundancy and capacity. Specifically, in the proof of this result the redundancy is linked directly, not only to the mathematical notion of capacity as the maximum mutual information, but also to the *operational* notion of capacity as the maximum attainable transmission rate that still enables reliable communication.

II. The Shannon Capacity Lower Bound

We first define some notation. $x^n = (x_1, \ldots, x_n)$ will denote a given string of symbols from a countable set A. The space of n-sequences will be denoted by A^n. A random vector in A^n will be denoted by $X^n = (X_1, \ldots, X_n)$. Let $\{P_\theta, \theta \in \Lambda\}$ be a class of probability mass functions (PMFs) of n-sequences in A^n, where the index set Λ, together with Borel subsets of Λ, form a measurable space. $E_\theta\{\cdot\}$ will denote the mathematical expectation w.r.t P_θ and the nth order entropy of P_θ is defined as $H_\theta(X^n) = -E_\theta \log P_\theta(X^n)$ where logarithms throughout the sequel will be taken to the base 2 unless specified otherwise. A uniquely decipherable (UD) encoder for n-sequences maps each possible source string x^n to a binary word whose length will be denoted by $L(x^n)$, where by Kraft's inequality, $\sum_{x^n \in A^n} 2^{-L(x^n)} \leq 1$. The redundancy associated with a given encoder for n-sequences is defined as $R_n(L,\theta) = \frac{1}{n}[E_\theta L(X^n) - H_\theta(X^n)]$.

For the sake of convenience, let us ignore the integer length constraint associated with the length function $L(\cdot)$ and allow any function from A^n to the nonnegative reals such that the Kraft inequality is satisfied. The minimax redundancy is defined as $R_n^+ = \min_L \sup_{\theta \in \Lambda} R_n(L,\theta)$. To define the maximin redundancy, let us assign a probability measure $w(\cdot)$ on Λ and let us define the mixture source $P(x^n) = \int_\Lambda w(d\theta) P_\theta(x^n)$. The average redundancy associated with a length function $L(\cdot)$, is defined as $R_n(L,w) = \int_\Lambda w(d\theta) R_n(L,\theta)$. The minimum expected redundancy for a given w is defined as $R_n(w) = \min_L R_n(L,w)$. Finally, the maximin redundancy is the worst case minimum expected redundancy among all priors w, i.e., $R_n^- = \sup_w R_n(w)$. It is easy to see [2] that the maximin redundancy is identical to the normalized capacity of the channel defined by the conditional probability measures $P_\theta(x^n)$, i.e., $R_n^- = \frac{C_n}{n} = \sup_w \frac{1}{n} I_w(\Theta; X^n)$, where $I_w(\Theta; X^n)$ is the mutual information induced by the joint measure $w(\theta) \cdot P_\theta(x^n)$. Gallager [5] was the first to show that if Λ along with its Borel subsets forms a measurable space and if $P_\theta(x^n)$ is a measurable function of θ for every x^n (henceforth, Gallager's measurability conditions), then $R_n^- = R_n^+$ and hence they are both equal to C_n/n. This means that the normalized capacity is an attainable lower bound on the redundancy both in the minimax sense and in the expected redundancy sense.

Suppose that the capacity C_n is attained by some prior w^*. Our first main result strengthens the above results by stating that C_n/n is also essentially a lower bound on $R_n(L,\theta)$ for all $\theta \in \Lambda$ except for a subset of points whose probability under w^* vanishes as $n \to \infty$ provided that $C_n \to \infty$ (which is normally the case).

Theorem 1 *For any length function L of a UD code and every $\epsilon > 0$, $R_n(L,\theta) > (1-\epsilon)C_n/n$ for all $\theta \in \Lambda$ except for points in a subset $B \subset \Lambda$ where $w^*(B) \leq e \cdot 2^{-\epsilon C_n}$, $w^*(B)$ being the probability of B under w^*.*

Proof. For a given length function L and $\epsilon > 0$, let $B = \{\theta : R_n(L,\theta) \leq (1-\epsilon)C_n/n\}$. Since $R_n(L,\theta) \leq (1-\epsilon)C_n/n$ for every $\theta \in B$, a-fortiori the minimax redundancy within B cannot exceed $(1-\epsilon)C_n/n$. But by Gallager's redundancy-capacity Theorem [5] the unnormalized minimax redundancy within B is equal to the capacity C_B of the channel from B to X^n. Let $Z = 1\{\Theta \in B\}$ where Θ is governed by w^*, namely, $\Pr\{Z = 1\} = w^*(B)$. Since $Z \to \Theta \to X^n$ is a Markov chain, we have

$$\begin{aligned} C_n = I_{w^*}(\Theta; X^n) &= I(Z; X^n) + I(\Theta; X^n|Z) \\ &= I(Z; X^n) + I(\Theta; X^n|Z=1) \cdot \Pr\{Z=1\} \\ &\quad + I(\Theta; X^n|Z=0) \cdot \Pr\{Z=0\} \end{aligned} \tag{1}$$

But $I(\Theta; X^n|Z=1) \leq C_B \leq (1-\epsilon)C_n$, and $I(\Theta; X^n|Z=0) \leq C_n$. Therefore, we have

$$\begin{aligned} C_n &\leq I(Z; X^n) + (1-\epsilon)C_n \cdot w^*(B) + C_n \cdot (1 - w^*(B)) \\ &\leq H(Z) + (1-\epsilon)C_n \cdot w^*(B) + C_n \cdot (1 - w^*(B)) \end{aligned} \tag{2}$$

where $H(Z) = h(w^*(B))$ is the entropy of Z, $h(\cdot)$ being the binary entropy function. Now elementary algebra yields

$$\log \frac{1}{w^*(B)} + \frac{1 - w^*(B)}{w^*(B)} \log \frac{1}{1 - w^*(B)} \geq \epsilon C_n, \tag{3}$$

which completes the proof by observing that the second term on the left-hand side of (3) never exceeds $\log e$.

Discussion: We would like to point out several aspects of the significance and the interpretation of Theorem 1.

Weighting the index set by the capacity-achieving prior. While Rissanen's lower bound [6] holds for the parametric case for most sources in the uniform measure sense, our result holds in the sense of the capacity-achieving prior w^*. At first glance, the Lebesgue measure formulation seems more plausible because there is no apparent reason to consider some parameter values as more important than others and hence, when scanning all points $\theta \in \Lambda$ and judging the performance of L at each point, every such point should weigh equally.

A closer look, however, tells us that this approach is not always justified and in some cases it might yield misleading or meaningless results. Consider the following extreme example. The index set is $\Lambda = \{1, 2, \ldots, M\}$, P_1 is a ternary dyadic memoryless source with letter probabilities $\Pr(0) = 1/2$, $\Pr(1) = \Pr(2) = 1/4$, and $P_2 = P_3 = \ldots = P_M$ all coincide with the memoryless source whose letter probabilities are $\Pr(0) = \Pr(1) = 1/4$, $\Pr(2) = 1/2$. Now, the capacity C_n of the channel corresponding to this class tends to $\log 2 = 1$ as $n \to \infty$, independently of M, because there are only two *distinct* sources in the class. However, if we choose L to be the length function of the Huffman code for $P_2 = ... = P_M$, then the redundancy is *identically* zero for these sources, and hence there is no nontrivial lower bound for most sources in the uniform counting sense, in spite of the fact that $C_n > 0$.

In contrast, if the indices $\{1, \ldots, M\}$ are weighted by the capacity-achieving prior, which assigns $w^*\{1\} = 1/2$ and $w^*\{2, 3, \ldots, M\} = 1/2$, there is a natural adaptation to the fact that there are effectively only two different sources. The general conclusion is that this happens because the capacity-achieving prior assigns higher probability to regions of Λ where there is a better discrimination among the sources $\{P_\theta\}$ (and hence X^n is more informative about θ), and smaller probabilities to "noisier" channel inputs where the sources of the class are closer to each other. In these noisier regions there is a weaker justification for treating the sources as distinct.

Achievability. In many examples it is known that a good choice of a universal code is a *mixture code*, i.e., $L(x^n) = -\log \int_\Lambda w(d\theta)P_\theta(x^n)$ for some weight function $w(\cdot)$ that integrates to unity. This turns out to be generally true in a fairly strong sense: For any universal code (i.e., independent of θ) $L(x^n)$ there exists a mixture code $L'(x^n)$ such that for *every* $\theta \in \Lambda$, $R_n(L', \theta) \leq R_n(L, \theta)$. This statement follows straightforwardly from certain properties of projections of probability measures on convex sets [1]. Specifically, assume that $K(x^n) = 2^{-L(x^n)}$ is a probability measure of n-vectors. Now construct $L'(x^n) = -\log Q(x^n)$ where Q is the I-projection of K on the set E of all possible mixtures $\int_\Lambda w(d\theta)P_\theta(x^n)$, i.e., $Q = \text{argmin}_{P \in E} D(P||K)$, and the minimizer is unique (if existent) because of the convexity of E. Now, by Theorem 2.2 of [1], $D(P||K) \geq D(P||Q) + D(Q||K) \geq D(P||Q)$ for every $P \in E$ and hence, in particular, for every $P = P_\theta$, $\theta \in \Lambda$. But $D(P_\theta||K)$ and $D(P_\theta||Q)$ are exactly the unnormalized redundancies $n \cdot R_n(L, \theta)$ and $n \cdot R_n(L', \theta)$, respectively, and therefore the claim follows. This means that when seeking universal codes, one can restrict himself to mixture codes without loss of optimality, virtually in any reasonable sense. Therefore, the minimax redundancy must take the form

$$\inf_L \sup_{\theta \in \Lambda} R_n(L, \theta) = \frac{1}{n} \inf_w \sup_{\theta \in \Lambda} \sum_{x^n \in A^n} P_\theta(x^n) \log \frac{P_\theta(x^n)}{\int_{\theta' \in \Lambda} w(d\theta')P_{\theta'}(x^n)} \tag{4}$$

which is known under Gallager's measurability conditions [5] to coincide with C_n. This means that the mixture code L^* corresponding to the best choice of w guarantees that $R_n(L^*, \theta) \leq C_n/n$ for every $\theta \in \Lambda$, namely, the upper bound and lower bound meet for almost every θ.

III. The Random Coding Capacity Lower Bound

In this section, we develop a variant of Theorem 1, in which the lower bound on the redundancy is given in terms of the random coding capacity, namely, the logarithm of the maximum number of randomly chosen points $\{\Theta_i\}$ that form a set of distinguishable sources. This capacity depends on the probability distribution $w(\cdot)$ under which the points are chosen, and the bound holds for all $\theta \in \Lambda$ except for a set whose measure vanishes w.r.t $w(\cdot)$. As mentioned in the Introduction, here, unlike in Theorem 1, $w(\cdot)$ can be any probability distribution, not necessarily the capacity achieving distribution.

The derivation of the bound follows from an analysis of a special case where $\Lambda = \{1, 2, \ldots, M\}$ and M is a finite integer being either fixed or growing with n. In other words, our class contains M known information sources $P_1, \ldots, P_M$. Let Ω_i denote the decision region associated with the ML rule, i.e.,

$$\Omega_i = \{x^n \in A^n : \quad P_i(x^n) > \max_{j \neq i} P_j(x^n)\} \tag{5}$$

and let the probability of error be defined as $P_e = \frac{1}{M}\sum_{i=1}^{M} P_i(\Omega_i^c)$, where the superscript c denotes the complementary set. Similarly to the notation in Section II, $R_n(L, i)$ will denote the redundancy of L w.r.t P_i.

Theorem 2 *For every $\epsilon > 0$, and every UD code, $R_n(L, i) \geq (1 - \epsilon)n^{-1} \log M$, for every $1 \leq i \leq M$ except for a subset of indices B where*

$$\frac{|B|}{M} \leq \frac{P_e \log M + 2}{\epsilon \log M}. \tag{6}$$

The Theorem tells us that if $M \to \infty$ (or just if M is very large) but still $P_e \to 0$ as $n \to \infty$, then the redundancy is essentially lower bounded by $n^{-1} \log M$ for all M sources except for a negligibly small fraction of them. The proof is omitted for the sake of brevity but the underlying idea is that this is a special case of Theorem 1 above because the capacity of the induced channel is about $\log M$ when the sources are well distinguishable (small P_e) and the uniform prior is nearly optimal, so the probability of B under the uniform prior (which is the same as $|B|/M$) is small.

We next show how Theorem 2 can be used to derive the more general desired result. Let us return to the general class of information sources $\{P_\theta, \theta \in \Lambda\}$ satisfying Gallager's measurability conditions. Let $w(\cdot)$ be an arbitrary probability measure on Λ and let $\Theta_1, \ldots, \Theta_M$ denote M independent random points selected from Λ under the probability measure w. Suppose, without loss of generality, that Θ_1 has generated X^n. Let $\bar{P}_e(M, n, w)$ denote the average error probability, namely, the probability that $\Theta_1, \ldots, \Theta_M$ and X^n are such that for some $2 \leq i \leq M$, $P_{\Theta_i}(X^n) \geq P_{\Theta_1}(X^n)$. Now let $M(n, \delta, w)$ be the largest integer M such that $\bar{P}_e(M, n, w) \leq \delta$ and finally, define the *random coding δ-capacity with respect to w* as $C_R(n, \delta, w) \triangleq \log M(n, \delta, w)$.

Theorem 3 *Let $\{P_\theta, \theta \in \Lambda\}$ satisfy Gallager's measurability conditions and let w be any probability measure on Λ. Then for every $\epsilon > 0$, $0 < \delta < 1$, and every UD code $R_n(L, \theta) \geq (1 - \epsilon)C_R(n, \delta, w)/n$ for every $\theta \in \Lambda$ except for a subset of points $B' \in \Lambda$ such that*

$$w(B') \leq \frac{\delta C_R(n, \delta, w) + 2}{\epsilon C_R(n, \delta, w)}. \tag{7}$$

Eq. (7) is of course meaningful if δ is kept very small compared to ϵ and if $C_R(n, \delta, w) \to \infty$. The tightest lower bound results from optimization of w in the sense of maximizing $C_R(n, \delta, w)$. The resulting maximum denoted $C_R(n, \delta)$, and henceforth referred to as the *random coding δ-capacity*, is essentially the lower bound for every θ except for a set whose probability under the *optimal* prior is small.

We shall not provide here the proof but the main idea is the following. Consider a two-step procedure of randomly selecting a point in Λ, where first, we select M independent random points $\Theta_1, \ldots, \Theta_M$ under $w(\cdot)$, and then, we randomly select an index $1 \leq i \leq M$ of θ_i with equal probabilities. On one hand, this is obviously equivalent to a direct random selection of Θ_i under $w(\cdot)$. On the other hand, under the above described two-step random selection, it will be convenient to show (using the result of Theorem 2), that the lower bound holds for most choices of Θ_i.

Two comments about Theorem 3 are in order.

Bounds for most sources in the uniform measure sense. Since the measure w in Theorem 3 is arbitrary, one can obtain a lower bound in the uniform measure sense and thereby extend more directly Rissanen's result [6]. This can be done by redefining $C_R(n,\delta)$ as the supremum of $C_R(n,\delta,w)$ over all priors w whose densities are bounded away from zero, i.e., all w such that $dw/d\mu \geq \Delta > 0$, where $dw/d\mu$ is the Radon-Nykodim derivative of w w.r.t the uniform probability measure μ. In this case, Theorem 3 holds, with $C_R(n,\delta,w)$ as a lower bound, outside B' with $\mu(B') \leq [\delta C_R(n,\delta,w) + 2]/[\epsilon \Delta C_R(n,\delta,w)]$. However, the restriction to w's that are uniformly bounded away from zero might result in a strictly smaller random coding capacity.

More general random coding distributions. The proof of Theorem 3 would continue to hold if rather than using M independent copies of a random variable governed by w, one would use any joint probability measure of $(\Theta_1, \ldots, \Theta_M)$ with the property that the mixture of its marginals, $M^{-1}\sum_{i=1}^{M} w_i(\cdot)$, agrees with $w(\cdot)$. For instance, let $\Lambda = [0,1]$ and consider the grid $\theta_i = i/M$, $i = 0, \ldots, M-1$. Now, let $\Theta_i = \theta_i + \alpha$, where α is uniformly distributed in $[0, 1/M]$. Then, the mixture of marginals of $\{\Theta_i\}$ is uniform on $[0,1]$. This might be useful when the evaluation of the capacity is easier with this constellation than with that of Theorem 3 (see Examples A and B in the next section). In spite of this fact, we preferred to formulate Theorem 3 with independent selections of $\{\Theta_i\}$ because this is in the spirit of conventional random coding techniques.

IV. Examples

In this section we demonstrate the applicability of our results in several specific examples of classes of sources.

A. Parametric Families

Let $\{P_\theta, \theta \in \Lambda\}$ be a parametric family, where Λ is a bounded subset of the k-dimensional Euclidean space. For Rissanen's lower bound [6] it is required that there exists an estimator $\hat{\theta} = \hat{\theta}(x^n)$ for θ, such that for every $\theta \in \Lambda$, every $c > 0$ and every

$n \geq n_0(c)$,

$$P_\theta \left\{ x^n : ||\hat{\theta}(x^n) - \theta|| > \frac{c}{\sqrt{n}} \right\} \leq \epsilon(c) \tag{8}$$

where $||\cdot||$ denotes the Euclidean norm (or the maximal component norm) and $\epsilon(c) \to 0$ as $c \to \infty$.

We next show that the existence of such an estimator *implies* that for the given parametric family, the maximum number of distinguishable randomly chosen points in Λ is proportional to $n^{k/2}$ and hence this condition is *weaker* than Rissanen's condition for the validity of the lower bound $0.5k \log n/n$.

In this case it is easier to apply Theorem 3 by using uniform grids with random offsets $\Theta_1, \ldots, \Theta_M$, rather than by independent random selection of the M points (see second comment after Theorem 3). Specifically, let $G_n = \{\theta_1, \ldots, \theta_M\}$ be the grid of k-dimensional vectors $\theta_i \in \Lambda$ whose components are all integer multiples of $2c/\sqrt{n}$. In our random set $\{\Theta_1, \ldots, \Theta_M\}$ let every Θ_i be given by $\theta_i + \eta$ where η is a random vector uniformly distributed within the k-dimensional cube whose all sides are $2c/\sqrt{n}$. By an argument similar to that of the proof of Theorem 3, if we show that Theorem 2 is applicable to $\{\Theta_1, \ldots, \Theta_M\}$ for *every* η, then this will imply that the lower bound holds for most points in Λ in the Lebesgue measure sense. This in turn is immediate if we consider the suboptimal decision rule which picks the ith source if $\hat{\theta}$ falls in the cube whose center is Θ_i, because then the probability of error is by definition less than $\epsilon(c)$ (independently of η), which in turn, can be made smaller than δ if c is sufficiently large. Since the number of grid points is proportional to $n^{k/2}$ the desired result follows.

B. Piecewise Fixed Sources

Let Q_1 and Q_2 be two given distinct probability assignments on data sequences, and for $i = 0, 1, \ldots, n$ let us define

$$P_i(x^n) = Q_1(x_1^i) \cdot Q_2(x_{i+1}^n) \tag{9}$$

where x_i^j denotes the substring $(x_i, \ldots, x_j)$ for $i \leq j$ and the empty string for $i > j$. The probability of the empty string (under both Q_1 and Q_2) is defined as unity. We shall show that if Q_1 and Q_2 are sufficiently "distant" the capacity associated with the class $\{P_i, i = 0, 1, \ldots, n\}$ behaves like $\log n$.

Assume that Q_1 and Q_2 are such that for every $\epsilon > 0$, $|i - j| > n^\epsilon$ implies that $P_i\{x^n : P_j(x^n) > P_i(x^n)\} = o(1/n)$. (For instance, if Q_1 and Q_2 are memoryless sources then $P_i\{x^n : P_j(x^n) > P_i(x^n)\}$ decays exponentially with $|i - j|$ and the assumption definitely holds). We shall use again the idea of a random grid similarly as in Example A.

Fix $\epsilon > 0$ and select $M = n^{1-\epsilon}$ integers $i_j = l + j \cdot n^\epsilon$, $j = 1, \ldots, M$, where l is uniformly distributed on the integers $\{1, \ldots, n^\epsilon\}$. Since $\{i_1, \ldots, i_M\}$ are such that $|i_j - i_k| > n^\epsilon$ for every $j \neq k$, then by the union bound, the probability of error is less than

$$(M-1)\max_{\{k:|i_k-i_j|>n^\epsilon\}} P_{i_j}\{P_{i_k}(x^n) > P_{i_j}(x^n)\} \le n \max_{\{k:|i_k-i_j|>n^\epsilon\}} P_{i_j}\{P_{i_k}(x^n) > P_{i_j}(x^n)\} \tag{10}$$

which vanishes with n (independently of l) under the above assumption. Therefore, $C_n > (1-\epsilon)\log n$. The bound is achievable by an encoder that seeks the best partitioning of the data in the sense of minimizing the total Shannon code length $[-\log Q_1(x_1^i)] + [-\log Q_2(x_{i+1}^n)]$ and adds $\log n$ bits to encode the best choice of i.

C. Arbitrarily Varying Sources

The memoryless arbitrarily varying source (AVS) is defined by

$$P(x^n|s^n) = \prod_{t=1}^{n} p(x_t|s_t) \tag{11}$$

where $s^n = (s_1, \ldots, s_n)$. The variable s_t, which is referred to as the *state* of the source at time t, is assumed to take on values in some finite set S. If we scan all possible state sequences s^n, we can view the AVS as a class of sources indexed by $\theta = s^n$ and the index set Λ is S^n. Thus, the problem of universal coding for the AVS is that of efficient data compression in the absence of knowledge about the underlying state sequence.

The AVS can be viewed also as a memoryless channel with transition probabilities $\{p(x|s)\}_{x\in A, s\in S}$, where the input is s^n and the output is x^n. Therefore the notion of capacity is more natural in this example than in the other examples. In order to use Theorem 1 in a meaningful manner in this example let us partition the state sequence space S^n into equivalence classes defined by the compositions (types) of the different state sequences. The type $T(s^n)$ of a state sequence s^n is the set of all state sequences $\sigma^n \in S^n$ for which the number of occurrences of every element $s \in S$ in σ^n is equal to the number of occurrences of the same element in s^n. The relative frequency of s in s^n will be denoted by $\hat{q}(s)$.

Now, if we treat every given type $T(s^n)$ as a separate index set, the best prior w^* is the uniform distribution μ on $T(s^n)$ which asymptotically achieves the per-symbol mutual information $I(s^n)$ associated with joint probability measure $p(s,x) = \hat{q}(s)p(x|s)$. Thus, asymptotically C_n/n is never less than $I(s^n)$ and hence, by Theorem 1, the normalized redundancy is lower bounded by $(1-\epsilon)I(s^n)$ for almost every state sequence in $T(s^n)$. This bound can be shown to be achievable for every s^n by a mixture code (see [4]).

D. Noisy Samples of Learnable Functions

An interesting special case of the AVS occurs when the the state variable s_i is given by some binary function f of another variable $z_i \in Z$, i.e., $s_i = f(z_i)$. For simplicity, let us assume that the channel corresponding to $p(x|s)$ is additive, namely, $x_i = f(z_i)+w_i$, where w_i is a binary random variable with $\Pr(w_i = 1) = p$ and the summation is modolu 2. Here $z_1, \ldots, z_n$ is some fixed sequence and the index set Λ is a certain class F of allowable binary functions f. This model has been widely studied in the context of computational learning theory.

It turns out that there is a relation between the learnability of functions in F and the existence of universal codes for the noisy labels $\{x_i\}$ given $\{z_i\}$ as side information. This happens because both these properties are connected to the *capacity* (or the Vapnik-Chervonenkis (VC) dimension) of F which is defined as the length n of the longest existing input sequence $z_1, \ldots, z_n$ for which all 2^n possible binary sequences $(f(z_1), \ldots, f(z_n))$ are obtained when f scans F.

Following [8] the maximum number of binary sequences $\{f(z_1), \ldots, f(z_n)\}$ that can be obtained by a class F whose VC dimension is d, is 2^n for $n \leq d$ and upper bounded by $\sum_{k=0}^{d} n!/[k!(n-k)!] = O(n^d)$ for $n > d$. Thus, following Example C, the best attainable normalized redundancy C_n/n is given by $1 - h(p)$ for $n < d$, and upper bounded by $(1 + o(1))d \log n/n$ for $n > d$. In other words, universal coding (in the sense of approaching the entropy) is possible if and only if the VC dimension of F is finite, and if this is the case the least attainable redundancy is essentially never larger than $d \log n/n$. For many parametric families the VC dimension d agrees with the dimension k of the parameter vector.

References

[1] I. Csiszár, "I-Divergence Geometry of Probability Distributions and Minimization Problems," *Ann. Probab.*, Vol. 3, No. 1, pp. 146-158, 1975.

[2] L. D. Davisson, "Universal Noiseless Coding," *IEEE Trans. Inform. Theory*, Vol. IT-19, No. 6, pp. 783–795, November 1973.

[3] L. D. Davisson and A. Leon-Garcia, "A Source Matching Approach to Finding Minimax Codes," *IEEE Trans. Inform. Theory,* Vol. IT-26, no. 2, pp. 166-174, March 1980.

[4] M. Feder and N. Merhav, "Universal Coding for Arbitrarily Varying Sources," in preparation.

[5] R. G. Gallager, "Source Coding with Side Information and Universal Coding," unpublished manuscript, Sept. 1976.

[6] J. Rissanen, "Universal Coding, Information, Prediction, and Estimation," *IEEE Trans. Inform. Theory*, Vol. IT-30, No. 4, pp. 629–636, July 1984.

[7] B. Ya. Ryabko, "Encoding a Source with Unknown but Ordered Probabilities," *Problems in Information Transmission*, pp. 134-138, October 1979.

[8] V. N. Vapnik and A. Ya. Chervonenkis, "On the Uniform Convergence of Relative Frequencies of Events to Their Probabilities," *Theory of Probab. and its Appl.,* Vol. XVI, pp. 264-280, 1971.

Differential State Quantization of High Order Gauss-Markov Process

Anurag Bist
Dept. of Electrical Engineering
University of Hawaii
Honolulu, HI 96822
e-mail : anurag@wiliki.eng.hawaii.edu

Abstract

We analyze a differential technique of tracking and quantizing a continuous time Gauss-Markov process using the process and its derivatives. By using fine quantization approximations we derive expressions for the time-average smoothed error. Analytical bounds are derived on the overall smoothed error and it is confirmed that the differential scheme outperforms vector quantization of the scalar process, state component quantization, and state vector quantization. It is shown that when the overall rate R in bits per second is high, the optimal smoothed error varies as $\frac{1}{R^3}$ for the differential scheme. This is better than the performance of DPCM and a modified vector DPCM, analyzed under the same framework. For both these schemes the asymptotic variation of the smoothed error is $\frac{1}{R^2}$ at rate R. For differential state quantization, the resulting optimal size of the vector quantizers are small and can be used in practice.

1 Introduction

We address the problem of tracking and differentially quantizing a continous time Gauss-Markov process by looking at an augmented state vector consisting of the process and its derivatives. Traditional approaches to analyze quantization systems rely on the discrete time domain analyses. In these analyses the measure of performance is the quantization error when the transmission rate is measured in bits per source symbol. If one assumes a finite bandwidth process, then the reconstruction errors in the discrete time domain and the continous time domain are equivalent. However, in real life all processes are of infinite bandwidth. Thus, we have to define a time-average smoothed error of our estimate, as done in [1] and [2]. Furthermore, for a higher order Gauss-Markov process, the sampled process is no longer Markov. For such cases, to do an exact analysis, we have to consider the process and its derivatives jointly as a vector. For a fixed transmission rate, for an infinite bandwidth random process, there always exist a tradeoff between sampling and quantization. In [2] we analyzed this tradeoff for several quantization systems for a high order Gauss-Markov process. In this paper we extend the analysis of [2] and analyze differential quantization of the state vector and compare its performance with other traditional differential systems.

We analyze and evaluate the performance of a quantization scheme which differentially quantizes an augmented vector, which we call the state vector, consisting of an n-th order

1068-0314/94 $3.00 © 1994 IEEE

Gauss-Markov process and its first $(n-1)$ derivatives. We show that for a second order baseband process the optimal smoothed error for the differential scheme varies approximately as $\frac{1}{R^3}$, where R is the overall rate in bits per second. The performance of this differential scheme is better than state vector quantization, state component quantization and vector quantization of the scalar process. The optimal vector quantizer size that we obtain is small and can be used in practice.

We consider the case of a bandpass spectrum and analyze the performance of the differential scheme as the bandwidth of the bandpass process varies. It is shown that the performance of all the quantization schemes deteriorates as the bandwidth of the bandpass process increases. The differential scheme still gives the best performance in terms of the optimal smoothed error among all the schemes analyzed.

Finally, we analyze two other known differential systems, DPCM and a modified vector DPCM, under the same framework. The smoothed error for both these schemes approximately varies as $\frac{1}{R^2}$, which is inferior to the $\frac{1}{R^3}$ variation in the differential state quantization.

This paper is organized as follows. In the next section we describe the state space model that we use for representing an n-th order Gauss-Markov process and evaluate the asymptotic expressions for the smoothed error. In Section 3 we describe differential quantization of the state. We give an example of a second order baseband process and compare the performance of the differential scheme with several previously analyzed schemes. In section 4 we consider a bandpass process and examine the performance of the differential scheme as the bandwidth of the bandpass process decreases. Section 5 compares the performance of two other differential systems. Finally, in section 6, we conclude giving the salient contributions of this work.

2 Gauss-Markov Model and Reconstruction Filters

Figure 1 shows a block diagram of a communication system which estimates and quantizes a vector random process. The input to the system is an n-th order stationary Gauss-Markov process and we estimate the state $\mathbf{S}(t)$, which is an augmented vector process consisting of the process and its first $(n-1)$ derivatives. The state space representation of the vector process $\mathbf{S}(t)$ is given, for $t > 0$, as

$$\dot{\mathbf{S}}(t) = A\mathbf{S}(t) + Bw(t), \tag{2.1}$$

where $A \epsilon \mathcal{R}^{n \times n}$, $B \epsilon \mathcal{R}^{n \times 1}$ and $w(t)$ is zero mean, white Gaussian noise. We can express the process to be quantized as $x(t) = C\mathbf{S}(t)$, where C is the output state space matrix. The covariance of the noise process $w(t)$ is given by $E\{w(t)w(s)\} = \delta(t-s)$, where δ is the Dirac delta function. The white noise $w(t)$ has intensity 1; this is without loss of generality because we can always scale our input with the vector B.

We are interested in finding an estimate of the state vector. As shown in [2], we can write down two such estimates : one which corresponds to a prediction filter and the other to a smoothing filter. When the sampling interval τ is small, both these estimates of the state $\hat{\mathbf{S}}(t)$ lead to nearly the same expression for the error covariance matrix $\mathbf{c_S}(t) = E\{(\mathbf{S}(t) - \hat{\mathbf{S}}(t))(\mathbf{S}(t) - \hat{\mathbf{S}}(t))^T\}$. Since the optimal sampling intervals are different for different source coding schemes, a fair measure of performance is given by averaging the reconstruction error over one whole sampling interval. This smoothed error is given by

$\zeta_{sm}(\tau) = \frac{1}{\tau}\int_0^\tau E\{(x(t) - \hat{x}(t))^2\}dt$. This can be rewritten as :

$$\zeta_{sm}(\tau) = \frac{1}{\tau}\int_0^\tau C\mathbf{c_S}(t)C^T dt \approx C\mathcal{E}C^T + C(A\mathcal{E} + \mathcal{E}A^T + BB^T)C^T\frac{\tau}{2}, \tag{2.2}$$

where $\mathcal{E}$ is the covariance matrix of the quantization error and $C = [1, 0, \cdots, 0]$ is a row vector. In all of our analysis we concentrate on evaluating the bounds for the smoothed error using this asymptotic expression (2.2).

3 Differential State Quantization

In this section we analyze the performance of a differential quantization of the state vector. The quantizer is shown in Fig. 2. To analyze the performance of an n-th order Gauss-Markov process $x(t)$, we consider the augmented state vector consisting of the process and its first $(n-1)$ derivatives. This augmented vector is now the input to the quantizer. We analyze this system in detail and use fine quantization approximations for the covariance matrix of the quantization error, $\mathcal{E}$, which results from the vector quantization of the error vector ϵ in Fig. 2. We use the filters of the preceding section to evaluate the time averaged smoothed error for the original scalar process $x(t)$. Finally, we find an optimal tradeoff between the number of levels N of the vector quantizer and the sampling interval τ.

3.1 Iterative equations for Differential State Quantization

The discrete time vector equations for the state vector are given by

$$\mathbf{S}_{j+1} = \alpha\mathbf{S}_j + \Gamma\mathbf{W}_{j+1}, \tag{3.3}$$

where $\alpha = e^{A\tau}$ and $\mathbf{W}_j$ is a zero mean Gaussian vector with identity autocorrelation matrix. If $\hat{\mathbf{S}}_j$ is the estimate of the vector $\mathbf{S}_j$ resulting from the Differential State Quantizer, then the governing equations for the quantizer (Fig. 2) can be written as

$$\hat{\mathbf{S}}_{j+1} = \alpha\hat{\mathbf{S}}_j + q_\epsilon(\epsilon_{j+1}); j \geq 0 \tag{3.4}$$

and

$$\epsilon_{j+1} = \mathbf{S}_{j+1} - \alpha\hat{\mathbf{S}}_j; j \geq 0. \tag{3.5}$$

Here $q_\epsilon(\epsilon_{j+1})$ is the quantized value of the error vector ϵ_{j+1} and we take the initial condition to be zero, that is, $\hat{\mathbf{S}}_0 = 0$. The above equations imply :

$$\mathbf{S}_{j+1} - \hat{\mathbf{S}}_{j+1} = \epsilon_{j+1} - q_\epsilon(\epsilon_{j+1}) = \gamma_\epsilon(\epsilon_{j+1}), \tag{3.6}$$

This says that the error between the discrete time vector $\mathbf{S}_{j+1}$ and its estimate is equal to that between the error vector ϵ_j and its quantized version. Another important relation between the error vector ϵ_j and the corresponding quantization error $q_\epsilon(\epsilon_{j+1})$ is :

$$\epsilon_{j+1} = \alpha\gamma_\epsilon(\epsilon_j) + \Gamma\mathbf{W}_{j+1}. \tag{3.7}$$

This is a non linear iterative equation driven by white noise. Finally, by using (3.7), we arrive at the following iterative equation for the covariance matrices

$$E\{\epsilon_{j+1}{\epsilon_{j+1}}^T\} = \alpha E\{\gamma_\epsilon(\epsilon_j)\gamma_\epsilon(\epsilon_j)^T\}\alpha^T + \Gamma\Gamma^T, \tag{3.8}$$

where the cross terms are zero because of the independence of the zero mean noise vector $\mathbf{W}_{j+1}$ and $\gamma_\epsilon(\epsilon_j)$. We can rewrite the above equation as

$$c_\epsilon(j+1) \quad = \quad \alpha c_{\gamma(\epsilon)}(j)\alpha^T + \Gamma\Gamma^T, \tag{3.9}$$

where $c_{\mathbf{S}}(j)$ is the autocovariance matrix of the random variable $\mathbf{S}$. Thus, equation (3.9) describes the evolution of the covariance matrix $c_\epsilon(j+1)$ with time. Eventually we are interested in the steady state behavior of our system which corresponds to a stationary state where $c_\epsilon(0) = c_\epsilon(j) = c_\epsilon(\infty)$. Thus, we have

$$c_\epsilon(0) \quad = \quad \alpha c_{\gamma(\epsilon)}(0)\alpha^T + \Gamma\Gamma^T \tag{3.10}$$

where $c_{\gamma(\epsilon)}(0)$ is the covariance matrix of the quantization error for the state $\mathbf{S}_j$.

3.2 Sampling and Quantization Tradeoff for Differential State Quantization

After having derived the equations which govern the differential state quantization structure, we derive an expression for the overall time averaged smoothed error. For this the covariance matrix of the quantization error $\mathcal{E}$ has to be evaluated. When each dimension of the vector $\mathbf{S}$, the input to the quantizer, is i. i. d unity variance Gaussian random variable, then the covariance matrix of the quantization error can be approximated as ([2])

$$\mathcal{E} = E\{(\mathbf{S}_j - \hat{\mathbf{S}}_j)(\mathbf{S}_j - \hat{\mathbf{S}}_j)^T\} = \frac{4}{(k+2)}\frac{\ln N}{(N^{2/k}-1)}I, \tag{3.11}$$

where N is the size of the k-dimensional vector quantizer. Here we are interested in deriving an expression for $\mathcal{E} = c_{\gamma(\epsilon)}(0) = E\{\gamma_\epsilon(\epsilon_j)\gamma_\epsilon(\epsilon_j)^T\}$, where the components of the vector ϵ, the input to the quantizer, are not i. i. d. Gaussian random variables. To use the approximation (3.11) we do an orthogonal transformation $\epsilon_j^{'} = T\epsilon_j$ such that $E\{\epsilon_j^{'}\epsilon_j^{'T}\} = I$. That is, the given transformation T results in a vector which has an identity matrix as the correlation matrix.

We can now use the fine quantization approximations of [2] to write the quantization matrix for the case when this vector is fed to the quantizer. We are eventually interested in the error covariance matrix of the vector ϵ for which we have the following relationship

$$E\{(\epsilon_j - \hat{\epsilon_j})(\epsilon_j - \hat{\epsilon_j})^T\} \quad = \quad T^{-1}E\{(\epsilon_j^{'} - \hat{\epsilon_j^{'}})(\epsilon_j^{'} - \hat{\epsilon_j^{'}})^T\}T^{-T}. \tag{3.12}$$

An approximation to ϵ can be found by solving the non linear iterative equation (3.9). The steady state result (for small τs) (and for $k=2$) is given by

$$E\{(\epsilon_j{\epsilon_j}^T)\} \approx \frac{1}{1-\frac{\ln N}{N-1}}\Gamma\Gamma^T. \tag{3.13}$$

Knowledge of the covariance matrix of ϵ allows us to determine the transformation T. This can then be used in equation (3.12) to calculate the required quantization matrix. We can then use this in equation (2.2) to get an expression for the smoothed error.

3.3 A Second Order Example

As an example we consider a second order system with $A = \begin{bmatrix} 0 & 1 \\ -\omega_n{}^2 & -2\zeta\omega_n \end{bmatrix}$ and $B = \begin{bmatrix} 0 \\ \sqrt{4\zeta\omega_n{}^3} \end{bmatrix}$. Following the analysis of previous section, the smoothed error for the Differential State Quantization (DSQ) structure (Figure 2) and for a two dimensional vector quantizer of size N is given by :

$$\zeta_{sm}(\tau') = \frac{8\zeta \ln 2\frac{R}{\omega_n}\tau'}{e^{2\ln 2\frac{R}{\omega_n}\tau'} - 1 - 2\ln 2\frac{R}{\omega_n}\tau'} \left(\frac{7\tau'^3}{6} - \frac{4\zeta\tau'^4}{3} + \frac{4\zeta^2\tau'^5}{9} \right) + 4\zeta\frac{\tau'^3}{12}, \quad (3.14)$$

where $\tau' = \omega_n\tau$. This expression is to be optimized with respect to N, or equivalently τ'. By expressing the smoothed error in terms of N and varying N from large values to small values, yields the optimum value to be $N = 2$. If we increase our quantizer levels more than this, the overall smoothed error will increase. Thus the optimal uniform vector quantizer for differential state quantization of this second order process is one having two quantizer levels. This is a simple quantizer to implement.

An interesting approximation results if we neglect the terms higher than τ'^3 in equation (3.14). The optimal smoothed error, neglecting the higher order terms in τ' and by substituting $N = 2$ in equation (3.14) ($N = e^{2\ln 2R\tau}$), is : $\zeta_{sm}(R) \approx a\zeta(\frac{\omega_n}{R})^3$, where $a = \frac{1}{24}[\frac{14\ln 2}{1-\ln 2} + 1] \approx 1.359$. Thus, the optimal smoothed error varies as $(\frac{\omega_n}{R})^3$. The ratio of the quantization error and the filtering error is constant, independent of the rate R, and is equal to $\frac{\zeta_{quant}(R)}{\zeta_{filt}(R)} = \frac{14\ln 2}{1-\ln 2} = 31.62$. The smoothed error can then be expressed as a sum of two terms: one due to the filtering error and the other due to the quantization error. A suboptimal solution for the vector quantizer size N can be obtained by equating these two error terms. The optimal N is the solution of the following transcendental equation :

$$15\ln N + 1 - N = 0. \quad (3.15)$$

Thus, $N^* = 63$ and $\tau^* = \frac{\ln N^*}{1.38R} \approx \frac{3}{R}$. The optimal smoothed error is :

$$\zeta_{sm}(R) \approx a\zeta(\frac{\omega_n}{R})^3, \quad (3.16)$$

where $a = \frac{2}{3}(\frac{\ln N^*}{2\ln 2})^2 = 18.04$. Thus, this approximate optimal smoothed error varies as $18.04\zeta(\frac{\omega_n}{R})^3$ and the suboptimal sampling time varies as $\frac{3\omega_n}{R}$.

Figure 3 gives a comparison of the performance of this differential scheme with state component quantization, state vector quantization and a vector quantization of the scalar process. These schemes were analyzed in [2]. In each of these schemes there exists a tradeoff between the size of the quantizers and the sampling rate. We have a different optimal sampling interval for each scheme. In state component quantization we quantize each component of the state vector and the overall smoothed error is proportional to $\frac{\omega_n}{R}$ for the second order process. Vector quantization of the scalar process performs slightly better than state component quantization. Finally, in state vector quantization, where we vector quantize the state vector, the optimal smoothed error varies approximately as $(\frac{\omega_n}{R})^3$ and thus is comparable, though still inferior, to this differential scheme. of the state outperforms all the other schemes considered. The figure also gives the relative performance of DPCM of the process which is discussed later. Figure 4 gives, for the same second order baseband process, a comparison of the optimal sampling time of the differential scheme with the other schemes previously analyzed in [2] and with DPCM of the process.

4 A Bandpass Example

Next we examine a bandpass process whose spectrum is given by

$$\psi_{xx}(\omega) = \frac{\beta^2(\frac{\omega}{\omega_n})^2\zeta^2}{(1-(\frac{\omega}{\omega_n})^2)^2 + (\frac{\omega}{\omega_n})^2\zeta^2}. \tag{4.17}$$

This normalized power spectrum has a zero at $\omega = 0$ and is centered at $\omega = \omega_n$. The parameter ζ is the 3 dB bandwidth of the process. Our interest lies in examining the performance of the different source coding schemes as the parameters of this bandpass process vary. We define $\beta = \frac{\omega_n}{\zeta}$.

Figure 5 gives the results for the second order bandpass process given by (4.17). This bandpass process has a zero at the origin and two complex poles. We study the variation of the performance of the systems as the shape of the spectrum changes. This can be done by varying the ratio $\frac{\omega_n}{\zeta}$. In this figure we show the performance of the differential state quantization with respect to state vector quantization for two different values of this ratio. Differential state quantization always outperforms the state vector quantization, as before. As the ratio $\frac{\omega_n}{\zeta}$ increases from 80 to 4000, corresponding to a more peaky spectrum, the performance improves for both the schemes.

5 A Comparison with Other Differential Systems

Having analyzed Differential State Quantization in detail, we now analyze some other differential systems in the same way. The objective is to compare the relative performance in terms of the time average smoothed error for different schemes. Two systems are analyzed. The first is a DPCM of the the original process and the second a vector DPCM of the same process. We will give the final results, refering the reader to [7] for details.

5.1 DPCM of the Original Process

DPCM can be viewed as a special case of the state quantization scheme where, for a second order example, the process is input to a DPCM loop and the derivative is not quantized at all ([7]).

Doing a similar analysis ([7]) we obtain, for a second order process, the following approximate expressions for the optimal sampling interval and the optimal smoothed error : $\tau^* \approx \frac{\nu}{R}$, and

$$\zeta_{sm}{}^* \approx \gamma(\frac{\omega_n}{R})^2, \tag{5.18}$$

where γ and ν are constants related to the dimension of the vector quantizer and the density function of the process. ζ and ω_n are the parameters of the second order process related to the width at the resonant frequency and the resonant frequency respectively. Thus, we see that the DPCM of a second order process gives a suboptimal smoothed error which varies as $(\frac{\omega_n}{R})^2$. The smoothed error varied as $(\frac{\omega_n}{R})^3$ for differential state quantization. Thus, everything else remaining same, differential state quantization performs roughly $10\log_{10} R$ dB better than DPCM for the second order process.

5.2 A Modified Vector DPCM

Now we compare another natural extension of the previous scheme, vector DPCM. We note that this is different from the state differential scheme where we were differentially quantizing a sampled vector consisting of the process and its derivatives. In this modified vector DPCM the vector that is differentially quantized consists of the sampled process and its past or future samples, not the process and its derivatives. For the same second order process the asymptotic expression for the smoothed error, following a similar analysis (see [7]) , is :

$$\zeta_{sm_{V-DPCM}}(\tau) \quad \approx \quad \frac{\ln N}{N-1}\tau^2\omega_n + \frac{{\omega_n}^2\tau^2}{3} + \frac{\zeta{\omega_n}^3\tau^3}{3}, \tag{5.19}$$

where ω_n and ζ are the paramters of the baseband second order process and N is the size of the vector quantizer. By using the fact that $N = e^{2\ln 2R\tau}$ we can then optimize this smoothed error with respect to τ, the sampling interval. Asymptotically this optimal smoothed error can be shown to be proportional to $\frac{1}{R^2}$. This smoothed error is approximately close to that obtained for the DPCM of the second order process in equation (5.18) and is inferior to that obtained for Differential State Quantization of the same process.

6 Conclusion

In this paper a differential technique of tracking and quantizing a continuous time high order Gauss-Markov process is studied. We use a state space representation and estimate a state vector consisting of the process and its first $(n-1)$ derivatives, where n is the order of the Gauss-Markov process. For any quantization scheme, for a fixed overall transmission rate in bits per second, there exists a tradeoff between the sampling rate and the resolution of the quantizer. This tradeoff is examined for this differential scheme and it is verified, both analytically and experimentally, that the differential quantization of the state (an augmented vector consisting of the process and its derivative) outperforms : i) vector quantization of the original process, ii) state component quantization, iii) state vector quantization, iv) DPCM of the original process, and v) vector DPCM of the original process. The optimal size of the vector quantizers for the differential scheme are small and can be used in practice. We analyze the variation of the input spectrum and how it affects the relative performance of different schemes. It is shown that for a second order process, the performance of all schemes improves as the input spectrum becomes more and more peaky. Differential state quantization still gives the best performance among all the schemes analyzed.

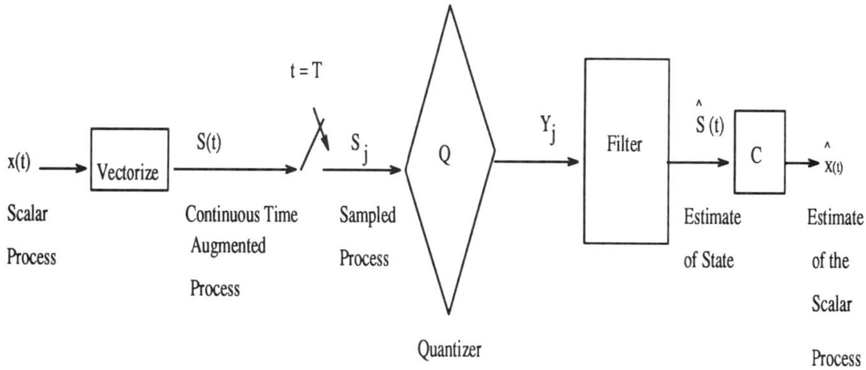

Figure 1: Block diagram of a communication system which quantizes a higher order Gauss-Markov process. $\mathbf{S}(t)$ is the state vector which is being quantized and $\hat{x}(t)$ is the estimate of the continuous time process $x(t)$.

Acknowledgements

The author wishes to thank Prof. N. T. Gaarder for suggesting the differential state quantization scheme and without whose help and guidance this work would not have been possible.

References

[1] D. Slepian, "On Delta Modulation," The Bell System Technical Journal, Vol. 51, pp.2101-2138, Dec. 1972 .

[2] A. Bist, "Analysis of Some Source Coding Schemes for a High Order Gauss-Markov Process," submitted to *IEEE Transactions on Communications* .

[3] N. S. Jayant, "Adaptive Delta Modulation with a One-Bit Memory," The Bell System Technical Journal, Vol. 49, pp.321-342, March 1970 .

[4] A. Hayashi, "Differential Pulse Coded Modulation of Stationary Gaussian Inputs," *IEEE Transactions on Communications*, Vol.COMM-26, pp. 1137-1147, Aug. 1978 .

[5] E. Janardhanan, "Differential PCM Systems," *IEEE Transactions on Communications*, Vol.COMM-27, pp.82-93, Jan. 1979 .

[6] H. Shankar, "Asymptotic Analysis of Digital Transmission Systems for a First Order Gauss-Markov Process," Ph.D Dissertation, University of Hawaii, Dec. 1991 .

[7] A. Bist, "Differential State Quantization of High Order Gauss-Markov Process," submitted to *IEEE Transactions on Communications* .

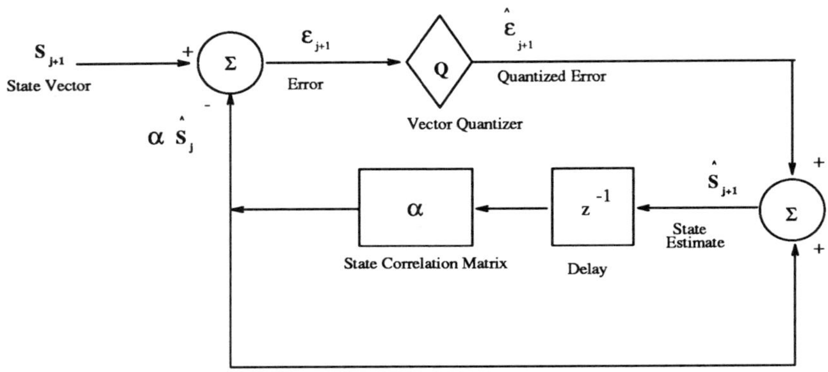

Figure 2: Differential State Quantization. The figure gives the standard DPCM loop through which the sampled state vector $\mathbf{S}_j$ is quantized.

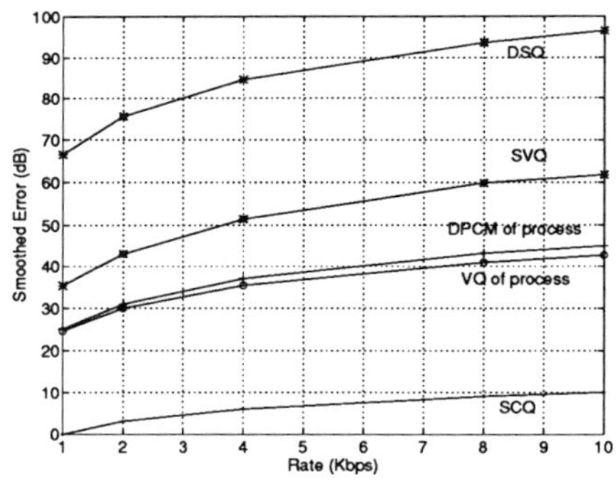

Figure 3: The optimal smoothed error (in dBs) for different quantization schemes. The process is the baseband process analyzed in section 3. The figure plots $10\log_{10}(\frac{\zeta_{sm_o}}{\zeta_{sm}})$, where ζ_{sm_o} is the smoothed error for scalar quantization of the state components at $R = 1Kbps$. The different curves are from top to bottom : i) Differential State Quantization, ii) State Vector Quantization, iii) DPCM of the scalar process, iv) VQ of the scalar process, and v) Scalar quantization of the state components.

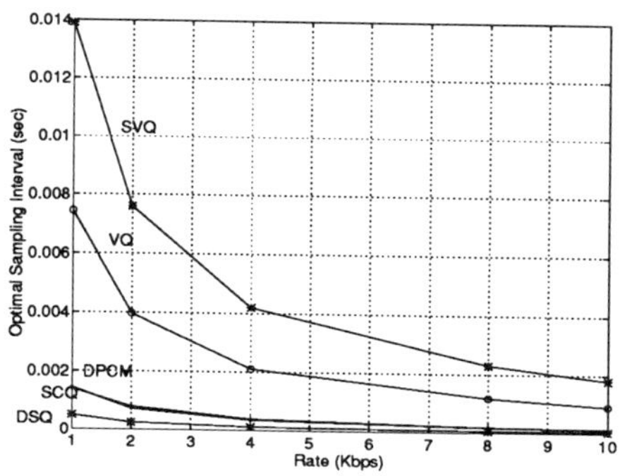

Figure 4: Comparison of the optimal sampling intervals of the differential scheme with others. The different curves are from top to bottom : i) VQ of the state, ii) VQ of the scalar process, iii) Scalar quantization of the state components, iv) DPCM of the scalar process, and v) Differential State Quantization.

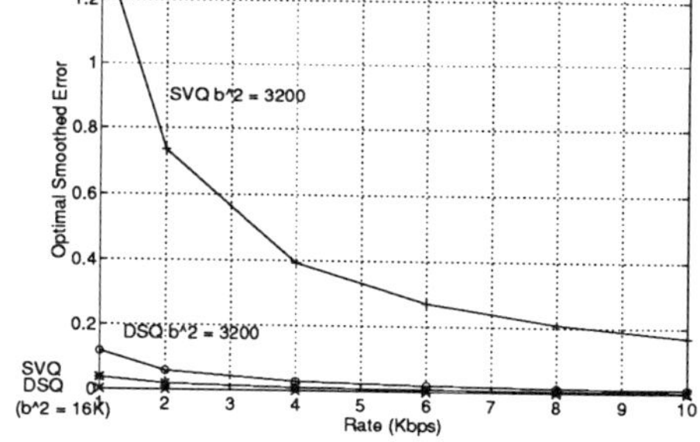

Figure 5: Comparison of the performance of the differential scheme with State Vector Quantization. The figure gives the optimal smoothed error for the bandpass spectrum for two different values of $\beta^2 = \frac{4\omega_n}{\zeta}$. The different curves are (from top to bottom) : i) State VQ at $\beta^2 = 3200$, ii) Differential State Quantization at $\beta^2 = 16000$, iii) State VQ at $\beta^2 = 3200$, and iv) Differential State Quantization at $\beta^2 = 16000$. The higher value of β^2 corresponds to a narrower bandwidth spectrum.

Data Compression Techniques for Stock Market Prediction

Salman Azhar, Greg J. Badros, Arman Glodjo
Ming-Yang Kao and John H. Reif[‡]

Abstract

This paper presents advanced data compression techniques for predicting stock markets behavior under widely accepted market models in finance. Our techniques are applicable to technical analysis, portfolio theory, and nonlinear market models. We find that lossy and lossless compression techniques are well suited for predicting stock prices as well as market modes such as strong trends and major adjustments. We also present novel applications of multispectral compression techniques to portfolio theory, correlation of similar stocks, effects of interest rates, transaction costs and taxes.

1 Stock market models

In this paper we address the applicability of modern data compression techniques for predicting future behavior of stock markets. Motivated by stock market theory, we find that most compression techniques are well suited for successful prediction. We introduce different market models and present compression techniques that work well under these models. A stock market provides a framework for investors to allocate funds into stocks, and to try to make profits by buying "under valued" stocks and selling "over valued" stocks. Stock markets are one of the most complex and rewarding systems to model accurately. Since their incorporation in the latter part of the last century, there have been a vast number of different techniques to predict their future behavior. Based on the market models we present in this section, we introduce several data compression based techniques for their prediction. We first present definitions of classical views 4f the markets, namely, the technical and the quantitative in Sections 1.1 and 1.2, respectively. In Section 1.3 we introduce a modern market model that admits non-efficiency. We analyze the applicability of data compression techniques under these different models. Lastly, in Section 1.4, we introduce the portfolio theory and implications thereof to data compression algorithms.

1.1 Technical analysis of stock markets

Stock market prices, as most other economic time series, have been modeled by examining how new information impacts the prices, and how much these prices reflect the true value of the underlying security. The most common market prediction techniques can be divided into two main categories: technical and quantitative. The technical view of the markets is that the prices are driven by investor sentiment and that the underlying sequence of prices can be captured and predicted well using data charting techniques [31, 30]. This method studies the action of the market as a *dynamical entity*, rather than studying the actual goods in which the market

[‡]Azhar is with Computer Science Dept., North Carolina A& T State University, Greensboro. All others are with Department of Computer Science, Duke University, Durham, NC. Reif is supported by DARPA/ISTO Grant N00014-91-J-1985, Subcontract KI-92-01-0182 of DARPA/ISTO prime Contract N00014-92-C-0182, NSF Grant NSF-IRI-91-00681, NASA subcontract 550-63 of prime Contract NAS5-30428, and US-Israel Binational NSF Grant 88-00282/2., Kao is in part supported by NSF grant CCR-9101385.

1068-0314/94 $3.00 © 1994 IEEE

operates. This is a science of recording the historical market data, such as prices of stocks and the volume traded, and attempting to predict the future from the past performance of the stock. This model implicitly admits a non-efficient market model, where the prices are not only a function of the underlying security valuation, but are also governed by investor sentiment, health of the economy and many other. This is a popular and highly contested market model. Terms like "primary", "secondary" and "minor" trends, "tides", "ripples", "head-and-shoulders top" patterns, and "triangles" were coined in the technical community by repeated observations of stock trends and their classification into more common patterns. Data compression techniques are therefore a perfect paradigm for algorithmic charting techniques. In Section 2 we present data compression techniques suitable for technical analysts.

1.2 The efficient markets hypothesis

No less controversial is the model of an efficient market. *Market efficiency* essentially states that the markets are priced in such a way that *all* public information available is already included in the price of a stock, and movements on the markets are only due to arrivals of new information [13, 14, 30]. Large numbers of investors insure that the prices on the market are fair, and always converge towards an equilibrium. The price history of the market does not affect the future, and consequently, the prices follow a random walk. Efficiency in capital markets implies that the time series of returns are identically and independently distributed (IID) random variables, and consequently, no investor can consistently beat that market. Hence, no predictive technique will be able to consistently outperform the buy-and-hold strategy. To quantify the above, we start by interpreting stock prices as a time series of data. Let P_t be the price of a particular stock at time t, where t can be measured in units of seconds, minutes, days, months or years. Under the efficient market hypothesis, the time series of prices P_t are a random walk, and the returns, $\frac{P_t}{P_{t-1}}$, of the stock are normally distributed. Under the efficiency hypothesis, no predictive technique is expected to consistently outperform the market. There is, however, considerable quantitative evidence that points to markets being non-efficient. Section 1.3 describes this evidence and defines the "nonlinear market model" used in this paper. We present data compression techniques suitable for this view of the markets in Section 2.4.

1.3 Nonlinear market models

A comprehensive study of stock daily returns [12] found that returns were negatively skewed, there were more observations in the left side of the tail, the tails were fatter than a Gaussian and the peak around the mean was higher. The distribution of returns was consistently behaved in this manner, pointing to a non-I.I.D. nature of returns. This condition was coined *leptokurtosis.* A novel and widely respected statistical technique, the Brock-Dechert-Sheinkman (BDS) statistic is one of many that rejects the null hypothesis of the IID nature of returns [32, 22, 37]. In other words, the markets have been analytically found to be inefficient, something that has empirically been obvious for some time(in view of the fact that considerable profit has been made from trades, such as arbitrage, exploiting market inefficiency). This degree of inefficiency is crucial to investors who compare dynamic "buy-sell" strategies (which are overwhelmed by transaction costs) to "buy-and-hold" strategies (which depend on accurate forecasting of long term trends), and off-set their risks by diversifying their investments. More on this in Section 2.3. The financial academic community(as opposed to the market community, e.g. Wall Street) has not, as of yet, completely accepted the failure of the EMH, but has largely agreed that the present investment techniques are in real danger of becoming obsolete [30]. Vaga and Paters [30, 35] postulate that the markets are multimodal, and that they continuously drift between the following four modes: (1)*Efficient Mode*, where current prices reflect all "available information" with history of prices and returns; (2)*Transition Mode*, where the level of coherent investor behavior increases due to new information and/or other factors, hence resulting in the impact of this information to extend for prolonged periods of time; (3)*Chaotic Mode*, where the investor sentiment is very strong but variations in groupthink are increased as well, which for example may arize before the release of company quarterly reports or shortly before election results; (4)*Coherent Mode*, where investors act as more or less one unit, resulting in very strong positive or negative market trends. So far this has been found to be a highly realistic view of the actual operation of the markets [30]. We introduce this model of the stock market. In Section 3.2 we present data compression techniques that are suitable for prediction of nonlinear market models under fixed time series memory. Section 3.4 addresses data compression techniques for dynamic memory models as defined below. Mandelbrot [26, 27] postulated and Lo [25] and Peters [30] have empirically shown that the distribution of returns on the stock market follows a fractal distribution, known as stable *Levy distribution*. These distributions have fatter tails and are peaked higher at the mean than the Gaussian, and their underlying time series can experience trends, cycles as well as catastrophes. The characteristic function $f(t)$ of a random variable, t, for the Levy distribution is given by $\log(f(t)) = i\delta t - \gamma|t|^{\alpha}(1 + \beta i(\frac{t}{|t|})\tan(\alpha\frac{\pi}{2}))$. This distribution has four characteristic parameters that are continuously changing: δ is the location parameter of the mean; γ a parameter to adjust for different granularity of data; β is a measure of skewness to the left or the right, valued from -1 to 1; α is a measure of the leptokurtosis of the distribution. For $\alpha = 2$, the distribution generalizes to the normal distribution. For example, if $\alpha = 2, \beta = 0, \gamma = 1, \delta = \mu$, we have $\log(f(t)) = i\mu t - (\frac{\sigma^2}{2})t^2$, the standard normal distribution $N(\mu, \sigma^2)$. The *nonlinear market hypothesis* [30] states that α can vary from 1 to 2. Noninteger values of α result in fractional Brownian motions of prices, which An important implication of this model is that a stock time series has a memory. Future prices are a function of new information as well as the past performance of the stock. For example, investors might be fairly reserved to invest in a company that is in financial crisis, even though the stock price is low. Estimation of the memory window can be tuned by adjusting the parameters of the underlying distribution. As the parameters of the Levy distribution are varying in time, in accordance with Vaga's multimodal model, the stocks have a continuously changing memory. The dynamic memory model of the stock market presents an intriguing problem for data compression. For example, the calculation of the memory for a particular stock is still an open question. But, following the works of Mandelbrot [27] described by Peters [30] and interpreting stock market time series as statistically self-similar fractals and using the tools of fractal geometry, one can get a very good approximation of the extent of current memory and hence, can form an appropriate window for our compression algorithm. We present this compression model in Section 3.4.

1.4 Modern portfolio theory

The efficient markets hypothesis was a fundamental driving force for development of the *modern portfolio theory*. Modern portfolio theory provides the toold for a quantitative analysis of risky assets such as stocks, based on the expected return, which under the EMH is the mean expected value, and the risk, under EMH defined as the variance of a portfolio. A portfolio is a vector-valued time series of stocks $X = \{X_i | i = 1, ..., n\}$ where n is the number of stocks and X_i is the stock "price relative" defined as $X_i = \frac{P_{it}}{P_{it-1}}$. For example, $X_5 = 1.05$ would imply that the fifth stock in our portfolio went up by 5 percent in one day. In this section we present the investment theory from the efficient hypothesis point of view, which assumes that X_i's independent and identically distributed random variables and that the time series of X's is a stationary ergodic vector-valued stochastic process. We adopt the notion of the distribution of X as normal, for the time being. As a part of our future work, we will re-examine this hypothesis and present portfolio allocation techniques under the non-efficient model. Define a portfolio as a vector representing the allocation of wealth over a collection of stocks: $b = (b_1, b_2, b_3, ..., b_m)$. Therefore, the ratio of wealth from start to the end of a trading day can be defined as: $\mathcal{S} = b^t X$. $\mathcal{S}$, itself is a random variable. As with most things associated with the stock markets, the distribution of $\mathcal{S}$ is also subject of a lot of controversy. The Sharpe-Markowitz [7] of stock market tries to maximize the expected value of S while minimizing its variance. In this model, one examines the so-called efficient frontier, a region in the variance-mean space, while assuming that there is a one-to-one correspondence between a true value of a stock and its variance. This is the so-called Capital Assets Pricing Model (CAPM). In Section 2.3 we present data compression techniques applicable for optimal portfolio allocation problems under the CAPM model.

2 Market prediction via data compression

Data compression (DC) is the task of efficiently encoding a data source to derive a more compact data representation by removing redundancy, while preserving the essential information in a retrievable format. DC explicitly assumes that the input has an a priori probability distribution that is exploited. DC algorithms have two distinct functions: encoding the source data and decoding the encoded data. An encoding phase of DC algorithms performs two distinct tasks: (1) learning the distribution of the source; (2) assigning codes based on this learning. These two tasks are usually employed in tandem: the learning phase generates a dictionary that is used to encode the source. The decoding phase reverses the dictionary look-up to recover the original source data (or a close approximation thereof). DC algorithms can be used as predictive schemes using the characteristics of the dictionary to predict the frequency of the source. This observed relationship between DC and prediction has been extensively used in [15, 9, 10, 8, 5, 16, 17, 36, 11], particularly for stationary sources. In this section, we examine basic issues in prediction for stationary sources. Later, we do present several new results for dynamic schemes, specifically in relation with the stock market. Cover and Thomas [6] provide a theoretical background to information complexity issues establishing a direct relationship between high compressibility and high predictability. Vitter and Krishnan [36, 11] prove this result for some particular lossless DC based prediction algorithms. Since the readers are likely to be experts in DC, our discussion of DC is brief. We shall note prediction can be done by various known DC techniques, all in the presence of a stationary source. DC schemes can be lossy or lossless. Lossy DC allows the algorithm to permanently lose non-essential information to achieve higher compression ratios, whereas lossless DC schemes insist that the decoded data should be identical to the source data. Lossy DC techniques can be used to represent a source by mapping each source item to one of finite number of dictionary elements that minimizes distortion under a suitable metric. Quantization is a fundamental example of lossy compression. Scalar Quantization (SQ) observes a single source datum and selects the nearest approximation value from a predetermined finite set of allowed numerical values [1]. Vector Quantization (VQ) [18] is a generalization of SQ to quantization of a vector, a point in n-dimensional Euclidean or any other metric space, according to some vector space metric such as the metric induced by the l^2 norm. VQ can be used for predicting by filtering primary components to maintain correlations among different values. Predictive VQ (PVQ) schemes were introduced by Fischer an Tinner [15] as well as Cuperman and Gersho [9]. Extensive studies were performed by Cuperman and Gersho [10, 8], Chang and

Gray [5], and Fischer and Tinnen [16, 17]. Lossless DC can be achieved by assigning shorter codes to frequently occurring source sequence, and vice versa. Lempel-Ziv algorithm [41, 34, 3] is an example of this technique. Analogously, prediction can be achieved by assigning higher probability to more frequently occurring sequences. Vitter and Krishnan [36, 11] use data compression based prediction to devise prefetching algorithms for theoretically optimal caching strategy. We present algorithms that use lossy and lossless schemes to predict movements on the stock market. Our algorithms are applicable for optimal portfolio allocation, technical analysis (charting) and other more advanced non-efficient market models. [33, 40, 4].

2.1 Vector quantization (VQ) based prediction

Vector quantization is a lossy DC technique is perfectly suited for market prediction under the technical and other nonlinear models. For example, lossy compression techniques will map a vector of a stock history to its representative under some desired metric, to form a collection of equivalence classes of market moves, and will reduce prediction complexity by orders of magnitude. All charting techniques can be viewed as implicit lossy compression schemes. VQ can be achieved by representing all source data using a dictionary consisting of representative vectors smaller in size and/or number than the original source. VQ maps an input vector to its closest neighbor in the dictionary based on a given distortion measure, and represents the input vector by the index to the dictionary [18]. We represent stock market time series data as a two dimensional space-time vector, where the rows of the vector contain, for example the securities' prices at the time indexed by the columns. Given a partial space-time vector, we can match it to the nearest space-time vector using an appropriate distortion measure. The matching vector is said to predict the unknown components as specified by it. *Tree Structured* VQ (TSVQ) is a variant of VQ that can reduce the time complexity of VQ from linear to logarithmic [19]. A TSVQ dictionary is implemented as a d-ary tree whose intermediate nodes represent the centroids of their children. TSVQ is most suited for our VQ-based prediction scheme for stock market indices for technical or other non-efficient market models. We therefore implement this variant of VQ for our empirical tests.

2.2 Lempel-Ziv based prediction

Lossless data compression can be regarded as a predictive algorithm applied to a set of quantized or raw stock market data. It is well-suited for optimal allocation of funds as given by CAPM in stock market portfolio theory. Lossless DC can be achieved by assigning shorter codes to frequently occurring source sequence, and vice versa. Lempel-Ziv (LZ) algorithm [41, 34, 3] is an example of this technique. LZ satisfies the unique parsing criteria: no two phrases in the parse of the source are identical. Cover and Thomas [6] show that LZ's unique parsing property makes it optimal for sources with stationary ergodic memoryless distributions. Vitter and Krishnan [36, 11] extend this result by proving that optimal compression algorithms can be converted in optimal prediction algorithms assuming stationary ergodic distribution.

2.3 Multispectral prediction

Multispectral compression (MC) algorithms exploit the high degree of redundancy among spectral bands to compress a multispectral image [29]. This spectral redundancy is similar to the redundancies among stock market indices: only limited portion of spatial information changes among bands. For example, stock indices from geographically close areas, stocks of similar companies, interest rates and housing stocks are pairwise related to each other. Lossy MC is a well-researched area [29, 20, 2]. The encoding phase of MC consists of the following steps: (1) Histogram equalization, (2) Spectral transform (such as cosine or more advanced techniques, e.g. wavelet transform), (3) Scalar or Vector Quantizer and (4) Lossless compressor such as LZ [41]. The decoding process reverses each one of the above steps in complementary order. The *histogram equalization* is a non-linear process that equalizes the probability distribution function (PDF) $p(t)$ of a random variable t with PDF $p_d(s)$ of a desired random variable s. It is accomplished by identifying a monotone non-decreasing map $s = T[t]$ that equalizes the cumulative PDFs of the two images [23], and identifying the image that needs to be modified. $P(t) = \sum_i^t p(i)$ is equalized to $P_d(t) = \sum_i^s p_d(i)$. This can be viewed as SQ mapping one set of quantized spectra into another using a table to specify the mapping. Prediction is achieved by breaking the source into blocks of different spectra and encoding it as a juxtaposed vector. MC affords an impressive treatment of capital markets where several indices, returns, averages, interest rates, etc. show strong correlation among one another. In fact, Fama [13] shows that returns from different stocks exhibit up to 97% correlation with each other. Consequently, we expect MC to yield high compression of various data associated with the stock markets such as indices, returns, interest rates, etc. This enables us to exploit more information and combine it efficiently. We are investigating the application of wavelet techniques and shall report our results in near future.

2.4 Distortion controlled prediction

Our prediction algorithms can also be used to find a particular mode of the stock market. Vaga and Peters [35, 30] describe a market to be in one of the following mode: efficient, transition, chaotic and coherent, as defined in Section 1.3. By looking at the time-series of the changing parameters of Levy distributed returns, we can predict new characteristic parameters of the distribution. Consequently, by looking at the α, we can see how close our series is to efficiency, and we can obtain precise measurements of predictive powers of our compression techniques. We can therefore quantitatively measure the expected accuracy of compression algorithms for prediction. Accordingly, we need different levels of granularity to preserve distortion. Traditionally lossy DC algorithms have focused on compressing data at fixed bit rates. Markas and Reif [28] present Distortion Controlled VQ (DCVQ) algorithms that comply with specified distortion measures. When the market is in the efficient and chaotic mode, the information loss is more tolerable. Hence, we used DCVQ algorithms [28] to relax the distortion control to smooth the insignificant changes. On the other hand, when the market is in transition or coherent mode, we can increase distortion control to some extent.

3 Prediction model

This section describes the development of prediction tables for stock market trends, so that knowledge the past trends of a stock can allow us to estimate the prediction probabilities of the stock's future performance. This is a memory-based model, and this type of models offers significant advantages when compared with memoryless techniques. The process of generating a model for predicting trends in stocks can divided into three phases: the generation of prediction tables, the prediction of trends based on the known information, and finally adaptation of the model based on new data.

3.1 Generation of prediction tables

During the generation step, data consisting of either a collection of correlated stocks and/or events that affect those classes of stocks are collected in a form of a discrete vector of fixed length, which we call a *stock-event*. A large selection of such vectors will be used to generate the VQ codebook vocabulary: each entry represents a sequence of events that indicate the past performance of a stock. Training can be accomplished based on one of the known VQ training algorithms (such as LBG method [24]). Since the traditional VQ algorithm is a memoryless technique, some memory that keeps track of sequences of events, as well as their transitions probabilities among different events must be implemented within the model. Given a particular window of time, we calculate the current probability distribution of returns, and quantize it into a dictionary of past distributions. For our analysis, we consider returns on the stock market to be stable-Levy. This two-stage quantization is necessary for prediction because the first stage will capture the deterministic components by deterministically weighing the past, and the VQ stage will codify the present distribution to a nearest distribution under the same conditions in a statistical sense.

3.2 Prediction

The prediction process can be seen as a predictive vector quantization(PVQ) algorithm [21]. PVQ consists of a series of discretization and matching operations that define the current state, and a prediction process that searches the prediction tree and identifies the probability tables for all possible transitions. The current state of a stock trend is defined as the sequence of the N past stock-events. The stock data sources that form an event are discretized at N-past time intervals, and a VQ process is initiated to identify their best-match vector from the existing codebook. The string that is generated during this process represents the current state of the stock. The complexity of the VQ algorithm is linear with respect to the size of the codebook. This step can become computationally prohibitive for large vocabularies, likely to be generated in stock market applications. The Tree-Structured Vector Quantization (TSVQ) [19] reduces the complexity of the VQ method from linear to logarithmic time. In TSVQ, the vocabulary is implemented in a d-ary tree form, whose intermediate nodes represent the centroids of their children nodes and the leaf nodes are the actual codewords. Once the current state has been computed, a sequence of events that exists in the prediction tree and matches with the current state needs to be identified. During this process, we search the past performance of a class of stocks to identify a sequence of trends that resemble the current performance of the stock. If such sequence is found, and if there exists enough statistical information concerning the possible trends of the stock, then we can predict how a stock is likely to behave in the next few periods. The identification of the current state is accomplished by identifying the maximum-length sequence of events that exists in the prediction tree. To achieve this, a string of past events is formed and search in the prediction table is initiated to identify a match for the current string. If a match is found, a new event is added to the sequence ($N = N + 1$) and a new matching process is initiated. If there is no match, the previous sequence is used as the current state. The matching process can be implemented efficiently using hashing tables similarly to the textual substitution [34, 38] algorithms used for data compression purposes of textual data. Once the maximum string has been identified, the prediction table for the future values of stock is predicted similar to the encoding process of arithmetic coders [39].

3.3 Adaptation

In this step, we use current information regarding the performance of a stock and prediction errors of our model dynamically adapt the prediction tree. This will improve the performance of our model. The adaptation part consists of modification of the transition tables so that the model learns new information: creation of new tree nodes in case that observed transitions do not exist in the current tables, and creation of new events once the distance between an observed event and its best-match vector is larger than a predefined threshold. This last step is similar to the splitting step that takes place during the creation of VQ codebooks for image or speech data. Once a vector (stock-event) whose distance from the best-match exceeds a certain threshold has been found, a new entry is created in the prediction tree. If a collection of vectors X_i, had B as the best-match vector, and a new vector Y has been encountered that has B as its best-match vector, but its distance from B exceeds a certain threshold, a new codevector B' is created. The X_i vectors will then be reassigned to either B or B' so that the quantization error for all X_i is minimized based on a given measure. It should be noted that a fair amount of computation is involved in this step since a large portion of the prediction tree will have to be readjusted.

4 Empirical results for Stock market prediction

4.1 Introduction

As noted earlier, data compression techniques are a perfect paradigm for stock market prediction. For our empirical tests we have adopted a notion of markets being multimodal [35], the prices obeying fractional Brownian motion and the returns distributed in accordance with stable-Levy distribution. This approach embodies the state of the art in nonlinear, chaotic, stock market models. It also presents some interesting compression issues. For example, we develop a dynamic memory VQ technique in order to quantize a vector that may have a variable window size. This window size is calculated by regarding the markets and statistically self-similar fractals and calculating its fractional dimension using the R/S statistic of Mandelbrot [30]. The R/S statistic adequately captures the long range memory of stock markets, and we can use this estimate to truncate the window appropriately. It is important to be able to precisely calculate this window, because if we quantized a price-time stock market vector that contained components that were not influencing the present, or for that matter, the future prices, our prediction and compression would be inaccurate. Once a memory window has been calculated, using lossy TVQ we map the price-time vector to its proper equivalence class, under a given market mode. From this data we can by the means of lossless LZ algorithm predict the next highest probable market mode, price of a stock or a group of stocks or any other parameter we are interested in. Preliminary experiments using only lossless techniques indicate a small, but significant degree of prediction.

4.2 Lossless compression - results

Below we present results of Lempel-Ziv for predicting rises and falls of all major world indices. We consider logarithmic returns, and apply uniform scalar quantization of the entries. We then run the LZ algorithm, and predict a rise or a fall from day to day returns. Each time we guess correctly we score a +1, and each time we guess incorrectly we score nothing. If we are at a leaf, we do not guess. The results, continent-wise, are tabulated below. Our lossless prediction scheme yields an average success of 55.06 percent, which we find very encouraging. It should be noted, however, that our results include periods where markets are stable(i.e. no price changes), and hence would in return yield higher compression ratios. These, although very few, instances do not significantly affect the results, and are discounted in our future work with lossy compression.

Simulation results - U.S. and Canada	
Market	**Percent Correct**
DowJones	51.10
Snp500	51.42
Toronto	54.83
Average	52.45

Europe	
Market	% Correct
Denmark	58.81
Germany	52.34
Finland	61.85
Netherla	51.48
Norway	56.07
Paris	57.11
Portugal	61.28
Spain	62.63
Sweden	55.80
Swtzrlnd	51.93
United Kingdom	52.85
Average	56.56

Asia and Africa	
Market	% Correct
Hongkong	50.95
Indonesia	60.03
Korea	53.98
Malasyia	52.33
Phillipines	53.97
Singapore	53.21
Taiwan	54.93
Thailand	52.58
Tokyo	51.93
South Africa	58.09
Average	54.20

References

[1] Gersho A and R. M. Gray. *Vector Quantization and Signal Compression.* Kluwer Academic Publishers, Norwell, Massachusetts, 1992.

[2] R. L. Baker and Y. T. Tse. Compression of high spectral resolution imagery. In *Proc. of SPIE: Applications of Digital Image Processing*, pages 255–264, August 1988.

[3] T. C. Bell, J. C. Cleary, and I. H. Witten. *Text Compression.* Prentice-Hall, 1990.

[4] Fischer Black, Michael Jensen, and Myron Scholes. The capital assets pricing model: some empirical tests. In Jenson, editor, *Jenson (ed.)*, pages 79–121, 1972.

[5] P. C. Chang and R. M. Gray. Gradient algorithms for designing predictive vector quantizers. *IEEE Trans. Accoust. Speech signal Processing*, ASSP-34:679–690, August 1986.

[6] T. M. Cover and J. A. Thomas. *Extensive Games and the Problem of Information.* John Wiley, 1991.

[7] T.M. Cover and J.A. Thomas. *Elements of Information Theory.* John Wiley and Sons, New York, NY, 1991.

[8] V. Cuperman. *Efficient waveform coding of speech using vector quantization.* PhD thesis, University of California, Santa Barbara, February 1983.

[9] V. Cuperman and A. Gersho. Adaptive differential vector coding of speech. In *Proceedings of GlobeCom*, pages 1092–1096, December 1982.

[10] V. Cuperman and A. Gersho. Vector predictive coding of speech at 16 kb/s. *IEEE trans. Comm.*, COM-33:685–696, 1985.

[11] K.M. Curewitz, P. Krishnan, and J.S. Vitter. Practical prefetching via data compression. *SIGMOD*, 1993.

[12] E.F. Fama. The behavior of stock market prices. *Journal of Business*, 38, 1965.

[13] E.F. Fama. *Foundations of Finance*. Basic Books, Inc., New York, New York, 1976.

[14] Eugene F. Fama. Efficient capital markets II. *Journal of Finance*, 46(5), June 1991.

[15] T. R. Fischer and D. J. Tinnen. Quantized control with differential pulse code modulation. In *Conference Proceedings: 21st Conference on Decision and Control*, pages 1222–1227, December 1982.

[16] T. R. Fischer and D. J. Tinnen. Quantized control using differential encoding. *Optimal Control Applications and Methods*, pages 69–83, 1984.

[17] T. R. Fischer and D. J. Tinnen. Quantized control with data compression constraints. *Optimal Control Applications and Methods*, 5:39–55, January 1984.

[18] R. M. Gray. Vector Quantization. *IEEE ASSP Magazine*, 1:4–29, April 1984.

[19] R. M. Gray and H. Abut. Full search and tree searched vector quantization of speech waveforms. *Proc. ICASSP*, pages 593–596, May 1982.

[20] S. Gupta and A. Gersho. Feature predictive vector quantization of multipsectral images. *Trans. on Geoscience & remote sensing*, 30(3):491–501, May 1992.

[21] H. Hang and J. W. Woods. Predictive vector quantization of images. *IEEE Trans. Acous. Speech and Sig. Proc.*, 33, Nov. 1985.

[22] D.A. Hsieh. Chaos and nonlinear dynamics: Application of financial markets. *J. Finance*, 46(5), 1991.

[23] J. S. Lim. *Two Dimensional Image and Signal Processing*. Prentice-Hall, 1990.

[24] Y. Linde, A. Buzo, and R. M. Gray. An algorithm for vector quantizer design. *IEEE Trans. on Commun.*, 28:84–95, Jan. 1980.

[25] A.W. Lo and C. MacKinlay. Stock prices do not follow random walks: Evidence form a simple specification test. *Rev. Finan. Stud.*, 1(1), 1988.

[26] B. Mandelbrot. The pareto-levy law and the distribution of income. *Inter. Nat. Econ. Rev.*, 1, 1960.

[27] B. Mandelbrot. Statistical methodology for non-periodic cycles. *Ann. Econ. Soc. Measr.*, 1, 1972.

[28] T. Markas and J. Reif. Image compression methods with distortion control capabilities. In *Proceedings of 1st Annual Data Compression Conference*, pages 121–130, April 1991.

[29] T. Markas and J. Reif. Mutispectral image compression algorithms. In *Proceedings of 3rd Annual Data Compression Conference*, pages 391–400, April 1993.

[30] E.E. Peters. *Chaos and Order in the Capital Markets.* John Wiley & Sons, 1991.

[31] J. Magee R.D. Edwards. *Technical Analysis of Stock Trends.* John Magee Inc., Boston, USA, 1992.

[32] Jose A. Scheinakman. Nonlinearities in economic dynamics. Technical report, Working paper, SFI Economics Research Program, 1989.

[33] William F. Sharpe. Capital asset prices: A theory of market equilibrium under conditions of risk. *Journal of Finance*, pages 425–442, September 1964.

[34] J. A. Storer. *Data Compression: Methods and Theory.* Computer Science Press, Rockville, MD, 1988.

[35] T. Vaga. The coherent market hypothesis. *Financial Analysts Jounral*, December/January 1991.

[36] J. S. Vitter and P. Krishnan. Optimal prefetching via data compression. In *Proceedings of 32nd Annual IEEE Symposium on FOCS*, pages 121–130, October 1991.

[37] B. LeBaron W.A. Brock, D.A. Hsieh. *Nonlinear Dynamics, Chaos, and Instability.* MIT Press, Boston, USA, 1991.

[38] T. A. Welch. A technique for high-performance data compression. *Commun. of ACM*, pages 8–19, June 1984.

[39] I. H. Witten, R. M. Neal, and J. G. Cleary. Arithmetic coding for data compression. *Commun. of ACM*, pages 520–540, June 1987.

[40] Holbrook Working. Capital asset prices: A theory of market equilibrium under conditions of risk. *American Economics Review*, 48:188–199, 1958.

[41] J. Ziv and A. Lempel. Compression of individual sequences via variable-rate coding. *IEEE Transactions of Information Theory*, 24:530–536, September 1978.

Huffman - type Codes for Infinite Source Distributions

Julia Abrahams
Mathematical Sciences Division
Office of Naval Research
Arlington, VA 22217-5660

Abstract

A new sufficient condition is given for an infinite source distribution to share a minimum average codeword length code with the geometric distribution. Thus some new examples of parametric families of infinite source distributions can be optimally encoded by Huffman - type codes.

I. Introduction

In the case of infinite sources for which the constructive Huffman algorithm does not apply, an indirect approach has been taken to obtain the minimum average codeword length code for certain parametric families of source distributions. For infinite sources, Gallager and Van Voorhis [3] find the optimal code for the geometric source, completing the solution to a problem first addressed by Golomb [4]. Humblet [6] solves the problem for the Poisson distribution. These results and the methods used to obtain them will be addressed further in the next section.

It also appears that a problem equivalent to coding the infinite geometric source and a finite distribution related to it arises in the statistics literature on group testing and in a search problem in the operations research literature where independent results appear. In particular, Hwang [7] gives explicit expressions for the minimum average binary codeword length for source probabilities $p_k = a^{k-1}(1-a)/(1-a^n)$ for n both finite and infinite where $0<a<1$. The codeword lengths themselves seem to be implicit. Explicit codeword lengths for the finite source are derived in Yao and Hwang [8] but only for $M = 2$ where M is the unique positive integer solution to $a^M + a^{M+1} \leq 1 < a^M + a^{M-1}$, that is for $0.618 \leq a \leq 0.755$. The case of $M = 1$, that is $a \leq 0.618$, is well known to be solved by $l_k = k$, $k < n$, $l_n = n-1$. Hassin [5] also discusses these problems in part.

In this note, a new sufficient condition for infinite sources to have minimum average codeword length codes of particular form are presented together with its application to example parametric source distributions. This generalizes the results of Gallager and Van Voorhis [3] and Humblet [6].

II. Sufficient Conditions for a Family of Infinite Codes to Minimize Average Codeword Length

Humblet [6] shows for probabilities $p_0 \geq p_1 \geq \ldots$ that for $p_k \geq p_{k+2} + p_{k+3} + \ldots$ for all k the corresponding codeword lengths in the optimal binary code are given by $l_k = k+1$. In addition, if Humblet's sufficient condition holds only for $k \geq m$, the optimal codeword lengths can be obtained from the Huffman algorithm applied to the reduced source with probabilities $p_0, p_1, \ldots, p_m, p_{m+1}+p_{m+2}+\ldots$; if the lengths of these codewords are l_k', $k = 0, 1, \ldots, m+1$, the lengths for the original source are $l_k = l_k'$, $k = 0, 1, \ldots, m$, $l_k = l_{m+1}' + k-m$, $k = m+1, m+2, \ldots$. In particular, the geometric distribution $p_k = a^k(1-a)$ satisfies the sufficient condition for all k for $a \leq (\sqrt{5}-1)/2 \approx 0.618$ (that is for a satisfying $a+a^2 \leq 1$) as does the Poisson distribution $p_k = (a^k e^{-a})/k!$ for $a \leq 1$. For $a > 1$, the Poisson distribution satisfies the condition for $k \geq m$ where m depends on a.

Gallager and Van Voorhis's [3] reduced source approach to the geometric distribution is the basis for Humblet's analysis as well as for the more extensive generalization to be given in this note. For the geometric distribution with M the unique integer solution to

$$a^M + a^{M+1} \leq 1 < a^M + a^{M-1}, \tag{1}$$

Gallager and Van Voorhis construct the reduced source with probabilities $p_0, p_1, \ldots, p_m, p_{m+1}+p_{m+1+M}+p_{m+1+2M}+\ldots, p_{m+2}+p_{m+2+M}+p_{m+2+2M}+\ldots, \ldots, p_{m+M}+p_{m+2M}+\ldots$ when $p_k = a^k(1-a)$. They binary Huffman code the reduced source making use of inequalities among the probabilities to determine the two lowest weight symbols to merge at each stage of the Huffman procedure and then examine the limiting situation as $m \rightarrow \infty$. The result is that $l_0, l_1, \ldots, l_{m-1}$ are determined according to the Huffman code for $p_0+p_M+p_{2M}+\ldots$, $p_1+p_{1+M}+p_{1+2M}+\ldots$, $\ldots$, $p_{M-1}+p_{2M-1}+p_{3M-1}+\ldots$, respectively and $l_k = l_\beta + \alpha$ for $k = \alpha M+\beta$.

The optimal codes have n_i codewords of length i, i = 1, 2, ..., given in Table 1. For convenient reference, denote a family of codes with these lengths for each M as M-codes.

The contribution of this note is to point out that Gallager and Van Voorhis's argument goes through not only for the geometric distribution but more generally. In particular, we have the

<u>Proposition</u>: The set of inequalities

$$p_{k+M-1} + p_{k+2M-1} + p_{k+3M-1}+\ldots \geq p_k \geq p_{k+M+1} + p_{k+2M+1} + p_{k+3M+1}+\ldots, \tag{2}$$

$k = 0,1,2,\ldots$, where $p_0 \geq p_1 \geq \ldots$, holding for some M is sufficient for the optimal binary code to be given by an M-code. (Note that this condition (2) for arbitrary probabilities reduces to Gallager and Van Voorhis's (1) for the geometric distribution.)

The derivation exactly follows Gallager and Van Voorhis. For the reduced source with m+1+M symbols, the Huffman algorithm first combines p_m and $p_{m+M}+p_{m+1+2M}+\ldots$ since $p_{m+M}+p_{m+2M}+\ldots$

$\leq p_{m-1}$ and $p_{m-1+M}+p_{m-1+2M}+\ldots \geq p_m$, because of the generalized sufficient condition (2). The combination gives a composite symbol with probability $p_m+p_{m+M}+p_{m+2M}+\ldots$, and the situation is now that of the reduced source with m+M letters. The process continues, and a limiting step as in Gallager and Van Voorhis completes the demonstration.

We also have as in Humblet's generalization of Gallager and Van Voorhis for M = 1, the

Corollary: If the generalized sufficient condition (2) holds for $k \geq m$, then the codeword lengths for the optimal binary code are determined according to the Huffman code for p_0, p_1, $\ldots$ p_m, $p_{m+1+M}+p_{m+1+2M}+\ldots$, $p_{m+2}+p_{m+2+M}+p_{m+2+2M}+\ldots$, $\ldots$, $p_{m+M}+p_{m+2M}+\ldots$; if the lengths of these codewords are l_k', $k = 0, 1, \ldots, m+M$, the lengths for the original source are $l_k = l_k'$, $k = 0, 1, \ldots, m$, $l_k = l_{m+\beta}' + \alpha$, for $k = \alpha M+\beta \geq m+1$.

III. New Examples of Optimal Codes for Infinite Sources

Because there are so few examples of infinite sources for which optimal codes are known, it is of interest to apply the sufficient condition (2) of the previous section to some parametric families. One example to which (2) applies at least in part is the distribution $p_{2k} = a^{k+1}(1-a)$, $p_{2k+1} = a^k(1-a)^2$, $k = 0,1,2, \ldots$ which is monotonically ordered as $p_0 \geq p_2 \geq p_4 \geq \ldots \geq p_{2(N-1)} \geq p_1 \geq p_{2N} \geq p_3 \geq p_{2(N+1)} \geq p_5 \geq \ldots$ where N is the unique positive integer determined by $a^{N+1} \leq 1-a < a^N$.

For N = 1, (2) holds with M = 2 whenever $(1-a)^2 \geq a^3$, and the vector of number of codewords of each length (0,2,2,2,...) is optimal for this distribution for a satisfying $0.5 \leq a \leq 0.57$. For N = 2, (2) holds with M = 3 whenever $(1-a^2-a^3)/(1-a^3) \geq 1-a \geq (1-a-a^3)/(1-a^3)$, $(a-a^2+a^5)/(1-a^3) \geq 1-a \geq (a^2-a^3+a^6)/(1-a^3)$, (this is the constraining pair of inequalities), and $(1-a+a^4)/(1-a^3) \geq a \geq (a-a^2+a^5)/(1-a^3)$; thus the length distribution vector (0,1,3,3,...) is optimal for this distribution for a satisfying $0.57 \leq a \leq 0.66$. The example distribution not been verified to satisfy (2) for other parameter values due to the complexity of the calculations involved. A mathematical computer package with symbolic manipulation capability should be effective in carrying out these calculations; this has not been pursued here.

However Golomb's [4] plausibility argument for the geometric distribution also can be used to suggest promising candidate codes for this example distribution for certain values of a. The candidate codes would need to be verified through (2). The argument is that for $a^j = 1/2$, the symbol with probability $a^{k+j}(1-a)$ is half as likely as the symbol with probability $a^k(1-a)$ and should require a codeword one bit longer. Similarly the symbol with probability $a^{k+j}(1-a)^2$ should require a codeword one bit longer than that with probability $a^k(1-a)^2$. Indeed this argument, together with the imposition of equality in the Kraft-McMillan inequality, $\Sigma n_i 2^{-i} = 1$, yields the codeword length distribution vectors (0,2,2,2,...) for a = 0.5, which has already been verified to satisfy (2), (0,1,2,4,4,...) for a = 0.707, that is the M = 4 case for $m \geq 3$, and (0,0,3,4,6,6,...) for a = 0.794, that is the M = 6 case for $m \geq 5$, and (2) should be able to be verified for these parameter values.

This particular example distribution arises in a run length coding problem. Assume the binary source generates 0's and 1's independently with probabilities $a \geq 0.5$ and 1-a respectively. In standard run length coding, runs of k 0's followed by a single 1 are each assigned a codeword. The runs are geometrically distributed so that M-codes encode them with minimum average codeword length. Consider instead runs of 0's punctuated by the occurrence of either the string 10 or 11. This nonstandard run length coding scheme leads to the example distribution discussed above. Clearly many highly structured nonstandard run length coding schemes lead to infinite source distributions of parametric form, however in general it appears difficult to identify parameter values for which (2) is satisfied.

Another example infinite source distribution to which (2) also applies at least in part is the two sided geometric distribution $p_k = a^{|k|}(1-a)/(1+a)$, $k = 0, \pm1, \pm2, \ldots$ used by Cheung et al. [1,2] in an image compression application. They propose a variant of M-codes in which $l_0 = 1$, l_k for $k > 0$ is obtained from the M-code plus one additional bit, and l_k for $k < 0$ is equal to l_k for $k > 0$. They find the minimum average codeword length possible over the class of M-code variants for the two sided geometric distribution. When the average codeword length for the Huffman code for a finite approximation to the two sided geometric distribution, obtained numerically, matches the minimum over the class of M-code variants, they conclude on the basis of numerical evidence that the optimal code has been found for particular values of a to be in fact one of the M-code variants. By using the corollary, it can be confirmed, for example, that the M-code variant for M = 2 is in fact the minimum average codeword length code for $0.618 \leq a \leq 0.707$ as the numerical evidence suggests, and, a new result, it can be seen that the M-code itself for M = 4 is the optimal code for $0.707 \leq a < 0.755$ for the two sided geometric distribution. Again, while numerical evidence in [1,2] suggests that the M-code variants are optimal for additional parameter ranges and while it may be that M-codes themselves are optimal for parameter ranges where the numerical evidence indicates that M-code variants are not optimal, the two sided geometric distribution has not been verified to satisfy (2) for other parameter values due to the complexity of the calculations involved.

If two sources satisfy sufficient conditions for the same optimal code, it is immediate that their convex combination satisfies the same conditions and therefore is optimally coded by the same code. Thus, for example, the distribution given by

$$p_{2k} = c\ a^{k+1}(1-a) + (1-c)b^{2k}(1-b),$$
$$p_{2k+1} = c\ a^{k}(1-a)^2+(1-c)b^{2k+1}(1-b)$$

for $a \in [0.5, 0.57]$, $b \in [0.618, 0.775]$, and $c \in [0,1]$ is optimally coded by the M-code with $M = 2$.

IV. Optimal Ternary Coding

The same approach can be used to find sufficient conditions for optimal full ternary codes. First, a plausibility argument based on Golomb's using $(a^2)^M = 1/3$ finds us candidate optimal codes for geometric sources and particular values of a. These codes suggest the form of the reduced source for which an argument along the lines of Gallager and Van Voorhis goes through both for geometric sources and the more general case addressed in this note for binary. The reduced sources are of the form

$$p_0,\ p_1,\ \ldots,\ p_m,\ p_{m+1}+p_{m+2}+p_{m+2M+1}+p_{m+2M+2}+\ldots,$$
$$p_{m+3}+p_{m+4}+p_{m+2M+3}+p_{m+2M+4}+\ldots,\ \ldots,\ p_{m+2M-1}+p_{m+2M}+p_{m+4M-1}+p_{m+4M}+\ldots.$$

The combination in the Huffman algorithm of p_{m-1}, p_m, and $p_{m+2M-1}+p_{m+2M}+p_{m+4M-1}+p_{m+4M}+\ldots$, which leads to a reduced source with two fewer symbols, is ensured if

$$p_{m+2M-1}+p_{m+2M}+p_{m+4M-1}+p_{m+4M}+\ldots \le p_{m-2}$$

and

$$p_{m+2M-3}+p_{m+2M-2}+p_{m+4M-3}+p_{m+4M-2} \ge p_{m-1}.$$

The overall sufficient conditions which imply this pair of inequalities are

$$p_{k+2M-2}+p_{k+2M-1}+p_{k+4M-2}+p_{k+4M-1}+\ldots \ge p_k \ge p_{k+2M+1}+p_{k+2M+2}+p_{k+4M+1}+p_{k+4M+2}, \quad (3)$$

$k = 0,1,2,\ \ldots.$ For the special geometric case, M is determined according to

$$a^{2(M-1)} \ge (1-a^{2M})/(1+a) \ge a^{2M+1}.$$

The optimal codes have n_i codewords of length i, i = 1, 2, ..., given in Table 2.

A ternary run length coding problem leads to a nongeometric distribution which can also be shown to satisfy (3) for certain parameter values. Here runs of $k > 0$ 0's followed by a single 1 or 2 are each assigned a codeword. If 0's occur with probability a_0, 1's with probability a_1, and 2's with probability a_2, where $a_0 + a_1 + a_2 = 1$, then the infinite source probabilities are a_1, a_2, a_0a_1, a_0a_2, $a_0^2a_1$, $a_0^2a_2$, ... in monotonically nonincreasing order whenever $a_1 \ge a_2 \ge a_0a_1$. For example, for $a_0 = .1$, $a_1 = .7$, $a_2 = .2$, we find that (3) is satisfied for $M = 1$, and the optimal code has the codeword lengths given in Table 2.

These seem to be the only nonbinary optimal codes known for infinite sources. It may well be that other parametric source distributions also satisfy the ternary sufficient conditions (3), but that has not been pursued here. Nor has the D-ary case been pursued, but the same general approach should apply.

V. Conclusion

A new sufficient condition which is useful in optimally binary coding some infinite source distributions is presented. Some new infinite source distributions are optimally coded using this condition. The generalization to ternary coding, particularly for the geometric distribution, is given.

References

1. K.- M. Cheung and P. Smyth, "A high-speed distortionless predictive image compression scheme," Proceedings 1990 International Symposium on Information Theory and Its Applications, Honolulu, Hawaii, pp. 467-470, Nov. 27-30, 1990.

2. K.- M. Cheung, P. Smyth, and H. Wang, "A high-speed distortionless predictive image - compression scheme," TDA Progress Report 42-102, Jet Propulsion Laboratory, Pasadena, CA, Aug. 15, 1990.

3. R. G. Gallager and D.C. Van Voorhis, "Optimal source codes for geometrically distributed alphabets," IEEE Trans. Inform. Theory, vol. IT-21, no. 2, pp. 228-230, Mar. 1975.

4. S. W. Golomb, "Run-length encodings," IEEE Trans. Inform. Theory, vol. IT-12, no. 4, pp. 339-401, Jul. 1966.

5. R. Hassin, "A dichotomous search for a geometric random variable," Operations Research, vol. 32, no. 2, pp. 423-439, Mar.-Apr. 1984.

6. P. Humblet, "Optimal source coding for a class of integer alphabets," IEEE Trans. Inform. Theory, vol. IT-24, no. 1, pp. 110-112, Jan. 1978.

7. F. K. Hwang, "On finding a single defective in binomial group testing," J. American Statistical Association, vol. 69, no. 345, pp. 146-150, Mar. 1974.

8. Y. C. Yao and F. K. Hwang, "On optimal nested group testing algorithms," J. Statistical Planning and Inference, vol. 24, pp. 167-175, 1990.

M	$(n_1, n_2, n_3, n_4, \ldots)$
1	(1, 1, 1, 1, ...)
2	(0, 2, 2, 2, ...)
3	(0, 1, 3, 3, ...)
4	(0, 0, 4, 4, ...)
5	(0, 0, 3, 5, 5, ...)
6	(0, 0, 2, 6, 6, ...)
7	(0, 0, 1, 7, 7, ...)
8	(0, 0, 0, 8, 8, ...)
9	(0, 0, 0, 7, 9, 9, ...)
...	...

Table 1: Optimal Binary Codes for Geometric Sources

M	$(n_1, n_2, n_3, n_4, \ldots)$
1	(2, 2, 2, 2, ...)
2	(1, 4, 4, 4, ...)
3	(0, 6, 6, 6, ...)
4	(0, 5, 8, 8, ...)
5	(0, 4, 10, 10, ...)
6	(0, 3, 12, 12, ...)
7	(0, 2, 14, 14, ...)
8	(0, 1, 16, 16, ...)
9	(0, 0, 18, 18, ...)
...	...

Table 2: Optimal Ternary Codes for Geometric Sources

On the redundancy of optimum fixed-to-variable length codes

Peter R. Stubley[1]
Bell-Northern Reserch

Abstract

There has been much interest in recent years in bounds on the redundancy of Huffman codes, given only partial information about the source word distribution, such as the probability of the most likely source. This work determines upper and lower bounds for the redundancy of Huffman codes of source words which are binomially distributed. Since the complete distribution is known, it is possible to determine bounds which are much tighter than other bounds in the literature, given only p, the probability of the most likely symbol of the binary source, and K, where there are 2^K source words. The upper and lower bounds will be shown to converge to the same value as K becomes large, resulting in a simple approximation which can be used to predict the redundancy of the Huffman code, given p and K, without constructing the code.

1 Introduction

Let S be an independent, identically distributed binary source, which generates a 0 with probability p, $p \geq 1-p$. Let $E[K]$ be the average code word length of the Huffman code of the alphabet obtained by taking K-bit blocks of input symbols, called source words, where the code words are also assumed to be binary, with equal cost symbols. The redundancy of the code is defined as

$$r(p,K) = E[K] - KH(S), \quad (1)$$

where $H(S) = -p\log p-(1-p)\log(1-p)$ (the logarithms are base 2). The compression ratio is

$$\rho = \frac{E[K]}{K} = H(S) + \frac{r(p,K)}{K}. \quad (2)$$

It is clear from Equation 2 that $\lim_{K\to\infty}\rho = H(S)$, since $0 \leq r(p,K) \leq 1$ for the Huffman code [7], and $\lim_{K\to\infty} 1/K = 0$. However, $\lim_{K\to\infty} r(p,K)$ is not as well understood. There have been numerous upper and lower bounds obtained for r in recent years (for example, [1, 2, 9, 10, 11]), given partial information about the source alphabet, such as the probability of the most likely source word. However, for the source words described above, obtained by taking K-bit blocks, the complete distribution is known, given p and K. The source words are binomially distributed, with probabilities of the form $p(i) = p^{K-i}(1-p)^i$, such that $\sum_{i=0}^{K}\binom{K}{i}p(i) = 1$. There are $\binom{K}{i}$ source words with probability $p(i)$.

[1]Bell-Northern Research Ltd., 16, Place du Commerce, Montréal, Québec, H3E 1H6, Phone: (514) 765-7818, Fax: (514) 761-8505, Email: stubley@bnr.ca.

Jakobssen [8] has analyzed $E[K]$ for the binomial distribution for a class of values of p, where

$$p \geq \frac{\binom{K}{\lceil K/2 \rceil} + 1}{\binom{K}{\lceil K/2 \rceil} + 2}. \tag{3}$$

However, observe that the values of p which satisfy Equation 3 become closer and closer to 1 as K becomes large. This approach does not allow us to consider the behaviour of a particular value of $E[K]$ for a particular value of p as K becomes large.

Huffman codes for binomially distributed source words have also been considered by Montgomery and Kumar [12]. They are particularly interested in the conditions which are necessary to ensure that Huffman code of a 2-symbol block is more efficient than simply constructing the Huffman code for the original source alphabet.

In this work, $r(p, K)$ is analyzed for the binomial distribution for arbitrary values of p, with simple closed forms for particular values of p. In particular, the problem of interest is what happens to $r(p, K)$ as K becomes large. The approach taken will be to derive upper and lower bounds on $r(p, K)$, and showing that the upper and lower bounds converge as K becomes large. Using this approach, it will be shown that $r(p, K)$ does not, in general, vanish, and does not monotonically increase or decrease, but tends to oscillate between values nearer and farther from 0.

2 Properties of Huffman codes of binomial distributions

This section assumes that a modified form of the Huffman algorithm is used (see Appendix). The modification ensures that the Huffman code produced by the algorithm is unique (there is only one code for a given source word distribution, which is not always the case for Huffman's original algorithm), and is constructed such that the longest code words have the shortest possible length. This assumption does not affect the optimality of the code produced by the modified algorithm, since all the Huffman codes for the same source word distribution have the same average length.

If there are M source words, each with probability $1/M$, then their code words will have length $\lfloor \log_2 M \rfloor$ or $(\lfloor \log_2 M \rfloor + 1)$ [4, 6]. A similar property holds for binomial distributions – if two source words have equal probabilities, then their code words will differ in length by at most 1, which follows from Gallager's sibling property [5]. Furthermore, the least likely source word, with probability $p(K)$, will have a code word with the same length as the source word with probability $p(K-1)$ with the longest code word, which is a direct result of the Huffman algorithm.

Let l_{c_j} be the length of the j-th source word, and let S_i be the set of source words with probability $p(i)$. Then,

$$E[K] = \sum_{j=1}^{2^K} p_j l_{c_j} \tag{4}$$

$$= \sum_{i=0}^{K} \binom{K}{i} p(i) L(i), \tag{5}$$

where p_j is the probability of the j-th source word, and

$$L(i) = \frac{1}{\binom{K}{i}} \sum_{j \in S_i} l_{c_j}. \tag{6}$$

Using Equation 4, the redundancy of the code is

$$r(p, K) = \sum_{i=0}^{K} \binom{K}{i} p(i) \left[L(i) + \log_2 p(i) \right]. \tag{7}$$

When $E[K]$ is expressed in the form of Equation 4, it is easily shown that the redundancy can be zero only if the source word distribution is dyadic; that is, $p_j = 2^{-z_j}$, for z_j a positive integer, and $l_{c_j} = z_j$. Equation 7 appears to relax this constraint, since zero redundancy may be obtained if $L(i) = \log_2 p(i)$ for all i, and $L(i)$ may take non-integer values. In fact, as will be shown, zero redundancy is not in general, attainable, unless $p = 1/2$.

2.1 Determining the code word lengths

In order to find the redundancy, it is necessary to determine the lengths of the code words. From the above properties of the code word lengths, the code words for S_i must have length $l(i)$ or $l(i)+1$, where $l(i)$ is a positive integer. Let n_i be the number of code words with length $l(i)+1$. Then, from the definition of $L(i)$, $L(i) = l(i) + \frac{n_i}{\binom{K}{i}}$, $i = 0, 1, \ldots, K$. It is neccessary to determine n_i and $l(i)$.

The Huffman code minimizes $r(p, K) = E[K] - KH(S)$. By removing all the constraints on $\{L(i), i = 0, 1, \ldots, K\}$, except $\sum_{i=0}^{K} \binom{K}{i} 2^{-L(i)} = 1$, then it is easy to show using Lagrange multipliers that $L_{opt}(i) = -\log_2 p(i)$ achieves the minimum solution, with $r = 0$. Similarly, letting $L(i) = l(i) + n(i)/\binom{K}{i}$, where $l(i)$ is a positive integer, and $0 \leq n(i) \leq \binom{K}{i}$, but with no integer constraint, then clearly, $l(i) = \lfloor -\log_2 p(i) \rfloor$ and $n(i) = \binom{K}{i} (-log_2 p(i) - l(i))$ is also an optimum solution, with $r = 0$. The integer values for $n(i)$ will be considered in the next section.

In fact, setting $l(i) = \lfloor -\log_2 p(i) \rfloor$ will only achieve a Huffman code if K is sufficiently large, and $p < 1$. If $p = 1$, then $r = 1$ for any K. When K is small, and p is near 1, then $p(K-1)$ may be much less than $2^K - 1$, which is the length of the longest possible Huffman code word for a block length of K. Since $p \geq 1/2$, then $2^K - 1$ grows faster than $p(K-1)$ decays, and the above value for $l(i)$ will become the Huffman code length, as K gets large, when $p < 1$. Also, using the properties of Huffman codes, $L(K) = l(K-1)$ or $l(K-1) + 1$.

3 Determining the redundancy

The number of code words of length $l(i)+1$, $n(i)$, will not be exactly determined, but will be upper and lower bounded, using the Kraft inequality. Let $d_i = \sum_{j\in S_i} 2^{-l_{c_j}}$. If $d_i \le \binom{K}{i}p(i)$ for all i, then the Kraft inequality will be satisfied, which will ensure that a prefix codes with lengths l_{c_j} exists. This code will be an upper bound on the Huffman code.

Note that from this point on, the constraint that $L(K)$ is determined from $\lfloor -\log_2 p(K-1)\rfloor$ and not $\lfloor -\log_2 p(K)\rfloor$ will be ignored. This approximation will simplify the ensuing development, but will not affect the final answer, since both $2^{-L(K)}$ and $p(K)\log_2 p(K)$ vanish as K becomes large.

Observe that

$$d_i \;=\; 2^{-l(i)}\left[\binom{K}{i} \;-\; \frac{n_i}{2}\right]. \tag{8}$$

If $n_i = \lceil 2\binom{K}{i}\left[1-p(i)2^{l(i)}\right]\rceil$, then $d_i \le \binom{K}{i}p(i)$, and the Kraft inequality will be satisfied. Let $f_i = l(i)+\log_2 p(i) = \lfloor -\log_2 p(i)\rfloor + \log_2 p(i)$, and let

$$L_U(i) \;=\; l(i) \;+\; \frac{1}{\binom{K}{i}}\lceil 2\binom{K}{i}(1-2^{f_i})\rceil, \tag{9}$$

and

$$L_L(i) \;=\; l(i) \;+\; \frac{1}{\binom{K}{i}}\lfloor 2\binom{K}{i}(1-2^{f_i})\rfloor. \tag{10}$$

If $L(i)$ is the value obtained by the Huffman code, then $L_L(i) \le L(i) \le L_U(i)$, $i \ne K$. From the definition of redundancy,

$$\begin{aligned}
&\sum_{i=0}^{K}\binom{K}{i}p(i)\left[f_i \;+\; \frac{1}{\binom{K}{i}}\lfloor 2\binom{K}{i}(1-2^{f_i})\rfloor\right] \;\le\\
&r(p,K) \le\\
&\sum_{i=0}^{K}\binom{K}{i}p(i)\left[f_i \;+\; \frac{1}{\binom{K}{i}}\lceil 2\binom{K}{i}(1-2^{f_i})\rceil\right]
\end{aligned} \tag{11}$$

and

$$\begin{aligned}
&\sum_{i=1}^{K-1}\binom{K}{i}p(i)\left[f_i+\frac{1}{\binom{K}{i}}\lfloor 2\binom{K}{i}(1-2^{f_i})\rfloor\right] \;+\; p(0)\left[f_0+\lfloor 2(1-2^{f_0})\rfloor\right] \;+\\
&p(K)\left[f_K+\lfloor 2(1-2^{f_K})\rfloor\right] \;\le\\
&r(p,K) \;\le\\
&\sum_{i=1}^{K-1}\binom{K}{i}p(i)\left[f_i+\frac{1}{\binom{K}{i}}\lceil 2\binom{K}{i}(1-2^{f_i})\rceil\right] \;+\; p(0)\left[f_0+\lceil 2(1-2^{f_0})\rceil\right] \;+\\
&p(K)\left[f_K+\lceil 2(1-2^{f_K})\rceil\right].
\end{aligned} \tag{12}$$

Observe that $-1 < f_i \le 0$, which implies that $\lfloor 2(1-2^{f_i})\rfloor = 0$, and $\lceil 2(1-2^{f_i})\rceil = 1$, and Equation 12 becomes

$$\sum_{i=0}^{K}\binom{K}{i}p(i)f_i + \sum_{i=1}^{K-1}\binom{K}{i}p(i)\left[f_i + \frac{1}{\binom{K}{i}}\lfloor 2\binom{K}{i}(1-2^{f_i})\rfloor\right] \le$$

$$r(p,K) \le$$

$$\sum_{i=0}^{K}\binom{K}{i}p(i)f_i + \sum_{i=1}^{K-1}\binom{K}{i}p(i)\left[f_i + \frac{1}{\binom{K}{i}}\lceil 2\binom{K}{i}(1-2^{f_i})\rceil\right] +$$

$$p(0) + p(K). \tag{13}$$

As K becomes large, for $p < 1$, the term $p(0) + p(K)$ becomes negligibly small. This, combined with the observation that $\lim_{a\to\infty}\frac{\lfloor ax\rfloor}{a} = \lim_{a\to\infty}\frac{\lceil ax\rceil}{a} = x$, implies that the upper and lower bounds of Equation 13 converge, and

$$\lim_{K\to\infty} r(p,K) = \lim_{K\to\infty}\left[\sum_{i=0}^{K}\binom{K}{i}p(i)f_i + \sum_{i=1}^{K-1}2\binom{K}{i}p(i)(1-2^{f_i})\right]. \tag{14}$$

Equation 14 is the fundamental result of this correspondence, but it is difficult to completely resolve the limit without further constraints on p.

3.1 Closed-form results for a class of values of p

Numerical results for $r(p,K)$ can be easily obtained from Equation 14 for any value of p. However, a more intuitive closed-form can be obtained for a particular class of values for p, where $p = (1+2^{-M})^{-1}$, for M a positive integer. For these values of p, $\log_2[(1-p)/p]$ is an integer, and $f_i = K\log_2 p + \lfloor -K\log_2 p\rfloor = f$ for all i. Equation 14 becomes

$$\begin{aligned}\lim_{K\to\infty} r(p,K) &= \lim_{K\to\infty}\left[f + 2(1-2^f)(1-p(0)-p(K))\right] \\ &= \lim_{K\to\infty}\left[f + 2(1-2^f)\right].\end{aligned}$$

It is clear that $\lim_{K\to\infty}[f + 2(1-2^f)]$ does not exist, and does not decay as K becomes large. Instead, it shows that $r(p,K)$ has a behaviour which is determined by the numerical properties of $K\log_2 p$, becoming closer to 0 when $-K\log_2 p$ is close to $\lfloor -K\log_2 p\rfloor$.

It is interesting to note that $\max_{-1<f\le 0}[f + 2(1-2^f)] = \log_2 2/(e\ln 2) \approx 0.086$, which is the number obtained by Gallager in [5] in determining upper bounds on r, given the probability of the most likely source word. Gallager obtains this value as the maximum of the function $H(q_1, q_2, \ldots, q_L)$, where the Huffman code tree is full at depth l, the q_i's are the probabilities of the nodes at depth l, $L = 2^l$, and $H()$ is the entropy function. The maximum value occurs at an extreme point, where $q_i = q_1$, for $i \le n$, for some $1 \le n \le L$, and $q_i = q_1/2$ for $n < i \le L$. A distribution of this form is similar to the binomial distributions which are being considered here, where there are blocks of nodes with the same probabilities.

K	$p = 0.666667$		$p = 0.8$		$p = 0.888889$	
	r	r_b	r	r_b	r	r_b
5	0.021690	0.021690	0.079960	0.079639	0.040585	0.040517
6	0.085561	0.085561	0.019919	0.019855	0.007377	0.007369
7	0.032377	0.032377	0.068795	0.068782	0.056676	0.056675
8	0.071710	0.071710	0.082401	0.082398	0.081623	0.081623
9	0.070551	0.070551	0.028906	0.028905	0.084917	0.084917
10	0.040517	0.040517	0.062732	0.062732	0.068966	0.068966

Table 1: Comparison of redundancy and bound.

As well, numerical results show that the redundancy of the Huffman codes for K-bit block converges quite quickly to $f + 2(1 - 2^f)$ (see Table 1), which makes it useful as a rule-of-thumb for estimating $r(p, K)$ with a simple calculation.

This approach extends naturally to source probabilities of a more general form, where $\log_2(1-p)/p = -A/B$, where A and B are positive, relatively prime integers. In this case, $p = (1 + 2^{-A/B})^{-1}$. Let

$$\begin{aligned} f_i &= K\log_2 p + i\log_2\frac{1-p}{p} + \lfloor -K\log_2 p - i\log_2\frac{1-p}{p}\rfloor \\ &= K\log_2 p - i\frac{A}{B} + \lfloor -K\log_2 p + i\frac{A}{B}\rfloor, \end{aligned}$$

for $0 \leq i \leq B-1$. Then, for large K, the redundancy converges to

$$\frac{1}{B}\sum_{i=0}^{B-1}\left[f_i + 2(1-2^{f_i})\right]. \tag{15}$$

4 Conclusions

This work has investigated the properties of the redundancy of Huffman codes for K-bit blocks of the binary source. It has been shown that for $p = (1 + 2^{-M})^{-1}$, the compression ratio for large K is

$$\rho = H(S) + \frac{f + 2(1-2^f)}{K}, \tag{16}$$

and that the redundancy of the code never goes to 0, no matter how large K becomes. Numerically, it has been shown that the redundancy of the Huffman code converges quite quickly to $f + 2(1-2^f)$, which means that the redundancy can be determined for a given K and p with only a simple calculation. In fact, the redundancies for abitrary values of p can also be approximated using Equation 15, since r is a continuous function of p, and A and B can be chosen to be as close to any p as required.

5 Appendix: The modified Huffman code

It is well-known that the Huffman code for a given source distribution is not necessarily unique. In fact, it is possible to construct a Huffman code which has code word lengths that are in some cases longer than the corresponding Shannon-Fano code word lengths (for example, see Problem 5.14 in [3]).

Recall that the Huffman code is an iterative algorithm, where the two lowest weight nodes are combined into a new node with a weight that is the sum of the weights of its two children. If at some point during the construction of the Huffman code, there are two or more nodes that have the same weight, then it is possible to construct more than one Huffman code. All the codes for the same distribution will have the same average length, but the topologies of their code trees may differ.

It is often convenient when studying the redundancy of Huffman codes to be able to use the Shannon-Fano code word lengths as upper bounds for the code word length of the Huffman code. If it is possible to construct Huffman codes that have code word lengths longer than the Shannon-Fano code words, then this approach is not feasible.

Fortunately, with a simple modification to Huffman's algorithm, it is possible to construct a Huffman code that does have average code words that are less than or equal to that of the Shannon-Fano code, by changing the algorithm so that the longest code words are as short as possible. This is achieved as follows. Assume that the nodes at each step of the Huffman algorithm are kept in a list which is ordered largest to smallest, in terms of weight, and, at each step, the bottom two nodes in the list are combined. The new node is moved up the list until the node which is immediately above it has a larger weight. Huffman's original algorithm specified that the new node should be moved up the list until the node which is immediately has the same or larger weight. If the modification is used, then the longest code words will have shortest possible length, and the lengths of the Huffman codes will indeed be less than or equal to those of the Shannon-Fano code.

References

[1] R.M. Capocelli, and A. de Santis, "Tight upper bounds on the redundancy of Huffman codes", *IEEE Trans. Inf. Theory*, Vol. 35, No.5, September 1989, pp. 1084-1091.

[2] R.M. Capocelli, and A. de Santis, "New bounds on the redundancy of Huffman codes", *IEEE Trans. Inf. Theory*, Vol. 37, No.4, July 1991, pp. 1095-1104.

[3] T.M. Cover, and J.A. Thomas, *Elements of information theory*, New York: Wiley, 1991.

[4] R.G. Gallager, *Information theory and reliable communication*, New York: Wiley, 1968.

[5] R.G. Gallager, "Variations on a theme by Huffman," *IEEE Trans. Inf. Theory*, IT-24, No.6, November 1978, pp. 668-674.

[6] N.C. Geckinli, "Two corollaries to the Huffman coding procedure," *IEEE Trans. Inf. Theory*, May 1975, pp. 342-344.

[7] D.A. Huffman, "A method for the construction of minimum redundancy codes," *Proc. IRE*, Vol. 40, 1952, pp. 1098-1101.

[8] M. Jakobssen, "Huffman coding in bit-vector compression," *Information Processing Letters*, Vol. 7, No. 6, October 1978, pp. 304-307.

[9] O. Johnsson, "On the redundancy of binary Huffman codes," *IEEE Trans. Inf. Theory*, IT-26, No.2, March 1980, pp. 220-222.

[10] D. Manstetten, "Tight upper bounds on the redundancy of Huffman codes," *IEEE Trans. Inf. Theory*, IT-38, No. 1, January 1992, pp. 144-151.

[11] B.L. Montgomery, and J. Abrahams, "On the redundancy of optimal prefix-condition codes for finite and infinite sources," *IEEE Trans. Inf. Theory*, IT-33, No. 1, January 1987, pp. 156-160.

[12] B.L. Montgomery, and B.V.K.V. Kumar, "On the average codeword length of optimal binary codes for extended sources," *IEEE Trans. Inf. Theory*, IT-33, No. 2, March 1987, pp. 293-296.

Adaptive variable-to-variable length codes

Peter R. Stubley[1]
Bell-Northern Reserch

Abstract

In the last several years, adaptive codes for fixed-to-variable length and variable-to-fixed length codes have been described. This paper examines two methods for implementing adaptive variable-to-variable length codes, which have not been considered before due to the difficulty of designing optimum variable-to-variable length codes. The two adaptive methods are based on dual-tree codes, where a source tree parses the input sequence into source words and a code tree assigns each source word a code word. One adaptive method uses a single dual-tree code, and uses an algorithm which requires a complex logic circuit to adjust the shape of the source and code trees. The second method, called state-tree codes, uses a fixed pool of dual-tree codes and a state machine to select which dual-tree code is used. State-tree codes require more memory than the first method, but only a trivial logic circuit is needed to implement the codes, which will result in a very fast circuit.

1 Introduction

Let S be a Bernoulli source that generates a zero with probability p, $p \geq 1-p$. A lossless, variable-to-variable length compression code maps blocks of source symbols, called source words, onto uniquely decodable code words. A dual-tree code (DTC) [2, 7] uses a complete binary tree, called the source tree, to parse the source sequence into source words, and a second complete binary tree, called the code tree, to assign a code word to each source word. There is a one-to-one mapping between the leaves of the source tree, T_s, and the leaves of the code tree, T_c.

Let $E[T_s]$ and $E[T_c]$ be the average depths of the source and code trees, respectively. The compression ratio, ρ, is defined as

$$\rho = \frac{E[T_c]}{E[T_s]} = H(S) + \frac{r}{E[T_s]}, \qquad (1)$$

where $H(S)$ is the entropy of the source S, and $r = E[T_c] - E[T_s]H(S)$ is the redundancy of the DTC. An optimum DTC is the source tree-code tree pair that has the minimum compression ratio over all pairs with the same number of leaves. The source probability p induces a distribution $P = \{p_1, p_2, \ldots, p_N\}$ on the leaves of T_s, where $p_i = p^{l_{s_i}-n_i}(1-p)^{n_i}$, where leaf i is at depth l_{s_i}, and there are n_i ones on the path from the root node to i. For a given source tree T_s, $E[T_c]$ (and hence ρ) is minimized by constructing the code tree T_c using Huffman's algorithm [3]. Since T_c is obtained deterministically from T_s, the optimum DTC is designed by finding the source tree

[1]Bell-Northern Research Ltd., 16, Place du Commerce, Montréal, Québec, H3E 1H6, Phone: (514) 765-7818, Fax: (514) 761-8505, Email: stubley@bnr.ca.

T_s that minimizes ρ. This paper addresses the problem of finding the optimum DTC, given p and N (the number of leaves). It also considers two methods of constructing the DTC adaptively, where p is not known beforehand.

The problem of finding the optimum DTC appears to be a difficult one. So far, the only known method is exhaustive searching over all possible source trees, although several suboptimal methods have been found. Tunstall considered this problem in 1968 [8], using an approach based on dynamic programming, which does not take advantage of the fact that T_c is the Huffman code of T_s. Freeman [2] derived an algorithm that uses this fact, and grows T_s from a root node by iteratively splitting leaves in an attempt to reduce r. Also, Fabris [1] recently constructed a DTC by combining a source tree, constructed using Tunstall's algorithm for maximizing $E[T_s]$, with a Huffman code, and then adjusting the two trees to reduce redundancy. From empirical observations of optimum DTC's [7], it appears that directly attempting to reduce r is more effective than maximizing $E[T_s]$. The problem of adaptive DTC's has not, to the author's knowledge, been considered elsewhere, and none of these approaches seems suitable for an adaptive implementation.

The next section summarizes some of the properties of optimum DTC's which make their use attractive, and describes a simple method, similar to Freeman's, for constructing nearly optimal DTC's when p is known, and adaptively when it is not. Section 3 shows another approach to adaptive coding with DTC's, which requires more memory to implement than the method of Section 2, but has a particularly simple and fast implementation.

2 An adaptive dual-tree code

Some of the properties of optimum DTC's have been described in [2] and [7]. In [2], it is shown, using Equation 1, that ρ converges to $H(S)$ as N goes to infinity. In fact, it is shown that any scheme which ensures that $E[T_s] \to \infty$ as $N \to \infty$, including splitting leaves at random, will guarantee that $\rho \to \infty$ as $N \to \infty$. Since the design of optimum DTC's involves several layers of non-linearities, it is difficult to say much more about the properties of optimum DTC's using analytical methods, including tight upper and lower bounds on ρ given p and N.

In [7], some properties of optimum DTC's are deduced from numerical results. For example, it is shown that it is not always possible to construct T_s for an optimum DTC with $N+1$ leaves from the DTC with N leaves simply by extending the source tree with N leaves. This is one of the properties that makes the design of optimum DTC's difficult. Fortunately, DTC's have several other properties which make their use attractive, even if the optimum DTC's cannot always be found, not the least of which is that even though it is difficult to design optimum DTC's, it is not hard to design codes which are near-optimal.

DTC's have two other particularly useful properties. The first is that ρ converges very quickly to values near $H(S)$, even for small N, and, after the initial rapid convergence, the approach to $H(S)$ is very slow (it is also not monotonic), so that larger DTC's do not perform much better than small DTC's, except in the region where p is near 1. If ρ is plotted versus p, then ρ remains very close to $H(S)$ until p approaches 1, when ρ breaks away from $H(S)$. This breakaway point moves closer to 1 as N increases. For example, when $N = 5$, the breakaway point is near $p = 0.85$, but for $N = 10$, it is near $p = 0.95$. The second useful property is that DTC's are robust to the estimate of p, since the same source tree is used for a range of p, which is an attractive feature for an adaptive code where the exact value of p is not necessarily known.

The remainder of this section examines methods of designing DTC's. To design an optimum DTC, it is necessary to minimize the right-hand side of Equation 1, which means minimizing $r/E[T_s]$. Since it is more difficult to minimize a ratio of two quantities, a natural simplification is to either maximize $E[T_s]$ without regard to r, or minimize r and ignore $E[T_s]$. It is easy to maximize $E[T_s]$, using Tunstall's algorithm [8], which is the approach chosen by Fabris [1]. However, this approach does not seem to produce DTC's which are very close to the optimum, and his method requires adjustment of the DTC to reduce redundancy. Minimizing r is more difficult, but seems to lead to better results. Although this has not been proven analytically, the source tree T_s which minimizes r also minimizes $r/E[T_s]$, and even simple heuristics for minimizing r achieve DTC's with smaller compression ratios than maximizing $E[T_s]$.

One example of a simple heuristic for minimizing r is Freeman's algorithm [2]. The redundancy r can be expressed as

$$r = \sum_{i=1}^{N} p_i \left[l_{c_i} + \log_2 p_i \right], \tag{2}$$

where l_{c_i} is the length of the code word assigned to leaf i. Freeman observed that $r = 0$ if and only if $l_{c_i} + \log_2 p_i = 0, \forall i$; that is, when p_i is dyadic, which means that $p_i = 2^{-l_{c_i}}$. His algorithm produces the DTC with $N+1$ leaves from the DTC with N leaves by splitting the leaf of T_s which is the least dyadic, in other words, the leaf with the largest $|l_{c_i} + \log_2 p_i|$, and recomputing T_c using Huffman's algorithm. This algorithm works well, but it has the disadvantage that the objective function is defined only at the leaves, which is a weakness for an adaptive implementation. In an adaptive implementation, when a leaf is reached and the code word sent, T_s and T_c are adjusted based on an updated estimate of p. To adjust the source tree, it is necessary to consider the effects of making a leaf an internal node, and making another leaf an internal node. If the objective function is defined only for the leaves, each possible adjustment must be tried and the objective function recomputed in order to find the best adjustment.

In [7], a similar approach to the Freeman algorithm is used, but with a different objective function which is defined for all the nodes of T_s, and does not actually require any knowledge of T_c while constructing T_s. Let T_s^O be the source tree of the optimum DTC with N leaves, for a given value of p, and let T_s^n be a sub-tree of T_s^O (in other words, T_s^O can grown from T_s^n by splitting leaves), $n < N$. An interative tree-growth algorithm produces T_s^{n+1} from T_s^n so that T_s^{n+1} is also a sub-tree of T_s^O. Let $r(i)$ be the minimum redundancy achievable if leaf i of T_s^n is split. The rule to determine T_s^{n+1} so that it is also a sub-tree of T_s^O is simple, at least in theory: split leaf j, where $j = \arg\min_i r(i)$. The difficulty is that it is not known how to determine $r(i)$ without actually constructing the final N-leaf tree.

To avoid this problem, bounds on $r(i)$ can be used as an approximation. Lower bounds have been shown to be a good choice for the objective function [7]. In particular, a bound on r given the probability of the most likely source word p_i [4],

$$r \geq F(p_i) \; = \; m \; - \; (1 - p_i)\log_2(2^k - 1) \; - \; h(p_i), \tag{3}$$

results in DTC's which are very close to optimum, where

$$m \; = \; \lceil \log_2 \frac{k-1}{2k-1} \rceil, \qquad k = 2^{1/(p_i - 1)}, \tag{4}$$

and

$$h(p_i) \; = \; -p_i \log_2 p_i \; - \; (1 - p_i)\log_2(1 - p_i). \tag{5}$$

The DTC is constructed by beginning with a root node, and at each iteration, splitting leaf i, where $F(p_i) > F(p_j), i \neq j$, until the source tree has N leaves, and then the code tree is constructed. Figure 1 shows an example of the performance of this algorithm compared to the optimum DTC's found by exhaustive search, for $N = 10$.

This algorithm is easily converted to an adaptive version. As compression of the source sequence proceeds, an estimate of p is maintained. This estimate of p allows $F(q_j)$ to be maintained, where q_j is the probability of internal node j of T_s, as well as $F(p_i)$ for the leaf nodes. As long as $F(q_j) \geq F(p_i)$, for all (i, j), then T_s does not need to be adjusted. When $F(q_j) < F(p_i)$ for some i and j, then node j is interchanged with leaf i. This algorithm works well, in terms of compression ratio, but, although it is simple in concept, the function $F()$ is still numerically complex, requiring the computation of exponents and logarithms.

This difficulty can be alleviated by several more approximations. The first is to assume that $m = \lfloor -\log_2 p_i + 0.5 \rfloor$, which is almost exactly equivalent to the definition in Equation 4, and eliminates one of the exponentiations. The next approximation is to observe that $\log_2(2^m - 1) \approx m$, if $m > 4$. For $1 \leq m \leq 4$, $\log_2(2^m - 1)$ can be tabulated, which eliminates the other exponentiation and one of the logarithms. With this approximation, Equation 3 becomes $F(p_i) = mp_i - h(p_i)$. There are several possible methods for simplifying $F()$ further. One way is to quantize p_i and tabulate the logarithms for each quantized value of p_i. Another way, which is described in more detail in [7], is to use Taylor series approximations of $\log_2 x$, and the fact that the node probabilities can be estimated as ratios of integer counts.

However, this algorithm has one further weakness which appears insurmountable. Each time a source word is encoded, it is necessary to update the objective function score at every node and leaf of T_s, not just for the nodes which are on the path of the source word. This increases the number of operations that must be performed each time a source word is coded, and makes an efficient, fast implementation in hardware more difficult. The next section describes a new approach to adaptive DTC's, which has an extremely fast hardware implementation.

3 State-tree codes

As was mentioned above, an optimum DTC remains the same over a range of p. Although the width of each interval has not been clearly defined, knowledge of which DTC is optimum provides an estimate of p - as the number of leaves in the code is increased, the width of the intervals decreases, and the precision of the estimate of p increases. This property can be used to construct an adaptive DTC that is optimum in the sense that, assuming the estimate of p is sufficiently accurate, the optimum DTC is used.

Assume that all of the optimum DTC's are available for $p \geq 0.5$. The encoder maintains a pointer to the DTC which is currently active. With each leaf of each T_s, a pointer to another DTC is associated, as well as the code word assigned to the leaf. This pointer indicates which DTC will be used to parse and code the next source word. In this scheme, the current DTC can be viewed as the state of the coder, and the next state is determined from the current state, and the next source word which is parsed. The basic principle of this scheme is that if the source word contains more zeros than ones, the state moves to the one for the next higher value of p. Otherwise, the state moves to the next lower value of p. In this manner, as with the Q-coder [5], the state tends to track the value of p. Also, since DTC's are symmetrical about $p = 0.5$, the assumption that $p \geq 1 - p$ can be removed by keeping track of whether a zero or one is more likely, and doing the parsing of the source sequence in terms of the most likely symbol, as with the Q-coder.

This scheme, although not very elegant, is simple to implement, as long as it is possible to store all the DTC's. In fact, the adaptive code is essentially a look-up table (LUT), and a buffer to collect the variable-length code words into fixed-length blocks. For the encoder, the LUT is defined by the input triple $[T_t, n_t, s_t]$, where T_t is the tree at time index t, n_t is the current node ot T_t, and s_t is the t-th input bit, and the LUT returns the quadruple $[T_{t+1}, n_{t+1}, cw_t, l_{c_t}]$, where T_{t+1} and n_{t+1} form part of the next address, cw_t is the output code word (if there is no code word at time t, cw_t is ignored), and l_{c_t} is the number of bits in cw_t (if $l_{c_t} > 0$, then cw_t is valid).

The decoder has virtually the same structure, except that the input to the LUT is c_t, a code bit, instead of s_t, and the output is sw_t and l_{s_t} to define the source words instead of code words. Both the encoder and decoder can be easily pipelined to make a very fast hardware implementation, so that the encoder and decoder will be equally fast. This is a significant advantage over some other approaches. For example, in [6], a pipelined implemenation of an arithmetic encoder, which is also based on a LUT, is described, but the decoder cannot be pipelined, and the resulting decoder is four times slower than the encoder. As well, the state-tree code has the advantage over arithmetic coding that there is no carry-bit propagation problem [5, 6] which complicates the design of arithmetic encoders/decoders.

As an example of this technique, consider a state-tree code which is based on 16-leaf DTC's, and assume that 32 DTC's are sufficient to adequately quantize p between 0.5 and 1. The size of the necessary LUT is determined as follows. Since each tree has 16 leaves, there are 15 internal nodes, which means that it takes 4 bits to retain

p	$H(S)$	16/32	8/16	8/16 (Est.)
0.6	0.971	0.989	0.989	0.977
0.65	0.934	0.967	0.964	0.938
0.7	0.881	0.908	0.915	0.885
0.75	0.811	0.821	0.840	0.817
0.8	0.722	0.734	0.745	0.725
0.85	0.610	0.621	0.630	0.613
0.9	0.469	0.480	0.480	0.473
0.95	0.286	0.293	0.312	0.310
0.975	0.169	0.178	0.226	0.226

Table 1: State-tree code results for randomly generated data of several values of p, for sequences of 100,000 bits.

the current node. With 5 bits to indicate the current tree, plus 1 bit for the current source bit, the LUT has 10 address bits, or 1024 locations. Each location requires 9 bits to indicate the next tree and node (with a little extra logic, it is possible to reduce the 9 bits to 6 bits, since the current tree only changes when a leaf is reached), 15 bits to represent the code or source word (15 bits is the maximum code/source word length), and 4 bits to indicate the code/source word length, for a total of 28 bits. The complete table requires 1024×28 bits, which is not inordinately large, given currently available off-the-shelf hardware.

The DTC's which are used in the table are constructed using exhaustive searches for each value of p, where the values of p are simply determined by partitioning the interval $[0.5, 1.0)$ into 32 points. Table 1 shows the performance of this method for several values of p, for randomly generated sequences of 100,000 bits. The first column of Table 1 shows the value of p, the second the source entropy, the third the compression ratio for the state-tree code based on 16-leaf DTC's, with 32 values of p, the fourth shows the state-tree code for 8-leaf DTC's and 16 values of p, and the last column uses the same table as column 4, but chooses the current tree by estimating p directly. As can be seen from the table, the state-tree code scheme works well. The last two columns give an indication of the cost of using the state-tree code scheme, instead of a more accurate method of estimating the source probability. These results show that there is a degradation in performance of using the state-tree code, but the degradation is not severe.

The results of the third column of Table 1, which gives the results for the state-tree codes based on 16-leaf DTC's, shows that there is not much improvement obtained by doubling the number of leaves, except as p approaches 1. Using this property, it is possible to reduce the size of the state-tree code by basing the DTC's for values close to 0.5 on a smaller number of leaves, and increasing the number of leaves for the DTC's closer to 1.

The state-tree code described here is only suitable for sources without memory, and is an example of a more general framework, which may be more suitable for sources with memory. For the more general framework, the LUT contains only a pool of DTC's. A state machine, separate from the DTC's, can provide the pointers to the currently active tree, and thus a more sophisticated estimate of p.

4 Conclusions

Although the problem of efficiently constructing optimal dual-tree codes is a difficult one that remains unsolved, it is possible to design nearly optimum codes easily. As well, adaptive dual-tree codes can be used, as shown by the method of Section 2 and the state-tree codes of Section 3. The adaptive codes of Section 2 require very little memory, but a complex logic circuit to implement the adaptation algorithm, while the state-tree codes require more memory to retain the pool of dual-tree codes, but the required logic circuit is trivial, and will provide a very fast implementation.

Two promising areas of investigation remain for the state-tree codes. The first is an extension to non-binary source alphabets, and particularly for bytes, which are useful for text compression. For non-binary source alphabets, the number of nodes in each dual-tree code becomes very large, although the size can be reduced by using incomplete source trees. It would be interesting to know if it is possible to construct a byte-level state-tree code, while still keeping the required memory manageable.

The second area of investigation is in the choice of which dual-tree codes should be included in the pool of trees for the state-tree code. This is a simple problem for memoryless sources, but if the more sophisticated state machine scheme described at the end of Section 3 is used to adaptively compress sources with memory, the choice of the dual-tree codes is much more difficult.

References

[1] F. Fabris, "Variable-length-to-variable-length source coding: a greedy step-by-step algorithm," *IEEE Trans. Inf. Theory*, vol. 38, no. 5, pp. 1609–1617, September 1992.

[2] G.H. Freeman, "Divergence and the construction of variable-to-variable-length lossless codes by source word extensions," *DCC '93 Data Compression Conference*, IEEE Computer Society Press, Los Alamitos, 1993, pp. 79–88.

[3] D.A. Huffman, "A method for the construction of minimum redundancy codes," *Proc. IRE*, Vol. 40, 1952, pp. 1098-1101.

[4] B.L. Montgomery, and J. Abrahams, "On the redundancy of optimal prefix-condition codes for finite and infinite sources," *IEEE Trans. Inf. Theory*, IT-33, No. 1, January 1987, pp. 156-160.

[5] W.B. Pennebaker, J.L. Mitchell, G.G. Langdon, Jr., and R.B. Arps, "An overview of the basic principles of the Q-coder adaptive binary arithmetic coder", *IBM Journal of Research and Development*, 32(6), November 1988, pp. 717-726.

[6] H. Printz, and P.R. Stubley, "Multialphabet arithmetic coding at 16 M/bytes/sec," Proceedings, DCC '93 Data Compression Conference, IEEE Computer Society Press, Los Alamitos, 1993, pp. 128-137.

[7] P.R. Stubley, "Adaptive data compression using tree codes," PhD. thesis, University of Waterloo, Waterloo, Ontario, 1993.

[8] B.P. Tunstall, "Synthesis of noiseless compression codes," PhD. thesis, Georgia Inst. Tech., Atlanta, Georgia, 1968.

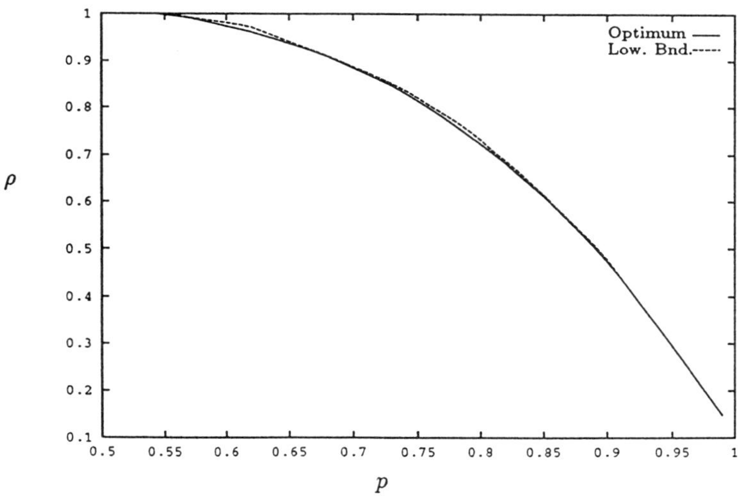

Figure 1: Lower bound algorithm compression ratios, $N = 10$.

Compression-based Template Matching

Stuart Inglis
Computer Science, University of Waikato, Hamilton, New Zealand.
email singlis@waikato.ac.nz

Ian H. Witten
Computer Science, University of Waikato, Hamilton, New Zealand.
email ihw@waikato.ac.nz

1 Introduction

Textual image compression is a method of both lossy and lossless image compression that is particularly effective for images containing repeated sub-images, notably pages of text (Mohiuddin *et al.*, 1984; Witten *et al.*, 1992). The process comprises three main steps:

- Extracting all the characters from an image;
- Building a library that contains one representative for each character class;
- Compressing the image with respect to the library.

The first step is to extract the "marks," or sets of connected black pixels, from the image. Marks correspond approximately to individual characters, except that characters with disconnected parts like "i" and "j" are represented by pairs of marks, one for the body and the other for the dot. (Due to the adaptive compression process that follows, this incurs a negligible penalty.) To build the library in the second step, the marks are clustered into self-similar categories. The intention is that all marks that represent a particular character fall into the same class. This effect is achieved by checking each new mark against the library and adding it as a new symbol if it is sufficiently different from all previous clusters. The final step compresses the image by coding the library symbols and then coding the sequence of symbols that correspond to the marks on the page. Because many marks in the image map to any one character, the mark that is stored in the library is an average of the original marks in the category. The use of a single representative introduces a small amount of noise in the reconstructed image, and an extra step can be used to make the compression lossless if desired. The result is an effective lossless/lossy method for compressing textual images.

A critical requirement in the second step is the ability to match marks accurately. This is really a process of pattern comparison, and is often called "template matching." Template matching in textual image compression differs from the matching required in an optical character recognition (OCR) system because there is no need to identify the actual character to which any particular mark corresponds. Nevertheless, it is important to match each new occurrence of a mark consistently with the cluster to which it belongs, because compression will deteriorate if the matching operation introduces errors.

Matching procedures generally work by aligning the two images in the position where we think the best match will be made, and then examining an *error map*, which is the bitwise exclusive-OR of the images. The most effective methods employ heuristics that are tailored

 1068-0314/94 $3.00

to the particular resolution of the input image. For example, the "combined size-independent strategy" defines measures that depend on the size and resolution of the marks and uses them to reject matches based on local criteria. For example, if any pixel in the error map has four black neighbors then the match is rejected.

This paper addresses the problem of pattern comparison by using an information or compression based approach. Following Mohiuddin *et al.* (1984), we use the amount of uncertainty or entropy between marks as the criterion for the matching process. Given a mark M consisting of binary pixels M_{ij}, the conditional information in M given the library pattern L is defined as

$$I(M|L) \quad = \quad -\log_2 \Pr[M|L] \quad = \quad -\sum_i \sum_j \log_2 \Pr[M_{ij}|L]$$

The pattern M is accepted as a match to that class L which minimizes $I(M|L)$, so long as

$$I(M|L) < T_L,$$

where T_L is a pre-defined threshold for acceptance to pattern class L.

In order to employ this method of classification it is necessary to estimate the probabilities $\Pr[m_{ij}|L]$. The idea is to find, for each unknown mark M, the library image L_k that best models it—in the sense that the amount of information required to specify M given L_k is minimized. This distance metric is called the *cross-entropy* between pairs of images, and can be approximated by compressing one mark relative to another. The entropy model we use is the context-based compression model proposed by Langdon & Rissanen (1981) and further developed by Moffat (1991).

There are two principal issues to investigate when studying template matching methods: their susceptibility to different kinds of noise, and how they respond to errors in the initial registration. Because of the computation-intensive nature of the comparison operation, many schemes have been devised to pre-filter or *screen* the marks in advance to determine those that will surely fail the match. We present a novel method of screening which uses a quad-tree decomposition and finds local centroids at each tree level.

2 Background

Previous models for template matching are divided into two categories: local and global matching. Local methods reject or accept matches based on pixels in a small portion of the image, while global methods generally return a value representing the overall goodness of the match. Local and global matching methods fulfill two different requirements. In the former the match either succeeds or fails, while the latter methods compute a score that can be used to rank the comparisons from best to worst. Of course, local methods can revert to a global matching scheme if a mark is not rejected, and global methods can use a threshold to accept or reject matches.

The evolution of previous methods of pattern-matching is as follows. The "combined symbol matching" (CSM) method of Pratt *et al.* (1980) computes a weighted sum of pixels in the error map, weighting error pixels more highly if they occur in clusters. A match is rejected if this exceeds a specified threshold. The "weighted and-not" approach (WAN) of Holt and Xydeas (1986) improves on this by distinguishing black-to-white errors from white-to-black ones. The "pattern matching and substitution" (PMS) method of Johnsen *et al.* (1983) rejects a match if any position in the error map is found to have four or more neighbors that are set. In order to detect mismatches due to the presence of a thin stroke or gap in one image but not the other, another heuristic is used. In an attempt to normalize for size, the "combined size independent strategy" (CSIS) of Holt *et al.* (1988) uses two different criteria to detect thin strokes or gaps—one for characters that exceed certain preset width and height thresholds, and the other for the remaining ones.

Langdon and Rissanen introduced the idea of context-based compression of binary images, in which the probability of a pixel being black or white is estimated and used to encode the pixel via arithmetic coding. The probabilities are conditioned on a certain context of preceding pixels, and they suggested that a good choice is the 10-bit context shown in Figure 1(a). (The word "template" is generally used in the literature to describe the particular size and shape of context that is to be used for prediction; however we use "context" instead to avoid confusion with the templates that are being matched.) A black dot marks each pixel included in the context and a bullseye marks the position of the pixel about to be coded. The light gray pixels are ones whose values are not yet known by the decoder and so cannot be included in the context, and the open circles indicate pixels whose values are known but are not included in the context.

For each different context, counts are recorded and used to predict black (c_b) and white (c_w) pixels in that context. The number of bits required to encode a particular black pixel is

$$-\log_2 \frac{c_b}{c_b + c_w} \text{ bits.}$$

Context-based image compression methods outperform well-known image compression methods for binary images such as CCITT Group 4.

Moffat (1991) pursued the idea further and investigated a number of variants. One was the notion of using a set of *surrounding* pixels as the context of the pixel being coded, rather than a set of *preceding* ones. An example is the template illustrated in Figure 1(b). This is of course a physically unrealizable configuration, but was introduced as a hypothetical "absolute best" compression scheme in order to estimate a bound on compressibility. We call these templates *clairvoyant*.

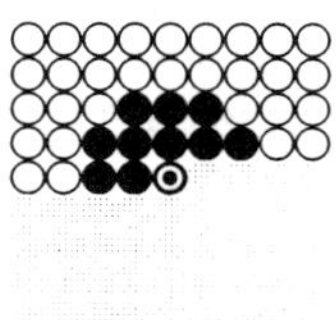

(a) Conventional

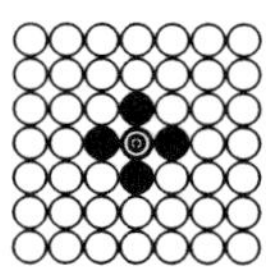

(b) Clairvoyant

Figure 1: Two different types of templates

3 Compression-based template matching: method & results

Compression-based template matching has been implemented and tested against several other approaches to template matching. This section describes the implementation, presents results obtained with the new method, and compares it with the previous state of the art. Before any template matching method can be applied the patterns to be matched must be aligned together, and we first discuss some experiments to determine the best method of alignment. Next we explain exactly how cross-entropy is calculated and compare its performance on a set of test patterns with that of other methods. In order to investigate the effect of noise on classification accuracy, we applied artificial noise models to corrupt the test patterns, and the results of this are examined next. Finally we look at the question of screening, describe our method for screening using quad-tree decomposition, and report on the results obtained.

In order to test the template matching methods, a large collection of marks was required, along with their correct classification. These were obtained by extracting connected groups of pixels from several test images. The test images were digitized pages of a library catalog from Trinity College, Dublin. They had been scanned at 400 dpi with no noticeable skewing, and with careful attention paid to contrast settings so that there was little fragmentation of characters or bleeding of one into another.

The marks were were labeled by hand, and ones that could not be identified easily were discarded. This left a collection of around 2500 marks, each with a well-defined, unambiguous classification. Most were in roman font but some were italicized, and were labeled as such so that they were assigned to a completely different class from the corresponding roman letter. Six marks were ligatures formed by two characters bleeding together—for example, "rt" occurred twice—and they were labeled as such. There was some minor variation in type size—for example, letters in a small capitals face were assigned to the same class as regular capital letters. In total, 80 different classifications were used with an average of just over 30 marks in each class. Twelve classes had just one member, while six contained over a hundred members.

3.1 Registration

Before marks can be compared, they must be aligned so that each pixel on one can be mapped to the other: this is the process of *registration*. The result of any matching method depends critically on the registration, and in particular, for those matching methods that use the error map, it is clear that this map is very sensitive to the precise alignment of the images. There are several possible methods of registration. Some previously-reported work aligns the upper left corner of the bounding boxes, while other work uses the lower left corner instead. A third possibility is to align the geometric center of the marks' bounding boxes, while a fourth is to use the marks' centroids—that is, the average position of the black pixels they contain.

We undertook a series of experiments to determine the best relative position of registration. Each of the marks was overlaid with a 7×7 grid, and each of the 49 grid points was considered to be a possible reference point for registration. A 50th possibility, namely the mark's centroid (which of course varies from mark to mark), was also included. For any particular choice of reference point, every pair of marks was aligned on the corresponding intersection.

Each pair of marks that were the same according to the hand-assigned labels was registered on each of the 50 positions, and the two templates were matched. (In fact the CSIS template-matching method was used because of its speed.) The result in each case was a binary decision, "match" or "no match," and the correct result in each case was "match." There were 487,000 pairs of marks that had the same label, and repeating the operation over all these gave an overall correctness classification for each of the 50 reference points.

The resulting scores were largest for centroid alignment. In fact, for our data the centroid was, on average, very close to the geometric center. Registering based on the upper left and lower left corners gave classification accuracies that were both 6% lower than when the centroid was used.

3.2 Cross-entropy

To calculate the cross-entropy between two marks, the context-based coding model of Section 2 was used. As it is not necessary to be able to compress and decompress the mark, a clairvoyant context can be used to estimate the information content of each pixel. Various different contexts were tested, and the 5-pixel clairvoyant mask of Figure 1(b) was found to give best results. Larger masks may be more suitable for larger marks, or for greater digitization resolutions.

As was explained earlier, the coding probabilities are based on counts associated with each context. In compression it is normal to use an adaptive model, accumulating the counts as compression proceeds, because otherwise the model must somehow be communicated to the decoder. However, when obtaining an entropy figure there is no need to communicate the model and so a static one can be used. Like the clairvoyant context, this provides a lower bound on the amount of compression that could possibly be achieved in practice. Preliminary experiments indicated that the static model gives a slight performance increase over an adaptive model.

The compression-based template matching procedure begins by building the model of one mark *with respect to* the other. It would be much faster to calculate a single model and use it for all matches. However, this was found to degrade performance very seriously. Suppose the two marks to be matched are L and M. For any particular pixel $L_{i,j}$ in the first, there is a corresponding pixel $M_{i+\Delta x, j+\Delta y}$ in the second, where $(\Delta x, \Delta y)$ is the displacement due to registration. Figure 2 shows two different marks with the 5-pixel clairvoyant mask superimposed. The values of the five pixels under the mask in the first mark L, taken together, determine a particular context. The value of the central mask pixel in the other mark M gives a color, black or white, and the corresponding count for that context value is incremented. The process is repeated for every pixel, to build a complete model. In fact the marks are assumed to be surrounded by white space, and, once they have been registered, the maximum extent in both the horizontal and vertical directions is used as the area over which the entropy is calculated.

Once the model has been created, a second pass is taken over the marks and the counts in the models are used to calculate the entropy of the second mark M with respect to the first one L. The process is not symmetric, and both model and entropy will depend on whether the calculation is done for mark M with respect to L, or for L with respect to M. Both are calculated and the maximum is taken as the final cross-entropy measure.

In order to to cluster marks into self-similar categories, a threshold is used to decide

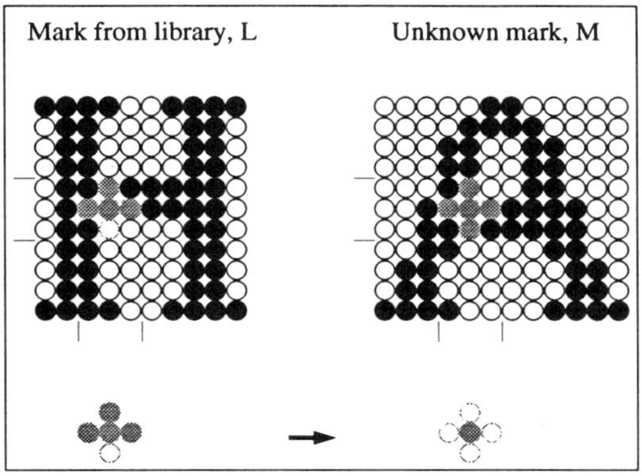

Figure 2: Using a five-pixel mask to build a model with respect to another mark

whether a match should be accepted or rejected. After some experimentation it was decided to use a two-part criterion based on both the entropy per pixel and the absolute cross-entropy value. A match was rejected if either the number of bits per pixel exceeded B, or the total number of bits exceeded T, where B and T are constants that were determined experimentally. The values used were $B = 0.4$ and $T = 300$.

It would be interesting to consider setting an absolute threshold based on whether one mark could be coded more effectively with respect to the other, or whether it would be coded more effectively if the other were ignored. This would avoids the arbitrariness of numeric thresholds, and has yet to be explored.

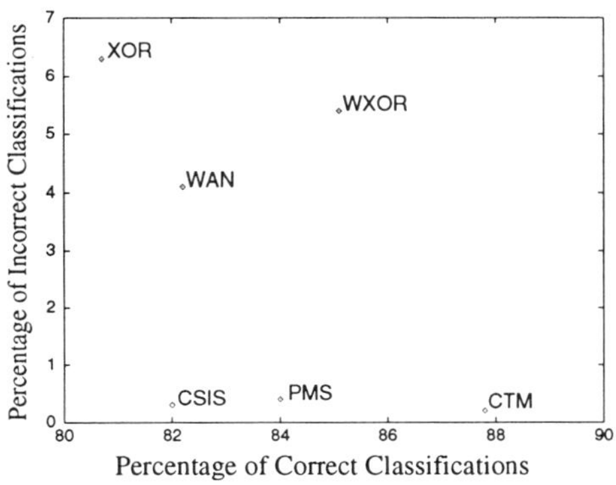

Figure 3: Results of each template matcher

3.3 Comparing CTM with other methods

The set of hand-labeled marks was used to compare the performance of compression-based template matching (CTM) with the other methods mentioned in Section 2. In order to test a particular template matching method, each mark was compared with every other mark using that matching method. The result of every comparison is a binary decision: "match" or "no match." In order to produce overall figures, only positive identifications are considered. If the true classification of the two marks according to the hand-assigned labels is the same, and the outcome is "match," this is counted as a correct positive identification. If the true classification is different and the outcome is "match," this is counted as an incorrect positive identification. The percentage of correct and incorrect positive identifications is used as a measure of the matching method's performance.

All the template matching methods have parameters that need to be chosen. Each of the methods was assessed under the most favorable possible conditions. Parameters were determined by searching within the parameter space to maximize the number of correct minus the number of incorrect identifications. For example, for the WXOR method the range of the rejection threshold was varied to get the best result, which was in fact 80.7% correct and 6.3% incorrect identifications. In both the PMS and CSIS methods, each localized criterion for rejecting matches was treated as a parameter which was then subjected to optimization. For example, the number of times an error pixel has more than a specified weight became a variable parameter.

Figure 3 shows the results. Compression-based template matching clearly outperforms the other methods. It obtains the best results in both of the classification dimensions. The percentage of correct classifications exceeds that of the closest competitor, WXOR, and the number of incorrect classifications is lower than the lowest of the other methods, PMS and CSIS.

3.4 Noise deterioration

Each method of template matching responds differently to different kinds of noise. Three types of noise were added to the marks to emulate results under noisy conditions. The first was salt-and-pepper noise, in which the polarity of a certain percentage (10%) of pixels within a mark's bounding box was reversed. The second was the kind of edge noise caused by variations in paper quality or evenness of inking. This was modeled by adding black pixels around the perimeter of the mark, with a certain probability (again chosen to be 10%) that each white pixel around the perimeter would be changed to black. The third type of noise was a more extreme kind of edge noise, intended to emulate the blurring that occurs when images are scanned at too high a contrast, and was obtained by repeating the previously-described edge-noise process four times.

The testing process of Section 3.3 was repeated for each noise type. Every mark was corrupted as described above, and the entire process of comparison was re-done (using the same parameters as before).

The results are shown in Table 1. Compression-based template matching (CTM) continues to achieve the highest number of correct matches under all conditions. However, it no longer achieves the lowest number of incorrect matches. The PMS and CSIS methods are consistently better at rejecting incorrect matches. However, their their performance with respect to correct

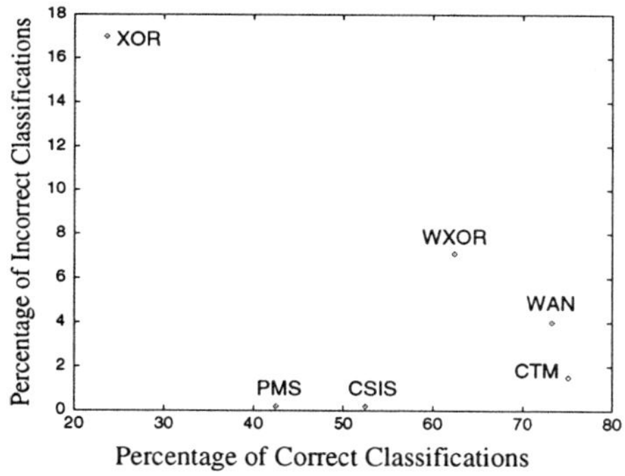

Figure 4: Average results with added noise

Method	Random Noise Correct	Random Noise Incorrect	Edge Noise Correct	Edge Noise Incorrect	High Edge Noise Correct	High Edge Noise Incorrect
XOR	24.4%	22.4%	38.2%	22.2%	8.3%	6.4%
WXOR	70.3%	7.3%	74.2%	5.7%	42.7%	8.4%
PMS	51.6%	0.3%	65.3%	0.3%	13.7%	0.1%
WAN	74.2%	4.7%	74.5%	4.1%	71.2%	3.3%
CSIS	64.3%	0.3%	68.7%	0.2%	24.6%	0.1%
CTM	74.9%	0.7%	76.3%	0.6%	74.1%	3.2%

Table 1: Susceptibility to different types of noise

matches is very much worse, reducing to only 25% for high edge noise, and CTM still seems to be the best choice overall.

Figure 4 shows the result of averaging the different kinds of artificial noise. CTM continues to classify more marks correctly than the other methods, and while the rate of incorrect classification is slightly higher than both PMS and CSIS, the latter methods make major sacrifices in correct classifications. The method with the closest number of correct classifications is the WAN method, but this has almost twice as many incorrect results.

3.5 Screening

Because of the high cost of the matching process, efficient methods for screening were investigated. Screening reduces the number of template matching operations that are undertaken, while simultaneously minimizing the number of matchable marks that are excluded. Many methods of screening have been investigated; including using features of the marks such as width, height, area, perimeter length, and number of internal black/white runs.

A novel approach to the screening problem is to register marks according to their centroids, and then divide them into quadrants defined by this position. At this stage a local centroid is calculated for each of the four quadrants, and for each of the four local centroids the distance between its position in the two marks is determined. Finally, these four distances are averaged.

Screening Method	Feature Space				Progressive centroids	
	Area	Perimeter	Horiz/Vertical Runs	Width/Height	Hamming	Euclidean
Screened matches	61.1%	67.3%	83.1%	84.3%	92.7%	93.4%

Table 2: Best screening percentages without affecting the classification

The process could be continued recursively, defining a distance at level 0 based on the original centroids (which is 0, since centroid registration is used), a distance at level 1 as described above, and further higher-level distances. However, excellent screening results were obtained with the level-1 distance and further elaboration seemed to be unnecessary.

Each of the screening methods mentioned above was used as a pre-filtering step to the compression-based template matcher. They work as follows. The screening method determines the value of a numeric parameter. If the parameters for the two marks differ by more than a predetermined threshold the match is rejected without further consideration, while if it differs by less, a full template matching operation is undertaken.

For each method an appropriate threshold was determined in a preliminary series of experiments. It was chosen to be as selective as it possibly could be without affecting the outcome of the classification process. For example, using area as a screening function, the best cut-off value for the threshold eliminated 61.1% of the matches from further consideration.

Results for each of the methods is shown in Table 2. Area was the least effective method, followed by perimeter. The simplest method—width and height of the mark—fared much better, as did the number of horizontal and vertical runs. The new progressive centroid method gave by far the best performance, achieving 93.4% screening. A faster version using Hamming instead of Euclidean distance performed only slightly worse.

4 Using CTM in a textual image compression system

Compression based template matching is a good choice for use in a textual image compression system. Not only does it give better results for the classification process, as detailed in Section 3, but also each library mark can be chosen to be the one that gives the greatest compression.

We have incorporated the CTM scheme in a textual image compression system and performed experiments on CCITT image 1 (as this image contains mainly type-written text). The results, shown in Table 3, show a very slight improvement in lossless compression ratio over all other methods. However, the real advantage of the new scheme is in lossy compression. Here the quality of template matching, as well as the amount of compression obtained, is of paramount importance, because matching errors produce errors in the reproduced document. The new method improves the lossy compression ratio by almost 15% over CSIS. Although other systems such as XOR and WXOR have high lossy compression figures, it is evident from Figure 3 that their accuracy is much lower.

5 Summary

Compression-based template matching uses as its basis the amount of information that one pattern contributes to the encoding of the other. This is measured by employing a context-based

Method	Library Size	Compression ratio	
		Lossless	Lossy
XOR	140	34.9	87.1
WXOR	135	35.8	91.1
PMS	180	35.9	79.3
WAN	126	31.6	76.8
CSIS	200	37.6	77.3
CTM	155	37.8	88.6

Table 3: Library size and compression ratios for TIC

compression method to approximate the cross entropy between images.

The resulting template matching procedure improves significantly on previous methods. Using it as a unsupervised classifier achieved 87.8% accuracy with 0.2% incorrect classifications, which is better in both dimensions than other methods. Combining this with the progressive screening of marks yields a method that is more accurate and involves less template comparisons than earlier methods. As an element of a textual image compression system, the matcher minimizes the number of bits required to encode a mark and achieves a slight overall gain in the lossless figures, as well as a 14% improvement in the lossy compression ratio.

References

Ascher, R.N. and Nagy, G. (1974) "A means for achieving a high degree of compaction on scan-digitized printed text," *IEEE Trans Computers* C-23(11): 1174–1179; November.

Bell, T.C., Cleary, J.G. and Witten, I.H. (1990) *Text Compression*. Prentice Hall, Englewood Cliffs, NJ.

Holt, M.J.J. and Xydeas, C.S. (1986) 'Recent developments in image data compression for digital facsimile,' *ICL Technical Journal*: 123-146; May.

Holt, M.J. (1988) 'A fast binary template matching algorithm for document image data compression,' in *Pattern Recognition*, J. Kittler (ed.) (Proc. Int. Conf., Cambridge). Springer Verlag, Berlin.

Johnsen, O., Segen, J. and Cash, G.L. (1983) 'Coding of two-level pictures by pattern matching and substitution,' *Bell System Technical J* 62(8): 2513-2545; May.

Langdon, G.G. and Rissanen, J. (1981) "Compression of black-white images with arithmetic coding," *IEEE Trans Communications* COM-29(6): 858–867; June.

Mohiuddin, K., Rissanen, J. and Arps, R. (1984) 'Lossless binary image compression based on pattern matching' *International Conference on Computers, Systems & Signal Processing* pp. 447-451, Bangalore, India; December.

Moffat, A. (1991) 'Two level context based compression of binary images,' in *Proc. DCC'91*, J.A. Storer and J.H. Reif (eds.), pp. 382-391. IEEE Computer Society Press, Los Alamitos, CA.

Pratt, W.K., Capitant, P.J., Chen, W.H., Hamilton, E.R. and Wallis, R.H. (1980) 'Combined symbol matching facsimile data compression system,' *Proc IEEE* 68(7): 786-796; July.

Witten, I.H., Bell, Harrison, James and Moffat, A. (1992) 'Textual Image Compression' in *Proc. DCC'92*, J.A. Storer and M. Cohn (eds.), pp. 42-51. IEEE Computer Society Press, Los Alamitos, CA.

Witten, I.H., Moffat, A. and Bell T.C. (forthcoming) *Managing gigabytes: Compressing and indexing large collections of documents and images*. Van Nostrand Reinhold, New York.

Markov Models for Clusters in Concordance Compression — Extended Abstract*

A. Bookstein
Center for Information
and Language Studies
University of Chicago
Chicago, IL 60637
a-bookstein@uchicago.edu

S. T. Klein
Dept. of Math. & CS
Bar Ilan University
Ramat-Gan 52900
Israel
tomi@bimacs.cs.biu.ac.il

T. Raita
Comp. Sci. Dept.
University of Turku
20520 Turku
Finland
raita@euroni.cs.utu.fi

Abstract

An earlier paper developed a procedure for compressing concordances, assuming that all elements occurred independently. In this paper, the earlier models are extended to take the possibility of clustering into account. We suggest several models adapted to concordances of large full-text information retrieval systems, which are generally subject to clustering.

1 Introduction and Background

The development of optical disk technology has made it possible to widely distribute large, full text databases. But large as the capacity of CD-roms may be, it still doesn't match our ambitions for storing data [5]. For example, it is often overlooked that to be able to access and manipulate text, auxiliary data-structures must also be created and stored, and these often occupy as much space as the original text itself. Thus, to distribute a functional, full-text information retrieval system, consideration must be given how to store these data structures efficiently.

Most large information retrieval systems are based on inverted files. In this approach, query processing does not directly involve the original text files (in which key words might be located using some pattern matching technique), but rather the auxiliary *dictionary* and *concordance* files. The dictionary is a list of all the different words appearing in the text and is usually ordered alphabetically. For each entry in

*Two of the authors (A.B. and S.T.K.) wish to acknowledge that the material in this paper is based upon research supported by the U.S. National Science Foundation under award number IRI-9307895, and by grant No. 92-00163 from the United States - Israel Binational Science Foundation (BSF), Jerusalem, Israel. T.R. acknowledges support by the Academy of Finland under grant No. 4964/30/93.

the dictionary, there is a pointer into the concordance, which lists each occurrence of the word.

Every occurrence of a word in the database can be uniquely characterized by a sequence of numbers that gives its exact position in the text. Typically, such a sequence would consist of the document number d, the paragraph number p (in the document), the sentence number s (in the paragraph) and the word number w (in the sentence). The quadruple (d, p, s, w) is the *coordinate* of the occurrence. The concordance contains, for every word of the dictionary, the lexicographically ordered list of all its coordinates in the text.

The concordance is generally of the order of magnitude of the text itself, its exact size depending on the omission or inclusion of the most frequent words, the so-called *stop-words*. Compressing it not only saves space, but also saves processing time by reducing the number of I/O operations needed to fetch parts of the concordance into main memory (see [5], [2], [8]).

We note that in a static information retrieval system, compression and decompression are not symmetrical tasks. Compression is done only once, while building the system, whereas decompression is needed during the processing of every query and directly affects the response time. One may thus use extensive and costly preprocessing for compression, provided reasonably fast decompression methods are possible. Moreover, in an information retrieval system, while we compress full files (text, concordance, etc.), we decompress only (possibly many) short pieces on demand; these may be accessed at random by means of pointers to their exact locations. This limits the value of adaptive methods based on tables that systematically change from the beginning to the end of the file.

Oddly, compared to full text, concordance compression has received relatively little attention. Some *ad-hoc* methods were used [3], [7], or simple models, assuming a structured entity in which term occurrences were distributed independently [1], [8]. In this paper we generalize the independence models to incorporate a tendency of the terms to cluster.

2 Modeling the Concordance

For our model of a textual database, we assume that the text is divided into documents and the documents are made up of words. We thus use only a two level hierarchy to identify the location of a word, which makes the exposition easier. The methods can, however, be readily adapted to more complex concordance structures, like the 4-level hierarchy mentioned above. In our present model, the conceptual concordance consists, for each word, of a series of (d, w) pairs, d standing for a document number, and w for the index, or offset, of a word within the given document. It is sometimes convenient to translate this model to an equivalent one, in which we indicate 1) the index of the next document containing the word, 2) the number of times the word occurs in the document, followed by 3) the list of word indices of the various occurrences:

$$
\begin{array}{ll}
\text{word}_1: & (d_1,\ m_1\ ;\ \ w_1, w_2, \ldots, w_{m_1}) \\
 & (d_2,\ m_2\ ;\ \ w_1, \ldots, w_{m_2}) \\
 & \ldots \\
 & (d_N,\ m_N\ ;\ \ w_1, \ldots, w_{m_N}) \\
\text{word}_2: & \cdots
\end{array}
$$

Our task is to model each of the components of the coordinate, and use standard compression methods to compress each entity. Below we assume that we know (from the dictionary) the total number of times a word occurs in the database, the number of different documents in which it occurs (N), and (from a separate table) the number of words in each document. We also know the value of D, the number of documents in the collection.

The model of [1] assumed that all documents are approximately of the same size, that there is no between-document clustering, and that within a single document, words are independently distributed. On the basis of these assumptions, three probability distributions were derived for each term, giving the location of the next document containing the term, the number of times the term occurs in this document, and the locations of the word within the document. Finally Huffman, arithmetic, or Shannon-Fano codes were generated for these probability distributions, and the codeword corresponding to the actually appearing value d, m or w was used in the encoding.

We now turn to the more realistic case in which the independence assumptions do not hold. For example, if the documents of an Information Retrieval system are grouped by author or some other criterion, the d-values of a many terms will tend to appear in clusters because of the specific style of the author, or because adjacent documents might treat similar subjects. Similarly, term-occurrences will cluster *within* documents, reflecting content variations over a document.

In the following section, we model the bit-generation process in a cluster prone environment by means of a Markov chain, and suggest how to exploit it for the compression of concordances. In Section 4 we report on some experimental results obtained by applying these methods on the concordance of the Hebrew Bible.

3 Models of Clustering

In our earlier examination of concordances, we first looked at the pattern of term occurrences over documents, and then at the distribution of terms within a given document. Formally, the analyses were identical. Since this remains true when clustering is considered, we shall here examine only the first case explicitly: that is, we have D documents, of which N are known to have at least one occurrence of the term being considered; our goal is to analyze the patterns of the gaps separating documents that contain the term. Formally, we shall represent each term by a bitmap, with a position for each document. If the term is present in a document, that document's bit position will be set to one; otherwise it will be zero. Below it is convenient to talk in terms of bitmaps rather than in terms of the concordance of which they are a component.

Should the tendency for clustering be pronounced, codes based on assumptions of term independence will produce poor compression. In this section we offer several models of clustering that potentially can be used to improve compression.

3.1 Full Markov Model

We investigate a family of n-state Markov chains as models of how our bitmap was generated: as we traverse the bitmap from beginning to end, at each position we are in a state, and that state determines the probability of being in any given state at the next location. The nature of the transition determines whether the next bit is a one or zero.

The simplest model is the independence model. This has two states, which, to be consistent with what follows, we denote by C (within cluster) and B (between clusters). In the independence model we assume the probabilities of the transitions $C \rightarrow C$ and $B \rightarrow C$ are equal. In this model, as in all the Markov models we consider, we assume that we are generating terms only when we are making a transition into a cluster, even if the cluster consists of only one document.

A simple, true Markov model is based on the same two states C and B, but in the true two-state model, the probability of a transition to C (that is, the probability of turning on a bit) differs depending on the state we are in. The state C indicates that we are in a cluster, and thus are more likely to generate occurrences of the designated term. We enter B as soon as we leave the cluster (that is, generate a zero-bit).

A limitation of the two-state model is that it doesn't recognize the possibility of spurious zeroes within a cluster: that is, we would like to incorporate the possibility that we may be in a cluster and generate a single zero bit without leaving the cluster. (For simplicity, we are neglecting the symmetric problem of spurious one's outside of a cluster; this can be dealt with in an identical manner.) We accommodate this possibility by introducing transitional states. For illustration, we describe in detail a 3-state model. The states are: **1.** Cluster State (C); **2.** Transitional State (X); and **3.** Between Cluster State (B).

The state X of the three-state model is introduced to permit us to be in a cluster and yet not generate any terms—it is a "maybe" state. However, if two consecutive documents do not contain the term, we have left the cluster—we are in state B *between* clusters. We can generalize this model by introducing a larger number of transitional states X_1, X_2, etc.

Within the three-state model, a term is generated whenever we enter state C. The transition probabilities are:

$$\begin{array}{ll} C \rightarrow C : \gamma_C, & C \rightarrow X : 1 - \gamma_C; \\ X \rightarrow C : \gamma_X, & X \rightarrow B : 1 - \gamma_X; \\ B \rightarrow C : \gamma_B, & B \rightarrow B : 1 - \gamma_B. \end{array}$$

We can encode each bit in a bitmap individually, using arithmetic coding based on the probability of a one-bit at each stage; alternatively, it may be more convenient to encode the gaps between one bits. To do this, we need the distribution of gap sizes, which is easily derived using the above model. Once we are in a document that contains an occurrence of the designated term, the probability, p_n, that the next n documents not have an occurrence is: $p_0 = \gamma_C$; $p_1 = (1 - \gamma_C)\gamma_X$; and for $n \geq 2$:

$$p_n = (1 - \gamma_C)(1 - \gamma_X)(1 - \gamma_B)^{n-2}\gamma_B.$$

The γ's are our model's basic parameters. But we will also consider a reparameterization that is suggestive: $\gamma_C \equiv \gamma$, $\gamma_X \equiv \theta_X\gamma_C$, and $\gamma_B \equiv \theta_B\gamma_X$, which define the parameters γ, θ_X, and θ_B. These parameters satisfy simpler constraints ($0 \leq \theta_X, \theta_B \leq 1$) independently of one another and of γ, which will ease problems of estimation. We also expect that regularities in the data will be more easily expressed in terms of the θ's than in terms of the γ's. It is also useful to define $\Theta \equiv \theta_X\theta_B$, so that $\gamma_B = \Theta\gamma_C$. Θ is a single value reflecting the strength of clustering: it indicates the relative likelihood of a term appearing if we are inside a cluster as compared to if we are outside a cluster.

More applications of Markov models to data compression can be found in [4] and [6].

3.2 Parameter Estimation

We can estimate the parameters directly. We assume that before generating the bitmap, we are in state B. The sequence of one's and zero's making up the bitmap completely determines the state at any bitmap position. Thus it is easy to tabulate the number, and hence probability, of each type of transition.

For illustration, consider the following bitmap:

$$0\ 0\ 1\ 0\ 1\ 1\ 0\ 0\ \cdots$$

Since we begin in state B, the initial zero indicates that the first transition is back to state B. Continuing in this manner we find the sequence of states corresponding to the above bitmap is given as follows (with the initial B preceding the colon):

$$B:\ B\ B\ C\ X\ C\ C\ X\ B\ \cdots$$

In this sequence, we are in state B four times, for which we have three transitions. Of these three transitions, one is to state C, so on the basis of the information given, we would estimate $\gamma_B \approx 1/3$; similarly $\gamma_C \approx 1/3$, and $\gamma_X \approx 1/2$. Thus each parameter is easily evaluated and these parameters can be used as the basis for compressing the bitmap. Further, the standard deviation of this estimate, for state S, is given by $\sigma_S = \sqrt{\gamma_S(1 - \gamma_S)/N_S}$, if we experience N_S transitions from state S in the pertinent bitmap. The standard deviations make it possible to compute confidence intervals and do tests of hypotheses.

For a large bitmap, the γ-values can be stored with the bitmap to permit decompression. But several mechanisms can be tried to reduce the cost of storing these parameters. For example, we can save the space for storing these parameters by evaluating them adaptively, beginning with reasonable initial values. We can also lower storage costs if we find the θ's are related in a regular manner over the terms. For example, since state X is intermediate between states C and B, we might find that γ_X is reasonably approximated by the average of γ_C and γ_B, that is, that $\theta_X = (1+\Theta)/2$.

It may also be possible, without serious deterioration in performance, to divide the parameters into a small number of categories. Thus, we might divide our terms into four clustering classes: one class would represent no clustering ($\Theta = 1$); the other three states would represent varying clustering strengths, with the values of the clustering parameter, Θ, for these states determined empirically. This simplification allows clustering strength to be represented with the cost of just two bits per term. We will explore the value of such simplifications.

3.3 Model Testing

The model allows us to make a number of predictions about the properties of the bitmaps, and these can be used to test the model.

Test 1: One such test predicts the density of one-bits, N/D; this can be compared to the actual values of N and D, which are available to us without extra cost. The relationship is defined as follows. We assume we first have a span of documents without the designated term; the size of this span is E. This is followed by N spans made up of a document containing the term followed by an inter-term gap (of size G) of documents, and a terminal span of approximate size E.

To derive our estimate, we assume that each internal span has a length equal to its expected value, and that the lengths of the terminal spans is of comparable size (say $E \approx \alpha G$, for $\alpha \approx 1$). As N gets large, the contribution of E becomes negligeable, allowing the following large-N relationship between D, N and the γ's:

$$\frac{N}{D} = \frac{\gamma_B}{\gamma_B + (1-\gamma_C)(1-\gamma_X+\gamma_B)}. \tag{1}$$

This relation, which can also be derived more formally in terms of Markov chain theory, provides our first test of the model.

The general theory of Markov chains allows us to derive the steady state probabilities π_C, π_X and π_B of being in states C, X, and B:

$$\pi_C = \frac{\gamma_B}{\gamma_B + (1-\gamma_C)(1-\gamma_X+\gamma_B)}, \tag{2}$$

$$\pi_X = \frac{\gamma_B(1-\gamma_C)}{\gamma_B + (1-\gamma_C)(1-\gamma_X+\gamma_B)}, \tag{3}$$

and,

$$\pi_B = \frac{(1-\gamma_C)(1-\gamma_X)}{\gamma_B + (1-\gamma_C)(1-\gamma_X+\gamma_B)}. \tag{4}$$

Since $\pi_C D = N$ equations 1 and 2 are very similar.

Test 2: As part of the development of test 1, we computed the average number of zeroes between two consecutive one-bits. A similar argument yields the useful relation that the average size, SZ, of an *actual* run of zeroes (that is, assuming at least one zero in the run) is given by $SZ = \gamma_X + (1-\gamma_X)(1+\gamma_B)/\gamma_B$. If there are NZ zeroes in the bitmap, we expect approximately NZ/SZ runs of zeroes. Further, since the number of runs of one's is within one of the number of runs of zeroes, NZ/SZ is also an estimate of the number of runs of one-bits. Each of these relations can be used as a test of the model.

3.4 Performance Estimates

If we are in state $S \in \{B, X, C\}$, we expect that we can encode the next bitmap element in $H(\gamma_S)$ bits (where $H(x) \equiv -(x\log(x) + (1-x)\log(1-x))$). Using eqs. 2, 3, and 4, we estimate that the D bits of the bitmap can be reduced to

$$B_M = (\pi_C H(\gamma_C) + \pi_B H(\gamma_B) + \pi_X H(\gamma_X))D$$

bits.

This estimate of performance can be used as a rough test of the Markov model. But even if the model is valid, we are left with the question of whether the savings of using the full model justifies the additional complexity relative to the independence model. The relative performance of the two models is easily computed.

Under the assumption of the independence model, the appearance of a one-bit is determined by a single parameter, p, and the size of the bitmap is reduced to

$$B_I = H(p)D$$

bits. But the probability p of generating a one-bit depends on which state S we are in (governed by the known probabilities π_S), and the probability of a transition to C from S. If the Markov model is valid, we could combine these to find:

$$\begin{aligned} p &= \pi_B\gamma_B + \pi_X\gamma_X + \pi_C\gamma_C \\ &= \pi_C. \end{aligned}$$

The equation $p = \pi_C$ could have been asserted directly: the probability of a one-bit is just the probability of going to state C from any of the states; but the long term probability of *going* to C is the same as the probability of *being* in C, as the last equation asserts.

The ratio B_M/B_I gives the relative advantage of using the full Markov model.

4 Partial experiment

We decided for technical reasons to continue testing our methods on the concordance of the Hebrew Bible, as we did in our earlier paper. The Bible consists of 309631 words which are partitioned into 929 chapters. The number of different words is 41197 and the number of coordinates of the form $(d, m; w_1, \ldots, w_m)$ is 192048.

The first step for applying the Markov model is to evaluate the values of the γ's and Θ. This was done by scanning the bitmaps generated from the concordance, simulating the B, X and C states, and counting the transitions. There is of course no sense in applying the Markov model to the full set of 41197 terms; most of these appear in very few documents, and 57% of the terms appear in one document only. Using the Markov model, one would need 9.35 bits on the average to encode the d-fields of terms that appear in less than 60 documents, while one could just use a fixed encoding, using 10 bits to designate in which of the 929 documents the term appears. We therefore restricted our test to the 426 terms appearing in at least 60 documents. Though these are only 1% of the terms, they account for 48% of the concordance.

	$N \geq 1$			$N \geq 60$		
Range	γ_C	γ_X	γ_B	γ_C	γ_X	γ_B
0.00 – 0.02	36779	37849	39751	0	0	1
0.02 – 0.1	896	1074	1284	4	34	263
0.1 – 0.2	1526	1357	117	137	192	117
0.2 – 0.4	1306	800	39	194	166	39
0.4 – 0.7	639	113	5	77	30	5
0.7 – 1.0	51	4	1	14	4	1

Table 1: *Distribution of γ values*

Table 1 shows the distribution of the values of the estimated parameters γ_C, γ_X and γ_B, both for the full set of coordinates and for the most frequent words. The table shows for each range, the number of terms having their value γ_S in the given range, for $S \in \{C, X, B\}$. We see a tendency of having more terms with γ_C in the higher ranges than with γ_X or γ_B. The large majority of terms have very low γ values (less than 0.02), because these terms are so rare that hardly any cluster is found. By comparing the two γ_B columns, one sees that no term with $N < 60$ has a γ_B value larger than 0.1. The average values, $\overline{\gamma_S}$, of γ_S in the given sets, are displayed in Table 2.

The last line of Table 2 gives the ratio B_M/B_I, which estimates the relative advantage of using the Markov model. The fact that these values are so close to 1 might at the first sight indicate that the expected gain is very small. It should, however, be noted that this is probably due to the fact that our test concordance is much too small. Most of the terms, even most of those appearing in more than 60 documents, are still relatively rare; on the other extreme, those few terms appearing in many documents are probably not content bearing words, which therefore will not exhibit any clustering tendency. But even if the B_M/B_I ratio is not very impressive, there is still evidence that clustering occurs, as suggested by the fact that

$\overline{\gamma_C} > \overline{\gamma_X} > \overline{\gamma_B}$, for both sets considered; if terms were distributed randomly, the various γ-values would tend to be equal.

Parameter	$N \geq 1$	$N \geq 60$
γ_C	0.1814	0.4105
γ_X	0.0713	0.2482
γ_B	0.0038	0.0945
Θ	0.0209	0.2302
B_M/B_I	0.986	0.947

Table 2: *Parameter values*

The compression results are listed in Table 3, giving the average number of bits needed to encode the document-field of a coordinate. The first line corresponds to the static independent model of [1], that is, N and D are fixed for each term. The second line are the results of the dynamic independent model of [1], where N and D are updated after each d-field encoded. The last line corresponds to the Markov model.

Model	$N \geq 1$	$N \geq 60$
Static indep.	7.0156	3.4808
Dynamic indep.	6.5093	3.4521
Dynamic Markov	8.3258	3.2817

Table 3: *Comparison of bit generation models*

The first column gives the averages on the full set. We see that using the Markov model would actually incur a loss. The second column gives the averages for the 426 terms appearing in at least 60 documents. These terms are not necessarily clustered, but because of their relatively high density, the Markov model shows here a moderate improvement over the earlier models. The denser the maps, the better does the Markov model perform. For instance, for the 79 words appearing in at least 200 documents, only 2.24 bits are needed on the average to encode the value in the document-field.

5 Final remarks

As noted already in our earlier paper, the Bible is not really a good example of a database on which to apply our new methods. The Bible is too small (just about 1.5 MB), so that hardly any concordance is needed. On real life concordances, of the size of hundreds of MB, the compression savings are usually much more substantial (about 40% by method POM of [3] on large data bases, versus 16% by POM here), so we expect there our method also to perform much better. The fact, however, that by restricting our action only to the most frequent words, we still cover a large part of the concordance, is true also for large systems. For instance, the 100 most frequent words of the *Trésor de la Langue Française* (TLF) account for 57% of the text. We are currently experimenting with the other tests and models, and shall apply these on the database of the TLF.

6 References

1. **Bookstein A., Klein S.T., Raita T.,** Model based concordance compression, *Proc. Data Compression Conference DCC–92*, Snowbird, Utah (1992) 82–91.

2. **Bookstein A., Klein S.T., Ziff, D.A.,** A systematic approach to compressing a full text retrieval system, *Information Processing & Management* **28** (1992) 795–806.

3. **Choueka Y., Fraenkel A.S., Klein S.T.,** Compression of Concordances in Full-Text Retrieval Systems, *Proc. 11-th ACM-SIGIR Conf.*, Grenoble (1988) 597–612.

4. **Cormack G.V., Horspool R.N.,** Data compression using dynamic Markov modeling, *The Computer Journal* **30** (1987) 541–550.

5. **Klein S.T., Bookstein A., Deerwester S.,** Storing Text Retrieval Systems on CD-ROM: Compression and Encryption Considerations, *ACM Trans. on Information Systems* **7** (1989), 230–245.

6. **Llewellyn J.A.,** Data compression for a source with Markov characteristics, *The Computer Journal* **30** (1987) 149–156.

7. **Wisniewski J.L.,** Compression of index term dictionary in an inverted file oriented database: some efficient algorithms, *Information Proc. & Management* **22** (1986) 493–501.

8. **Witten I.H., Bell T.C., Nevill C.G.,** Models for compression in full-text retrieval systems, *Proc. Data Compression Conference DCC–91*, Snowbird, Utah (1991) 23–32.

Static Compression for Dynamic Texts *

(Extended Abstract)

Alistair Moffat† Neil Sharman‡ Justin Zobel§

1 Word-Based Compression

The use of a word-based zero-order compression model to represent English text has been considered by several authors [1, 3, 5, 6]. It is particularly appropriate for compressing full-text document collections, an application in which large quantities of text are stored but individual documents must be independently decodable [2]. In this case a semi-static approach that makes a preliminary pass over the text before compressing it in a second pass is appropriate, and when the word-based model is coupled with static Huffman coding, it yields the three necessary properties: good compression, fast decoding, and random access.

There are, however, two drawbacks to the use of this combination. First, a great deal of decode-time memory space might be required to store the tokens of the compression alphabet. In our experience the number of distinct "words" in a text grows as an almost linear function of its size, without the tailing-off effect often predicted. If for no other reason, this happens because new misspelt words occur at a reasonably constant rate, and these are all regarded as novel by the compression system. As part of the international *trec* information retrieval experiment we have been dealing with several corpora of English text, each of approximately 500 Mb [4]. One of the collections is several years of articles from the *Wall Street Journal*, and this 508.15 Mb *wsj* database uses 289,101 distinct words totalling 2,159,044 characters; and 8,912 distinct non-words requiring in total 77,882 bytes. Allowing a 4-byte string pointer for each word, and ignoring for the moment the possibility of storing the words compressed in memory, the total requirement during decompression is about 3.3 Mb, a non-trivial amount even by workstation standards. Moreover, there is only limited overlap when these parts are combined to make the 2 Gb *trec* collection. Using the same method of calculating space, to decode *trec* more than 11 Mb of memory is required.

The second problem is that use of a semi-static model assumes the complete text is known in advance. In full-text applications this will often be the case, for example, when databases are being mastered onto CD-ROM. However there are also many situations in which there is a need for new documents to be appended to the

*This work was supported by the Australian Research Council and the Collaborative Information Technology Research Institute.

†Department of Computer Science, The University of Melbourne, Australia 3052. Facsimile: +61 3 3481184. Internet: alistair@cs.mu.oz.au.

‡Department of Computer Science, The University of Melbourne, Australia 3052.

§Department of Computer Science, RMIT, GPO Box 2476V, Melbourne 3001, Australia.

collection. One obvious example of this is a newspaper archive, to which articles are added almost continuously. In this case the compression scheme must permit the text to be dynamic, since it is clearly unreasonable to suppose that the entire collection should be recompressed after each insertion, or even once a day.

We have considered both of these problems. To solve the first, use is made of a subsidiary character-level model to code words deliberately omitted from the word-level model. We give details of one simple selection algorithm that allows the decoder memory requirement to be held to a few hundred kilobytes with almost no impact on compression rates.

Our solution to the second problem is to permit the static model some small and controlled amount of leeway to modify itself during document insertion. In a sense, the model is best described as taking "one and a bit" passes, since it is neither one-pass nor two-pass. We again describe a suitable strategy for maximising compression, and show that the "bit" can be as small as one part in a thousand with almost no loss of efficiency. That is, we demonstrate that a compression model developed on some text can be usefully employed to compress a text 1,000 times larger. Hence the title, static compression for dynamic texts.

Throughout the following we will describe how the "words" of the compression model are handled; the same treatment is, of course, applied in parallel to the intervening non-words. All compression figures given here include both the words and the non-words, and are for lossless compression of the source text.

2 Reducing the Memory Requirements

One simple way to reduce the decode-time memory requirement is to omit some of the words from the lexicon. When non-lexicon words are encountered during the compression pass, they must be represented in some other way; and so a subsidiary character-based model—with only modest demands on main memory—is used to "spell" these out. If a full first pass is made over the text, statistics for the character model can be accumulated based upon knowledge of the rejected words and their frequencies. Three different methods for selecting words have been explored, and these are described below. In all cases an escape code must be provided, appearance of which in the compressed text signals the decoder to receive the next word in character by character mode rather than as a single token. To actually spell the word, a Huffman coded length is issued, and then a sequence of Huffman coded characters. In a semi-static model both of these codes, and the escape code itself, can be based upon the actual probabilities of occurrence.

2.1 Method A

If a bounded amount of model space is to be used then some of the word tokens need to be discarded. The first method considered for choosing which words to accept and which to reject is to allow the first pass to accumulate words only until the memory limit is reached. The remainder of the first pass continues to accumulate frequencies for words that made it into the lexicon, but novel words are recorded as a sequence of characters, and no attempt is made to determine whether they might themselves warrant the allocation of space in the lexicon and the assignment of a word code.

There is a single major reason why this simplistic approach can be useful: it means that the amount of memory required in the encoder is also bounded. Furthermore, despite its simplicity, it can also be expected to give reasonable compression, since intuitively one expects that frequent words will benefit most by being included in the lexicon, and the first appearance of each should be encountered relatively early in the text.

2.2 Method B

If the encoder is permitted enough memory to retain all words, then a more disciplined approach is to record all word frequencies, and select into the lexicon those with the highest probability of appearance. This ensures that only rare words are spelt out in the relatively inefficient subsidiary model, and so overall compression should be better than that achieved by Method A. This method supposes that encoding is performed on a better endowed machine than is decoding, a situation that will often be the case for text retrieval.

2.3 Method C

Both Method A and Method B are approximations of the "optimal" selection of words into the bounded amount of memory space. Ideally, the selection of words should be such that no exchange between the *accepted* list and the *rejected* list decreases the length of the compressed text. To identify an almost optimal selection, the following technique is used.

First, the accepted list is seeded with words using Method B. Then the Huffman code on words, and the Huffman code on characters are established. Each accepted word occupies $l+4$ bytes of lexicon, where l is its length in bytes and a string pointer requires 4 bytes; and it contributes some known number of bits to the compressed output stream, calculable from its frequency and the length of the corresponding codeword. On the other hand, if it were to be moved to the rejected list, then, according to the character codes, it would contribute some greater number of bits to the output file. Thus, the bytes of lexicon currently occupied by this word can be *priced* at the difference between these two quantities, divided by $l + 4$.

Similarly, each currently rejected word would save some number of output bits were it to be transferred into the lexicon, and so it can be regarded as *bidding* for entry at a certain price in terms of bits in the output per byte of lexicon occupied. In this case, however, the length of the word Huffman code can only be estimated, since it does not currently have a codeword assigned. This estimate is taken to be the negative logarithm of its probability.

At each iteration of the selection process, all of the bids and prices are evaluated, and any rejected words that on a per byte basis bid higher than any currently accepted prices are swapped into the lexicon, until the least price in the lexicon is greater than the highest bid. Then all of the Huffman codes are reevaluated, and the prices and bids recalculated. The process is continued until, immediately after the code recalculation, there are still no bids greater than any of the prices. This establishes a lexicon where no words can be exchanged from the rejected to the accepted state without increasing the total output bitlength.

2.4 RESULTS

All three methods have been implemented and tested against *wsj*. Figure 1 shows the effect each of these three strategies has upon compression rate, plotted as a function of decoding model size. Throughout this paper compression rates are given as a percentage remaining of the original input text size, and include all auxiliary lexicon files necessary for decoding. The latter are, by and large, stored using a simple zero-order character-based model, and account for less than half a percentage point in all of the compression figures listed. The memory requirements shown on the horizontal axis are exclusive of the space required by the character-level model, which adds about 1 Kb to the memory requirements. There are a number of other small in-memory tables (totalling less than 1 Kb) that have not been included, and the domain in Figure 1 is purely the memory required by the word tokens. As above, this is calculated based upon the generous estimate of 1 byte for each character of each accepted token, plus one four byte string pointer per token. This is generous because front coding (also known as prefix omission) can be used to reduce the space required by the bytes of each string, and the strings can be indexed in blocks, with one pointer per block. Experiments have shown that front coding can halve the cost of storing the compression lexicon, but double the decoding time [7].

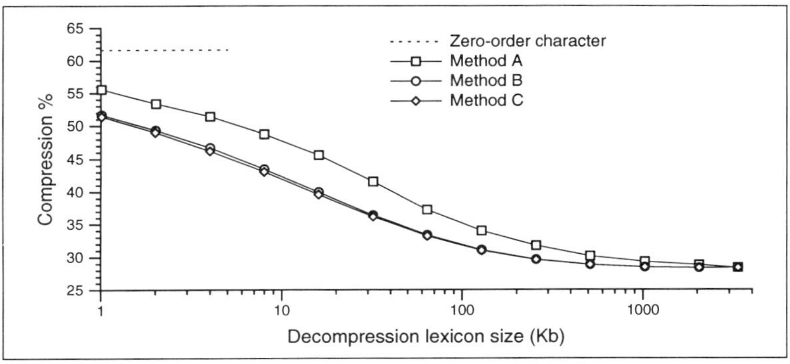

Figure 1: Effect on compression for *wsj* of reduced model size

As expected, Method A is outperformed by Methods B and C. More surprising is the excellent performance of Method B, which is only marginally inferior to Method C. Choosing the most frequently appearing terms is an excellent heuristic. Using either Method B or Method C the decode-time memory requirement can be reduced to well under 1 Mb with only minimal degradation of compression. Figure 1 also shows the compression achieved by a zero-order character model, which, by this method of calculation, requires 0 Kb.

Table 1 shows in detail some of the points on the curve for Method C. When no memory is allocated for word storage the model is effectively a zero-order character model. The first 10 Kb of word storage improves the compression rate by nearly 20 percentage points, whereas the last 2000 Kb gain only a final 0.1 percentage points.

Memory Allowed	Words #	Words Kb	Non-words #	Non-words Kb	Hit rate %	Compression %
0.0	0	0.0	0	0.0	0.0	61.7
10.0	983	9.3	80	0.7	78.0	42.0
100.0	9,207	97.7	255	2.3	95.0	31.7
1024.0	91,028	1002.7	1,891	21.3	99.7	28.5
3348.6	289,102	3237.7	8,913	110.9	100.0	28.4

Table 1: Compression with restricted model size, Method C

One of the advantages of the word-based model is its fast decoding, resulting from the use of multi-byte symbols. Use of a restricted lexicon means that some fraction of the text is coded in a character model, and that decompression speed suffers. The loss, however, is small, because most of the frequently appearing symbols are still allocated word codes. For example, with a 100 Kb model just 5% of the tokens are coded in the auxiliary character model, and even with a 10 Kb model nearly 80% of the tokens were lexicon words—the "hit rate" in Table 1. Exact values for decoding speed are presented in the full paper [7].

3 Catering for Dynamic Collections

The second problem we consider is that of providing extensibility. Some text archives are intrinsically static, but many are dynamic, with new documents frequently added and a collection growing by perhaps many orders of magnitude during its lifetime. In this case it is not at all clear that a semi-static model should be relied upon for text compression, since, if applied strictly, the entire text should be completely recompressed after every document insertion. In this section we consider three methods for extending a collection without recourse to recompression, assuming that some amount of seed text is available.

3.1 Method A

One obvious way in which the model can be made open-ended is to supply an escape code and a subsidiary character model, so that novel words in new text can still be encoded. The only difference is that the probabilities of the escape symbol and in the character level model must be estimates rather than exact values, since the text they are called upon to represent is, at time of model creation, still unknown. The latter can, however, be assumed to be similar to the character probabilities already observed in the text available, provided only that every symbol is allocated a code whether or not it has occurred. Method XC of Witten and Bell [8] was used to estimate the probability of a novel word. This technique assigns the escape symbol a "frequency" of t_1, where t_1 is the number of symbols that have occurred once. That is, the number of symbols of frequency zero is approximated by the number of symbols of frequency one.

Figure 2 shows the "instantaneous" compression achieved on *wsj* for three models. The data points are the compression rate achieved for each 4 Mb chunk of input text, and so the overall compression rate for the file is the area under the curve plus the cost of storing the lexicon. No limitations on decoding memory were assumed.

The darkest line shows the compression assuming that a complete first pass over *wsj* is made, meaning that the model used during the second compression pass truly reflects the text being compressed. The compression rate is uniform, although the second part of the text does appear to be a little less compressible than the first. The other two lines show the instantaneous compression rates achieved when models built assuming knowledge of the first 25% of *wsj* (dark grey) and 6.25% of *wsj* (light grey) are used to compress the whole text. That is, they represent the compression that would be achieved if an initial collection of about 125 Mb was expanded to 500 Mb by the insertion of new text; and the compression that would result if an initial text of 35 Mb was available at time of model creation, and then the database grew.

Notice how the two partial models give *better* compression on the initial text they have "seen", but are worse on the text that they have no foreknowledge of. In particular, the changes at about 230 Mb and then again at 370 Mb catch these two unawares, and compression suffers. Nevertheless, the degradation is small. The compression rates for the two partial models, including the lexicon, are 29.9% and 30.5%, only fractionally worse than the compression rate reported in the last line of Table 1.

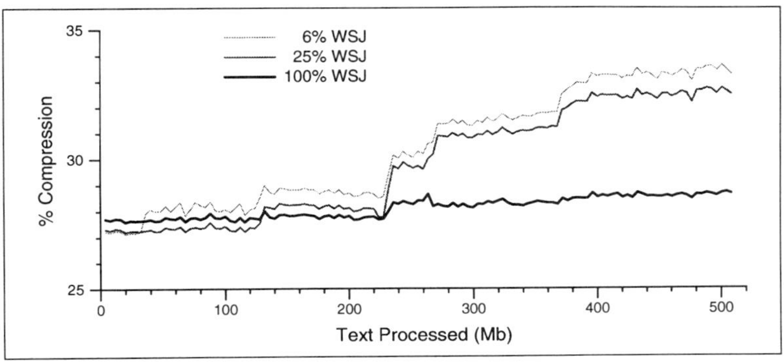

Figure 2: Instantaneous compression for *wsj*

3.2 Method B

Assuming a semi-static model and only a certain amount of known seed text, it might seem that there is little more that can be done. However, for this application there are actually *two* channels of communication between encoder and decoder. The first is the compressed text, stored in the indexed file in the normal way. Once compressed it cannot be changed, because each document might be requested and decoded at any time.

The second channel is the lexicon of words used to control the compression. It is much smaller than the text, and, provided that the codes for existing words are not changed, new words can be appended to it without rendering unreadable previously compressed documents. Moreover, if the encoder installs words into the lexicon as they are discovered during document insertion operations, they will certainly be there before the decoder can ever be called upon to emit them, and there is no need for them to ever be spelt out. All that is required is an agreed-upon set of codewords to indicate arbitrary positions in an auxiliary lexicon of "escaped" words. Then, rather than escaping to a subsidiary character model when it encounters a non-lexicon word, the compressor escapes to an auxiliary list of words, and, even if the word is not in that list either, is free to add it and emit the corresponding code. Now locations in the auxiliary lexicon must be coded.

Method B1 One possibility is to use Elias's C_δ code (see [1]) for positive integers. Each word in the auxiliary lexicon is assigned a code based upon its ordinal number: the first, a 1-bit code; the second and third, 4-bit codes; and, in general, the n'th a code of approximately $1 + 2\log\log n + \log n$ bits. The lexicon grows each time a novel word is encountered, but this is a simple append operation, and in the compressed text this first appearance and all subsequent occurrences of this word are coded as an offset in the auxiliary lexicon.

Method B2 The C_δ code is biased heavily in favour of small values—for example, it assigns an implicit probability of 0.5 to symbol "1". A flatter distribution of codes might better match the actual distribution of novel words, and so a binary code is also a possibility. Because binary is not an open-ended code, the number of novel words applicable to this document must be prefixed to the document's representation in the text file. During decoding, if r of the novel words have been encountered to date, then binary codes in the range 1 to $r+1$ are emitted, with $r+1$ indicating that the next novel word is now in play and that r should be incremented. The latter strategy is effective because the novel words are installed in the lexicon in appearance order by the encoder. The drawback of this method is that the implicit probabilities are now perhaps *too* even.

Method B3 As a third possibility, a hybrid code was implemented. The C_δ code in effect assigns symbols to *buckets*, with 1 symbol in the first bucket; 2 in the second; 4 in the third; etc. The code for a symbol in this scheme is generated as a C_γ coded bucket number, and a binary "position-within-bucket" value. To flatten the probability distribution, we placed r_{dict} symbols in the first bucket rather than 1, where r_{dict} is the number of words in the compression lexicon that are assigned proper

Huffman codes. The second bucket is given $2r_{\text{dict}}$ symbols, the third $4r_{\text{dict}}$, and so on. This hybrid code is more skewed in favour of low values than a binary code, but not as biased as C_δ; and does not require an upper bound on the size of the auxiliary lexicon of novel words.

3.3 METHOD C

The model can be even more flexible than is allowed in Method B. The requirement for synchronisation is only that at the *start* of each document the model be in some consistent and known state, and there is no reason why it cannot be adaptive *within* each document.

Bentley et al. [3] describe a "Move-to-Front" (MTF) heuristic for assigning codes to symbols. We considered the use of this strategy for reorganising the list of words in the auxiliary lexicon, but discarded it because of the relatively high cost of tracking list positions. Instead a simpler rule was used, which we call "Swap-to-Near-Front" (SNF). At the commencement of decoding of each document the list of auxiliary terms is assigned codewords in order of their first appearance in the collection. This satisfies the synchronisation requirement. A pointer p is initialised to zero, indicating that no words have been swapped; at any given time during the processing of each document words with codes of p or less have occurred at least once.

Then the document is encoded. When each non-lexicon word is encountered it is encoded as a location within the auxiliary lexicon, using the hybrid code. Immediately after being encoded, its current location x is checked against the pointer p. If $x > p$ then it has not yet been swapped, and so p is incremented, and words x and p exchanged. On the other hand, if $x \leq p$ no action is taken, since word x has already been moved forward at least once, and to move it again would only displace some other word which is also known to have already occurred within this document.

At the end of the document, all of the swaps are undone in the reverse order to that they were applied in so that the model returns to the "standard" state ready to commence the processing of the next document. This is easily accomplished by maintaining a list S of values x for which swaps have occurred, and applying them in reverse order, decrementing p after each such swap. Swapping two strings by pointer exchange is a substantially faster operation than reorganising a dynamic search structure such as the splay tree required by the MTF policy, and the SNF approach has no effect on encoding and decoding rates.

This then is Method C: a Huffman coded lexicon based upon whatever seed text is available; an escape code assigned a probability using method XC; an open-ended auxiliary lexicon containing all of the non-lexicon words in order of first appearance; a modified C_δ code with which locations in the auxiliary lexicon are represented, parameterised in terms of r_{dict}, the number of words assigned Huffman codes; and the SNF strategy to allow the codewords within the auxiliary lexicon to be self-modifying. Although complex in description, all of the essential features of the word-based model are retained, and this mechanism provides both synchronisation and fast decoding. Moreover, as is demonstrated in the next section, it handles quite astounding text expansions with exemplary compression ratios.

3.4 RESULTS

Figure 3 shows the application of these methods to the *wsj* collection. The horizontal axis shows the fraction of the original text used to build the model. For example, at an expansion factor of 100, the first 1%—a little over 5 Mb—of the text of *wsj* is assumed to be available to the encoder to be used to establish a compression model, and then this plus the other 99% is compressed according to the model constructed at that time. The minimum amount of seed text used was a little under 32 Kb, to obtain an expansion ratio of 16,384.

The uppermost line shows the result of using a subsidiary character-level model, with every appearance of each novel word spelt out in full, Method A. The first, third, and fifth points on this curve correspond to the three lines plotted in Figure 2. This method provides reasonable compression for expansion ratios of up to about 10, but compression steadily degrades thereafter. Note the sudden change in compression rate between expansion factors 1 and 2 common to all of the methods; this is caused by the sharply different nature of the two halves of the *wsj* collection, demonstrated in Figure 2. Despite its poor compression performance, Method A does has one clear advantage over all of the other approaches: the decode-time memory requirement is fixed, regardless of expansion in the collection.

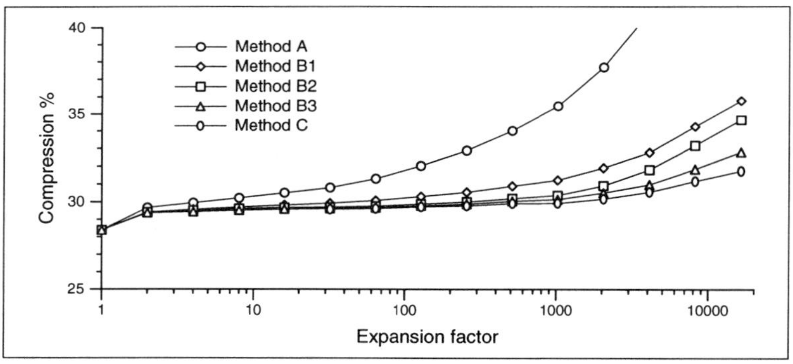

Figure 3: Simulated expansion of *wsj*

The next three lines show the effect of allowing novel words to be inserted into the lexicon and assigned simple codes using methods B1, B2, and B3. As expected, all give markedly better compression than Method A. Method C then provides further improvement. Quite remarkably, this final method allows the compression degradation to be restricted to less than 2 percentage points, even in the face of a 4,000-fold expansion in the size of the collection. A collection that starts at 1 Mb will reach 1 Gb before the compression gets even slightly worse; a recompression then to establish a new model sets the scene for expansion beyond 1 *tera*byte.

4 Other Considerations

The full paper [7] includes further results for other large collections and for cross-compression, when a model based upon one corpus is used to compress another; for the memory savings achieved by front coding and blocking; and a performance comparison showing that the mechanisms described here provide compression efficiency at a decoding speed unmatched by other algorithms, both static and adaptive.

5 Summary

We have explored the particular needs of large information retrieval systems, in which hundreds of megabytes of data are stored, retrieval is non-sequential, and new text is continually being appended. It has been shown that the word-based model can be adapted to cope well both with dynamic environments, and with situations in which decode-time memory is limited. In the latter case as little as 100 Kb of main memory is sufficient to achieve excellent compression, provided a suitable choice of tokens is used as the compression lexicon. To solve the former problem a new paradigm of compression has been introduced, in which some components of the compression model are required to remain static to ensure that all parts of the text can be decoded, and some parts are extensible, so that new text can also influence the assignment of codewords. An additional heuristic—Swap-to-Near-the-Front—allows collections to be seeded with as little as 1/1000 of their final text with minimal loss of compression efficiency. The resulting "almost static" compression method is ideal for large dynamic collections.

References

[1] T.C. Bell, J.G. Cleary, and I.H. Witten. *Text Compression.* Prentice-Hall, Englewood Cliffs, New Jersey, 1990.

[2] T.C. Bell, A. Moffat, C.G. Nevill-Manning, I.H. Witten, and J. Zobel. Data compression in full-text retrieval systems. *Journal of the American Society for Information Science*, 44:508–531, October 1993.

[3] J. Bentley, D. Sleator, R. Tarjan, and V. Wei. A locally adaptive data compression scheme. *Communications of the ACM*, 29:320–330, April 1986.

[4] D.K. Harman. Overview of the first text retrieval conference. In *Proc. TREC Text Retrieval Conference*, pages 1–20, Gaithersburg, Maryland, November 1992. National Institute of Standards Special Publication 500-207.

[5] R.N. Horspool and G.V. Cormack. Constructing word-based text compression algorithms. In *Proc. IEEE Data Compression Conference*, pages 62–81, Snowbird, Utah, March 1992. IEEE Computer Society Press, Los Alamitos, California.

[6] A. Moffat. Word based text compression. *Software—Practice and Experience*, 19:185–198, February 1989.

[7] A. Moffat, N.B. Sharman, and J. Zobel. Static compression for dynamic texts. Technical Report 93/28, Department of Computer Science, The University of Melbourne, Parkville 3052, Australia, November 1993.

[8] I.H. Witten and T.C. Bell. The zero frequency problem: Estimating the probabilities of novel events in adaptive text compression. *IEEE Transactions on Information Theory*, 37:1085–1094, July 1991.

Parsing Algorithms for Dictionary Compression on the PRAM

Daniel S. Hirschberg and Lynn M. Stauffer
Information and Computer Science Department
University of California, Irvine
Irvine, CA 92717-3425
dan@ics.uci.edu, stauffer@ics.uci.edu

Abstract

Parallel algorithms for lossless data compression via dictionary compression using optimal and greedy parsing strategies are described. Dictionary compression removes redundancy by replacing substrings of the input by references to strings stored in a dictionary. Given a static dictionary stored as a suffix tree, we present a PRAM CREW algorithm for optimal compression which runs in $O(M + \log M \log n)$ time with $O(nM^2)$ processors, where it is assumed that M is the maximum length of any dictionary entry. We also describe an $O(M + \log n)$ time and $O(n)$ processor algorithm for greedy parsing given a static or sliding-window dictionary. For sliding-window compression, a different approach finds the greedy parsing in $O(\log n)$ time using $O(nM \log M / \log n)$ processors. Our algorithms are practical in the sense that their analysis elicits small constants.

1. Introduction

We present parallel algorithms for dictionary compression using optimal and greedy parsings. Dictionary compression methods, also called textual substitution and Ziv-Lempel compression, achieve compression by replacing strings with references to some dictionary of strings [ZL77, ZL78]. In this paper, we consider algorithms for dictionary compression on the parallel random access memory (PRAM) model of parallel computation. The PRAM model consists of a number of identical general-purpose sequential processors that communicate through a large shared, random access memory. Variants of the PRAM model differ in their handling of simultaneous reading and writing of the global memory. The Concurrent-Read, Concurrent-Write (CRCW) model allows processors to read and write the shared memory simultaneously, while the Concurrent-Read, Exclusive-Write (CREW) model forbids simultaneous writes. CRCW models are further distinguished by their methods for handling write conflicts. The Common CRCW permits concurrent writes only when all processors are attempting to write the same value to the same block; the Arbitrary CRCW allows an arbitrary processor to succeed in a concurrent write; the Priority CRCW assumes processors are assigned unique ordered priorities and, when several processors attempt to write to a single location, the processor with the highest priority carries out its write instruction.

In the parallel environment, dictionary compression schemes have been developed using a systolic array [GS85, SR91, SH92, SH93]. A systolic array consists of a collection of linearly-connected processors where input enters at one end of the array and output exits at the other [L92]. This model requires linear time to handle input and output. The PRAM models allow blocks of data to be read or written in a single time step, and so sublinear time data compression is possible. In this paper, we improve previously known dictionary compression algorithms which utilize optimal and greedy parsing heuristics. We refer the reader to [S88A], [BCW90], and [W91] for a thorough coverage of sequential text compression and to [SH93] for a survey of parallel text compression.

Dictionary compression methods can be static or adaptive. A *static* method creates a fixed dictionary before compression begins. An *adaptive* (also called *dynamic*) method allows changes to the dictionary during compression. A popular adaptive approach based on the work of Lempel and Ziv [ZL78] (often called LZ78 or LZ2 compression) parses the input into phrases which are compared to a dynamic dictionary. The discovery of $\mathcal{NC}$[1] algorithms for LZ78 is unlikely since LZ78 and two LZ78 variations are known to be P-complete[2] [D91]. The P-complete LZ78 variants implement different parsing and dictionary update strategies [W84, S88A]. Ziv and Lempel's earlier approach limits references to a window of input characters preceding the input position being considered for encoding [ZL77]. The dictionary is implicitly represented by a window that slides continuously over the input. Encoding references consist of (*position, length*) pairs that indicate a substring in the window. These methods are referred to variously as LZ77, LZ1, and *sliding-window* compression.

Once the dictionary has been selected, the input stream must be parsed to determine which substrings are to be replaced by dictionary indices or references. A position in the input stream is a *breakpoint* if a substring starting at that position is to be replaced by a dictionary reference. A *parsing* of the input determines the set of breakpoint positions and the corresponding sequence of substrings that will be represented by references and results in determining the sequence of dictionary references. An *optimal* parsing of the input is a parsing whose resulting sequence of dictionary references has the most succinct representation. If it is assumed that dictionary references are of fixed-length then an optimal parsing is one with the fewest number of references. For variable-length references, an optimal parsing is not necessarily one with the fewest number of references. We consider optimal parsing

[1] The class $\mathcal{NC}$ is the collection of problems that are solvable by deterministic parallel algorithms that operate in time bounded by a power of the logarithm of the input size using a polynomially-bounded number of processors [J92].

[2] If an $\mathcal{NC}$ algorithm for any P-complete problem could be found then all problems in $\mathcal{P}$ would have similar $\mathcal{NC}$ solutions. Although it has not been proven, it is strongly believed that $\mathcal{P} \neq \mathcal{NC}$ [J92].

with both fixed and variable-length pointers. A more straightforward approach is *greedy* parsing where iteratively the encoder finds the longest dictionary phrase that matches a prefix of the uncoded portion of the input stream and the index of that dictionary entry is used to encode the input prefix.

Greedy parsing is not necessarily optimal. However, to compute an optimal parsing, a sequential encoder must perform two passes over the input or be capable of looking at arbitrarily large prefixes of the input. Consequently, greedy parsing is widely used in sequential compression systems since it requires only limited look-ahead and is computed on-line. The PRAM model lifts the performance limitations of optimal parsing by making the entire input string available for computation in a single step.

In this paper, we describe parallel algorithms for static dictionary compression subsequent to the selection of strings represented in the dictionary (see [CL82] and [SH73] for discussions of the dictionary creation problem). We assume that the dictionary contains d entries, each of length less than or equal to some maximum length M. We also assume that the input string is processed in blocks of n characters. To guarantee a feasible compressed representation, the dictionary is required to include all members of the input character set.

Table 1 summarizes previously known results and those presented in this paper. Some algorithms assume that the dictionary satisfies the prefix property (notated "Pref" in Table 1), i.e., all prefixes of each dictionary entry are present in the dictionary. Many of the results assume that the dictionary is represented as a suffix tree. (These results are notated by "*" in Table 1.) A suffix tree for a dictionary D is a trie composed of all the strings in D. Every string in D corresponds to a path in the suffix tree in a natural way. Associated with each node in the tree is the substring (not necessarily in D) consisting of the concatenation of the substrings of the edges along the path from the root to the node. For our purposes, we require that a node corresponding to a string in D stores a pointer into a table of references. This information can be easily added in the suffix tree construction stage which builds the suffix tree representing the static dictionary in $O(\log(dM))$ time using $O(dM)$ processors on the Arbitrary CRCW [AILSV88].

The remainder of the paper is organized as follows. Section 2 presents an $O(M + \log M \log n)$ time and $O(nM^2)$ processor algorithm for optimal dictionary compression with respect to a static dictionary satisfying the assumptions stated above. Greedy parsing is described in Section 3, for both static and sliding-window dictionary compression. We conclude the paper with a discussion of other aspects of parallel compression and possible extensions to this work.

Notation:

d	=	number of strings in the dictionary
M	=	maximum length of any dictionary entry
n	=	input size
Pref	=	prefix property
*	=	requires suffix tree dictionary
exp.	=	expected time complexity (randomized algorithm)

Parsing	Model/Assumptions	Time	Processors	Reference
STATIC DICTIONARY				
Optimal	Common CRCW, Pref, *	$O(M + \log n)$	$O(n^2)$	[DS92]
		$O(M + \log^2 n)$	$O(n)$	[DS92]
	Common CRCW, Pref	$O(\log M + \log n)$	$O(n^2 d)$	[DS93]
	CREW, *	$O(M + \log^2 n)$	$O(n^3)$	[DS92]
		$O(M + \log n)$	$O(n^4)$	[DS92]
		$O(M + \log M \log n)$	$O(nM^2)$	[§2]
	Arbitrary CRCW, Pref	exp. $O(\log M + \log n)$	$O(dM + n)$	[DS93]
Greedy	CREW	$O(M + \log n)$	$O(n)$	[§3.1]
	Arbitrary CRCW, *	exp. $O(\log M + \log n)$	$O(dM + n)$	[DS93]
UNRESTRICTED SLIDING-WINDOW				
Greedy	CREW	$O(M + \log n)$	$O(n)$	[§3.2]
		$O(\log n)$	$O(n^2 \log M / \log n)$	[§3.3]
		$O(M + \log n)$	$O(n^2)$	[DS92]
		exp. $O(\log n)$	$O(n)$	[N91]
	Priority CRCW	$O(M + \log n)$	$O(n)$	[DS93]
FIXED-SIZE SLIDING-WINDOW				
Greedy	CREW	$O(\log n)$	$O(nM \log M / \log n)$	[§3.3]

Table 1

Parallel parsing results for static and sliding-window compression

2. Optimal Parsing

In this section, we describe PRAM algorithms for optimal compression. We assume that the static dictionary is arbitrary and is represented as a suffix tree.

Computing the optimal parsing can be transformed into the problem of finding a shortest path in a graph [BCW90]. The optimal parsing can be computed in $O(M + \log^2 n)$ time using $O(n^3)$ processors or in $O(M + \log n)$ time using $O(n^4)$ processors using that reduction [DS92]. For input $X = x_1 \cdots x_n$, the transformation views each character as a vertex in a graph and a directed edge from x_i to x_j is in the graph if the string $x_i \cdots x_j$ is in the dictionary. We show how to obtain improved complexity bounds. We first consider fixed-length dictionary references and the shortest path is in terms of the number of edges that have to be traversed. In the case of variable-length references, edges are assigned weights equal to the length of the corresponding dictionary reference and the shortest path is in terms of the sum of the edge weights of the edges traversed.

The input is divided into n/M blocks, $B_1, \ldots, B_{n/M}$. Block B_l, $1 \leq l \leq n/M$ consists of M characters, $x_{M(l-1)+1} \cdots x_{Ml}$. The first step of the algorithm determines the matches between strings beginning at each input position and the dictionary. This is equivalent to adding the directed edges to the associated graph. This can be done in $O(M)$ time using $O(n)$ processors by assigning a processor to each position and stepping sequentially down the suffix tree. Define C to be an $n \times n$ matrix which is updated in a sequence of $O(\log(n/M))$ iterations. C is initialized using the dictionary match information. That is, if $x_i \cdots x_j$ is in the dictionary, then $C[i,j] = 1$. Otherwise, $C[i,j] = 0$. Next, the shortest path is computed for all pairs of positions belonging to the same or adjacent blocks. For all pairs (i,j), within one block or one pair of blocks, this can be done in $O(\log^2 M)$ time using $O(M^3)$ processors. For all n/M groups, this computation can be done in $O(\log^2 M)$ time using $O(nM^2)$ processors.

At this point, $C[i,j]$ is the length of the shortest path between x_i and x_j for $1 \leq i \leq n$ and $i \leq j \leq \min\{i+M, n\}$. The remainder of the algorithm consists of an iterated step. Within each iteration, the search for paths is extended to consider all paths between positions with up to twice the number of intermediate blocks of the previous iteration. In the first iteration the shortest path between vertices in blocks B_l and B_{l+2} is computed. The maximum dictionary entry length, M, forces the shortest path from any position in B_l to pass through a vertex in B_{l+1}. Since the shortest path between every position in B_{l+1} and every position in B_{l+2} is known, the shortest path between any x_i in B_l and x_j in B_{l+2} is computed considering all positions in B_{l+1} as intermediate vertices and taking the minimum over the resulting paths. More formally,

$$C[i,j] = \min_{t \in B_{l+1}}\{C[i,t] + C[t,j]\}$$

In iteration k, the shortest paths between blocks B_l and B_{l+2^k} passing through block $B_{l+2^{k-1}}$ are computed and added to matrix C. In each iteration, the minimum computation can be completed in $O(\log M)$ time using $O(M^3)$ processors for each group. Totaling over all n/M groups, each iteration runs in $O(\log M)$ time using $O(nM^2)$ processors. All $O(\log(n/M))$ iterations require $O(\log M \log n)$ time.

Combining this with the initialization phase, the shortest path or, equivalently, the optimal parsing, can be computed in in $O(M + \log M \log n)$ time using $O(nM^2)$ processors.

The algorithm for fixed-length dictionary references, described above, essentially computes the shortest path in terms of the number of edges. In the case of variable-length references, the edge joining x_i to x_j is assigned a weight equal to the length of the dictionary reference for dictionary entry $x_i \cdots x_j$. The algorithm above can be generalized to compute the shortest path in terms of the sum of the weights of the edges traversed. Thus, the optimal parsing with variable-length references can be computed in $O(M + \log M \log n)$ time using $O(nM^2)$ processors.

3. Greedy Parsing

Greedy parsing sequentially scans the input, locating and removing the longest dictionary entry occurring as a prefix of the uncoded portion of the input. In this section, we consider both static and sliding-window dictionaries. We describe an algorithm for determining the greedy parsing given a static dictionary in $O(M + \log n)$ time using $O(n)$ processors. Later in this section we describe two algorithms for sliding-window compression. Using an approach similar to the one taken for the static dictionary model, the first approach yields an $O(M + \log n)$ time and $O(n)$ processor algorithm on the CREW. The second algorithm runs in $O(\log n)$ time using $O(nM \log M / \log n)$ processors on the CREW.

3.1 Static Dictionary

For greedy parsing, we must determine the longest match between the input beginning at each position and the dictionary. We assume that the dictionary is in the form of a suffix tree. Using $O(M)$ time, a processor assigned to each input position can determine the longest match information by stepping down the suffix tree, beginning at the root.

By assigning a processor to each input position, the breakpoint positions in the parsing are marked as follows. Position 1 is automatically a breakpoint and, by viewing the match lengths as pointers (i.e., if the match length at position i is j, processor P_i is pointing at position $i+j$), the standard pointer doubling technique is used to mark all breakpoints on the path from position 1 to position n in logarithmic time [J92]. Thus, the greedy parsing can be computed in $O(M + \log n)$ time using $O(n)$ processors.

3.2 Sliding-window Dictionary with unrestricted window

In sliding-window compression, the dictionary is implicitly represented for each input position by the characters preceding the position. Many variations of sliding-window compression are possible by imposing restrictions on the size of the window and the set of allowable dictionary strings. When the size of the window is unrestricted, better compression is possible but often at the expense of increased complexity. We describe an algorithm for sliding-window compression with an unrestricted window. This algorithm uses a suffix tree representation of the input string to carry out compression. In Section 3.3, we describe an algorithm that obtains largest match information based on a fixed-sized window consisting of the previous M characters.

Our algorithm for sliding-window compression with an unrestricted window uses an approach similar to the one described above for static dictionary compression. Here, a suffix tree representation of the *input string* is used to compute the longest match information. The suffix tree is augmented to store the index at each node of the earliest occurrence of the node's corresponding substring[3]. It is not necessary to store the indices of each occurrence of the node's corresponding substring since the earliest occurrence is included in the window of each input string occurring after it. As the longest match computation for a particular input position proceeds, only nodes storing indices less than the input position are considered. Using the augmented suffix tree, the longest match between an input position and the strings in its window can be computed in $O(M)$ time. Thus, all positions can determine their longest match in $O(M)$ time using $O(n)$ processors.

At this point, the greedy parsing is obtained by marking the input positions in the path from position 1 to n (as described earlier). This marking requires $O(\log n)$ time. So, the greedy parsing is computed in $O(M + \log n)$ time using $O(n)$ processors. Using the method shown in Section 3.3, the greedy parsing for an unrestricted sliding window can be computed in time $O(\log n)$ using $O(n^2 \log M / \log n)$ processors.

3.3 Sliding-window Dictionary with fixed-sized window

For input string $X = x_1 \cdots x_n$ and a fixed-sized window of size M, the dictionary at character x_i consists of the previous M characters, $x_{i-M} \cdots x_{i-1}$. Our algorithm for greedy parsing using a fixed-sized sliding-window proceeds in 3 phases. In Phase 1, the length of the longest match between the string beginning at x_i and the strings beginning at each position in x_i's window is computed for all i, $1 \leq i \leq n$. Observe that the matches for x_i are required to begin in x_i's window but may overlap a prefix of the string beginning at x_i. Define L to be an $n \times M$ table which is updated in a series of $\log M$ rounds to compute the longest match information. At the end of round k, $1 \leq k \leq \log M$, $L_k[i,j]$ stores the length of the longest match between the prefixes of strings $x_i \cdots x_{i+2^k-1}$ and $x_{i-j} \cdots x_{i-j+2^k-1}$.

Initially, $k = 0$ and each input character is compared to each character in its window. In constant time, processors $P_{i,1}, \ldots, P_{i,M}$ compare x_i to each character in x_i's window. If $x_i = x_{i-j}$ then $P_{i,j}$ sets $L_0[i,j] = 1$. Otherwise, $P_{i,j}$ sets $L_0[i,j] = 0$. Using nM processors, table L is initialized for all pairs (i,j) in $O(1)$ time. In round k, $1 \leq k \leq \log M$, matches of length up to 2^k are built from matches of lengths up to 2^{k-1}. For x_i, if $L_{k-1}[i,j] = 2^{k-1}$ then the match between $x_i \cdots x_{i+2^{k-1}-1}$ and

[3] Naor describes this augmentation in [N91].

$x_{i-j} \cdots x_{i-j+2^{k-1}-1}$ is concatenated with the match between the string beginning at $x_{i+2^{k-1}}$ and the string in x_i's window beginning at $x_{i-j+2^{k-1}}$. Observe that $x_{i-j+2^{k-1}}$ is the jth character in $x_{i+2^{k-1}}$'s window. Otherwise, if $L_{k-1}[i,j] < 2^{k-1}$ then the maximum match between the string beginning at x_i and the string in x_i's window beginning at x_{i-j} cannot be extended. Thus, the following recurrence represents the computation in round k:

$$L_k[i,j] = \begin{cases} L_{k-1}[i,j] + L_{k-1}[i+2^{k-1},j], & \text{if} \quad L_{k-1}[i,j] = 2^{k-1} \\ L_{k-1}[i,j], & \text{if} \quad L_{k-1}[i,j] < 2^{k-1} \end{cases}$$

and each round can be completed in constant time by assigning a processor to each (i,j) pair. So, Phase 1 requires $O(\log M)$ time and nM processors.

In Phase 2, the longest match of the string starting at x_i among all strings beginning in its sliding-window can be computed in $O(\log M)$ time using $O(M)$ processors by a standard maximum computation of the values in the ith row of table L. Using $O(nM)$ processors, the longest match information can be computed for all positions $x_1, \ldots, x_n$.

In the final phase, standard pointer doubling techniques (as mentioned above) are used to determine the parsing containing the set of longest matches that begins at location 1. Phase 3 can be completed in $O(\log n)$ time using $O(n)$ processors.

Thus, using the sliding-window, we can find the greedy parsing in time $O(\log M + \log n)$ using $O(nM)$ processors. When $M = O(\log n)$, this solution takes $O(\log n)$ time and $O(n \log n)$ processors.

It is possible to reduce the number of processors by spending additional time in Phases 1 and 2. By Brent's Theorem [GR88], increasing the time in Phases 1 and 2 to $O(\log n)$ reduces the processor requirements to $O(nM \log M / \log n)$.

Using this method, the greedy parsing for an unrestricted sliding window can be computed in time $O(\log n)$ using $O(n^2 \log M / \log n)$ processors by noting the following. Phase 1 can be performed in $\log M$ time using n^2 processors or, by Brent's Theorem, in the claimed time-processor bounds. Phase 2 requires a prefix maximum computation (as opposed to a maximum over a fixed-size window) which can be done in time $O(\log n)$ using $O(n)$ processors.

4. Other Considerations

In this section, we describe how to produce the compressed output from the parsing, decompression, and possibilities for further research.

We have addressed the parsing problem in dictionary compression. After the input string has been parsed, the compressed output consists of the concatenation of the dictionary references corresponding to the substrings in the parsing. A processor, assigned to the start position of each substring in the parsing, can determine where in the output stream to write its corresponding dictionary reference by performing a prefix sum computation. This can be done optimally in parallel in time $O(\log n)$ using $O(n/\log n)$ processors [GR88].

Decompression replaces each dictionary reference in the compressed string by its corresponding dictionary entry. If dictionary references are all of fixed-length, the parsing of the compressed stream into individual dictionary references is straightforward (the ith reference starts after stream byte $c(i-1)$, where each reference is c bytes in length). If P_i is assigned to the ith reference, it can determine in time $O(M)$ the length of its represented string and, using a prefix sum computation, the location for each represented string in the original input stream can be computed in $O(\log n)$ time. In $O(M)$ time, each processor writes its represented string to the recovered original stream. For variable-length dictionary references, assigning processors to dictionary references in the output stream, requires additional work. Let r be the maximum length of any dictionary reference. Assign a processor to each output byte and in $O(r)$ time each processor can determine its complete dictionary reference in a way similar to recognition of references in sequential decompression. By treating the reference length information as pointers, the parsing of the output stream into dictionary references can be done using pointer doubling in $O(\log n)$ time and $O(n)$ processors. Now, the decompression problem is the same as for fixed-length references and the method above combined with the preprocessing yields the recovered original stream in $O(r + M + \log n)$ time using $O(n)$ processors.

Since dynamic dictionary compression of the Lempel and Ziv variety is P-complete, dynamic methods differing from this approach are of interest. List compression, where a dictionary of words is maintained using a self-organizing heuristic, seems amenable to parallelization. Also, parallel parsing strategies other than those used for sequential compression may lead to improved parallel systems.

References

[AILSV88] Apostolico, A., Iliopoulos, C., Landau, G. M., Schieber, B., and Vishkin, U. Parallel construction of a suffix tree with applications. *Algorithmica 3*, 3 (1988), 347–365.

[BCW90] Bell, T. C., Cleary, J. G., and Witten, I. H. *Text Compression*, Prentice-Hall, Englewood Cliffs, New Jersey, 1990.

[CL82] Cooper, D. and Lynch, M. F. Text compression using variable- to fixed-length encodings. *J. Amer. Society for Information Science* (Jan., 1982), 18–31.

[D91] De Agostino, S. P-Complete problems in data compression. Tech. Rep. URLS-DM/NS-90/001(INFO). Dept. of Mathematics, University of Rome "La Sapienza", Italy (1991).

[DS92] De Agostino, S. and Storer, J. A. Parallel algorithms for optimal compression using dictionaries with the prefix property. In *Proceedings IEEE Data Compression Conference*, Snowbird, Utah, IEEE Computer Society Press, 1992, pp. 52–61.

[DS93] De Agostino, S. and Storer, J. A. Parallel algorithms for optimal compression using dictionaries with the prefix property. Manuscript (1993).

[GR88] Gibbons, A. M. and Rytter, W. *Efficient Parallel Algorithms*, Cambridge University Press, Cambridge, 1988.

[GS85] Gonzalez-Smith, M. E. and Storer, J. A. Parallel algorithms for data compression. *J. ACM 32*, 2 (Apr., 1985), 344–373.

[J92] JaJa, J. *An Introduction to Parallel Algorithms*, Addison-Wesley, 1992.

[L92] Leighton, F. T. *Introduction to Parallel Algorithms and Architectures: Arrays, Trees, Hypercubes*, Morgan Kaufmann Publishers, 1992.

[N91] Naor, M. String matching with preprocessing of text and pattern. In *Proceedings ICALP, LNCS 510*, Springer-Verlag, 1991, pp. 739–750.

[SH73] Schuegraf, E. J. and Heaps, H. S. Selection of equifrequent word fragments for information retrieval. *Inform. Stor. Retr. 9* (1973), 697–711.

[SH92] Stauffer, L. M. and Hirschberg, D. S. Transpose coding on the systolic array. In *Proceedings IEEE Data Compression Conference*, Snowbird, Utah, IEEE Computer Society Press, 1992, pp. 162–171.

[SH93] Stauffer, L. M. and Hirschberg, D. S. Parallel text compression. Technical Report 91-44, Revised. Info. and Comp. Sci. Department, University of California, Irvine (1993).

[S88a] Storer, J. A. *Data Compression Methods and Theory*, Computer Science Press, Rockville, MD, 1988.

[SR91] Storer, J. A. and Reif, J. H. A parallel architecture for high-speed data compression. *J. Parallel and Distr. Comp. 13* (1991), 222–227.

[W84] Welch, T. A. A technique for high-performance data compression. *IEEE Computer 17*, 6 (June, 1984), 8–19.

[W91] Williams, R. N. *Adaptive Data Compression*, Kluwer Academic Publishers, Norwell, MA, 1991.

[ZL77] Ziv, J. and Lempel, A. A universal algorithm for sequential data compression. *IEEE Trans. Inf. Theory 23*, 3 (1977), 337–343.

[ZL78] Ziv, J. and Lempel, A. Compression of individual sequences via variable-rate coding. *IEEE Trans. Inf. Theory 24*, 5 (1978), 530–536.

Syntax-constrained encoder optimization using adaptive quantization thresholding for JPEG/MPEG coders

Kannan Ramchandran
Department of Electrical and Computer Engineering
University of Illinois at Urbana-Champaign

Martin Vetterli
Department of Electrical Engineering and Computer Science
University of California at Berkeley

January 17, 1994

Abstract

We show a rate–distortion optimal quantization technique to threshold the DCT coefficients in the industry image and video coding standards JPEG and MPEG respectively. Our scheme achieves a decent thresholding gain in terms of both objective SNR (about 1 dB) as well as perceived quality and uses a fast dynamic programming recursive structure which exploits certain monotonicity characteristics of the JPEG and MPEG codebooks to drastically reduce the complexity. The primary advantage of our encoding algorithm is that it is completely compatible with the baseline JPEG and MPEG decoders.

1 Introduction

Recent advances in digital image and video compression techniques have culminated in the formulation of the popular CCITT standards for still–image and video compression formats, JPEG [1] and MPEG [2] respectively. Although the *syntax* of these coding formats is constrained by the proposed standards, there remains considerable freedom to optimize the coder while being syntax-constrained. This leads to the paradigm of decoder-compatible encoder optimization, which has obvious applications to the optimal use of "existing" decoders. In this paper, as an extenion of our work in [6], we address decoder-compatible encoder optimization applied to the JPEG and

MPEG coders, with the obvious advantage being that the user does not have to change his existing decoder, an important practical consideration in light of the ever-increasing volume of existing JPEG and MPEG decoders in the market today.

It must be pointed out that though this paper is directed at the optimization of the JPEG and MPEG coding formats, its scope of application (i.e. the use of quantization thresholding) is broad, and encompasses general coding systems. In particular, wavelet based coding methods have received considerable attention in the literature lately due to their good performance [7]. The use of quantization thresholding methods to the wavelet coder has recently been applied to a wavelet-based coder with considerable success [9, 10].

JPEG and MPEG are based on the Discrete Cosine Transform (DCT). Non–overlapping 8x8 blocks of the image or video frame are 2–D DCT transformed, quantized using a perceptually weighted quantization matrix, scanned in a zigzag order, and subjected to a 2–D variable length code (VLC) using Huffman coding tables. Refer to [1, 2] for details. The widely–used "default" Huffman coding tables of JPEG and MPEG are derived from statistics of typical training images and video sequences respectively, and are not customized for arbitrary inputs. While the standards allow for custom Huffman codebooks for each input source, this represents, in most cases, an expensive overhead (as the Huffman table has to be sent). This therefore provides the motivation to investigate ways of introducing adaptivity of the coding tables *without actually changing the default codebook,* i.e. without incurring the overhead of sending the customized codebook information.

A key to good compression when using these standards *while still being compatible with the standard decoder* lies in sending "smart" subsets of the transform coefficients used to represent the image or video sequence. This could be viewed as an application of entropy-constrained quantization [4] to the existing JPEG/MPEG codebooks. Thus, from the existing set of all possible quantization levels that can be applied to the transform coefficients, we are interested in picking the choice which minimizes the distortion subject to the rate constraint, as dictated by the use of the JPEG/MPEG codebooks.

Thus, our goal consists in determining which DCT coefficients are "significant" enough to be coded and which ones are better off being thresholded or dropped. Dropping or thresholding of the less significant coefficients may be desirable in the rate–distortion sense, as it may lead, at a marginal sacrifice of coded quality, to a significant reduction in expended bit rate, due to fewer coefficients needing to be transmitted. This is especially so when deciding the last non–zero coefficient, which is typically followed by an inexpensive "end–of–block" code [1, 2]. Thus, it may especially pay to get rid of compression–hindering sparsely interspersed insignificant coefficients that represent the last non–zero values before the end–of–block. In the case of JPEG, where the standard does not permit variable scaling of the different image blocks, intelligent adaptive thresholding of the coefficients would tantamount to changing the quantization scales at the block level, without violating the syntax rules.

We formulate an optimal strategy to drop or threshold the quantized DCT coefficients using a fast recursive technique employing dynamic programming (DP). While in [6], we restricted ourselves to "hard" thresholding (i.e. making a binary decision on keeping or dropping a coefficient), in this work, we consider "soft" thresholding methods also (i.e. we allow for coarser but non-zero quantization while being syntax-compatible). The optimality is in a rate–distortion (R–D) sense, for the fixed scale quantization performed prior to thresholding. Thus, starting from the "highest quality point" after quantization at a fixed scale (for JPEG) or QP–level (for MPEG [2]), one can sweep the entire thresholding R–D curve over a continuous range of target bit rates (or equivalently target coding qualities) by thresholding insigificant coefficients in the image or video frame. Thus, our algorithm could find all points that reside on the convex hull [1] [3] of the R–D curve. The appeal of the strategy lies in its combination of R–D optimality, speed of operation, and its complete compatibility with standard JPEG and MPEG decoders, which remain blissfully oblivious to the thresholding gymnastics performed by the encoder. A point to note is that the algorithm described in this work exploits the monotonic nature of bit rate versus the zero run–length count preceding a non–zero coefficient inherent in the Huffman tables of JPEG and MPEG, to specify a fast "pruning" operation in the DP recursion. Thus, the computational complexity of the algorithm (at least for the hard thresholding case) becomes low enough for it to be implementable.

This paper is organized as follows. Section 2 states the problem formally, while Section 3 gives the basic idea of the optimal algorithm. Coding applications using JPEG and MPEG are presented in Section 4.

[1] i.e. the convex boundary of R-D points (see Fig. 3)

2 Problem statement

We wish to find that optimal set of post-quantization DCT coefficients to be retained for every 8x8 block of an image or video frame such that the mean-squared-error (MSE) distortion (any additive distortion metric is feasible in general, e.g. weighted MSE) between the original image and the thresholded version is minimized *subject to a maximum target coding bit rate constraint* or equivalently, the coding bit rate is minimized subject to a maximum allowable distortion constraint.

See Figure 1. Thus, if X is the input signal, $\hat{X}$ the quantized output corresponding to a fixed scale or "anchor" level representing the maximum quality operating point, and $\tilde{X}$ the thresholded version of $\hat{X}$, we seek to minimize the MSE distortion between X and $\tilde{X}$ given the quantized image $\hat{X}$, subject to a total coding bit budget of R_{budget} for $\tilde{X}$. That is, our goal is to find:

$$\min[\mathcal{D}(X, \tilde{X})|\hat{X}] \text{ subject to } \mathcal{R}(\tilde{\mathrm{X}}) \leq \mathrm{R_{budget}}. \quad (1)$$

3 Basic idea of solution

R–D optimality: the constant slope condition

The "hard" constrained thresholding problem of Eq.(1) can be solved by being converted to an "easy" equivalent unconstrained problem by "merging" rate and distortion through the Lagrange multiplier λ [8]. The unconstrained thresholding problem becomes the determination (for a fixed λ) of that set of coefficients, which results in the minimum total Lagrangian cost defined as $J(\lambda) = D(X, \tilde{X}) + \lambda R(\tilde{X})$.

The optimal coefficient search for the image *can be done independently* for every 8x8 image block for the fixed quality "slope" λ, which trades off distortion for rate. This is because it can be shown [8, 5] that, at R–D optimality, all blocks *must operate at a constant slope point λ on their R–D curves.* The desired optimal constant slope value λ^* is not known *a priori* and depends on the particular target budget or quality constraint. Fortunately, however, the search for λ^* is a fast convex one, and it can be obtained using a fast convex recursion in λ using the bisection algorithm [5].

Fast dynamic programming algorithm

Since the optimal solution can be obtained by finding the minimum-Lagrangian-cost operating point for each block independently, it suffices to consider a single block for analysis. The problem is solved using a dynamic programming approach.

The zigzag scan that is part of the standards [1, 2] is used to order the 2–D coefficients. As an initialization, one has to gather the $\Delta J_{j,k}$'s associated with the incremental Lagrangian cost of going from coefficient j to coefficient k (i.e. dropping all the coefficients between them) for all non–zero valued (j,k) coefficient pairs with $j < k$. The optimal operating point, for a fixed value of λ, can be done in a recursive fashion by finding (i) the minimum Lagrangian cost, $J^*(k)$ and (ii) the optimal predecessor coefficient, $predecessor(k)$, associated with choosing coefficient k as *the last non–zero coefficient* for all $k = 1, 2, \ldots, 63$. Then, starting from that coefficient k^* which is the cheapest to retain as the last non–zero coefficient, i.e. minimum $J^*(.)$, the optimal set can be "backtracked" from the optimal predecessor chain calculated for all predecessors of k^*. See Figure 2.

In finding the optimal predecessor at a particular iteration k as described above, one generally has to consider as candidates ALL coefficients $i < k$. However, for the particular case of monotonicity of $R_{i,k}$ in the zero runlength count $(k - i - 1)$, which is true for the coding tables of JPEG and MPEG, a fast pruning algorithm can be used to speed up the search. This leads to a substantial decrease in computational complexity, and leads to a fast optimal algorithm. The above optimal DP algorithm is performed independently on all blocks. The composite R–D point for the picked λ is obtained simply as the sum of the optimally obtained R–D points for each block for that λ. Finally, the optimal slope λ^* which solves the desired budget or quality constraint is found with a fast convex search using the bisection algorithm [5].

Soft thresholding

While the above discussion describes the optimal algorithm for doing "hard" thresholding –i.e. in reaching a binary decision on whether or not to drop a coefficient, it can be modified to include soft decisions as well. Thus, it may pay, in the rate-distortion sense, to quantize some coefficients coarser but not zero them out altogether. Thus, the hard thresholding algorithm would become a special case of the soft thresholding paradigm, though the latter has significantly more computational complexity. Experiments of the soft thresholding technique are ongoing, though preliminary results indicate that the benefit of using soft thresholding for JPEG/MPEG applications is probably unprofitable in the complexity-performance tradeoff sense, as we are dealing with codebooks which are optimized for zero runlengths. However, the gain of applying soft thresholding techniques to other coding environments which are not zero run-length coders (e.g. the wavelet-based entropy coder of [10] may be significant.

4 Application

The optimal algorithm outlined in Section 3 can be used to quantify the benefits of adaptive thresholding applied to the JPEG and MPEG coding environments. R–D curves are obtained by sweeping the Lagrange multiplier λ through all positive values for typical quantization scales of interest. Figure 3 shows the R–D curves for a typical image ("House") using JPEG for pre–thresholding quantization scales of 1.0 and 0.7. Note the significance of Figure 3. Point X on curve (a) is the unthresholded "reference" obtained for a scale of 1.0. Let us fix the bit rate for the problem at the reference X's bit rate of 0.615 bits per pixel (bpp). Now, to see the advantage of optimal thresholding, observe curve (b) corresponding to a finer quantization scale of s=0.7 instead of 1.0. For this finer scale, the non–thresholded bit rate, corresponding to point Z, is obviously greater than that of X. However, if we now start thresholding optimally until the bit budget constraint imposed by curve (a) is satisfied, *we will get an adaptive thresholding gain in terms of increased SNR for the same bit rate.* Thus, point Y enjoys a 0.7 dB gain at the same bit rate over X. Alternatively, if we fix the PSNR according to that of X (35.17 dB), point W enjoys a compression advantage at the same PSNR of roughly 15 %. Coding results show that for typical images and video sequences, a gain of 0.5-0.8 dB is obtainable while being completely compatible with the decoder!

References

[1] JPEG technical specification: Revision (DRAFT), joint photographic experts group, ISO/IEC JTC1/SC2/WG8, CCITT SGVIII, August

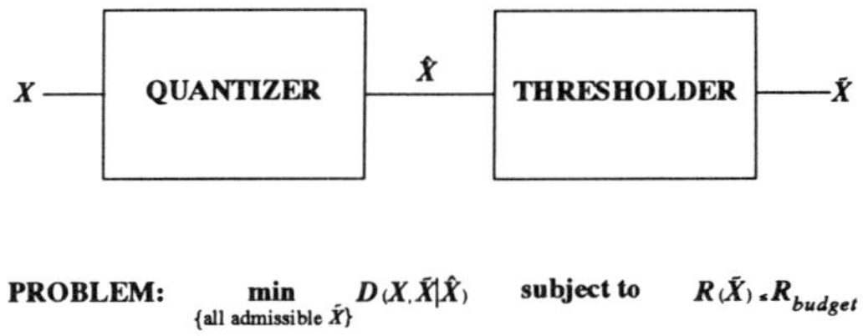

Figure 1: Block diagram of problem statement: X is the input image, $\hat{X}$ is the quantized pre–thresholded version (after JPEG or MPEG), and $\tilde{X}$ the output of the thresholder. We want to minimize the distortion, for a fixed quantizer, between the original and the thresholded images subject to a bit budget constraint.

1990.

[2] MPEG video simulation model three, ISO, coded representation of picture and audio information, 1990.

[3] P. A. Chou, T. Lookabaugh, and R. M. Gray. Optimal pruning with applications to tree-structured source coding and modeling. *IEEE Trans. on Inform. Theory*, IT-35:299–315, March 1986.

[4] P. A. Chou, T. Lookabaugh, and R. M. Gray. Entropy-constrained vector quantization. *IEEE Trans. on Acoust., Speech, Signal Proc.*, 37(1):31–42, January 1989.

[5] K. Ramchandran and M. Vetterli. Best wavelet packet bases in a rate–distortion sense. *IEEE Trans. on Image Proc.*, 2(2):160–175, April 1993.

[6] K. Ramchandran and M. Vetterli. Rate–distortion optimal fast thresholding with complete JPEG/MPEG decoder compatibility. In *PCS'93, Lausanne, Switzerland*, 1993.

[7] J. M. Shapiro. An embedded wavelet hierarchical image coder. *Proc. of ICASSP*, pages 657–660, March 1992.

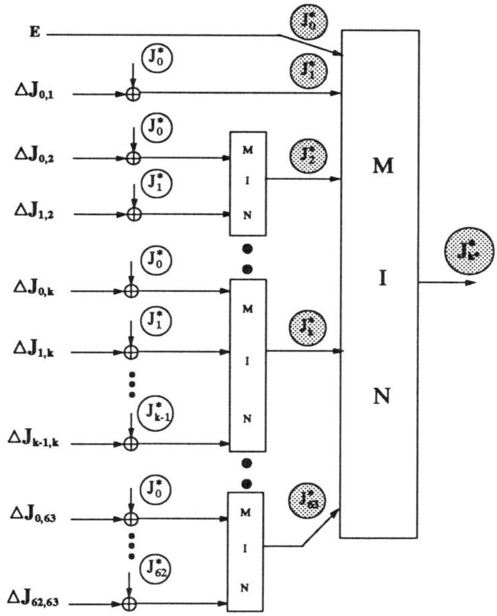

Figure 2: Block diagram of the dynamic programming recursion of the optimal algorithm for each 8x8 image block. E is the A.C. energy, $\Delta J_{i,j}$ is the incremental Lagrangian cost of going from coefficient i to coefficient j while dropping all coefficients in between, and J_k^* is the minimum Lagrangian cost associated with ending at coefficient k. Note that $k^* = \min^{-1}_{0 \leq k \leq 63}$ is the optimal "last" coefficient.

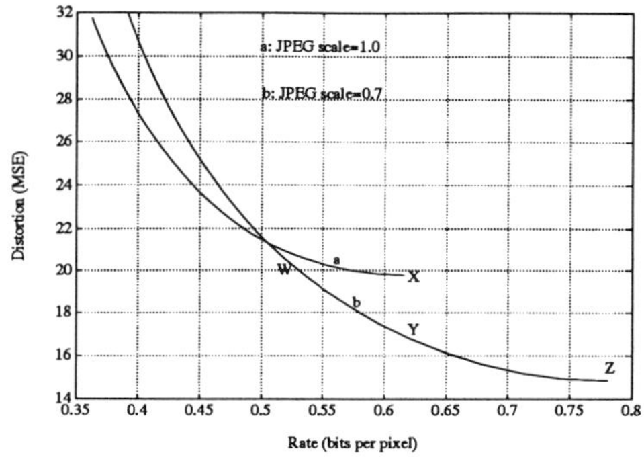

Figure 3: Optimal thresholding R-D curves for "House" image using JPEG. Curve (a) corresponds to a JPEG quantization scale of 1.0, while curve (b) to a finer scale of 0.7. Note that if we fix the reference at point X on curve (a) corresponding to a scale of 1.0, we can achieve point Y by "backing off" to a finer scale of 0.7 (point Z on curve b) and then thresholding optimally to point Y at the same bit rate as X. Note that the thresholding gain for this example (reference X) is approximately 0.7 dB at a bit rate of 0.615 bpp (point Y), or alternatively about 15% reduction in bit rate (point W of curve b) at the same PSNR of 35.17 dB.

[8] Y. Shoham and A. Gersho. Efficient bit allocation for an arbitrary set of quantizers. *IEEE Trans. on Acoust., Speech, Signal Proc.*, 36(9):1445–1453, September 1988.

[9] Z. Xiong, N. P. Galatsanos, and M. T. Orchard. Marginal analysis prioritization for image compression based on a hierarchical wavelet decomposition. In *Proc. of ICASSP'93*, pages 546–549, April 1993.

[10] Z. Xiong, K. Ramchandran, and M. T. Orchard. Joint optimization of scalar and tree-structured quantization of wavelet image decomposition. In *Asilomar conference on signals, systems and computers*, November 1993.

Customized JPEG Compression for Grayscale Printing

Rick A. Vander Kam*   Ping Wah Wong

Hewlett-Packard Laboratories, 1501 Page Mill Road, Palo Alto, CA 94304 USA

Abstract

We describe a procedure by which JPEG compression may be customized for grayscale images that are to be compressed, halftoned, and printed. Our technique maintains 100% compatibility with the JPEG standard, and is applicable with any halftoning algorithm. The JPEG quantization table is designed using frequency-domain characteristics of the halftoning patterns and the human visual system, and the Huffman tables are optimized for low-rate coding. We present experimental results demonstrating that the customized JPEG encoder offers a significant performance advantage over a coder that uses the default quantization and Huffman tables. Our results also show that the customized encoder typically achieves rates in the range 0.13–0.25 bits per pixel (image dependent) with practically no visible compression artifacts in the printed images.

1 Introduction

The purpose of this investigation is to explore the possibility of customizing or optimizing the JPEG lossy compression algorithm [1] for use with grayscale images that will eventually be halftoned. The goal is to minimize the amount of data prior to decompression and halftoning, while simultaneously eliminating or minimizing any visible compression artifacts. A possible application would be a pipeline in which JPEG compression is performed at the host computer, while decompression and halftoning are done at the printer.

The motivation for this work has come from two fairly simple intuitive arguments. First, because halftoning changes an image's spectral content in a way that can be measured and predicted, and because JPEG acts as a type of sub-band coder, it should be possible to obtain better compression performance (while maintaining the quality of the halftoned image) by allowing JPEG to throw away more information in those frequency bands that are likely to be "corrupted" by halftoning anyway. That is, since halftoning tends to introduce significant errors in certain frequency bands, JPEG would only be wasting bits by trying to preserve the original grayscale image content in those bands. Second, because the human eye has varying sensitivity to errors and artifacts in different spatial frequency bands, we would like to take advantage of this by allowing more encoding errors where the eye can tolerate them.

*Rick Vander Kam is now a student in the Dept. of Electrical Engineering, Stanford University, Stanford, CA 94305-4055

1068-0314/94 $3.00 © 1994 IEEE

Neuhoff and Pappas have proposed a sub-band coding scheme that seeks to minimize the visible compression artifacts in halftoned images [2]. Their sub-band coder is designed open-loop on the basis of measurements of human visual perception. We, too, take the eye's sensitivity into account, but our approach differs in that it specifically uses an error profile depending on both the halftone and human perceptual characteristics. Furthermore, we propose a closed-loop design algorithm that maintains 100% compatibility with standard JPEG compression. Our customization affects only the quantization table and the dc and ac Huffman coding tables, all of which are transmitted as header information in the compressed data stream.

We shall first examine the characteristics of halftoning and the human visual system in more detail, and then describe how the JPEG tables can be modified for our purposes. Roughly speaking, we allow the JPEG encoder to make more errors (via coarser quantization, or larger quantization table entries) in those frequency bands where the halftoning introduces more distortion or where the eye is more tolerant.

2 Distortion Due to Halftoning

Halftoning itself may be viewed as a type of lossy data compression. In converting a continuous-tone image at 8 bits per pixel (bpp) to a binary image at 1 bpp, halftoning effectively discards $\frac{7}{8}$ of the information in the orignal image, and it is usually impossible to perfectly reconstruct the grayscale original from a halftoned version [3].

It is well known that different halftoning algorithms have different spectral "signatures" [4, 5]. Each algorithm tends to introduce artifacts, or distortion, in a way that can be predictably characterized in the frequency domain. Moreover, these spectral characteristics are directly related to the visual appearance of the halftone patterns.

Our work to date has focused on the clustered-dot halftoning algorithm with an 8×8 dither matrix. This algorithm produces very regular, periodic dot patterns, hence its spectral signature consists of distinct spikes with significant energy at low frequencies. Such strong spikes are usually not present in the spectra of natural grayscale images, and consequently we expect that most of the distortion due to clustered-dot dithering will be at the locations of the spikes in the frequency domain.

We have used the following procedure to *quantify* the frequency-domain distortion due to halftoning. Note that in the computation of the error spectrum, no assumption is made about the particular halftoning algorithm being used. As a result, the same approach can be applied with any chosen halftoning algorithm.

Algorithm 1: Computation of the Halftoning Error Spectrum

1. Start with an arbitrary collection of "typical" grayscale (8 bpp) images, and halftone each image in the collection.
2. Compute the difference between each original image and its halftone. The result is an image whose pixel values are in the range $[-255, 255]$.
3. Convert each difference image to a "grayscale error image" with unsigned 8-bit pixel values. This is done by remapping the range $[-255, 255]$ to $[0, 255]$ using straightforward linear operations.
4. Parse each "error image" into 8×8 blocks, and compute the DCT for each block.

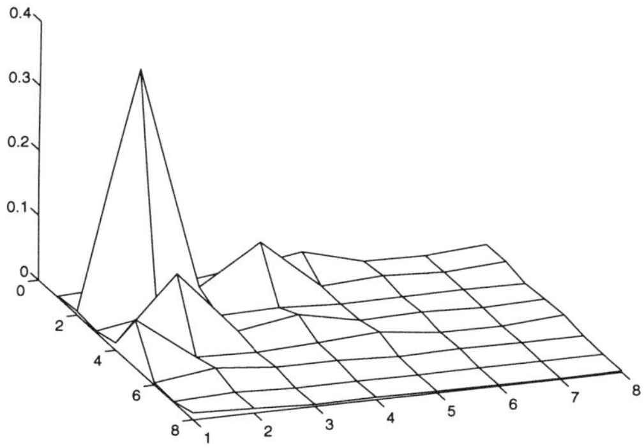

Figure 1: Error spectrum for 8 × 8 clustered-dot halftoning, shown in the DCT frequency domain. The location of dc is at (1,1) in this view.

5. For each component in the 8 × 8 block, compute the *average squared value* of the DCT coefficient at that location, taking the average over all the blocks in all the images. This provides a measure of the "strength" of the halftoning error at each component location in the 8 × 8 DCT.

A typical error spectrum for clustered-dot halftoning, computed using five images, is shown in Figure 1.

3 Frequency Response of the Visual System

It is well known that the eye is less sensitive to image patterns with high spatial frequency content than to those with low frequency content. We have sought to exploit the eye's increased tolerance for high-frequency errors by combining a quantitative human visual system (HVS) model with the halftoning error spectrum computed in the previous section. There are many examples in the literature of HVS models and their application to image processing and coding (see [6], [7], [8], and [9], for example). Previous research has also considered the use of a HVS model in the design of JPEG quantization tables [10, 11]. The novelty in our approach is the combination of the halftoning error spectrum with the HVS response, in designing the quantization table specifically for images that will be *printed*.

The particular HVS model that we have used is that of Mannos and Sakrison [9], with one modification: the sensitivity function is assumed to be flat from the location of the peak down to dc, instead of rolling off at the low frequencies. A one-dimensional slice of the radially symmetric Mannos and Sakrison sensitivity function is shown in Figure 2, along with our modified version. Note that the frequency axis units are cycles/degree, allowing the function to be tuned for different printing resolutions and viewing distances.

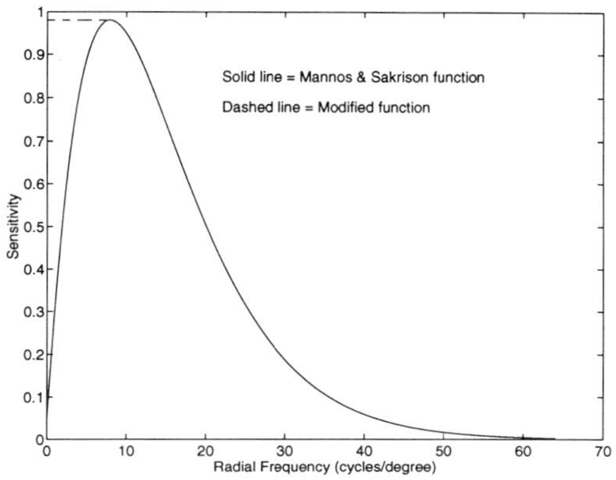

Figure 2: Human visual sensitivity functions. The modified function is different only at low frequencies.

4 Quantization Table Design

We have devised a heuristic procedure for designing a JPEG quantization table that takes into account the halftoning error spectrum and human visual response. Before describing it, we briefly discuss previous research that has influenced our technique.

4.1 Traditional Bit Allocation

Our goal of customizing the JPEG quantization table is closely related to the problem of *bit allocation*, which has been studied widely in data compression circles (see chapter 8 of [12] for an introduction and more references). A general bit allocation algorithm based on a tree-pruning technique can be found in [13]. Our manipulation of the JPEG quantization table is roughly equivalent to varying the bit allocation in a DCT-based transform coder, because it similarly controls how much quantization error is allowed for each DCT component. At first glance, it would appear that previous solutions to the bit allocation problem could be applied directly to our situation.

Unfortunately, the usual bit allocation techniques do not carry over in a straightforward manner to the design of the JPEG quantization table. There are several reasons for this. Perhaps most importantly, the bit allocation solutions assume that the designer has more control over the component quantizers than JPEG allows.

- Because each component quantizer is described by a single parameter (the quantization table entry), it is impossible to independently specify the number of quantizer levels and their spacing.

- Standard JPEG does not allow the designer to force any quantizer to have "zero rate," i.e., a single constant output. This is because the quantization table entries can be no larger than 255, whereas the DCT coefficients can range from -1023 to $+1023$ prior to quantization. Thus each component quantizer in the JPEG encoder has no less than 9 output levels (four positive, four negative, and one at 0), assuming that arbitrary input images are allowed.

- It is impossible to specify or predict the exact bit rate for any of the JPEG component quantizers individually. JPEG's Huffman coding of the quantizer outputs mixes all of the components together in such a way that their individual bit rates are lost (see [1] for more details).

- The high-rate (asymptotic) assumptions used to derive many of the bit allocation results do not necessarily hold in our case.

4.2 Design Procedure

Despite the aforementioned problems with existing bit allocation schemes, there remains a close similarity between their intended use and our goals. The design procedure that we have devised maintains the flavor of the bit allocation approaches, but glosses over some of the mathematical difficulties. At the moment, we have no proof that the following procedure is "optimal" in terms of producing the least possible distortion for a given compression ratio. However, it does reliably generate a quantization table that causes JPEG to behave the way we have argued that it should in our printing pipeline.

We first combine the information about the halftoning error spectrum and the HVS response to quantitatively determine how much quantization error should be allowed for each of the 64 DCT components.

Algorithm 2: Computation of the Desired Error Profile

1. Compute the halftoning error spectrum and the HVS response. The error spectrum in the DCT domain is obtained as described in Section 2 above. The 8×8 HVS response is computed by mapping the modified Mannos and Sakrison sensitivity function [9] to the DCT grid according to the desired printing resolution and viewing distance. (Note that the frequencies of the DCT basis functions are multiples of one-half cycle per 8 *pixels*, which must be converted to cycles per degree.)

2. Normalize the measured halftone error spectrum and the HVS response. The exact normalization is somewhat arbitrary; in our algorithm, we normalize the error spectrum so that the sum of its 64 values is 1, and separately normalize the HVS response array so that its smallest value is 1. Each term in the normalized HVS response is then squared. We shall refer to the values in the resulting error spectrum array as e_n, and to those in the HVS response as h_n, where n ranges from 0 to 63[1].

3. Compute a "rate" for each of the 64 DCT components according to the formula

$$R_n = \frac{1}{2}\left[\lambda \log_2(h_n) - (1-\lambda)\log_2(e_n)\right], \quad n = 0, 1, \ldots, 63.$$

   The parameter λ can range from 0 to 1, controlling the mixture of the error spectrum and HVS information. We expect that the best results will be obtained when λ is set to values near the middle of this range, rather than the extreme

---

[1] We have tacitly converted from two-dimensional indexing in the 8×8 block to one-dimensional indexing. If the block indices are i and j, then n can be obtained according to $n = 8i + j$, for example.

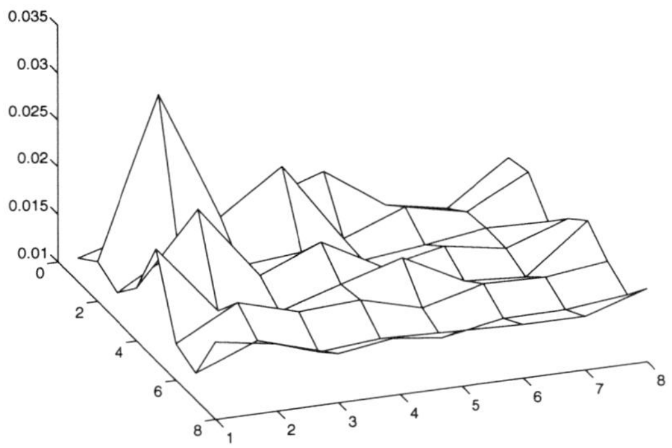

Figure 3: Desired quantization error profile, from a combination of the halftoning error spectrum and the HVS response. The location of dc is at (1,1) in this view.

values 0 (where only the halftoning error enters the computation) and 1 (where only the HVS response is used). Although the R_n are not actual bit rates, we are mimicking the basic strategy of allocating fewer bits to components where the eye's sensitivity is small or halftoning errors are large. Any zero rates are set to a small positive number to avoid division errors in the next step.

4. Compute the desired JPEG quantization error profile as the reciprocal of the rates: $W_n = \frac{1}{R_n}$, $n = 0, 1, \ldots, 63$. The W_n values are then normalized so that they sum to 1.

The result is the array of W_n, which specifies for each DCT component the proportion of the total quantization error that is desired in that frequency band. Figure 3 contains a plot of an example error profile. The desired quantization error profile will provide us with a "target" as we design the JPEG quantization table. However, we would like to have some additional flexibility. Even if we design the quantization table so that it produces errors in exactly the desired proportions for all components, we would have no control over the resulting *compression ratio*.

By scaling the entire desired error profile up or down (by a multiplicative constant), we can control the design rate while maintaining the correct error proportions. The components of the scaled profile will sum to a number either greater than or less than 1. If we scale up, allowing more distortion for every component, the design rate will decrease; if we scale down, the design rate will increase. This scaling can also be used to compensate for the unequal distribution of energy between low- and high-frequency bands that is usually found in natural images. We have found experimentally that to obtain useful design rates of 0.50 bpp and lower, we must scale the desired error profile up by a factor between 1.5 and 10.

We are now ready to design the quantization table. We will iteratively improve the table entries in a way such that the actual quantization error profile will more closely approximate the desired profile.

Algorithm 3: Quantization Table Design

1. Initialize the quantization table, setting each entry to an allowed integer value

in the range $[1, 255]$. Our experiments have shown that the initial table values are not important—any valid starting table will yield the same results.

2. Run the JPEG encoder on one or more "typical" images, keeping track of the total squared quantization error for each of the 64 DCT components.

3. Normalize the array of quantization error values so that their sum is 1. This gives the *actual* quantization error profile. We shall refer to these values as D_n, with n ranging from 0 to 63. Before proceeding to the next step, we multiply the value of D_0 (the proportion of error in the dc component) by 2 to compensate for the fact that the dc component is encoded differentially.

4. Replace table entry Q_n with an updated value according to $Q_n \longleftarrow Q_n\sqrt{\frac{W_n}{D_n}}$. The intuitive reasoning behind this step is that we would like to increase or decrease the squared quantization error for the nth component by the ratio of the desired error proportion (W_n) to the actual error proportion (D_n). Because each Q_n is the divisor used to quantize the nth component, the replacement specified above would provide the proper correction if the quantization errors were distributed uniformly. Although this will not be the case in practice, the behavior is still approximately correct under the assumption that the quantizer *inputs* have a Laplacian distribution [14]. In the case where $\frac{W_n}{D_n} > 1$, we must also check whether increasing Q_n actually yields the desired increase in quantization error. If the original images do not have sufficient energy in the nth frequency band to produce the desired proportion of quantization error there, then increasing Q_n will accomplish nothing. When this situation occurs, we mark Q_n, and then set it to the maximum of the other table entries after they all have been updated.

5. Using the updated quantization table, return to step 2, and continue in the loop until the design converges. Convergence is indicated when the "update factors" $\frac{W_n}{D_n}$ all approach 1.0, or when the file sizes of the encoded images change very little after additional iterations.

This completes the design of the JPEG quantization table. Although we have no proof that convergence will occur in every case, the above procedure has been very stable in our experiments, converging without exception after no more than about 30 iterations.

An additional consideration related to the dc entry is that the 8×8 clustered-dot algorithm can produce 33 levels of gray in "flat" regions of an image. Taking into account the fact that JPEG encodes the dc coefficient of the DCT differentially, we found that a value of about 32 for the dc entry in the quantization table will result in 33 quantization levels. Thus we would expect that in customizing JPEG for the clustered-dot algorithm, the dc quantization table entry should be kept to values of about 32 or lower for good image quality. Our experiments have indeed shown that contouring artifacts become noticeable in the halftoned image when the dc quantization table entry takes on values of about 40 and above, i.e., when quantization results in a smaller number of "flat" gray levels than the halftoning algorithm can reproduce.

5 Huffman Table Design

Our customization of the JPEG Huffman tables is influenced by several factors. Perhaps the most important fact to note is that the "default" tables published in [1] are *not* optimized for low-rate coding. In particular, the default tables do not exploit the fact that in the low-rate case, most of the quantized coefficient values will be zero. We also note that the Huffman tables do not affect image quality in any way, but do strongly influence the bit rate that can be achieved at a given level of image quality.

In general, we can design the Huffman tables according to the following procedure.

Algorithm 4: Optimization of Huffman Tables

1. Begin with a collection of "typical" images and a chosen JPEG quantization table, and run the JPEG encoder on all of the images in the collection, keeping track of statistics on the quantized DCT coefficient values and their locations within the 8×8 block. The coefficient values and their locations are used to form the input symbols for the Huffman coder.

2. Use a standard technique (see, for example, [15]) for designing Huffman tables according to the collected statistics. In the tables, the output symbols with the shortest lengths (fewest bits) are generally assigned to the input symbols with the highest probabilities of occurrence, and longer output symbols are assigned to less probable input symbols.

It is possible to incorporate the above procedure into the JPEG encoder, so that the Huffman tables are statistically optimized for each image as it is encoded. This is seldom done in practice, however, because of the required extra computation and resultant delay in the encoding.

Good generic Huffman tables designed by the above procedure for a given quantization table and a given class of images will perform only slightly worse than tables optimized for individual images in the class. Moreover, our experiments have shown that generic Huffman tables designed for low-rate coding can easily produce bit rates 5–10% lower than the "default" tables at a given level of image quality.

6 Experimental Results

We have tested our design procedure in the following way. The halftoning error spectrum for the 8×8 clustered-dot algorithm was computed using five natural images from the USC database, and the HVS response was adjusted for 300 dpi resolution and a viewing distance of 8 inches. The value of the parameter λ in the quantization table design procedure was swept from 0 to 1, and quantization tables were designed for several different rates (below 0.30 bpp) at each value of λ. Generic low-rate Huffman tables were designed using some of these quantization tables with the USC images. The customized Huffman tables were used with the different customized quantization tables to compress the USC images as well as several others from the JPEG test set. Our purpose in these experiments was to compare the performance of the customized JPEG encoder against an encoder using the "default" tables, and to determine typical bit rates at which compression artifacts would become noticeable for the customized encoder.

Figure 4: "Lena" images printed at 300 dpi. Left: Halftoned original, 8 bpp grayscale; center: compressed to 0.24 bpp using "default" JPEG, then halftoned; right: compressed to 0.20 bpp using customized JPEG, then halftoned.

Figure 5: "Lena" images printed at 600 dpi. Left: Halftoned original, 8 bpp grayscale; center: compressed to 0.171 bpp using "default" JPEG, then halftoned; right: compressed to 0.137 bpp using customized JPEG, then halftoned.

We determined that setting λ to values in the range 0.4–0.6 gave the best results. The custom encoder consistently gave a significant performance advantage over the default encoder for all images that were tested. Typically, the custom encoder resulted in noticeably better halftoned image quality at a given bit rate, and maintained superior quality at rates 20–40% lower, depending on the specific image being encoded. Compression artifacts became noticeable at rates in the range 0.13–0.25 bpp, corresponding to compression ratios of 32:1–64:1 in the grayscale domain and 4:1–8:1 in the binary domain. A typical result is shown in Figure 4.

We have also done some preliminary work with 600 dpi printing. Keeping λ set to 0.4, we tuned the HVS response for 600 dpi resolution, designed new tables, and encoded a few images from the previous test set after scaling them up (using bilinear interpolation) by a factor of 2 in each dimension. The results in this experiment were about the same as before: our customized encoder again produced significantly better halftoned image quality at a given rate, and maintained the advantage to rates 20–40% lower than the default encoder. Moreover, because larger image files contain more redundancy and are, in that sense, easier to compress, we achieved lower rates (compared to the 300 dpi case) before artifacts became visible. An example is shown in Figure 5.

References

[1] W. B. Pennebaker and J. L. Mitchell, *JPEG Still Image Data Compression Standard.* New York: Van Nostrand Reinhold, 1993.

[2] D. L. Neuhoff and T. N. Pappas, "Perceptual coding of images for halftone display," in *Proc. of Int'l Conf. on Acoustics, Speech, and Signal Processing,* (Toronto, Canada), pp. 2797–2800, IEEE, May 1991.

[3] P. W. Wong, "Inverse halftoning and kernel estimation for error diffusion," *IEEE Transactions on Image Processing.* To appear.

[4] R. Ulichney, *Digital Halftoning.* MIT Press, 1987.

[5] Q. Lin, "Halftone image quality analysis based on a human vision model," in *Proceedings of IS&T/SPIE Symposium on Electronic Imaging,* (San Jose, CA), February 1993.

[6] A. J. Ahumada, Jr., "Computational image-quality metrics: a review," in *SID Int'l. Symp. Dig. of Tech. Papers,* vol. XXIV, (Seattle, WA), pp. 305–308, Soc. for Info. Display, May 1993.

[7] S. Daly, "Quantitative performance assessment of an algorithm for the determination of image fidelity," in *SID Int'l. Symp. Dig. of Tech. Papers,* vol. XXIV, (Seattle, WA), pp. 317–320, Soc. for Info. Display, May 1993.

[8] T. D. Lookabaugh and M. G. Perkins, "Application of the Princen-Bradley filter bank to speech and image compression," *IEEE Trans. Acoustics, Speech, and Signal Processing,* vol. ASSP-38, pp. 1914–1926, November 1990.

[9] J. L. Mannos and D. J. Sakrison, "The effects of a visual fidelity criterion on the encoding of images," *IEEE Transactions on Information Theory,* vol. IT-20, pp. 525–536, July 1974.

[10] A. B. Watson, "Visually optimal DCT quantization matrices for individual images," in *Proc. Data Compression Conference,* (Snowbird, UT), pp. 178–187, IEEE Computer Society, Mar. 1993.

[11] D. M. Monro and B. G. Sherlock, "Optimum DCT quantization," in *Proc. Data Compression Conference,* (Snowbird, UT), pp. 188–194, IEEE Computer Society, Mar. 1993.

[12] A. Gersho and R. M. Gray, *Vector Quantization and Signal Compression.* Boston: Kluwer, 1992.

[13] E. A. Riskin, "Optimal bit allocation via the generalized BFOS algorithm," *IEEE Transactions on Information Theory,* vol. IT-37, pp. 400–402, March 1991.

[14] R. C. Reininger and J. D. Gibson, "Distributions of the two-dimensional DCT coefficients for images," *IEEE Trans. Comm.,* vol. COM-31, pp. 835–839, June 1983.

[15] R. G. Gallager, *Information Theory and Reliable Communication.* New York: John Wiley & Sons, Inc, 1968.

Lossless Image Compression with Lossy Image Using Adaptive Prediction and Arithmetic Coding

Seishi Takamura and Mikio Takagi
Institute of Industrial Science, University of Tokyo

Abstract

Lossless gray scale image compression is necessary in many purposes, such as medical image, image database and so on. Lossy image is important as well, because of its high compression ratio. In this paper, we propose a lossless image compression scheme using a lossy image generated with JPEG-DCT scheme. Our concept is, send a JPEG-compressed lossy image primaly, then send residual information and reconstruct the original image using both the lossy image and residual information. 3-dimensional adaptive prediction and an adaptive arithmetic coding are used, which fully uses the statistical parameter of distribution of symbol source. The optimal number of neighbor pixels and lossy pixels used for prediction is discussed. The compression ratio is better than previous work and quite close to the originally lossless algorithm.

1 Introduction

Today there are many studies on image compression, particularly on lossy and very low bit rate compression. For image database, such high compression ratio is important for storage and also for quick transmission, but to deal with various kinds of users demand, lossless image transmission is indispensable.

In this paper, we propose an effective lossless compression algorithm for gray image using lossy compressed image. The lossy compression scheme uses the Joint Photographic Experts Group discrete cosine transform (JPEG-DCT) algorithm as the lossy coding algorithm.

First we search the similar pairs of pixels (*contexts*), according to their neighbor pixels. For such pixels which have contexts, we predict their values from the contexts and the neighbors. On the other hand, for each pixel which doesn't have its context pairs, we calculate the *edge level* according to the difference of adjacent pixel values. For each edge level of pixels, we calculate the predictive coefficients of linear combination under the least square error criterion. Not only the pixels which have already processed but also the pixels of the lossy image is used for prediction.

For every pixel, the difference between predicted value and real value is calculated, and the difference is converted to a non-negative value before being encoded, according to their distribution. In entropy coding stage, we use the arithmetic coding. It is made adaptive, and initial error distribution is given only by one parameter, which is specific for each edge level's statistical distribution. The pixels belonging to the different edge levels are encoded independently.

Experimental results and good performance are shown. Like the other LPL(Lossy Plus Lossless) approaches, our compression ratio is less than that of originally lossless scheme, but the difference is slight. Of all things, however, users get the great merit that they can browse the image before the lossless decompression. Many such schemes have been proposed in the literature, but most of them treat the lossy image and its lossless residual as independent symbol source. One of the exceptions is Memon's algorithm[6]. We utilize the lossy data thoroughly, and much better result is obtained.

1.1 Pixel estimation

Normally the image data is scanned along the scan-line direction. In figure 1, current pixel is '▒', processed pixels are '□'.

Ordinal pixel estimation method predicts the value of current pixel using $P_1 \ldots P_4$. Then calculate the prediction error $e = \hat{x} - x$. Normally the linear combination is used for prediction as follows, where $r_1 \ldots r_4$ are the coefficients. This is the extrapolative prediction.

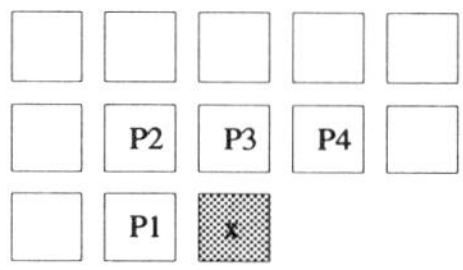

Figure 1: Current pixel and processed neighbor pixels

$$\hat{x} = r_1 P_1 + r_2 P_2 + r_3 P_3 + r_4 P_4 + C \tag{1}$$

Usually, the zero-order entropy of set $\{e\}$ is lower than that of set $\{x\}$. Therefore, after entropy coding scheme such as Huffman coding[1] or Arithmetic coding[2] or Lempel-Ziv coding[3], data size is reduced.

2 Our Method

Principally, we also use the linear combination like equation (1) for prediction, but the process is more adaptive than normal prediction method. And we use more neighbor pixels (up to ten), also using the pixels of lossy image and prediction error e is converted to another form before encoding.

2.1 Grouping the pixels

Each image pixel has different property under certain criterion. From a point of image compression, grouping similar pixels and encode them together causes effective result. For grouping the pixels, we use the Q value:

$$Q \equiv |P_2 - P_1| + |P_3 - P_1| + |P_4 - P_1| + |P_5 - P_1| \tag{2}$$

Using this Q value, we classify each pixel into several groups according to table 1.

Table 1: Grouping table

Q	0–1	2–4	5–8	9–16	17–32	33–64	65–128	129–
Group #	0	1	2	3	4	5	6	7

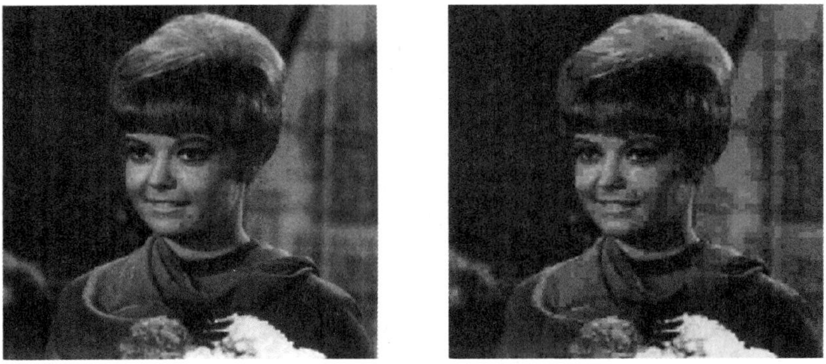

(a) (b)

Figure 2: (a)Original image 'Girl' and (b)JPEG compressed image(quality value=5)

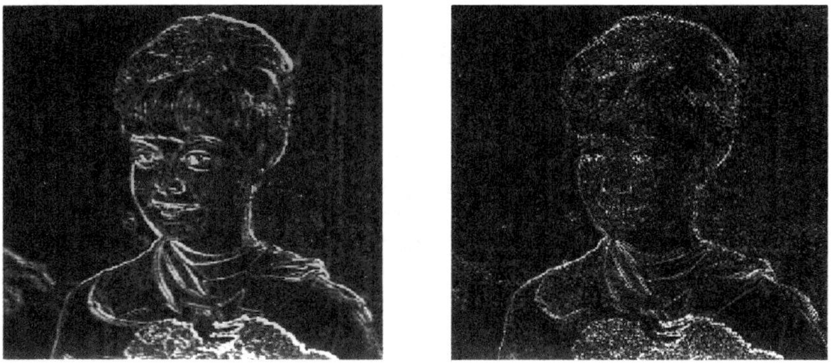

(a) (b)

Figure 3: (a)Image of Q value, (b)Image of prediction error of simple prediction

Figure 3(a) shows the Q value and (b) shows the error of simple prediction. As can be seen from them, the value Q correlate closely with the prediction error. Therefore the prediction coefficients are calculated independently in each group.

2.2 Context search

Table 2 shows each group's final zero-order entropy of prediction result of image 'Girl'. Obviously, the upper groups are more difficult to be compressed than the lower groups. We use the context-based prediction method to deal with such upper groups.

The region where we search the similar area (we denote this *"context"*) is shown in figure 4. This is restricted within already processed pixels' area. The procedure is described below:

1. Scan the area and find points that satisfy

$$Q(x') > 70 \quad \text{and} \quad |Q(x) - Q(x')| < 10 \tag{3}$$

2. Within such points, find one that minimizes

$$C = ||b' - a'| - |b - a|| + ||c' - a'| - |c - a|| \tag{4}$$

3. If the C_{min} is smaller than 12, treat it as the context of the current point. Otherwise, return failure (not found).

2.3 Prediction

2.3.1 Prediction of normal groups

For each group, we predict the value of a current pixel by linear combination of its neighbors' pixel values. The coefficients are calculated by least square error method. The neighbor pixels used for prediction are shown in figure 5 ($P_1 \ldots P_{10}$). Number of pixels are variable (up to 10 pixels), and afterwards we will choose it optimumly. The priority is shown by the suffix number in the figure. The most effective number will be discussed later.

Table 2: Group v.s. Entropy (image 'Girl')

Group #	0	1	2	3	4	5	6	7
Entropy	3.0182	3.3405	3.5378	3.9016	4.4358	4.9533	5.5070	6.1044

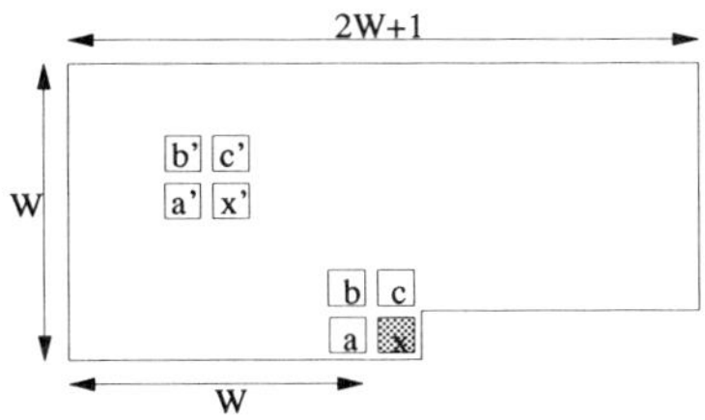

Figure 4: Context-search region

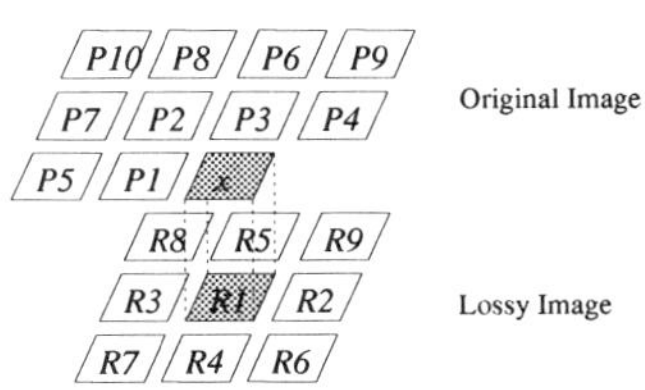

Figure 5: Pixels used for prediction

Here, some of the lossy pixels ($R_1 \dots R_9$) got from JPEG-compressed image are also used. Using these pixels, something like interpolative prediction is achieved. This prediction contributes the reduction of compressed size.

2.3.2 Prediction of context

Under the criterion of condition (3) and (4), a pair of context have the similar shapes of height. Therefore, we predict the value $\hat{x}$ from $\{a', b', c', x', a, b, c\}$ (see figure 4). We also use the least square error estimation. The most different point from prediction of non-context pixels is, not only using the values of neighbor pixels but also using the closest context. This scheme is effective for continuous edges, because nearby an edge there is a sequence of similar looking pixels.

2.4 Error conversion

If each pixel has 8 bits, the prediction error $e(= \hat{x} - x)$ can have the real number between -255 and +255 (roughly). After prediction, e should be expressed as an integer. One easy way for conversion is, simply round the value off the integer (calculate $\lfloor e + 0.5 \rfloor$) and consider it as the 2's complement 8-bit number.

Our conversion algorithm is totally based on Taniguchi's method[5]. After this conversion, we can also get the 8-bit non-negative integer E. First we obtain the upper and lower bound of the group (max, min). Then, according to the figure 6, convert the actual pixel value into integer. (In this figure, if actual pixel is equal to 'max', $E = 9$.) For each group, we get the maximum and minimum pixel value and convert the prediction error respectively.

This conversion is reversible. If you get the predicted value and the converted number E (and also upper and lower bound), you can obtain the actual pixel value from similar numerical line.

2.5 Adaptive arithmetic coding

2.5.1 Fitting of the distribution of E

According to the experimental result, the distribution of E(figure 7(a)), after error conversion, looks very close to the right half of a Gaussian distribution:

$$f_{\sigma^2}(x) = \frac{1}{\sqrt{2\pi\sigma^2}} \exp(-\frac{x^2}{2\sigma^2}) \tag{5}$$

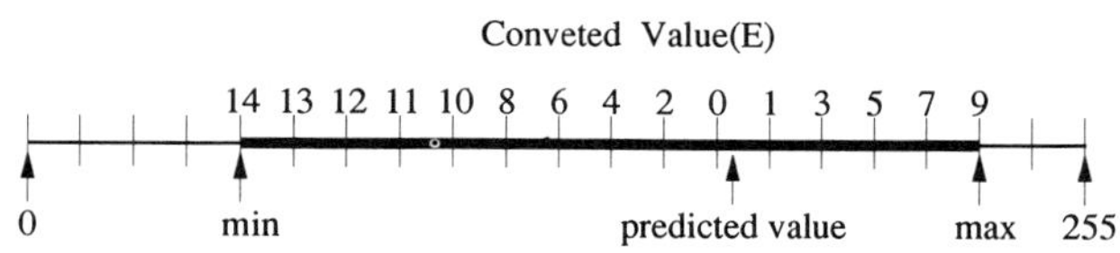

Figure 6: Algorithm of error conversion (example)

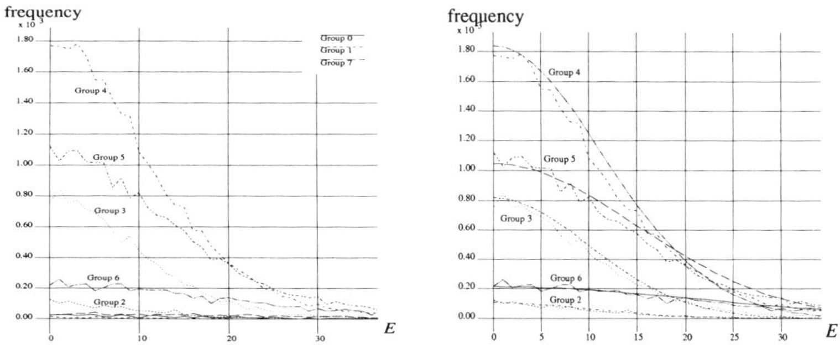

(a) (b)

Figure 7: (a)Distribution of E (image='Moon'), (b)Fitting of E

where the variance is σ^2.

As this distribution is limited right half, σ^2 is equal to $\sum x^2/N$, where N is the number of samples. The fitting line (estimated frequency) of E's distribution is calculated $2Nf_{\sigma^2}(x)$.

Their graphs are shown in figure 7(b). You can see that using this Gaussian model, the distribution of E is approximated well.

2.5.2 Adaptive arithmetic coding

The probability density function of this fitting curve can be expressed by only one parameter, σ^2. This distribution is used to generate the initial distribution table for encoder (and also for decoder), instead of passing the large amount of actual frequency table. For this purpose, arithmetic coding is very suitable. For this purpose, our coder is made adaptive, each symbol from the data stream renews the frequency table. By using σ^2 and adaptive arithmetic coder, even small amount of data is coded with high coding rate.

3 Experimental Results

To generate a lossy image, we adopt the JPEG compression scheme. The reason is that JPEG is the standard scheme for still image compression and users can find JPEG-tools easily.

We use the tools named 'cjpeg' and 'djpeg', which is the products of Independent JPEG Group. To create the JPEG image,

cjpeg -quality *quality-value* -optimize *filename*

and to decompress the JPEG file,

djpeg *jpegfile*

is invoked. The option '-optimize performs optimization of entropy encoding parameters. It usually makes the JPEG file a little smaller. 'djpeg' has the option

Table 3: Effect of context search (N=9, NL=4, quality=5)

Image	without context search	with context search
Girl	4.61182	4.61169
Couple	4.05957	4.05481
Moon	5.04614	5.04419

'-blocksmooth', which performs cross-block smoothing, but from experimental results, it made the compression ratio worse, therefore this option is not used.

Parameters which are necessary for decompression are put together and also encoded by adaptive arithmetic coder. Only several percent compression is achieved, but better than doing nothing.

3.1 Effect of context search

We use three test images 'Girl', 'Couple' and 'Moon', which are chosen from SIDBA(Standard Image DataBase).

For these images, the bit rate of compressing with and without context search is compared. The results are shown in table 3. NL is the number of lossy pixels used for prediction. N is the number of lossless neighbor pixels.

3.2 Effect of the quality value on compression ratio

JPEG provides a fine tuning factor (*quality value*), which corresponds to different qualities of the compressed images. For typical image data, a low quality value such as 20 provides high compression with poor image fidelity. As the quality value increases the fidelity improves at the expense of compression ratio.

Figure 8 shows the bit rate and quality value. As the quality value decreases, the total bit rate decreases, too. Later we use the image quality value of 5, which is enough for undersanding the image roughly (see figure 2(b)).

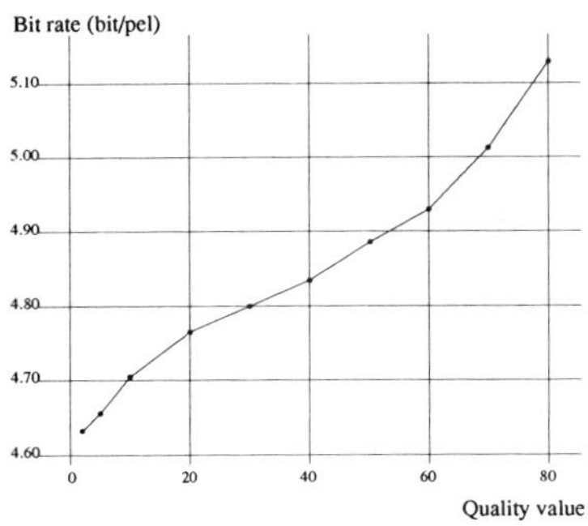

Figure 8: Bit rate V.S. Quality value (N=10, NL=9, image='Girl')

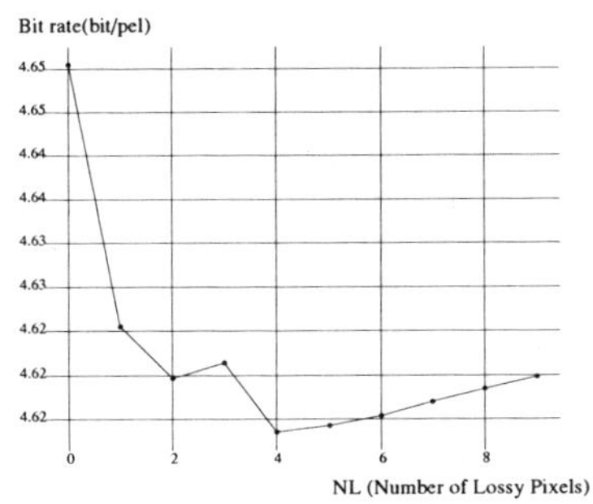

Figure 9: Bit rate V.S. NL (N=10, quality=5, image='Girl')

Table 4: Result of bit rate (quality=5, N=9, NL=4)

Image	Taniguchi	MAW (entropy)	Our method
Girl	4.494	5.10	4.612
Couple	3.978	4.56	4.055
Moon	5.019	—	5.046

3.3 Effect of using a lossy image

There might be a doubt that the lossy image looks similar with the original to our eyes, but differs much from a standpoint of pixel-value, therefore it hardly helps the prediction.

Figure 9 shows the bit rate and the number of lossy pixels used for prediction (NL). From this figure, it is known even the poor image (quality=5) helps the compression ratio considerably. The reason why the bit rate increases gradually where NL is greater than 4 is, that additional parameter (coefficients) is necessary for each pixel position. The optimum NL is 4. Moreover we conducted experiments to find the optimum number of N, and obtained 9.

3.4 Comparison with the other methods

Table 4 shows the result of the compression. Taniguchi's method[5] is originally lossless oriented one, therefore the results are slightly better than ours. In our method, N and NL are set optimally.

MAW method is proposed by Memon[6]. It also uses a lossy JPEG image to reconstruct a lossless image. Our result is about 0.5 bit/pel better than MAW, and 0.03 to 0.12 bit/pel worse than Taniguchi's method. As the MAW's result is given only by entropy, the difference of performance from ours might be bigger.

4 Conclusion

In this paper, we proposed the algorithm of lossless image compression. Unlike other literatures, we have discussed not only the entropy of residual, but how to encode it efficiently and the final size of the compressed product. This provides an attractive option in applications that have need for quick transmission on the one hand and exact reconstruction on the other. Furthermore, using this lossy image thoroughly, the total bit rate is considerably low.

Searching the contexts and using it for prediction is proved to work. We will research more effective way of using context.

Our algorithm is applicable for originally lossless oriented one (not using lossy image). In some images, we have obtained better results than Taniguchi's method. We are proceeding the investigation in this standpoint.

We are examining if there is a more suitable algorithm for lossy compression other than JPEG. And also speculating the more accurate error distribution fitting other than Gaussian model.

References

[1] D. A. Huffman: "A method for the construction of minimum redundancy codes", Proceedings of IRE 40, pp. 411–420, 1951

[2] J. J. Rissanen et al.: "Arithmetic coding", IBM Journal or Research and Development, 23(2), pp. 188–193, 1976

[3] J. Ziv and A. Lempel: "A Universal Algorithm for Sequential Data Compression", IEEE Transactions on Information Theory, IT-23(3), pp. 337–343, May 1997

[4] Paul G. Howard and Jefferey Scott Vitter: "New Methods for Lossless Image Compression Using Arithmetic Coding", Proceedings of Data Compression Conference '91, pp. 257–266, 1991

[5] Takayuki Taniguchi et al.: "Variable-Length-Code-Selective Reversible Predictive Coding for Multi-Level Images", The Transactions of the Institute of Electronics, Information and Communication Engineers, Vol.J70-B, pp.654–663, Jun. 1987

[6] Nasir D. Memon et al.: "Simple method for enhancing the performance of lossy plus lossless image compression schemes", Journal of Electronic Imaging 2(3), pp. 245–252, Jul. 1993

[7] Dmitry A. Novik: "Compression Through Decompression into Browse and Residual Images", Proceedings of 1993 Space and Earth Science Data Compression Workshop, NASA Conference Publication 3191, pp. 7–12, Apr. 1993

Explicit Bit Minimization for Motion-Compensated Video Coding

(extended abstract)

Dzung T. Hoang*   Philip M. Long†   Jeffrey Scott Vitter‡

Department of Computer Science
Duke University
Box 90129
Durham, NC 27708–0129

Abstract

We compare methods for choosing motion vectors for motion-compensated video compression. Our primary focus is on videophone and videoconferencing applications, where very low bit rates are necessary, where the motion is usually limited, and where the frames must be coded in the order they are generated. We provide evidence, using established benchmark videos of this type, that choosing motion vectors to minimize codelength subject to (implicit) constraints on quality yields substantially better rate-distortion tradeoffs than minimizing notions of prediction error. We illustrate this point using an algorithm within the $p \times 64$ standard. We show that using quadtrees to code the motion vectors in conjunction with explicit codelength minimization yields further improvement. We describe a dynamic-programming algorithm for choosing a quadtree to minimize the codelength.

1 Introduction

The typically strong correlation between successive frames of a video sequence makes video highly compressible, since the pixels of the previous frame can be used to predict the intensities of the current frame. The difference between the predicted and the true frame often is small and can be encoded efficiently, for example, by a lossy transform coder using the two-dimensional discrete cosine transform (2D DCT).

Improved compression is readily obtained by first estimating what portions of the current frame correspond to moving objects and then transmitting *motion vectors*

*Affiliated with Brown University. Supported in part by an NSF Graduate Fellowship and by Air Force Office of Strategic Research grant F49620–92–J–0515.

†Support was provided in part by Air Force Office of Strategic Research grant F49620–92–J–0515.

‡Support was provided in part by Air Force Office of Strategic Research grant F49620–92–J–0515, Army Research Office grant DAAH04–93–G–0076, and by an associate membership in CESDIS.

that tell the decoder where to look on the previous frame for predictions of the intensity of each pixel in the current frame. The most popular method for estimating these motion vectors originated with Jain and Jain [8] and is called block matching. In their approach, the current frame is divided into blocks (usually 8×8) whose pixels are assigned the same motion vector. (Carpentieri and Storer [2] group together blocks with the same motion vector into *superblocks*, and describe a method for keeping track of which block is in which superblock, in order to reduce the encoding of the motion vectors.) Jain and Jain's approach is taken by the CCITT in Recommendation H.261 (also known as the $p \times 64$ standard) [3, 10]. The motion vector for a given block B is usually obtained by (approximately) minimizing, from among candidates $\vec{v}$ within a limited search area, some norm of the difference between B and the prediction obtained from $\vec{v}$. The mean squared error (which is the square of the ℓ_2-norm) is a commonly used measure, although for example the mean absolute difference is often substituted because it can be implemented efficiently. This is done, for example, in the implementation of the $p \times 64$ standard made available by the Portable Video Research Group (PVRG) [6].

In this paper, we report on work in progress investigating the use of heuristics that more directly estimate the effect of the choice of a given motion vector on the total codelength. Our experimental results give evidence that this approach yields substantially better rate-distortion tradeoffs. While the error-minimization approach enables one to separate into modules the tasks of predicting the current frame and coding the resulting error, our experiments suggest that this separation comes at a substantial cost: integrating the two can lead to a better coder. We illustrate this point using three programs. The first two implement this idea within the $p \times 64$ standard, and the third adds the idea of using a quadtree to transmit the motion vectors to exploit spatial redundancy in the estimated motion field.

In this paper, our emphasis is on codelength and quality, not on computation time, in order to determine the limits on the compressibility of video. We can initially use computationally intensive coders to set a standard against which more efficient algorithms can be judged, such as those obtained, for example, by modifying the computationally intensive coders. Furthermore, our algorithms are highly parallelizable, and special-purpose chips are already available for many subroutines used by our algorithm.

The $p \times 64$ standard is intended for applications like videophone and video conferencing, where very low bit rates are required, not much motion is present, and frames are to be transmitted essentially as they are generated. Unlike the case of the MPEG standard, we cannot first compress a subsampling of frames, and then use frames both before and after a given frame to predict it. Our experimental results are for benchmark videos typical of the type for which the $p \times 64$ standard was intended: they consist of a single speaker sitting at a table.

Using the block-matching approach, we create only a crude, but concise, model of the motion. For video coding, we do not necessarily want to find the "correct" motion vectors, in contrast to a goal of research in optic flow, for example [13]. If a motion vector field that does not correspond to the actual motion in the scene yields the shortest description, that is sufficient for purposes of compression. However, an accurate motion field is desirable for motion interpolation, where a non-coded frame is interpolated from two successive coded frames by performing motion compensation using an interpolated motion field. We plan to apply our techniques to the compression-related optic flow techniques of [12], which should result in improved motion estimates.

In the next section, we describe the PVRG implementation of the $p \times 64$ standard, and then show how to modify the PVRG implementation, but remain within the $p \times 64$ standard, to choose motion vectors that more directly minimize codelength. For comparable quality, at the level roughly required for transmitting 15 CIF frames at 128 Kbits/sec, explicit bit minimization reduces the codelength by about 17% on average for a particular benchmark video. In the $p \times 64$ standard, two binary decisions must be made from time to time (for details, see Section 2). In the PVRG implementation, heuristics based on prediction error are used to make these decisions. When the explicit bit minimization philosophy is also applied here, the improvement becomes a significant 33%. Rate-distortion plots appear in Section 2.

In Sections 3 and 4, we present a non-standard approach based on quadtree decompositions using the explicit bit minimization paradigm in which coding improvement for interframe prediction at low bit rates can reach about 40%. (A rate-distortion plot for this experiment is given in Section 3.) Such an improvement suggests that this approach has potential in the related field of optic flow motion estimation.

To the best of our knowledge, ours is the first work investigating the effect of minimizing codelength subject to quality constraints to choose motion vectors. Puri and Hang [11] considered using transform coding for the error, adaptively choosing a transform for each block from among those in a given list by taking the one that resulted in the shortest code.

2 Within the $p \times 64$ standard

In this section, we compare the performance of three algorithms which conform to the $p \times 64$ standard [3, 10]. The first algorithm[1] chooses motion vectors to minimize a notion of the prediction error. The second is the same as the first, except that motion vectors are chosen in order to minimize a local approximation to the contribution of the choice of the given motion vector to the total codelength. In the third, certain binary decisions made in the first algorithm using heuristics based on error are instead made again to minimize total codelength.

2.1 Overview of the $p \times 64$ standard

We first provide a brief overview of key components of the $p \times 64$ standard. The $p \times 64$ standard specifies a three-component color system as the format for the video data. The three components are a luminance band Y and two chrominance bands C_B and C_R. Since the human visual system is more sensitive to the luminance component and less sensitive to the chrominance components, C_B and C_R are subsampled by a factor of 4 compared to Y. The image is decomposed into *macroblocks* (MB) each consisting of four 8×8 Y blocks, one 8×8 C_B block and one 8×8 C_R block. Motion prediction and compensation are performed by treating each macroblock as an atomic entity; that is, there is one motion vector per macroblock.

[1] The code for this algorithm was obtained via anonymous ftp from PVRG. We modified this code for the other implementations of algorithms operating within the $p \times 64$ standard.

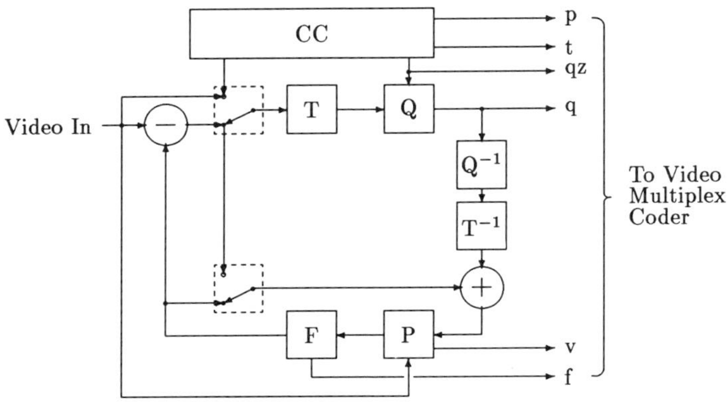

T: Transform
Q: Quantizer
P: Picture Memory with motion-compensated variable delay
F: Loop Filter
CC: Coding Control

p: Flag for INTRA/INTER
t: Flag for transmitted or not
qz: Quantizer indication
q: Quantizing index for transform coefficients
v: Motion vector
f: Switching on/off of the loop filter

Figure 1: Block Diagram of the $p \times 64$ Source Coder [3]

Figure 1 shows a block diagram of the $p \times 64$ coder. At a high level, the basic process is as follows. The macroblocks are scanned in a linear order. For a macroblock M, the encoder chooses a motion vector $\vec{v}$ (how this is done is left unspecified), and the difference between $\vec{v}$ and the motion vector for the previous macroblock is transmitted, using a static Huffman code. For each 8×8 block B contained in M, a lossy version of the block of prediction errors obtained by using $\vec{v}$ to predict B is then transmitted. This is done by applying a 2D DCT to the block of prediction errors, quantizing the resulting coefficients, and sending the result using a run-length/Huffman coder, where the coefficients are scanned in a zigzag order.

As indicated in the diagram, the encoder has the option of changing certain aspects of the above process. First, the encoder might simply not transmit the current macroblock; the decoder is then assumed to use the corresponding macroblock in the previous frame in its place. If transmitted, the macroblock can be transform coded with motion compensation (interframe coding) or without (intraframe coding). If motion compensation is used, there is an option to apply a linear filter to the previous decoded frame before using it for prediction.

2.2 PVRG implementation of $p \times 64$

In the PVRG implementation, a motion vector $\vec{v}$ is determined for each macroblock M by means of block matching. Only the luminance blocks are compared to the determine the best match, with the mean absolute difference being used as the measure of similarity. The variance V_P of the resulting prediction errors for the luminance blocks in M by using $\vec{v}$ is compared against the variance of the luminance blocks in M to determine whether to perform intraframe or interframe coding. The loop filter in interframe mode is enabled if V_P is below a certain threshold.

The decision of whether to transmit a transform-coded block is made individually for each block in a macroblock by considering the sum of absolute values of the quantized transform coefficients. If the sum falls below a predefined threshold, the block is not transmitted.

2.3 Algorithm M1

A good first place to apply the bit-minimization principle is in choosing the motion vectors. Instead of performing block matching to minimize the mean absolute difference, we minimize the actual number of bits needed to code the current macroblock. In computing the codelength, we make the same coding decisions as the original PVRG $p \times 64$ implementation and perform the appropriate encoding steps for each choice of motion vector within the search area, picking the motion vector that results in the minimum codelength for the entire macroblock. The computed codelength includes the coding of the transform coefficients, the motion vector, and all other side information. We call this algorithm M1.

When choosing the motion vector to minimize the coding of the current macroblock, we use the fact that the motion vectors for previous macroblocks (in scan order) have been determined to compute the codelength. However, since the choice of a motion vector for the current macroblock affects the codelength of future macroblocks, this is a greedy minimization procedure, and we may not obtain a globally minimal codelength.

Since we are explicitly attempting to minimize the codelength, we are almost assured to have higher prediction error than if we attempted to minimize the prediction error. Instead of attempting to deal with quality directly, we rely on the transform coder and quantizer to deliver a desired level of quality; that is, the M1 coder may require a finer quantization step size to deliver the same quality as the PVRG coder. As we will see in the results section, bit-minimization does indeed result in consistently better rate-distortion curves.

2.4 Algorithm M2

In Algorithm M1, the decisions of whether to use a filter and whether to use motion compensation are made the same way as in the PVRG $p \times 64$ implementation. In algorithm M2, however, these decisions are also made to minimize codelength: All three combinations of the decisions are tried, and the one resulting in the smallest codelength is used. Here, even more than with M1, we rely on the transform coder and the quantizer to code the prediction errors with adequate quality. Our hope is that the gain in compression efficiency will offset the decrease in reconstruction quality for a given quantization step size; that is, to achieve a certain quality level, we may be able to use finer quantization and still get improvements in compression.

Since M2 is able to make decisions on how to code each macroblock, it is able to take into account the coding of side information in minimizing the codelength. For low bit rates, where the percentage of side information is significant compared to the

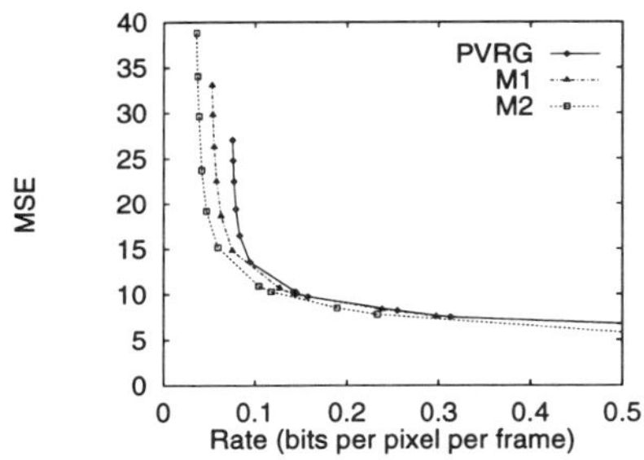

(a) Low Bit Rates

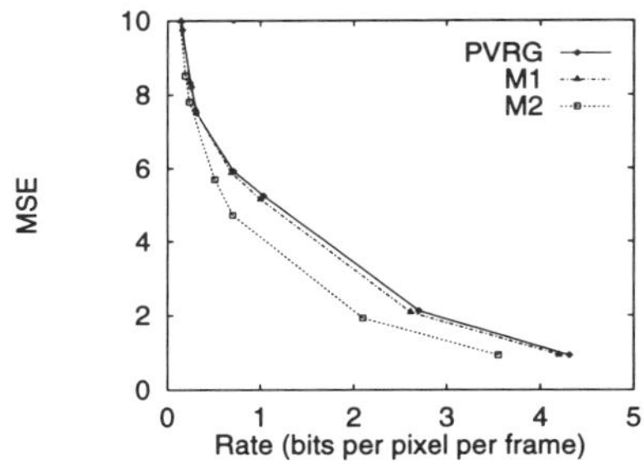

(b) High Bit Rates

Figure 2: MSE vs. Rate for Miss America

coding of motion vectors and transform coefficients, one would expect that M2 will be able to reduce the codelength of side information.

2.5 Experimental results

We performed experiments using 150 frames of the "Miss America" sequence in CIF (352×288) format. We ran the three $p \times 64$ algorithms for various quantization step sizes. The search region used for block matching is ± 7 in both directions. Rate-distortion curves are plotted in Figure 2.

As indicated in the plots, M1 performs slightly better than the PVRG implementation and M2 significantly better. For instance, transmitting a CIF-format video sequence at 15 frames per second (fps) on a 128 kbits-per-second line would allow for 8,738 bits per frame. For the same distortion achieved by the PVRG codec at this rate, the M1 and M2 coders would require 17% and 33% less bandwidth, respectively. Equivalently, for the same bandwidth, M1 would be able to code a sequence at 17.5 fps and M2 at 20 fps.

It is interesting to note that, for the one quantization level for which we did this experiment, increasing the search range from ± 7 to ± 15 yielded an improvement only for the M2 coder. The codelength actually increased for the PVRG coder and was unchanged for the M1 coder. This result points out one property of the bit-minimization approach: increasing the search range can never increase the codelength.

Though the experiments were performed with no rate control, we expect similar relative performance even with rate control.

In summary, for one particular test sequence both M1 and M2 exhibit significantly better rate-distortion curves than the PVRG $p \times 64$ coder at low bit rates. In addition, M2 has better performance at high bit rates.

3 Quadtrees for motion vector coding

Like the underlying image data that they are computed from, motion vector fields exhibit an appreciable amount of spatial correlation. Approaches such as the $p \times 64$

standard exploit this observation by coding the differences between successive motion vectors in a one-dimensional scan order. Potentially better results can be achieved by directly exploiting the two-dimensional correlation of motion vectors. A quadtree data structure can be used for this purpose by encoding a hierarchical decomposition of a frame into variable-sized regions of uniform motion [4]. For video sequences where there are large regions of uniform motion, a quadtree decomposition could reduce the number of bits required to encode the motion field compared to a method which used fixed-sized blocks.

In this section, we consider the instantiation of the bit-minimization principle in an algorithm which uses a quadtree to code motion vectors, thereby departing from the $p \times 64$ standard.

3.1 Previous work

Puri and Hang [11] considered an algorithm for motion-compensated video coding which, when an 8×8 block B is not coded well (that is, when coding it requires a lot of bits), chooses a separate motion vector for each of B's four 4×4 subblocks. Bierling [1] described a hierarchical algorithm for choosing motion vectors in which initially motion vectors are chosen for large blocks (64×64) by minimizing the prediction error.[2] Then for each large block B, motion vectors are chosen for subblocks of B again by minimizing prediction error, except looking only at motion vectors close to the motion vector chosen for B. This process results in a smoother motion field, and experiments suggest that it is closer to the "true" motion than is a motion field obtained by separately minimizing error on the small blocks. While Bierling did not discuss how to code motion vectors obtained through by his method, Chan, Yu, and Constantinides [4] described a method where motion vectors are again chosen in a top-down fashion, starting with large blocks and refining with smaller blocks, except when the average squared prediction error for a given block B is below a given threshold, the algorithm does not refine the motion vector chosen for B by looking at subblocks of B. Similarly, if the use of separate motion vectors for the subblocks of B does not reduce the error significantly, the subblocks of B are "merged" with B. After this process is completed, the tree obtained by making a given block the parent of its subblocks is transmitted, together with motion vectors for each of the leaves. Methods for taking a tree structure like the above (except expanded completely) and then "smoothing" the motion vectors by making children tend to be like their parents and vice-versa, were discussed by Dufaux and Kunt [5]. Zhang, Cavenor, and Arnold [15] considered various ways of using quadtrees to code the prediction error.

3.2 Description of our algorithm

In [4], Chan, Yu, and Constantinides describe several coding schemes using quadtrees in which the split/merge operations used to construct the tree are controlled by prediction error criteria. We propose to use a quadtree to encode motion vectors for a block-matching motion-compensated video coder in which the tree is constructed using the bit-minimization principle. The basic coder design is similar to the $p \times 64$ coder shown in Figure 1. The difference is that now motion vectors are coded with a quadtree whose leaves represent regions of uniform motion. Conceptually, one might

[2] In fact, a heuristic search [8, 9] was used to only approximately minimize the error.

associate a motion vector with each *node* of the quadtree, which, for internal nodes, is refined further down the tree. Using this viewpoint, for each node other than the root, the difference between the node's and its parent's motion vectors is transmitted. Thus, one can construct the motion vector for each leaf by adding the root's motion vector to the sum of the differences encountered along the path from the root to the given leaf.

Given a particular quadtree decomposition, we code the structure of the tree using an adaptive arithmetic code to code whether each node is a leaf or not (a different adaptive coder is used for each level). The motion vector differences at each node are coded using another adaptive arithmetic code (again, using a different coder for each level). For each leaf node, the 8×8 transform coded blocks subsumed by the node are transmitted in scan order. The decision of how to code the block (choosing from among alternatives similar to those in the $p \times 64$ standard) is also transmitted using an adaptive arithmetic coder. If the quantized transform coefficients are transmitted, this is done using the run-length/Huffman coding method from the $p \times 64$ standard. The counts for the adaptive arithmetic coder are updated once at the end of each frame.

The quadtree coding structure just described has several nice properties that make a dynamic-programming solution possible for finding an optimal set of motion vectors that minimizes the sum of the codelengths needed to encode the motion vectors and the transform-coded prediction error. Since the code used for the motion vector differences at each node doesn't change during the coding of a particular frame, the optimum number of bits to code the motion vector differences for any subtree is independent of the coding of any other disjoint subtree. Similarly, the transform coding of the prediction errors is independent for disjoint subtrees.

We now describe a dynamic-programming algorithm for choosing an optimal quadtree. For each node in the tree, we store a table indexed by the (absolute) motion vector of the node's parent. This table, for each possible motion vector $\vec{v}$ of the parent, gives the minimum codelength to code the subtree rooted at the current node given that the parent's motion vector is $\vec{v}$. Also stored with each table entry is a motion vector giving the minimum codelength. Construction of the tables is performed in a bottom-up fashion, starting at the 8×8 block level. For a node p, the table is constructed by finding, for each possible motion vector $\vec{v}'$ of the parent of p, a motion vector for p that results in the minimum codelength for the subtree rooted at p. If p is at the 8×8 block level, this is done by computing the transform codelength of the prediction error for each motion vector in the search range S and noting the minimum codelength and the corresponding motion vector. Otherwise if p is not an 8×8 block, we consider for each motion vector $\vec{v}$ in S the codelength needed to transform-code the prediction errors if the quadtree is pruned at p. (This quantity can be computed in a preprocessing step.) We also consider the codelength if the quadtree is not pruned at p. This codelength is computed by indexing the tables of children of p with $\vec{v}$ and summing. The minimum of these two quantities is added to the number of bits to code $\vec{v}' - \vec{v}$. The result is the minimum codelength required to code the subtree rooted at p given motion $\vec{v}'$ at p's parent node.

Once the minimum codelength is computed for the root of the quadtree, the motion vectors for each node in the tree are determined by going back down the tree, using the tables constructed on the way up. The optimal motion vector for the root

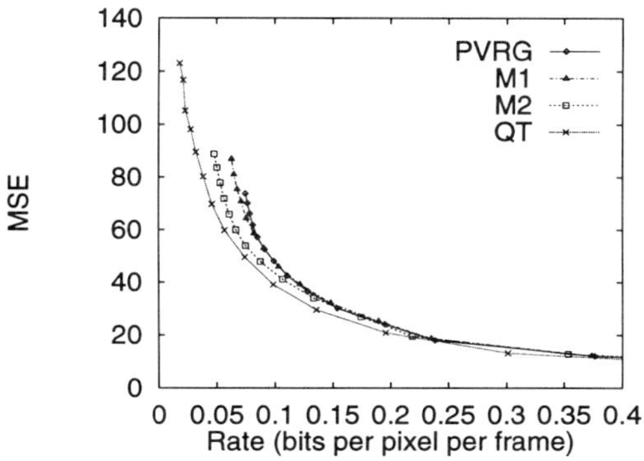

Figure 3: MSE vs. Rate for Trevor

node is made known to its children. Each child uses this to index its table to find its optimal motion vector. Pruning of the tree is also performed as a result.

The dynamic-programming algorithm requires $O(N|S|^2)$ time, where N is the number of 8×8 blocks in the frame and S is the search area for block-matching. The space requirement is $O(N|S|)$.

We performed experiments using 50 frames of the grayscale 256×256 "Trevor" sequence. The $p \times 64$ coders were modified to accept input at 256×256 resolution. A rate-distortion plot for the quadtree and $p \times 64$ coders is given in Figure 3.

4 Ongoing research

The current quadtree algorithm uses a bottom-up dynamic programming approach, except that the "bottom" level is defined as the 8×8 block level used for DCT coding. More efficient encoding can be obtained by allowing the quadtree decomposition to go all the way to the pixel level. The most promising approach within reason is to "freeze" the quadtree resulting from the "bottom-up" approach starting at the 8×8 level, and then use a heuristic to expand non-pruned nodes at the 8×8 level. Another use for the top-down heuristic is as a fast approximation to the bottom-up dynamic programming approach.

The same motion estimation methods we discussed in this paper should work as well for MPEG, in which interframe coding can be both forwards and backwards. The MPEG approach is more suitable for computationally intensive encoding methods, as long as decoding is fast, as in the case at hand.

We are also interested in adapting the optic flow algorithms of Shvaytser [12], which use the Occam paradigm of minimizing code length in order to get better estimates of the motion. However, the algorithms in [12] only approximately minimize code length, since they ignore the coding of the error signal. The approach we advocate in this paper, when combined with the prediction framework in [12] should yield better motion estimates.

References

[1] M. Bierling. Displacement estimation by hierarchical blockmatching. *SPIE Vol. 1001 Visual Communications and Image Processing*, pages 942–951, 1988.

[2] B. Carpentieri and J. Storer. A split-merge parallel block matching algorithm for video displacement estimation. In *Proceedings of the 1992 IEEE Data Compression Conference*, pages 239–248, Snowbird, UT, April 1992.

[3] CCITT. Video codec for audiovisual services at $p \times 64$ kbit/s, 1990. Study group XV – Report R 37.

[4] M.H. Chan, Y.B. Yu, and A.G. Constantinides. Variable size block matching motion compensation with applications to video coding. *IEE proceedings*, 137(4):205–212, 1990.

[5] F. Dufaux and M. Kunt. Multigrid block matching motion estimation with an adaptive local mesh refinement. *SPIE Vol. 1818 Visual Communications and Image Processing*, pages 97–109, 1992.

[6] Portable Video Research Group. Pvrg-p64 codec 1.1, 1993. Available from Stanford University by anonymous ftp.

[7] P. G. Howard and J. S. Vitter. Analysis of arithmetic coding for data compression. *Information Processing and Management*, 28(6):749–763, 1992. Special issue on data compression for images and texts.

[8] J.R. Jain and A.K. Jain. Displacement measurement and its application in interframe coding. *IEEE Transactions on Communications*, COM-29(12):1799–1808, 1981.

[9] T. Koga, K. Iinuma, A. Hirano, Y. Iijima, and T. Ishiguro. Motion-compensated interframe coding for video conferencing. *Proceedings of the NTC 81*, pages G5.3.1–G5.3.5, 1981.

[10] M. Liou. Overview of the $p \times 64$ kbit/s video coding standard. *Communications of the ACM*, 34(4):60–63, 1991.

[11] A. Puri and H.-M. Hang. Adaptive schemes for motion-compensated coding. *SPIE Vol. 1001 Visual Communications and Image Processing*, pages 925–935, 1988.

[12] H. Shvaytser. Occam algorithms for computing visual motion. In *Proceedings of ICCV*, 1993.

[13] A. Singh. *Optic Flow Computation.* IEEE Computer Science Press, 1991.

[14] P. Strobach. Quadtree-structured interframe coding of hdtv sequences. *SPIE Vol. 1001 Visual Communications and Image Processing*, pages 812–820, 1988.

[15] X. Zhang, M.C. Cavenor, and J.F. Arnold. Adaptive quadtree coding of motion-compensated image sequences for use on the broadband isdn. *IEEE Transactions on Circuits and Systems for Video Technology*, 3(3):222–229, 1993.

Online Compression of Video Sequences using adaptive VQ codebooks *

Xiaomei Wang Sunil M. Shende
Khalid Sayood
University of Nebraska-Lincoln, Lincoln, NE 68588.

Abstract

We propose a novel approach that combines the space covering property of high rate lattice VQ with the pattern matching ability of clustering VQ. The proposed scheme encompasses a broad range of *online* algorithms that use suitable VQ encodings and fixed-size, adaptive codebooks. The generic baseline algorithm for the scheme has the following desirable characteristics.

The distortion per individual vector is guaranteed to be less than a user specified threshold. Secondly, the algorithm is amenable to fast realtime implementation and requires minimal statistical assumptions for analysis. Finally, with careful analysis, the coding rate can be bounded with respect to some theoretical benchmark.

1 Introduction

Vector quantization (VQ) is one of the more popular compression techniques to appear in the last twenty years [1]. Numerous compression techniques, which incorporate VQ, have been proposed. The basic technique is simple. The source sequence is blocked into vectors. These vectors are compared to a set of representative vectors called a codebook. The index of the vector in the codebook which provides the closest match (generally in the sense of the L_1 or L_2 norm) is then transmitted. The codebook is usually generated using a clustering algorithm [7].

The traditional VQ approach to image compression has several disadvantages. Choosing an appropriate training set for the initial codebook, the actual construction of the codebook from the training set, and the analysis of the rate/distortion characteristics of a proposed VQ algorithm, are performed, for the most part, in the context of specific images or classes of images and specific bandwidth constraints. When the bandwidth constraints and/or the source statistics change this can result in severe degradation in the quality of the reconstructed output.

*This work was supported in part by the NASA Lewis Research Center under grant NAG 3-806.

To alleviate this problem a number of approaches have been proposed to adapt the VQ to changing source statistics [4, 3]. However, inherent in these approaches is the assumption of slowly changing statistics. While this assumption could be justified when coding still images or video sequences with minimal motion, when coding more typical video sequences the situation is much more dynamic. In such dynamic situations, somewhat different approaches need to be considered. One approach is to use a very large "universal" codebook which has been trained using a very diverse set of images [12]. Unfortunately, due to the size requirements this can exacerbate the search and memory requirements. These problems can be somewhat alleviated by using only a subset of the universal codebook at any given time [10]. The composition of this subset depends on local statistics and is transmitted to the decoder as side information. This reduces the search problem while retaining the "universality" of the codebook. This approach essentially involves replacement of the codewords of the codebook, however, the set from which the replacements are chosen are somewhat restrictive. It would make sense to examine the possibility of codeword replacement without any *apriori* restrictions. There have been some attempts in this direction for very low rate speech coding [11] as well as image coding [5, 6, 2]. The empirical evaluations of these heuristics are promising, but rigorous theoretical analyses are often inadequate and do not provide any provable guarantees of performance.

A second drawback of the traditional VQ technique arises from the need to maintain fairly low rates of compression. This restricts the size of a VQ codebook; as a consequence, the input space may be inadequately covered. This is especially true if while most of the input vectors tend to cluster in one particular region of the input space, there is a small yet significant number of input vectors which fall outside the region. As the VQ algorithms are designed to minimize some average measure of error, all VQ output points may be clustered in the high probability region. This means that the occurrence of the low probability vector will lead to large errors which can be devastating, particularly if they are perceptually important. At sufficiently high rates, lattice VQs can alleviate the problem by providing wider coverage of the range of the data. However, the lattice VQs are designed without reference to the patterns in the data, therefore there is a significant loss in compression efficiency.

We propose a new VQ algorithm which does not suffer from these drawbacks. In sections 2 and 3, we outline the baseline algorithm and present a fairly detailed analytical framework for our approach. In section 4 we describe a specific implementation of the proposed approach. Simulation results for this approach are presented in section 5, along with some conclusions and observations.

2 The Baseline Algorithm

For simplicity, we shall first describe a simple baseline scheme using VQ along with fixed-size, adaptive codebooks. In a two-dimensional image with L^2 pixels, we perform quantization over $(n \times n)$-blocks ($n << L$) with each pixel being represented by an integer value in the range $[0, M-1]$. The codebook, $\mathcal{V}$, is considered to be some labeled data structure of *fixed* size K, containing output vectors. The space of codewords, $\mathcal{C}$, is explicitly chosen based on the value of n^2, the block size, M, the range of values in any dimension, and on D, a *distortion bound* chosen in advance. The codebook size, K, is much smaller than the number of codewords, $|\mathcal{C}|$. For the sake of concreteness, we describe the VQ scheme using a standard n^2-dimensional *lattice code*, $\mathcal{C}$, over the space M^{n^2}, with *minimum distance* between codewords depending on D, the chosen distortion bound. In the baseline scheme, both the receiver and the transmitter start with some initial (possibly empty) codebooks containing codewords in $\mathcal{C}$.

Transmitter's Algorithm:

1. Obtain the next $(n \times n)$-block, B, and find the closest match, $C(B)$, in the current codebook to B. If the relative distortion between B and $C(B)$ is bounded above by D, then transmit the *label* of $C(B)$ and repeat.

2. Quantize B to the unique codeword $f(B) \in \mathcal{C}$, and proceed to step 4.

3. If the codebook is not full, then choose an available label, l, for $f(B)$. Otherwise, select some existing codeword for *replacement*, and transfer the label, l, of that codeword to $f(B)$.

4. Install $f(B)$ in the codebook with the label l chosen in the previous step. Transmit $f(B)$ *and* l, and go to step 1.

Receiver's Algorithm:

1. If the received string is a label l, then reproduce the codeword from the current codebook with that label, and repeat.

2. Otherwise, the received string is a codeword, $f(B)$, followed by its label, l. Install $f(B)$ with label l in the codebook (replacing the previous codeword with that label if necessary).

3. Reproduce $f(B)$, and go to step 1.

The algorithm always ensures that the *worst-case* distortion error per block is bounded above by D. Secondly, the rate of transmission varies from block to block, and depends crucially on the correlations in the data and on the nature of the *replacement* strategy in step 3 of the transmitter's algorithm. Thus, at any stage, a block that is located in the current codebook can be transmitted at a rate of $(\log K)$ bits, whereas an absent block needs an extra n^2 bits to update the codebook. However, a very significant point of departure from existing quantization schemes is that the algorithm need not explicitly assume any *apriori* distribution on the pixel values, and hence may lend itself to distribution-free analysis.

3 Analytical Framework

Traditional analysis of adaptive VQ schemes pre-supposes a source distribution: once the distribution is assumed, the goal is to compute the rate-distortion in the limit as the block size tends to infinity. We propose a different approach that has been used often in mainstream computer science. The goal is to consider an online algorithm to be *in competition with* an *idealized, optimal* algorithm. This notion of *competitive* analysis (for e.g., see [9]) has yielded very powerful results for a wide class of online problems. One such problem is the cache management problem. Most computers organize their memory resources into two categories: fast, short-term memory (the *cache*) residing in the CPU chip, and slow, massive-storage devices like disk drives which communicate with the CPU via a data bus. Efficient memory management algorithms (called *paging algorithms*) try to manage pages in cache in such a way that disk accesses (called *cache misses*) are minimized. This is done by implementing some *cache replacement* policy, viz. whenever the cache is full and a page from disk is accessed, the algorithm may choose to replace some page in cache with the newly accessed page.

In practice, the sequence of page requests is not known *apriori* and does not follow any fixed distribution, and any candidate algorithm must be *online*. The idea is then to compare an online algorithm with an ideal (perhaps, offline) one on any given sequence of page requests. This is done by computing the *worst-case* ratio, or the *competitive factor*, of the number of cache misses suffered by the proposed algorithm to the number of cache misses suffered by the idealized, optimal algorithm. Such competitive analysis can provide a very strong indicator of the effectiveness of an online algorithm, especially if the above ratio (the *competitiveness*) is bounded above. We suggest the following approximate analogy between the image compression with adaptive codebook VQ problem and the paging problem. The space of possible codewords is the space of requested pages, the fixed size codebook is the cache, and the sequence of encoded blocks in an image or set of images is the online sequence of requested pages. Using a certain codeword to encode the next block in sequence corresponds to managing a page request. In particular, it is easy to see from our baseline algorithm that *the rate/distortion of the transmitted codeword corresponds to the frequency of cache misses.* As a consequence, any incarnation of the baseline VQ algorithm, with a well-defined replacement strategy, seems to be amenable to competitive analysis.

For example, there are simple, randomized paging strategies for adaptive codebook replacement which are $O(\log K)$-competitive [8]. Using the correspondence suggested earlier, we could analyze an adaptive VQ algorithm obtained from the baseline algorithm as follows. If L^2 is the number of pixels with pixel values in the range $[0, M-1]$ and n^2 is the size of a VQ block, then the baseline algorithm has bounded distortion D and rate R per image given by $R \leq c \times R_{\mathrm{OPT}}$, where R_{OPT} is the optimal rate of an adaptive VQ quantizer for the same image with bounded distortion D, and c approximately equals the ratio

$$\frac{P + Q\log Km}{P + Qm}$$

where $P = L^2 \log K / n^2$, $Q = (n^2 \log M - \log K)$ and m equals the number of codewords replaced by the optimal algorithm. This translates to *a performance guarantee on rate with bounded distortion.* It is prudent to interpret these calculations cautiously, because these are really *expected ratios* and may vary from image to image. Nevertheless, the analysis is distribution-free and in the long run, the performance will tend to fall in the expected range. It should also be noted that the approach consistently underestimates the cost to the optimal algorithm. The optimal algorithm is assumed to have a degree of omniscience which in practice would significantly increase the complexity and rate of the VQ. As indicated by our simulation results, the main contribution of the present approach is two-fold. The baseline algorithm, even with simple adaptive replacement strategies, obtains good rate/distortion and is amenable to fast realtime implementation. Secondly, it may be possible to analyze the compression parameters under minimal statistical assumptions using competitive analysis.

4 Implementation

In this section, we report on an implementation of our adaptive scheme as applied to *video sequence coding.* Like other lossy coding schemes for image sequences, we have incorporated some enhancements like motion compensation into our baseline algorithm to accomplish the task of source coding. Figure 1 is a diagram of our video coding scheme. Briefly, each image is divided into blocks, with each block treated as an input vector. The *activity* of each block determines the distortion thresholds used for the block. With these thresholds, we can decide whether blocks can be motion compensated or can be coded by the adaptive vector quantizer. The basic idea is to adjust the distortion threshold based on the local activity. This has the effect of smoothing out the distortion; more noise is introduced where it is less visible, while ensuring that sensitive areas are relatively finely quantized. By calculating the variance, which is an indicator of activity, either a low, high or medium distortion threshold is applied to the block. Block matching motion compensation is used. This technique is well-known and hence, will not be discussed here. Instead, we shall focus on the choice of replacement strategy used in the baseline algorithm.

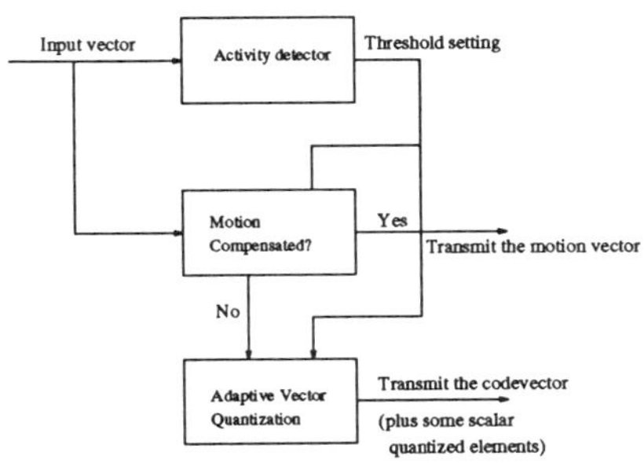

Figure 1: Video Coding Scheme

Our baseline algorithm can be initialized arbitrarily. At any stage, if the current input vector (encoded block) cannot be represented by any of the existing codevectors in the codebook, then the new vector is installed in the codebook, perhaps replacing a former codevector. This forces the codebook to reflect the local statistics of the image. This codebook will be relatively stable if there is not much change in the image sequence.

Codeword updating is necessary only when the quantization error exceeds the distortion threshold. In this case, we perform some local fine-tuning: instead of transmitting a new codevector immediately, we try to use the closest codevector while updating those components which cause relatively large errors. We update these components by replacing them with the scalar quantized values of the corresponding components of the input vector.

The receiver can determine the representation from the new vector after receiving the label for the closest codevector followed by some scalar quantized components. Since the closest codevector from the codebook is used, we usually need only a few components to be updated to satisfy the distortion criteria. Transmitting these components cost much less than a whole new vector. For instance, for an 8×8 (64-dimensional) block, with 6 bits per element, a total of 384 bits are needed for a whole new vector. To transmit an element separately, we need 6 bits for the value and another 6 bits for its position. Although this sounds worse, only a few component need to be transmitted. Hence, along with overhead information, a total of about 60 bits suffices for four components. In case of drastic change, the number of components that need to be updated may be excessive. In this situation, we transmit the entire new vector. Overall, we achieve two goals simultaneously: the overhead for updating information is minimized, and both the transmitter and the receiver can maintain identical codebooks.

We do not need an initial codebook since it is generated as we encode the input sequence. The codeword updating (or updating of codevector components) can occur as often as necessary. This is especially useful when there is drastic change from the input, like in TV program there are a lot of scene cuts. Other fixed interval adaptation schemes cannot perform well in such environments. Our codebook adaptation strategy, in contrast, can be performed very rapidly.

We tested several on-line cache replacement algorithms as part of our baseline scheme. Because of lack of space, we only present the simulation results for the *least recently used* (LRU) strategy : replace the codevector that has been used least recently in the past. In our implementation, the codebook is treated like a circular array. Hence, the LRU strategy is equivalent to the *move-to-front* rule: move the currently used codevector (whether newly installed or previously used) to the front of the codebook while shifting all other codevectors one position. In the process, the least recently used codeword will automatically be replaced. This can be accomplished simultaneously by the transmitter and the receiver without information about the labels for the current codevector and the replaced codevector. As we mentioned in the general baseline algorithm, we will have to transmit these labels if other replacement rules are used instead of the LRU rule.

The detailed algorithm is summarized in Figure 2. In the figure, X is the in-

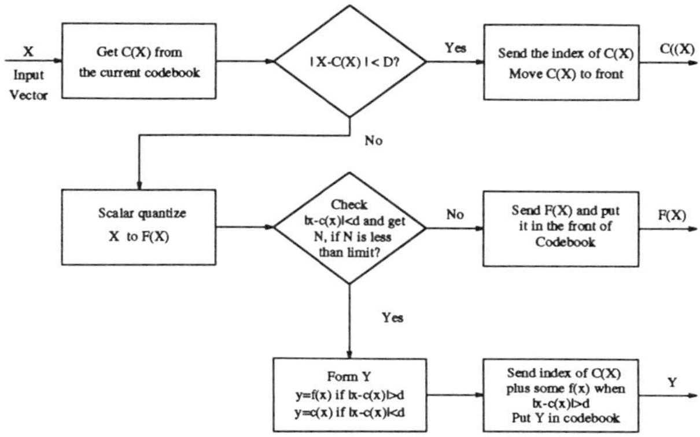

Figure 2: Adaptive Vector Quantization Scheme

put vector, $C(X)$ is the closest codevector from the current codebook, $F(X)$ is the uniformly quantized value of X, Y is the new codevector, D is the block distortion threshold, and N is the number of over-threshold elements in the error vector. The corresponding lower case letters represent the components of the vector, in particular d is the pixel error threshold.

5 Experiments and results

We tested the above algorithm with a video sequence consisting of 150 frames of black and white images, each of size 480 × 720. The image sequence (called "Susie") represents a typical video conferencing situation, with a person speaking on a telephone. In Figure 3-(a) and (b), we present, respectively, the bit-rate and SNR of the coded "Susie" sequence. The SNR is given by:

$$SNR(db) = 10 \log 256^2 - 10 \log \frac{1}{N} \{ \sum_{i=1}^{N} (x_i - y_i)^2 \}$$

with x_i the input pixel value, y_i the coded pixel value and N the size of one frame of the sequence.

To calculate the bit rate, let N_c be the codebook size, N_v the number of dimensions in a codevector, N_s the scalar quantizer level, and N_l the upper limit on the number of pixels which could be updated for a codevector. Then the number of bits needed to transmit each vector is either $1 + \log N_c$ if only the label is transmitted, or $1 + \log N_c + M(1 + \log N_v + \log N_s)$ where M is the number of scalar quantized pixels, or $N_l + N_v \log N_s$ if the whole quantized input vector needs to be transmitted.

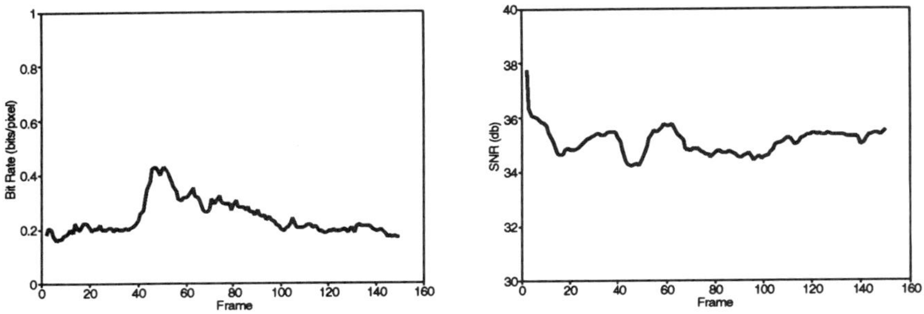

Figure 3: (a) Bit Rate, and (b) SNR of Coded "Susie" sequence

It may be observed that the bit rate is relatively high in the middle portion of Figure 3-(a), which corresponds to some frames during which a lot of movement takes place (Susie shakes her head etc.). We can also see that the SNR is quite stable except for some initial frames. This can be attributed to the fact that it takes the codebook some time to stabilize, but thereafter, our scheme *limits* the distortion regardless of local activity. This is exactly what we anticipated: achieving "smooth" quality with variable rate coding with modest variance.

Of course, typical video sequences encountered in everyday situations, need not always have stable or low activity. Often quite drastic changes can be seen, for instance, in regular TV programming where scene-cuts to commercials can cause local abruptness in the activity levels. Many well-studied schemes like predictive coding and transform coding cannot work well in such situations; indeed, it is reasonable to expect that any fixed-interval adaptive scheme will also suffer a temporary loss in quality for a short period. In order to test the adaptiveness of our scheme, we simulated the scene-cut situation by interleaving portions of the "Susie" sequence with another sequence called "Football" (the latter sequence contains substantially complex motion scenes against a low activity background).

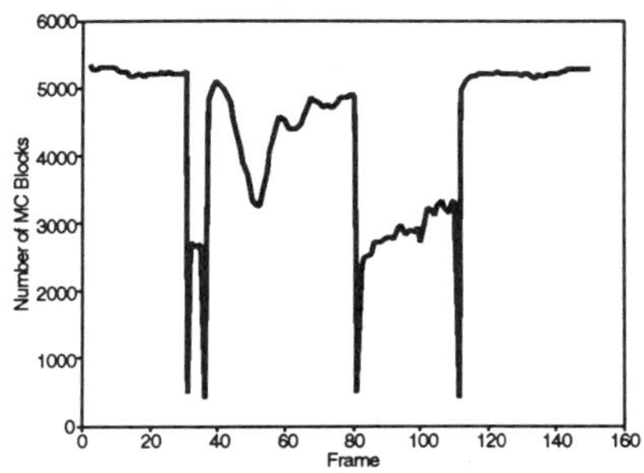

Figure 4: Motion compensated blocks vs. Frames (Scene Cut)

As can be seen from Figure 4, motion compensation does not work when the scene cuts from one sequence to the other (observe the intermittent decrease in the number of motion compensated blocks in Figure 4). Nevertheless, our scheme is still very robust during scene cuts as evidenced by the respective plots of bit rate and SNR versus frame number shown in Figure 5-(a) and (b). Figure 6 shows some of the original frames from the scene cut sequence.

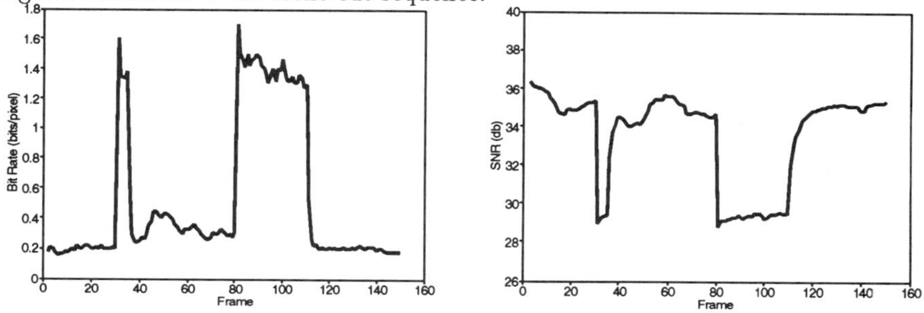

Figure 5: (a) Bit rate, and (b) SNR vs. frame number in a scene cut

In summary, we see that the scheme adapts itself rather well in the presence of very different scenes. It should be noted that maintaining a quasi-constant overall SNR with scene-cut video sequences may not necessarily be desirable for human visual perception. This has been incorporated by adjusting distortion thresholds depending on local activity (the "Football" sequence has higher thresholds). By doing so, the adaptively encoded images have far fewer quantization artifacts like blockiness or dirty background, as compared to other coding methods like predictive or transform coding. Combined with other obvious advantages like ease of implementation, absence of codebook training, and genuine "real-time" behavior, we believe that the proposed online scheme is worth further investigation. In particular, a more rigorous analysis will be the focus of a forthcoming paper.

References

[1] H. Abut, editor. *Vector Quantization.* IEEE Press, 1990.

[2] O.T-C. Chen, Z. Zhang, and B.J. Shen. An Adaptive High-Speed Lossy Data Compression. In *Proc. Data Compression Conference '92*, pages 349–355. IEEE, 1992.

[3] C. Fong and M. Baraniecki. Adaptive Transform Coding with Multi-Band Vector Quantization for Video Signals. In *Proceddings ICASSP '88.* IEEE, 1988.

[4] A. Gersho and R.M. Gray. *Vector Quantization and Signal Compression.* Kluwer Academic Publishers, 1991.

[5] A. Gersho and M. Yano. Adaptive Vector Quantization by Progressive Codevector Replacement. In *Proceedings ICASSP.* IEEE, 1985.

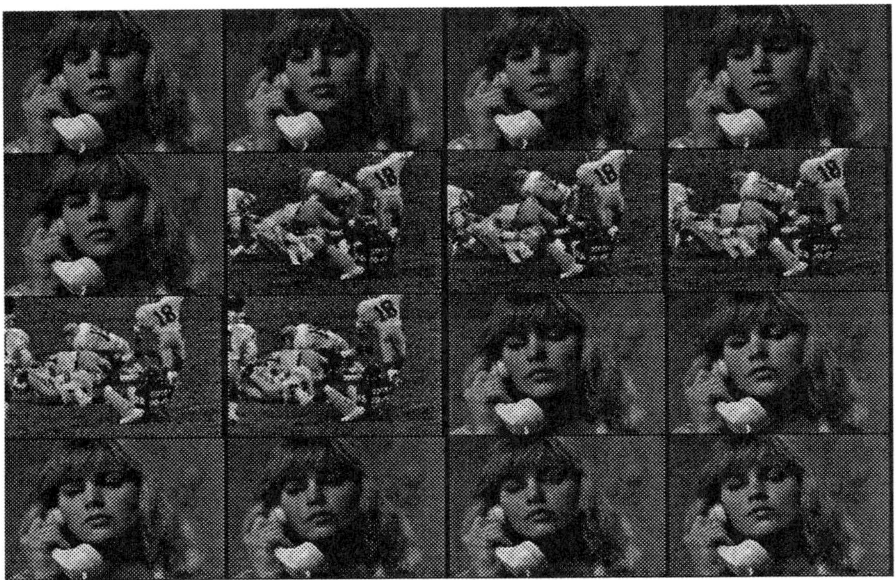

Figure 6: 16 frames from the scene cut sequence.

[6] M. Goldberg and H. Sun. Image Sequence Coding ... *IEEE Transactions on Communications*, COM-34:703–710, July 1986.

[7] Y. Linde, A. Buzo, and R. M. Gray. An algorithm for vector quantization design. *IEEE Transactions on Communications*, COM-28:84–95, Jan. 1980.

[8] Mark S. Manasse, Lyle A. McGeoch, and Daniel D. Sleator. Competitive algorithms for server problems. *Journal of Algorithms*, 11:208–230, 1990.

[9] Lyle A. McGeoch and Daniel D. Sleator, editors. *On-Line Algorithms: Proceedings of a DIMACS Workshop*, volume 7 of *DIMACS Series in Discrete Mathematics and Theoretical Computer Science*, February 1991.

[10] S. Panchanathan and M. Goldberg. Adaptive Algorithm for Image Coding Using Vector Quantization. *Signal Processing: Image Communication*, 4:81–92, 1991.

[11] D. Paul. A 500-800 bps Adaptive Vector Quantization Vocoder Using a Perceptually Motivated Distortion Measure. In *Conference Record, IEEE Globecom*, pages pp. 1079–1082. IEEE, 1982.

[12] Y. Yamada, K. Fujita, and S. Tazaki. Vector Quantization of Video Signals. In *Proceedings Annual Conference of IECE.* IECE, 1980.

COMPRESSION OF HDTV SIGNALS FOR LOW BIT-RATE TRANSMISSION USING MOTION COMPENSATED SUBBAND TRANSFORM CODING AND A SELF-ORGANIZATION NEURAL NETWORK

R. Bhaskaran & S. C. Kwatra
Dept. of Electrical Engineering, The University of Toledo
2801, W. Bancroft street, Toledo, Ohio 43606.

ABSTRACT

The quality of visual communications has greatly improved with the introduction of HDTV, because of its high quality and very high picture resolution. Due to the inherent advantages of digital communications, and the global trend towards it, it is desirable to develop a cost effective digital codec for HDTV signals. One of the criteria in the transmission of digital signals via satellites is the transmission bandwidth which dictates the transmission costs. Apart from development of good compression schemes, due consideration should also be given to the ease of hardware implementation, which is crucial in deciding factors like processing delay and the level of encoder/decoder complexity. With the above mentioned factors in mind a cost-effective HDTV codec is proposed in this paper.

Few US organizations have addressed the problem of HDTV distribution via communication satellites. Majority of the efforts in the development of an HDTV codec are aimed at 100 to 140 Mbits/sec data rate for the purpose of BISDN [1] - [3]. To facilitate cost effective satellite transmission, the DS3 rate of 45 Mbits/sec, will be desirable. The purpose of this research is to compress the HDTV signals to around 20 Mbits/sec so that 2 HDTV channels can be transmitted through the DS3 rate channel. To achieve this degree of compression a new scheme is proposed. First subband coding is used to decompose the image into different frequency bands. Next motion compensation is applied to the low band, and the resulting interframe difference is discrete cosine transform (DCT) coded. The high bands are also DCT coded. The DCT coefficients of the difference signal of the low band and the DCT coefficients of the high band are then vector quantized.

1068-0314/94 $3.00

Subband coding has been extensively applied to encode the speech signals and has produced satisfactory results [4,5]. Since perfect reconstruction filters for image coding were not available, the application of subband coding to video compression was delayed. Recently, many researchers have proposed very low reconstruction error analysis/synthesis filters for the uncoded image data [6,7]. They are broadly classified as quadrature mirror filters (QMF) and generalized quadrature mirror filters (GQMF). A class of perfect reconstruction QMFs are short kernel filters (SKF). The QMFs used in the commonly proposed schemes [8] - [11] usually have a large number of coefficients and are computation intensive for implementation. The SKFs have very small number of coefficients and can usually be implemented by simple shift operations [7]. They keep the implementation complexity at a very low level. The class of GQMFs [8] require fewer number of FFT and IFFT operations as compared to the QMFs. This results in a smaller delay which is of great importance in high data rate applications such as HDTV. A study of low complexity GQMF schemes with high quality reconstructed still images in the range 25 - 45 Mbits /sec is reported in [12]. Apart from QMF filters, there has recently been an accruing interest in a class of filters called wavelet filters [13] -[16]. Like the SKFs, these filters too can be designed to have a small number of taps. In this paper two types of perfect reconstruction filters are studied. The first is a seven band decomposition of a 24 tap 4 band GQMF developed by Cox [9]. The second is a seven band decomposition of a biorthogonal wavelet filter presented in [16].

Apart from using efficient analysis/synthesis filters, schemes that reduce the bit rate considerably are required. Motion compensation is a temporal coding scheme that takes advantage of the interframe redundancy to achieve high data compression. Among the various techniques proposed for motion compensation, the block matching method [17] is less computation intensive. In the block matching motion compensated coding technique, the trajectory of moving objects between two successive frames is tracked using blocks of data. The direction as well as the amount of motion vector and the quantized motion differential signal are coded and transmitted. The interframe difference for the low band and the subband coded signal for the high bands are quantized using vector quantization with the self organization neural network.

Digital image coding using vector quantization (VQ) based techniques provide low bit rates and high quality coded images, at the expense of intensive computational demands. The computational requirement which is due to the encoding search process, has hindered application of VQ to real time high-quality coding of images. Reduction of the encoding search complexity has been proposed in [18]. However, VQ algorithms using neural networks, that use efficient search techniques have been proposed [19,20]. Recently a new VQ algorithm using self-organization neural networks was proposed [21]. In this research the VQ algorithm is applied to subband transform coded images.

In this paper, two independent studies are performed, one for the GQMF and the other for a biorthogonal wavelet filter. A block diagram of the proposed HDTV codec is shown in Fig. 1. The image is, first, decomposed into seven bands using either of the two filters mentioned. Then the motion compensation technique using a block-matching three stage motion search algorithm [17] is applied on the low band (or base band) which contains highly correlated information. The interframe difference signal is then DCT coded using 4 x 4 subblocks. The DC coefficient is transmitted using an 8 bit uniform quantizer. The rest of the 15 ac coefficients are vector quantized. The 15 ac coefficients are first divided into 8 classes depending on their energies (See Table I). To identify which of the 8 classes the 15 ac coefficients belong to, they are fed to 8 neurons as shown in Fig 2. Each of the 8 neurons compute the ac energy of the subblock. The output of each of these neurons is fed to 8 hardlimiting neurons. Depending on the ac energy of the subblock, one of the hardlimiting neurons will have an output of logic '1', while all other hardlimiting neurons will have an output of logic '0'. Thus only one of the 8 frequency-sensitive self-organization (FSO) neural networks shown in Fig. 2 are activated. The FSO neural network architecture is given in [21]. Only that FSO neural network which is activated by one of the hardlimiting neurons will be active in VQ of the ac coefficients. Each FSO neural network has 32 code vectors. Therefore to transmit a 4 x 4 subblock for the low band 8 bits are needed for the dc coefficient, 3 bits to select the FSO neural network and 5 bits to transmit the code vector. This makes a total of 16 bits per 4 x 4 subblock, not including the bits required to transmit the motion vector.

The high bands are intraframe DCT (4 x 4 block size) encoded. Since the high bands have a much lesser variance than the low band, each band has only one set of code vectors. The number of code vectors to be used depends on the quality of the image required. By statistical tests, the number of code vectors required for each band were precalculated. The number of code vectors for each band for GQMF and wavelet filters are given in Tables II and III respectively. The information regarding the quantized code vectors is transmitted using a Huffman code. This entropy coding assures that less bits are allocated to code vectors that have a higher probability of occurrence.

The test data was studied and it was determined that for 20 Mbits/ sec encoded rate, the luminance component will have to be encoded at around 0.387 bits/pixel. It is assumed that the color difference components U and V can be encoded using the same algorithm as used for encoding the luminance (Y) component. Computer simulations are carried out using HDTV signals. Apart from objective evauluations of reconstructed images with the computations of signal-to-noise ratios (SNR), subjective evaluations of the reconstructed images are also done by visually comparing them with their respective original (uncompressed) images. Simulation results show that the proposed scheme has the capacity to reduce the bit rate to about 0.35 bpp with a medium complexity compared to other familiar QMF schemes [9] - [11] while retaining very good picture quality. The algorithm is designed based on three HDTV test sequences SEQ10Y, FRAME51 and MIT. To examine its performance, the algorithm is tested on two HDTV test sequences, namely the MIT sequence and the KIEL HARBOR sequence. The simulation results presented here are for these two sequences.

The results for the GQMF filters are as follows. For the MIT sequence, the interframe coding algorithm developed reconstructs the low band with about 47 dB SNR and at about 1.2 bpp. The simulation results (Table IV) show that the scheme renders very good quality images with an average bit rate around 0.3298 bpp at an average SNR of about 39.42 dB. The interframe coding algorithm reconstructs the low band of the KIEL HARBOR image sequence with about 46 dB SNR at a bit rate of 1.1 bpp. The simulation results given in Table V for the KIEL HARBOR sequence also show that it can be reconstructed with an average bit rate around 0.3277 bpp at an average SNR of about 39.51 dB.

The results for the biorthogonal wavelet filters are as follows. For the MIT sequence, the interframe coding algorithm developed reconstructs the low band with about 47 dB SNR and at about 1.2 bpp. The simulation results (Table VI) show that the scheme renders very good quality images with an average bit rate around 0.3598 bpp at an average SNR of about 38.75 dB. The interframe coding algorithm reconstructs the low band of the KIEL HARBOR image sequence with about 46 dB SNR at a bit rate of 1.1 bpp. The simulation results from Table VII show that very good quality images can be reconstructed with an average bit rate around 0.3544bpp at an average SNR of about 39.33 dB.

The results show that the performance of the GQMF filters and the biorthogonal wavelet filters is close. The GQMFs have filter lengths of 24, and the biorthogonal wavelet filters have lengths of 9 and 7. But the GQMF filters need only 16 FFT operations for a 7 band image decomposition and reconstruction, while the wavelet filters require 24 FFT operations for the same procedure. The wavelet filters are easier to design than the GQMFs, since no computer program is required to optimize filter coefficients as is done in the GQMF case. These tradeoffs give an idea about which filter should be used depending on the type of implementation needed. If lower number of taps are needed, the wavelet filter should be considered. On the other hand if the number of FFT operations required is the criterion, then the GQMF is a better choice.

To effectively transmit the HDTV signal via a satellite, an error-correcting coding scheme (ECCS) is employed to combat channel errors. For an ECCS, a fixed code, with a certain code rate and error correction capability matched to the protection requirement of all the data to be transmitted, and adapted to the average or worst channel conditions is desired [22]. The compression scheme proposed in this paper has the capability of compressing the HDTV signals to 20 Mb/sec or less. If it is desired to transmit two HDTV signals via the DS3 rate 45 Mb/sec channel, then 5 MBits out of 45 Mbits remain, that can be effectively employed for error correction coding purposes. Therefore a rate 8/9 ECCS is required.

The complexity of the desired rate 8/9 ECCS should be kept minimal. This can be achieved by using punctured convolutional codes. The simplicity of punctured codes originates from the fact that high rate codes can be obtained by puncturing a lower rate code [23]. Thus all encoding and decoding operations are performed on the lower rate code, which reduces the complexity. The performance of these codes is close to that of the best known general convolutional codes of the respective rates. Further a rate-compatibility restriction on the punctured tables ensures that all code bits of high rate codes are used by the lower rate code. These codes are termed rate-compatible punctured convolutional codes (RCPC). Simulation results from [23] indicate that for a rate 8/9 RCPC code, a BER of 10^{-8} can be achieved with a bit energy to noise ratio (E_b/N_o) of less than 8 dB for Gaussian channels. This means that for the proposed codec an average of 0.23 errors per frame (less than one error for 4 frames) will occur, which is acceptable for good quality images. This justifies the choice of the rate 8/9 RCPC code as an error control coding scheme for Gaussian channels.

REFERENCES

1. P. J. Tourtier, Thomson-CSF/LER "A Compatible Approach on Digital HDTV Coding Based on Subband Techniques," Proc. of the Third Int'l Workshop on HDTV, Torino, Italy, Aug. 1989.
2. Y. Yashima, and K. Sawada, NTT, "100 Mb/s HDTV Transmission by a High Efficiency Codec," Proc. of the Third Int'l Workshop on HDTV, Torino, Italy, Aug. 1989.
3. P. Elmer, BTRL, UK, "The Design of High Bit Rate HDTV Codec," Proc. of the Third Int'l Workshop on HDTV, Torino, Italy, Aug. 1989.
4. R. E. Crochiere, S. A. Webber and J. L. Flanagan, "Digital Coding of Speech in Subbands," Bell Systems Technical Journal, vol. 55, pp. 1069-1085, Oct. 1976.
5. R. E. Crochiere, R. V. Cox and J. D. Johnston, "Real Time Speech Coding," IEEE Transactions on Communications, vol. 30, pp. 621-634, Apr. 1982.
6. J. D. Johnston, "A Filter Family Designed for Use in Quadrature Mirror Filter Banks," Proc. of ICASSP, Denver, CO, pp. 291-294, April 1980.
7. Didier Le Gall and Ali Tabatabai, "Sub-band Coding of Digital Images Using Symmetric Short Kernel Filters and Arithmetic Coding Techniques," Proc. of ICASSP, New York, NY, pp. 761-764, April 1988.

8. Richard V. Cox, "The Design of Uniformly and Nonuniformly Spaced Pseudoquadrature Mirror Filters," IEEE Trans. on ASSP, vol. ASSP-34, no. 5, pp. 1090-1096, Oct. 1986.
9. H. Gharavi and Ali Tabatabai, "Sub-band Coding of Digital Images Using Two-Dimensional Quadrature Mirror Filtering," SPIE Visual Communications and Image Processing, vol. 707, Cambridge, MA, pp. 51-61, Sept. 1986.
10. G. Karlsson and M. Vetterli, "Sub-band Coding of Video for Packet Networks," Optical Engineering, vol. 27, pp. 574-586, July 1988.
11. Mark J. T. Smith and Steven L. Eddins, "Sub-band Coding of Images with Octave Band Tree Structures," Proc. of ICASSP, Dallas, TX, pp. 1382-1385, April 6-9 1987.
12. N. Coppisetti, S. C. Kwatra and Awad Al Asmari, "Low Complexity Subband Encoding for HDTV Images," Proc. of Data Compression Conference, Snow Bird, UT, pp. 415, March 22-26, 1992.
13. I. Daubechies, "Orthonormal bases of compactly supported wavelets II. Variations on a theme," AT & T Bell Lab., tech. Rep. TM 11217-89111617, 1990.
14. S. G. Mallat,"A Theory for Multiresolution Signal Decomposition: The Wavelet Representation," IEEE Transactions on Pattern Analysis and Machine Intelligence, vol. 11, No. 7. pp. 674-693, July 1989.
15. M. Vitterli and C. Herley,"Wavelets and Filter Banks: Theory and Design", IEEE Transactions on Signal Processing, vol. 40, No. 9, pp. 2207-2232, Sept. 1992.
16. M. Antonini, M. Barlaud, Pierre Mathieu and I. Daubechies, "Image Coding Using Wavelet Transform", IEEE Transactions on Image Processing, vol. 1, No. 2, April 1992.
17. S. C. Kwatra, Chow-Ming Lin and Wayne A. Whyte, "An Adaptive Algorithm for Motion Compensated Color Image Coding," IEEE Transactions on Communications, vol. COM-35, no. 7, pp. 747-754, July 1987.
18. K. Dezhgosha, M. M. Jamali and S. C. Kwatra,"A VLSI Architecture for Real-Time Image Coding Using a Vector Quantization Based Algorithm", IEEE Transactions on Signal Processing, vol. 40, No. 1, pp. 181-189, Jan. 1992.

19. S. C. Ahalt, A. K. Krishnamurthy, P. Chen and D. Melton,"Competitive Learning Algorithm for Vector Quantization," Neural Networks, vol. 3, pp. 277-290, 1990.
20. N. M. Nasrabadi and Y. Feng,"Vector Quantization of Images Based upon the Kohonen Self-Organizing Feature Maps," in Proc. Int. Joint Conf. Neural Networks, San Diego, CA, vol. I, pp. 101-108, June 1988.
21. W. Fang, B. J. Sheu, O. T. C. Chen and Joongho Choi,"A VLSI Neural Processor for Image Data Compression Using Self-Organization Networks", IEEE Transactions on Neural Networks, Vol. 3, No. 3,pp. 506-517, May 1992.
22. G. C. Clark and J. B. Cain,"Error-Correction Coding for Digital Communications", New York: Plenum, 1981.
23. J. Hagenauer,"Rate-Compatible Punctured Convolutional Codes (RCPC) and their Applications", IEEE Transactions on Communications, vol. 36, no. 4, April 1988.

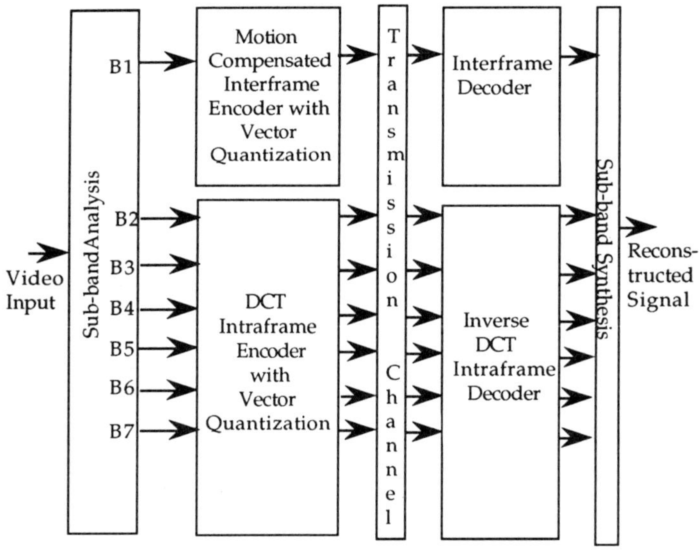

Figure 1. System Block Diagram.

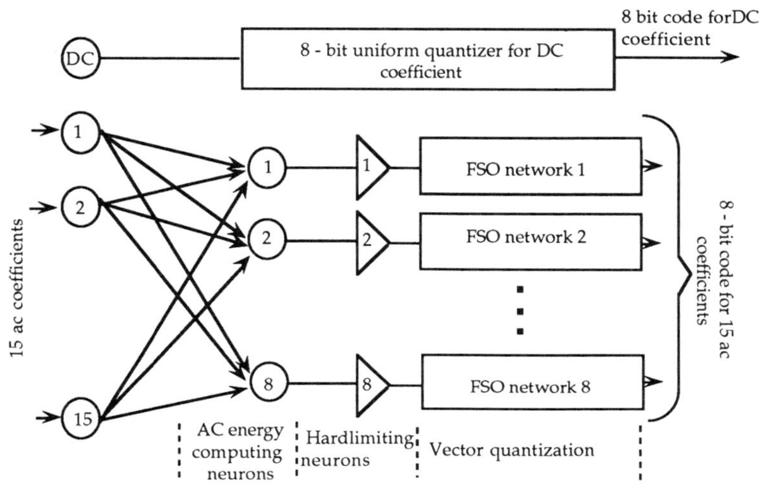

Figure 2. Architecture of the system required to quantize and code the low band.

TABLE I: Range of AC energies for the 8 different classes for the low band.

Class 1	Class 2	Class 3	Class 4	Class 5	Class 6	Class 7	Class 8
0-32	32-96	96-160	160-224	224-320	320-400	400-600	>600

TABLE II : Number of code vectors per band for vector quantization (4 band GQMF filter).

Band	B2	B3	B4	B5	B6	B7	Total
no: of vectors	30	37	36	27	10	6	146

TABLE III : Number of code vectors per band for vector quantization (biorthogonal wavelet filter).

Band	B2	B3	B4	B5	B6	B7	Total
no: of vectors	18	43	24	42	28	9	164

TABLE IV : Simulation results for the 4 band GQMF (MIT sequence)

Frame	bpp	MSE	SNR
MIT01	0.3306	7.67	39.28
MIT02	0.3290	7.31	39.48
MIT03	0.3300	7.25	39.52
Average	0.3298	7.41	39.42

TABLE V : Simulation results for the 4 band GQMF (KIEL HARBOR sequence)

Frame	bpp	MSE	SNR
KIEL01	0.3290	7.34	39.47
KIEL02	0.3280	7.21	39.54
KIEL03	0.3261	7.23	39.53
Average	0,3277	7.26	39.51

TABLE VI : Simulation results for the biorthogonal wavelet filter (MIT sequence)

Frame	bpp	MSE	SNR
MIT01	0.3601	8.884	38.64
MIT02	0.3588	8.629	38.77
MIT03	0.3605	8.456	38.85
Average	0.3598	8.656	38.75

TABLE VII : Simulation results for the biorthogonal wavelet filter (KIEL HARBOR sequence)

Frame	bpp	MSE	SNR
KIEL01	0.3539	7.56	39.34
KIEL02	0.3544	7.60	39.32
KIEL03	0.3538	7.55	39.34
Average	0.3544	7.57	39.33

Differential Vector Quantization of Real-Time Video

James E. Fowler   Stanley C. Ahalt
Department of Electrical Engineering
The Ohio State University
Columbus, Ohio 43210

Abstract

This paper describes hardware that has been built to compress video in real time using full-search vector quantization (VQ). This architecture implements a differential-vector-quantization (DVQ) algorithm and features a special-purpose digital associative memory, the VAMPIRE chip, which has been fabricated in 2μm CMOS. We describe the DVQ algorithm, its adaptations for sampled NTSC composite-color video, and details of its hardware implementation. We conclude by presenting images drawn from real-time operation of the DVQ hardware.

Introduction

Vector quantization has become well-known and widely studied since Shannon first established the merits of quantizing vectors rather than scalars [1]. Since that time, vector quantization (VQ) has been shown to be useful in the realm of data compression, particularly attracting attention for its efficient compression of digitized speech and image data. Meanwhile, as digital data has become more prevalent, the demand for real-time image-coding hardware has increased dramatically. The design of real-time vector quantizers for image coding has been particularly difficult due to the inherent computational complexity of VQ encoders and the extremely fast speeds demanded by real-time video applications. While much of the research effort directed at image compression via VQ has not been directly applicable to real-time hardware coding architectures, some recent proposals have been put forward [2, 3, 4, 5]. Unfortunately, the actual performance of VQ of real video signals in real time has not been sufficiently demonstrated. The work presented here represents a real-time demonstration of the merits of VQ.

In this paper, we begin with a review of previously proposed hardware VQ architectures. Next, we give a description of an algorithm for video compression called differential vector quantization (DVQ), a combination of differential-pulse-code modulation (DPCM) and full-search VQ. We present an architecture that, having been constructed in hardware, implements this algorithm in real time. This architecture is centered around a special-purpose digital associative memory, the VAMPIRE chip, which has been fabricated with a 2μm CMOS n-well process and is described briefly here. We conclude with examples drawn from the actual operation of the hardware.[1]

[1]The results presented here are stills taken from the real-time, processed video stream. We have, however, produced a video tape that demonstrates the system's real-time behavior.

1068-0314/94 $3.00

Vector Quantization

Despite the promising performance of VQ in theory, practical hardware VQ architectures for image coding have been somewhat scarce in the literature. The first hardware VQ encoders were designed for speech; however, real-time video encoding requires significantly faster processing. Rather than attempt full-search VQ at these rates, several proposed architectures for real-time video VQ are based on suboptimal techniques. These suboptimal alternatives typically restrict the codeword search to a subset of the codebook or split the quantization into separate steps that each use smaller codebooks. For example, Dezhgosha et al. [2] propose an architecture based on mean/residual VQ and Ramamoorthy et al. [6] propose using multi-stage VQ.

Recent advances in VLSI technology have made full-search VQ at video rates possible. For example, Panchanthan and Goldberg [3] propose an architecture based on an exact-match content-addressable memory (CAM). More recently, analog VQ encoding chips have been fabricated by Fang et al. [4] and Tuttle et al. [5]. However, none of the above have actually demonstrated performance of VQ on real-time video. A number of papers (e.g. [2], [6], and [3]) have presented *proposals* for hardware architectures, but few have actually fabricated their designs. The analog designs of [4] and [5] suffer from limited precision and conclusive operational behavior for real-time video has not been proven for either.

Below, we present an algorithm for VQ of real-time sampled NTSC video. The architecture which implements the algorithm is described and results which were obtained from real-time operation of the hardware are given. The heart of the design features a digital associative memory, the VAMPIRE chip, which is described below with the hardware implementation of the DVQ algorithm.

Algorithm Description

Differential vector quantization (DVQ) combines the methods of VQ and DPCM. DVQ replaces the scalar quantizer in the DPCM framework with a vector quantizer, and consequently has many of the compression advantages of both VQ and DPCM. DVQ has been presented previously in [7], where it was called vector DPCM, and in [8], where it was called predictive VQ (PVQ). One of the first applications of prediction to VQ for image coding was [9], which also featured a delayed-decision encoding tree. Our DVQ algorithm has been explored in detail previously [10, 11], so only a brief overview is given here.

Fig. 1 shows the general block diagram of our DVQ algorithm. In the encoding process, the predictor uses previously reconstructed tiles to predict the pixel values of the current tile. This predicted tile, PV, is subtracted pixel by pixel from the actual tile, PIX. The resulting difference tile, $DIFF$, is vector-quantized and the index, $INDEX$, is broadcast via the transmission channel to the decoder. The encoder inverse vector-quantizes $INDEX$, producing a reconstructed tile, $\widehat{PIX}$, to be used in later predictions. Note that, since the vector quantizer processes difference tiles, the VQ codebook must be appropriately derived from "difference images."

DVQ has several advantages over both scalar DPCM and VQ. Primarily, the quantization of vectors yields better compression performance than that of scalars.

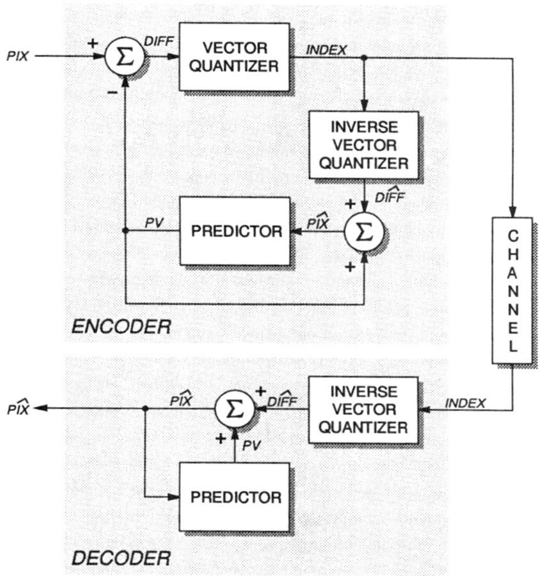

Figure 1: Block diagram of DVQ algorithm

Additionally, since the VQ is performed on difference values rather than on the image itself, the resulting image is less "blocky" [7]. Finally, the codebooks for DVQ tend to be more robust and more representative of many images than codebooks designed for VQ because the difference tiles in a DVQ codebook are more generic than the image tiles in a VQ codebook [7].

There are many decisions to be considered in the design of a DVQ algorithm, such as tile size, distortion criterion, and method of prediction. These issues have been discussed in previous publications and so are omitted here. For more detail, refer to [10, 11].

The hardware implementation of our DVQ algorithm processes NTSC composite-color video signals. Generally, color video is comprised of three signals: one luminance signal and two separate color signals. In composite-color video, the two color signals are combined in quadrature, modulated by a specially chosen frequency called the color subcarrier, and added to the luminance signal. Finally, horizontal and vertical synchronization pulses are included to produce the baseband composite-color video signal.

In typical discussions of image compression, compression is performed on red-green-blue pixel arrays (ppm-format images), and, consequently, nearest-neighbor pixels can be used in prediction. In contrast, the hardware implementation of our DVQ algorithm processes sampled NTSC composite-color video signals. To correctly

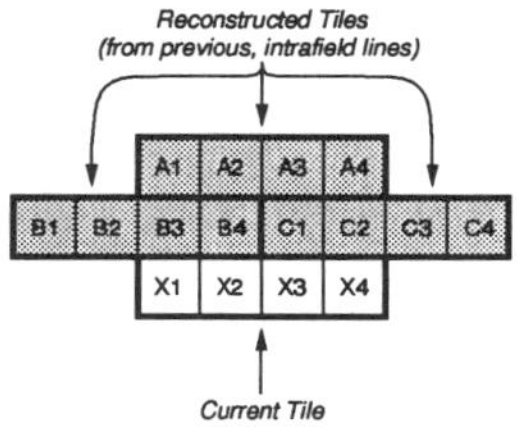

Prediction: $\tilde{X}_i = ((B_i + C_i)/2 + A_i)/2$

(a)

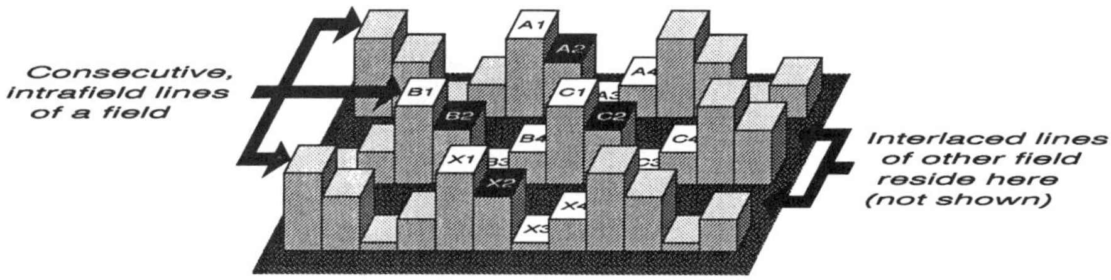

(b)

Figure 2: Prediction of sampled NTSC composite-color video. (a) Prediction from reconstructed tiles of previous, intrafield lines. (b) Phase considerations.

perform prediction on sampled composite-color video, one must consider the phasing of the color subcarrier.

Fig. 2 illustrates the prediction scheme of our DVQ algorithm and how it accounts for the phase of the color subcarrier. Note that only those samples that have the same phase as the current pixel may be used in prediction. Thus, our prediction scheme accounts for the phasing of the color information in the video signal at the expense of using pixels which are farther away from the current pixel than the nearest neighbors. Fig. 2a shows the prediction used in the hardware implementation of our DVQ algorithm in relation to the tiling of the pixels by the vector quantizer. The NTSC video signal is sampled at four times the color-subcarrier frequency (14.31818MHz). The vectors for VQ are tiles of 4×1 samples. Note that, as shown in Fig. 2b, consecutive intrafield lines of NTSC video have a phase difference of 180°.

The VAMPIRE Chip

The Vector-quantizing Associative Memory Processor Implementing Real-time Encoding (VAMPIRE) is a special-purpose, digital associative memory designed for video-rate vector quantization. The details of the design and operation of this chip are found elsewhere [12], so only a brief overview is given here. Fig. 3 shows the general structure of the VAMPIRE chip.

The VAMPIRE chip is designed to quantize vectors at video rates. The input to the chip is 32 bits representing a 4-dimensional vector with each vector component having 8 bits of resolution. Since these vectors are composed of four video samples, the designed throughput is that of the NTSC colorburst (3.579545MHz, or one vector every 280ns). Each VAMPIRE chip holds 32 codewords. The chips can be operated alone (for codebooks of 32 or less codewords) or can be linked together to accommodate codebooks of greater than 32 codewords.

The VAMPIRE chip calculates the l_1 metric (also known as absolute distance or city-block distance) between the input vector and each of the 32 codewords stored in its memory. These distortion calculations are done digitally and in parallel by 256 computation cells (8 computation cells for each of the 32 codewords, see Fig. 3). A priority encoder selects the codeword with the lowest distortion and places the address on the output bus. Additionally, the distortion is placed on a wired-NOR compare bus. This bus is used to compare each chip's minimum internal distortion to the overall minimum distance as broadcast among chips when several chips are connected together for codebooks of greater than 32 codewords. Each chip "disqualifies" itself if it doesn't hold the winning codeword; the address of the winning codeword is then placed on the address bus.

System Details

Fig. 4 shows the organization of the hardware constructed to implement our DVQ video-compression algorithm. The system is composed of the following logical units: controller and interface; A/D converter and frame buffer; encoder; and decoder. Discussion of these units follows. To meet the speed requirements of real-time operation, FAST Advanced Schottky TTL logic was used in most of the units.

The controller routes the flow of data between the units of the system. In addition, it drives a SCSI-bus interface which allows communication with a PC. The SCSI bus is used to transfer commands to the system and also to upload or download single frames of video.

The A/D converter samples the incoming video at four times the color-subcarrier frequency (14.31818MHz). In addition to the active-video portion of the signal, all horizontal and vertical synchronization pulses are sampled and processed. Thus, one frame of sampled video consists of 910×526 samples.

The frame buffer consists of a 512×8 dynamic RAM and associated addressing and synchronization circuitry. The frame buffer is used to store a frame of video from the A/D converter for output through the SCSI bus. Additionally, it can receive a frame from the SCSI bus and output it repeatedly to the D/A converter or to the encoder. The synchronization circuitry analyses the incoming video and provides the frame buffer with information indicating the starting and stopping points of a frame.

Fig. 5 shows a block diagram of the architecture of the encoder. The encoder consists of the following units: predictor, vector quantizer, and inverse vector quantizer. The encoder runs in real-time without buffering, processing input pixel samples and outputting reconstructed pixels at the sample rate (14.31818MHz).

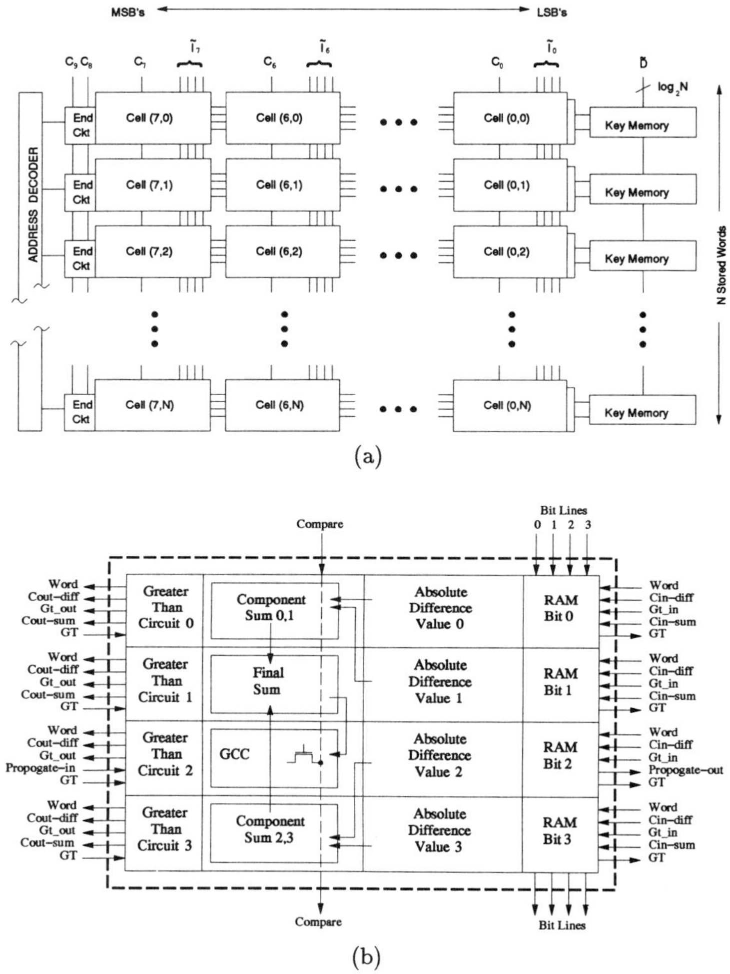

Figure 3: General structure of the VAMPIRE chip. (a) Detailed floorplan. (b) Structure of a single computation cell.

The predictor calculates predicted values at the sample rate. At this rate, the predictor has 69ns to generate each predicted value. The prediction process involves extracting three 8-bit reconstructed pixel values from FIFO memory and performing two 8-bit additions and two divisions-by-2. High-speed, CMOS FIFOs (size $= 2048 \times 9$, access time = 10ns) are used. Each 8-bit addition is accomplished with two 74F283

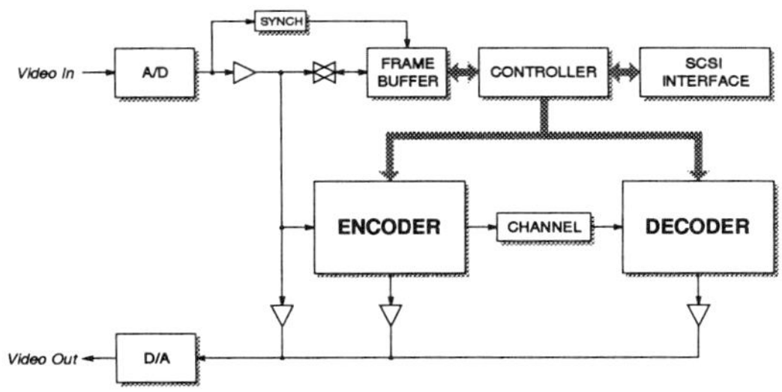

Figure 4: Block diagram of the DVQ system

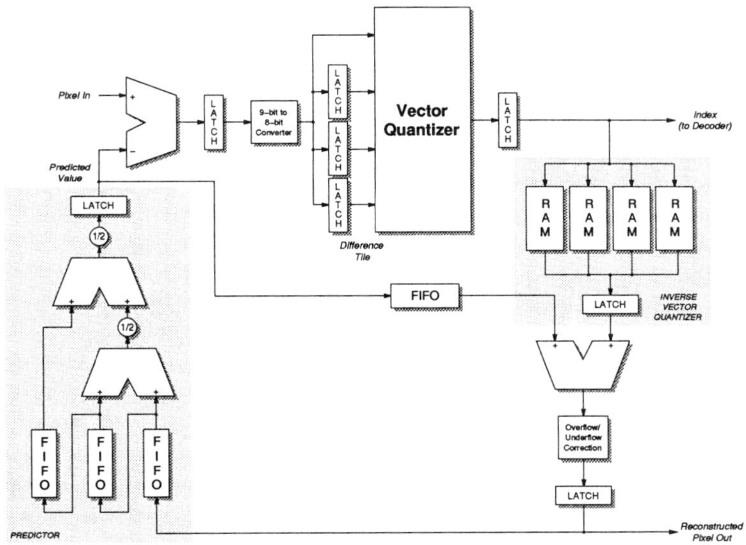

Figure 5: Encoder block diagram

4-bit adders. The divisions result from ignoring the least-significant bit.

The inverse vector quantizer is composed of 4 dynamic RAMs, one for each of the four vector components. The VQ codebook is stored in both the vector quantizer and the inverse vector quantizer (This storage is done via the SCSI bus by circuitry not shown in Fig. 5). The inverse vector quantizer performs a table lookup into the codebook given the index value generated by the vector quantizer.

As seen in Fig. 1, the architecture of the decoder is simply a replication of a subset of the encoder architecture. In the absence of channel errors, the output of the decoder is the same as the reconstructed values found within the encoder. Thus, for proof of principle, only the encoder was constructed.

Table 1: Summary of VAMPIRE Chip Characteristics

Die size	4.6×6.8mm
Technology	2μm CMOS n-well
Vector Rate	3.57×10^6 vectors/sec
Encoding delay*	approx. 1μs
Codebook size	32 codewords on one chip; expandable to 256 with 8 chips
Vector dimension	Four 8-bit components
Power supply	5V

*Encoding delay is for the VAMPIRE chip operating in the DVQ architecture

Results

Fig. 6 presents the results obtained during real-time operation of our hardware DVQ implementation on NTSC video. Fig. 6(a) shows one frame from the original video sequence. Fig. 6(b) shows that same frame from the output video sequence, which has been compressed and reconstructed by the DVQ hardware using 32 codewords (a compression ratio of 6.4:1). Some "blocky" effects on the edges, along with some color distortion, are visible.

The output video represented here is not quite of broadcast quality. However, these experimental results are confined to vector quantization using only 32 codewords. Computer simulations of the algorithm at 256 codewords have indicated that significantly better quality can be obtained at this lower compression.

Conclusions and Future Work

In this paper, we have described our DVQ algorithm, presented a hardware architecture implementing it, and demonstrated real-time operation of this hardware on NTSC video. The heart of this compression system is the VAMPIRE chip, whose characteristics are summarized in Table 1. Digital associative memories, such as the VAMPIRE chip, will certainly play a role in bringing VQ to prominence in practical, real-time applications. It should be noted that the vector dimension provided by the VAMPIRE chip, 4 components, may be too small for some applications. Proposals have been made for modifications to the VAMPIRE design to expand this maximum number of vector components [12].

The main goal of this work has been to demonstrate VQ in real time on real video, not to provide a design immediately applicable to commercial broadcasting. Since, in this implementation, we were limited to 32 codewords, the quality we obtained, although reasonable and as expected from computer simulations, was not sufficient for broadcast applications. The first improvement we plan to make to our design is to increase the codeword capacity to 256 codewords, which will done when new, updated VAMPIRE chips complete fabrication. There are several additional modifications that would improve the picture quality and compression performance. First, compression should be performed on only the active-video portion of the signal. To this end, a digital television chip set, such as the one made by Philips, could be used to strip out

(a)

(b)

Figure 6: Output of the DVQ hardware on real-time video. (a) Original video frame. (b) Frame from output video compressed using VQ with 32 codewords.

the sync information. Additionally, these digital TV chips could also demodulate the color signals from the luminance. These color signals could be processed separately, yielding better edge and color fidelity. And finally, the predictor should incorporate temporal information in the form of motion estimation. These ideas are the topics of further research which we hope will extend the utility of our architecture.

Acknowledgements

The VAMPIRE chip was designed by Ken Adkins. We thank him for the use of Fig. 3.

References

[1] C. E. Shannon, "A mathematical theory of communication," in *Key Papers in The Development of Information Theory* (D. Slepian, ed.), pp. 5–18, New York: IEEE Press, 1948.

[2] K. Dezhgosha, M. M. Jamali, and S. C. Kwatra, "A VLSI Architecture for Real-Time Image Coding Using a Vector Quantization Based Algorithm," *IEEE Transactions on Signal Processing*, vol. 40, pp. 181–189, January 1992.

[3] S. Panchanathan and M. Goldberg, "A content-addressable memory architecture for image coding using vector quantization," *IEEE Transactions on Signal Processing*, vol. 39, pp. 2066–2078, September 1991.

[4] W.-C. Fang, B. J. Sheu, O. T.-C. Chen, and J. Choi, "A VLSI Neural Processor for Image Data Compression Using Self-Organization Networks," *IEEE Transactions on Neural Networks*, vol. 3, pp. 506–518, May 1992.

[5] G. T. Tuttle, S. Fallahi, and A. A. Abidi, "A Low-Power Analog CMOS Vector Quantizer," in *Proceedings of the IEEE Data Compression Conference* (J. A. Storer and M. Cohn, eds.), (Snowbird, UT), pp. 410–419, IEEE Computer Society Press, 1993.

[6] P. A. Ramamoorthy, B. Potu, and T. Tran, "Bit-Serial VLSI Implementation of Vector Quantizer for Real-Time Image Coding," *IEEE Transactions on Circuits and Systems*, vol. 36, pp. 1281–1290, October 1989.

[7] C. W. Rutledge, "Vector DPCM: Vector Predictive Coding of Color Images," in *Proceedings of the IEEE Global Telecommunications Conference*, pp. 1158–1164, September 1986.

[8] A. Gersho and R. M. Gray, *Vector Quantization and Signal Compression.* Kluwer international series in engineering and computer science, Norwell, MA: Kluwer Academic Publishers, 1992.

[9] H.-M. Hang and J. W. Woods, "Predictive Vector Quantization of Images," *IEEE Transactions on Communications*, vol. COM-33, pp. 1208–1219, November 1985.

[10] J. E. Fowler, M. R. Carbonara, and S. C. Ahalt, "Image Coding Using Differential Vector Quantization," *IEEE Transactions on Circuits and Systems for Video Technology*, vol. 3, pp. 350–367, October 1993.

[11] J. E. Fowler and S. C. Ahalt, "Robust, Variable Bit-rate Coding Using Entropy-biased Codebooks," in *Proceedings of the IEEE Data Compression Conference* (J. A. Storer and M. Cohn, eds.), (Snowbird, UT), pp. 361–370, IEEE Computer Society Press, 1993.

[12] K. C. Adkins, *The VAMPIRE Chip: A Vector-quantizer Associative Memory Processor Implementing Real-time Encoding.* PhD thesis, The Ohio State University, 1993.

The MVP: A Highly-Integrated Video Compression Chip

Robert J. Gove

Texas Instuments, Inc.
Dallas, Texas 75265

ABSTRACT

We introduce a new highly-integrated processing chip for performing a variety of functions, however this chip is particularly well suited for video compression algorithms. Applications include multimedia PCs, virtual reality 3D graphics, full-duplex videoconferencing, HDTV, and color hardcopy. We have architected the Multimedia Video Processor, or MVP, to provide a yet unattainable level of *performance* from a single chip, although with the *programmability* typically found in today's general-purpose computers. While advanced semiconductor design and process techniques have been used for its design, the *key* to the advantage of this component lies in optimization of the architecture for real-time video and graphics processing. This paper will analyze video compression application requirements, describe the MVP architecture, and pose its potential as a very capable solution for a wide range of markets.

INTRODUCTION

The computer and consumer video industries are pursuing varied paths to offer cost-effective computing products which provide new forms of information and entertainment. Products are emerging from cable TV delivery of interactive digital movies to digital mobile offices. Digital compression and video processing at a reasonable cost are spurring this revolution. While algorithm developments have been important, most of the enabling advances lie in the availability of high-density memory and high-performance processing ICs. With the pending general availability of the Multimedia Video Processor, or MVP, in 1994, a yet unattained level of digital signal processing performance will be available and with all the flexibility of present day programmable computers. Standard-based video-conferencing and playback of compressed digital video and audio (using Px64, JPEG or MPEG "multi-standard" codecs systems) with a single MVP processor will be possible, as well as codecs with yet-to-be-defined algorithms like model-based compression. However, not only will the MVP support compression, it will also handle processing of high-resolution video, full-motion video processing from sources like camcorders, digital audio processing, hardcopy raster image processing, and 3D graphics, and all under software control and generation. From this wide range of functions, we calculated that several billion operations per second are required to provide video-based applications on the desktop. Current and soon to appear desktop host processors like X86, Pentium, Alpha, and MIPS do not have the computational power to meet these demands.

KEYS TO THE MVP ARCHITECTURE

The MVP's unique architecture and computational power enables users to integrate these varied functions on a single processing component. The keys to obtaining both exceptional processing speeds and fully-programmable features with the MVP include the use of:

(1) *an efficient parallel processing architecture,*
(2) *fast pixel processing tuned to image, video, and graphics processing,*
(3) *intelligent control of image data flow throughout the architecture,*
(4) *single-chip integration without slower chip-to-chip communications.*

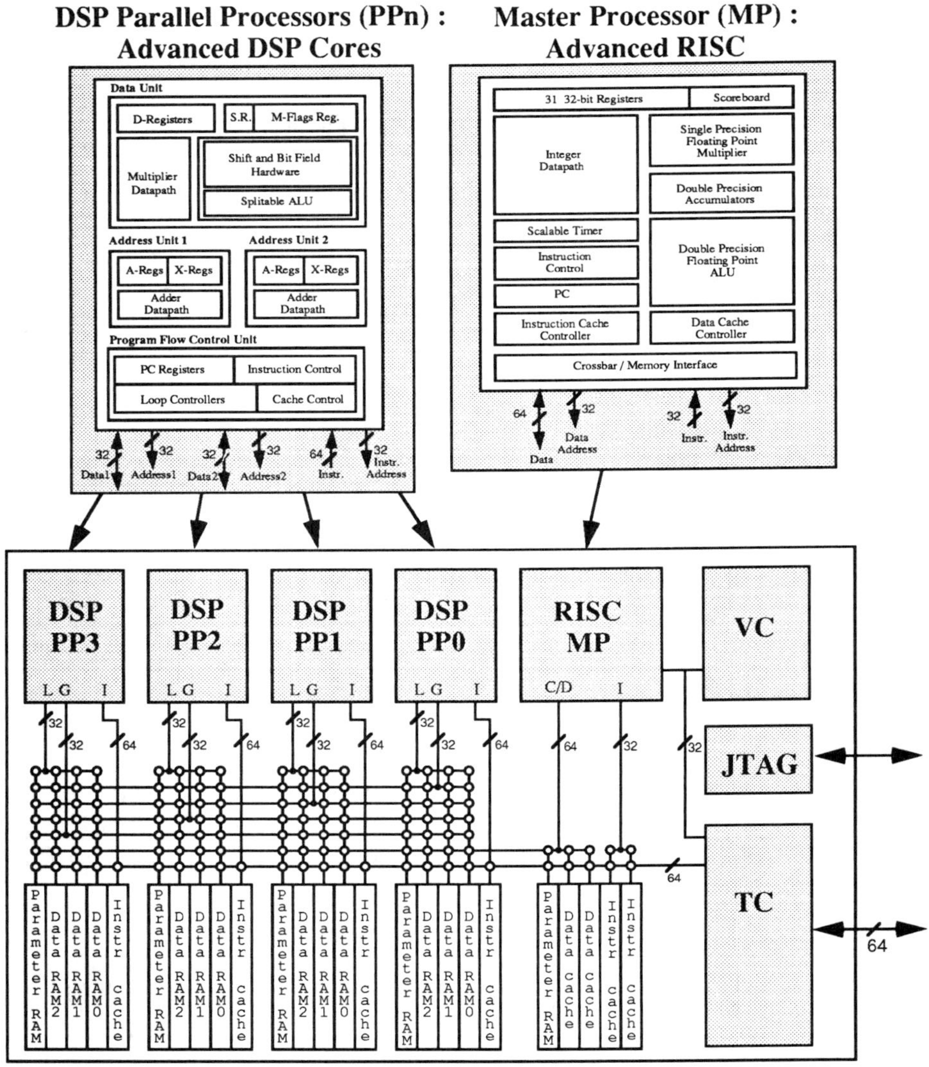

Figure 1: MVP Block Diagram:

(A Single-Chip Parallel Processor)

ALGORITHM-DIRECTED ARCHITECTURE DEFINITION

Processing Requirements

Today's proposed international video compression standards use common frequency domain, quantization, and entropy coding techniques to (de)compress small portions (8x8) of each image. While these functions demand a great deal from the encoder/decoder, many other varied functions remain, each with dynamic requirements which vary based on the type of image compressed as well as the channel rate required to maintain real-time operation. For optimal efficiency a processor must adapt to these dynamic needs. A typical average of the processing demands of the Px64 video-conferencing standard appears in the following table.

RISC vs. MVP-PP Processing Requirements for Px64

Px64 (H.261) FULL-DUPLEX, FULL-CIF, 30Hz Functions	**RISC Execution Speed (average % of time) ***	**MVP Execution Speed (average % of time)**	**Speed-up of MVP-PP vs. RISC Processors**
Motion Estimation - Block Matching (encode)	0.51	0.29	14
Encoding Decisions - (1) Inter w/motion vectors, (2) Inter w/coded diff.,(3) Intra	0.034	0.039	7
Loop Filtering (both)	0.092	0.116	6
Difference image (current - predicted)	0.18	0.013	9
Fast DCT (encode)	0.062	0.077	6
Threshold/Quantization/Zig-Zag Run-length	0.042	0.071	5
Bitstream Encode	0.014	0.045	3
IDCT (both)	0.161**	0.226	6
Reconstruction (both) (predicted + diff. image)	0.052	0.077	5
Bitstream Decode & Dequantization (decode)	0.018	0.045	3
TOTAL CYCLES (MIPS)	**1.00 = 1,193 MIPS**	**1.00 = 155 PP MIPS *** **	**AVERAGE SPEED-UP = 7.7**

* Multiply counted a one instruction even though most RISCs require many cycles.
** If the "Truncated-IDCT" algorithm was used, IDCTs speed-up again (see later).
*** The total is equivalent to 3 MVP-PP processors (see below PP section).
**** Audio standards concurrently execute on the MVP-MP (see below MP section).

As we studied the computational requirements for motion estimation (51%) and DCTs (22%) it became quite apparent that a programmable image processor must excel at these functions. It is important to recognize that what's done poorly in a processor can dominate its performance. Since most architectural improvements would not uniformly accelerate all functions uniformly, we looked for special architectural features for these critical functions, while maintaining enough flexibility to benefit a larger class of algorithms. In final analysis, a much more uniform distribution of computational loading resulted after the changes.

As seen in the table, the programmable image processor must perform many other functions well, including: bit manipulation and table look ups for entropy encoding, and multiply and accumulate for various types of filtering operations. To obtain good image quality at any channel rate and 30 frames per second, the image processor must compute over 1.2 billion operations per second (BOPS).

The addition of audio compression (which requires higher precision integer and possibly floating point algorithms) and network communication, necessary for video conferencing (G.728 or G.711, H.242, H.230, H.221), further increases the scope of computational requirements. Reducing the system cost, we propose to include support in the architecture for the required non-standard functions like color space conversion (YCrCb to RGB), decimation of the source image to CIF resolution and variable scaling of the decompressed sequence. Complete implementation of compression applications such as video-conferencing requires over 2 BOPS of the programmable image processor.

ARCHITECTURE CHOICES

We considered several candidate parallel architectures for implementation of this single-chip video processor [Gove-92, Guttag-92]. An architecture with a mix of dedicated and programmable processors was initially evaluated, then subsequently discounted when no single dominant function was found that was necessary almost all of the time. Besides, we predicted that by the time the chip was completed, that a new *important* algorithm would emerge. From the standpoint of loss of silicon efficiency by dedicated resources to any one function (like a DCT), we felt compelled to seek a general-purpose well-balanced system solution. Several other candidates existed, however the mix of algorithms and practical implementation limitations focused us on SIMD and MIMD architectures. These differ by the autonomy of the processors functions with MIMD -- a desirable feature for any data dependent algorithm operating in parallel.

With MIMD desirable, the choice of a processor and memory interconnection architecture remained. Pipelined, shared bus memory, communication port (mesh/array/hypercube), and crossbar fully-shared memory were considered. Pipeline memory and processors (systolic arrays) are typically used for video, however they're too restrictive in the sense that one must a priori know the size of the memory and dynamics of the algorithm to prevent data contention and processor stalls. With our varied needs, this would lead to inefficiencies. A shared-bus memory structure would also have bottleneck problems with highly variable instruction and data streams and moving of results from one processor to the other. The n-way connected communication port requires a very ordered flow of data, like a systolic or wavefront flow of data, or the application of a pixel per processor (not practical in a single chip). This approach works for large arrays of simple processors which can operate uniformly on images, however we wanted more complex processors which could adapt to varying types of data, from bit graphics to floating-point representations. The crossbar fully-shared memory is ideally suited to these needs, minimizing contention, data movement and providing flexibility for many types of algorithms. In fact, since the crossbar operations at the processor instruction rates, this architecture can functionally emulate the other approaches (pipeline, shared bus...).

We not only wanted to provide this order of magnitude performance increase, but the goal was to apply a *traditional* computer model of programmable processing and a large memory to applications with integrated image, graphics, video and audio processing, or image computing. As shown in Figure #2 titled *"MVP System Architecture"*, replacing the processing and memory pipeline of conventional video systems with the single video processor and large memory system model yields tremendous application flexibility. In effect the system can re-configure itself with software from video conferencing to playing CD movies, just as a PC would re-configure from a spreadsheet to a video game.

Figure 2: The MVP "System" Architecture.

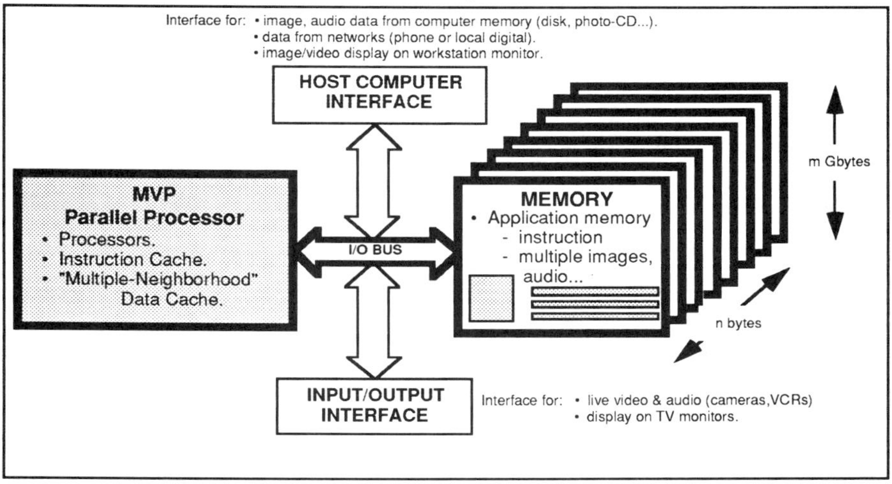

THE MVP ARCHITECTURE

The Multimedia Video Processor, or MVP, represents the next-generation of digital signal processors. The MVP can be technically described as a single-chip crossbar shared memory heterogeneous MIMD multiprocessor. It combines RISC and advanced DSP processing in one parallel architecture with unique features for each. Current RISC processors typically use instruction pipelining, numerous registers and a detached floating point processor. On the other hand, current DSPs are optimized for one dimensional multiply-accumulate functions. Newer DSPs have floating-point capabilities, yet most imaging and video only needs integer operations. DSPs usually have fewer registers than RISC and have direct memory accesses (DMA) with limited capabilities.

The MVP combines the best features of RISC and DSP in parallel and adds other features to offer unprecedented *Power* and *Flexibility*. The heart of an image or video chip is its capability to process 2D signals. The MVP has features for 2D DSP-like processing, including multiply-accumulate operations. The on-chip memory and register characteristics of the MVP were optimized for image computing algorithms, preventing time consuming cache misses or swapping of register contents. Multidimensional external memory access and double buffering minimizes the typical memory bottleneck of current DSP solutions. An internal memory crossbar provides extremely efficient synchronization and communication of multiple processors. A very high-performance RISC processor is integrated on the chip, providing intelligent control of the DSP-like processors. Also integrated into the chip, a new floating-point architecture can act as a co-processor to any of the DSP-like processors or the RISC processor. By analysis of the algorithms, the required mix of integer ops to floating-point ops was somewhere between 8:1 and 4:1 -- a balance which the MVP supports. The entire collection of processors and memory is configured as a MIMD architecture for ease of programming and high performance for all image and video computing applications. This MIMD data and control supports both data dependent algorithms like object feature matching or Huffman coding and also supporting traditional data independent SIMD operations like convolution.

To prevent contention for memory or register access, a very wide instruction set in the DSPs and a large on-chip crossbarred memory is used in the MVP. This flexibility permits the programmer to produce highly-parallel optimized code. A performance penalty may result if only one highly-serial task is performed continuously, however, the very nature of image, video, graphics, and audio processing, with varied concurrent and complex processing, prevents this from occurring. The MVP integrates more functions than ever before into one chip, while avoiding the compromises of other architectures.

Detailed Architecture Description:
Figure #1, titled *"MVP Block Diagram"*, shows the MVP chip architecture. The Master Processor (MP) provides a RISC processor for simple user interface, sequential processing, and orchestration of multiple concurrent tasks operating on the entire MVP. The DSP Parallel Processors (PP), of which 4 will be designed in the first version of the MVP, provide highly-optimized image/video/graphics/audio processing capabilities. The Transfer Controller (TC) intelligently moves data and instructions on and off the MVP. All of these processors are locally interconnected with a crossbar to 25 on-chip 2Kbyte SRAM modules. Other features include dual video frame timing generators (VC) and JTAG test and emulation circuits.

With five 32+bit programmable processors operating at one targeted state rate of 50MHz and numerous parallel operations performed in each processor, over 2 billion operations per second result. In addition, 100 MFLOPS (fully IEEE-754) can occur. The peak data transfer rate is then 400 MBytes/second, adequate for many video applications. The internal bandwidth over the crossbar between on-chip memory and processors is 2.4 GBytes/second.

DSP PARALLEL PROCESSORS (PP)

The PP has many powerful features beyond those found in conventional DSPs. Practically all video algorithms benefit from these features. Most of the features were added to permit scalability within the PP to support many simple functions (like bit ops) in one cycle or fewer operations with the same hardware at higher precision (like 32-bits). The following describes the feature and advantage:

- 44 user registers:
    - ease of programming/compiling and fast parallel functions.
- Single-cycle access into crossbar memory expands effective registers to 34K:
    - flexibility.
- Three-level, no overhead instruction looping:
    - programming flexibility and faster tight loops (usually 20-30%)
- Double parallel transfer from memory with address update:
    - most algorithms need two pixels loaded per cycle.
- Three-operand ALU arithmetic and logical operations:
    - double speed correlation and windows support.
- Splitable multiply (8x8=16 or 16x16=32):
    - double speed pixel operations.
- Word/Halfword/Byte multiple arithmetic:
    - 4x on algorithms like motion estimation and 2x on fast DCTs.
- Flexible data path:
    - masking, merging, rotating... for bit stream coding (like Huffman).
- General-purpose use of address adders:

- up to 6x number of adds in one cycle.
- Conditional operations prevent need for branching (and possible pipeline stalls):
  - adaptive algorithms will operate faster (like adaptive thresholding).

As a result, as many as 15 RISC operations will be performed in one PP cycle. When multiplied by the number of PPs and added to the MP and FPU operations, a formidable number results. In addition, since the C-compiler also influenced the architecture of the PP, many of these features will automatically compile into fast code -- many users of the MVP will not need to understand the PP architecture to take advantage of its performance.

MASTER PROCESSOR (MP)

The MP is a general-purpose RISC processor with an integral IEEE-compatible floating-point unit. A 32-bit instruction is accessed from a 4KByte instruction cache. Data loads can be 8, 16, 32, or 64 bits from a 4KByte data cache or from any data module via the crossbar. The MP has thirty-one 32-bit usable registers. Uncommon features include:

- Register files common to floating-point & integer operations.
- Scoreboard keeps track of result of loads and FPU, preventing use until updated.
- Addressing modes support optional updating of base-address register with results of the address computation.
- Special FPU instruction permits new multiply, add/subt, & increment each cycle.
- Left-most and Right-most one logic.
- Both endians supported.

Since the MP was designed to efficiently execute C programs and has added hardware for bitstream processing, it performs exceptionally well as the controller and data interpretation processor. The floating point capability accelerates and simplifies programming of high precision applications like medical imaging and 3D graphics.

SHARED MEMORY & TRANSFER CONTROLLER (TC)

Much of the advantage of the MVP architecture lies in the memory and data I/O architecture. Each processor and memory is fully interconnected through the crossbar and switchable at instruction rates. With greater than 500 signal lines switching at nanosecond speeds, the crossbarred memory architecture is *only* possible with single-chip implementation. With adequate on-chip memory and the ability to reconnect the next processor to the data memory, rather than moving the data to another memory, the data on-chip is not required to move as often. In effect, the original requirement of billions of bytes/second data transfer is reduced to only 100's of Mbytes/second. This model works well as long as the algorithm uses localized regions of data (patches, blocks, neighborhoods, rows...), each of which "fit" into the on-chip memory, and are accessed in repeated or predictable patterns. While this usually occurs with image processing, an extremely intelligent transfer controller was architected to aid in insuring the validity of this assumption. The TC has numerous modes of transferring data on- or off-chip, each optimized for a particular type of dataflow (block, patch, fat line, indexed or guided patches...). Most importantly, the on-chip SRAM memory was architected with sufficient size and modularity to permit double-buffering of data I/O on and off the chip, while the on-chip processors access the other on-chip memory modules. In effect, practically no overhead is required for video I/O. Many convenient methods were designed into the TC to prioritize these accesses. In addition, we included support for most commodity memory components (VRAM, SRAM, DRAM). Finally, we devised several methods to mitigate any contention between the processors for a particular memory module. Both round-robin and fixed-robin priority schemes are available to permit developers flexibility in structuring their algorithms to reduce contention. For the many image and video algorithms currently developed for the MVP thus far, contention has not been a problem.

Another advantage of the crossbar architecture is expandability. We can design many different MVP chips, as a function of the number of PPs. We simply slice the architecture, cutting or adding PPs and memory modules. Conceptually, the advantage of this approach is that, with the same package and pin-out, several different performance and price points can be used. A range of applications may require a range of different MVP chips. Applications which require CCIR 601 studio quality video and/or multifunction processing (graphics / audio / video) would most-likely require an MVP with 4 processors. On the other hand, a more dedicated or single-function application like graphics may require fewer PPs. In addition, if only limited resolution video (QCIF) processing is necessary, again a small number of PPs could suffice. We anticipate various versions of the MVP in the future.

VIDEO CONTROLLER (VC)

In addition, the MVP has two programmable timing controllers for generation of video and other timing signals. As an example, video frame grabbing and display requires may pixel, horizontal, and vertical signals for synchronization of the external logic in the system. The MVP has internal logic to generate those signals under program control, relieving the system designer from design of external logic to perform those functions.

NEW DCT ALGORITHMS FOR COMPRESSION SPEED-UP WITH USE OF A PROGRAMMABLE ARCHITECTURE

One advantage of the programmable compression chip is the optimization possible by selecting the least computationally demanding DCT algorithm that will meet the accuracy required of the application. For example, fast DCT algorithms like those of Lee and Chen [Lee-84, Chen-77] have considerable advantage with respect to traditional matrix multiply approaches (with a factor of 5 or more speedup). Seperability of the 2D DCT is generally used for decomposition of DCTs (with successive processing of the individual rows & columns of an image) . The size of the DCT directly influences the benefit of seperability, however with the 8x8 DCTs of most standards, a definite speedup results. The Lee algorithm tends to be easy to implement and achieve faster computation, although has accuracy issues. The Chen algorithm is harder to implement and is computational slower, but with good accuracy. Depending on the available processing bandwidth, the encoder can select an appropriate DCT or IDCT algorithm to perform the task. If errors result, different coding decisions result and either lower SNRs or compression ratios occur.

In addition, we devised a "Truncated-IDCT" algorithm to utilize the advantages of a programmable architecture. Since the DCT, quantizer and threholding operations seek to minimize the population of selective frequency coefficients (for high compression), statistically, most of the high frequency coefficients are zero valued. Therefore, the conventional IDCT will act on 8x8 matrixes with a high percentage of zero valued inputs. We can then significantly reduce the amount of IDCT operations performed by not executing the zero valued multiplies and adds (similar work has been reported[McMillan-92]). This is only possible with software-based IDCTs. In implementation, the program adaptively truncates the 8x1 IDCT summation in the vertical direction based on the run-length encoded input values. Further reductions by selecting 4x1 summation when appropriate also shortens the process, although not as frequently. With this approach a factor of 3 or more speed-up on IDCTs will usually occur.

TOOLS

Advances in video compression have been limited by the availability of tools to develop software and hardware. With the MVP, TI offers a range of software tools and direct on-chip support for in-circuit debug. A real-time executive, C++ compilers, algebraic assembler, windowed high-level language debugger (with JTAG emulation hardware on chip) and library of primitives/applications, all the tools familiar to computer application developers, will now be available for development of video applications.

The software model for the MVP is based on two levels. The primary level includes the Master Processor acting as a director and scheduler of the MVP's parallelism. The *Executive* operates on the MP, performing those supervisory tasks. The *Executive* can dispatch tasks for operation in pipeline, parallel or any other arrangement on any processor within the MVP. Under that, a level which actually performs the tasks on each processor is accessed by either: (1) a library of primitives, (2) application tools for programming in assembly or (3) a high-level language compiler. Each of these methods have advantages, with varying performance and skill level required to code the chip, as a function of the particular application. Although nothing restricts the use of any processor as the master or slave processor, only software convention.

COMPETING VIDEO COMPRESSION CHIP ARCHITECTURES

Several semiconductor companies have reported activity in video compression chip or chip set solutions ([Bolton-93][Konstantinides-92]). Most chip manufacturers are proposing hardwired or paramaterized architectures, without C-level programmability. Our MVP is an exception. In addition, most of the other "programmable" approaches are based on an architecture which integrates dedicated logic modules, like DCTs and Motion Estimators, with only the controller programmable. This limits their efficiency since the silicon devoted to those functions must always keep busy with those functions to justify their cost. On the contrary the MVP architecture has no dedicated logic, permitting user *balancing* of silicon based on the varied and dynamic computational demands of compression. Other researchers have recently described simulations which support our position that universally programmable architectures are competitive solutions when compared with dedicated or hybrid architectures for video decompression (Mayer-93).

Many different architectures are proposed, in development, or currently available, however none except the MVP has the flexibility nor computational performance to meet the complete demands of *truly* integrated digital video on the desktop, including the complete concert of real-time video & audio compression, with image & 3D graphics processing. Not only compression and decompression, but system-level bit-stream control, video scaling, error correction and even audio echo cancellation. Architecture limitations and transistor counts limit other chips to subsets of these functions.

CONCLUSION

The MVP is a monolithic single-chip parallel processor that performs compression processing, audio & video processing, 3D graphics and others, and even at the same time. Over 2 billion operations are performed per second. This dramatic performance boost will enable a wide range of new applications, including desktop interactive digital video. Integrating fully-programmable parallel DSP processors with a RISC processor on one chip provides software flexibility and system adaptability. A new parallel architecture, using a crossbar network to couple the processors and large on-chip SRAMs, and with MIMD (Multiple Instruction Multiple Data) operations, yields extremely high efficiency for most image, graphics, and video algorithms. Software tools like real-time executives, assemblers and compilers all help bring a familiar computer programming model to multidimensional signal processing. This new technology frees developers of compression algorithms to optimize implementations of standard video & audio compression algorithms, without the restrictions found in today's compression chips (those which are limited to current interpretations or versions of the standards). In addition, algorithm developers can implement future compression algorithms, without the difficulties of developing new chips or adapting existing chips.

The MVP supports a wide range of open standards for video compression and image computing. The variation within each standard to promote creative and distinguishing advantages in the market place and the constant urge to optimize the standard to a particular range of markets, each work to prevent fixed hardware solutions. This programmable, integrated solution gives flexibility to system designers to develop competitive algorithms as well as adapt to emerging standards.

ACKNOWLEDGMENTS

The author wishes to thank Jeremiah Golston, Dr. Chris Read, and Dr. V. Venkateswar for compression algorithm work relating to the MVP. In addition, thanks to the MVP Program Manager, Walt Bonneau, for developing and motivating a "world-class" team. A special thanks to my original co-MVP-architects, Keith Balmer, Karl Guttag, and Nick Ing-Simmons. Finally, thanks to the entire "Team-MVP"!

REFERENCES

[Bolton-93] Bolton, M. "A Family of MPEG Video Encoder and Decoder Chips", IEEE Proceeding of Conference on Hot Chips, 1993.

[Chen-77] Chen, W.H., C.H. Smith, and S.C. Fralick, "A Fast Computational Algorithm for the Discrete Cosine Transform", IEEE Transactions of Communication, Vol. 25, pp. 1004-1009, Sept. 1977.

[Gove-92] Gove, R.J., "Architectures for Single-Chip Image Computing", SPIE Proceedings of Conf. on Image Processing and Interchange, San Jose, Ca., Feb 1992.

[Guttag-92] Guttag, K.M., R.J. Gove, & J.R. Van Aken, "A Single-Chip Multiprocessor For Multimedia: The MVP", IEEE Computer Graphics & Applications, pp.53-64, 11/92.

[Konstantinides-92] K. Konstantinides & V. Bhaskaran, *"Monolithic Architectures for Image Processing & Compression"*, IEEE Computer Graphics & Applications, pp 75-86, Nov. 1992.

[Lee-84] B.G. Lee, "A New Algorithm for the Discrete Cosine Transform", IEEE Trans. on Acoustics, Speech, and Signal Processing, Vol. 32, pp. 1243-1245, 1984.

[Mayer-93] A. C. Mayer, "The Architecture of a Processor Array for Video Decompression", IEEE Trans. on Consumer Elect.,Vol39, No.3, pp 565-569, Aug. 1993.

[McMillan-92] McMillan, L.& L. Westover, "A Forward-Mapping Realization of the Inverse Discrete Cosine Transform", IEEE Proc. of the Data Compression Conference, pp 219-228, 1992.

A Hybrid Approach to Text Compression

Peter C Gutmann
Computer Science, University of Auckland, New Zealand
Telephone +64 9 426-5097; email pgut1@cs.aukuni.ac.nz

Timothy C Bell
Computer Science, University of Canterbury, Christchurch 1, New Zealand
Telephone +64 3 364-2352; fax 364-2569; email tim@cosc.canterbury.ac.nz

1 Introduction

Text compression schemes have sometimes been divided into two classes: *symbolwise* methods, which form a source model, typically using a finite context to predict symbols; and *dictionary* methods, which replace phrases (groups of symbols) in the input with a code. Symbolwise methods tend to give better compression because they form more accurate models of text, while dictionary methods tend to be faster because multiple symbols are coded at once.

It is possible to decompose some dictionary methods into equivalent symbolwise methods (Langdon 1983, Bell & Witten in press). The decomposed method gives identical compression performance, but is slower because more coded symbols are transmitted. This decomposition is of interest primarily because it is helpful in making comparisons of the two methods. In this paper we explore a hybrid approach based on the opposite of this decomposition: the predictions of a symbolwise method are grouped together so that several characters can be coded at once. The objective is to combine the good compression of symbolwise methods with the high speed of dictionary methods. The hybrid allows tradeoffs to be made in terms of compression speed, compression performance, and memory usage. More importantly, investigating a hybrid method gives extra insights into the relationship between dictionary and symbolwise methods, and reveals that they are more closely related than might be expected.

The primary goal in the design of the hybrid method described here was to create a very fast system that is based on context modelling. We therefore begin by surveying techniques that have been used in the literature to achieve fast compression.

The current method of choice for very fast adaptive compressors is to use some variant of the LZ77 method (Ziv & Lempel 1977) in which the extent of the search for repeated strings is limited. In general this is accomplished by terminating the search after a predetermined number of potential matches have been checked. An extreme example of

1068-0314/94 $3.00 © 1994 IEEE

this is LZRW1 (Williams 1991a), which hashes the next few characters of the input into a table of pointers that point back into the sliding window. A new phrase entering the window is added by overwriting any existing phrase that is stored at the same location in the hash table. Consequently, only the most recent occurrence of a phrase is stored, and even this may be lost if another phrase collides with it in the hash table. This very simple replacement strategy achieves very fast compression. The output is packed into 16-bit words to make coding even faster, with 12 bits of position information (corresponding to a window size of 4K characters), and 4 bits of length information.

LZRW2 (Williams 1991b) extends LZRW1 by storing a table of selected phrases instead of referencing the sliding window directly. The hash table entries point to a phrase table that contains pointers to the sliding window. Since the window size is no longer limited by the hash table size (the phrase table entries can point back an arbitrarily large distance), a much larger window is available, and the index can access 4K phrases instead of 4K characters. The price paid is that the decompressor has the extra overhead of maintaining the same hash table and phrase table used in the compressor, and an extra level of indirection is introduced.

LZRW3 is another refinement, which merges the hash and phrase table into one unified lookup table (Williams 1991b). In addition, LZRW3 variants store multiple pointers at each hash table location, with a commensurate decrease in the number of hash buckets so that the table is the same size. Although the reduced number of buckets leads to more collisions, the increased bucket size means that more strings can be searched for a given hash value than in the simpler versions. A bucket size of 4 or 8 phrases seems to be the best tradeoff for an overall table size of 4K entries.

Several strategies can be used to decide which entry in a bucket should be overwritten. Methods such as overwriting the least-recently used entry could be applied, but a particularly simple strategy that performs well is to simply overwrite a random entry. Rather than using a random number generator, a single counter can be maintained that is incremented each time a pointer is stored into a bucket. This achieves a combination of cyclic and random overwrite.

Schemes based on this idea can outperform the standard Unix *compress* utility in terms of both compression and (generally) speed, while using an order of magnitude less memory. The *compress* program only outperforms LZRW3 methods on larger files in which its enormous dictionary is able to contain a more accurate model of the source statistics.

Hash tables are currently widely used for Ziv-Lempel methods because they provide very fast searching for prior phrases. The number of references stored at each hash table location can be limited (saving storage and time), or this limit can be applied at search time by simply only searching the first few references (saving time but not storage). Collision resolution can be ignored if desired because the price paid is simply poorer compression, and not failure of the system. Hash tables can also be used for symbolwise methods, in this case to locate information about previous occurrences of contexts (Raita & Teuhola 1987). Again, the speed can be improved by ignoring collisions or limiting the extent of a search, giving a trade-off against the amount of compression.

2 A hybrid symbolwise/dictionary method

Many dictionary methods can be decomposed into a symbolwise method in which a context is identified for each character coded. In the symbol-wise equivalent of Ziv-Lempel methods, the first character in a phrase is coded using a zero-order context, the next with a first-order context, and so on, until an end-of-phrase message is sent, and the context reverts to zero-order again (Bell 1987, Langdon 1983). This contrasts with conventional symbol-wise methods, where zero-order contexts are usually only used as a last resort.

The approach that we have used to create a hybrid method is to reverse this decomposition. The general idea is to identify some sort of "current context", and then predict a sequence of characters that is likely to come next. This could be done by storing likely sequences, and their respective probabilities. A special case of this has been described by Raita (1987), where a context predicts *two* symbols at once instead of one. An approximation to this is to store only the sequences, and assume that all are equally probable. This simplifies the book-keeping that must go on during coding, and also means that a "flat" code is appropriate.

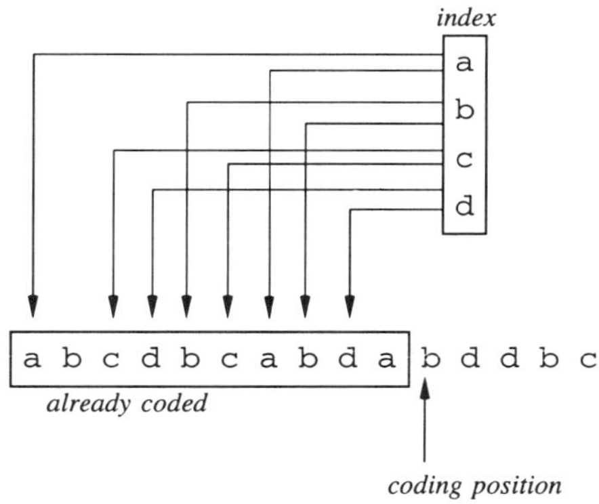

Figure 1: Index to prior text

Rather than maintain an explicit data structure of contexts and phrases, our hybrid method keeps a window of previously-coded text (see Figure 1). An index to the window is used to locate the phrases that are available in each context. The index could be a hash table of contexts; however, an even faster approach is to use a straight look-up table using a single symbol as the context[1]. The look-up table contains a maximum of k pointers for each symbol, allowing k phrases to be stored for each context. This means that not all occurrences of a context will necessarily be indexed—for example, the earliest occurrence of the context "b" in Figure 1 is not indexed.

[1] Larger contexts could be used with a lookup table, but the cost in memory increases exponentially with the size, and a hash table would be better for larger contexts because such an index would be very sparse.

At each coding step, the symbol that has just been encoded (an "a" in Figure 1) is used as the context. Previous occurrences of the context are located using the index, and the longest sequence of characters that has occurred in that context is located. In the example, the longest previous sequence is the second phrase indexed by "a". This phrase is then identified in the output. This can be done using $\log_2 k$ bits, since at most k prior contexts are indexed. Typically k is around eight, so only three bits are required to transmit the location. The number of characters that match is then transmitted. If the number of matching characters is zero, then an "escape" message is sent, and the next character is transmitted explicitly.

Decoding is very fast. The decoder maintains the same index structure, and simply copies the appropriate phrase from the current context. If suitable codes are used, this involves very few instructions for each symbol decoded.

The above is a very general description of the hybrid method. In the following section we describe some specific implementations.

3 Variations of the hybrid method

The main aspects of the hybrid method described previously that are yet to be specified are the codes used for the output, and the method of updating the pointers.

There are several components of the output that must be coded. The encoder must identify which of the k previous contexts is to be used. If we assume that each is equally likely then a simple code of $\log_2 k$ bits is appropriate. Variable length codes could be used to favour more recent phrases, although this was not investigated because of the speed penalty of the extra book-keeping required.

Coding the length of matches is more critical to compression performance, because shorter matches are considerably more likely than longer ones. One strategy is to limit the length of matches to, say, m symbols, and to code the length in $\log_2 m$ bits. We have also investigated a variable length code for this purpose. The best compression would be obtained by codes generated by Huffman's algorithm from sample length distributions, but this would incur a significant speed penalty.

When a context cannot be used for coding because the next symbol has never occurred in that context, an "escape" symbol must be transmitted. This can be represented by a single bit that is sent at each coding step, although this assumes that the probability of an "escape" occurring is 50%. Better compression can be obtained by transmitting the length of a match before identifying the phrase, and using a zero length to indicate an escape. If this is represented by a variable length code then a more appropriate length can be used. An advantage of the single-bit flag is that they can conveniently be stored eight to a byte, which admits a faster implementation.

An alternative that eliminates the need for escape codes is to always transmit the context symbol explicitly. This means that progress will be made at each coding step even if the match length is zero. Another possibility is for the escape code to switch to a "literal" mode, where symbols are transmitted explicitly until a second escape code switches back to the context coding mode. This approach has been used for some Ziv-Lempel methods (e.g. Fiala and Greene 1989), but it is not suitable in this situation because escape symbols do not tend to occur in clusters.

Another possibility is to use multi-bit flags at each coding step (Fenwick 1993). Such a flag could indicate more than one literal symbol, or could select from more than one representation of phrases.

A final possibility is to use a fast statistical coder (such as a table-driven Huffman coder) to represent the encoder output. This approach is used by the more successful Ziv-Lempel compression systems, which use a two-pass Huffman code to represent the output. A two-pass Huffman code gives similar compression to a single pass adaptive one, but is many times faster for both encoding and decoding if a table-driven canonical code is used (e.g. Siemiński 1988). Other methods, such as arithmetic coding, could be used, but these tend to be slower and require relatively complex models to be maintained (Gutmann 1992).

The choice of method for updating pointers in the table of contexts also requires a compromise between compression and speed. In initial experiments we stored pointers to the k most recent occurrences of each context. The amount of book-keeping can be reduced by simply overwriting a randomly chosen pointer instead of the oldest one. The probability of consistently overwriting useful pointers is relatively low, and so this approach has relatively little effect on the compression performance. As with LZRW3, a suitable pseudo-random overwrite is achieved by a single counter that cycles through 1 to k to determine which pointer is to be replaced next.

4 Performance of the hybrid method

In this section we evaluate the effect of the different choices suggested in the previous section.

In order to determine how the parameters k (the number of pointers stored for each context) and m (the maximum match length) should be chosen, a simple hybrid compressor was implemented with a one-bit escape code followed by an 8-bit representation of the next character. The k pointers for each context were maintained using the pseudo-random cyclic overwrite. The system was used to compress the files of the "Calgary corpus" (Bell *et al.* 1990). Figure 2 shows how the compression performance of this method depends on k and m. The graph shows the average (unweighted) compression over all the files in the corpus.

Figure 2 shows that compression improves as the number of phrases stored in each context increases, although the returns are diminishing by the time $k = 64$. The disadvantage of increasing k is that it causes a corresponding increase in encoding time due to the overall increase in the number of strings to search for matches, and it also requires more memory. If k is large and encoding speed is a problem then a more complex strategy than the simple linear search of the k entries could be used. The compression performance is relatively insensitive to the maximum match length, m, provided that it is greater than 8. The degradation in compression for longer matches could be avoided by using variable length codes for the match lengths, and we explore a simple form of this later.

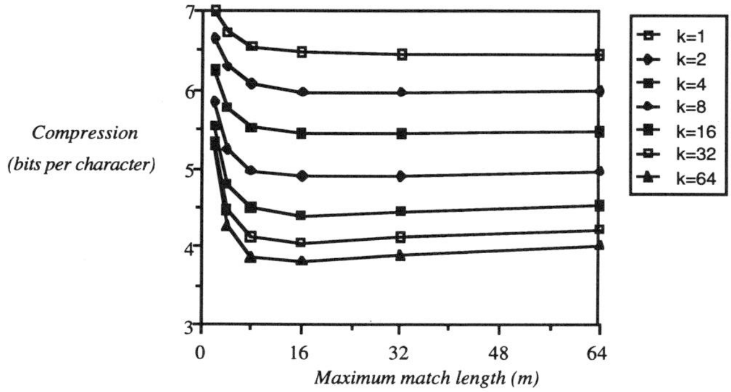

Figure 2: Compression of a simple hybrid coder averaged over the Calgary corpus (k = number of phrases per context)

To simplify coding, it is convenient if the phrase identifier and the match length can fit into one byte, that is, $\log_2 k + \log_2 m = 8$. The best compression that satisfies this constraint occurs when $k = 32$ and $m = 8$, where the corpus files are compressed to 4.12 bits per character on average (that is, files are reduced to approximately half their original size). This is remarkably good performance considering the speed and simplicity of the scheme, particularly for decoding.

A multi-bit encoding has been evaluated, where a *two*-bit flag is sent at each coding step. Table 1 shows how the four values of the flag are interpreted. Two of the values correspond to the two values of the one-bit flag used previously; the other two values are used for shorter encodings of literals and codewords respectively. The short literal coding represents characters in six bits. These characters are selected from an adaptive list of the 64 most recently used symbols. The short codeword still has $\log_2 k$ bits to choose the phrase, but has fewer bits to represent the length. This takes advantage of the high frequency of short lengths.

Flag	Use
00	8 bits: Literal
01	6 bits: 64 most recently used literals
10	8 bits: Index + length
11	6 bits: Index + short length

Table 1: Interpretation of the two bit flag

The size of the flags have been chosen so that they can conveniently be packed into bytes to enable processing to be fast (Fenwick 1993). Four flags are packed into one byte, and they are also stored in the two remaining bits of the 6-bit literals and codewords. Using two-bit flags is equivalent to a two-level coding method for characters and lengths, and so indicates the kind of improvement that can be expected from moving to variable length codes.

The use of two-bit flags achieves compression of 3.57 bits per character (bpc) averaged over the Calgary corpus. This compares with 3.83 bpc for the best parameters using single-bit flag. Table 2 shows comparable results achieved by other fast compression methods.

Method	Compression (bits per character)
Hybrid, 2-bit flags	3.57
Compress	3.21
Gzip	2.70

Table 2: Compression performance of fast methods, averaged over the Calgary corpus.

The compression of the hybrid method is not quite as good as that of Unix *compress*, but it has the advantage that the output fits conveniently into bytes and so is able to operate faster. The "Gzip" method is one of the best Ziv-Lempel based methods currently available, implemented by GNU. The version reported here was set for best compression. It achieves superior compression to the hybrid method at the expense of a more extensive search for matching phrases, and using two passes to generate Huffman codes for the output.

The hybrid method described here is very fast for both encoding and decoding. Searching for matches involves evaluating just k matches, where k is typically between 8 and 64. Even faster coding is possible by reducing k. Decoding requires just two indirections to locate the phrase to be copied. Input and output is fast because no codes cross byte boundaries, and are easily inserted and extracted within bytes.

The memory requirements of the hybrid method are relatively low. Most of the memory is consumed by the window of prior characters and the index structure. A window of about 8Kbytes is suitable (the experiments reported above used a window of 32K, which is slightly better). If $k = 32$ then the index uses 16 Kbytes of memory.

Analysing the output of the hybrid method reveals that the "literal" characters (i.e. escapes to zero-order) occur frequently—often more frequently than coded phrases. Presumably this is because phrases tend to end when a novel character occurs, and so the first character at each coding step is less likely to have occurred in the first-order context. This suggests the possibility of *always* encoding a literal character, eliminating the need for the escape flag. Initial experiments have indicated that this degrades compression by just a few percent.

5 Conclusion

The idea of a hybrid between dictionary and symbol-wise methods has several consequences. It demonstrates that the two approaches are more closely related that might be expected. The implementation described here suggests analogies between the two classes. For example, the "escape" symbol used by context coders performs a function that in analogous to that of the literal flag used by Ziv-Lempel methods. Characters that are difficult to predict cause a phrase boundary to occur in the hybrid method, indicating a correlation between low probability symbols and phrase boundaries in Ziv-Lempel coders. The index that is used to locate previous occurrences of phrases for a Ziv-Lempel method is closely related to the data structure used by a context-based method for keeping statistics about the contexts. Ziv-Lempel coders use several different strategies to determine which phrases will be made available for coding; likewise, symbolwise models must determine which contexts are the most useful to store. These issues also get caught up with compromises caused by the choice of data structure used, such as a hash table, a trie (digital search tree), or a simple look-up table.

These relationships raise the possibility of a very general model that includes the two approaches—and hybrid methods—as special cases. This in turn will help to formalise the continuum of tradeoffs between compression performance, memory usage, and speed.

In our investigation we have pursued speed rather than compression performance, and have created a context-based method that is extremely fast. Many other trade-offs between speed and compression performance are possible, and work is continuing on this. For example, using a Huffman code for the output is likely to give significantly better compression. Fast approximate arithmetic coders might also be used for this purpose.

Acknowledgements

The authors are grateful to Timo Raita and Ross Williams for helpful comments on this work.

References

Bell, T. C., "A unifying theory and improvements for existing approaches to text compression", Ph.D. thesis, Department of Computer Science, University of Canterbury, New Zealand: 1987.

Bell, T.C., Cleary, J.G. and Witten, I.H. (1990) *Text compression*. Prentice Hall, Englewood Cliffs, NJ.

Bell, T. C. and Witten, I. H., "The relationship between greedy parsing and symbolwise text compression", J. ACM, in press.

Fenwick, P. "Ziv-Lempel Coding with Multi-bit Flags", Proceedings of DCC'93, April 1993, p.138.

Fiala, E. R. and Greene, D. H., "Data compression with finite windows", Comm. ACM, 1989. 32(4): p. 490-505.

Gutmann, P. "Practical Dictionary/Arithmetic Data Compression Synthesis", University of Auckland MSc thesis, February 1992.

Langdon, G. G., "A note on the Ziv-Limpel model for compressing individual sequences", IEEE Transactions on Information Theory, 1983. 29(2): p. 284-287.

Raita, T. and Teuhola, J., "Predictive text compression by hashing", Proceedings of the Tenth Annual International ACMSIGIR Conference, New Orleans, 1987.

Raita, T., (1987) "Generalized Coding Algorithms for Predictive Text Compression", Report AY7, Department of Computer Science, University of Turku, Finland.

Siemiński, A. "Fast Decoding of Huffman Codes", Information ProcessingLetters, Vol.26, No.5 (January 1988), p.237.

Williams R.N. (1991a) "An Extremely Fast Ziv-Lempel Data Compression Algorithm", Proceedings of DCC'91, p.362.

Williams R.N (1991b). "Notes on the LZRW3 Algorithm", posted to the Usenet comp.compression newsgroup in June 1991.

Ziv, J. and Lempel, A., "A universal algorithm for sequential data compression", IEEE Transactions on Information Theory, 1977. IT-23(3): p. 337-343.

Highly Efficient Universal Coding with Classifying to Subdictionaries for Text Compression

Yasuhiko NAKANO, Hironori YAHAGI, Yoshiyuki OKADA and Shigeru YOSHIDA

Holography and Color-Imaging Laboratory, Electronic Systems Laboratories, Fujitsu Laboratories Ltd.
10-1 Morinosato-Wakamiya, Atsugi 243-01, Japan

{nakano, yahagi, yokada, per241}@flab.fujitsu.co.jp

Abstract

This paper describes a practical, locally adaptive data compression algorithm of the LZ78 class. According to the Lempel-Ziv incremental parsing rule, the boundary of a string is not related to the statistical history modeled by finite-state sources. We have already reported an algorithm classifying to subdictionaries (CSD), which uses multiple subdictionaries and conditions the current string by using the previous one to obtain a higher compression ratio for image compression.
In this paper, we present a practical implementation of this method for any kinds of data, and show that CSD was more efficient than LZC used as the UNIX utility compress. The compression performance of CSD was about 10% better than LZC with the practical dictionary size, an 8K-entry dictionary when the test data were used form Calgary Compression Corpus. Using hashing, processing speed of CSD became as fast as LZC, though the CSD algorithm was more complicated than LZC.

1. Introduction

Data compression is important for file storage and distributed communication systems. Text compression algorithms can be divided into two classes, statistical and dictionary. Statistical methods obtain nearly optimal compression performance, but they take a long time to compute. Dictionary methods do not compress as well as statistical methods, but they are easy to implement on a personal computer, using only a modest amount of computer time and memory. We developed a dictionary compression method that has a high compression ratio and is practical to implement. According to the Lempel-Ziv incremental parsing rule, the boundary of a string is not related to the statistical history modeled by finite-state sources. Our algorithm, named CSD, based on a state-conditioned incremental parsing rule, uses multiple subdictionaries to correlate previous and current substrings. We have already used the basic CSD design for image compression[1,2]. Plotnik

1068-0314/94 $3.00 © 1994 IEEE

et al. discussed the CSD concept and proved its efficiency[3]. Ohmine et al. simulated CSD and concluded that multiple dictionaries without memory limitations are more efficient than conventional methods when the input data exceeds 10K bytes[4]. However, there was no practical methods and its evaluation about CSD implementation with memory limitations. Our aim was to realize classifying to subdictionaries (CSD) with a reasonably-sized dictionary, such as 8K entries which is well suited for personal computers. CSD with this dictionary can be implemented on a single LSI IC, or used as software residing in main memory. Both versions provide high-speed compression.

2. CSD Concept

2.1. Why CSD?

The two main types of dictionary method are LZ77 and LZ78. Our algorithm, CSD is based on LZ78 class. Although the LZ78 has a slightly lower compression performance than LZ77, it is better suited for high-speed applications. We chose LZ78 and improved its compression performance. The algorithm LZC, a popular conventional LZ78 dictionary method works by dividing an input data string into variable-length substrings that are assigned constant-length codewords. These substrings are the longest match those stored in the dictionary. Only the dictionary addresses are transmitted. The dictionary is initially loaded with all strings of length 1. A transmitted string is processed by an *incremental parsing rule* that appends the next symbol to it, then is stored in the dictionary. Each stored string is unique. So, the more frequently a substring occurs, the longer becomes. According to the Lempel-Ziv incremental parsing rule, the boundary of a string is related to the greedy longest matching, and does not depend on the statistical history modeled by finite-state sources. However, adjacent substrings have strong correlations in text and may correspond to some statistical states. In fact, their redundancy remains in encoded data. To enhance the compression ratio, we used this fact to reduce redundancy. We devised an algorithm classifying to subdictionaries (CSD), which uses multiple subdictionaries and conditions the current string by using the previous one to obtain a higher compression ratio.

2.2 Algorithm

CSD uses multiple subdictionaries to correlate the previous and current substrings. The multiple subdictionaries classify the current string into states. The subdictionary used to encode the current substring is selected based on the last symbol of the previous substring (Fig. 1). Every subdictionary is initially loaded with all strings of length 1 (the same as LZC). If we uses 256 subdictionaries, we consumes 256*256 strings as a initially loaded strings. Actually, it incurs a overhead. After a string is transmitted, the next symbol is appended to it and it is stored in the subdictionary indexed by the last symbol of the previous string in what is called *state-conditioned incremental parsing*. Each stored string in a subdictionary is unique. So, the more frequently a substring occurs, the longer it becomes in each subdictionary. Figure 1 illustrates how this method works. The current substring S_i , "ca", is stored in subdictionary Dc_{i-1} because the last symbol of the previous substring S_{i-1} , "ab", is C_{i-1}, "b". It is encoded by address A_i, "257", of the longest matching string S_i, "ca", in subdictionary Dc_{i-1}. Each address is encoded by using the bit length corresponding to the number of strings stored in the selected subdictionary. The current substring is thus classified by the previous symbol and is encoded by a variable-to-fixed-length code related to the previous substring. Since the subdictionary is determined by previous data, dictionary selection in the decoder does not require additional data. Encoding is the same as the original LZC but uses individual dictionaries for each state. CSD thus obtains a higher compression ratio than LZC by using state-conditioned plural dictionaries.

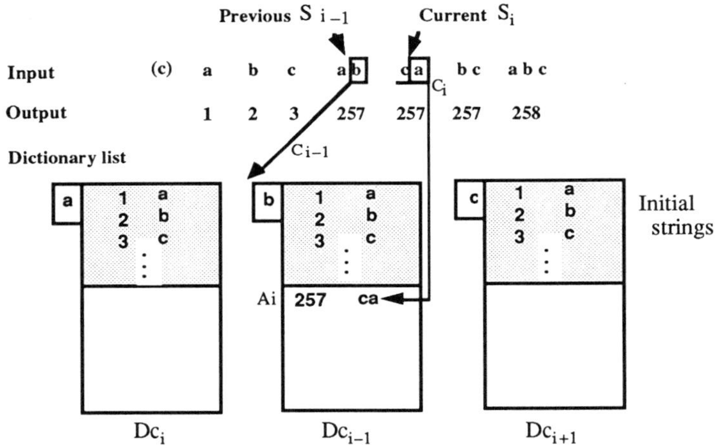

Figure 1 **Basic CSD Algorithm**

3. Problems about Dictionary size

Two problems are caused by the small, plural subdictionaries as memory required for practical use is around 8K-entry.

Initializing the subdictionaries:

LZC initially stores all strings of length 1 in a dictionary. If each subdictionary initially contains 256 strings of length 1, up to 64K entry may be used. Also, not so many initial strings are referenced during the encoding process. The 8K entry dictionary cannot have the 64K entry of initial strings. (We can reduce the initial strings by cutting down the number of subdictionaries. However, it also degrade the compression performance. It is discussed in 4.2.2 and 5.1 again) We should devise the new method without initial strings to solve this problem.

Designing the plural subdictionaries:
Using the last one-byte symbol in the previous string gives plural subdictionaries such as 256 (8bit), but, these are not used uniformly, and some subdictionaries are not used at all. Besides, if a fixed maximum size of subdictionaries is assigned initially, they can be fragmented. We should devise a dictionary structure with flexible size of subdictionaries.

4. Implementation

In this section, we address the implementation of new CSD design. To enhance the basic CSD, briefly, we reduce the dictionary size following three points without degrading compression performance.

Initializing the subdictionaries: We propose two-mode coding which deals with literals (the rare data) and string numbers independently to solve the initially strings problem.

Designing the plural sub-dictionaries: We devised variable-sized subdictionaries to avoid fragmentation. The whole dictionary can be used without loss. We also devised high-speed processing using hashing.

Clearing dictionaries: We reviewed some kinds of methods for clearing dictionary, because such a small-sized dictionary must be cleared for efficient compression.
In the next section, we give the precise scheme in order.

4.1 Subdictionary Initialization

4.1.1 Initial Dictionary Reduction

In two-mode coding, CSD eliminates initial strings and encodes literals and strings independently. Literals are distinguished from string numbers by a special flag. It gives restricted strings of length 1 appeared in the input stream, instead of initially storing all strings of length 1, which leaves dictionary space for new strings that will actually appear in the input stream. This differs from LZC. For the delimiter, CSD needs to store only one pair of strings of length 1 to the dictionary initially like LZC. It may take up as little as 256 entry (Fig. 1). The CSD string number starts a string number at the smallest number assigned in advance because there is no initial dictionary. CSD string numbers start at 1 except for special function codes, such as end-of-file and dictionary clearing. A string of length 1 must be sent as a literal code. Figure 2 illustrates how this method works. The current substring Si , "ca", is stored in subdictionary Dc_{i-1} because the last symbol of the previous substring S_{i-1} , "ab", was C_{i-1}, "b". It is encoded by string number A_i, "2", of the longest matching string S_i, "ca", in sub-dictionary Dc_{i-1}. Each string number is encoded by using the bit length corresponding to the number of strings stored in the selected subdictionary. The current substring is thus classified by the previous symbol and is encoded by variable-to-fixed-length coding related to the previous substring. Since the subdictionary is determined by previous data, dictionary selection in the decoder does not require additional data.

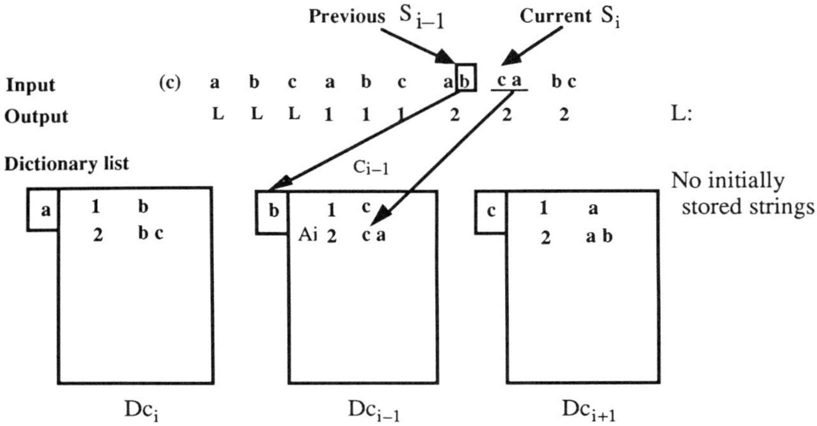

Figure 2 **CSD without initial dictionary**

4.2 Subdictionary Design

4.2.1 Structure

A conventional 1M-entry dictionary is divided the dictionary into fixed-size subdictionaries of 4K entries each (Fig. 3(a)). Each subdictionary initially contains 256 strings of length 1 and special function codes end-of-file (EOF) and dictionary clearing (CLR). The dictionary may be as large as 64K entries. Strings to be stored are numbered after the initial 258 entries. Each subdictionary string numbers (SD numbers) are only biased to the total dictionary numbers by equal entries of subdictionaries. The conversion from SD numbers to total dictionary numbers and the reverse are both calculated easily. Equally sized subdictionaries cause fragmentation, however, which degrades the compression ratio because, when dictionaries are full, no more strings can be stored in them even if other dictionaries have space for new strings.

We developed a subdictionary structure to avoid fragmentation (Fig. 3(b)). The key is to use one dictionary (OD) for all subdictionary strings. The OD has 256 entries both for previous symbols and the delimiter of encoding and decoding, which only occupies 256 words. Strings are numbered from 256 just after the previous symbol entries in the dictionary. Also, strings in the same subdictionary are numbered from 2 which contains two special flag codes. In encoding, the last symbol of the previous string is added as the first character, and its OD string number is increased one by one, the same as in conventional LZC methods. After that, the OD string number is converted to the corresponding SD string number, which is easier than decoding. In decoding, the SD string number is converted to the corresponding OD string number, which is reversed operation of encoding. The coded SD string number and subdictionary determined by the last symbol of previous decoded string are used to calculate the OD string number. This is complicated because OD numbers must be traced. We used hashing to simplify and speed up this operation. The original string, with the first symbol discarded, is then retrieved with the OD string number.

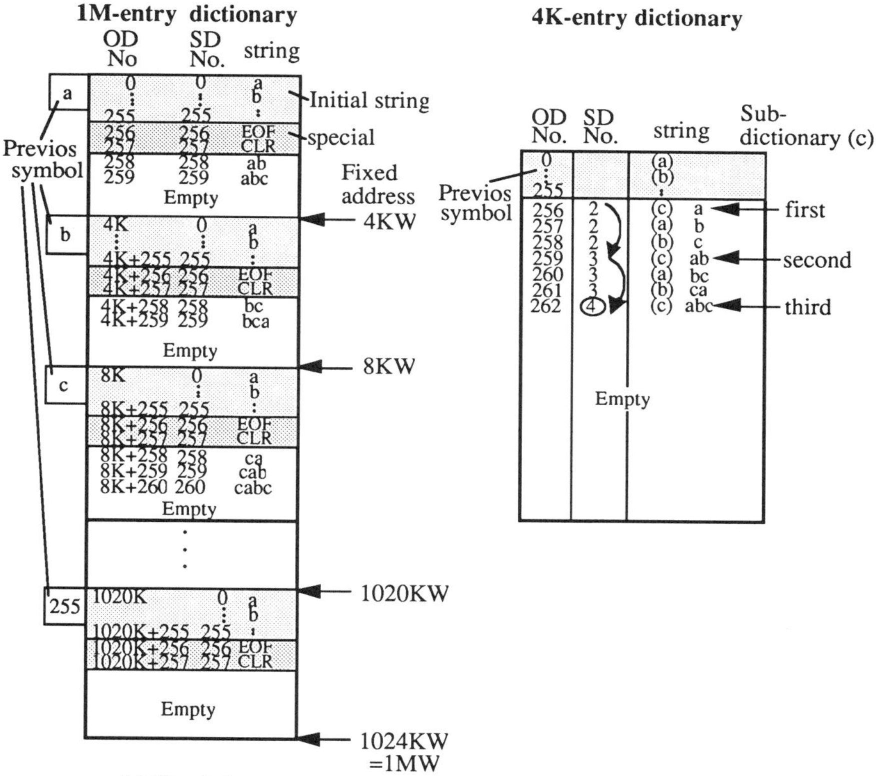

(a) Fixed size

(b) Variable size

Figure 3 **Subdictionary Structures**

Here, the input stream is "(c) a b c a b c a b c"

4.2.2 Number of Subdictionaries

We can reduce the number of subdictionaries to cut down the initially stored strings. For example, if we use only 16 subdictionaries, only the 16*256 strings are required as initially stored strings. And, It may be better when the dictionary size is small around 4K-8K entry because a each subdictionary is not so large enough to compress efficiently. However, the number of condition-state gets smaller if the number of subdictionaries becomes small. Therefore, the state-conditioned incremental parsing rule seems not to work well. It has trade-off. In respect to this point, we have a simulation in section 5 to decide how to divide dictionaries.

4.2.3 String Number Search by Hashing

Variable-sized subdictionaries reduce memory space for stored strings, but also degrade the processing speed, especially during decoding. In encoding, SD string numbers are easily found as output code because the table which maps OD string numbers to SD string numbers is constructed in order. During decoding, however OD string numbers are found by tracing all SD string numbers, which consumes a lot of time. As shown by figure 3(b), for example, when decoding subdictionary (c) and the SD string number 4 as "(c) abc", we must trace all OD string numbers. Instead of this, we constructed on inverse table using hashing which maps SD string numbers onto OD numbers. (Fig. 4(a) and (b)). Encoding uses a string number and the next matching symbol. The last symbol of the previous substring may also be included. Decoding uses a string number and the last symbol of the previous substring. Such hashing, dramatically reduces computer time, especially during decoding.

Figure 4 Hashing

4.3 Dictionary Clearing

A practical-sized dictionary of 8K entries becomes full when several tens of kilobytes of data are input. For a small dictionary, management when adopting new input characteristics is very important in maintaining the compression ratio. Once the dictionary is full, LZW, a predecessor of LZC, uses the filled dictionary until encoding ends. This makes the dictionary inefficient when the statistical characteristics of input data change. This is two ways avoided:

One is clearing the dictionary, i.e., reinitializing it. The dictionary clear, only when the filled dictionary brings deteriorated compression ratio, obtain better performance than the one just after the dictionary is full (LZW). This method is adopted to LZC. The other is least recently used (LRU) replacement. Once the dictionary is full, the space is made for new string by discarding the least recently used string. In terms of compression ratio and processing speed, we adopted the dictionary clear when deteriorated compression ratio.

5. Performance

5.1 Compression ratio

We evaluated performance on a SPARCstation LT, 17.5 MIPS machine based on a 25 MHz SPARC CPU (Figure 5 and Table 1). We chose the Calgary Compression Corpus and a Japanese manual as test data. These contain the following: Two books and papers (book1, book2, paper1 and paper2) are natural English, both fiction and nonfiction. A bibliography (bib) and a batch of unedited news articles (news) are written in more unusual styles of English. Three computer programs represent artificial languages (progc, progl, progp). A transcript of a terminal session (trans) was also included. We also included some non-ASCII files. Two executable files (obj1, obj2), geographical data (geo), and a bit-mapped, black-and-white picture (pic). We also used Kanji data, lha.doc, which is the Japanese language manual of LHarc ver. 2.12 dated March 21, 1991.

Figure 6 indicates the compression efficiency due to the subdictionaries number. We have simulated no divide, 16, 64, and 256 subdictionaries when the total dictionary size is 8K entry. In overall tendency, the 256 subdictionaries has the best performance. According to this result, with such small dictionary size, 8K entry, it is useful to divide the dictionary into 256 to collect the state condition. In table 1, we compared the compression performance of LZC and CSD. CSD compressed about 5-10% better than its predecessor, LZC. CSD did not compress pseudo-random data (geo) well because adjacent substrings have little correlations in input stream and may correspond to only one statistical state. Overall, CSD with a dictionary larger than 4K entries compressed better than LZC.

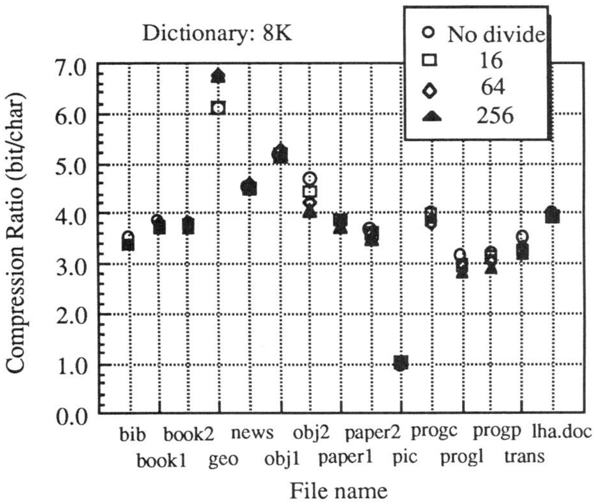

Figure 5 Number of Subdictionaries

Table 1 Compression Performance

file	Size Kbyte	LZC	CSD	LZC	CSD	LZC	CSD
		Dictionary: 4K		Dictionary: 8K		Dictionary: 16K	
bib	111	3.85	3.94	3.61	3.51	3.52	3.22
book1	769	4.04	4.13	3.85	3.80	3.68	3.59
book2	611	4.16	4.11	3.89	3.70	3.66	3.37
geo	102	6.09	7.02	6.15	6.83	6.12	6.74
news	377	4.83	4.94	4.54	4.48	4.30	4.13
obj1	22	5.01	5.29	5.16	5.14	5.23	5.12
obj2	247	4.54	4.28	4.44	3.95	4.29	3.80
paper1	53	4.22	4.02	3.98	3.74	3.77	3.43
paper2	82	3.94	3.97	3.72	3.60	3.63	3.28
pic	513	1.02	1.07	1.01	1.03	0.99	1.00
progc	40	4.22	4.21	4.06	3.76	3.86	3.42
progl	72	3.38	3.09	3.17	2.87	3.03	2.70
progp	49	3.46	3.23	3.26	2.97	3.11	2.66
trans	94	3.87	3.58	3.61	3.19	3.36	2.91
lha.doc	26	4.27	4.28	4.04	3.90	4.05	3.57
Average		4.06	4.08	3.90	3.76	3.77	3.53

Average file size: 211 Kbytes

5.2 Processing Speed

We compared the processing speed of LZC, CSD, and CSD with hashing (Table 2). The programs were written in C and executed on SPARCstation LT. Several files of the Calgary Compression Corpus were used as test data. The processing speeds were calculated for ten consecutive operations from the *user time* given by the unix *time* command. CSD required a little more computer time than LZC, but CSD with hashing reduced the computer time, especially during decoding. CSD consumes more computer time because it stores more strings than LZC, and the complicated two-mode algorithm has more steps to execute. Using hashing, CSD encoding speed became fast as almost same as LZC. Decoding of CSD took more time than LZC decoding because the searching and storage of distinguishing literals from string numbers takes more time.

Table 2 Performance Speed SPARCstataion LT, 17.5 MIPS (Dictionary: 8K)

File		LZC	CSD	CSD with hashing
bib	Coding	2.27	2.72	2.30
	Decoding	1.55	4.97	2.14
book1	Coding	15.85	19.14	16.31
	Decoding	11.04	44.71	15.46
paper1	Coding	1.16	1.27	1.17
	Decoding	0.79	2.70	1.14

6. Conclusion

We implemented CSD practically, based on a state-conditioned incremental parsing rule, and realized CSD with a small dictionary of approximately 8K entries. The key techniques were how to initialize and how to design the plural sub-dictionaries for practical use. We devised two-mode coding and variable-sized subdictionary. In two-mode coding, CSD eliminates initial strings and encodes literals and strings independently to leave space for new string. In variable-sized subdictionary, CSD uses only one dictionary for all subdictionary to avoid fragmentation.

We also used hashing to speed up coding. The compression performance of CSD is 5-10% better than LZC with an 8K-entry dictionary. Processing speed of CSD became as fast as LZC, though the CSD algorithm is more complicated than LZC.

CSD does not work better with little input data size because encoding ends before the dictionary accumulates enough string to be effective. Ohmine et al reported that multiple dictionaries without memory limitations are more efficient than conventional methods when the input data is exceeds 10K bytes. This is because CSD is slow at storing string. We will boost the speed by AP (All Prefix) or ID (Identity) method[6]. We considered two counter measures. One is to increase the number of strings to be stored. The other is to switch the conventional dictionary to CSD when the subdictionary accumulates enough strings. The switching types will give the equal to better performance than LZC, regardless of input data types, even if the statistical data (geo).

References

(1) S. Yoshida, Y. Okada, Y. Nakano, H. Chiba, and M. Mori, "New binary image compression scheme for various kinds of images," Proc. SPIE/IS&T Symp. on Electro. Imag. Sci. & Tech. , 1657-15, 1992.

(2) S. Yoshida, Y. Okada, Y. Nakano, H. Chiba, and M. Mori, "Study of universal coding to achieve a good compression rate," Proc. Inst. of Electro. Inform. Commun. Eng. Conf., Autumn 1991, A-138, Sep. 1991 (in Japanese).

(3) E. Plotnik, M. J. Weinberger, and J. Ziv:, "Upper bounds on the probability of sequences emitted by finite-state sources and on the redundancy of the Lempel-Ziv algorithm," IEEE Trans. on Inform. Theory, Vol. 38, No. 1, Jan. 1992.

(4) M. Ohmine, and H. Yamamoto," Universal data compression algorithms with multiple dictionaries," Tech. Repo. of Inst. of Electro. Inform. Commun. Eng. , pp. 1-6, IT92-134, Mar. 1993 (in Japanese).

(5) T. C. Bell, J. G. Cleary, and I. H. Witten, "Text compression," Prentice-Hall Inc., 1990.

(6) J. A. Storer, "Data Compression," Computer Science Press Inc., 1988.

(7) T. A. Welch, "A Technique for High-Performance Data Compression," Computer pp. 8-19, Jun. 1984

(8) R. N. Williams, "Adaptive Data Compression," Cluwer Academic Publishers, 1991.

Compression by Induction of Hierarchical Grammars

Craig G. Nevill-Manning
Computer Science, University of Waikato, Hamilton, New Zealand
Telephone +64 7 838–4021; email cgn@waikato.ac.NZ

Ian H. Witten
Computer Science, University of Waikato, Hamilton, New Zealand
Telephone +64 7 838–4246; email ihw@waikato.ac.NZ

David L. Maulsby
Computer Science, University of Calgary, Calgary T2N 1N4, Canada
Email maulsby@cpsc.UCalgary.CA

1 Introduction

Adaptive compression methods build models of symbol sequences. In many areas of computer science, models of sequences are constructed for their explanatory value. In contrast, data compression schemes use models that are *opaque* in that they do not provide descriptions of the sequence that can be readily understood or applied in other domains. Statistical methods that compress text well invariably generate large models that are not so much a structural description of the sequence as a record of frequencies of short substrings. Macro models replace repeated text by references to earlier occurrences and generally work within a small moving window of symbols so that any implicit model is transient. In both cases the models are flat and do not provide abstractions by combining references into higher level phrases.

This paper describes a technique that constructs models of symbol sequences in the form of small, human-readable, hierarchical grammars. The grammars are both semantically plausible and compact. The technique can induce structure from a variety of different kinds of sequence, and examples are given of models derived from English text, C source code and a sequence of terminal control codes.

The grammar for a particular text can be encoded using a simple arithmetic code and transmitted in its entirety, yielding a compression rate that rivals the best macro techniques. Alternatively, the sequence can be transmitted adaptively by using the grammar to select phrases for a macro scheme; this gives a compression rate that outperforms other macro schemes and rivals that achieved by the best context models. Neither of these techniques operate on-line: they both involve building a model for the entire sequence first and then coding it as a second stage.

This paper explains the grammatical induction technique, demonstrates its application to three very different sequences, evaluates its compression performance, and concludes by briefly discussing its use as a method for knowledge acquisition.

2 Induction of the grammar

The idea is simple. Given a string of symbols, a grammar is constructed by replacing any repeated sequence of two or more symbols by a non-terminal symbol. For example, given a string S ::= a b c d e b c d f, the repeated 'b c d' is condensed into a new non-terminal, say A:

S ::= a A e A f
A ::= b c d.

Sequences that are repeated may themselves include non-terminals. For example, suppose S was augmented by appending 'b c d e b c d f g'. First, the two occurrences of 'b c d' would be replaced by A, yielding S ::= a A e A f A e A f g, and then the repeated sequence 'A e A f' would be replaced by a new non-terminal, say B:

S ::= a B B g
A ::= b c d
B ::= A e A f.

Because every repeated sequence is replaced by a non-terminal, grammars produced by this technique satisfy the constraint that *every digram in the grammar is unique*.

In order to implement this method efficiently, processing proceeds from left to right, and greedy parsing is used to select the longest repetition at each stage. This will not necessarily produce the smallest grammar possible. To do this would require finding two things: the best set of productions, and the best order in which they should be applied. The latter is called 'optimal parsing', and can be implemented by a dynamic programming algorithm [1]. Parsing is dependant upon the set of productions, or dictionary, and this technique builds a dictionary and performs parsing simultaneously. Unfortunately, the selection of the best dictionary can be shown to be NP-complete, [4, 7]. It is not known how much better this technique would perform if an optimal dictionary could be constructed and optimal parsing performed using this dictionary, but the process would be at least NP-complete.

Although this technique for grammar induction is simple and natural in concept, it is—surprisingly—not obvious how to implement it efficiently. The problem is that at any one time there may be several partially matched rules at different levels in the hierarchy. Suppose that the string in the example above continues 'b c d e b c'. At this point rules A and B are both partially matched in anticipation that 'd' will occur next. However, if the next symbol is not 'd' both partial matches have to be rolled back and two new rules created, one for the sequence 'b c' and the other for 'A e'. The algorithm must keep track of a potentially unbounded number of partial matches, and when an unexpected symbol occurs it must roll them back and create new rules. To decide whether the next symbol continues the partial matches or terminates them, it is necessary to consider all expansions of the matching rules at all levels. Furthermore, at any particular point in time, the grammar may not satisfy the 'digram uniqueness' constraint, as there are repeated digrams pending the match of a complete rule.

The solution to these problems is to create rules as early as possible, and to extend them when appropriate. As soon as a new symbol is appended to the first rule (S) it forms a new digram with the preceding symbol. If the new digram is unique, no further action is necessary: all digrams are still unique. If the digram matches another in the grammar, there are three possibilities. It may

1. be replaced by a non-terminal which heads a matching two-symbol rule,
2. result in the creation of a new two-symbol rule, or
3. extend an existing rule.

The first action is performed if the matching digram is the entire body of an existing production. In this case, the non-terminal which heads the matching rule replaces the new digram.

The second action is performed if the first rule does not apply and serves to create new rules. However, if the first symbol in the digram is a non-terminal that appears exactly twice in the body of the rules in the grammar, the third action is performed. This is because the only two places in which the non-terminal appears are in the new digram and in the matching digram. As the digrams are identical, the rule that the non-terminal heads can be extended by incorporating the second symbol in the digram. For example, in Figure 1, after the second ocurrence of 'b c d', rule A is extended by appending 'd', and the two occurrences of 'd' are removed from rule S, rather than creating a new rule B ::= A d.

To illustrate the algorithm, the earlier example is reworked in Figure 1. Whenever a new digram matches an existing one, the action is explained on the right in terms of the three possibilities identified above.

a	S ::= a	
b	S ::= a b	
c	S ::= a b c	
d	S ::= a b c d	
e	S ::= a b c d e	
b	S ::= a b c d e b	
c	S ::= a b c d e b c ⇓ S ::= a A d e A A ::= b c	The repeated 'b c' creates a new rule (case 2)
d	S ::= a A d e A d A ::= b c ⇓ S ::= a A e A A ::= b c d	A only appears twice in the body of the grammar, so instead of creating a new rule B ::= A d, A is extended (case 3)
f	S ::= a A e A f A ::= b c d	
b	S ::= a A e A b A ::= b c d	
c	S ::= a A e A f b c A ::= b c d ⇓ S ::= a A e A f B A ::= B d B ::= b c	The repeated 'b c' creates a new rule (case 2)
d	S ::= a A e A f B d A ::= B d B ::= b c ⇓ S ::= a A e A f B A ::= B B ::= b c d ⇓ S ::= a A e A f A A ::= b c d	B has only been used twice, so it is extended (case 3) As A has only one symbol on the right-hand side, it is expanded, and B is removed (see text)

e	S ::= a A e A f A e A ::= b c d ⇓ S ::= a B A f B A ::= b c d B ::= A e	The repeated 'A e' creates a new rule (case 2)
b	S ::= a B A f B b A ::= b c d B ::= A e	
c	S ::= a B A f B b c A ::= b c d B ::= A e ⇓ S ::= a B A f B C A ::= C d B ::= A e C ::= b c	The repeated 'b c' creates a new rule (case 2)
d	S ::= a B A f B C d A ::= C d B ::= A e C ::= b c ⇓ S ::= a B A f B C A ::= C B ::= A e C ::= b c d ⇓ S ::= a B A f B A A ::= b c d B ::= A e ⇓ S ::= a B f B A ::= b c d B ::= A e A	C has only been used twice, so it is extended (case 3) As the rule for A has only one element, it is expanded and C is removed (see text) Now that A has been matched, the digram 'B A' causes B to be extended (case 3)
f	S ::= a B B A ::= b c d B ::= A e A f	The repeated 'B f' extends B (case 3)
g	S ::= a B B g A ::= b c d B ::= A e A f	This is the final grammar

Figure 1: Execution of the induction algorithm

A slight complication may occur in the application of the third action. If it results in the matching digram being reduced to a rule of length one, the non-terminal that was just extended is removed from the grammar, and its contents substituted in the two places in which it appeared. This occurs when a rule longer than two symbols has been completely matched. The resulting creation and deletion of rules seems inefficient, but requires little processing, and ensures that the digram uniqueness constraint is maintained at all times, even during partial matches.

3 Examples of structure discovery

To illustrate the structures that can be discovered using this technique, Figure 2 shows a sample from three grammars that are inferred from different sequences. In each case the rules are expanded to demonstrate how symbols are combined to form higher level rules.

3.1 English Text

Figure 2(a) represents the decomposition of part of the grammar induced from Thomas Hardy's novel *Far from the Madding Crowd.* The darkest bar at the top represents one non-terminal that covers the whole phrase: 'uncle•was•a•very•fair•sort•of•man. •Did•ye •know'. The existence of this rule indicates that the whole phrase occurs at least twice in the text. Bullets are used to make the spaces explicit.

The top-level rule comprises nine non-terminals, represented by the nine lighter bars on the second line. These correspond to the fragments 'uncle•was•', 'a•', 'very•', 'fair•', 'sort•of•', 'man', '.•D', 'id•ye' and '•know'. These fragments include two phrases ('uncle•was•' and 'sort•of•'), five words, and two fragments '.•D' and 'id•ye'. It is interesting that the letter at the start of the phrase 'Did•ye•know' is grouped with the preceding period. Although this is different from normal word boundaries in English, without being aware of the equivalence of lower- and upper-case letters the relationship between the period and the capital letters is stronger than with the rest of the word. If the representation of the text had included capitalization as a separate 'upper-case' marker that prefixed capital letters then it would be quite correct to associate it with a preceding period rather than with the letters that followed.

At the next level, the phrase 'uncle•was•' is split into its two constituent words, and 'id•ye' is also split on the space. The other phrase, 'sort•of•', is split after 'sor', which indicates that the word 'sort' has not previously been seen in any other context. The other words are split into less interesting digrams and trigrams. In other parts of the text prefixes and suffixes can be observed being split from the root, for example 'play' and 'ing', 're' and 'view'.

3.2 C Source Code

Figure 2(b) shows the structure of a model formed from a C source file—in fact, in the true spirit of recursive presentation, the file is part of the source code for the actual modeling program. The top level shows four rules which expand to

for•(k•=•0   ;•k•<•   MAX_RULES   ;•k•++)•{\n••••.

The first and last fragments correspond to the beginning and end of a C 'for' statement with k as the counter variable. The middle two fragments identify a less-than comparison involving k, and a constant MAX_RULES.

At the next level, 'for•(k•=•0' is split into 'for•(k•' and '=•0', indicating that something other than an assignment has followed 'for•(k•' in the past. The phrase ';•k•<•' is split into the variable and the operator ';•k•' and '<•', indicating that other comparisons have been made on k.

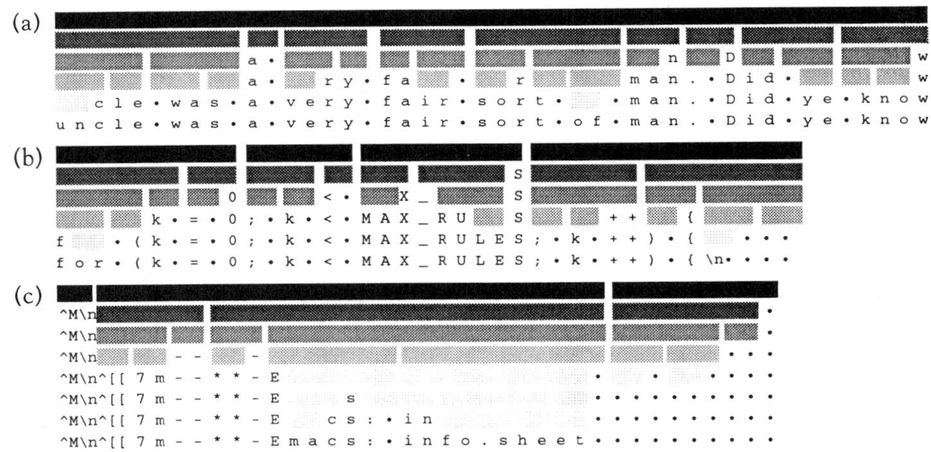

Figure 2: Structure derived from (a) English text,
(b) C source code, and (c) a sequence of terminal control codes

The third line separates 'for•(', the standard beginning of a C 'for' statement, from 'k•', the specification of the counter variable.The assignment operator '=•' is separated from the value '0'; the operator '++' is separated from ';•k•' and ')•{' is separated from the following white space '\n•••'.

Overall, the divisions make structural sense in terms of the syntax of C, combining terminal symbols into groups on boundaries that coincide with meaningful blocks within the language.

3.3 Transcript of an Emacs Editing Session

Figure 2(c) is a part of a shell transcript, which included the user editing a file using the Emacs editor. The top line shows three rules which expand to

^M\n ^[[7m--**-Emacs:•info.sheet• ••••••••••

The first rule is the sequence to send terminal cursor to the left-most column of the next line. The second rule draws part of the Emacs status line, and the last rule is a run spaces. The decomposition of the last rule shows how runs of symbols are combined into one rule, and it is clear that some way of expressing runs even more concisely would improve the modeling process in some cases.

The next line splits the escape sequence and hyphens '^[[7m--' from the rest of the status line. The split is made just before the '**' which indicate that buffer has not been saved. The prescence of a split here indicates that the same sequence without the asterisks has occurred elsewhere in the sequence (probably when the file was first loaded).

On the next line, the VT100 escape code for reverse video text is separated from the hyphens. Also the '**-' status indicator is split from 'Emacs:•info.sheet•'. Next, '**' is split from the hyphen and 'Emacs:•' is split from the file name 'info.sheet•'.

The technique has identified the new-line-carriage return sequence, a run of spaces, the saved buffer indicator, the reverse-video escape sequence, the word 'Emacs:•' and the file name. Each of these constitute major structural components of the original sequence.

4 Transmission of the grammar

There are two ways in which the induced grammar can be used to transmit a compressed version of the original sequence. The grammar itself can be transmitted, or it can be used to parse the sequence so that the latter can be transmitted adaptively.

4.1 TRANSMITTING THE GRAMMAR

The simplest way of transmitting the sequence compactly is to encode the grammar directly. Most compression schemes are adaptive in that the encoder and decoder build a model simultaneously, and the sequence is transmitted relative to the current model. It has been shown that adaptive modeling is at least as good as sending a static model and then sending the sequence relative to that model [1]. The present technique represents an interesting variation: rather than describing some characteristics of the sequence, the model describes the sequence *exactly*. No more information is needed once the model has been sent; the decoder simply expands the first rule in the grammar, and continues recursively.

First, the complete grammar is formed by processing the entire sequence. The grammar can be viewed as a sequence of terminals, non-terminals and end-of-rule markers. This sequence can be coded efficiently using a zero-order model together with an arithmetic coder [10]. Recall that every digram in the grammar is unique. This implies that each symbol is unique in the context of the preceding one, and so models of higher order cannot contribute any useful predictions. Similarly, macro schemes will not achieve any compression, as no phrase appears more than once.

The compression performance of the scheme was measured on the Calgary corpus. This corpus contains fourteen files ranging in content from English text to object programs [1]. The sizes of the files after being compressed by this technique are given in the column labeled 'Grammar' in Table 1. Results are also shown for Unix *compress* [1], a standard macro scheme, LZFG [3], an excellent macro scheme, and a high-performance context scheme, PPMC [6]. The second grammar induction column, labeled 'Adaptive', is discussed below. Compression rates in bits per character are given for each scheme on each file. The average rate is shown at the bottom of the column for each scheme. This gives an indication of compression performance over a broad range of file types.

Compress performs poorly relative to the other methods, but is a practical and widely used macro scheme. Macro methods achieve compression by replacing repeated sequences with references to earlier occurrences, either by explicit reference to a segment of the sequence already transmitted in the case of LZ77 [11], or by referring to a phrase in a list of phrases extracted from the sequence in the case of LZ78 [12]. LZFG is a macro scheme based on LZ78 principles, but with improved selection of phrases and correspondingly improved compression performance. PPMC, on the other hand, is based on statistical context modeling, where the next symbol is predicted based on the preceding symbols. This prediction indicates the amount of information conveyed by the next symbol, and arithmetic coding is used to transmit exactly this number of bits. PPMC achieves the best overall compression rate of any known general-purpose compression method.

The mean compression achieved by transmitting the grammar as above is 19% better than *compress* and only 3.7% worse than LZFG. It is still 23% worse than PPMC, which might be expected from its similarity in approach to the macro schemes. The performance relative to the macro schemes is gratifying given that this is a static model, and one that explains the sequence structure in a useful way.

4.2 ADAPTIVE TRANSMISSION

The grammatical inference method can be used in a different way to achieve even greater compression. First, a grammar is constructed for the whole sequence as before. The first rule, S, consists of a sequence of symbols which can be expanded to reproduce the original text. This rule is transmitted from left to right. When a non-terminal appears, there are three possibilities:

- if it has not appeared before, the right-hand side of its rule is transmitted;
- if it has been seen exactly once before, a pointer to the first occurrence is transmitted;
- if it has been seen two or more times before, it is transmitted as a symbol.

If a non-terminal has not appeared before, then the rule it heads must be transmitted explicitly. At the start of the sequence a marker is transmitted which indicates a position in the sequence that will be referred to when the rule appears for the second time. The markers are numbered implicitly by both encoder and decoder so that they can be referred to later. The cases above for rule S apply equally to the transmission of the contents of the new rule; if the new rule contains any novel non-terminals, then contents of *these* rules will be transmitted, and so on recursively. An order-zero model with arithmetic coding is used to transmit both symbols and markers.

If the non-terminal has appeared exactly once before, it is communicated simply by specifying the number of the marker that was transmitted on its first occurrence, together with the length of the rule's contents. This is similar to LZ77, which represents repeated sequences by referring to earlier occurrences. Markers are deleted once they are used, and the implicit marker numbers are adjusted accordingly. Given a certain number of markers which have been transmitted but not used, say k, the number of bits in which a marker number will be transmitted is $\log_2(k)$. The length of the new rule is transmitted using an adaptive arithmetic code, using fewer bits to transmit shorter lengths.

Once a non-terminal has been seen twice, the rule it heads has been completely specified with a marker and a length and so can be fully reconstructed by the decoder. It is now sufficient to transmit the non-terminal as an ordinary symbol. This is similar to LZ78,

		Grammar induction		Other methods, for comparison		
File	**Description**	**Grammar**	**Adaptive**	**PPMC**	**LZFG**	**Compress**
bib	bibliography	3.03	2.56	2.12	2.90	3.35
book1	fiction book	3.21	2.86	2.52	3.62	3.46
book2	non-fiction book	2.93	2.51	2.28	3.05	3.28
geo	geophysical data	4.87	4.78	5.01	5.70	6.08
news	electronic news	3.41	2.92	2.77	3.44	3.86
obj1	object code	4.43	3.89	3.68	4.03	5.23
obj2	object code	3.28	2.72	2.59	2.96	4.17
paper1	technical paper	3.52	2.93	2.48	3.03	3.77
paper2	technical paper	3.41	2.91	2.46	3.16	3.52
pic	bilevel image	1.08	0.94	0.98	0.87	0.97
progc	C program	3.51	2.90	2.49	2.89	3.87
progl	Lisp program	2.50	2.02	1.87	1.97	3.03
progp	Pascal program	2.45	1.97	1.82	1.90	3.11
trans	shell transcript	2.21	1.78	1.75	1.76	3.27
	Average	**3.13**	**2.70**	**2.49**	**2.95**	**3.64**

Table 1: Compression performance of several techniques (bits per character)

a	S ::= a	
♦	S ::= a ♦	marker 1
♦	S ::= a ♦ ♦	marker 2
b	S ::= a ♦ ♦ b	
c	S ::= a ♦ ♦ b c	
d	S ::= a ♦ ♦ b c d	
e	S ::= a ♦ ♦ b c d e	
↑(2, 3)	S ::= a ♦ A e A A ::= b c d	creates a rule of length 3 starting at marker 2
f	S ::= a ♦ A e A f A ::= b c d	
↑(1, 4)	S ::= a B B A ::= b c d B ::= A e A f	creates a rule of length 4 starting at marker 1
g	S ::= a B B g A ::= b c d B ::= A e A f	

Figure 3: Incremental transmission of the example sequence

where the list of phrases is the set of rules identified so far. Again an order-zero arithmetic code is used.

Figure 3 shows how the earlier example would be represented for transmission. On the left is what is actually coded, and on the right is the grammar built up by the decoder. The symbol ♦ represents a marker, and markers are unparameterized, although both encoder and decoder refer to them by number. The symbol ↑ represents a pointer and has two parameters, marker number and length. It causes the creation of a rule, and rules are labeled (by convention) A, B, C, ... so that they can be referred to later on. Although it does not occur in the example, subsequent references to the non-terminals A and B are transmitted as simply 'A' and 'B'.

This technique has two advantages over other macro schemes. First, because the sequence up to the current point contains non-terminals in place of longer terminal sequences, it is shorter than the equivalent sequence that LZ77-based schemes refer to. As there are fewer symbols sent, the proportion of markers is higher, and the number of bits needed to specify the marker is correspondingly smaller. Also, given that the sequence is compressed, the lengths of the rules can be transmitted in fewer bits. Second, because the rules are chosen to be as long as possible, and all rules are used, there are fewer rules than there are phrases in most LZ78 schemes, so the rule number can be transmitted in fewer bits. In many LZ78 techniques, phrases are extended by only one symbol at a time, so rules grow slowly and prefixes of long phrases may only be used once.

The compression performance of this technique is given in the column labeled 'Adaptive' of Table 1. It achieves a mean compression rate of 2.7, which is 9.3% better than that of LZFG. It represents an improvement of 13% over sending the grammar using an order-zero model, and is only 8.4% worse than PPMC. For file *geo*, the grammar induction methods both outperform LZFG and PPMC. For file *pic*, the grammar induction method outperforms PPMC when adaptive transmission is used. However, PPMC is best on all the other files. Grammar induction using adaptive transmission wins out over LZFG for most files, the exceptions being the image, the programs, and the shell transcript.

The superior compression performance of the new method (using adaptive transmission) over LZFG, may be partly due to the use of arithmetic coding to encode the numbers and symbols in the exact fractional number of bits dictated by the frequency models. The use of arithmetic coding extracts a penalty in execution time, and to rectify this an integral-bit coding technique could be considered instead. However, experiments with such methods have not been conducted.

5 Application to knowledge acquisition

One of the key advantages of this modeling technique is that it is capable of identifying interesting structure in diverse sequences, and presenting the structure in a form that is easily understood and readily applied to problems in other research areas. Specific applications for this technique are still being investigated, and four of the more promising possibilities are briefly presented here.

5.1 Programming by Demonstration

The grammar modeling technique was originally conceived as a way of modeling a sequence of user actions, in order to induce a program that would perform the same actions in a different context automatically. This process is called *programming by demonstration*, and is a burgeoning area of research in human-computer interaction [9]. The ability of the new method of grammar inference to identify repeated sequences of actions, and to abstract these into higher level 'tasks,' simplifies the identification of control structures such as loops or branches. For example, a loop appears as a repeated non-terminal at some level in the grammar. Moreover, if user actions are only available at a very low level of abstraction, this method can identify more interesting, meaningful actions as non-terminals higher in the hierarchy of rules.

5.2 Analysing Natural Language

The identification of words, phrases, suffixes, prefixes and roots of natural language text could form a basis for the analysis of language without a priori assumptions of the nature and morphology of words. Furthermore, the inclusion of a small amount of domain knowledge, such as the role of white space as a word separator, may improve the accuracy with which this technique identifies significant structural features of text. Leaving written languages aside, it could also help in the identification of words and phrases in new languages where only a phoneme-level transcript is available, grouping phonemes together into meaningful utterances.

5.3 Characterising Music

Repetition of note phrases, and recombination of phrases at various levels, is fundamental to musical composition—even at the simplest level of the ubiquitous verse, chorus, verse structure. It has been shown that there is considerable redundancy in note sequences, and this has been successfully captured by a statistical modeler [8]. The statistical approach is, however, unable to identify the recursive and iterative structure that humans recognise in music [5]. This technique may provide a way of identifying these regularities.

5.4 DNA SEQUENCES

Molecular analysis of DNA strands produces DNA sequences in symbolic form. Each strand consists of a sequence of nucleotides, which can be one of four types: adenine, cytosine, guanine and thymine. This technique could offer a way of extracting some of the structure from DNA sequences to offer a higher-level view of the patterns of nucleotides [2].

6 Conclusion

Data compression takes advantage of regularities in a symbol sequence to reduce its size. Researchers in machine learning and artificial intelligence are also interested in identifying the structure of sequences. The technique for inferring hierarchical grammars serves both purposes. The grammars induced from a variety of different sequences correspond to the structure that we would expect, and sometimes suggest novel relationships that offer insight into the nature of the sequence and the effect of notation. The compression performance of methods based on the induced grammar indicate that the models, while readable and semantically plausible, also approach the best compression techniques in their predictive ability.

7 Acknowledgments

We gratefully acknowledge Tim Bell for helping us to develop our ideas. This work is supported by the New Zealand Foundation for Research, Science and Technology.

8 References

[1] Bell, T.C., Cleary, J.G. and Witten, I.H. (1990) *Text Compression*. Prentice Hall, Englewood Cliffs, NJ.

[2] Chan, P.K. "Machine Learning in Molecular Biology Sequence Analysis," *CUCS-011-91*, Department of Computer Science, Columbia University.

[3] Fiala, E.R., Greene, D.H. (1989) "Data compression with finite windows," *Communications of the ACM*, *32*(4) 490–505

[4] Fraenkel, A.S. Mor, M. and Perl, Y. (1983) "Is text compression by prefixes and suffixes practical?," *Acta Informatica*, (20) 371–389.

[5] Manzara, L.C., Witten, I.H., James, M., 1992 "On the entropy of music: an experiment with Bach Chorale melodies," *Leonardo Music Journal* *2*(1) 81–88

[6] Moffat, A. (1990), "Implementing the PPM data compression scheme," *IEEE Transactions on Communications* COM-*38*(11), 1917–1921

[7] Storer, J.A. and Szymanski, T.G. (1978) "The macro model for data compression," *10th Annual Symposium of the Theory of Computing*, 30–39.

[8] Conklin, D., Witten, I.H. (1990), "Prediction and Entropy of Music," *Technical report 91/457/41* (Calgary: Department of Computer Science, Univ. of Calgary).

[9] Witten, I.H., Mo, D. (1993) "TELS: Learning text editing tasks from examples," *Watch what I do: programming by demonstration*, A. Cypher (Ed.), MIT Press, Cambridge, Massachusetts, 182–203

[10] Witten, I.H., Neal, R., Cleary, J.G. (1987) "Arithmetic coding for data compression," *Communications of the* ACM 30(6), 520–540

[11] Ziv, J., Lempel, A. (1977) "A universal algorithm for sequential data compression," *IEEE Transactions on Information Theory IT-23*(3), 337–343

[12] Ziv, J., Lempel, A.(1978) "Compression of individual sequences via variable-rate coding," *IEEE Transactions on Information Theory IT-24*(5), 530–536

Architectural Advances in the VLSI Implementation of Arithmetic Coding for Binary Image Compression

Gennady Feygin, Patrick Glenn Gulak, and Paul Chow[1] [2]
Department of Electrical and Computer Engineering
University of Toronto, Toronto, Ontario, Canada M5S 1A4

Abstract

This paper presents some recent advances in the architecture for the data compression technique known as Arithmetic Coding. The new architecture employs loop unrolling and speculative execution of the inner loop of the algorithm to achieve a significant speed-up relative to the Q-Coder architecture. This approach reduces the number of iterations required to compress a block of data by a factor that is on the order of the compression ratio. While the speed-up technique has been previously discovered independently by researchers at IBM, no systematic study of the architectural trade-offs has ever been published. For the CCITT facsimile documents, the new architecture achieves a speed-up of approximately seven compared to the IBM Q-coder when four lookahead units are employed in parallel. A structure for fast Input/Output processing based on run length pre-coding of the data stream to accompany the new architecture is also presented.

1 Introduction

Data compression has found widespread use in data storage, and audio and video transmission. In all of the above cases it is advantageous to compress data to conserve scarce resources (disk space in storage, bandwidth in sound and image transmission).

Arithmetic Coding [1, 2] is a data compression technique that represents the source data as a fraction that assumes a value between zero and one. The encoding algorithm is based upon recursive subdivision of an interval and retaining one of the created subintervals as a new interval for the next step of the recursion. The advantages of Arithmetic Coding include working directly with symbols, without resorting to construction of multi-symbol sequences (extensions of the source alphabet). This makes Arithmetic Coding particularly well suited to the encoding of binary images, where the probabilities of occurrence of two symbols are frequently skewed.

[1]Many thanks to Dr. Joan Mitchell and Dr. Ronald Arps for their thoughtful comments on an earlier version of this paper. Financial support for this research was provided by NSERC and ITRC.

[2]e-mail:gfeygin@eecg.toronto.edu

1068-0314/94 $3.00 © 1994 IEEE

A group at IBM has reported a CMOS realization of an Arithmetic encoder/decoder for binary images in [3]. An updated version of the system, known as the Q-coder, appeared in [4]. The simplified encoding and decoding processes are described in Figures 1 and 2 respectively. The variable C keeps track of the code string, while the variable A keeps track of the interval as it is being subdivided. Q_e is the probability of the Less Probable Symbol. An efficient mechanism for adaptively varying the value of Q_e based on the frequencies of occurrence of ones and zeros in the data stream is suggested in [5].

In Section 2 we apply loop unrolling to the Q-coder algorithm and demonstrate how the Q-coder algorithm can be made faster through processing multiple source pels at a time. Section 3 discusses the techniques that must be applied to eliminate the bottleneck at the input to the encoder (and symmetrically at the output of the decoder). Section 4 discusses the trade-offs inherent in designing and implementing a high-performance arithmetic coder. Finally, Section 5 gives a summary of research and indicates possible directions for future work.

2 Loop Unrolling

We present a scheme for achieving parallelism in Arithmetic Coding using a variant of a common technique used in compiler optimization called *Loop Unrolling* [6], which exposes more parallelism to the hardware. This technique was investigated in [7], and in this paper we extend their investigation and consider an optimum hardware implementation of the technique. For instance, the encoder described in [4, 5] considers the source symbols sequentially, one symbol at a time. We may place at the encoder a second unit that considers input symbols two at a time. When the probability of the *More Probable Symbol* (MPS) is much greater than the probability of the *Less Probable Symbol* (LPS), the probability of two MPS's in a row is much greater than the sum of the probabilities of all other two-symbol combinations. Thus the most likely sequence of events will be as follows:

1. Examine the first input bit; detect an MPS. Update A and C: $A \leftarrow A - Q_e$, $C \leftarrow C - Q_e$.
2. Compare A against $A_{\mathrm{min}} = 0.75$. Find that $A > A_{\mathrm{min}}$, therefore no renormalization (which causes Q_e to be updated) is required.
3. Examine the second input bit; detect an MPS. Update A and C: $A \leftarrow A - Q_e$, $C \leftarrow C - Q_e$.

Thus the most likely outcome of the sequence of processing two input bits is simply the following update: $A \leftarrow A - 2 \times Q_e$, $C \leftarrow C - 2 \times Q_e$. These computations are easy to perform (multiplication by 2 is implemented by wiring, with no circuitry required). It is natural to combine the two updates into one, thus saving one iteration. This is analogous to *loop unrolling*, with two iterations of the updates of the variables A and C combined into a single iteration of the new algorithm. What makes this modification of the basic algorithm particularly appealing is the possibility of combining the two operations that must be performed on each of the variables A and C into only a single operation on each variable. Of course there will be a small number of cases where advancing by two bits is not possible, due either to the presence of an LPS in the second bit position, or the need to re-normalize A and C, and update Q_e following the $A \leftarrow A - Q_e$ computation. Thus we must preserve the ability to perform the original one-bit update — our attempt to combine two iterations into one must be treated as *speculative*. The best technique is to compute both $A_1 \leftarrow A - Q_e$ and $A_2 \leftarrow A - 2 \times Q_e$, while simultaneously checking for the LPS and the re-normalization required, and selecting A_1 or A_2 as the new, updated value of A. The input data stream is also updated by removing one or two bits from the input stream, as appropriate. If $p(\text{MPS}) \gg p(\text{LPS})$, then the two-bit updates will dominate, allowing the processing rate to increase by a factor of almost two.

Of course there is nothing magical about examining the input stream two bits at a time. In principle, we could choose to examine k bits at a time and increase the processing speed by a factor of approximately k. There are obvious practical limitations on what values of k are worth considering — for instance in computing $A_k \leftarrow A - k \times Q_e$ we must restrict k to be a power of two, if we are to avoid the expense and delay of a true multiplication. As k grows larger it becomes increasingly difficult to get k input bits and to verify whether or not they are all MPS's. Yet this verification must be fast enough to keep up with the circuitry used to update A and C. The technique for providing fast I/O will be discussed at length in Section 3.

A technique described in [7] requires that an integer quotient $(A - 0.75)/Q_e$ be computed to calculate the value k. Although this may be perfectly acceptable in a software implementation running on a general-purpose computer, a fast division operation is expensive in hardware[3] and would add significantly to the cycle time (since it must precede the actual update of the A and C registers).

Thus we propose a modification of the approach of [4]. This modification consists of allowing simultaneous lookahead by multiple powers of two $(2, 4, \ldots 2^{k_{\max}})$ to be performed. While occurrences of a large number of MPS's in a row are less frequent than those of the smaller number of MPS's in a row, each incidence of accepting a long string gives greater benefit than accepting a short string. Thus maintaining separate circuitry for large lookahead values may be advantageous, even if used only infrequently. Any string of length $N < 2^{k_{\max}+1}$ can be processed in $O(\lfloor \log_2(N) \rfloor)$ iterations using $O(\lfloor \log_2(N) \rfloor)$ adders for updating A and C. In the original Q-Coder, N iterations are required using one adder for A and one for C.

The pseudo-code describing the operation of the proposed encoder is presented in Figure 3. Note that the operation of lookahead by two is slightly different from all other powers of two. Since we know that $Q_e < 0.75$, we can accept lookahead by two even when re-normalization is caused by *the second MPS*. This is easily verified by considering A_1. If $A_1 \geq 0.75$ then we can guarantee that the re-normalization is not required until at least the second MPS. Thus we can always take advantage of lookahead by two. A similar enhancement for any other power of two is impossible:

[3]Recall that the Q-coder is designed to be multiplication-free.

for instance, to guarantee that lookahead by eight is acceptable, we must ensure that the re-normalization occurs after the eighth bit at the earliest. For this we must know $A_7 = A - 7 \times Q_e$. Since computing A_7 requires (expensive) multiplication, we avoid it by slightly tightening the constraint and verifying that re-normalization is not required until the ninth bit at the earliest ($A_8 \geq 0.75$). Occasionally, we may miss an opportunity to perform lookahead by the maximum amount possible, but we avoid the penalties (time and circuitry) required to perform the multiplication. For the case of lookahead by two, where the result of the "multiplication" is available for free, we use it.

As we process our input data stream, we frequently encounter long strings of MPS's with only a few LPS's, however, each LPS contains a large amount of information, while each MPS contains only a little. In the original Q-Coder, either a single MPS or a single LPS was processed in one iteration, resulting in an encoded output whose rate was uneven. In our scheme with lookahead, we process a single LPS or *multiple* MPS's in one iteration. Thus the amount of *information* being processed per iteration is more nearly balanced. Since the number of output bits must be (in the ideal case) proportional to the amount of information being transmitted, our design with lookahead results in reduced jitter at the encoded output end. The situation at the decoder end is similar.

3 Input Data Stream Processing

As lookahead is introduced into the *Interval Update Core* (IUC) of the encoder, the speed of the encoder will become increasingly limited by the speed at which uncompressed data can be supplied and examined for the presence of an LPS in the data stream. Some kind of buffering must be provided to examine up to $2^{k_{\max}}$ input symbols at one time. A simple solution is to use a simple form of run-length codes. Whenever a run is terminated, a number indicating the length of the run is deposited in a FIFO that is placed between the run-length encoder and the IUC. This also removes input processing from the critical path of the IUC iteration, and allows all input processing to be pipelined. The IUC "consumes" run lengths from the FIFO and loads them into its own counter, and proceeds to encode the run. At each step of the IUC operations an internal counter is decremented by an appropriate amount. It is advantageous to generate packets that correspond to the number of MPS's followed by an LPS in a manner similar to that of [8]. Thus i MPS's followed by one LPS followed by j MPS's followed by one LPS will require only two packet locations inside the FIFO (i, j). This scheme is superior to the usual run-length encoding, since the probability of two or more LPS's in a row is very low (if the source information is compressible), and since processing more than one LPS at a time is impossible (the IUC performs re-normalization following every LPS). This scheme also has certain shortcomings, primarily the need for an escape sequence to indicate the occurrence of a string of MPS's that is longer than can be stored inside the counter.

4 Performance Driven Design

As discussed previously, IUC performance can be immproved by employing lookahead into the input sequence. To determine precisely how much speed-up can be obtained, we have encoded the eight CCITT FAX images [9, 10]. The seven-pel predictor with *context* used in [10] was employed.

4.1 Speed-up Evaluation

The methodology of examining the speed-up that can be obtained with various arrangements of the IUC is quite simple. We begin by running a simulation that assumes a fully parallel IUC, with a lookahead by every power of 2 up to a maximum[4] of 1024. We record the number of iterations in which lookahead by $1, 2, \ldots, 1024$ MPS's was employed. The results for such an experiment are summarized in Table 1 for the CCITT1 image.

Note that the three largest lookahead values account for for well over 50% of the processed bits, but under 2% of the number of iterations. This gives a clear indication that the better encoder configurations will not be confined to using only the smallest lookahead values. It is also important to note that the processing of single LPS's and single MPS's together account for over 75% of the iterations of the encoder. Thus any additional speed-up improvement must involve reducing the number of iterations spent processing single pels.

It is convenient to represent an encoder by assigning a 12-bit binary number that has a one in position i if lookahead by 2^i is provided and a zero if lookahead by 2^i is not provided. Thus, under this classification, the Q-coder encoder is 000000000001 (or $0X001$ in hexadecimal notation), the fully parallel encoder/decoder is 111111111111 or $0XFFF$, and the decoder with lookahead by $1024, 64, 8, 1$ pel is 010001001001 or $0X449$. It is then relatively simple to perform an exhaustive search of all possible combinations, noting the best encoder and the number of iterations required when using the system with $1, 2, \ldots,$ lookahead units for each of the eight CCITT images. We have determined the "best" encoders for each CCITT image when $1, 2, \ldots, 12$ lookahead units are employed. The results are summarized in Figure 4, with each curve corresponding to one of the CCITT documents (indicated by a number).

We make the following observations: even in the worst case (least-compressible, CCITT7 document) up to four lookahead units may be employed with approximately linear speed-up and is therefore a reasonable choice for a lookahead value. Only one question remains outstanding: which particular encoder with four lookahead units is the best? Unfortunately, there is no one encoder for a particular value of lookahead[5] that is best for all eight CCITT documents. We can narrow our choice by looking at candidate encoder configurations that have been found to be optimum for at least one of the eight CCITT documents. The results are summarized in Table 2.

[4]The maximum is the highest power of two that is less than or equal to $\frac{A_{\min}}{\min(Q_e)}$

[5]Except, of course, for the trivial cases of one and twelve lookahead units.

The configuration $0X95$ is a clear winner, with the best average speed-up of 8.48. It is the optimum encoder configuration for *three* out of the eight CCITT documents. It is also important to note that the worst encoder configuration, $0X2b$, is on average only 8% slower than the best configuration. Thus any one of the four configurations shown in Table 2 can be expected to perform reasonably well. Yet another criterion that must be considered when choosing an encoder configuration is keeping the largest lookahead value used in an encoder as small as possible, since it reduces the wiring required to provide shifted (i.e., multiplied by powers of two) copies of the Q_e. The configurations $0X4b$ and $0X55$ require one bit less shifting than the configuration $0X95$. The diagram of a four-lookahead unit encoder with configuration $0X95$ is shown in Figure 5.

4.2 Single-Cycle Processing of Multiple Pels in an Area with Changing Context

Consider again Table 1. We have already pointed out that the lion's share of the clock cycles are spent in processing the pels one at a time. Even if all the time spent processing two, four, etc. pels at a time was reduced to zero, 75% of the clock cycles would still be required to continue processing single MPS's and single LPS's (Amdahl's Law [11]). Table 3 gives a summary of the causes that prevent the processing of multiple pels.

In those cases where the context is changing and where an MPS is followed by another MPS, it may be possible to process two MPS's in a single clock cycle, providing the Q_e values are available in time for both contexts. This may be accomplished through employing a double-ported storage for the Q_e values. A better alternative may be pre-fetching of the Q_e values. For instance, suppose an encoder is processing a run of zeros and the present context[6] is also zero $\begin{smallmatrix}00000\\00\end{smallmatrix}$. There is only one possible context following an all-zero context, namely $\begin{smallmatrix}00001\\00\end{smallmatrix}$, that might allow two MPS's to be processed in the same clock cycle. Thus, when processing an all-zero run, the encoder begins to fetch the Q_e value of the contexts $\begin{smallmatrix}00001\\00\end{smallmatrix}$, $\begin{smallmatrix}00011\\00\end{smallmatrix}$, $\begin{smallmatrix}00111\\00\end{smallmatrix}$ etc. always selecting the more likely successor context to pre-fetch. As successive Q_e values are fetched, they are stored in a cache and are made available to the interval and code point update circuitry as required. Note that the Q_e values cannot change in the interim and the cache is guaranteed to have the correct Q_e values.

The speed-up that may be achieved if this change is implemented is shown and compared to the default scheme in Table 4. A speed-up gain of up to thirty percent is consistent with our analysis of the default configuration, where advancing by a single MPS accounted for approximately 60% of the cycles, with the lion's share of these being convertible into pairs of MPS pels that can be processed in a single cycle.

---

[6]We adopt the notation $\begin{smallmatrix}XXXXX\\XX\end{smallmatrix}$ to describe the seven-pel context determined by the values of five pels in the previous line and two pels in the current line of the image being processed

5 Summary

This paper has presented new architectures for the data compression technique known as Arithmetic Coding based on loop unrolling and speculative execution of the inner loop of the algorithm that is a generalization of the Q-Coder [4] architecture. Multiple lookahead units are employed, with each unit attempting to process a different number of input bits (output bits in the case of the decoder) in one iteration. For the set of CCITT documents, the coder achieves a speed-up of approximately eight compared to the IBM Q-coder when four lookahead units are employed in parallel. A structure for fast Input/Output processing based on Run-Length encoding of the data stream to accompany the new, faster IUC is also suggested.

Additional speed-up using single-cycle processing of multiple pels with different contexts was also investigated.

References

[1] N. Abramson. *Information Theory and Coding*, pages 61–62. McGraw-Hill, New York, NY, 1963. Refers to unpublished work of Elias.

[2] J. J. Rissanen and G. G. Langdon. Universal Modelling and Coding. *IEEE Transactions on Information Theory*, 27(12):12–23, 1981.

[3] G. G. Langdon and J. J. Rissanen. A Simple General Binary Source Code. *IEEE Transactions on Information Theory*, 28(5):800–803, 1982.

[4] J. L. Mitchell and W. B. Pennebaker. Optimal hardware and software arithmetic coding procedures for the Q-Coder. *IBM Journal of Research and Development*, 32(6):727–736, November 1988.

[5] W. B. Pennebaker et al. An overview of the basic principles of the Q-Coder adaptive binary arithmetic coder. *IBM Journal of Research and Development*, 32(6):717–726, November 1988.

[6] John L. Hennessy and David A. Patterson. *Computer Architecture A Quntitative Approach*, chapter 6, page 315. Morgan Kaufmann Publishers, Inc., 1990.

[7] W. B. Pennebaker and J. L. Mitchell. *JPEG Still Image Data Compression Standard*, chapter 13.7, pages 231–232. Van Nostrand Reinhold, 1993.

[8] R. B. Arps. Binary image compression. In William K. Pratt, editor, *Image Transmission Techniques*, pages 222–276. Academic Press Inc, New York, 1979.

[9] R. Hunter and A. Robinson. International Digital Facsimile Coding Standards. *Proceedings of the IEEE*, 68, July 1980.

[10] R. B. Arps, T. K. Truong, D. J. Lu, R. C. Pasco, and T. D. Friedman. A Multi-Purpose VLSI Chip for Adaptive Data Compression of Bilevel Images. *IBM Journal of Research and Development*, 32(6):775–794, November 1988.

[11] G. M. Amdahl. Validity of the Single Processor Approach to Achieving Large Scale Computing Capabilities. In *Proceedings of the AFIPS 1967 Spring Joint Computer Conference*, pages 483–485, Atlantic City, New Jersey, April 1967.

```
if MPS is encoded
   C ← C + Q_e      A ← A − Q_e
   while A ≤ 0.75 do
         A ← A × 2      C ← C × 2
         decrement Q_e
   end do
else       LPS encoded
         A ← Q_e
   while A ≤ 0.75 do
         A ← A × 2      C ← C × 2
         increment Q_e
   end do
end if
```

Figure 1: Pseudo-code Description of Arithmetic Encoding

```
if C ≥ Q_e       MPS decoded
   C ← C − Q_e      A ← A − Q_e
   while A ≤ 0.75 do
         A ← A × 2      C ← C × 2
         decrement Q_e
   end do
else       LPS decoded
         A ← Q_e
   while A ≤ 0.75 do
         A ← A × 2      C ← C × 2
         increment Q_e
   end do
end if
```

Figure 2: Pseudo-code Description of Arithmetic Decoding

```
do      par
        C_1 ← C + Q_e       A_1 ← A − Q_e       FLAG_1MPS ← 1 symb. =? MPS
        C_2 ← C + 2 × Q_e   A_2 ← A − 2 × Q_e   FLAG_2MPS ← 2 symb. =? MPS
        C_4 ← C + 4 × Q_e   A_4 ← A − 4 × Q_e   FLAG_4MPS ← 4 symb. =? MPS
                                  ⋮
        C_{2^kmax} ← C + 2^kmax × Q_e ...FLAG_{2^kmax MPS} ← 2^kmax symb. =? MPS
end     par
if       ( FLAG_{2^kmax MPS} ∧ A_{2^kmax} ≥ 0.75 )   { C ← C_{2^kmax}   A ← A_{2^kmax} }
else if  ( FLAG_4MPS ∧ A_4 ≥ 0.75 )                  { C ← C_4          A ← A_4 }
else if  ( FLAG_2MPS ∧ A_2 ≥ 0.75 )                  { C ← C_2          A ← A_2 }
else if  ( FLAG_1MPS )                               { C ← C_1          A ← A_1 }
else                                                 { C ← C            A ← Q_e }
end if
do      par
        if (( FLAG_{2^kmax MPS} ∨ ... ∨ FLAG_2MPS ∨ FLAG_1MPS ) ∧ A < 0.75 )   decr Q_e
        else if ( A < 0.75 )                                                 incr Q_e
        end if
        while ( A ≤ 0.75 ) do { A ← A × 2     C ← C × 2 }
        end do
end     par
```

Figure 3: Pseudo-code Description of an Arithmetic Encoder with Lookahead by Multiple Powers of 2.FLAG $\leftarrow a \stackrel{?}{=} b$ means that FLAG will be set to TRUE if a equals b.

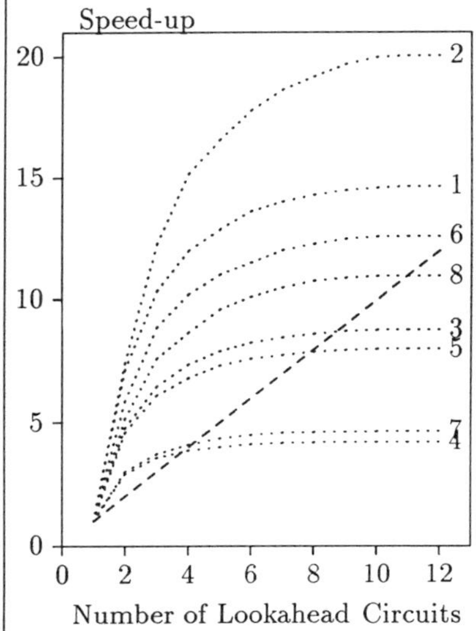

Figure 4: Maximum Speed-up versus Number of Lookahead Units for all eight CCITT FAX documents The dashed line corresponds to Speed-up linear in number of Lookahead Units.

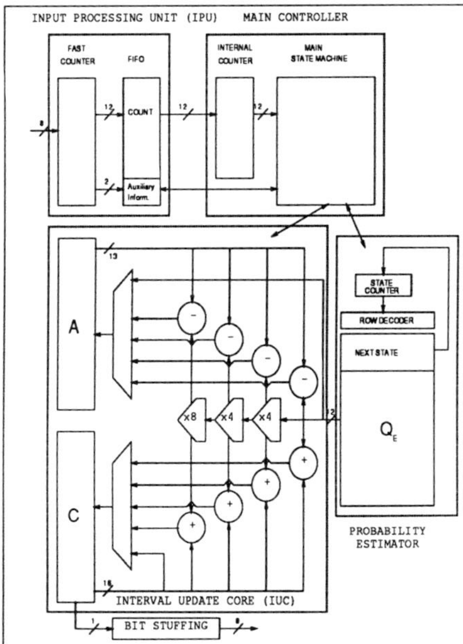

Figure 5: A block diagram of an arithmetic encoder with four lookahead units (configuration $0X95$).

Advance by	No. of Iterations	% of total	No. of Bits Encoded	% of total
1 LPS	34640	12.35	34640	0.84
1 MPS	182233	64.98	182233	4.44
2 MPS	22174	7.91	44348	1.08
4 MPS	12946	4.62	51784	1.26
8 MPS	7307	2.61	58456	1.42
16 MPS	5574	1.99	89184	2.17
32 MPS	3835	1.37	122720	2.99
64 MPS	3609	1.29	230976	5.63
128 MPS	3030	1.08	387840	9.45
256 MPS	1698	0.61	434688	10.59
512 MPS	2008	0.72	1028096	25.04
1024 MPS	1407	0.50	1440768	35.09
Total	280461	100%	4105728	100%

Table 1: Applying Lookahead to the CCITT1 image encoded with a seven-pel predictor employing context.

Speed-up for Coder Configuration	CCITT Document								Average
	1	2	3	4	5	6	7	8	
0X95	**12.00**	**15.17**	7.37	3.76	6.79	**10.21**	3.98	8.53	8.48
0x4b	11.61	14.45	**7.39**	**3.87**	**6.82**	10.10	4.02	8.31	8.32
0x2b	10.33	12.81	7.10	3.81	6.63	9.39	**4.09**	8.59	7.84
0x55	11.50	14.78	7.35	3.76	6.79	10.17	4.04	**8.68**	8.38
Compression Ratio	34.0	57.4	21.7	9.1	19.0	36.5	8.8	32.8	

Table 2: Speed-up for all eight CCITT documents that is obtained using four different encoder configurations and a seven pel predictor with context. Speed-up values corresponding to the optimum encoder configuration for a particular CCITT document are highlighted. The compression ratio is independent of the encoder configuration.

Advance by	No. of bits processed
Single LPS	34640
MPS followed by renormalization	25085
MPS followed by LPS	2634
MPS in a changing context followed by an LPS	23580
MPS in a changing context followed by an MPS	130934

Table 3: Frequency breakdown of the case of advancing by a single pel for the CCITT1 image encoded with a seven-pel predictor employing context.

	Average Speed-up			
Configuration	$0X95+$	$0X95$	$0XFFF+$	$0XFFF$
CCITT (1-8)	10.34	8.48	13.46	10.49

Table 4: Speed-up averaged over eight CCITT documents for the fastest four-adder configuration, $0X95$, and twelve-adder configuration $0XFFF$. The "+" indicates that pairs of MPS's with different context are processed in parallel, where possible.

MULTIPLICATION AND DIVISION FREE ADAPTIVE ARITHMETIC CODING TECHNIQUES FOR BI-LEVEL IMAGES

Linh Huynh
Department of Computer Science, CITRI-RMIT
723 Swanston St., Carlton, Victoria 3053, Australia
linh@kbs.citri.edu.au

1 INTRODUCTION

Arithmetic coding is an attractive method for data compression. The main advantage of arithmetic coding is its optimality: it is capable of encoding any source at a bit rate close to the source entropy [2, 12]. However, arithmetic coding tends to be slow, because in simplest form it requires at least one multiplication per input symbol. Moreover, if used adaptively, desirable in many applications, an extra division may be needed at every coding step. To reduce this cost, approximate arithmetic coding techniques, which replace the multiplication operations by a small number of less expensive operations such as shifts and additions, have been used [1, 2, 4, 7, 8, 9]. In this paper, we propose two new approximate methods for coding binary alphabet with negligible loss of compression efficiency.

In Section 2 we briefly overview arithmetic coding and bi-level image modelling. Then, in Section 3 we describe the proposed methods, followed by the implementation in Section 4. Next, Section 5 discusses the compression performance theoretically, and finally in Section 6 we empirically evaluate the proposed techniques. The focus throughout is on encoding; the decoding process is similar.

2 OVERVIEW

2.1 ARITHMETIC CODING

Conceptually, arithmetic coding is a data compression technique whereby an input data string is represented by a fractional value between 0 and 1. Before any symbol in the data string is encoded, the initial range of values for coding the data string is the entire interval $[0, 1)$. As each new symbol is processed, the coder partitions the current interval into a number of subintervals. Each possible input symbol is given a subinterval whose size is proportional to the probability of that symbol. The coder then retains as the current interval the subinterval that corresponds to the symbol being coded. As the input data string becomes longer, the interval that represents it becomes smaller and the number of bits needed to specify that interval increases. The more probable symbols reduce the interval by less, and thus add fewer bits to the encoded data. At the end of the input, any value within the current interval can be used to represent the compressed data.

2.2 BI-LEVEL IMAGE MODELLING

Accurate source modelling is essential to any compression scheme since performance bounds are established with respect to that model. The effectiveness of a model is determined by how accurately it predicts the symbol probabilities. In context based bi-level image modelling, the probability of the pixel to be encoded is estimated by using m neighbouring pixels to form a *context* or *template* [4]. The template is moved along the scan line from left to right and from top to bottom of the image being processed. Each time the template is shifted to a new position, the pixels under the template are evaluated to form an m bit pattern called the *state*. These states are used to condition the probability of the pixel being encoded, and the probability of pixel i occurring in state s is estimated as $p(i|s) = c_{s,i}/N_s$, where $c_{s,i}$ is number of occurrences of pixel i in state s, and N_s is the total number of times state s has occurred so far in the image. If the context has never occurred before, the coder does not know how to code a pixel in that context. The simplest solution is to start all counts at non-zero values.

Generally, larger templates result in better prediction of pixel probabilities and render more efficient coding but at the expense of increased running time in both encoder and decoder. The use of variable order contexts has been investigated by Moffat [5].

Figure 1 shows the ten-bit template which has been used for modelling [3]. In Figure 1, '*' denotes the pixel to be encoded; 'X' marks the pixels included in the template, the values of which are already known; '?' marks pixels whose values are not known by the encoder and so cannot be included in the template; and '.' indicates pixels whose value are known but are not included in the template.

```
. . X X X . .
. X X X X X .
. X X * ? ? ?
```

Figure 1: Ten-bit template

3 APPROXIMATE ARITHMETIC CODING

The practical implementation of arithmetic coding has a major difficulty: calculating the range of the new interval requires the multiplication of the current range by the probability of the symbol being encoded. An alternative method for avoiding the time penalty of multiplication is to use approximate arithmetic coding in which multiplication operations are replaced by a small number of less expensive operations such as shifts and additions. Approximate arithmetic coding works by using a number of special form to approximate either the range of the current interval or the probability of the symbol to be encoded. For example, Langdon and Rissanen [4] approximate the probability of the less probable symbol (LPS) by a value 2^{-Q}, where Q is a positive integer. Rissanen and Mohiuddin [9] scale the total count N and the occurrence count of the LPS by the same power of two such that the scaled total count is close to the current range R. The range allocated for the LPS is then approximated by the scaled LPS occurrence count. Thus, the multiplication and the division become unnecessary. Neal [7] suggests that the value R/N be approximated by a power of two, and allows the accuracy of the result to be controlled by a precision parameter. The IBM Q-coder [8] scales the current range R in the interval $[0.75, 1.5)$ so that R can be approximated by one in decimal representation, the multiplication is thus avoided. Chevion, Karnin and Walach [1] approximate R by $1/2 + \delta$ where δ is either zero or a negative power of two. The Quasi-arithmetic coder of Howard and Vitter [2] replaces arithmetic operations by a table lookups.

In this paper, we suggest alternative approximate arithmetic coding techniques whereby the probability of the more probable symbol (MPS) is approximated by a number of special form whose value is determined by the subinterval in which the ratio of the LPS probability to the MPS probability lies.

Let p and q be the probabilities of the LPS and the MPS respectively ($p \leq q$). The possible interval $(0, 1]$ in which p/q lies is partitioned into n subintervals whose end points are $a_0, a_1, \ldots, a_n$ where $0 = a_0 < a_1 < \ldots < a_n = 1$. The question to be answered is that if the actual ratio p/q lies in the subinterval $(a_i, a_{i+1}]$ where $i = 0, 1, \ldots, n-1$; what the approximate probability of the MPS, $\hat{q}_i$, should be used in order to minimise the average excess code length.

In the light of the noiseless source coding theorem [10], if the MPS is encoded using its exact probability q, the average code length is equal to the source entropy H:

$$H(q) = -(1-q)\log_2(1-q) - q\log_2 q$$

However, if the MPS is encoded using its approximate probability $\hat{q}$ instead of the exact value q, the average code length, $\hat{H}$, is

$$\hat{H}(q, \hat{q}) = -(1-q)\log_2(1-\hat{q}) - q\log_2 \hat{q}$$

Let X be the ratio p/q, that is $q = 1/(1+X)$. Substituting this into the above equations yields

$$H(X) = \frac{1}{1+X}\log_2 X - \log_2\left(\frac{X}{1+X}\right) \tag{1}$$

$$\hat{H}(X, \hat{q}) = \frac{1}{1+X}\log_2\left(\frac{1-\hat{q}}{\hat{q}}\right) - \log_2(1-\hat{q}) \tag{2}$$

Suppose that the probability that X takes on a value in the subinterval $(a_i, a_{i+1}]$ is z_i and that X is uniformly distributed in that subinterval, the probability distribution function of the variable X, $f_X(x)$, is then given by

$$f_X(x) = \begin{cases} z_i/(a_{i+1} - a_i) & \text{if } a_i < x \leq a_{i+1} \\ 0 & \text{otherwise} \end{cases} \tag{3}$$

Let $D = \hat{H} - H$. The expected value of D, the excess code length per pixel, is defined as $E(D) = \int_{-\infty}^{+\infty} f_X(x)D(x)dx$. Substituting Equations 1, 2, and 3 into $E(D)$ gives

$$E(D) = \sum_{i=0}^{n-1} w_i \int_{a_i}^{a_{i+1}} \left\{\frac{-1}{1+x}\log_2\left(\frac{x\hat{q}_i}{1-\hat{q}_i}\right) + \log_2\left[\frac{x}{(1+x)(1-\hat{q}_i)}\right]\right\} dx \tag{4}$$

where $w_i = z_i/(a_{i+1} - a_i)$. Note that the general value $\hat{q}$ in the function $\hat{H}$ is now replaced by $\hat{q}_i$ since $\hat{q}$ takes different values in different subintervals.

Integrating the first term in Equation 4 using integration by part and series expansion techniques yields

$$\int_{a_i}^{a_{i+1}} \frac{-1}{1+x}\log_2\left(\frac{x\hat{q}_i}{1-\hat{q}_i}\right) dx = \frac{1}{\ln 2}\left\{\sum_{k=1}^{\infty}\frac{(-1)^{k-1}x^k}{k^2} - \ln\left(\frac{x\hat{q}_i}{1-\hat{q}_i}\right)\ln(1+x)\right\}_{x=a_i}^{x=a_{i+1}} \tag{5}$$

Integrating the second term in Equation 4 using a table of integrals [11] gives

$$\int_{a_i}^{a_{i+1}} \log_2\left[\frac{x}{(1+x)(1-\hat{q}_i)}\right] dx = \frac{1}{\ln 2}\left\{x \ln\left[\frac{x}{(1+x)(1-\hat{q}_i)}\right] - \ln(1+x)\right\}_{x=a_i}^{x=a_{i+1}} \tag{6}$$

Substituting Equations 5 and 6 into Equation 4 results in

$$E(D) = \sum_{i=0}^{n-1} E_i \tag{7}$$

where

$$E_i = \frac{w_i}{\ln 2}\left\{x \ln\left(\frac{x}{1-\hat{q}_i}\right) - \ln(1+x)\left[\ln\left(\frac{x\hat{q}_i}{1-\hat{q}_i}\right) + 1 + x\right] + \sum_{k=1}^{\infty}\frac{(-1)^{k-1}x^k}{k^2}\right\}_{x=a_i}^{x=a_{i+1}} \tag{8}$$

Since $D = \hat{H} - H \geq 0$ (from the noiseless source coding theorem [10]), and $w_i \geq 0$, $E_i \geq 0$. Consequently, function $E(D)$ is minimum if each element E_i is minimum. Solving $dE_i/d\hat{q}_i = 0$ for $\hat{q}_i$ yields

$$\hat{q}_i = \frac{1}{(a_{i+1} - a_i)} \ln\left(\frac{1 + a_{i+1}}{1 + a_i}\right) \tag{9}$$

A further test, omitted here, indicates that function E_i has an absolute minimum at $\hat{q}_i$, given by Equation 9. Thus, if the ratio p/q lies in the subinterval $(a_i, a_{i+1}]$, the MPS probability can be approximated by Equation 9 in order to minimise the excess bits.

The approximation in Equation 9 is more complicated than the original problem: the multiplication and division used in calculating the new range are replaced by an even more expensive computation. However, if the interval $(0,1]$ is partitioned in a special way, then Equation 9 yields surprisingly simple method for determining $\hat{q}_i$.

4 IMPLEMENTATION

There are two problems with the implementation: (1) how to partition the interval $(0,1]$ into subintervals so that finding the subinterval in which the ratio p/q lies does not require a division, and (2) how to approximate $\hat{q}_i$ (Equation 9) by a number of special form.

INTERVAL PARTITIONING The possible interval $(0,1]$ in which p/q lies is partitioned into $f+1$ subintervals where f is the number of bits being used to represent the occurrence counts. The end points of the subintervals are zero and 2^{-i} where $i = f, f-1, \ldots, 0$.

In adaptive coding techniques using a model with multiple contexts, the symbol occurrence counts are often used to estimate the probabilities of symbols: $p = c_{s,LPS}/N_s$ and $q = c_{s,MPS}/N_s$. Thus, $p/q = c_{s,LPS}/c_{s,MPS}$. The problem of finding the subinterval in which p/q lies becomes the problem of determining the value i so that the condition $2^{-i} < c_{s,LPS}/c_{s,MPS} \leq 2^{-i+1}$ is satisfied without actually dividing $c_{s,LPS}$ by $c_{s,MPS}$. By observation, the value i is, at least, equal to the difference between the number of significant bits of $c_{s,MPS}$ and that of $c_{s,LPS}$; and, at most, equal to the difference plus one.

The straightforward method is to implement a look-up table, called *SizeOf*, to store numbers of significant bits of all possible occurrence counts. The table has 2^f entries; each requires a byte, thus, the total memory requirement is 2^f bytes. In binary arithmetic coding, f is typically from 12 to 14, thus, the memory usage is not large. The algorithm for determining the value i is illustrated in step 2 of Figure 3.

Alternatively, if memory is scarce, a smaller look-up table T, consists of only f entries, can be implemented. The kth entry is equal to $2^k - 1$ where $k = 1, 2 \ldots, f$. If a number c satisfying $T[k-1] < c \leq T[k]$, then k is the number of significant bits of c. For bi-level images, the value of $c_{s,LPS}$ is usually small, thus, in order to find the number of significant bits of $c_{s,LPS}$ quickly, the table is searched linearly starting from the first entry. Conversely, the number of significant bits of $c_{s,MPS}$ is found by searching the table in the opposite direction.

$\hat{q}_i$ APPROXIMATION Since the values a_i and a_{i+1} are in the interval $(0, 1]$, Equation 9 can be expressed as a MacLaurin series [11]:

$$\hat{q}_i = \frac{1}{(a_{i+1} - a_i)} \sum_{k=1}^{\infty} \frac{(-1)^{k-1}(a_{i+1}^k - a_i^k)}{k} \tag{10}$$

If a_{i+1} is much smaller than one, the MPS probability can be approximated by the first two terms of the series without appreciable error:

$$\hat{q}_i \approx q_i' = 1 - \frac{a_{i+1} + a_i}{2} = 1 - \frac{(2^{-i+1} + 2^{-i})}{2} = 1 - \frac{1.5}{2^i} \tag{11}$$

Consequently, the approximate range allocated for the MPS is calculated as $R_{MPS} = R \times q_i' = R - (1.5 \times R)/2^i$. The multiplication by a factor of 1.5 can be implemented by one right shift and one addition; the division by 2^i is done by a single shift. Thus, the multiplication and the division in the original problem are now replaced by two shifts, one addition and one subtraction.

In the proposed methods, the value q_i', given by Equation 11, is considered to be a good approximation of $\hat{q}_i$ if $i > 4$. Otherwise, the MPS probability is approximated manually. Denote the binary representation of a number c rounded to six binary digits as $B(c)$. The approximate MPS probability is chosen as either $B(\hat{q}_i)$ or $1 - B(1 - \hat{q}_i)$, which ever has the fewer 1-bits. In summary, the approximate MPS probabilities are given by

$$q_i' = \begin{cases} 2^{-1} + 2^{-4} + 2^{-6} & \text{if } i = 1 \\ 1 - 2^{-2} - 2^{-6} & \text{if } i = 2 \\ 1 - 2^{-3} - 2^{-5} & \text{if } i = 3 \\ 1 - 2^{-4} - 2^{-6} & \text{if } i = 4 \\ 1 - 1.5/2^i & \text{otherwise} \end{cases} \tag{12}$$

The algorithm used to calculate the MPS range, R_{MPS}, is illustrated in Figure 2.

if $(i > 4)$ **then**	$R_{MPS} \leftarrow R - (R + R/2)/2^i;$
else if $(i = 4)$ **then**	$R_{MPS} \leftarrow R - R/2^4 - R/2^6;$
else if $(i = 3)$ **then**	$R_{MPS} \leftarrow R - R/2^3 - R/2^5;$
else if $(i = 2)$ **then**	$R_{MPS} \leftarrow R - R/2^2 - R/2^6;$
else	$R_{MPS} \leftarrow R/2 + R/2^4 + R/2^6;$

Figure 2: The approximate MPS range

It is interesting to note that a wide range of the MPS probabilities can be condensed to just a handful of single cases. The values expressed in Equation 12 allow two different implementations.

4.1 METHOD B1

The algorithm described in Figure 2 can be used to approximate the multiplication and division in calculating new intervals. The complete algorithm for encoding a pixel *pel* in state s is illustrated in Figure 3.

In a practical implementation of arithmetic coding, the current interval at each coding step is specified by two integers L and R where L is the lower bound and R is the range (width) of the interval. Thus, any interval can be represented by $[L, L+R)$. Suppose that b bits are being used to represent L and R, which are initialised to 0 and $2^{b-1}-1$ respectively. Step 5, as described by Moffat et al. [6], is used for scaling the current interval in the range $[2^{b-2}, 2^{b-1})$ and for outputting encoded data. A description of this step and the use of *bitplusfollow* and *bitstofollow* can be found in [6, 12]. Steps 6 and 7 might be part of the modelling module, but are included here for convenience of discussion. The $increment_s$ in step 6 can be one or a non-unit amount. Step 7 is necessary because arithmetic coding routines typically have an upper limit on the maximum frequency count that can be handled, caused by the use of fixed length registers. Suppose that the total count N_s is less than 2^f for some integer f, and the individual count may be as small as one. This requirement can be met by *count scaling*—reducing both symbol counts by the same factor, taking care that neither symbol is assigned a count of zero. One obvious way to do this is to halve the counts $c_{s,0}$ and $c_{s,1}$. To ensure that no symbol is assigned a count of zero, one is added to each count before halving (step 6). By reducing all symbol counts by the same factor, the relative frequencies and thus the probabilities are kept approximately the same while using only a fixed amount of storage for each count. For example, in an extreme case to save storage, each count might be assigned four or eight bits. Count scaling also introduces a *locality of reference*, which often improves compression [2]. In the experiments described in Section 6, the values of $c_{s,0}$ and $c_{s,1}$ are initialised to a quarter of the count limit, that is 2^{f-2}, the initial increment $increment_s$ is equal to half of the count limit, 2^{f-1}, and then getting smaller through scaling as in step 7. To prevent it getting too small, the lower bound $increment_{min}$ is introduced. Note that the divisions by two in steps 3 and 7 and the multiplication by two in step 5 can be performed by shifting.

4.2 METHOD B2

In Method B1, the current range R is used directly in the approximation process. However, in Method B2, a smaller value is used in the hope that the approximation error can be reduced.

The MPS range can be expressed as

$$R_{MPS} = \frac{Rc_{s,MPS}}{N_s} = 2^{b-f-1}c_{s,MPS} + \frac{(R - 2^{b-f-1}N_s)c_{s,MPS}}{N_s}$$

The smaller value used in the approximation is $R' = |R - 2^{b-f-1}N_s|$. In order that $R' < R$, the total occurrence count is required to be partially normalised, that is $2^{f-1} \le N_s < 2^f$. This requirement together with the condition $2^{b-2} \le R < 2^{b-1}$ [6] results in $R' < R$. The term $R'c_{s,MPS}/N_s$ can be approximated by the same technique used in Method B1. The algorithm for Method B2 is the same as Figure 3 except that step 3 is replaced by Figure 4.

5 COMPRESSION PERFORMANCE ANALYSIS

The upper bound of the relative increase in code length for Method B1, resulted from the approximation of the multiplication and division, is derived in this section.

1. **if** $(c_{s,1} \leq c_{s,0})$ **then** *MPS* $\leftarrow 0$; — *Identify the MPS*
   else *MPS* $\leftarrow 1$;
   LPS $\leftarrow 1 -$ *MPS*;

2. $i \leftarrow SizeOf[c_{s,MPS}] - SizeOf[c_{s,LPS}]$; — *Determine the subinterval in which the ratio p/q lies*
   if $(c_{s,MPS} \geq 2^i c_{s,LPS})$ **then** $i \leftarrow i + 1$;

3. Use Figure 2; — *Calculate the MPS range*

4. **if** (*pel* = *MPS*) **then** $R \leftarrow R_{MPS}$; — *Calculate the new interval*
   else $L \leftarrow L + R_{MPS}$; $R \leftarrow R - R_{MPS}$;

5. **while** $R < 2^{b-2}$ **do** — *Output bits and adjust the range*
   if $L + R \leq 2^{b-1}$ **then** *bitplusfollow*(0)
   else if $L \geq 2^{b-1}$ **then** *bitplusfollow*(1); $L \leftarrow L - 2^{b-1}$
   else *bitstofollow* $\leftarrow$ *bitstofollow* $+ 1$; $L \leftarrow L - 2^{b-2}$;
   $L \leftarrow 2 \times L$; $R \leftarrow 2 \times R$.

6. $c_{s,pel} \leftarrow c_{s,pel} + increment_s$; — *Update the count*

7. **if** $(c_{s,0} + c_{s,1} \geq 2^f)$ **then** — *Halve the counts and increment if necessary*
   $c_{s,0} \leftarrow (c_{s,0} + 1)/2$; $c_{s,1} \leftarrow (c_{s,1} + 1)/2$;
   $increment_s \leftarrow (increment_s + increment_{min})/2$;

Figure 3: B1 algorithm

The relative increase in code length is defined as $E(D)/H$ where $E(D)$ and H were given by Equations 7 and 1 respectively. Since functions $E(D)$ and H are independent—they do not have any common variable—$E(D)/H$ is maximum if H is minimum and $E(D)$ is maximum.

MINIMUM OF FUNCTION H Differentiating Equation 1 with respect to X yields

$$\frac{dH}{dX} = \frac{-\log_2 X}{(1+X)^2} \geq 0 \quad \text{since} \quad 0 < X \leq 1$$

It implies that H is a monotonically increasing function of variable X in the interval $(0, 1]$. Thus, in the subinterval $(2^{-i}, 2^{-i+1}]$, function H has an absolute minimum at $X = 2^{-i}$.

MAXIMUM OF FUNCTION $E(D)$ By definition, Equation 3 must satisfy $\int_{-\infty}^{\infty} f_X(x)dx = 1$ or $\sum_{i=0}^{n-1} z_i = 1$. This implies that $z_i \leq 1$ or

$$w_i \leq \frac{1}{a_{i+1} - a_i} = \frac{1}{2^{-i+1} - 2^{-i}} = 2^i$$

Suppose that w_i takes on the maximum value 2^i (effectively X is assumed to be uniformly distributed in only one subinterval: $(2^{-i}, 2^{-i+1}]$), then $E(D) = E_i$.

Substituting $\hat{q}_i$, given by Equations 9, and q'_i, given by Equation 12, into Equation 7 obtains functions $\hat{E}(D)$ and $E'(D)$ respectively. The corresponding functions $\hat{E}(D)/H$ and $E'(D)/H$ are evaluated for different subintervals using $X = 2^{-i}$, $a_i = 2^{-i}$, $a_{i+1} = 2^{-i+1}$,

3a $N' \leftarrow 2^{b-f-1}N_s$;

3b **if** $(R > N')$ **then**
$R' \leftarrow R - N'$;
Use Figure 2 but R is replaced by R';
$R_{MPS} \leftarrow 2^{b-f-1}c_{s,MPS} + R_{MPS}$;
else
$R' \leftarrow N' - R$;
Use Figure 2 but R is replaced by R';
$R_{MPS} \leftarrow 2^{b-f-1}c_{s,MPS} - R_{MPS}$;

Figure 4: B2 algorithm

and $w_i = 2^i$. The results, tabulated in Table 1, shows that the relative increases in code length by using $\hat{q}_i$ and q'_i are not much different except at $i = 4$, corresponding to the interval $(2^{-4}, 2^{-3}]$, the difference is largest. The reason is that $q'_4 = 0.921875$, given by Equation 12, is not close to the 'true' value $\hat{q}_4 = 0.914535$, evaluated from Equation 9. Overall, the maximum relative increase in code length is less than 1% and decreases as i is getting larger.

i	$\hat{E}(D)/H\%$	$E'(D)/H\%$	i	$\hat{E}(D)/H\%$	$E'(D)/H\%$
1	0.740	0.742	7	0.473	0.474
2	0.753	0.766	8	0.426	0.426
3	0.719	0.720	9	0.387	0.387
4	0.658	0.821	10	0.354	0.354
5	0.591	0.630	11	0.325	0.325
6	0.528	0.536	12	0.301	0.301

Table 1: The relative increase in code length

6 Experimental Results

The two approximate coding methods were written in C and compiled using gcc. The exact method, called Method E, which employs multiplication and division operations in calculating new intervals was used as a benchmark for evaluating the compression performances of the proposed methods. All experiments were performed on a lightly loaded SPARCstation2. The test documents were the eight CCITT standard bi-level images scanned with a resolution of 3.85 lines/mm. Each image has 1726 pixels/line and 2376 pixels in the vertical direction gives total of 4,105,728 pixels. Ten-bit template (Figure 1) was used for modelling.

The proposed methods used 12 bits of precision for f, and the value b was varied. For precision reason, the smallest value of $b - f$ is two. The reader is referred to [6] for discussion of this. Both values $c_{s,0}$ and $c_{s,1}$ were initialised to 2^{f-2}, $increment_s$ to 2^{f-1}, and $increment_{min}$ to 64.

Speed Figure 5(a) shows the average time, measured as CPU usage in seconds, required for encoding a CCITT image by using the exact and approximate methods. The results

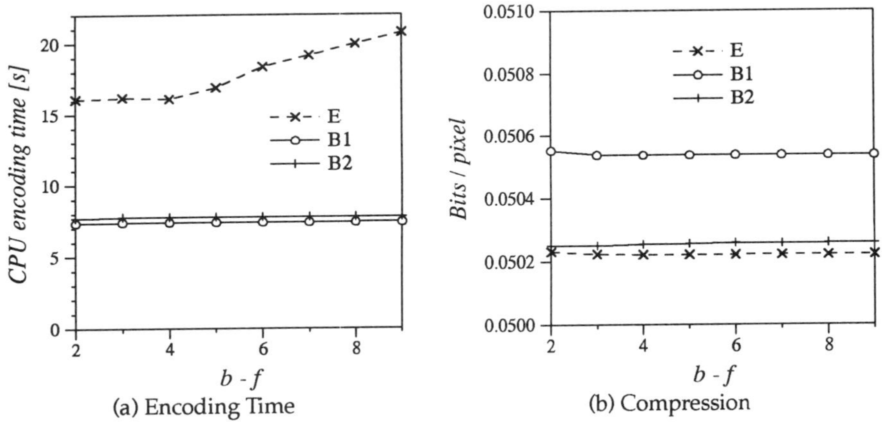

Figure 5: Encoding Time and Compression

indicate that both proposed methods run about twice as quickly as Method E. Since the approximation is independent of b, the speed of Methods B1 and B2 remains constant over the large range of b. This feature is desirable since there is no worst case even if the 'wrong' parameter b is chosen. Although an extra number of arithmetic operations used, Method B2 does not run significantly slower than Method B1.

MEMORY REQUIREMENT The look-up table *SizeOf* has $2^f = 2^{12}$ entries; each requires a byte. Thus, the memory required by the table is 2^{12} bytes or 4 Kbytes which is quite small.

COMPRESSION Figure 5(b) shows the average number of bits required to represent a pixel using the exact and approximate coding methods. The analysis shows that even in the worst case the coding is about 1% inefficient. In bi-level images, the MPS probability is usually close to one, and so p/q is small, thus the performances of the approximate coders are expected to be comparable to the exact one. Indeed, the relative increase in code length is less than 0.6% for Method B1, and 0.1% for Method B2. The smallest average bit rate, achieved by Method B2, is 0.05025 bits/pixel which corresponds to the average compression factor of 19.9:1 (calculated as the ratio of the total of the original file sizes to the total file size of the compressed files). This is comparable to the compression reported by Langdon and Rissanen [4] and for the Q-coder [8].

7 CONCLUSION

Two approximate arithmetic coding methods have been presented that improve the speed of binary arithmetic coding. They replace the expensive multiplication and division operations by a small number of shifts, additions and subtractions and run twice as fast as an exact method in trading off for negligible loss of compression efficiency. Analysis shows that even in the worst case, the relative excess code length is less than 1%. Experiments on the eight CCITT standard images demonstrate that the relative increase in code length is less than 0.6% for the first method, and less than 0.1% for the second one. Both methods are straightforward to implement and suitable for coding bi-level data using adaptive models.

ACKNOWLEDGEMENTS

The author thanks Alistair Moffat and Ron Sacks-Davis for their assistance during the course of this investigation. This work is supported by an Australian Industry Post-graduate Research Award in conjunction with Kodak Australia and the Collaborative Information Technology Research Institute (CITRI).

REFERENCES

[1] D. Chevion, E.D. Karnin, and E. Walach. High efficiency, multiplication free approximation of arithmetic coding. In J.A. Storer and J.H. Reif, editors, *Proceedings of the IEEE Data Compression Conference*, pages 43–52, Snowbird, Utah, April 1991. IEEE Computer Society Press, Los Alamitos, CA.

[2] P.G. Howard and J.S. Vitter. Practical implementations of arithmetic coding. In J.A. Storer, editor, *Image and Text Compression*, pages 85–112. Kluwer Academic, Norwell, Massachusetts, 1992.

[3] ISO/IEC Draft International Standard 11544 WG9-S1R5.1. *Coded Representation of Picture and Audio Information—Progressive Bi-level Image Compression*, April 1992.

[4] G.G. Langdon Jr. and J. Rissanen. Compression of black-white images with arithmetic coding. *IEEE Transactions on Communications*, COM-29(6):858–867, June 1981.

[5] A. Moffat. Two-level context based compression of binary images. In J. A. Storer and R. H. Reif, editors, *Proceedings of the IEEE Data Compression Conference*, pages 382–391, Snowbird, Utah, April 1991. IEEE Computer Society Press, Los Alamitos, CA.

[6] A. Moffat, N. Sharman, I.H. Witten, and T.C. Bell. An empirical evaluation of coding methods for multi-symbol alphabets. In J.A. Storer and M. Cohn, editors, *Proceedings of the IEEE Data Compression Conference*, pages 108–117, Snowbird, Utah, March 1993. IEEE Computer Society Press, Los Alamitos, CA.

[7] R.M. Neal. Fast arithmetic coding using low-precision division. Code implementing this method is available by anonymous ftp from ftp.cpsc.ucalgary.ca, 1987.

[8] W.B. Pennebaker, J.L. Mitchell, G.G. Langdon Jr., and R.B. Arps. An overview of the basic principles of the Q-coder adaptive binary arithmetic coder. *IBM Journal of Research and Development*, 32(6):717–726, November 1988.

[9] J. Rissanen and K.M. Mohiuddin. A multiplication free multialphabet arithmetic code. *IEEE Transactions on Communications*, 37(2):93–98, February 1989.

[10] C.E. Shannon and W. Weaver. *The Mathematical Theory of Communication*. University of Illinois Press, Urbana, Illinois, 1949.

[11] G.B. Thomas and R.L. Finney. *Calculus and Analytic Geometry*. Addison-Wesley Publishing Company, eighth edition, 1992.

[12] I.H. Witten, R.M. Neal, and J.G. Cleary. Arithmetic coding for data compression. *Communications of the ACM*, 30(6):520–540, June 1987.

Bayes Risk Weighted Tree-structured Vector Quantization with Posterior Estimation

Keren O. Perlmutter Robert M. Gray Karen L. Oehler *
Richard A. Olshen†

Information Systems Lab, Stanford University, Stanford, CA 94305-4055
†Division of Biostatistics, Stanford University, Stanford, CA 94305-5092

Abstract

We investigate a method that combines compression and low-level classification of images by designing codes that contain implicit information regarding classification. The design consists of a tree-structured vector quantizer (TSVQ) that incorporates a Bayes risk term into the distortion measure used in the quantizer design algorithm in order to permit a tradeoff of mean squared error and classification error. Once designed, the quantizer can operate to minimize the Bayes risk weighted distortion measure by incorporating the posterior probabilities into the encoding process. A completely nonparametric design algorithm is constructed by estimating these posterior distributions using a TSVQ that incorporates the classification error into the splitting criterion. This approach is used to analyze simulated data and to identify tumors in CT lung images. Comparisons are made with other vector quantizer based classifiers, including Kohonen's "learning vector quantizer." For the examples considered, our method provided classification superior to the other methods while simultaneously providing close to or superior compression performance.

1 Compression and Classification

Compression and classification play important roles in making digital images useful. The goal of image compression is to speed transmission or minimize storage of the image while preserving the best possible quality of reproduction. Image classification can assist human observers in differentiating between the features of an image. For example, special areas of interest in the image can be highlighted to draw attention to them. Often both of these digital signal processing techniques are desired, and consequently both good compression and good classification performance must be achieved. Because two of the design components of vector quantization (VQ), clustering and

*Dr. Oehler is now with Texas Instruments, Incorporated, Dallas, Tx 75265

tree-structured classification methods, have obvious applications to both the pure classification problem and the compression problem [1], it is a natural technique to use in pursuing this combined compression/classification goal. A simple approach to accomplish both of these goals is to separately and independently design the VQ and classifier. In the high rate case, simply designing a minimum mean squared error VQ and applying an empirical Bayes classifier to the output will provide performance near that of the Bayes classifier provided the training set is sufficiently large [6, 7, 8]. We are interested in the low or modest bit rate case, however, where this independent design of VQ and classifier may not provide good performance. An alternative approach is to design a VQ encoder as a classifier. For example, Kohonen et al. [3] have proposed "learning vector quantization" (LVQ), a technique in which the encoder operates as an ordinary minimum mean squared error selector of a representative from the codebook, but the codebook is designed to attempt to reduce classification error implicitly rather than reduce the mean squared error. In addition, Kramer [5] and Oehler et al. [9] provided algorithms for designing TSVQs for classification. A recent technique for combining compression and low-level classification explicitly incorporates a Bayes risk component into the distortion measure used for the full search VQ code design in order to permit a tradeoff of mean squared error with classification error [10, 11, 15]. In both the design and implementation of this algorithm, knowledge of the posterior class probabilities is required. In the nonparametic case, however, these probabilities are not known outside the training set. Consequently, although the modified distortion measure is used in the code design, only ordinary Euclidean nearest neighbor encoding is used in the encoding process. In the parametric case, it was shown in [10] that the incorporation of these probabilities into the encoding process can improve both classification and compression performance. It is thus desirable to estimate the posterior probabilities so that they can be used in the encoding process.

In this paper we describe a technique that estimates these posterior probabilities and then incorporates these estimates into a Bayes risk weighted tree-structured VQ (Bayes TSVQ) design. Several examples are given and comparisons made with other methods.

2 Bayes Risk Weighted TSVQ

Consider a joint distribution $\{X(n), Y(n)\}$, where the $X(n)$ are k-dimensional vectors and $Y(n)$ represent membership in a class and take on values in the set $\mathcal{H} = \{0, \cdots, M-1\}$. We assume that $\{X(n), Y(n)\}$ is stationary and ergodic. The system consists of the encoder, which views only X and outputs a binary index vector $i = \alpha(X)$, and a decoder which produces both a reproduction $\hat{x} = \beta(i)$ for compression and a classifier $\hat{y} = \delta(i)$.

The average ordinary distortion corresponding to (α, β) is $D(\alpha, \beta) = E[d(X, \beta(\alpha(X))]$. Typically the distortion measure used is the mean squared error (MSE), defined as $d(X, \hat{X}) = ||X - \hat{X}||^2$.

The classification performance can be measured by the Bayes risk [11]

$$\begin{aligned} B(\alpha,\delta) &= \sum_{k=0}^{M-1}\sum_{j=0}^{M-1} C_{jk}\Pr(\delta(\alpha(X))=k \text{ and } Y=j) \\ &= \sum_{i=0}^{N-1}\Pr(\alpha(X)=i)\sum_{k=0}^{M-1}1(\delta(i)=k)\sum_{j=0}^{M-1}C_{jk}\Pr(Y=j|\alpha(X)=i), \quad (1) \end{aligned}$$

where 1 (expression) is defined as 1 if the expression is true and 0 otherwise. Cost C_{jk} represents the cost incurred when a class j vector is misclassified as class k. Typically, $C_{jk}=0$ when $j=k$.

The encoder is designed to produce small MSE and Bayes risk simultaneously by using a Lagrangian formulation of a modified distortion measure which includes both ordinary distortion and classification error:

$$J_\lambda(\alpha,\beta,\delta) = D(\alpha,\beta) + \lambda B(\alpha,\delta)$$

Intermediate values of $\lambda \geq 0$ enable the encoder to vary the relative importance of classification and compression. The goal of the quantizer design is to minimize this functional J_λ for a given value of λ. This is accomplished by the following descent algorithm which iteratively optimizes α, β, and δ for each other:

Step 1 Choose $\delta^{(t+1)}$ to minimize $J_\lambda(\alpha^{(t)},\beta^{(t)},\delta^{(t+1)})$.

Step 2 Choose $\beta^{(t+1)}$ to minimize $J_\lambda(\alpha^{(t)},\beta^{(t+1)},\delta^{(t+1)})$.

Step 3 Choose $\alpha^{(t+1)}$ to minimize $J_\lambda(\alpha^{(t+1)},\beta^{(t+1)},\delta^{(t+1)})$.

The Bayes full search VQ described in [11] can be computationally intensive in both the codebook generation and encoding processes. Both VQ and classification algorithms, however, can be implemented with a tree-structure, which greatly reduces encoding complexity. Tree-structured vector quantization (TSVQ) replaces a full nearest neighbor search of the codebook of reproduction vectors available to the decoder with a sequence of binary nearest neighbor selections, or, equivalently, hyperplane tests. Bayes risk weighted VQ can be implemented as an unbalanced TSVQ by combining it with known tree growing and pruning techniques [13]. By incorporating the modified distortion measure J_λ rather than the ordinary distortion D into the splitting criterion and codeword design methods, both classification ability and compression can be achieved with a TSVQ.

3 Posterior Estimation

Both the design and implementation of the algorithm require knowledge of the posterior probabilities $\Pr(Y|X)$. In the parametric case, when the conditional probabilities $\Pr(Y=l|X=x)$ are known, the encoder, decoder, and classifier are exactly as produced in the final iteration of the design algorithm of Section 2. In the nonparametric case, however, these probabilities must be replaced by estimates based on the learning set. We denote these estimates as $\hat{P}(l|x)$, $l \in \mathcal{H}$.

We design a competely nonparametric algorithm that estimates the posterior probabilities required by the optimal encoder. In particular, the modified distortion measure uses these estimates for $\Pr(Y = l|\alpha(x) = i)$ in (1), the classifier becomes $\delta_{\text{Bayes}}(i) = \min_k{}^{-1} \sum_j C_{jk}\hat{P}(l|x)$, where $i = \alpha(x)$, and the encoder is given by

$$\alpha(x) = \min_i{}^{-1} \left\{ d(x, \beta(i)) + \lambda \left[\sum_{k=0}^{M-1} 1(\{\delta(i) = k\}) \sum_{j=0}^{M-1} C_{jk}\hat{P}(l|x) \right] \right\}.$$

We note that this incorporation of the estimates into Steps 1-3 in section 2 yields a descent algorithm for code design. We also note that the posterior estimation TSVQ is used in the encoding process but is not used in the decoding process. As a result, no additional bits need to be sent to transmit this information.

There are many ways to form these estimates. Because the Bayes TSVQ is designed based on a learning set of empirical data, $\mathcal{L}$, this same set can be used to estimate the posteriors during design by using relative frequencies. In particular, $\Pr(Y = l|X = x)$ can be estimated by t_l/t, where t_l is the number of times x occurred with class label l and t is the number of occurences of x [11].

This estimate, which we denote by $P_{\mathcal{L}}(l|x)$, was used in [11, 15] within the training set for code design, but it does not immediately provide a useful estimate of the conditional probabilities outside the training set. Although some form of multidimensional interpolation or kernel estimation technique can be used, the computational complexity required is extreme. The classification and regression tree algorithm CART^{TM} could be used to estimate the posterior probabilities, but it is likely that an estimator that operates on the entire vector x at each step and not on separate coordinates (as traditional CART^{TM} does) would provide better results. A Euclidean nearest neighbor (MSE) encoder [11] provides a simple nonparametric encoder outside the training set, as do most other VQ classification techniques including LVQ. An even better approach in some applications would be to form a "smoother" estimate of the posterior probabilities that can be used inside or outside the training set [2].

We wish to develop an estimator that is simple to compute and that results in the best possible overall combined compression and classification performance. Because this goal is not easy to formally quantify and implement, we instead use the following heuristic. An estimator will be good if it is (1) simple to compute, and (2) provides an estimate $\hat{P}$ that is "close" to the empirical estimator $P_{\mathcal{L}}$. This second property entails smoothing the binary empirical estimate. If the training set is enormous, the empirical estimator suitably smoothed will be close to the true distribution, and hence so too should the given estimator. We will use relative entropy as a measure of closeness.

We first note that any given TSVQ with a minimum Euclidean distance encoder can be used to estimate posteriors. In particular, an input vector is encoded using this TSVQ, and when a leaf is reached, the estimate for $P(l|x)$ is the relative frequency of the class in the node. This is in fact the "centroid" of the node with respect to the relative entropy distortion [14, 12], and it is asymptotically good if the VQ is designed to minimize squared error and the rate is asymptotically large [7, 8].

We define the overall average distortion between the learning set distribution and the estimate as the relative entropy

$$D(P_{\mathcal{L}}||\hat{P}) = \sum_{x:x\in\mathcal{L}} p(x) \sum_{l\in\mathcal{H}} P_{\mathcal{L}}(l|x) \log \frac{P_{\mathcal{L}}(l|x)}{\hat{P}(l|x)}. \tag{2}$$

By assumption, the estimate $\hat{P}$ depends on the input x only through the leaf containing it, and thus we can write that $\hat{P}(l|x) = \hat{P}(l|\text{leaf}(x))$. Since the latter quantity is the relative frequency of class l in the leaf, we also have that $\hat{P}(l|x) = \sum_{x:\text{label}(x)=l} p(x|\text{leaf})$. In the case where training vectors are unique, (2) reduces to

$$D(P_{\mathcal{L}}||\hat{P}) = \sum_{\text{all leaves}} p(\text{leaf}) \sum_{l\in\mathcal{H}} \hat{P}(l|\text{leaf}) \log \frac{1}{\hat{P}(l|\text{leaf})}. \tag{3}$$

Thus the overall relative entropy is the conditional entropy of the class given the leaf or, equivalently, the weighted sum over all leaves of the TSVQ of the class entropy given the individual leaf.

There are many ways in which the distortion measure in (3) can be incorporated into the splitting criterion of the TSVQ [12]. In this paper, we consider the following two splitting criteria:

Criterion 1: Split the leaf with the largest value of $p(\text{leaf}) \sum_{l\in\mathcal{H}} \hat{P}(l|\text{leaf}) \log \frac{1}{\hat{P}(l|\text{leaf})}$. Note that "pure" leaves will not be split since they have zero entropy.

Criterion 2: Split the leaf with the greatest reduction in $D(P_{\mathcal{L}}||\hat{P})$ between the leaf and its children per increase in rate. We note that this approach is greedy.

4 Examples

Simulated Data

We consider two simulated examples where the distributions are known. In both cases the input vector is a mixture of two equally likely distributions (i.e. the priors are equal) of two-dimensional data. Equal costs are assumed so that Bayes risk is simply probability of error. The codebooks were designed using 10,000 randomly chosen vectors and we evaluated the codebooks using 10,000 additional vectors. The simulations were carried out five times and the averages are reported.

The following design methods were compared:

Parametric Bayes TSVQ with optimal encoding: The true probabilities are used in both the codebook design and the encoding process, as in [2, 10]. We include this method in order to illustrate the achievable performance when the posterior probabilities are known and can be used.

Parametric Bayes TSVQ with nearest neighbor (MSE) encoding: During the codebook design process, the true probabilities are used in the codebook design. Euclidean nearest neighbor encoding is used in the encoding process, as is done in [11, 15].

Bayes TSVQ with posterior estimation: TSVQ-estimated posteriors are used in both the codebook design and the encoding process.

A fixed value of λ is used throughout the Bayes TSVQ designs.

Kohonen's LVQ: The codebook is initialized using the LVQ_PAK *eveninit* algorithm [4]. The codebook is designed with *olvq1* using 50,000 iterations.

Ordinary TSVQ (Independent classification and compression design): Only mean squared error is considered in the design of the code. A Bayes classifier is then applied. Nearest neighbor encoding is used. Note that in the limit of large rate and training set, this scheme should do asymptotically well [6, 7, 8].

Diamond Example

We consider the vectors $X = (X_1, X_2)$ belonging to Class 0 to be uniformly distributed over the diamond $|x_1| + |x_2| \leq 1$ and the vectors belonging to Class 1 to be uniformly distributed over $|x_1| + |x_2| > 1$ where $|x_1| \leq 1$ and $|x_2| \leq 1$. The ideal classification is a diamond shape as illustrated in Figure 1. Vectors within the white center region belong to Class 0, whereas vectors belonging to the gray corner regions belong to Class 1. We note that it is possible to differentiate perfectly between the two classes.

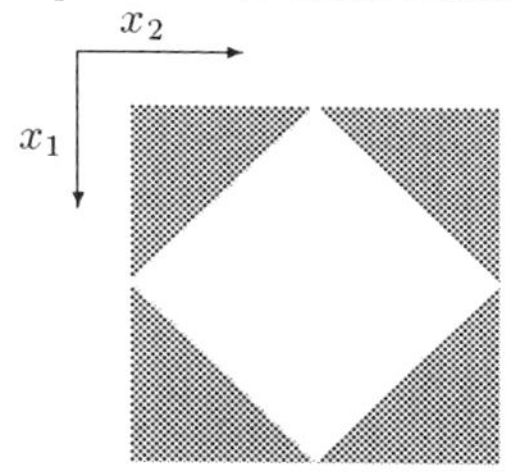

Figure 1: Ideal classification: Class 0 shown as white, Class 1 shown as gray

Classification and compression results are given in Tables 1 and 2, respectively. We investigated average compression code rates between 1.5 and 3.0 bpp. The posterior estimation TSVQ was grown to 3.19 bits per pixel (bpp) by greedily splitting the leaf with the greatest distortion reduction per increase in rate (Criterion 2). Recall that these bits are not actually sent to the decoder, but are only used in producing the posterior estimator that is used by the compression code encoder. Only the bits from the compression code are actually sent since the decoder does not need to know the posterior estimates used in encoding. $\lambda = 100$ for all Bayes TSVQ designs.

Incorporating the posterior class probabilities into the encoding process produces improved classification and compression performance as compared to the performance with ordinary Euclidean nearest neighbor encoding. When the optimal encoder is used for both the design and the encoding process, we obtain perfect classification at all rates investigated. When Bayes TSVQ with posterior estimation is used, 98.77% of the vectors are classified correctly at all bit rates considered. This yields as much as 15% improved classification performance as compared to the Bayes TSVQ design with nearest neighbor encoding. The difference in classification performance is illustrated in the partitioning and classification diagrams of Figure 2. In addition, the compression performance using posterior estimation is also superior to the performance

Codebook design method:	Ave. codebook rate: 1.5	2.0	2.5	3.0
Param. Bayes TSVQ, Opt. enc.	100.0	100.0	100.0	100.0
Param. Bayes TSVQ, MSE enc.	83.40	90.24	93.96	95.36
Bayes TSVQ with post. est.	98.77	98.77	98.77	98.77
Kohonen LVQ	87.19	93.32	95.39	96.59
Ordinary TSVQ	78.70	81.02	87.23	91.15

Table 1: Percentage of vectors correctly classified.

Codebook design method:	Ave. codebook rate: 1.5	2.0	2.5	3.0
Param. Bayes TSVQ, Opt. enc.	0.0530	0.0257	0.0124	0.0064
Param. Bayes TSVQ, MSE enc.	0.0641	0.0267	0.0129	0.0065
Bayes TSVQ with post. est.	0.0535	0.0256	0.0125	0.0064
Kohonen LVQ	0.1502	0.0539	0.0256	0.0127
Ordinary TSVQ	0.0476	0.0220	0.0118	0.0057

Table 2: Mean squared error per pixel.

obtained using MSE encoding at all rates investigated. Both the Bayes TSVQ with optimal encoding and the Bayes TSVQ with posterior estimation provide classification and compression performance superior to Kohonen's LVQ. We note that this is in contrast to the Bayes TSVQ with MSE encoding which is outperformed in classification ability (but not compression ability) at some of the rates investigated. In addition, the Bayes TSVQ with posterior estimation also yields significant improvement in classification performance while providing compression close to that of the independent compression and classification TSVQ design.

Gaussian Example

We also consider an example from Kohonen [3]. The two classes are each bivariate (two-dimensional) normal random vectors with iid components having 0 mean and equal variance. The variances are $\sigma_0^2 = 1$ and $\sigma_1^2 = 4$ for Classes 0 and 1, respectively.

We note that the two distributions overlap, and thus there is no decision rule providing perfect classification. The Bayes decision rule that minimizes the Bayes risk is a circle about the origin of radius 1.923. This optimal decision rule will classify 73.624% of vectors correctly on average.

The posterior estimation tree was grown to a rate of 3.0 bpp by splitting the leaf with the largest relative entropy (Criterion 1). $\lambda = 100$ for all of the Bayes VQ designs. For this example, optimal encoding and posterior estimation encoding yielded similar classification performance but improved compression performance as compared to results obtained using the nearest neighbor encoding design. All three methods outperform Kohonen's LVQ in both classification and compression. In contrast to results obtained with the Bayes TSVQ design with MSE encoding, the Bayes TSVQ

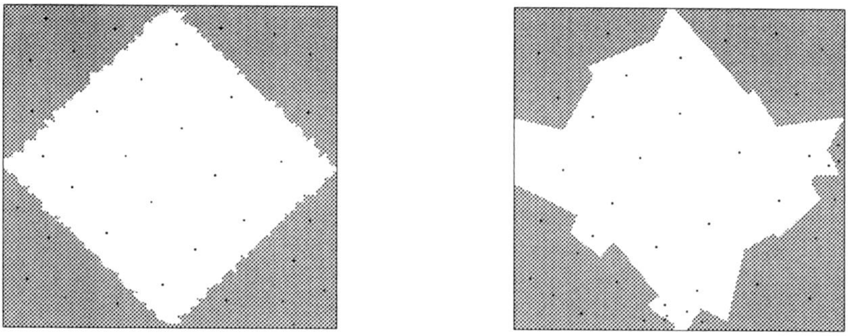

Figure 2: Voronoi regions of Bayes TSVQ with posterior estimation (left) and MSE encoding (right). Average rate = 2.5 bpp.

design with posterior estimation provided both superior classification and superior compression as compared to the ordinary TSVQ design.

Medical Images

The Bayes TSVQ algorithms with posterior estimation and with MSE encoding were also applied to 512×512 12-bit grayscale CT lung images, where the goal was to both compress the image and to identify tumors.

The training sequence consisted of ten images plus tumor vectors from an additional five images. Vectors consisted of 2×2 pixel blocks. We denote nontumors as class 0 and tumors as class 1. We assign different costs to C_{10} and C_{01} in order to signify that misclassifying a tumor is more important than misclassifying a nontumor. The compression codes were grown to an average rate of 2 bpp. The posterior estimation tree was grown to 3 bpp and its nodes were split according to Criterion 1. We used a fixed value of $\lambda = 500$, $C_{10} = 100$, and $C_{01} = 1$. The compression performance of the encoded images was measured by SNR, where $\text{SNR} = 10\log_{10}(D_0/D)$, D is the distortion measured by mean squared error, and D_0 is the distortion at rate 0. The classification performance of the encoded images was measured by the following four parameters: sensitivity, predictive value positive, specificity, and overall Bayes risk. Sensitivity is the percentage of tumor vectors that are correctly classified as tumor. Specificity is the percentage of nontumor vectors that are correctly classified as nontumor. Predictive value positive (PVP) is the percentage of vectors classified as tumor that are actually tumor vectors. The sensitivity is particularly valuable in judging classification performance on the CT images because of the importance of identifying all suspicious regions. Table 3 compares the classification and compression performance of the Bayes TSVQ designs when used with the posterior estimation and when used with nearest neighbor encoding. Figure 3 illustrates the compressed test image and the combined compressed and classified test image using Bayes TSVQ with posterior estimation. The intensities of these images have been "windowed" in order to improve the contrast in the pixel value region of interest. The highlighted regions in Figure 3 (right) represent vectors classified as tumors. We observe that the design using posterior estimation identifies substantial portions (84.8 %) of each of the three tumors. The design with MSE encoding, however, only identifies 14.4 % of the tumor vectors correctly. We note that using other λ and cost values can yield slightly better performance (i.e. up to 22 % sensitivity) with MSE encoding, but the results are still significantly inferior to those obtained with posterior estimation.

Codebook design method:	SNR(dB)	Sensitivity	Specificity	PVP	Bayes risk
Bayes TSVQ, MSE enc.	32.46	14.4	99.1	3.1	0.181
Bayes TSVQ w/ post. est.	32.48	84.8	97.0	5.4	0.060

Table 3: Statistical results of algorithm on CT test image using posterior estimation and MSE encoding.

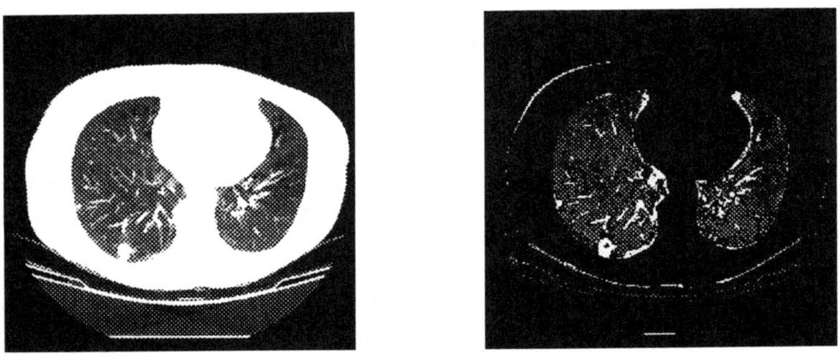

Figure 3: Compressed CT image (left) and Compressed/Classified CT image (right) using Bayes TSVQ with posterior estimation.

5 Conclusions

A completely nonparametric Bayes TSVQ algorithm can be implemented by incorporating posterior probability estimation into the processes of design and encoding. The resulting system yields superior classification performance and close to or superior compression performance to the Bayes TSVQ design with MSE encoding. In addition, the Bayes TSVQ with posterior estimation outperforms Kohonen's LVQ in both classification and compression for all examples considered in this paper.

6 Acknowledgements

This work was supported in part by the National Science Foundation under grants MIP-9016974, MIP-9311190, and DMS-9101548 and the National Institutes of Health under grant CA55325.

References

[1] A. Gersho and R. M. Gray. *Vector Quantization and Signal Compression.* Kluwer Academic Publishers, Boston, 1992.

[2] R. M. Gray, K. L. Oehler, K. O. Perlmutter, and R. A. Olshen. Combining tree-structured vector quantization with classification and regression trees. In *Proceedings of the 27th Asilomar Conference on Circuits Systems and computers*, Pacific Grove, CA, 1993.

[3] T. Kohonen, G. Barna, and R. Chrisley. Statistical pattern recognition with neural networks: benchmarking studies. In *IEEE International Conference on Neural Networks*, pages 61–68, July 1988.

[4] T. Kohonen, J. Kangas, J. Laaksonen, and K. Torkkola. LVQ_PAK: The learning vector quantization program package, version 2.1. Technical report, Helsinki University of Technology, Laboratory of Computer and Information Science, Finland, Oct 1992. Available via anonymous ftp to cochlea.hut.fi (130.233.168.48).

[5] J. Kramer. Tree structured neural net classifier. Technical report # 19900805, Stanford University Center for Design Research, 1990.

[6] G. Lugosi and A. B. Nobel. Consistency of data-driven histogram methods for density estimation and classification. Beckman institute technical report UIUC-BI-93-01, University of Illinois U-C, 1993. Submitted for publication.

[7] A. B. Nobel. Histogram regression estimation using data-dependent partitions. In preparation.

[8] A. B. Nobel and R. A. Olshen. Termination and continuity of greedy growing for tree structured vector quantizers. Submitted for publication.

[9] K. L. Oehler, P. C. Cosman, R. M. Gray, and J. May. Classification using vector quantization. In *Conference record of the Twenty-Fifth Asilomar Conference on Signals, Systems, and Computers*, pages 439–445, Pacific Grove, CA, Nov. 1991.

[10] K. L. Oehler and R. M. Gray. Combining image compression and classification using vector quantization. Submitted to IEEE Trans. PAMI, 1993.

[11] K. L. Oehler and R. M. Gray. Combining image classification and image compression using vector quantization. In J.A. Storer and M. Cohn, editors, *Proceedings of the 1993 IEEE Data Compression Conference (DCC)*, pages 2–11, Snowbird, Utah, March 1993. IEEE Computer Society Press.

[12] K. O. Perlmutter, R. M. Gray, K. L. Oehler, and R. A. Olshen. Bayes risk weighted vector quantization with estimated class posteriors. Paper in progress, 1994.

[13] E. A. Riskin and R. M. Gray. A greedy tree growing algorithm for the design of variable rate vector quantizers. *IEEE Trans. Signal Process.*, 39:2500–2507, Nov. 1991.

[14] J. E. Shore and R. M. Gray. Minimum-cross-entropy pattern classification and cluster analysis. *IEEE Trans. Pattern Anal. and Mach. Int.*, PAMI-4:11–17, Jan. 1982.

[15] R. D. Wesel and R. M. Gray. Bayes risk weighted VQ and learning VQ. To appear, 1993.

Fast Bintree-Structured Image Coder for High Subjective Quality

Xiaolin Wu* and Yonggang Fang
Department of Computer Science
University of Western Ontario
London, Ontario, Canada N6A 5B7.

Summary– A practical, fast, bintree-structured variable size block image coder is proposed. The inability of current segmentation-based image coding methods using piecewise functional approximation to represent textures is overcome by a generalized BTC encoding of approximation errors in texture areas. This new texture encoding technique significantly enhances subjective image quality at small extra costs to compression ratio and algorithm complexity.

1 Introduction

Recently, there has been some renewed interest in segmentation-based image coding [1, 6, 7, 9, 10, 11, 12], abbreviated to SIC hereafter. SIC was first proposed by Kunt *et al.* [5] a decade ago as what they called "second generation image coding". The above papers demonstrated that SIC can be a viable and competitive alternative to well-studied image coding techniques such as DCT and VQ. For most types of images, SIC is superior to DCT and VQ at bit rates lower than 0.2 bits/pil. However, at bit rates around 0.8 bits/pil when high subjective image quality is required, SIC loses its advantage over DCT and VQ on images with excessive textures. Our SIC coder [11] becomes inefficient in texture areas. We found two main causes for this drawback of SIC: 1) piecewise functional approximation scheme cannot model texture compactly, yielding too many small segments without much gain in SNR, and 2) the least-squares criterion used by the functional approximation does not characterize the subjective redundancy such as contrast masking in high texture areas. In this extended abstract, we will propose a simple solution to these two problems, and enhance the subjective quality of the images compressed by SIC with a small number of extra bits.

*Supported by grants from the Natural Sciences and Engineering Research Council of Canada.

1068-0314/94 $3.00 © 1994 IEEE

Our second concern is with the efficiency and simplicity of SIC algorithm. Although our earlier SIC algorithm based on optimal four-way bipartition [11] is more scene-adaptive than regular tessellation such as quadtree, and its computational complexity is significantly lower than its predecessor [5], its logic and data structures are still too complicated for hardware implementation at a reasonable cost. In this research we also try to simplify our previous SIC algorithm with negligible loss in compression ratios.

An important issue in designing a SIC coder is how to spatially partition neighboring pixels of similar characteristics into segments. An accurate and structured segmentation itself offers a compact high-level image description, thus it contributes directly to image compression. In fact, image segmentation may also play a role in VQ and transform coding, where one can at least adapt the block sizes, if not block shapes, to the different levels of details in different areas of an image [2, 9]. There are various segmentation techniques that can be used for image coding, ranging from the complex split-and-merge strategy to simple quadtree-based regular tessellation. These techniques offer different trade offs between the compactness of segmentation description, the scene adaptability of the segmentation, the complexity of the segmentation algorithm, and ease of implementation.

After a careful evaluation of all existing segmentation techniques, we decide to use a bintree-structured bottom-up merge (BBUM) process to form the segmentation framework in which the image is encoded by piecewise least-squares polynomials and texture masks. The computations involved in piecewise least-squares approximation can be efficiently integrated into the BBUM process, resulting in a very fast encoding algorithm. The BBUM process is also simple in its logic and data structure, hence it is much easier to implement than our previous algorithm [10] which uses a generalized bintree.

In what follows, we will develop a fast bintree-structured image coder for high subjective quality by elaborating on this intuition. First, fit pixel values by a low-order (linear or quadratic) polynomial in least-squares sense to form a largest possible block, as long as the approximation error is below a given threshold. If the block is large in size, then we hypothesize that the intensity function is smooth in that area, which semantically represents a large smooth surface in the scene. This is the situation where SIC will outperform DCT or VQ. Perceptually in this context, human eyes are sensitive to the tone continuity, thus higher quantization precision is required, consequently more bits are allocated to code the approximation coefficients. On the other hand, when pixel values cannot be satisfactorily approximated by a low-order polynomial in a small block, we hypothesize that the intensity function contains rich high-frequency components in that area. This is the situation where SIC of functional approximation is ineffective. We can of course break the block into even smaller cells or increase the order of polynomials to get a good approximation. But this approach defeats the purpose of data compression with too many approximation coefficients to be encoded. Instead, we will use BTC-like binary texture masks to approximate the high-frequency components to visual satisfaction. In the areas of high texture, our eyes become less sensitive to the absolute signal amplitude. Thus we can make the intensity quantization very coarse in the presence of high image activities without introducing objectionable distortion. But traditional BTC needs at least one bit per pixel just to encode the pattern. To increase code efficiency, on a 4×4 block, we use a simple, fast VQ technique to create 16 typical texture patterns rather than 2^{16} patterns as allowed by BTC.

Our presentation in this extended abstract follows the development outlined above with more details filled in. In the end, empirical results are given to demonstrate the subjective performance of the proposed new SIC coder.

2 Piecewise Approximation via BBUM Merge

The bintree data structure was first introduced by Knowlton for progressive image coding [4]. It is the same as the quadtree in principle, and differs from the quadtree only in that the bintree recursively partitions image into two equally-sized rectilinear blocks instead of four. Admittedly, a bintree-structured segmentation, with its rectilinear mid-point bipartition scheme, is less adaptive to scene structure than the segmentation proposed by [10], but it is more adaptive than quadtree-structured segmentation. The latter creates only square segments, while the former can generate rectangular segments as well. For images of prolonged features, the bintree will have fewer leaf nodes than the quadtree, hence the image is approximated by fewer polynomials. This added freedom of bintree, as illustrated by Fig. 1, can translate to higher compression ratio. The bintree gains better segmentation flexibility than the quadtree without complicating the segmentation description. In terms of algorithm complexity, bintree-structured segmentation is as simple as quadtree-structured segmentation.

To form an image segmentation, we can either split the entire image top-down or merge primitive blocks bottom-up, corresponding to top-down or bottom-up bintree construction. But there is a computational advantage to the bottom-up bintree construction, if a piecewise least-squares approximation is to be embedded into the bintree. By merging smaller blocks, we do not unnecessarily solve the least-squares problem in large image blocks which cannot possibly be leaf nodes. This is why we adopt the bintree-structured bottom-up merge (BBUM) process to create variable size rectangular blocks for coding.

We are now ready to introduce the piecewise least-squares linear approximation algorithm in the framework of BBUM. Denote the intensity function of the input

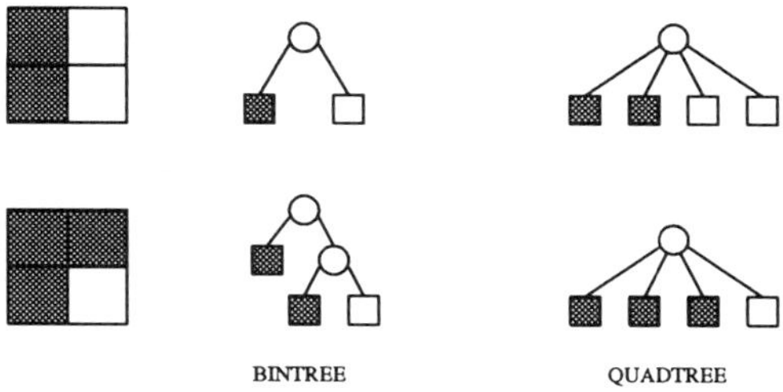

Figure 1: Situations in which bintree has few leaf nodes than quadtree.

image by $f(x,y)$. Let $g(x,y) = ax + by + c$ be the least-squares approximation of $f(x,y)$ in a rectangular $w \times h$ block B. To simplify the computations, we choose the center of B to be the origin. Then one can show that

$$a = \frac{\sum_B x f(x,y)}{\sum_B x^2}, \quad b = \frac{\sum_B y f(x,y)}{\sum_B y^2}, \quad c = \frac{\sum_B f(x,y)}{\sum_B 1}, \tag{1}$$

and the mean-squares error of the approximation is

$$E(B) = \sum_B f^2(x,y) - a \sum_B x f(x,y) - b \sum_B y f(x,y) - c \sum_B f(x,y). \tag{2}$$

We use an approximation error threshold σ to control the subjective image quality. If $E(B) \leq \sigma$, then block B is considered to be in a smooth region. We will merge B with its sibling node B' in the bintree, if $E(B \cup B') \leq \sigma$ also holds, in an attempt to reduce the number of leaf nodes. If $E(B \cup B') > \sigma$, then B and B' become two separate leaf nodes. During BBUM merge process, we either merge two horizontally adjacent blocks or two vertically adjacent blocks. In order to compute $E(B \cup B')$, we need to compute the least-squares coefficients a, b, and c for the newly created block $\text{ß} = B \cup B'$. In turn we need to evaluate Eq(1) for block ß. Remember that we should now consider the origin to be the center of ß, because in Eq(1) the origin is always the center of the block in question. It is easy to show that $\sum_{\text{ß}} x f(x,y)$, $\sum_{\text{ß}} y f(x,y)$, and $\sum_{\text{ß}} f^t(x,y)$, $t = 1,2$, can be obtained from the corresponding values for B and B', namely,

$$\begin{aligned}
\sum_{\text{ß}} f^t(x,y) &= \sum_B f^t(x,y) + \sum_{B'} f^t(x,y), \quad t = 1,2. \\
\sum_{\text{ß}} x f(x,y) &= \sum_B x f(x,y) + \sum_{B'} x f(x,y) + \\
& \begin{cases} w\left(\sum_{B'} f(x,y) - \sum_B f(x,y)\right) & \text{horizontal merge} \\ 0 & \text{vertical merge} \end{cases}
\end{aligned}$$

$$\sum_{\mathcal{B}} yf(x,y) = \sum_{B} yf(x,y) + \sum_{B'} yf(x,y) + \begin{cases} h\left(\sum_{B'} f(x,y) - \sum_{B} f(x,y)\right) & \text{vertical merge} \\ 0 & \text{horizontal merge} \end{cases} \tag{3}$$

We can see from the above equations that the updating of the summations $\sum xf(x,y)$, $\sum yf(x,y)$, and $\sum f^t(x,y)$, $t = 1, 2$, requires only four additions and one multiplication per merge. If w and h are power of 2, which is usually the case, then that multiplication can be done by bit shifting. The other quantities $\sum_{\mathcal{B}} x^2$, $\sum_{\mathcal{B}} y^2$, $\sum_{\mathcal{B}} 1$ in Eq(1) are independent of the input image, and they can be precomputed and stored. Then in the BBUM process, the algorithm can look up a table to get their values. By counting the number of operations in Eq(1) and Eq(2), one can see that the least-square linear approximation requires only seven multiplications and eight additions per merge, among which two multiplications can be converted to bit shifting if the height and width of block B and B' are power of 2. In our implementation, the merge process starts not from pixel level rather from 4×4 blocks for high compression ratio and for efficient texture encoding as we will see later. So the merge cost is shared by at least 32 pixels, resulting in a very low operation count per pixel. For the primitive 4×4 blocks, the computations of $\sum xf(x,y)$, $\sum yf(x,y)$, and $\sum f^t(x,y)$, $t = 1, 2$, can be done very fast by table look up without multiplications. Because in the 4×4 block, $|x| = 0.5, 1.5$, $|y| = 0.5, 1.5$, and $0 \leq f(x,y) \leq 255$, $xf(x,y)$ (equivalently $yf(x,y)$), and $f^2(x,y)$ can be precomputed for all possible combinations and stored in two tables of sizes 512 and 256 respectively. By now we can conclude that the bintree-based least-squares linear approximation has lower time complexity than DCT or VQ. Since the BBUM process involves only merging of two rectangles, no sweeping and merging of polygons of various shapes are required as in [10], the algorithm becomes much simpler and more suitable for hardware implementation.

If the size of a merged block becomes large, say exceeding 8×8, it pays, in terms of subjective image quality, to increase the order of least-squares approximation from linear to quadratic. Quadratic approximation retains tone subtlety better and subdues possible blocking effect, while not increasing the time complexity significantly. The underlying least-squares quadratic approximation problem is to minimize

$$E(B) = \sum_{B} [f(x,y) - c_5x^2 - c_4y^2 - c_3xy - c_2x - c_1y - c_0]^2, \tag{4}$$

where (x,y) are the coordinates with the origin being the center of block B. We can obtain, by setting $\partial E/\partial c_i = 0$, three of the least-squares coefficients c_i by solving the following simple linear system

$$\begin{pmatrix} \sum x^4 & \sum x^2y^2 & \sum x^2 \\ \sum x^2y^2 & \sum y^4 & \sum y^2 \\ \sum x^2 & \sum y^2 & \sum 1 \end{pmatrix} \begin{pmatrix} c_5 \\ c_4 \\ c_0 \end{pmatrix} = \begin{pmatrix} \sum x^2 f(x,y) \\ \sum y^2 f(x,y) \\ \sum f(x,y) \end{pmatrix}. \tag{5}$$

And the other three coefficients are

$$c_3 = \frac{\sum xyf(x,y)}{\sum x^2 \sum y^2}, \quad c_2 = \frac{\sum xf(x,y)}{\sum x^2}, \quad c_1 = \frac{\sum yf(x,y)}{\sum y^2}. \tag{6}$$

Here all $\sum$ are with respect to B. The summations $\sum x^m$ and $\sum y^m$ can be looked up from a table as in the linear approximation case. Also we note that $\sum_B x^2y^2$ can be reduced to $\sum_x x^2 \sum_y y^2$ since $\sum_B x^2y^2$ is separable for rectangle B. We have just shown how to update $\sum xf(x,y)$, $\sum yf(x,y)$, $\sum f^t(x,y)$ efficiently during merge in bintree. The same strategy can be applied to derive efficient updating formulas for $\sum x^2 f(x,y)$, $\sum y^2 f(x,y)$, and $\sum xyf(x,y)$. We omit the tedious derivations in this extended abstract due to the space limitation, instead just claim that the least-squares quadratic approximation requires about twice as many operations as its linear approximation counterpart.

3 Efficient Texture Encoding

After the BBUM-based piecewise least-squares approximation process completes, we have an approximation of the input image that can be reconstructed at the decoder side, if the approximation coefficients are quantized, coded, and transmitted. However, as we pointed out in the introduction, this functional approximation tends to smooth out fine details. In order to improve the subjective quality of decoded images, we have to recover the prominent textures to the degree of visual satisfaction. The problems are how to identify, model and compactly encode textures.

The size of a leaf block is a fair indicator for the existence of prominent textures. If the size is smaller than 8×8, we will encode the residual function $e(x,y) = f(x,y) - g(x,y)$ in B to add higher frequency components to the linear function $g(x,y)$. Note that $e(x,y)$ is a zero-mean function. Either DCT or VQ can be used to encode $e(x,y)$. However, we propose a much simpler, efficient, and effective alternative. Our solution is a generalization of the block truncation coding technique [3]. We map $e(x,y)$ in B to a binary pattern, called texture mask $m(x,y)$, where $m(x,y) = 0$ if $e(x,y) \geq 0$ and $m(x,y) = 1$ if $e(x,y) < 0$. Then we quantize $e(x,y)$ to two levels: $-s$ or s, depending on $m(x,y) = 0$ or $m(x,y) = 1$. Thus, the texture in B is modeled by the binary texture mask $m(x,y)$ and the texture strength s. Visually, this simple texture model

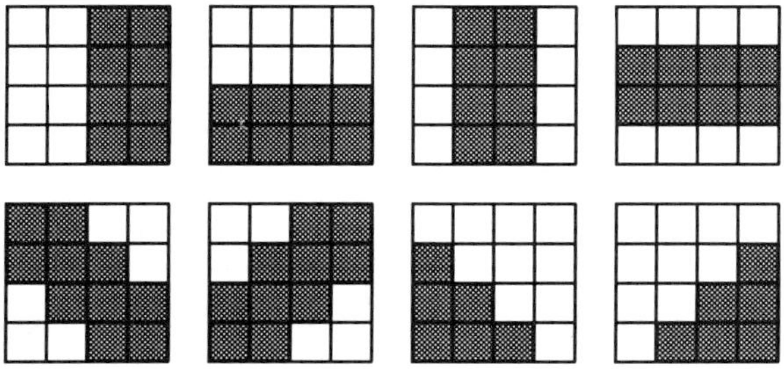

Figure 2: Sixteen typical texture masks. Only eight are listed and other eight are just inverse of the listed eight.

is very good, because in high texture areas our eyes pick up spatial resolution much better than intensity resolution. Also semantically, the rapid and sharp variation of pixel values conveys more subjective information than the pixel brightness. Thus we can trade intensity resolution for spatial resolution by a coarse quantization of $e(x, y)$.

As to image decoding, we may send the bit stream of $m(x, y)$ and quantized s to the decoder. The decoder can then synthesize the texture. The image reconstructed by this scheme looks excellent, but the compression ratio is not competitive against VQ or DCT because more than one bit is spent on each pixel. Fortunately, we can predict the texture strength s based on the merge threshold σ used in BBUM and the size $|B|$ of the leaf node in question. The reason that the leaf block B survives the merge operation is because $E(B \cup B') > \sigma$. So the decoder estimates $E(B) \approx \sigma$, and predicts s to be $\sqrt{\sigma/|B|}$. Then the DPCM technique can be used to encode quantized s at about 2 bits per block. Since both parameters σ and $|B|$ are available to the decoder, no side information is required. Another possibility is not to transmit s at all. The decoder simply lets $s = \sqrt{\sigma/|B|}$. If the texture strength is too strong, the viewer can interactively set it lower until reaching a satisfactory point. This can be naturally done if a soft dial in the user interface is provided to the viewer to adjust s as a contrast parameter.

In terms of transparent subjective image quality, a lossless encoding of the texture mask $m(x, y)$ is wasteful. Instead, one can vector-quantize $m(x, y)$ in a similar way as Udpikar and Raina quantize the BTC bit patterns [8]. For easy VQ implementation, we form 4×4 input texture masks, and fill 4×8 blocks with two masks. Because we quantize bit vectors, Hamming distance is used in the clustering process. This gives us computational advantage in nearest neighbor encoding. Computing distance between an input mask $m(x, y)$ and a codeword $c(x, y)$ becomes a simple bitwise exclusive OR operation, which can be done by a single instruction.

To pursue further in the direction of removing subjective redundancy, we find that in a 4×4 block, 16 texture masks as listed in Fig. 2 cover the most distinguishable texture patterns. Interestingly, when we used the LBG algorithm to cluster training bit vectors taken from five images using the 16 masks in Fig. 2 as initial codewords, the clustering process converged in three iterations with only minor changes to the patterns in Fig. 2. This means that the 16 patterns form a codebook that is close to a local optimum. If we use a codebook of 16 bit vectors for quantizing 4×4 masks, 0.25 bits are spent on each pixel in texture areas to encode the spatial information of the texture. Since Hamming distance between two 16-dimensional bit vectors can be done in only one XOR operation, it becomes computationally feasible to design an image-dependent VQ codebook on line. The entire resulting locally optimal codebook, if transmitted as it is, requires only 32 bytes, a negligible overhead. We can still do better by using the bit patterns in Fig. 2 as the initial codewords, and encode the differences between the resulting locally optimal codewords and the corresponding initial codewords.

It is helpful to consider the texture encoding as a postprocessing to our SIC technique. The goal of this postprocessing is to model and encode the residual image $e(x, y) = f(x, y) - g(x, y)$ to be a simpler function $t(x, y)$ under a subjective criterion such that $g(x, y) + t(x, y)$ is a visually good reproduction of $f(x, y)$. The separation of overall image approximation and local texture encoding can be convenient in some applications, for instances, progressive transmission and feature extraction. At the postprocessing stage, we may add an intensity interpolation cross the boundaries of local blocks to alleviate blockiness artifacts. Sometimes, the representation of smooth shades by mathematical surfaces may appear too contrived to the viewer. In this case, adding "salt-and-pepper" noise will add certain naturalness to the compressed image. The end-user can perform cross-boundary interpolation and the "salt-and-pepper" rendition without any side information, and do so interactively to his/her taste.

4 Empirical Results and Remarks

In Fig. 3 we present a set of photos of test images "Zelda". The set contains (a) the original image, (b) the image compressed by JPEG at the compression ratio 16.3 : 1, (c) the image compressed by our BBUM-based SIC coder without texture encoding at the compression ratio 23.5 : 1, and (d) the image by our method after the postprocessing of texture encoding at the compression ratio 19.1 : 1 which is slightly higher than (b). The image in (c) is noticeably fuzzier than the original. Pay attention to the regions of hair and eyes. The image (d) restores much of the texture lost in image (c), hence improves the subjective quality with a modest reduction in the compression ratio. In fact, images (a), (b) and (d) are hardly distinguishable from each other. We succeeded in making the subjective image quality of our SIG coder comparable to that of JPEG at bit rates around 0.5 bits/pil. Considering that the SIC coder can outperform JPEG at very low bit rate and the simplicity and low computational cost of the BBUM process, we have made some progress.

References

[1] V. Bhaskaran, B. K. Natarajan, and K. Konstantinides, "Optimal piecewise-linear compression of images," *Proc. DCC'93*, pp. 168-177, April, 1993.

[2] C. -T. Chen, "Adaptive transform coding via quadtree-based variable block size DCT," *Proc. Int. Conf. ASSP*, pp. 1854-1857, May 1989.

[3] E. J. Delp and O. R. Mitchell, "Image compression using BTC," *IEEE Trans. on Comm.*, vol. 27, no. 9, pp. 1335-1342, Sept. 1979.

[4] K. Knowlton, "Progressive transmission of grey-scale and binary pictures by simple, efficient, and lossless encoding schemes," *Proceedings of IEEE*, vol-68, no. 7, pp. 885-896, July 1980.

[5] M. Kunt, A. Ikonomopoulos, and M. Kocher, "Second generation image coding techniques," *Proc. IEEE*, vol. 73, pp. 549-574, Apr. 1985.

[6] H. Radha, R. Leonardi, and M. Vetterli, "A multiresolution approach to binary tree representations of images," *Proc. of ICASSP'91*, pp. 2653-2656, 1991.

[7] P. Strobach, "Image coding based on quadtree-structured recursive least-squares approximation," *Proc. IEEE ICASSP*'89, pp. 1961-1964, Glasgow, 1989.

[8] V. R. Udpikar and J. P. Raina, "BTC image coding using vector quantization," *IEEE Trans. on Comm.*, vol. 35, no. 3, pp. 352-356, Mar. 1987.

[9] J. Vaisey and A. Gersho, "Image compression with variable block size segmentation," *IEEE Trans. on Signal Proc.*, vol. 40, no. 8, pp. 2040-2060, Aug. 1992.

[10] X. Wu, "Image coding by adaptive tree-structured segmentation," *IEEE Trans. on Information Theory*, vol. 38, no. 6, pp. 1755-1767, Nov. 1992.

[11] X. Wu and Y. Fang, "Progressive image coding by hierarchical piecewise linear approximation," *J. of Info. Proc. and Manag.* (to appear).

[12] X. Wu and Y. Fang, "A segmentation-based predictive multiresolution image coder," *IEEE Trans. on Image Processing*, Jan., 1995 (to appear).

Figure 3: Test results (clockwise from the top-left corner): (a) the original, (b) JPEG compressed image at 0.491 bits/pil, (c) BBUM compressed image without texture encoding at 0.340 bits/pil, and (d) BBUM compressed image with texture encoding at 0.419 bits/pil.

A High Performance Fixed Rate Compression Scheme for Still Image Transmission

Michael J. Ruf
German Aerospace Research Establishment (DLR)
Institute for Communications Technology
D – 82234 Wessling, Germany
Phone: + 49 - 8153 - 282868
Fax: + 49 - 8153 - 281442
e-mail: ruf@holmes.nt.op.dlr.de

Abstract

It is well known that variable length source coding schemes, despite their excellent compression properties, have a very painful drawback when it comes to transmission of those compressed images. That is why we restricted ourselves to fixed rate source coding schemes, that do not have the problems of re-synchronization or complete loss of information in case of uncorrectable transmission errors. In this paper, a high performance source coding scheme based on the Discrete Wavelet Transform (DWT) with an additional DCT for the low frequency subimage and a Product Pyramid Vector Quantizer (PPVQ) utilizing Trellis Coded Quantization (TCQ) is proposed, which gives close to optimum results compared to variable length coding (VLC). This together with the ability to calculate the bit-sensitivity of the compressed image data enables one to perform a highly efficient unequal error protection for image transmission over noisy channels. Simulation results show a source coding degradation of only 0.5 - 0.7 dB in PSNR due to fixed rate coding compared to the best found VLC scheme. In addition, applying combined source and channel coding and looking at the performance after transmission over an additive white Gaussian noise (AWGN) channel, the proposed scheme outperforms all other known fixed rate schemes, even a sophisticated VLC scheme based also on the DWT and especially has gains of up to 5 dB in PSNR and up to 3.5 dB in E_s/N_0 compared to JPEG.

1 Introduction

The advantage of fixed rate source coding schemes like the Product Pyramid VQ [1] is the robustness of the compressed image data to channel errors. While variable length schemes like JPEG [2] or others based on VLC or RLC [3] suffer from problems in synchronization in case of bit corruption during transmission and, therefore, must be protected with a very powerful channel code, which of course reduces the available source rate R_S, fixed length schemes can handle bit errors much better, due to the fact that the effect of an error is limited to one codeword. With a method of calculating very precisely the mean square error caused by source coding mse_S before transmission [4] and the knowledge of the average contribution $\bar{A}_i$ of an error of bit i of the compressed image data, one is able to perform an a-priori optimization matched to the condition of the transmission channel, in order to share the available bits for source- and channel-coding in an optimum way. This is done by unequal error protection (UEP). This paper is organized as follows: Section 2 explains the implementation of the source coding scheme based on the DWT, DCT, PPVQ and TCQ, and shows simulation results of the compression performance. Section 3 shows the derivation of the bit-sensitivities and the optimization of source and channel coding is described. Section 4 is devoted to simulation results followed by conclusions.

2 Source Coding

2.1 Transformation

As in other source coding schemes, the image first undergoes a transformation before quantization, to decorrelate the energy. This could be done by a discrete cosine transform (DCT) or a subband transform (SBT). Hence, multiresolution representations or discrete wavelet transforms (DWT) have been applied very successfully in image coding and showed a superior performance for both low and high rate compression, this technique is combined with the fixed rate quantizer, the PPVQ, to build a base for applying the joint optimization of source and channel coding.

The basic idea of the discrete wavelet transform (DWT) [5] is the approximation of an image $\tilde{A}_0 f$ by its discrete detail representations $\tilde{D}^0_{-1}f$, $\tilde{D}^1_{-1}f$, $\tilde{D}^2_{-1}f$ and the subimage at resolution $r = 1$, $\tilde{A}_{-1}f$, where a successive approximation of $\tilde{A}_{-1}f$ by $\tilde{A}_{-2}f$ and $\tilde{D}^0_{-2}f$, $\tilde{D}^1_{-2}f$, $\tilde{D}^2_{-2}f$ can be applied again and so on. So one obtains the mapping at resolution r

$$\tilde{A}_0 f \mapsto (\tilde{A}_{-r}f, \tilde{D}^0_{-r}f, \tilde{D}^1_{-r}f, \tilde{D}^2_{-r}f, \tilde{D}^0_{-r+1}f, \tilde{D}^1_{-r+1}f, \tilde{D}^2_{-r+1}f, ..., \tilde{D}^0_{-1}f, \tilde{D}^1_{-1}f, \tilde{D}^2_{-1}f) \quad , \tag{1}$$

that corresponds to an orthogonal transform, where $\tilde{D}^0_{-r}f$, $\tilde{D}^1_{-r}f$ and $\tilde{D}^2_{-r}f$ are the detail representations (see fig. 1) of $\tilde{A}_{-r+1}f$ at resolution r.

For images, the discrete representations $\tilde{D}^0_{-r}f$, $\tilde{D}^1_{-r}f$, $\tilde{D}^2_{-r}f$ and the subimage $\tilde{A}_{-r}f$ at resolution r can be computed from the subimage $\tilde{A}_{-r+1}f$ at resolution $(r-1)$ by applying the elementary steps of filtering first to the rows and then to the columns of $\tilde{A}_{-r+1}f$ followed by subsampling by a factor of 2. So the discrete representation of the original image at resolution r consists of $K := 3r + 1$ subimages. The two filters $(g_m)_{m\in Z}$ and $(h_m)_{m\in Z}$ which are used, are related by the condition $g_m = (-1)^{1-m} \cdot h_{1-m}$. Furthermore, wavelet theory shows that $|H(\omega)|^2 - |H(\omega+\pi)|^2 = 2$, so the filters have the characteristics of quadrature mirror filters (QMF). Finally the inverse wavelet transform can be performed by upsampling $\tilde{D}^0_{-r}f$, $\tilde{D}^1_{-r}f$, $\tilde{D}^2_{-r}f$ and

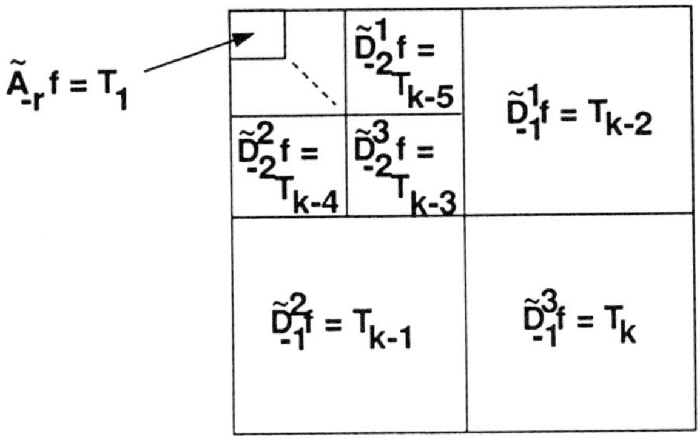

Figure 1: The disposition of the wavelet transformed image

$\tilde{A}_{-r}f$ by a factor of 2 and filtering. In the simulation, the Johnston 16 tab (b) filter [6] was used for the elementary steps. In the following let us denote the subimages of the wavelet transformed image matrix T as $T_1 = \tilde{A}_{-r}f$, $T_2 = \tilde{D}^0_{-r}f$, $T_3 = \tilde{D}^1_{-r}f$, $T_4 = \tilde{D}^2_{-r}f$, $T_5 = \tilde{D}^0_{-r+1}f$, etc. Though the low frequency subimage T_1 still is highly correlated, it undergoes a (2,2) DCT for further decorrelation.

2.2 Quantization and Coding

As shown in [4], the fixed rate product pyramid vector quantization of transformed image data, that is approximately Laplacian distributed, performs very well with respect to the obtained peak signal-to-noise ratio $PSNR = 10\log(\frac{255^2}{mse})$. Furthermore, the (L-K)-thresholding of the components of the vector $\vec{X}$ as introduced in [7], where K denotes the maximum lattice size in one dimension and L the dimension of the vector$\vec{X}$, can significantly improve the quantization performance.

Denoting by $\tau_{L-K}(\vec{X})$ the $(L-K)$-thresholded vector $\vec{X}$, denoting by $\rho(\vec{X})_{L-K} = \| \tau_{L-K}(\vec{X}) \|_1$ its $\| \, . \, \|$-radius and by $Q(\rho(\vec{X}))$ the quantized radius, the quantization error, that can be calculated before compression can be written as [4]

$$\begin{aligned} mse_S(\vec{X}) &= \mathbb{E}(\| \vec{X} - \tau_{L-K}(\vec{X})_p \|_2^2) = \frac{\mathbb{E}((Q(\rho(\vec{X})_{L-K}) - \rho(\vec{X})_{L-K})^2)}{K} \quad + \\ &+ \quad \frac{\varepsilon_K \cdot \mathbb{E}(Q(\rho(\vec{X})_{L-K})^2)}{K^2} + \mathbb{E}(\| \vec{X} \|_2^2 - \| \tau_{L-K}(\vec{X}) \|_2^2) \ , \end{aligned} \tag{2}$$

with the resulting pyramid lattice point $\tau_{L-K}(\vec{X})_p$.

Here, the PPVQ is applied to vectors $\vec{X}$ formed out of amplitudes a of the subimages T_i, $i = 1, ..., K$ after DWT. To keep the variance $var(\rho(\vec{X}))$ of the radii as low as possible (to quantize with a minimum amount of bits) a random forming of vectors is advised (see figure 2), which improves the performance compared to forming vectors out of neighboring elements (scan_n) within the subimages. Another way to

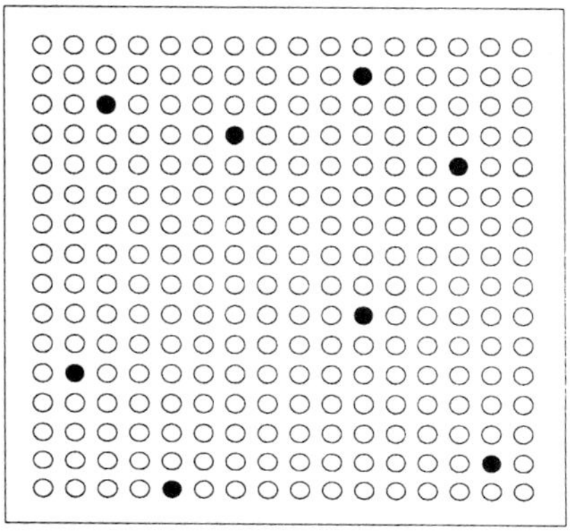

Figure 2: Random forming of vectors

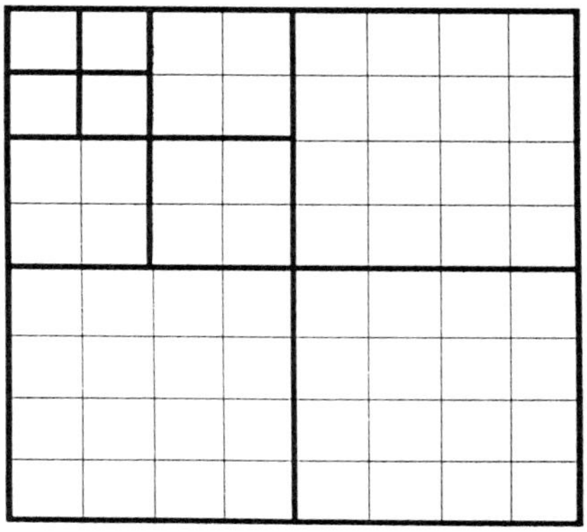

Figure 3: Decomposition into fields

significantly improve the coding performance is to exploit the different local activities within the subimages. Therefore, all subimages $T_i (i = 4, .., K)$ were decomposed into fields of the size of the lowest resolution subimage T_1 (see figure 3). In this way, the bit allocation [8] using formula (2) could perform a local adaptivity when allocating (for a given compression rate R_S) the bits for coding the radii and the pyramid numbers, when assigning different rates to the fields within one subimage T_i. Other ways to improve the performance and the estimation of the quantization error mse_S, is to use the true second moment when the amplitudes of one field or subimage are set to zero, and to apply Trellis Coded Quantization (TCQ) [9] for coding the radii, that performs Maximum Likelihood encoding with the Viterbi algorithm (VA).

2.3 Performance of Source Coding Scheme

Coding simulations were performed with the 8-bit grayscale LENA image of size 512 x 512. The resolution of the DWT was chosen as $r = 5$. The vectors $\vec{X}$ had dimension L=8, the trellis of TCQ had memory $\nu_T = 6$. The bit allocation was done for all fields, and the forming of the vectors was done by a random scheme (scan_rand). This together with the DWT and the DCT in addition for the low frequency subimage T_1 gives the results shown in table 1. Though a fixed rate coding scheme was employed, the obtained bit rate differed from the constrained bit rate by less than 3%. The side information to be transmitted accounts for less than 5% of the compressed data and thus is neglected.

One can see the very close matching of estimation and real performance for the proposed scheme, which is the base for further joint optimization of source and channel coding. In comparison with other schemes, one can note the excellent properties of the proposed fixed-length coding (FLC) scheme, either in comparison with other FLC-schemes based on different transforms like the 16 x16 discrete cosine transform

(DCT + PPVQ) [4] with scan_n (see 2.2), or the subband transform (SBT ($r = 5$) + PPVQ) [10] with scan_nn that gives one the maximum regular distance between the amplitude-positions, or in comparison with VLC-schemes like the image compression standard JPEG [2] or the best found scheme also based on the DWT (Filip) [3]. The gain compared to JPEG varies from 1 dB (0.5-1.0 bpp) up to 3 dB (0.2 bpp). The reduction in coding performance due to FLC compared to VLC (Filip) is only about 0.6 dB in the range from 0.1 - 0.7 bpp, getting smaller with lower compression rates, but having the advantage of the much less sensitive behavior to channel errors.

Source Coding Performance Comparison (PSNR)					
	fixed rate coding			variable length coding	
bit rate (bpp)	DWT PPVQ scan_rand	DCT PPVQ scan_n	SBT PPVQ scan_nn	DCT JPEG	DWT Filip
0.1	29.148 (29.24)	26.986	28.717		29.8
0.2	32.060 (32.14)	29.704	31.159	28.8	32.7
0.3	33.873 (33.81)	31.383	32.751	31.8	34.6
0.5	36.307 (36.28)	33.661	34.914	35.1	36.8
0.7	37.974 (37.92)	35.324	36.517	36.9	38.2
1.0	39.792 (39.67)	37.248	38.367	38.6	40.0

Table 1: Performance for 512 x 512 LENA image, estimated values in brackets

3 Combined Source and Channel Coding

3.1 Bit Sensitivities after Compression

In order to be able to calculate the effects of channel errors and to sufficiently protect the compressed data according to their priority, one has to know their sensitivity $\bar{A}_i$. Though the TCQ was applied for radius quantization, one has to calculate the sensitivities of the **path-bits** specifying the path through the trellis and the **level-bits** which choose the right value of the specific subset. In addition, the **pyramid-bits** that code the vectors $\tau_{L-K}(\vec{X})$ of dimension $L = 8$ are of interest.

As shown in [11], the radius error can be written as

$$\| \hat{X}_1 - \hat{X}_2 \|_2^2 = \frac{2}{L+1} \cdot (\hat{\rho}_1 - \hat{\rho}_2)^2 = \frac{2}{L+1} \cdot mse_{rad} \ , \tag{3}$$

where $\hat{X}_1 = \frac{\hat{\rho}_1}{K} \cdot X_p$ and $\hat{X}_2 = \frac{\hat{\rho}_2}{K} \cdot X_p$ are two lattice points on the fixed pyramid. With (3) the sensitivities of a path-bit is

$$\bar{A}_{path} = \frac{2}{L+1} \cdot (3 \cdot 2^{(\nu_T - 1)} - 1) \cdot Q_{TCQ}^2 \cdot \alpha \cdot \beta \cdot \gamma \ , \tag{4}$$

with ν_T the code memory and Q_{TCQ} the average quantization distance of TCQ and with $\alpha = 1/L$ (if $K \geq L$, i.e. no thresholding) or $\alpha = 1/K$ (else), $\beta = 1/$(number of fields)$= 2^{2r}$ and $\gamma = 1/$(number of vectors per field)=L/M (M is the number of amplitudes in a field or subimage).

When quantizing the level of a certain subset with $r' = (\tilde{r} - 1)$ bits, due to the subset division, we obtain with (3) the bit-sensitivity of a level bit

$$\bar{A}_{i,level} = \frac{2}{L+1} \cdot Q^2_{TCQ} \cdot 2^{2(\nu_T+i)} \cdot \alpha \cdot \beta \cdot \gamma \qquad \text{with} \quad i = 0, ..., (r'-1) \,. \qquad (5)$$

Finally the bit-sensitivity of a **pyramid bit** can be expressed as [11]

$$\begin{aligned} \bar{A}_{pyr} &= \frac{4}{(L+1)} \cdot \mathbb{E}(\rho(\vec{X})^2) \cdot \alpha \cdot \beta \cdot \gamma \\ &= \frac{4}{(L+1)} \cdot (var(\rho(\vec{X})) + \mathbb{E}(\rho(\vec{X}))^2) \cdot \alpha \cdot \beta \cdot \gamma \,. \end{aligned} \qquad (6)$$

To confirm the formulas, we induced errors in the compressed image data, to simulate all bit-sensitivities. The comparison with the analytical sensitivities is shown in a significance ordered way in figure 4. For better representation of the wide range of the $\bar{A}_i$ we plotted the $snr_i = 10 \cdot \log_{10}(\frac{255^2}{(\bar{A}_i + mse_S)})$ instead of the $\bar{A}_i$. One can see that the simulated snr_i almost never falls below the estimated snr_i, which would cause insufficient protection in the following channel rate allocation process and would thus correspond to a higher overall mse after transmission than estimated.

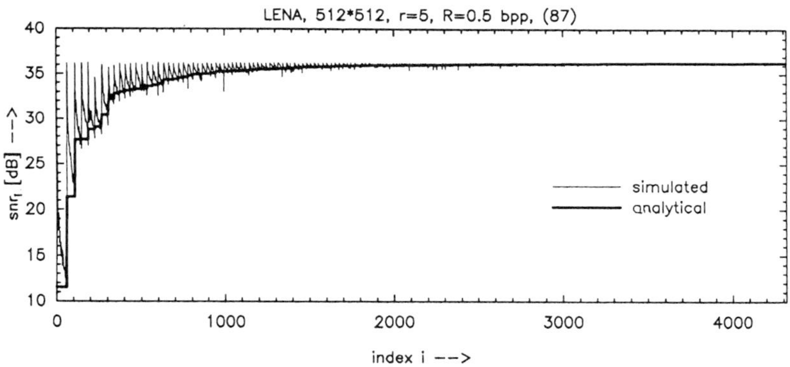

Figure 4: SNR_i vs. coding unit index i

3.2 Performing Unequal Error Protection

For a given (or estimated) signal-to-noise ratio E_S/N_0 on the channel we can calculate the bit-error probability p_b for a channel corrupted by additive white Gaussian noise (AWGN) or the remaining bit-error probability if using some error correcting codes.

The expected overall $mse = mse_S + mse_C$ can be evaluated by using (2) and

$$mse_C = \sum_{j=0}^{(n_{path}-1)} \bar{A}_{j,path}\frac{p_{b,j}}{\gamma} + \sum_{k=0}^{(n_{level}-1)}\sum_{i=0}^{(r'-1)} \bar{A}_{k,i,path}\frac{p_{b,k,i}}{\gamma} + \sum_{l=0}^{(n_{pyr}-1)} \bar{A}_{l,pyr}\frac{p_{b,l}}{\gamma}\cdot a_l \quad , \tag{7}$$

before transmitting the image, with n_{path}, n_{level} and n_{pyr} the number of fields coded with path-, level- and pyramid-bits respectively, a_l the number of pyramid bits used for one vector $\vec{X}$ in field l and p_b the associated bit error probability assigned to the particular bits. It is easy to see that we are able to calculate the resulting mse for every possible assignment of source and channel rates, so we can optimize the source to channel rate ratio in order to obtain the lowest mse.

The optimization starts with the allocation of the evaluated channel code rates (with different error probabilities p_b) to the different bit-sensitivities for given source code rates R_S. This is done by applying an adapted allocation algorithm [8] as done earlier for the PPVQ-bit allocation, to optimally allocate the available channel bits. Then we search for the optimum source to channel rate ratio with $R = R_S + \bar{R}_C$ which is easy, because as is clear from figure 5, the $mse = f(\bar{R}_C)$ is a convex function.

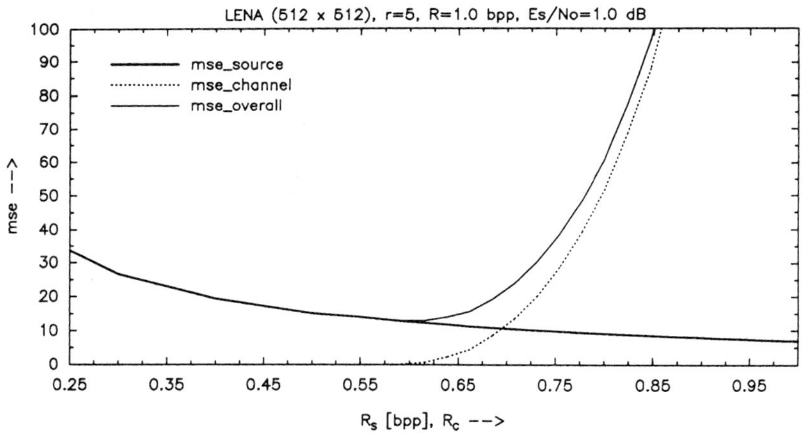

Figure 5: mse vs. R_S [bpp] and $\bar{R}_C$ for R=1.0 bpp

4 Simulation Results

To show the benefits of the a-priori ability to calculate the mse caused by image compression **and** channel errors and thus the a-priori optimization, we simulated the transmission system. It consisted of the source coder, the DWT at resolution $r = 5$, the DCT for T_1, a TCQ with $\nu_T = 6$ and the PPVQ with $L = 8$ plus (L-K)-thresholding. The channel coder was a concatenated system with a $\nu = 6$ RCPC code [12] and a $(255, 255 - 2t)$-Reed-Solomon code. This fixed length scheme was compared with two other fixed length schemes using either a (16 x 16) DCT or the SBT (resolution r=4) [10] together with the PPVQ (scan_n and scan_nn respectively) and to show the benefits of FLC, with the variable length schemes, the image compression standard JPEG with inserted synch data and a DWT based scheme [13] with unequally distributed synch data to obtain equal sensitive data. All three FLC schemes were protected by UEP, and both VLC schemes with EEP, that guaranteed a BER $p_b \leq 10^{-10}$. The test image was the well known LENA image in the (512,512) pixel format with 8-bit resolution. The overall rate was R = 1.0 in bits per pixel (bpp). Figure 6 shows large gains of up to 5 dB in PSNR or up to 3.5 dB in E_S/N_0 of the proposed scheme compared to JPEG for a Gaussian channel, especially for a very low channel SNR. This gain is more significant for lower overall rates R. One can furthermore see the better performance of the DWT compared to the SBT and DCT respectively. Even with complex pre-processing of VLC images, the performance of the proposed scheme cannot be reached.

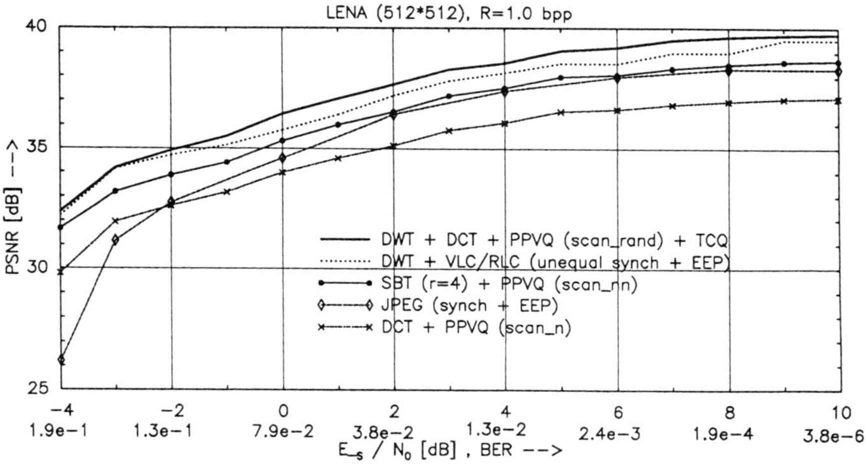

Figure 6: Comparison of PSNR vs. E_S/N_0 for various schemes

5 Conclusions

In this paper we pointed out the close to optimum performance (0.5 - 0.7 dB degradation in PSNR compared to the best found VLC compression method) of a fixed length source coding scheme based on the discrete wavelet transform, the DCT, the product pyramid vector quantizer and trellis coded quantization. Furthermore, we showed how to perform an a-priori overall-mse-calculation and -optimization for a Gaussian channel, which can be easily adopted to other channel models (e.g. Rayleigh fading channel, [11]). This not only allows us to transmit images at very low E_S/N_0 when conventional variable length schemes (JPEG, etc.) deliver poor image qualities, it is even possible to adapt the source and channel coding to the channel SNR in a way as to increase the image throughput for a given maximum-mse to save channel SNR or so to transmit images with a lower mse for a given overall rate R. For the latter application we demonstrated the superiority of the a-priori processing of the proposed scheme with gains compared to JPEG of up to 3.5 dB in E_S/N_0 and up to 5 dB in PSNR when transmitting the compressed images over a Gaussian channel.

Acknowledgement

The author likes to thank Pavel Filip for helpful hints.

References

[1] T. R. Fischer, "A pyramid vector quantizer," *IEEE Trans. Inform. Theory*, vol. IT-32, pp. 568–583, July 1986.

[2] Joint Photographic Experts Group, *JPEG Technical Specification, Revision 5*, January 1990.

[3] P. Filip, "An efficient method for image compression in the wavelet transform domain," in *Proc. of SPIE Int. Symp. on Optics, Imaging and Instrumentation*, (San Diego, Ca), 1993.

[4] P. Filip and M. J. Ruf, "A fixed-rate product pyramid vector quantzation using a Bayesian model," in *Proc. of IEEE Globecom '92*, (Orlando, Fl.), pp. 240–244, 1992.

[5] S. G. Mallat, "A theory for multifrequency signal decomposition: the wavelet representation," *IEEE Trans. Pattern Anal. Machine Intell.*, vol. PAMI-11, pp. 674–693, July 1989.

[6] J. D. Johnston, "A filter family designed for use in quadrature mirror filter banks," in *Proc. IEEE ICASSP*, pp. 291–294, 1980.

[7] M. E. Blain and T. R. Fischer, "A comparison of vector quantization techniques in transform and subband coding of imagery," *Signal Processing: Image Communication*, vol. 3, pp. 91–105, Feb. 1991.

[8] P. H. Westerink, J. Biemond, and D. E. Boekee, "An optimal bit allocation algorithm for sub-band coding," in *Proc. IEEE ICASSP*, pp. 757–760, 1988.

[9] M. W. Marcellin and T. R. Fischer, "Trellis coded quantization of memoryless and Gauss-Markov sources," *IEEE Trans. Com.*, vol. COM-38, pp. 82–93, Jan. 1990.

[10] M. Maurer, *Kombinierte Quell- und Kanalcodierung fuer Subband-Transformierte Bilder*. Dipl.-Ing. thesis, Technical University Munich, Germany, 1993.

[11] M. J. Ruf and P. Filip, "Combined source and channel coding for transmission of pvq compressed images over gaussian and rayleigh fading channels," in *Proc. Picture Coding Symposium, Lausanne*, p. 9.7, 1993.

[12] J. Hagenauer, "Rate-compatible punctured convolutional codes (RCPC codes) and their applications," *IEEE Trans. Commun.*, vol. COM-36, pp. 389–400, Apr. 1988.

[13] B. Blumentritt, *Kombinierte Quellen- und Kanalcodierung fuer Wavelet-Transformierte Bilder*. Dipl.-Ing. thesis, Technical University Munich, Germany, 1993.

A Nonlinear VQ-based Predictive Lossless Image Coder

Marko J. Slyz

David L. Neuhoff

Electrical Engineering and Computer Science
University of Michigan
Ann Arbor, MI 48109

Abstract

A new lossless predictive image coder is introduced and tested. The predictions are made with a nonlinear, vector quantizer based, adaptive predictor. The prediction errors are losslessly compressed with an arithmetic coder that presumes they are Laplacian distributed with variances that are estimated during the prediction process, as in the approach of Howard and Vitter.

I. Introduction

Predictive coding is a common way of losslessly compressing originally analog data. A block diagram of a typical system is shown in Figure 1.

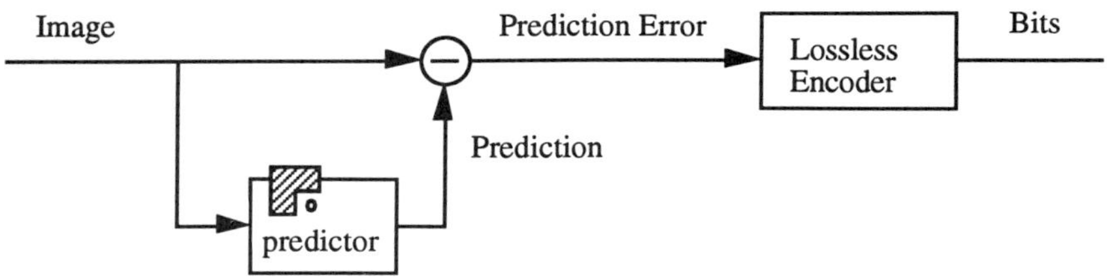

Figure 1: A Predictive Lossless Image Coder

In such systems, a prediction for each sample to be coded is generated using the sample values previously transmitted to the decoder. This prediction is subtracted from the sample to produce an error value, which is then compressed with a lossless encoder such as a Huffman coder or an arithmetic coder. The decoder can make the same prediction as the coder since it has access to the same samples that were used by the coder. It then adds its prediction to the decoded error value to reconstruct the original sample.

 1068-0314/94 $3.00

The better the predictor, the smaller the errors and the fewer bits needed to represent them. The principal goal of this paper is to investigate a VQ based strategy for designing nonlinear adaptive predictors. The lossless error encoder is taken to be a Howard-Vitter style arithmetic coder [1,2] that presumes the errors are Laplacian distributed with variances that are estimated by some method. In our case, the variance estimates are a natural adjunct to the prediction process.

Section II of this paper discusses the basic form of our predictors, which can be improved by introducing the ideas in Section III. The lossless encoding of the prediction errors is described in Section IV. Section V gives results and discusses future research.

II. The Basic Prediction Method

The fundamental principle behind our predictor is that if we are trying to predict a random vector Y using a random vector X, then the optimal prediction, Y'(X), in the sense of minimizing $E\,|Y - Y'(X)|^2$ is $Y'(X) = E[Y|X]$. The trouble with this is that E[Y|X] cannot be easily calculated for real-world data because the conditional distribution of Y given X is usually not known. Even so, it is fairly straightforward to produce an approximation to E[Y|X] using a vector quantizer as follows [3-6]: Design a vector quantizer for X that partitions the X sample space into N fairly small cells $\{c_1,\ldots,c_N\}$. Let C(x) be the function that classifies each incoming X vector according to the cell in which it lies; i.e. C(x) = i when $x \in c_i$. As an approximation to the best prediction of Y based on X, we produce the best prediction of Y based on C(X), which if C(X) = i, is $y_i = E[Y|C(X) = i]$. The y_i's are called the *potential predictions*. Standard VQ methods can be used to design both the partition $\{c_1,\ldots,c_N\}$ and the potential predictions $\{y_1,\ldots,y_N\}$. For example, for a given partition, the y_i's are calculated by a training set method: get a bunch of actual (X,Y) pairs from the source and set y_i equal to the arithmetic mean of all the Y's whose corresponding X lies in the ith cell, c_i.

To be specific to the case of predictive coding, consider the case of a two-point predictor consisting of the pixel above and the pixel to the left of the current pixel (shown with a y in Fig. 2).

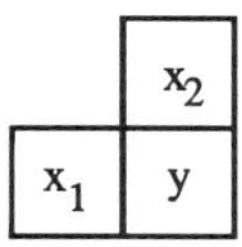

Fig. 2: Two point predictor

We go through a typical picture and obtain many ordered pairs (one for each pixel except, possibly, the ones on the top and left edges) of the form ([x1 x2], y). Using some good method (c.f. [5]), we design a partition for the X = [x1 x2] vectors, which might look like the one in Figure 3:

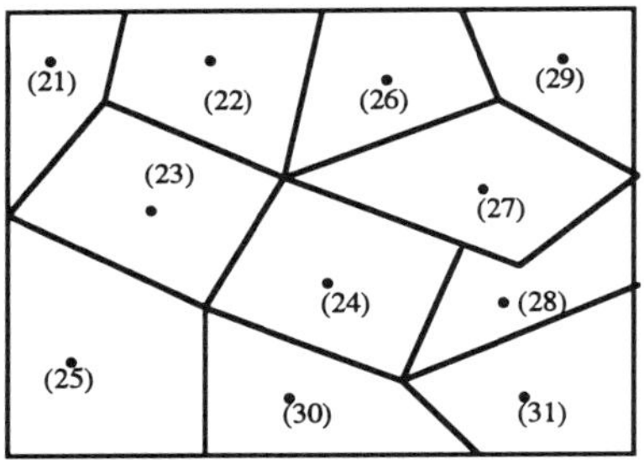

Fig. 3: Sample VQ partition and potential predictions (in parentheses).

Finally, we go through all the pixels and average the y's of all the [x1 x2]'s that get classified into a particular cell. When we are done we have both a partition $\{c_1,\ldots,c_N\}$ and a set of potential predictions $\{y_1,\ldots y_N\}$.

Actually, we use predictors based on more than just two pixels. We describe them in terms of the following terminology: a pixel's *context* is some fixed shaped grouping of pixels that are near it. These are the pixels upon which the prediction is based; i.e. it is the "contexts" that are classified by the partition $\{c_1,\ldots,c_N\}$. The *origin* is the pixel for which we are obtaining a prediction. We typically use y to denote the value of the origin and x to denote the vector-valued contents of the context.

One common method of operation is to design the predictor for a representative set of pictures, and to then use it on future pictures. But we wish to explore adaptive methods that work well even on pictures that come from non-representative data. Designing a predictor for each picture or each part of a picture and encoding the predictor(s) as part of the compressed output is one possibility, but this involves the question of overhead. Instead we decided to focus on the following backward adaptive scheme: for each pixel, look at a training region, e.g. the 30x30 block of pixels above it as illustrated by Figure 4, and perform the described design procedure. Since the decoder has the same training region it can do an identical design.

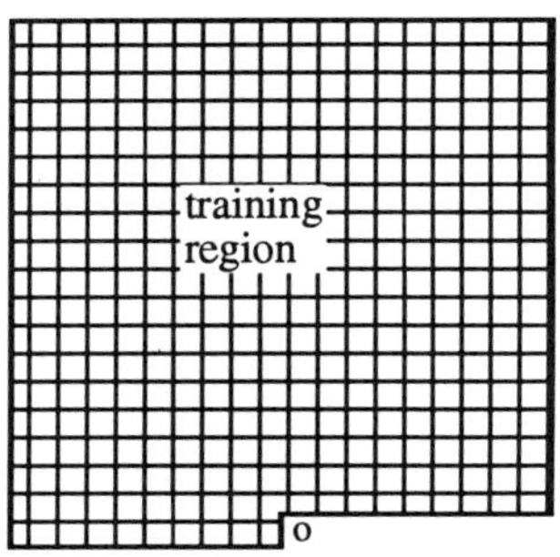

Fig. 4: Training region to design a VQ to predict
the pixel marked with an "o" for "origin".

The trouble with this method is that it is too expensive to design a new VQ-type estimator at every single pixel of the image. Instead we realized that we only need to use a single cell for every pixel we are going to predict, namely the cell in which that pixel's context lies. Therefore we should just average all the y's whose contexts lie in the same cell as the origin's and not bother figuring out what the rest of the VQ is. The trouble with this is that VQ design methods require the same amount of effort to produce one small cell as to produce many small cells. So instead we somewhat arbitrarily decide on a cell shape, an n-dimensional sphere (where n is the number of pixels in the desired context), for example. Then we can classify all the contexts that lie in the training region as being either inside or outside of the cell and then average the y's of all the pixels that are inside.

Actually, it is hard to predict ahead of time the diameter of this sphere, so instead we specify that its population size -- the number of contexts in the training region that fall inside the sphere -- should be some constant. 11 seems to work well. So to summarize, we predict each pixel with the following algorithm:

1) Calculate the Euclidean distance between the context of each pixel in the training region and the origin's context. For example, if one is using a two point predictor as above, and the origin's context is $[x_1\ x_2]$ while the context of some arbitrary pixel in the 30×30 training region is $[x_1'\ x_2']$, then the distance between the two is $(x_1 - x_1')^2 + (x_2 - x_2')^2$.

2) Identify the contexts with the 11 smallest distances.

3) Average their "y" pixels and use this as a prediction for the origin.

As a test case, we tried this method on the image *lena* with various context sizes, population sizes, and training region sizes. For the best choice of parameters the first-order entropy of the prediction errors is about 4.38 bits/pixel. An improved method is described in the next section.

III. Length-Normalization for Increasing the Number of Matches

The estimates for $E[Y|C(X) = i]$ would be more accurate if we averaged more y pixels to obtain them. Unfortunately, simply increasing the cell population size does not work since that soon forces us to start averaging y's belonging to contexts which are too distant from the origin's context and therefore not legitimately in the VQ cell. Fortunately, there is an idea from a structured VQ technique called Shape-Gain VQ (c.f. [5]) which applies here.

The idea is that contexts that have different amplitudes, but which are otherwise similar, can be counted together after being normalized in the obvious way. For example, in Figure 5 context A would ordinarily be considered quite far from context B if just the usual Euclidean distance is computed. But if each element in context A is divided by the Euclidean length of context A and each element in context B is divided by the Euclidean length of context B, then they will be quite near.

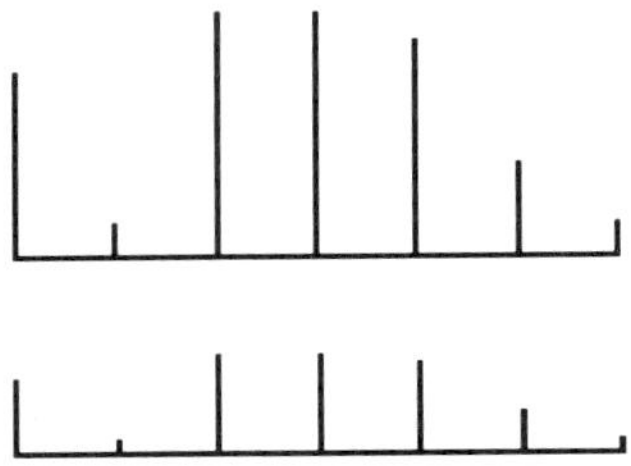

Figure 5: Two contexts with the same shape, different gains.

Normalizing all the context vectors effectively projects them onto the surface of a unit sphere. This space will be more densely populated than the original one and so there will usually be more vectors within a given distance of the origin's context.

The one caveat is that of course the y's must also be scaled. We first normalize each y by the length of its context, and then multiply it by the length of the origin's context. This gives us a set of adjusted y's which we can then average in the usual way to get our prediction.

This technique improves the compression of lena by about .07 bits/pixel. The best compression occurs when there are about 21 matches in the quantizer cell, a population size too large to give good compression if the length-normalization technique were not being used. As we shall see, having larger cell populations will also be important when it comes time to code the errors.

IV. Howard & Vitter's Error Coding Method

After we make a prediction, we must still code the error between it and the actual pixel value. To do this we implemented a method similar to that described in [1]. In this method the prediction errors are encoded using arithmetic coding, which requires that we supply a probability distribution for each error. As prediction errors have often been found to be Laplacian, the probability distributions are assumed to be discretized Laplacians (symmetric two-sided exponential). The Laplacian distribution has one parameter -- the variance. To obtain the variance associated with a given pixel we looked at all the contexts in the training region that were nearest to the origin's context, and were used to generate the prediction in the first place. We remember the errors that occurred when predicting the y's in each of these contexts and find their variance. Having a larger cell population means that we have more samples with which to estimate the variance and, therefore, obtain better estimates. The variance is then quantized to one of 37 values which, together with the actual error, are fed to an arithmetic coder that generates the coded representation.

Our variance estimation technique is somewhat similar to the one used in the PPPM method of [1]. One difference is that the distance measure in [1] is less discriminating since two contexts which match in their high-order bits would be considered to be equivalent by the

[1] distance measure, but might still be meaningfully distinguished by a Euclidean measure. On the other hand, we are not aware of a theoretical reason why the context classification performed in [1] is worse than any other, and doing it explicitly this way allows for lazy updating of context statistics, which may improve variance estimation.

V. Results and Future Work

Table 1 contains the results in bits per pixel for running three different coders on the 7 bands of the Landsat Thematic Mapper data set originally used in [1]. PPPM is [1]'s method. It is the best performing lossless image coder that we are aware of. JPEG is the Joint Photographic Experts Group Coder being run in its lossless mode. The data for the PPPM and JPEG columns both come from [1]. VQ-pred is the algorithm described in this article being run with cell populations of size 26.

Band	PPPM	JPEG	VQ-pred
1	3.67	3.86	3.77
2	2.87	3.00	2.96
3	3.31	3.51	3.42
4	4.15	4.42	4.26
5	4.47	4.76	4.60
6	1.09	1.01	0.98
7	3.62	3.81	3.73

Table 1

In an effort to discover why PPPM -- which inspired our research into context matching for image coding -- is generally better than our current coder, we investigated the respective predictors and found that our predictor generates about .3 bits/pixel less than the two-point average used by PPPM. Therefore the advantage of PPPM must lie in its variance estimation, which we are currently studying.

We can also compare our coder to adaptive *linear* predictors that generate a linear predictor for each pixel using some sort of least squares method, and then use that predictor on the pixel. These are also quite successful in compressing images and, when used with sufficiently high-order predictors, can obtain compression ratios as good as the nonlinear systems discussed here. The advantage of the context-search type methods in this paper and in [1] over linear predictors is in complexity: our nonlinear VQ coders obtain their results significantly faster than an adaptive linear coder set for this quality level. This is because to achieve this level of performance, adaptive linear coders must design a different linear predictor for each pixel, whether recursively or with batch least-squares, and that turns out to be time consuming. In contrast, to predict a particular pixel VQ-pred must mainly do a distance calculation for each point in that pixel's training region, which is easier. Furthermore, there exist techniques, some of which are similar to the hashing done for context matching in PPPM, that can potentially speed this up.

We hope to further improve the performance of this nonlinear VQ method by using better cell shapes, perhaps with a variant of the method in [6]. We are also studying the performance of these nonlinear predictors on other kinds of data. Images are well modeled by autoregressive sources and so may be especially well suited to linear prediction. It may be that other kinds of data have structure that's less obvious but that can still be exploited by these nonlinear predictors. Also, in our research we have considered the VQ-pred's use of relatively few pixels in making a prediction -- compared to least squares methods, which generally use all the points in their training region -- a liability, since in a sense they are throwing away data that might be useful. But for sources whose statistics rapidly change with time, paying such close attention to the relevancy of data may be an advantage.

References

[1] P. Howard, J. Vitter, "New Methods for Lossless Image Compression Using Arithmetic Coding", *Proc. Data Compression Conference*, J. Storer and J. Reif, eds., Snowbird, Utah, Apr. 8-11,1991, pp. 257-266. A more complete version appeared in *Inform. Proc. & Management*, vol. 28, no. 5, pp. 765-779, 1992.

[2] P. Howard and J. Vitter, "Error Modeling for Hierarchical Lossless Image Compression," *Proceedings of 1992 Data Compression Conference*, J. Storer and M. Cohen, eds., pp. 269-278.

[3] A. Gersho, "Optimal Nonlinear Interpolative Vector Quantization", *IEEE Trans. on Communications*, vol. 38, no. 9, Sept. 1990.

[4] S. Wang, E. Paksoy, A. Gersho, "Performance of Nonlinear Prediction of Speech," *Proc. Int. Conf. Spoken Language Processing*, Kobe, Japan, Nov. 1990, pp. 29-32.

[5] A. Gersho and R. Gray, *Vector Quantization and Signal Compression*, Boston, Kluwer Academic Publishers, 1992.

[6] A. Gersho, "Optimal Vector Quantized Nonlinear Estimation," *Proc. 1993 IEEE Int. Symp. on Information Theory*, Jan. 17-22, 1993, p.170.

Band Ordering in Lossless Compression of Multispectral Images

(*Extended Abstract*)*

Stephen R. Tate†

Department of Computer Sciences
University of North Texas
P.O. Box 13886
Denton, TX 76203–6886

E-mail: srt@cs.unt.edu

1 Introduction

Multispectral satellite images require enormous amounts of space, and with NASA's project EOS (the Earth Observing System) data will be generated at an unprecedented rate. The estimates are that over a terabyte (10^{12} bytes) of data will be generated every day by the EOS satellites, most of it being multispectral image data. Largely due to this fact, a lot of attention has recently been focussed on compression of multispectral images [3, 8, 11]. However, most of the compression methods that exploit spectral as well as spatial redundancy have been lossy compression algorithms, and for archival storage and for certain applications it is important to use lossless compression in order to preserve all of the data that is collected.

In this paper, we study lossless compression of multispectral images. Spectral redundancy is extracted by coding each band of the multispectral image by making use of a second "prediction band". In much the same way that standard single-image lossless compression is separated into the two separate components of prediction and coding, we divide the lossless compression of multispectral images into three components: band ordering, prediction, and coding. The new stage, band ordering, refers to selecting a permutation of the bands in which the bands that are coded first act as good predictors for the later bands in the ordering. The band ordering phase is independent of the other phases of the compressor, and the computational problems associated with this phase are identified and studied in this paper. In particular, given any particular predictor and coder, we give an efficient algorithm for computing the optimal ordering of the bands for compression performance. For an n-band multispectral image, our algorithm runs in $O(n^2)$ time, which is a vast improvement over the obvious $\Omega(n!)$ solution. In timing tests performed on a DEC

*The full version of this paper is available as University of North Texas Technical Report N-93-003.

†This research was supported by NASA subcontract 550-63 of prime contract NAS5-30428, and a substantial part of the experiments were conducted when the author was affiliated with Duke University and visiting the CESDIS office at the Goddard Space Flight Center.

Alpha workstation, our algorithm computed the optimal ordering from the input matrices (see Section 2) of a 12 band image in 1/100 of a second, whereas the naive algorithm took 87 minutes.

Unfortunately, in some cases the optimal ordering may not be a practical archival format for large numbers of bands (see Section 3 for more information on this), so we consider the natural restriction on band orderings that overcomes this problem. We refer to the restricted ordering as the *optimal compression order with bounded prediction*. Unfortunately, this new problem is shown to be NP-hard except in the most trivial case, so is computationally infeasible.

Next, we examine various possibilities for the prediction phase for multispectral data. Most predictors for image data use some form of linear prediction, and most of these use fixed coefficients for the prediction (or a small set of fixed coefficients as in lossless JPEG compression). With multispectral images it is vital that the linear prediction coefficients be chosen adaptively, and different methods for doing this are discussed in Section 4.

The coder for multispectral images is the simplest part, and is discussed in Section 5. We investigate the use of various configurations of an arithmetic coder, using data within both the current band and the previous, "prediction band", as context for the coder.

Finally, in Section 6 we present some experimental results using the techniques and algorithms presented in this paper on real multispectral data obtained from NASA. The experiments show that the compression methods developed in this paper can have a substantial practical impact on compression performance. In addition, our experiments show that a fixed band ordering can achieve almost optimal performance on a large class of data; therefore, using a pre-computed band ordering can give a very fast, high-performance compression system for multispectral images.

2 Terminology and Notation

Just as single-image data can be represented by a two-dimensional array $S[x,y]$, the data of a multispectral image may be represented as a three-dimensional array, with entry $M[b,x,y]$ representing the pixel from in band b, row x, column y. In traditional single-image compression, when coding pixel $S[x,y]$ the previously coded neighboring pixels may be used to predict the value of the current pixel. Likewise, when coding pixel $M[b,x,y]$ for a multispectral image, the previously coded neighboring pixels may be used for prediction, but we also allow neighboring pixels to come from a previously coded band. In other words, for any band b, we choose a *prediction band* $p(b)$ and use pixel values from band $p(b)$ in the encoding of $M[b,x,y]$.

The compression methods described in this paper all code the pixels of a band in scan order. At any point in time, the pixel $M[b,x,y]$ that the compression algorithm is predicting or coding is called the "current pixel", which comes from the "current band" (band b). As mentioned above, we also designate a separate band $p(b)$ as the "prediction band" for the current band. Just as in single-image compression, all pixel values used in prediction must be coded before the current pixel, including pixel values from the prediction band. Thus we may use the prediction band's pixel location corresponding to the current pixel (i.e., $M[p(b),x,y]$) if and only if band $p(b)$ is coded before band b. Clearly, the ordering of the bands determines what bands may be selected as the prediction band for the current band, and determining an ordering of the bands that maximizes compression over all possible orderings is an important problem.

For any given predictor/coder pair, and two bands b_1 and b_2, we can define the following two values:

B_{b_1,b_2} is the compressed size of band b_2 if band b_1 is used for prediction, but $M[b_1, x, y]$ is *not* used in the prediction of $M[b_2, x, y]$. In other words, this is the compressed size for band b_2 using b_1 for prediction, even if band b_2 is encoded *before* band b_1.

A_{b_1,b_2} is the compressed size of band b_2 if band b_1 is used for prediction, and the current pixel location from band b_1 is used in the prediction. This is the compressed size possible for band b_2 if band b_2 is encoded *after* band b_1.

We will represent the A and B values for a multispectral image as matrices. In the next section, we will discuss various ways of choosing a band ordering when given matrices A and B.

3 Determining Band Compression Order

In this section, we examine the following problem: In what order should we compress the bands of a multispectral image to achieve the best compression? For example, if band 2 acts as a good predictor for band 1, substantial savings may be achieved by compressing band 2 first. We will show that, given the matrices as defined in the previous section, the optimal ordering of the bands can be found very efficiently. For multispectral data with a small number of bands, this result shows that optimal ordering is both simple and practical.

However, for data with a large number of spectral bands (such as the 210 band AVIRIS data), the optimal ordering can be computed, but may not be what is desired. In particular, given a compressed file containing all 210 bands of AVIRIS data, it may be desirable to be able to extract one particular band from the compressed data. Unfortunately, the band dependencies of the optimal ordering may be a single, long chain, which would mean that *all* bands would have to be uncompressed in order to uncompress the last single band in the chain. A good solution to this problem would be to partition the bands into small sets, each containing at most b bands, and then when compressing one band, the only other bands that may be used for prediction are those within the same set. With this method at most b bands would have to be uncompressed in order to extract a single band from the compressed file. For a particular partition size bound b, we will call the optimal solution to this problem the *optimal compression order with bounded prediction.*

We will show that finding the optimal compression order with bounded prediction is easy if $b = 2$, but is NP-hard for any $b \geq 3$.

3.1 Unconstrained Optimal Ordering. In this section we consider the problem of finding an optimal compression order, with no constraints on how many bands are necessary for uncompression of a single band. This ordering is the best possible ordering for encoding bands, and is practical when either there are a small number of bands (such as the 5 bands of CZCS data or the 7 bands of TM data), or if extraction of a single band is never needed (an archive of AVIRIS data may require uncompression of all 210 bands when it is accessed).

We will transform the problem of finding an optimal compression ordering into a problem on weighted directed graphs which has a known efficient solution. The directed graph $G = (V, E)$ is constructed so that each edge $E_{i,j}$ has a corresponding weight $W_{i,j}$ that represents the compression savings attainable by compressing band i before band j. To construct this graph, define $B_{\text{min},j}$ to be

$$B_{\text{min},j} = \min_{1 \le i \le n} B_{i,j}.$$

$B_{\text{min},j}$ represents the minimum compressed size of band j if the current pixel location is not used from any other band. In particular, a compressed size of $B_{\text{min},j}$ is attainable for band j regardless of the order in which the bands are compressed.

Of course, if the bands are ordered such that band i is encoded before band j, then the current pixel location from band i can be used to predict the current pixel of band j. In some cases, the resulting compressed size may be substantially smaller than the size that was attainable without considering ordering. We define the edge weights of our graph in terms of the savings possible by encoding band j using the current pixel location from band i for prediction. In particular,

$$W_{i,j} = \begin{cases} 0 & \text{if } A_{i,j} \ge B_{\text{min},j}, \\ B_{\text{min},j} - A_{i,j} & \text{otherwise.} \end{cases}$$

The problem of finding an optimal compression order is equivalent to finding a maximum weight directed spanning forest of G. The resulting spanning forest defines a partial order on the vertices, and since the spanning forest is maximum weight, the partial order represents the maximum compression savings of any band ordering, or the optimal compression order of the bands of the multispectral image. It is known that a maximum weight directed spanning forest (also known as an "optimal branching") can be found in $O(|V| \log |E| + |E|)$ time on sparse graphs and $O(|V|^2)$ time on dense graphs [13, 2], so it follows that an optimal compression order can be found in $O(n^2)$ time. We summarize the result of this section in the following theorem.

Theorem 3.1 Given values $A_{i,j}$ and $B_{i,j}$ for all pairs of bands (i, j) from an n-band multispectral image, the optimal compression ordering can be computed in $O(n^2)$ time.

3.2 Optimal Ordering with Bounded Prediction. As mentioned at the beginning of this section, the optimal ordering is not always practical. In particular, if it is necessary to be able to extract and uncompress a single band of the image efficiently, the optimal compression ordering does not always make this possible. Consider a case where the directed spanning tree obtained as in the previous subsection is actually a long directed path. In a 210 band data set, it would be possible for band 210 to be coded using band 209 for prediction, band 209 to be coded using band 208, etc. Thus, in order to extract band 210, all of the 209 other bands would have to be uncompressed in addition to band 210.

For data sets with a large number of bands, a reasonable approach would be to partition the bands into small sets (containing, say, b bands each), and then compress each set using its optimal compression ordering. In this case, if a single band needs to be extracted, only the other bands in the same set as the requested band will possibly need to be uncompressed. We call such an ordering the *optimal compression order with bounded prediction*, and prove the following theorem regarding the complexity of computing such an ordering.

(a) 2–neighborhood (b) 4–neighborhood

Figure 1: Neighboring pixels used in prediction phase.

Theorem 3.2 Given values $A_{i,j}$ and $B_{i,j}$ for all pairs of bands (i, j) from an n-band multispectral image, the problem of finding an optimal compression order with bounded prediction is NP-hard if $b \geq 3$, but can be computed in $O(n^3)$ time if $b = 2$.

Proof: The NP-hardness result is proved by reducing the PARTITION INTO PATHS OF LENGTH TWO to a decision problem dealing with the existence compression order with bounded prediction. The algorithm for $b = 2$ is by a reduction to maximum weight graph matching. Details of these proofs can be found in the full paper. ∎

4 Prediction for Multispectral Images

The vast majority of lossless image compression algorithms are made up of a prediction stage in which pixel values are predicted, and a coding stage in which the difference between the actual pixel value and the predicted value is coded (for recent examples, see [9, 15]). The predictor typically uses a linear function to predict the current pixel value, based on the values of previously coded pixels (the "neighborhood" of the current pixel). In compression algorithms that code the pixels in scan-order, the neighborhood is usually a subset of the 4-neighborhood shown in Figure 1(b), where the current pixel is marked with the solid circle. For example, we may predict the current pixel by computing the average of its two nearest neighbors: $(A + C)/2$. The lossless JPEG scheme has 8 different possible linear prediction functions of A, B, and C, and is free to use any of those eight [15].

Since the relationship between different bands of a multispectral image is not known ahead of time, we must find a good prediction function by examining the image data. In particular, in our experiments, we consider both 2-neighborhoods and 4-neighborhoods for pairs of bands (see Figure 1), and use the actual image data to determine the coefficients of the linear function of neighborhood values that minimizes the variance of the prediction error. Determining the coefficients in this way is similar (although not exactly the same) to standard linear prediction methods (see for example [10]), and can be done using least squares approximation algorithms.

The experiments of this paper were done with a predictor that finds linear coefficients for the 2-neighborhood and 4-neighborhood of the current pixel location, where values from both the current band and the prediction band are used in the prediction function. Both the 2-neighborhood and 4-neighborhood are then used for a second pass on the data using the computed coefficients, and whichever resulted in a smaller compressed size is reported. The program computes the coefficients both with and without the current pixel location in the prediction band, and the resulting compressed sizes are used for the A and B matrix values, respectively.

5 Coding for Multispectral Images

The coder has the responsibility of turning the predicted values into an output bitstream. Various approaches have been taken in different compression systems, including Huffman coding, Rice coding, and arithmetic coding (or variants such as Q-coding). A good explanation of coding in general, including Huffman coding and arithmetic coding, can be found in [1]; Rice coding is described in [12], which is similar to Golumb coding as described in [6]. Huffman coding performs poorly on small alphabets or when the prediction phase produces very small (or low entropy) errors, and Rice coding performs poorly when the errors are not generated according to a Laplacian distribution. While the distribution of errors is usually close to Laplacian, it was discovered in our experiments that CZCS data produced very markedly non-Laplacian error distributions (the other sensors did produce prediction errors that were more or less Laplacian).

Our final choice for a coder was an adaptive arithmetic coder, with three neighboring prediction errors used as context for the coder (the two nearest neighbors in the current band, and the current pixel location from the prediction band when possible). While the actual prediction errors could easily be used for neighboring pixels in the same band, the prediction error for the current location in the prediction band was estimated by using the simple single-image linear prediction formula $X - \lfloor (A+C)/2 \rfloor$, where X is the prediction band pixel in the current location, and A and C are neighboring pixels in the prediction band as defined by Figure 1(a). The prediction errors were bucketed (similar to [14]) into "zero", "small" (1-2), "medium" (3-8), and "large" (over 9), with the sign of the error also used in the context. Since the context is computed from 3 prediction errors with 7 possible values each, the coder used 343 contexts.

The actual prediction errors are encoded by first encoding a tag denoting negative, positive, or zero error, and then encoding the error magnitude two bits at a time. This method substantially reduces the amount of storage required for maintaining the error frequency statistics, since frequency tables only need to be maintained for a 4 symbol alphabet (the 2-bit blocks). For example, in an image with 16 bit pixels, the error can range from -65,535 to +65,535, so directly coding the prediction error would require 131,071 frequency counts per context (for a total of almost 4.5 million counts over all contexts). On the other hand, keeping statistics only for the error sign and the two-bit blocks of the error magnitude requires only 35 frequency counts per context (for a total of 12,005 frequency counts over all contexts). It is very significant to note that when the errors are Laplacian distributed (the majority of cases), encoding the errors in this significantly more efficient way is fully as efficient as keeping separate frequency counts for all possible error values. Furthermore, when the errors are not Laplacian distributed (such as for the CZCS data), this method greatly outperforms true Laplacian coders such as the Rice coder, and performs almost as well as the arithmetic coder with full frequency counts.

6 Experimental Results

We performed many experiments using the algorithms described in this paper and real multispectral satellite data. Our experiments show that band reordering can substantially improve compression performance for certain data sets, and that using a fixed, pre-computed band ordering works well for entire classes of data, giving a

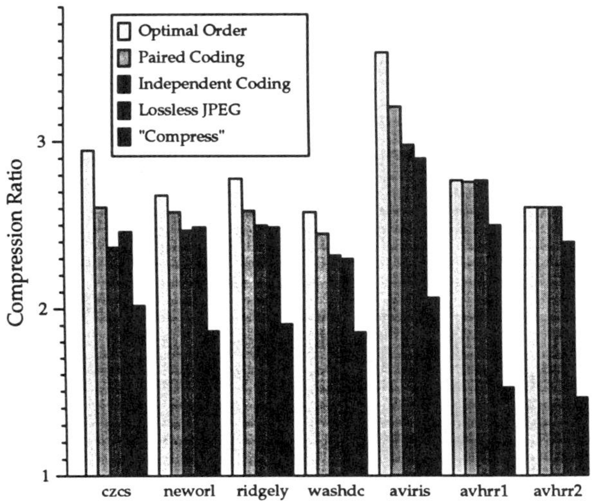

Figure 2: Compression ratio for some sample data files

very fast and high-quality compression system for multispectral images. The data for our experiments came from several types of sensors: images "neworl", "ridgely", and "washdc" come from the 7-band Thematic Mapper (TM); images "czcs" and the series "czcsl-7" come from the 6-band Coastal Zone Color Scanner (CZCS); images "avhrrl" and "avhrr2" are from the 6-band Advanced Very High Resolution Radiometer (AVHRR); and image "aviris" comes from the 210-band Airborne Visible Infrared Imaging Spectrometer (AVIRIS).

To compute the A and B matrices, the matrix entries were computed in parallel on a CM-5 parallel computer. Once these values were computed, the A and B matrices were fed into implementations of the algorithms described in section 3 for finding the optimal band ordering, and for finding the optimal paired ordering. The resulting compression ratio for the various sample images is shown in Figure 2. The compression ratio using our prediction and coding phases, but with no inter-band prediction, is shown as "Independent Coding" (meaning that the bands are coded independently of other bands). In addition, the compression ratios using lossless JPEG (with each band coded independently of the others) and the UNIX compress command are included for comparison purposes. The performance of lossless JPEG compares well with the best lossless single-image compressors. The UNIX compress results are included since many installations currently choose this method for compressing their multispectral data sets, and these results emphasize how poor this choice is.

As can be seen from Figure 2, the effect of band ordering seems to rely heavily on the source of the data. In particular, large gains were seen by selecting the optimal band ordering for the AVIRIS and CZCS data, moderate gains were seen in the TM data sets, and almost nothing was gained by band-ordering in the AVHRR data. What this suggests is that the individual bands of the AVHRR data are more independent than the bands of the other sensors, which is supported by the technical specifications of the sensor.

It is interesting to note that for data sets in which band ordering made a difference, the performance of paired ordering is only a moderate improvement over independent coding. This implies that the band dependencies are of a more global nature than pairs of bands. In light of our proof that computing the optimal partitioning into blocks of size three or more is NP-hard, it seems that close-to-optimal performance is not possible without using the absolute optimal ordering and risking long dependence chains. To examine the importance of selecting a good partitioning, we divided the 210 bands of AVIRIS data into blocks of 5 adjacent bands per block, without regard for the content of those bands. In other words, the blocks consisted of bands 1-5, bands 6-10, bands 11-15, etc. Within each block, the bands were optimally ordered, but there is no reason to believe that the chosen blocks bear any resemblance to the optimal partioning. The results are shown in the following table.

Blocking Method	Compression Ratio
No blocking (optimal order)	3.53
Blocks of 5 adjacent bands	3.39
Optimal partitioning of 2-band blocks	3.21
Block size 1 (independent coding)	2.98

It can be seen from this table that simply picking blocks of adjacent bands for the partitioning seems to work well for AVIRIS data. While the compression ratio does not quite match the performance of the optimal ordering, the added benefit of being able to efficiently extract a single band from the compressed archive may be worth sacrificing some compression.

The next experiment we tried was to determine how much the band ordering depends on the sensor, and how much it depends on the individual data sets. For this test, we obtained seven independent data sets from a single sensor (CZCS) and ran all of the previous tests, in addition to the following test: for any particular data set, the optimal compression ordering for the *other* six data sets is computed, and then that ordering is used for the data set being tested. The results, with the last type of test labeled as "Pre-computed Order", are shown in Figure 3.

As can be seen from the figure, in most cases the order computed from the other images gave a compression ratio that was competitive with the optimal order computed specifically for that image. This suggests that, at least for CZCS data, the band ordering is more a function of the sensor than of the individual image; therefore, a reasonable approach to a production compression package would be to compute the optimal ordering from a large, representative set of images, and hard code this band ordering into the compressor. To compress a multispectral image with this approach, no band-ordering has to be computed, and the A and B matrices do not need to be computed, so the compression is very efficient. The results of this last experiment show that this approach should yield almost optimal compression.

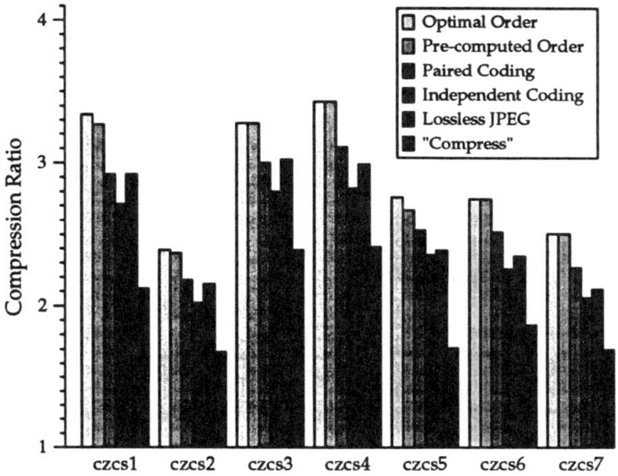

Figure 3: Compression ratio for sample CZCS data files

7 Conclusions

In this paper, we have extensively studied the benefits and problems associated with reordering the bands of a multispectral image for performing lossless compression. Under a reasonable model of inter-band prediction, we have shown how to efficiently compute the optimal compression band ordering. In addition, we have formalized the restrictions that arise when bands need to be extracted individually from a compressed archive, and have shown that computing the optimal ordering under these restrictions is NP-hard, except in the most simple case.

Our experiments show that for certain data sources (such as CZCS or AVIRIS satellite imagery), the band ordering algorithms of this paper can substantially improve compression performance. Interestingly, some data sources (such as the AVHRR data) don't benefit from the techniques of this paper at all, implying that the bands are independent, and can be treated separately (as if the data was not a multispectral image at all). By computing the band ordering as described in this paper, and evaluating the compression results, it is easy to determine if band re-ordering is going to have a substantial benefit for a particular data set.

While computing the optimal band ordering may be efficient (i.e., polynomial time), it is certainly not fast, requiring that all pairs of bands be tested as prediction-coding pairs. An alternative is to compute a fixed band ordering for a class of data, and use that fixed ordering when coding all data sets in that class. For instance, a fixed "CZCS ordering" could be pre-computed and used for all CZCS data sets. This has the benefit of being extremely fast (similar in speed to simply ignoring inter-band correlation); furthermore, our experiments have shown that for CZCS data, the results are almost indistinguishable from the optimal ordering results. Thus, this last approach of using a fixed band reordering seems to be a very promising lossless multispectral compression method.

8 Acknowledgements

The author would like to thank Doreen Revis for her help with various aspects of the CM-5, Jim Tilton and Manohar Mareboyana for supplying a wide range of test data, Gene Feldman for supplying the CZCS data, and Mary James for supplying the AVHRR data.

References

[1] T. C. Bell, J. G. Cleary, and I. H. Witten. *Text Compression*, Prentice Hall, Englewood Cliffs, NJ, 1990.

[2] P. M. Camerini, L. Fratta, and F. Maffioli. "A Note on Finding Optimum Branchings," *Networks*, Vol. 9, pp. 309–312, 1979.

[3] B. R. Epstein, R. Hingorani, J. M. Shapiro, and M. Czigler. "Multispectral KLT-Wavelet Data Compression for Landsat Thematic Mapper Images," *Proc. of the Data Compression Conference (DCC '92)*, pp. 200–208, 1992.

[4] H. N. Gabow. "An Efficient Implementation of Edmonds' Algorithm for Maximum Matching on Graphs," *JACM*, Vol. 23, No. 2, pp. 221–234, 1976.

[5] H. N. Gabow and R. E. Tarjan. "Faster Scaling Algorithms for General Graph-Matching Problems," *JACM*, Vol. 38, No. 4, pp. 815–853, 1991.

[6] R. G. Gallager and D. C. Van Voorhis. "Optimal Source Codes for Geometrically Distributed Integer Alphabets", *IEEE Transactions on Information Theory*, Vol. IT–21, pp. 228–230, March 1975.

[7] M. R. Garey and D. S. Johnson. *Computers and Intractability: A Guide to the Theory of NP-Completeness*, W. H. Freeman and Company, New York, 1979.

[8] S. Gupta and A. Gersho. "Feature Predictive Vector Quantization of Multispectral Images," *IEEE Transactions on Geoscience and Remote Sensing*, Vol. 30, No. 3, May 1992.

[9] P. G. Howard and J. S. Vitter. "New Methods for Lossless Image Compression Using Arithmetic Coding", *Information Processing and Management*, Vol. 26, No. 6, pp. 765–779, Nov. 1992.

[10] J. Makhoul. "Linear Prediction: A Tutorial Review," *Proceedings of the IEEE*, Vol. 63, No. 4, pp. 561–580, April 1975.

[11] T. Markas and J. Reif. "Multispectral Image Compression Algorithms," *Proc. of the Data Compression Conference (DCC '93)*, pp. 391–400, 1993.

[12] R. F. Rice. "Some Practical Universal Noiseless Coding Techniques", *JPL Publication 79–22*, Jet Propulsion Laboratory, Pasadena, CA, Mar. 1979.

[13] R. E. Tarjan. "Finding Optimum Branchings," *Networks*, Vol. 7, pp. 25–35, 1977.

[14] S. Todd, G. Langdon, J. Rissanen. "Parameter Reduction and Context Selection for Compression of Gray-scale Images", *IBM J. Res. Develop.*, Vol. 29, No. 2, pp. 188–193, March 1985.

[15] G. K. Wallace. "The JPEG Still Compression Standard", *Communications of the ACM*, Vol. 34, No. 4, pp. 30–44, April 1991.

Enhancement of Block Transform Coded Images Using Residual Spectra Adaptive Postfiltering

Irving Linares[1] Russell M. Mersereau Mark J. T. Smith

School of Electrical Engineering
Georgia Institute of Technology
Atlanta, GA 30332 USA

Abstract – Image block transform techniques usually introduce several types of spatial periodic distortion which are mostly noticeable at low bit rates. One way to reduce these artifacts to obtain an acceptable visual quality level is to postfilter the decoded images using *nonlinear space-variant adaptive filters* derived from the structural relationships and residual spectral information provided by the Discrete-Time Fourier Transform (DTFT) of block transforms such as the Discrete Cosine Transform (DCT) and the Lapped Orthogonal Transform (LOT). A method for analyzing and filtering the DCT *blocking* noise and the LOT *ringing* noise for moderate and highly compressed images is described and several test cases are presented. A generalized Fourier analysis of the block transform distortion as seen in the frequency domain is discussed in conjunction with an outline of a separable adaptive postfiltering algorithm for decoded image enhancement.

1 Introduction

Clearly, image enhancement using linear space-invariant postfiltering of block transform coded images is not adequate because of its inflexibility to adapt to the varying spatial frequencies found in most images. Block transform methods usually introduce some type of spatial periodic distortion which is particularly noticeable at low bit rates. In order to improve the quality of the decoded image we would like to minimize these spatial periodic artifacts introduced in the coding process.

One of the earliest methods capable of attenuating one of such distortions, the blocking problem of DCT coded images, was proposed by Reeve and Lim [1] in 1983. Their method, based on *overlap prefiltering*, had the disadvantage of requiring a 13% increase in the bit rate in order to reduce the blocking distortion. They also proposed an alternative *postfiltering* method based on a 3x3 Gaussian low pass filter which was applied only to pixels adjacent to block boundaries after decoding. This second method had the disadvantage that it could indiscriminately blur true image edges located at the block boundaries.

In 1986, Ramamurthi and Gersho [2] proposed a nonlinear space-variant *postfilter* to reduce the blocking effect. This algorithm was applicable to Transform Coded (TC) images, Block Truncation Coded (BTC) images and Vector Quantized (VQ) images. It used 1-D and 2-D Parks-McClellan FIR filters. The 2-D separable filters were used in areas away from edges while the one-dimensional filter was adaptively aligned parallel to image edges. Edge blocks were categorized as containing one of four spatial edge orientations: 0°, 45°, 90° and 135°. This method was able to increase

[1]This work was supported by the NASA Goddard Space Flight Center Part-Time Graduate Study Program and the NASA Goddard Research and Study Fellowship Program. The author is also with the NASA Goddard Space Flight Center in Greenbelt, MD 20771 USA.

both the subjective quality and the Peak Signal-to-Noise Ratio (PSNR)[2] by about 0.4 dB in several test cases without increasing the bit rate.

The LOT on the other hand, attempts to solve the blocking problem from the *prefiltering* perspective [3, 4, 5, 6, 7]. It uses *orthonormal overlapped* basis functions which mimic the shape of the DCT basis functions but extend their spatial coverage into adjacent blocks. However, *ringing* is observed in LOT coded images at moderate to high compression ratios. The LOT reduces the blocking effect, but it does so at the expense of introducing ringing.

More recently, the JPEG Still Image Compression Standard [8, 9], a very popular and well known method that exploits intrablock correlation through the *Adaptive Discrete Cosine Transform* (ADCT), addresses the block-to-block discontinuities by modeling a 3x3 array of 8x8 blocks by a two-dimensional second-degree polynomial (Section 13.10, ref.[9]). By imposing certain constraints, the low frequency AC coefficients for the block under consideration can be predicted and used to diminish the blocking artifacts observed at low bit rates.

We propose a new alternative *nonlinear space-variant adaptive postfilter* applicable to block transforms such as the ADCT and LOT that can reduce the distortion created by the independent coding of each block subimage at low bit rates. It is an *optional supplementary* method for image enhancement that not only improves the subjective quality of gray scale images, but also can significantly increase the objective PSNR measure by approximately 1 dB over non-postfiltered decoded images *without* increasing the bit rate.

2 Block Transform Coding

Image transform coding using block subimages has the advantage of capturing the high correlation that exists among neighboring pixels within a small block, usually of 8x8 pixels. This high correlation is generally transformed into a set of coefficients, some of which pack most of the energy content of the block. The coefficients are then adaptively quantized according to their spatial frequencies, coded and transmitted. At the receiver, the image is decoded, dequantized and inverse transformed to obtain an approximation $\hat{x}[n_1, n_2]$ of the original image.

Adaptive quantization is based on the fact that the human visual system is more tolerant to errors introduced by coarse quantization in the high frequencies (*perceptual error masking*) than it is to quantization errors in the low frequencies. Generally, the low frequency coefficients are finely quantized while the high frequencies are coarsely quantized according to some *Quantization Table.* This JPEG-style *lossy* scheme allows moderate bit pixel rates with little perceptual degradation of the image quality. For our purposes, *moderate* compression refers to average pixel rates down to 1.0 BPP and *high* compression refers to pixel rates of less than 1.0 BPP based on 256x256 pixel 8-BPP gray-scale images. Under 1.0 BPP, however, it is usual to begin noticing some block discontinuities due to the independent processing of each block when using DCT coded images.

If we look at the 16:1 and the 32:1 JPEG[3] compressed images of Lena in Figure 1(a) and 1(b), we notice that some blocking is noticeable, particularly in the smooth areas. The blocking of Figure 1(b) is of course more objectionable than that of 1(a)

---

[2] $\mathrm{PSNR} = 10 \log \frac{(N)^2 (255)^2}{\sum_{n_1=0}^{N-1} \sum_{n_2=0}^{N-1} (x[n_1,n_2] - \hat{x}[n_1,n_2])^2}$ dB,
where x is the original image, $\hat{x}$ is the decoded image and N is the image size.

[3] We used Lempel-Ziv (UNIX *compress*) lossless entropy coding instead of Huffman Coding and a Graphical User's Interface (GUI) to interactively modify the DCT coefficient Quantization Table.

(a)

(b)

Figure 1: ADCT Coded Lena images (a) 0.5 BPP, 29.54 dB PSNR and (b) 0.25 BPP, 26.17 dB PSNR, *no postfiltering.*

due to the doubling of the compression ratio. Our objective is to remove the block-to-block discontinuities present in the *spatial* domain. We will make the blocking removal *analysis* in the frequency domain and use this information to perform the actual filtering of the blocking noise in the spatial domain. The filter is implemented as a pixel-by-pixel adaptive convolution as explained in next section.

We now ask the following: If we can see the *spatial* blocking distortion or noise caused by coarse quantization of the coefficients of a highly compressed DCT image, then, how are these periodic block discontinuities represented in the spatial *frequency* domain? This very important question is the basis for the foregoing discussion.

3 Fourier Analysis of Spatial Periodic Distortions and Frequency Domain Adaptive Postfiltering

We must first observe the behavior of the Discrete-Time Fourier Transform (DTFT) of each of the basis functions of an orthonormal block transform such as the DCT. To simplify the analysis, consider the magnitude of the 1-D case and ignore its phase since we will be using non-causal (zero-phase) filters for the actual postfiltering process. Extension to the 2-D case is easily achieved by defining 2-D separable filters.

Let's analyze the *magnitude* of the Fourier Transform of the first DCT basis function $F_0(\omega)$[4] shown in Figure 2(a) for N=8 samples. Based on a standard DTFT analysis ([10], Section 7.4, Ref. [11]), the *main lobe* of $F_0(\omega)$ shown as a *solid* line approaches an appropriately scaled $\delta(\omega)$ impulse function as the number of constant-value DC samples is extended let's say from N=8 to N=256. The *ripples* or secondary sidelobes shown as *dashed* lines, simultaneously decrease in magnitude relative to the main lobe as the number of constant amplitude samples increases toward 256. The number of ripples also increases in direct proportion forcing each ripple to inversely decrease its width in a $2\pi/N$ proportion. A careful analysis of the relationship between DCT blocking and its Fourier Transform soon reveals that the *ripples* are the frequency representation of the spatial *block discontinuities* in the transform domain. These ripples also contain most of the *out-of-band* quantization noise[5] while the *main*

[4] $F_0(\omega) \equiv F_0(e^{j\omega})$

[5] Ref. [2] is a more detailed treatment of the in-band and out-of-band noise spectral analysis.

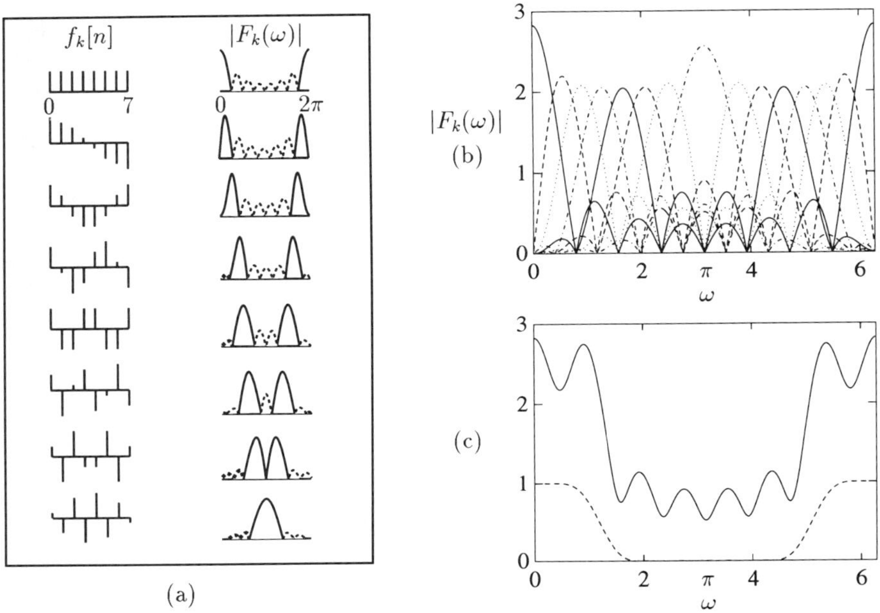

Figure 2: (a) DCT Basis Functions $f_k[n]$ and the magnitudes of their DTFTs $|F_k(w)|$, $k = 0..7$, in top to bottom order. (b) Superposition of the magnitude of the DTFTs of the DCT Basis Functions, N=8, $k = 0..7$ (c) Magnitude of the DTFT of the $\sum(f_0[n] + f_1[n] + f_2[n])$, N = 8

lobe represents the local block near-DC low spatial frequency content and contains most of the *in-band* low frequencies.

This analysis not only applies to $F_0(\omega)$ but also to $F_k(\omega), k = 1..7$, i.e., to all the basis functions. The dashed ripples of $|F_k(\omega)|$ represent out-of-band noise for AC coefficients while the solid main lobes represent in-band frequency content. The main lobe locations are at $3\pi/16, 5\pi/16, ..., 13\pi/16$ for $k = 1..6$ and at π for $k = 7$. The main lobe -3 dB bandwidths are approximately $\pi/4$ for $|F_k(\omega)|, k = 1..6$ and $3\pi/8$ for $|F_0(\omega)|$ and $|F_7(\omega)|$. Figure 2(b) shows a superposition of all the DTFTs of the DCT basis functions for N=8.

After image decoding we know the *exact* dequantized coefficient values $\hat{C}_i(k_1, k_2)$ for each 8x8 block i of the reconstructed image $\hat{x}[n_1, n_2]$. Therefore, we have a very clear idea of the approximate frequency content $\hat{X}_i(k_1, k_2)$ of each individual block. We lack however, an overall method for obtaining a *global* frequency content approximation $\hat{X}(\omega_1, \omega_2)$ for the entire image. We will approach this problem by postulating a *non-isotropic* 2-D separable bandwidth $B_{\omega_1,\omega_2}[n_1, n_2]$ for *each* pixel $x[n_1, n_2]$ and its immediate surrounding region R. Typical regions considered were 9x9, 17x17 and 25x25-pixel squares. Let us also define a corresponding *estimated* 2-D bandwidth $\hat{B}_{\omega_1,\omega_2}[n_1, n_2]$ associated with the decoded image $\hat{x}[n_1, n_2]$. We will limit our analysis to separable 2-D block transforms, thus each frequency variable ω_1 and ω_2 will be analyzed separately.

3.1 ADCT Coded Images

Let's assume that a decoded 1-D block has the following dequantized DCT basis functions and its corresponding Discrete-Time Fourier Transform

$$f_0[n] + f_1[n] + f_2[n] \underset{\text{DTFT}}{\Longleftrightarrow} F_0(\omega) + F_1(\omega) + F_2(\omega) \tag{1}$$

We observe from Figure 2(c) that the half power point or -3 dB bandwidth for a typical low frequency content 1-D block like this is about $3\pi/8$ or 0.375π. If we filter the high frequency ripple with a low pass filter with a cutoff frequency $\omega_c = 3\pi/8$ as shown, we will be removing most of the blocking noise and leaving most of the in-band frequencies present in the $[0..3\pi/8]$ range. The ripple component present in the $[0..3\pi/8]$ frequency range is *masked* by the larger low frequency content while the ripple component between $(3\pi/8..\pi]$ is almost completely suppressed. Indeed, if we assume that the coded blocks mostly contain low frequency coefficients as it is usually the case, after an analysis similar to that of Figure 2(c) we obtain the following relationships between the non-zero DCT coefficient content and the in-band bandwidth of the block.

DCT Coefficients Present	Approx. Norm. Bandwidths
c_0	0.125π
c_0, c_1	0.250π
c_0, c_1, c_2	0.375π
c_0, c_1, c_2, c_3	0.500π
c_0, c_1, c_2, c_3, c_4	0.625π
$c_0, c_1, c_2, c_3, c_4, c_5$	0.750π
$c_0, c_1, c_2, c_3, c_4, c_5, c_6$	0.875π
$c_0, c_1, c_2, c_3, c_4, c_5, c_6, c_7$	1.0π

It is not necessary to have all the coefficients present, some of them may be zero. What is important to determine is the current block spectral bandwidth which is found by *inspection* of the highest 2-D frequency present. To obtain a non-isotropic bandwidth for each 8x8 block we simply look for the highest 2-D coefficient of the DCT transform in each block and assign a 2-D bandwidth according to the above table. For example, if the decoded block's highest coefficient is $C(2,5)$, we say in a deterministic way, that the *vertical* bandwidth is 0.375π and the *horizontal* bandwidth is 0.750π. We will also assume that this 2-D local bandwidth, denoted $L_B(i)$ is spatially *centered* in the middle of the 8x8 block. After doing this we obtain two 32x32 frequency images: the Non-Interpolated DCT *Vertical* Frequency Image and the Non-Interpolated DCT *Horizontal* Frequency Image shown in Figures 3.a and 3.b respectively. The vertical component of $L_B(i)$ is denoted $L_B^V(i)$ while its horizontal component is denoted $L_B^H(i)$.

The next step of the algorithm relies on a *Frequency Continuity* Heuristic to obtain an approximated local pixel bandwidth $\hat{B}_{\omega_1,\omega_2}[n_1,n_2]$ from the array of local bandwidths $L_B(i), i = 0..1023$ for a 256x256 image. If the digitized image $x[n_1,n_2]$ represents a continuous signal, then its DTFT $X(\omega_1,\omega_2)$ must also be continuous. Thus, we can *interpolate* the Non-interpolated Horizontal and Vertical Frequency images to the original image size of N=256 to find a frequency approximation $\hat{X}(\omega_1,\omega_2)$

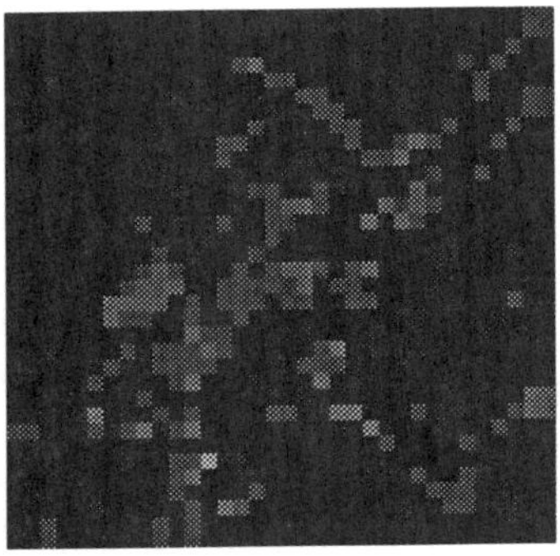

(a)

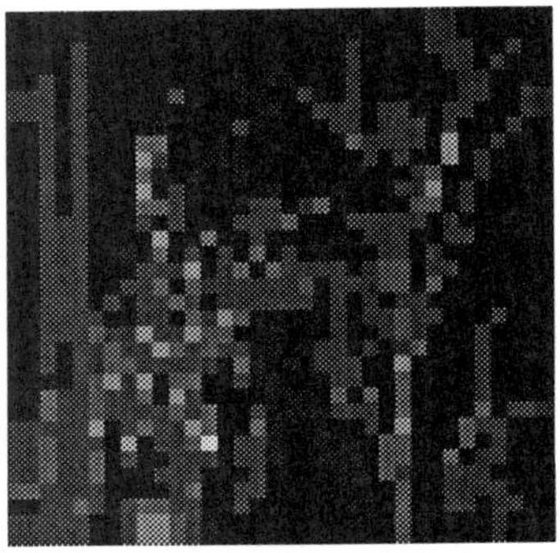

(b)

Figure 3: (a) Non-Interpolated Vertical Frequency Image for Lena @ 0.25 BPP and (b) Non-Interpolated Horizontal Frequency Image for Lena @ 0.25 BPP.

for the decoded image. Doing so we obtain the interpolated vertical frequency image

$$\hat{B}_{\omega_1}[n_1,n_2] \;=\; \sum_{i=0}^{(\frac{N}{8})^2-1} L_B^V(i) \;\times$$

$$\left(8.0 \sum_{n_1=-\infty}^{+\infty} \frac{\sin\frac{\pi}{8}(n_1-d_{1_i})}{\pi(n_1-d_{1_i})}\right)\left(8.0 \sum_{n_2=-\infty}^{+\infty} \frac{\sin\frac{\pi}{8}(n_2-d_{2_i})}{\pi(n_2-d_{2_i})}\right) \tag{2}$$

where (n_1, n_2) are restricted to the mid-block values (... -3/2, -1/2, 1/2, 3/2, 5/2, ...) and (d_{1_i}, d_{2_i}) are displacement values for each mid-block point given by $d_{1_i} = (i/32) * 8 + 3.5$ and $d_{2_i} = (i * 8) \bmod 256 + 3.5$. The division $i/32$ is an *integer* truncated division.

Similarly, the interpolated horizontal frequency image $\hat{B}_{\omega_2}[n_1, n_2]$ can be obtained by just substituting the $L_B^V(i)$ term by $L_B^H(i)$ in the above equation. The results of these operations are shown in Figures 4(a) and 4(b) for the 0.25 BPP ADCT-Coded Lena's image example under consideration.

Now that we have estimated the approximated local 2-D bandwidth $\hat{B}_{\omega_1,\omega_2}[n_1, n_2]$, it is possible to adaptively postfilter the decoded image using an adaptive bandwidth for *each* pixel. We designed a set of 128 Non-causal Hamming Window 1-D Low Pass Filters with cutoff frequencies ranging from $\omega_c = [1/128\pi..128/128\pi]$ to closely match the in-band interpolated bandwidths between the decoded blocks. These 128 LPF bandwidths provided enough frequency resolution to prevent any noticeable frequency quantization effects. If the highest interpolated 2-D frequencies present in a decoded pixel $\hat{x}[n_1, n_2]$ are $(\hat{\omega}_1, \hat{\omega}_2)$, which are proportional in turn to the index pair (d_1, d_2) by

$$\hat{\omega_1} = (d_1/128)\pi, \quad \hat{\omega_2} = (d_2/128)\pi \tag{3}$$

with $1 \le d_{1,2} \le 128$, then filter (convolve) the current pixel $\hat{x}[n_1, n_2]$ with the 2-D non-causal separable adaptive filter

$$h[n_1, n_2] = h_{d_1}[n_1] \;\; h_{d_2}[n_2] \tag{4}$$

shown in Figure 5(a). These filters can be pre-computed or read as an ASCII file during program initialization.

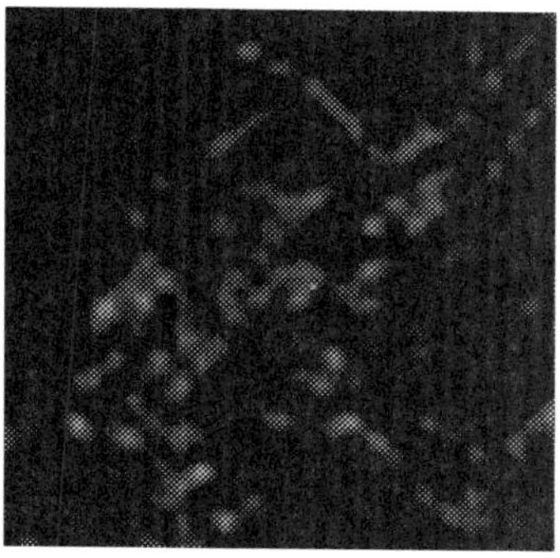

(a)

(b)

Figure 4: (a) Interpolated Vertical Frequency Image for Lena @ 0.25 BPP and (b) Interpolated Horizontal Frequency Image for Lena @ 0.25 BPP.

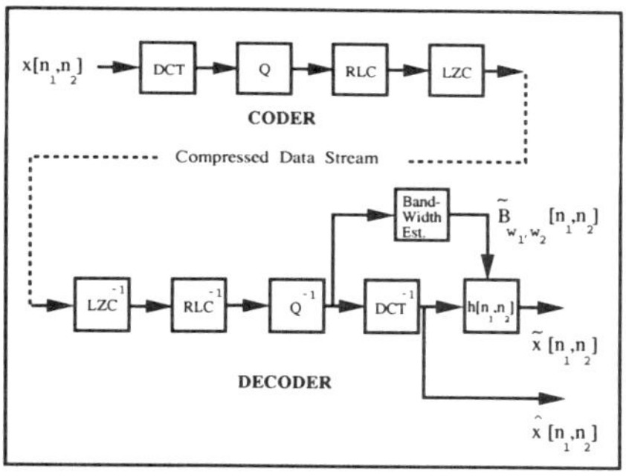

(a) (b)

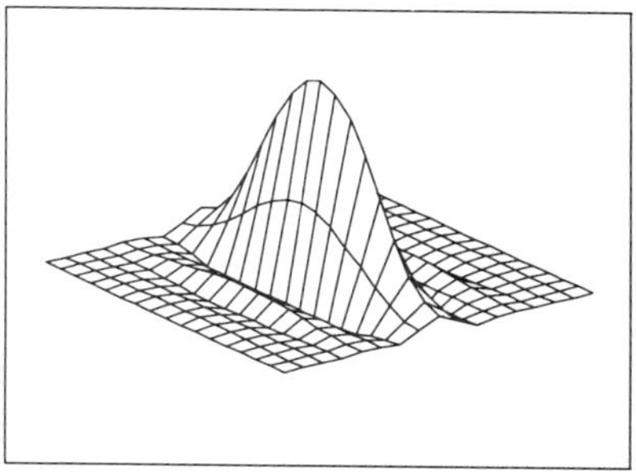

Figure 5: (a) Block diagram of the *Residual Spectra Adaptive Postfiltering* Algorithm extension to the JPEG DCT coder where $\tilde{x}$ is the postfiltered image and $\hat{x}$ is the non-postfiltered decoded image. (b) Separable adaptive $h[n_1, n_2]$ postfilter example for $(d_1, d_2) = (1, 85)$.

Figure 5(b) shows a typical adaptive postfilter $h[n_1, n_2]$ example for the index pair $(d_1, d_2) = (1, 85) \sim (\hat{\omega_1}, \hat{\omega_2}) = (0.0078\pi, 0.6641\pi)$. Figures 6(a) and 6(b) show the adaptively postfiltered ADCT coded images corresponding to the non-postfiltered images in Figures 1(a) and 1(b).

3.2 Adaptive LOT (ALOT) Coded Images

Basically, adaptive postfiltering of adaptively quantized LOT images is no different from adaptive postfiltering of adaptively quantized DCT images. Noting the similarity of the DTFT{ DCT } in Figure 2(b) with the DTFT{ LOT } in Figure 7, we can extend the same adaptive DCT postfiltering algorithm previously discussed to ALOT coded images. The ALOT non-postfiltered images and their corresponding adaptively postfiltered images are shown in Figures 8(a) through 8(d).

(a) (b)

Figure 6: Adaptively *postfiltered* ADCT Coded Lena's images (a) 0.5 BPP, 30.20 dB PSNR and (b) 0.25 BPP, 27.09 dB PSNR using 17x17 adaptive filters.

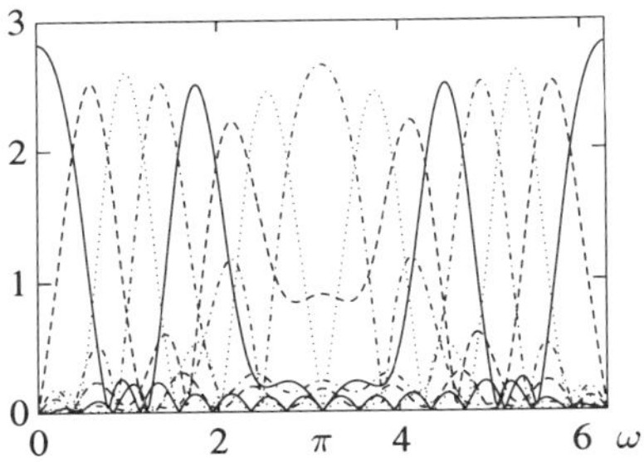

Figure 7: Magnitude of the DTFTs of the LOT Basis Functions, N=8, L=4.

4 Results

It was found during this work that the adaptive pixel-by-pixel bandwidth $\hat{B}_{\omega_1,\omega 2}[n_1, n_2]$ derivable from the DTFT interpretation of block transforms is the most important factor to obtain a significant reduction of the Inverse ADCT blocking and Inverse ALOT ringing. This bandwidth modulates a *shrinking-dilating* quasi-sync function unitary-gain two-dimensional low pass filter that effectively adapts itself to the varying spatio-frequency characteristics of a block-transformed image. It filters most of the out-of-band quantization noise while retaining most of the in-band signal present in the immediate surrounding region R of a decoded pixel $\hat{x}[n_1, n_2]$. However, it is still necessary to further increase the pixel-by-pixel 2-D passband when filtering high frequency areas such as image edges to preserve the decoded image crispness. We are considering additional alternatives to achieve this goal.

The following results were obtained for the grey-scale Lena test image:

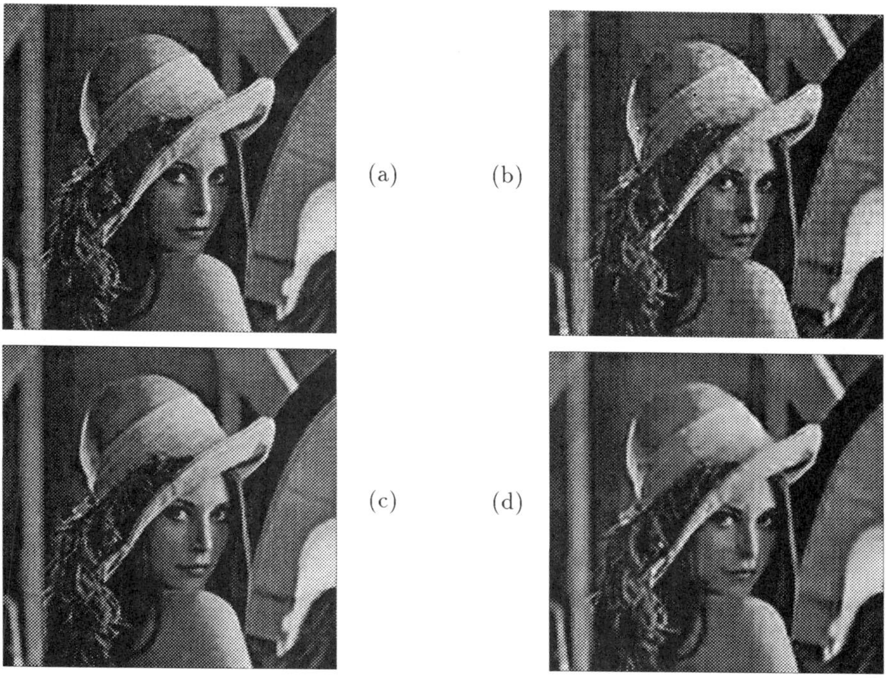

Figure 8: ALOT Coded Lena's images (a) 0.5 BPP, 29.18 dB PSNR, *no postfiltering.* (b) 0.25 BPP, 26.44 dB PSNR, *no postfiltering.* (c) Adaptively *postfiltered* @ 0.5 BPP, 30.05 dB PSNR using a 17x17 filter. (d) Adaptively *postfiltered* @ 0.25 BPP, 27.38 dB PSNR using a 17x17 filter.

Figure	Description	PSNR (dB)
1(a)	0.5 BPP, DCT, NPF[6]	29.54
6(a)	0.5 BPP, DCT, APF[7]	30.20
1(b)	0.25 BPP, DCT, NPF	26.17
6(b)	0.25 BPP, DCT, APF	27.09
8(a)	0.5 BPP, LOT, NPF	29.18
8(c)	0.5 BPP, LOT, APF	30.05
8(b)	0.25 BPP, LOT, NPF	26.44
8(d)	0.25 BPP, LOT, APF	27.38

We also experimented with 9x9 and 25x25 filters. The 9x9 filters did not filter as well as the 17x17 filters due to their limited spatial coverage. Essentially, they were unable to remove the blocking of the DCT and the ringing of the LOT. Extending the region to 25x25 did not improve the PSNR nor the subjective quality either. The effect of using 25x25 filters was to lower the PSNR by approximately 0.06 dB and it

[6]NPF = No Postfiltering.

[7]APF = Adaptively Postfiltered using a 17x17 filter $h[n_1, n_2]$.

also introduced some contouring in the background areas.

5 Conclusion

We have presented a new nonlinear space-variant adaptive postfiltering algorithm capable on enhancing DCT and LOT block coded images both subjectively and objectively without increasing the bit rate. We obtained PSNR gain improvements in the range of 0.66 to 0.94 dB over the non-postfiltered image for several test cases.

The Residual Spectra Adaptive Postfiltering Algorithm is based on the DTFT interpretation of the blocking and ringing spatial distortions of the DCT and LOT transforms as seen in the frequency domain. We found that these distortions appear as sidelobes or ripples in the frequency domain when analyzed from the perspective of non-causal filters spatially centered at each decoded image block. We computed an approximated pixel-by-pixel adaptive bandwidth using a frequency continuity heuristic and by interpolating the 2-D bandwidths obtained from the highest frequency indexes (k_1, k_2) of each 8x8 block.

The disadvantage of this method is the expensive computational complexity of the postfiltering process implemented as an adaptive convolution. The number of multiplications and additions varied as $\mathcal{O}((\mathrm{NM})^2)$ where N and M are the image and filter sizes respectively. Also the 2-D local pixel bandwidth $\hat{B}_{\omega_1,\omega_2}[n_1, n_2]$ computation could require as much as $\mathcal{O}(\mathrm{N}^4)$ for fully interpolated horizontal and vertical frequency images. However, limiting the size of the interpolation to $N/2$, which in our case represents a 128x128 region, reduces the complexity to $\mathcal{O}(\frac{(N^4)}{4})$. All the images presented were obtained using a 128x128 interpolation region.

References

[1] H. C. Reeve III and J. S. Lim, "Reduction of Blocking Effect in Image Coding", IEEE *ICASSP*, Boston MA, 1983, pp. 1212-1215

[2] B. Ramamurthi and A. Gersho, "Nonlinear Space-Variant Postprocessing of Block Coded Images" IEEE *Trans On Acoustics, Speech, and Sig Proc*, ASSP-34, No.5, pp.1258-68, October 1986

[3] P. H. Cassereau and D. H. Staelin, "A New Class of Optimal Unitary Transforms for Image Processing", Master of Science Thesis, *MIT*, 1985

[4] H. S. Malvar and D. H. Staelin, "Reduction of Blocking Effects In Image Coding With a Lapped Orthogonal Transform, IEEE Abstract *M2.8* 1988

[5] H.S.Malvar and D.H.Staelin, "The LOT: Transform Coding Without Blocking Effects", IEEE *Trans on Acoustics, Speech and Sig Proc*, Vol.37, No.4, April 1989

[6] P. M. Cassereau, D. H. Staelin and G. DeJager, "Encoding of Images Based on a Lapped Orthogonal Transform", IEEE *Trans on Comm*, Vol.37, No.2, Feb 1989

[7] A. N. Akansu and F. E. Wadas, "On Lapped Orthogonal Transforms", IEEE *Transactions on Signal Processing*, Vol. 40, No. 2, February 1992

[8] G. K. Wallace, "The JPEG Still Picture Compression Standard", *Communications of the ACM*, Vol. 34, No. 4, April 1991

[9] W. B. Pannebaker, "Joint Photographic Experts Group (JPEG) Specification", Rev. 8, *ANSI* ISO/IEC JTC1/SC2/WG8, August 17, 1990

[10] R. J. Clarke, "Spectral response of the discrete cosine and Walsh-Hadamard transforms", IEE *Proceedings*, Vol. 130, Pt. F, No. 4, June 1983

[11] A. V. Oppenheim and R. W. Schafer, "Discrete-Time Signal Processing", Prentice Hall *Signal Processing Series*, 1989

Self-similarity of the Multiresolutional Image/Video Decomposition: Smart Expansion as Compression of Still and Moving Pictures*

Oleg Kiselyov and Paul Fisher
Department of Computer Science
PO Box 13886
University of North Texas
Denton Texas 76203-3886

Phone: (817) 565-2767, FAX: (817) 565-2799
Email: oleg@ponder.csci.unt.edu, fisher@gab.unt.edu

Index words: image compression, video compression, lossy compression, self-similarity, multiresolutional analysis, wavelet decomposition, loose wavelet bases.

Abstract

The paper introduces a new combined fractal/multiresolutional image compression based on the observed property of self-similarity of the pyramidal image transform. The gist of the method is zooming out from a (possibly shrunken) low-resolution image producing a sharp and crisp "natural looking" high-resolution view, without blockiness and jaggedness. It is demonstrated that the technique possesses features of preserving thinness of lines on expansion, translational invariance and providing a perfect high-resolution representation of the gradient fill. The multiresolutional transform algorithms and 'smart' image magnification developed for still images have been generalized to deal with moving pictures as a three-dimensional, spatio-temporal frame sequence, which permits rapid compression, smooth motion interpolation, and has potential for use in video transmission in real time.

I. Introduction

The present paper deals with an alternative scheme to eliminate the redundant information from the image/video on compression and to fill it in on decompression. The technique is based on, and makes extensive use of the property of self-similarity. However, unlike the IFS Fractal Image Compression algorithm [BARN93], we are estimating and exploring the self-similarity within a multiresolutional pyramidal decomposition of the image rather than within the image as it is. Specifically, the redundant information in an image, which comes mainly from local correlations in pixel intensities, can be effectively reduced by simply squeezing (or decimating) the picture. This by itself can be regarded as a very fast compression. Indeed, squeezing an image 4 times in each dimension reduces the amount of required storage 16 times. Compressing the

---

* This work supported in part by US Navy SPAWAR Grants N-0003993-C-0048 "Video Compression" and N-0003992-C-0063 "Compression of Geophysical Data".

shrunken picture at least 10:1 (which as we saw [KIFI93] introduces little visual loss) would result in a hefty overall compression of 160:1! Unfortunately, a dumb expansion of the squeezed image back to its original size gives a very jagged and blocky picture. Therefore, the problem is to explore the remaining (mostly high-level) correlations in the squeezed image to perform a smart image magnification, which ought to result in a smooth and 'natural looking' picture.

Thus, our goal is to find a way to estimate the self-similarity of the multiresolutional image decomposition and perform an image expansion based upon that. We have developed an idea of a formula of self-similarity to estimate the self-similarity in the pyramidal decomposition. The next section illustrates the idea on a very simple example of a self-similar image. We will next introduce a concept of *local* self-similarity in a complex image and consider its application to a 'smart' image expansion. Simple images of straight lines, gradient fills and other basic elements that constitute a complex realistic picture will help to clarify the potential of this approach and its implementations. It is demonstrated that the multiresolutional decomposition of frame sequences also possesses the property of self-similarity, which (as in case of still pictures) can be used to perform smooth inter- and intraframe interpolation. In conclusion, we will show how the method works in the case of realistic complex images. It is significant that the algorithm is very fast, much faster than that based on the Iterative Function System Fractals [BARN93].

II. A Simple Example of Self-similarity in the Multiresolutional Image Decomposition

We start the discussion of self-similarity and how it emerges in the multiresolution decomposition by examining a simple self-similar image, Fig. 1. Each small square on the figure stands for a pixel of an 8x8 image.

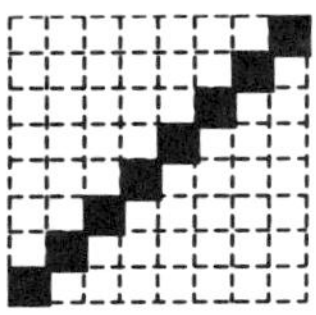

Fig. 1. A simple test image.

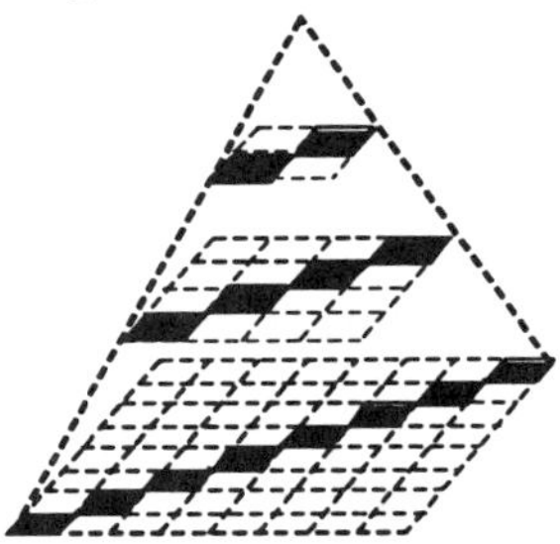

Fig. 2. Gaussian pyramid for the simple fractal image.

Fig. 2 demonstrates a set of views of the image at different resolutions, which are stacked one upon another to build a pyramid-like structure, a Gaussian pyramid [BURT83].

The bottom of the pyramid is the original image itself. The layer just above it is a view of the image at a coarser resolution, obtained by replacing a 2x2 square of 4 pixels by one pixel. The middle layer is, in turn, reduced to give the top layer of the pyramid. From this example we can easily see that all image views at different resolutions 'look alike'. This behavior is similar to that of images of clouds and coastlines, where "In a rough approximation, the small and large details of coastlines are geometrically identical except for scale. When each piece of a shape is geometrically similar to the whole, both the shape and the mechanism that generates it are called *self-similar*" [MAND83]. This notion can be given a more precise meaning. Consider the first two top layers of the pyramid. The top 2x2 image represents the entire image at a very coarse resolution; but it is identical to, say, the left lower quadrant of the layer below it, which represents only a part of the original image. Thus, we are able to map an entire image into a part of itself at a finer resolution. A set of mappings of a low resolution picture onto all four quadrants of a higher-resolution view constitutes a formula of the self-similarity, which in our case looks like—

quadrant #0 of a high-resolution image is equal to 0 * low-resolution image
quadrant #1 of a high-resolution image is equal to 1 * low-resolution image
quadrant #2 of a high-resolution image is equal to 0 * low-resolution image
quadrant #3 of a high-resolution image is equal to 1 * low-resolution image

Exactly the same relationship holds between any two adjacent layers of the pyramid, Fig. 2. Consequently, the formula above is a unique description of the image, and captures all its essence. It opens up a possibility of expanding the image to get an image at even finer resolution. Indeed, applying the formula to the original image in Fig. 1 gives us Fig 3a.

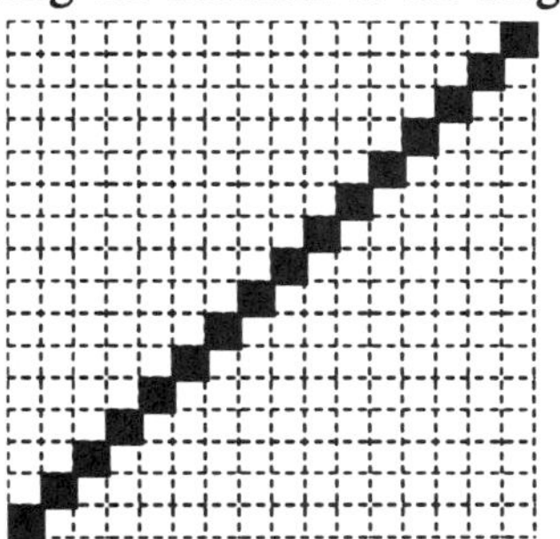

Fig. 3a. 'Smart' expansion of the original image, Fig. 1, based on the formula of self-similarity.

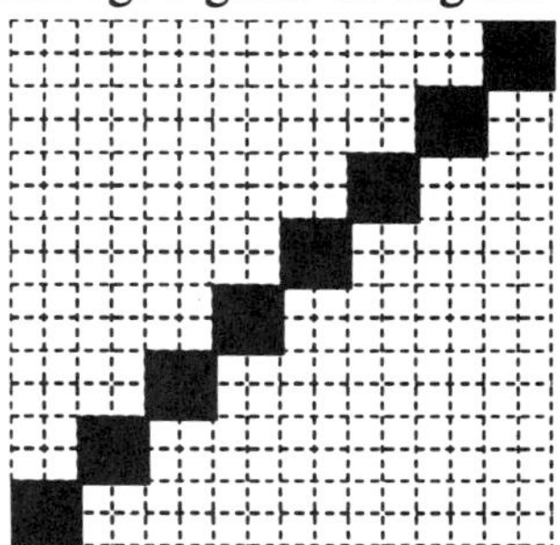

Fig. 3b. 'Dumb' expansion of the original image, Fig. 1.

Fig. 3b depicts the result of a 'dumb' expansion; i.e., inflating each pixel into a 2x2 square. Obviously the expansion based on the property of self-similarity looks less jagged and blocky, and goes along with our intrinsic feeling as to how the expansion of Fig. 1 should look.

In general, the relation between the image and a quadrant of itself at a finer resolution may be more complicated than in the simplest case shown above. First, a quadrant of the finer resolution image may be darker or brighter than the entire coarse resolution image by some specific factor. Moreover, we might need to rotate a low-resolution view and/or perform the reflection before trying to match it with quadrants of the high-resolution one. Thus the formula of the self-similarity between two images is defined to be a set of the four pairs. Each pair $\{x,y\}$ in the set tells the relation between the entire smaller picture and the corresponding quadrant of the larger image. The first number in the pair, x, specifies that the image A is to be rotated by $|x| \times 90°$ clockwise and, if $x < 0$, reflected in y-axis. The second number, y, tells that the intensity of all the pixels of the low-resolution view is to be increased y times. After rotation, flipping, and intensity scaling, the image then matches a corresponding quadrant of a larger picture. Apparently, it is not always possible to get a perfect match; i.e., no rotation and scaling of the intensity of a 2x2-pixel square can give an image that looks *exactly* like some quadrant of a 4x4-pixel square. However, we are content with a match which is rather good, though it might not be perfect. At present, we are using a scaled projection of one image considered as a multi-dimensional vector onto another as a criterion to choose among non-perfect matches.

Realistic images with which we are concerned are a bit more complicated than the test example, Fig. 1. One can hardly expect that, say, a frame of the weather broadcast video can be described entirely by a single simple formula as we have discussed earlier. However, we believe that a small separate part of the complicated picture does possess that property. Indeed, one small piece of an image may well be a segment of the straight line, which as we saw is very well described by the formula of self-similarity. Moreover, clouds, flowers, rugged views of mountains, and other well-known examples of self-similar images can make up a (significant) part of a realistic picture. In other words, although the property of self-similarity normally holds only for fractal images, one can hope that it applies *locally* for usual images as well. Local self-similarity can be estimated by comparing quadrants of the 4x4 square of the bottom level of the pyramid with the 2x2 pixel square of the higher level that is a view of the original 4x4 square at a coarser resolution.

III. Smart Expansion of Pictures

In the present section, we will demonstrate how the method works for simple images. Note that the figures throughout the section show the pixel value as the number rather than the shade of gray. For example, a pixel with value 8 is displayed as the number eight. A zero pixel is shown as a dot for clarity. The selected test images are indeed very simple, but one can consider them as a tiny part of a complex picture. Therefore, if expansion of the simple images seems indeed 'smart', one can expect good results for realistic images, too.

Figures 4 and 5 are segments of the straight line, which is the atomic part of any picture. In these examples, we are interested to see if the expansion of a *thin* line looks as thin rather than bloated. Thinness of the line is very important here, because if this property is preserved upon expansion, the magnified image would look as crisp and sharp as does the original. In Fig. 5, which is a shifted version of Fig. 4, we are also looking at whether the property of keeping thin lines thin upon magnification is preserved through translation, the bane of the pyramidal transforms [MALL89]. As one can see, surprisingly it does. This result is indeed astonishing since the reduced resolution representations can be severely distorted when the input is shifted. The problem is known in the quadtree literature as the shift-dependence of the description. In the worst case, a one-pixel shift of the input image can lead to a significantly modified pyramid structure [see refs. in MONT91]. As it turns out, even though the multiresolution decomposition is altered by the shift, it still preserves the property of self-similarity.

```
8 . . .
8 . . .
8 . . .
8 . . .
```

Fig. 4a. Original image.

```
8 8 . . . . . .
8 8 . . . . . .
8 8 . . . . . .
8 8 . . . . . .
8 8 . . . . . .
8 8 . . . . . .
8 8 . . . . . .
8 8 . . . . . .
```

Fig. 4b. Dumb expansion.

```
8 . . . . . . .
8 . . . . . . .
8 . . . . . . .
8 . . . . . . .
8 . . . . . . .
8 . . . . . . .
8 . . . . . . .
8 . . . . . . .
```

Fig. 4c. Smart expansion based on Gaussian pyramid.

```
12 4 . . . . . .
12 4 . . . . . .
12 4 . . . . . .
12 4 . . . . . .
12 4 . . . . . .
12 4 . . . . . .
12 4 . . . . . .
12 4 . . . . . .
```

Fig. 4d. Smart expansion based on Laplacian pyramid.

```
. 8 . .
. 8 . .
. 8 . .
. 8 . .
```

Fig. 5a. Original image.

```
. . 8 8 . . . .
. . 8 8 . . . .
. . 8 8 . . . .
. . 8 8 . . . .
. . 8 8 . . . .
. . 8 8 . . . .
. . 8 8 . . . .
. . 8 8 . . . .
```

Fig. 5b. Dumb expansion.

```
. . 8 . . . . .
. . 8 . . . . .
. . 8 . . . . .
. . 8 . . . . .
. . 8 . . . . .
. . 8 . . . . .
. . 8 . . . . .
. . 8 . . . . .
```

Fig. 5c. Smart expansion based on Gaussian pyramid.

```
. . 12 4 . . . .
. . 12 4 . . . .
. . 12 4 . . . .
. . 12 4 . . . .
. . 12 4 . . . .
. . 12 4 . . . .
. . 12 4 . . . .
. . 12 4 . . . .
```

Fig. 5d. Smart expansion based on Laplacian pyramid.

8	10	12	14
8	10	12	14
8	10	12	14
8	10	12	14

Fig. 6a. Original image.

8	8	10	10	12	12	14	14
8	8	10	10	12	12	14	14
8	8	10	10	12	12	14	14
8	8	10	10	12	12	14	14
8	8	10	10	12	12	14	14
8	8	10	10	12	12	14	14
8	8	10	10	12	12	14	14
8	8	10	10	12	12	14	14

Fig. 6b. Dumb expansion.

6	7	9	10	8	10	12	14
6	7	9	10	8	10	12	14
6	7	9	10	8	10	12	14
6	7	9	10	8	10	12	14
6	7	9	10	8	10	12	14
6	7	9	10	8	10	12	14
6	7	9	10	8	10	12	14
6	7	9	10	8	10	12	14

Fig. 6c. Smart expansion based on Gaussian pyramid.

7	8	9	10	11	12	13	14
7	8	9	10	11	12	13	14
7	8	9	10	11	12	13	14
7	8	9	10	11	12	13	14
7	8	9	10	11	12	13	14
7	8	9	10	11	12	13	14
7	8	9	10	11	12	13	14
7	8	9	10	11	12	13	14

Fig. 6d. Smart expansion based on Laplacian pyramid.

Figure 6 presents the results for a stripy image with a horizontal gradient fill. One astounding feature of the smart image expansion based on the Laplacian pyramid is its ability to reproduce an utterly perfect, smooth gradient fill upon magnification. Indeed, Fig. 6d shows gradual smooth transitions from one stripe to another, which is precisely how a high-resolution picture of the gradient fill is supposed to look.

Since our method of expansion is based on the self-similarity, it ought to work perfectly for 'classical' self-similar images. To demonstrate that this is really the case, we chose one such picture, a Sierpinski gasket [MAND83]. It turns out that all the various implementations of the smart image magnification produce a perfect correct view of the gasket at the finer resolution.

Finally, Fig. 7 demonstrates the expansion technique on a realistic example. The picture of clouds was squeezed 4 times in each dimension, and then expanded back to the original size using the dumb and smart expansions. Comparison of the original image with a shrunken/expanded one then gives an idea how good the expansion procedures are.

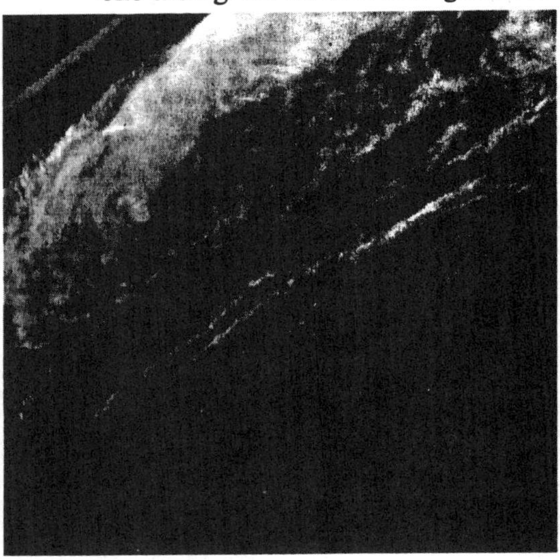

Fig. 7a. Original Clouds. Printed at scale 2:1 after the contrast enhancement of the inverted LUT.

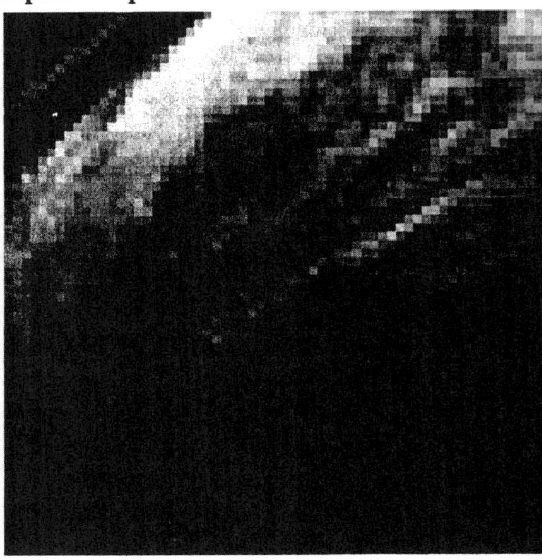

Fig. 7b. Shrunken/dumb expanded.

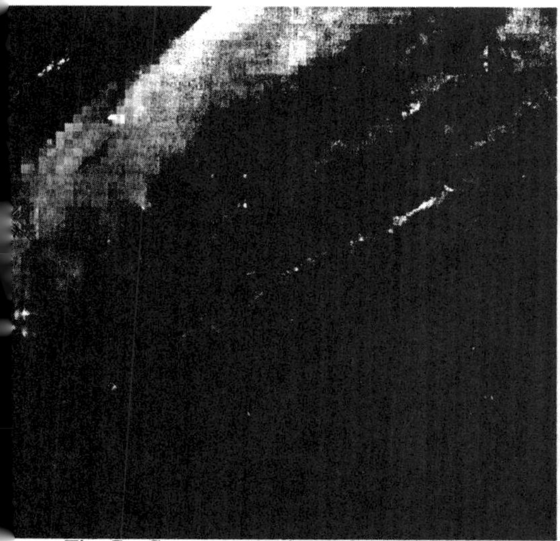

Fig. 7c. Smart expansion using the Laplacian pyramid.

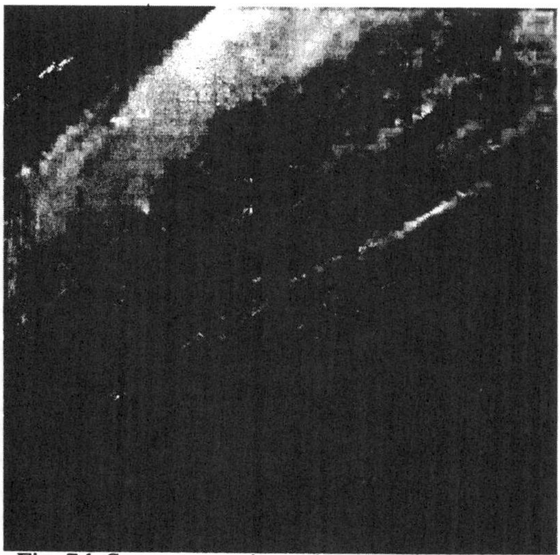

Fig. 7d. Smart expansion using the smooth Laplacian pyramid.

IV. Self-similarity in the Multiresolutional Video Decomposition and Motion Interpolation

Another feature of the present study is the generalization of the multiresolutional pyramidal approach to deal with moving pictures. We have developed and experimented with algorithms of wavelet pyramidal decomposition of a three-dimensional spatio-temporal frame sequence. Moreover, we have discovered that the transform coefficients arranged in the form of a four-dimensional octpyramid possess the property of self-similarity that we observed for the pyramidal decomposition of still images. This leads to the idea of a 'smart' magnification both in space and in time, which allows one to restore fairly accurately a high resolution video sequence from the low resolution one, producing crisp, sharp looking individual frames as well as smooth motion between the adjacent frames. This concept permits rapid compression, and has potential for use in video compression in real time.

Similarly to the two-dimensional case, we start the discussion of self-similarity in the spatial-temporal multiresolutional decomposition by examining the following test frame sequence, which is composed of snapshots of a single moving vertical line.

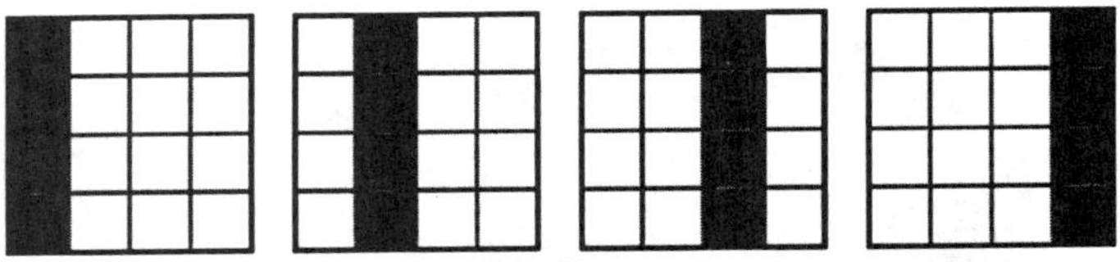

Fig. 8. A simple self-similar test frame sequence.

The Laplacian pyramid decomposition of the sequence (using a simple δ-function wavelet basis) is depicted on Fig. 9. Cross-hatched cubes on the picture stand for the pyramidal nodes with the value of minus one.

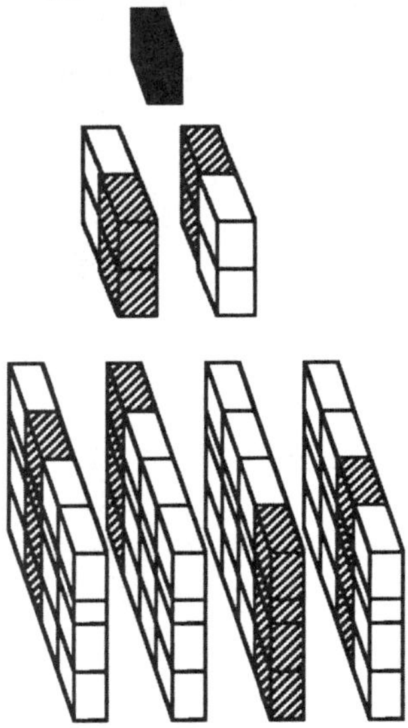

Fig. 9. Laplacian pyramid for the test frame sequence.

The formula of the self-similarity in the three-dimensional case can be derived then as follows: The bottom level of the pyramid on Fig. 9 describes the frame details and the motion that are discernible at the resolution 1:1; the level just above it contains larger scale details and refers to a coarser motion, corresponding to the resolution 2:1. Obviously, the former sequence is 8 times bigger than the latter. The high resolution sequence can be split into eight octants, each of them having exactly the same size (dimensions) as the entire low resolution sequence, so that it is possible to consider a mapping between the latter and the octants of the former. These mappings define a formula of the self-similarity of the moving picture, similar to the two-dimensional case. The formula allows us to extend the Laplacian pyramid one level deeper. Converting the extended

Laplacian pyramid back to the Gaussian one and taking the bottom level of it gives a magnified original sequence:

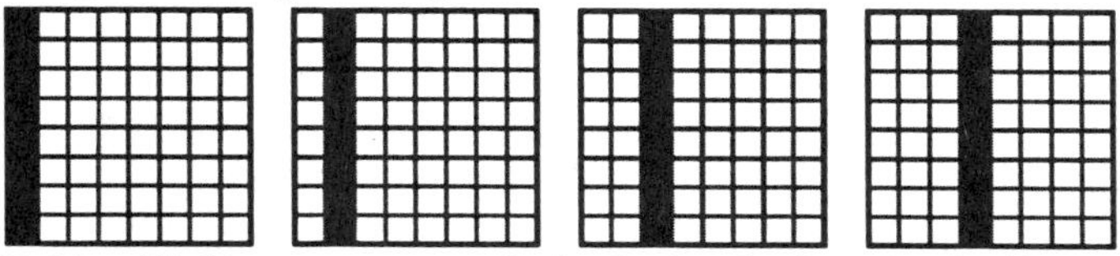

Fig. 10. Magnified image sequence obtained using the formula of self-similarity.

Figure 11 displays for comparison the frame sequence obtained by the 'dumb' magnification:

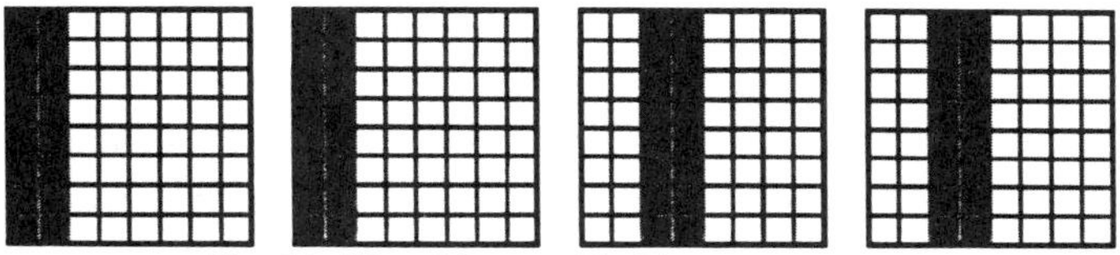

Fig. 11. "Dumb" magnified image sequence.

Let us consider another, more complex example of the movie, which is a translation of a simple object against the static background. Four consecutive frames of the sample movie are presented below:

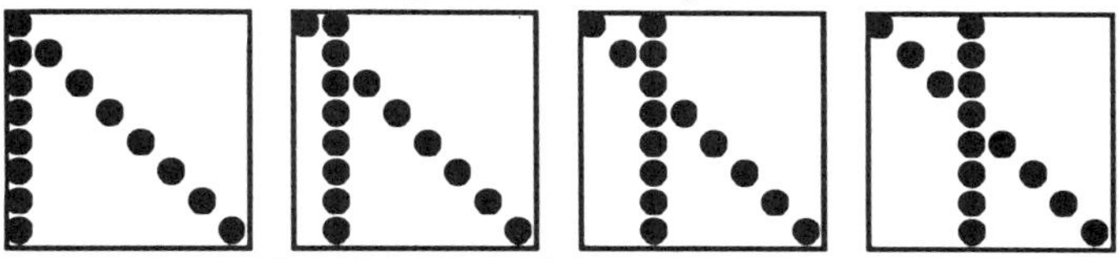

Fig. 12. Frames of the sample movie.

The following figure shows the results of the smart magnification of the sequence; only the first 5 frames are shown, but it is easy to imagine the rest.

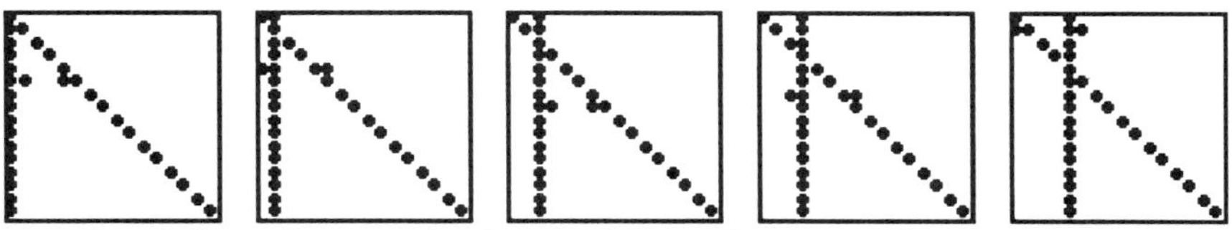

Fig. 13. Several consecutive frames of the predicted magnified sample movie.

The paper provides other examples as well. Though predictions for the high resolution sequence are not exact, they are quite close to what one would expect. It should be noted here that a prediction does not have to be perfect, as one can always encode the error separately. If the prediction is quite accurate, the error will be small and can be transmitted at a low bit rate. As shown in Fig. 13, this is the case here. It must be stressed that the motion in the predicted frame sequence is indeed gradual and smooth as it should be.

A real-time video compression of 128x128 frames at the rate of 4-5 frames/sec with fairly good quality has been achieved as the outcome of the present research. A VHS tape of a weather briefing has been produced that contains the original video clip and those compressed and re-expanded using several developed algorithms, playing side-by-side. The tape is available upon request.

References

[BARN93] Barnsley, M.F., Hurd L.P., Fractal Image Compression, AK Peters Ltd., 1993, 244 p.

[BURT83] Burt, P., Adelson, E., "The Laplacian Pyramid as a Compact Image Code," *IEEE Trans. Comm.*, Vol. 31, No. 4, pp. 532-540, April 1983.

[KIFI93] Kiselyov, O. and P. Fisher, "Pyramidal Image Decompositions: A New Look," in *Proc. DCC'93, 1993 Data Compression Conference*, Snowbird, Utah, p.479, March 30-April 2, 1993.

[MALL89a] Mallat S., "A Theory for Multiresolutional Signal Decomposition: the Wavelet Representation," *IEEE Trans. on Pattern Analysis and Machine Intell.*, Vol. 11, No. 7, pp.674-693, July 1989.

[MAND83] Mandelbrot, B.B., The Fractal Geometry of Nature, W.H. Freeman and Co., 1983.

[MONT91] Montanvert, A., Meer P., and A. Rosenfeld, "Hierarchical Image Analysis Using Irregular Tessellations," *IEEE Trans. on Pattern Analysis and Machine Intell*, Vol. 13, No. 4, pp. 307-316, April 1991.

An investigation of wavelet-based image coding using an entropy-constrained quantization framework

Michael T. Orchard and Kannan Ramchandran
Beckman Institute, University of Illinois at Urbana-Champaign
405 N. Mathews Ave., Urbana, IL 61801

January 17, 1994

Abstract

Wavelet image decompositions generate a tree-structured set of coefficients, providing an hierarchical data-structure for representing images. Several recently proposed image compression algorithms have focused on new ways for exploiting dependencies between this hierarchy of wavelet coefficients. This paper presents a new framework for understanding the efficiency of one such algorithm as a simplified attempt to design a global entropy-constrained image quantizer. The principle insight offered by the new framework is that improved performance is achieved by more accurately characterizing the joint probabilities of arbitrary sets of wavelet coefficients. The specific algorithm described is designed around one conveniently structured collection of such sets. The efficiency of hierarchical wavelet coding algorithms derives from their success at identifying and exploiting dependencies between coefficients in the hierarchical structure. The second part of the paper presents an empirical study of the distribution of high-band wavelet coefficients, the band responsible for most of the performance improvements of the new algorithms.

1 Introduction

Applications of hierarchical decompositions to image compression have received considerable attention over the past five years, motivated by their ability to offer space-frequency resolution tradeoffs well matched to the characteristics of real images. However, until recently, algorithms based on hierarchical image decompositions have shown performance only marginally better than standard block-based algorithms. A recently introduced class of hierarchical-based compression schemes [1, 2, 3] has attracted attention because its high performance appears to confirm the promised benefits of hierarchical representation. This class couples standard approaches for quantizing frequency coefficients individually or in groups (e.g. scalar or vector quantization) with tree-structured quantization schemes aimed at exploited spatially localized phenomena. This paper explores the efficiency of these new algorithms, first offering a new framework for describing their operation, and then empirically investigating those aspects of the distribution of wavelet coefficients exploited by the algorithm.

Wavelets provide a tool for decomposing images into a hierarchy of frequency components, each represented with spatial resolution proportional to frequency. The resulting hierarchical image representation provides an attractive tradeoff between spatial and frequency resolution, with promising application to image compression. Low frequency coefficients with large spatial support provide the ability to efficiently represent large low-frequency regions found in many images. At the same time, high-frequency coefficients with small spatial support provide the ability to compactly represent spatially-local phenomena such as edges found in most images. Thus, the wavelet offers the potential to compactly represent the diverse space-frequency phenomena found in typical images. The challenge of wavelet coding is the efficient management of the information in the complex space-frequency data structure. Early wavelet coding algorithms managed the wavelet transform coefficients with conventional bit-allocation methods, driven by distinct statistical characterizations of each frequency band. Recent wavelet-based algorithms propose more complex coefficient quantization strategies, aimed at exploiting both frequency and spatial characterization of coefficients.

The next section develops a framework for describing the operation of a recently proposed wavelet-based compression algorithm, offering insights into the algorithm's excellent performance and suggesting possible directions for future investigation. The new algorithm involves both frequency-domain scalar quantization and spatial-domain quantization of sets of wavelet coefficients. We describe the operation of the new algorithm as a special case of the global application of entropy-constrained image quantization methods developed in [9]. ¿From this perspective, we learn that the performance advantages of the new algorithm are tied to an improved characterization of the probability of sets of zeros in the hierarchy of wavelet coefficients. Section 2 presents an empirical study of the joint distribution of those coefficients, aimed at exploring the coefficient dependencies responsible for the effectiveness of the proposed coding algorithm. In particular, it suggests a model for partitioning coefficients into sets exhibiting different statistical properties. Section 3 discusses the relationship between the coding framework presented in the next section and the empirical studies of section 2.

The wavelet decomposition of an image can be viewed as a tree-structured set of coefficients. The detailed parent-children relationships defining this tree can be found in [1, 2, 3]. Here we give a brief high-level description of this tree. Figure 1 illustrates the N^2 coefficients generated by a 4-level wavelet decomposition of the Lenna image. High-frequency bands are located at the bottom and to the left. Low-frequency bands are located towards the upper, right corner. The wavelet tree is generated by grouping coefficients in different bands which describe a common spatial region of the image. Consider a fixed spatial region of the Lenna image, and identify all coefficients in figure 1 carrying information about that region. For a region identified with one coefficient in the lowest band, we find multiple coefficients in the next higher band, and still more in yet higher bands. More detailed definition of the wavelet tree will not be needed in this paper (the reader is referred to [3]), but it suffices to note that the wavelet decomposition lends itself to two types of groupings of coefficients: a frequency grouping of coefficients in the same band, and a spatial grouping of coefficients from the same region.

The key issue in the development of any wavelet-based image compression algorithm is the strategy used for quantizing this tree-structured set of wavelet coefficients. Several researchers have proposed separately quantizing each band (or level) of coefficients using scalar [6] or vector quantizers [7] optimized for the distribution of coefficients (or joint distribution of groups of coefficients). While these algorithms have demostrated slightly better performance than block-based algorithms, they fail to exploit certain wavelet-tree dependencies which allow improved performance. Before empirically exploring these dependencies in section 2, we describe how an algorithm that applies optimal scalar quantization to wavelet coefficients using a statistical characterization of the probability distribution of frequency bands can be iteratively improved to produce more efficient algorithms. We apply a simplification of entropy-constrained vector quantization design from [9], described in the following section.

1.1 Entropy-constrained quantization

Chou, Lookabaugh, and Gray [9] proposed an iterative descent algorithm for designing vector quantizers having minimum distortion subject to an entropy constraint. Though we refer the reader to [9] for a detailed description of this work, we briefly summarize here the steps of their iterative algorithm, since it provides the basis for our approach to improving the performance of wavelet-based compression algorithms.

Let $\{\beta(i)\}_{i\in\mathcal{I}}$ denote an L-dimensional VQ codebook ($\beta(i) \in \mathbb{R}^L$) indexed by index set $\mathcal{I}$, and let $\{\gamma(i)\}_{i\in\mathcal{I}}$ denote the transmitted symbol lengths of the codewords. Let a stationary vector source generate vectors $\{X^n\}$ from $\mathbb{R}^L$ independently with distribution P_{X^n}. Let λ be a Lagrange multiplier controlling the entropy constraint, and let $\rho(x, y)$ specify a distortion measure. Each iteration of the design algorithm consists of three steps (here we ignore processing associated with checking conditions for stopping the iteration).

1. define an entropy-constrained mapping of input vectors:

$$\alpha(x) = \arg\min_{i\in\mathcal{I}} \rho(x, \beta(i)) + \lambda|\gamma(i)|. \tag{1}$$

2. update transmitted symbol lengths to reflect codeword entropy

$$|\gamma(i)| = -\log_2 P_{X^n}\{\alpha(X^n) = i\}. \tag{2}$$

3. optimize reproduction codebook

$$\beta(i) = E[X^n|\alpha(X^n) = i]. \tag{3}$$

4. iterate until stopped

While the above algorithm is reasonable for the design of low-dimensional VQ coders, the approach becomes impractical when the VQ dimension and codebook size get very large. In the following discussion, we analyze a wavelet coding scheme as $N \times N$ dimensional VQ, where N is the image size (e.g. $N \times N = 262144$). Due to the large dimension, direct application of the above algorithm would produce a VQ algorithm too large to implement, even if it were possible to design. Instead, we consider simplifications of the above algorithm that ensure reasonable encoder and decoder complexity. We should emphasize that the following discussion is not intended to accurately detail the steps of the algorithm, but only to provide a framework for understanding its operation. The VQ characterization of the new algorithm provides insights into how it works, and what statistical features of images it exploits well. The actual coding algorithm does not involve $N \times N$ dimensional VQ codebooks, but implements recursive tree-pruning procedures that perform optimizations equivalent to those described below. Thus, at times the discussion below will grossly mischaracterize the computational complexity of the actual algorithm. We refer to [3] for implementation details.

An algorithm that applies scalar quantization to wavelet coefficients can be viewed as a special case of an $N \times N$-dimensional VQ coder. If K-level scalar quantizers are applied to each coefficient, the VQ codebook contains exactly $K^{N\times N}$ codewords. If uniform scalar quantizers are used, codewords lie on a $N \times N$-dimensional lattice. Note: if we consider arbitrary scalar quantizers (e.g. entropy-constrained scalar quantizers), the codewords possess a separable structure, but do not lie on a regular lattice. The algorithm of [3] uses uniform quantizers, though arbitrary scalar quantizers can be incorporated with no conceptual difference. In addition to constraining $\{\beta(i)\}$ to possess a separable structure, the scalar-equivalent VQ coder also constrains how transmitted symbol lengths $\{\gamma(i)\}$ can be assigned to codewords. Specifically, for each codeword $\beta(i)$, the transmitted symbol length $\gamma(i)$ must equal the sum of symbol lengths for the component scalar coefficients. Given these constraints on $\{\beta(i)\}$ and $\{\gamma(i)\}$, scalar quantization of wavelet coefficients can be viewed as optimal VQ coding with respect to either a distortion measure $\rho(x, \beta(i))$ or entropy-constrained distortion measure $\rho(x, \beta(i)) + \lambda|\gamma(i)|$, depending on whether we apply scalar quantization or entropy-constrained scalar quantization to the coefficients.

Starting at this initial scalar-equivalent VQ coder, let us consider improving performance by applying the Chou, Lookabaugh, and Gray iterative descent algorithm. To motivate our modifications to that algorithm, we consider the computational significance of each of its three steps, starting with step 3 and working backward. Given Voronoi regions associated with the initial lattice-structured codebook, step 3 repositions each codeword from its position on the lattice to the centroid of its Voronoi region. For arbitrary Voronoi regions, we can expect the resulting codebook to neither lie on a lattice nor to possess a general separable structure. The task of scalar quantizing $N \times N$ coefficients is thus transformed into a virtually impossible general nearest-neighbor mapping in $\mathbb{R}^{N*N}$. Consequently, we propose to skip step 3, forcing the final codebook to be identical to the initial codebook, and implementable as simple scalar quantization.

Step 2 calls for updating the lengths of the transmitted symbols to reflect codeword entropy. As mentioned earlier, the initial lengths of all symbols are given by the sum of the lengths of each of the scalar symbols composing the codeword. If the lengths of the scalar symbols reflect the true entropy of the coefficients of X_n, and if the coefficients in X_n are independent, this initial assignment of symbol codelengths truly reflects the codeword entropy. However, if the coefficients are not independent, step 2 of the original algorithm requires the impossible task of estimating the entropy of all $K^{N\times N}$ codewords. We propose a dramatic simplification of step 2 to allow efficient implementation while exploiting relevant dependencies. We continue to constrain most codelengths to be assigned as the sum of scalar symbol lengths. However, for a few prespecified sets of coefficients we allow a specific group of scalar symbols on those sets to be represented with an arbitrary codelength. For example, consider one arbitrary fixed set B of coefficients, and consider treating the case of all-zeros on B as a special symbol. Then, any codeword having a nonzero coefficient anywhere in B is assigned codeword length as the sum of scalar symbol lengths (as before). However, for codewords with all-zeros in B, codeword length is assigned as the sum of scalar symbol lengths of coefficients outside B, plus the codelength assigned to the special symbol. For selecting special symbols, we intend to identify groups of scalar symbols which we believe to be much more likely than would be characterized by the product of the marginal probabilities, thus deserving a codelength much lower than the sum of scalar symbol lengths. Our simplified step 2 requires updating the codelength for the special symbols, and updating the scalar symbol codelengths.

Finally, we consider the implementation of step 1 of the original algorithm. Because the codebook is constrained to a lattice, and the rates of most codewords are simply the sum of scalar symbol lengths, the mapping defined in step 1 can almost be implemented as simple entropy-constrained scalar quantization ECSQ (i.e. each scalar is quantized by minimizing a scalar Lagrangian cost analagous to (1)). (In practice, we replace this ECSQ with uniform quantization.) That is, the minimum Lagrangian cost, over all codewords not containing special symbols, can be determined by independently scalar quantizing all coefficients. However, even if the scalar quantized result contains no special symbols, the relatively small codelength of special symbols raises the possibility that a nearby codeword (necessarily larger distortion) containing a special symbol (lower rate) might have a lower Lagrangian cost than the optimal scalar-quantized codeword. Thus, in addition to scalar quantization, a systematic and exhaustive search of codewords with special symbols must be conducted to implement the entropy-constrained mapping of step 1. The complexity of this search motivates us to limit the number and allowable location of special symbols.

1.2 Basic idea of algorithm

The previous section described a two-step simplification of the ECVQ design procedure of [9] allowing its implementation in a huge dimensional vector space. Here we address a number of high-level issues arising in the design of a coding algorithm based on this iterative procedure. Refer to [3] for mathematical and implementation details of the algorithms.

The first step towards designing a coding algorithm based on the above iterative procedure is to define good special symbols. As described earlier, these symbols should be selected as groups of symbols whose probability is much larger than that characterized by an independent probability model. Based on empirical modeling of wavelet coefficients discussed in section 2, we define special symbols as groups of all-zero values on selected sets of wavelet coefficients. Although there is no statistical reason for distinguishing between a very large collection of possible sets of coefficients (i.e. all 2×2, 3×3, 4×4, etc. blocks) the complexity associated with exhaustively searching all such sets in the mapping stage of step 1 leads us to limit the number and structure of those we consider. For example, non-overlapping sets can be evaluated with much lower complexity than overlapping sets. Certain collections of embedded overlapping sets allow searches to be performed with efficient tree-structured pruning algorithms. Thus, [3] uses a specific collection of embedded sets, called *zerotrees*, designed to exploit the tree structure of wavelet coefficients, in order to reduce computational complexity.

We should emphasize that the coding gain realized by the special symbols is far larger than that achieved by efficiently coding only groups of zeros. While it is true that groups of zeros are coded with much lower symbol lengths, the iterative design algorithm achieves its advantage over a much larger group of symbols that get mapped to the special symbols in step 1. Specifically, because the probability of zeros is greatly underestimated by the independent probability model, the special symbol is coded with a much smaller codelength than its neighbors. The lower codelength lowers the Lagrangian costs of the special symbol for all neighboring groups of symbols (e.g. groups with many zeros and a few small values), and many of these codewords are mapped to the special symbol. Since the probability of all these symbols is also highly underestimated by the independent probability model, the codelength of the special symbol decreases further. Eventually, when the codelength of the special symbol becomes too small to experience further large decreases, the Lagrangian cost of potential additional neighboring codewords becomes dominated by distortion, which does not change because we omit step 3.

For a fixed scalar quantizer of step size q defining the lattice of codewords, the Lagrange multiplier λ in (1) controls the bitrate of the coder. For $\lambda = 0$, the efficient coding of the special symbol is ignored by nearby codewords, and the rate of the coder is determined by the q. As λ is increased, more coefficients are mapped to special symbols, and both the codelengths of the special symbols and the overall rate of the coder decrease until, at $\lambda = \infty$, a rate of zero is realized. Clearly, both q and λ influence the rate of the coder, and there are many (q, λ) pairs corresponding to the same rate. This raises the question of which (q, λ) pair optimizes performance for a given target rate. A necessary condition for a given (q, λ) pair to be optimal for achieving a fixed rate R is that λ should equal the slope of the rate-distortion function of the scalar quantizer at its operating point. This is, however, a difficult condition to analytically insure, since the performance of the scalar quantizer (and therefore its rate-distortion function) depends on what coefficients it operates on. Note: the distribution of these coefficients is biased by the use of the special symbol, since mostly small-valued coefficients are represented by the special symbols. Thus, the algorithm in [3] iteratively refines the quantization step q until the condition is met.

Though the details of the algorithm in [3] are not the subject of this paper, we include in Table 1 performance results for the standard 512×512 greyscale Lena image, using a 4-level wavelet decomposition with the biorthogonal spline variant filters of [6]. The algorithm shows exceptional coding efficiency, among the best in the published literature. Based on the discussion above, it is apparent that the significant statistical dependencies are exploited by the zerotree special symbols. The following section presents an empirical study of the high-band wavelet coefficients, intended to characterize the statistical dependencies responsible for the algorithm's excellent performance.

bit rate (b/p)	PSNR (dB)	total bytes
0.25	33.95	8168
0.50	37.06	16379
1.00	40.40	32760

2 Empirical statistical study

This section describes an empirical study of the joint probabilities (first-order correlations) of wavelet coefficients (using the wavelet filters of [3]) for the 512 x 512 grayscale Lenna image. See Fig. 1 for the wavelet decomposition of Lenna. Fig. 2(a) depicts the 2-D correlation characteristics of the unquantized LH^1 (high frequency) band for a lag window of absolute value 3 in each dimension. As can be seen, there is some spatial correlation around the neighborhood of each coefficient, with the absolute value of the correlation decaying quickly with increased lag distances. Fig. 2(b) shows the covariance of the *magnitudes* of the coefficients, assuming them to be identically distributed. As can be seen, the magnitudes are more correlated than the original values, indicating dependence among intrabrand wavelet coefficients. The presence of dependencies other than those captured by correlation leads us to conclude that some form of non-linear processing may be beneficial. Figure 1 offers some intuition into the nature of these complex dependencies. Although the high-frequency bands may be uncorrelated (it is difficult to imagine how one visually recognizes lack of correlation), the magnitude of coefficients around edges appears to be quite correlated. Alternatively, we recognize that the energy in high-frequency bands is spatially clustered around regions corresponding to edges of the original image. Motivated by this observation, we attempt to characterize the spatial clustering of energy by applying a non-linear partitioning of the coefficients.

We propose the following classification to explore the potential coding gain achievable by partitioning the original wavelet coefficients into distinct sets with dissimilar statistical properties. First, we identify regions having non-negligible coefficient energy (indicating the presence of edges). by applying an appropriate threshold. Then, we apply a morphological dilation [10] of this edge region to identify a deterministic neighborhood of these significant coefficients. The morphological filtering thus enlarges the significant coefficient "islands" to include neighborhoods around them, essentially dividing the wavelet coefficients into two sets, with one set having relatively significant coefficients and the other set having relatively insignficant ones. The order of the filter, as specified by the size of the dilation's structuring element, determines the size of this neighborhood. The lowest order filter merely preserves the original edges, the first-order structuring element includes the four immediate nearest neighbor locations in 2-D, and the higher order filters correspond to monotonically increasing neighborhood regions, with the 6th order filter referring to a neighborhood of magnitude 3 in 2-D centered around each coefficient. Note that the number of coefficients in the zero-order region (those exceeding a threshold) will roughly match the number predicted by the common i.i.d. model for high-frequency coefficients (although they will be much more clustered than predicted). However, if the number of neighboring coefficients added by the first-order filter is K_1, the independence assumption predicts that the average energy of those coefficients should equal the average energy of all remaining coefficients. Evidence of the disparity in the probabilities of the coefficients in the two different sets is borne out by Fig. 3(a), which shows the variances of the residue sets (insignificant coefficients) as the order of the morphological filter is varied. Fig. 3(b) shows the magnitude correlation of the residue set after applying morphological filtering. Note that the correlation has decreased compared to the plot in 2(b), but is not zero.

3 Discussion and conclusions

The simulations results described in Section 2 verify the presence of two statistically distinct sets, those around edges and those which are zero-valued or insignificant, identified with relative ease by using morphological filtering. The intraset dependencies evident from the magnitude correlations observed in the simulations further highlight the inefficiency of modelling the joint entropy of certain groups of coefficients as the sum of their individual entropies. Although complex coding schemes can be designed for optimally exploiting these dependencies, adopting the framework of the previous section, we seek to exploit these dependencies by identifying "good" sets of coefficients for special symbols (as described in Section 1.1) whose entropies are the most grossly misrepresented as the sum of the entropies of their individual components. The relatively small variance of the residue sets and their relatively high correlation point to the potential coding gain obtained by selecting groups of zeroes as *zerotree* special symbols in the entropy-constrained dictionary, as described in Section 1.1. In our algorithm of [3], the specific special symbol chosen (viz., the zerotree) is consistent with the expectation of high misrepresentation (and hence increased coding gain) of trees of insignificant coefficients. The scope of application of this paradigm is obviously more general.

A framework to describe the new class of high-performance coding algorithms based on wavelet decompositions has been developed in this paper. In particular, the high-performance image compression algorithm of [3] has been cast in this framework of a specialized form of entropy constrained vector quantization codebook design. This framework clearly identifies the coding advantage of this approach over that of conventional scalar quantization schemes as being due to the latter's misrepresentation of the joint probabilities of certain sets of coefficients (like the all-zeroes), as verified using empirical statistical analysis of real image data. The entropy-constrained quantization interpretation is useful as it introduces a framework on which extensions of recent successful wavelet based coding algorithms can be conceptually easily developed.

References

[1] A. Lewis and G. Knowles, "Image Compression Using the 2-D Wavelet Transform", *IEEE Trans. on Image Processing*, Vol. 1, 2, pp. 244-250, April, 1992.

[2] J. M. Shapiro, "An Embedded Wavelet Hierarchical Image Coder", *Proc. ICASSP'92*, pp. 657-660, 1992.

[3] Z. Xiong, K. Ramchandran and M. T. Orchard, "Joint Optimization of Scalar and Tree-structured Quantization of Wavelet Image Decomposition," *Proc. 27th Ann. Asilomar Conf. on Sig., Syst., and Comp.*, Pacific Grove, CA, November, 1993.

[4] K. Ramchandran and M. Vetterli, "Rate-distortion optimal fast thresholding with complete JPEG/MPEG decoder compatibility", *preprint*, October, 1992.

[5] Y. Shoham and A. Gersho, "Efficient Bit Allocation for an Arbitrary Set of Quantizers", *IEEE Trans. Acoustics, Speech, and Signal Processing*, Vol. 36, pp. 1445-1453, Sept., 1988.

[6] M. Antonini, M. Barlaud, P. Mathieu and I. Daubechies, "Image Coding Using Wavelet Transform", *IEEE Trans. Image Processing*, Vol. 1, 2, pp. 205-221, April, 1992.

[7] T. Senoo and G. Girod, "Vector Quantization for Entropy Coding of Image Subbands," *IEEE Trans. Image Processing*, Vol. 1, 4, pp. 526-533, October, 1992.

[8] I. Witten, R. Neal and J. Cleary, "Arithmetic Coding for Data Compression", *Communications of the ACM*, 30, 6, pp. 520-540, 1987.

[9] P. A. Chou, T. Lookabaugh, and R. M. Gray, "Entropy-constrained vector quantization," *IEEE Trans. Acoustics, Speech, and Signal Processing*, Vol. 37, pp. 31-42, Jan., 1989.

[10] P. Maragos and R. W. Schafer, "Morphological systems for multidimensional signal processing," *Proceedings of the IEEE*, Vol. 78, pp. 690-710, April 1990.

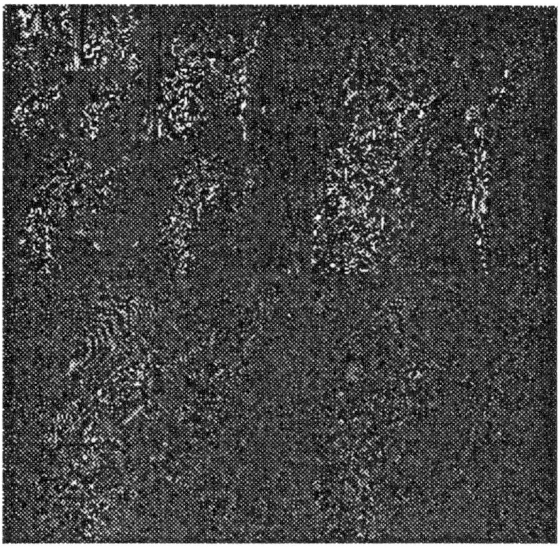

Figure 1: 4-level wavelet decomposition of 512 $\times$ 512 Lena Image

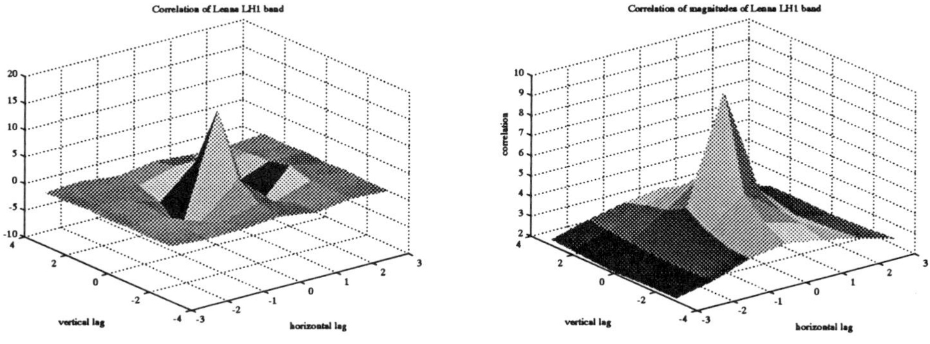

(a) (b)

Figure 2: (a) Correlations of the LH1 band unquantized wavelet coefficients for the "Lenna" image; (b) Correlations of the *magnitudes* of the unquantized coefficients.

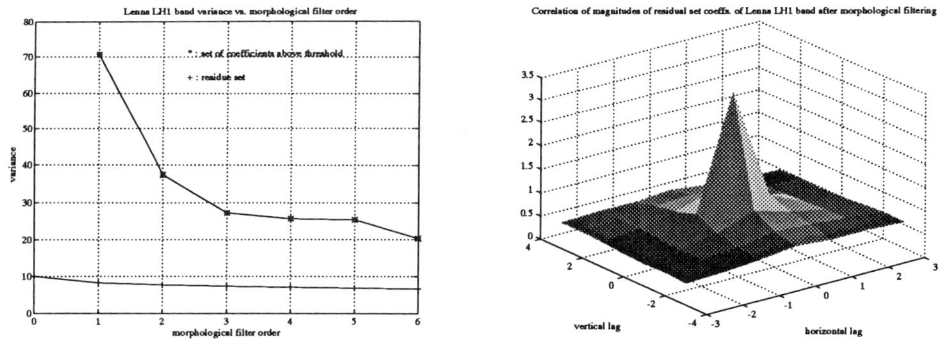

(a) (b)

Figure 3: (a) Variances of the sets of significant and insig nificant (residue) coefficients respectively as a function of the morphological filter order. Significance is with respect to an absolute threshold of 16 for the LH1 band coefficients of the Lenna image. Note the marked disparity in variances between the two sets. (b) Post-morphological filter (6th order) correlation of magnitudes of the residue set. Compare to Fig. 3(b) and note the decrease in the correlation compared to that for the original unquantized set.

Filter Evaluation and Selection in Wavelet Image Compression

John D. Villasenor, Benjamin Belzer, and Judy Liao
Electrical Engineering Department
University of California, Los Angeles
405 Hilgard Avenue
Los Angeles, CA 90024-1594

Abstract

Choice of filter bank in wavelet compression is a critical issue that affects image quality as well as system design. Although regularity is sometimes used in filter evaluation, its success at predicting compression performance is only partial. A more reliable evaluation can be obtained by considering an L-level synthesis/analysis system as a single-input, single-output, linear shift-variant system with a response that varies according to the input location modulo $(2^L, 2^L)$. *By characterizing a filter bank according to its impulse response and step response in addition to regularity, we obtain reliable and relevant (for image coding) filter evaluation metrics. Using this approach, we have evaluated all possible reasonably short (less than 34 taps in the synthesis/analysis pair) minimum order biorthogonal wavelet filter banks. Of this group of over 4300 candidate filter banks, we have selected and present here the filters best suited to image compression. While some of these filters have been published previously, others are new and have properties that make them attractive in system design.*

I. Introduction

Wavelet transforms have received significant attention recently due to their suitability for a number of important signal and image processing tasks including image coding. The principle behind the wavelet transform, as elaborated in a number of recent papers [1, 2, 3, 4], is to hierarchically decompose an input signal into a series of successively lower-resolution reference signals and their associated detail signals. At each level, the reference signal and detail signal (or signals in the separable multidimensional case) contain the information needed to reconstruct the reference signal at the next higher resolution level. Efficient image coding is enabled by allocating bandwidth according to the relative importance of information in the reference and detail signals, and then applying scalar or vector quantization to the transformed data values [5, 6].

Many issues relating to the choice of filter bank for image compression remain unresolved. Regularity [11] has been suggested as a criterion for filter evaluation, but as a recent author noted in reference to wavelet transforms, "the importance of regularity for signal processing applications is still an open question" [7]. Furthermore, there is only a partial correlation between filter regularity and reconstructed image quality. Wavelet choice has been considered by other authors [10, 12] but the methods of these papers rest on the assumption of orthogonality, which can be incompatible with other desirable filter characteristics. The techniques we present make no assumptions regarding filter orthogonality; we are concerned instead with the relationship between data in the input signal, their representation in the reference signal and the reconstruction to which it leads.

Wavelet filter banks are characterized in terms of their associated continuous scaling functions and wavelets derived under iteration. This viewpoint is crucial and indeed constitutes a basis for the work presented here. However, since a biorthogonal filter bank has associated with it four such functions (the scaling functions and wavelets for the analysis and synthesis stages) it is difficult to intuitively relate the reconstructed image quality to the form of these functions. In the past, conclusions regarding the suitability of various filter banks for image coding have been made on a somewhat ad-hoc basis by compressing a set of images using several different filters. The reconstructed images with the best subjective and NMSE quality are then identified, and the properties of the scaling functions of the filter banks furnishing the best reconstruction observed. By contrast, we adopt an end-to-end approach to the wavelet decomposition/reconstruction based on the lowest-level reference signal. This allows a more intuitive input-output description in terms of a shift-variant linear system to be elaborated, and clearly explains observations by previous authors regarding the greater importance of the synthesis (versus analysis) scaling function in compression performance. Our approach still requires that compression be performed experimentally on a series of impulse and step functions, but it furnishes a unified framework involving classical criteria such as impulse response, sidelobe strength, and shift-variance minimization to the characterization, evaluation and comparison of candidate filter banks. Although one previous author [13] has proposed evaluating filter banks based on reconstruction from the reference signal, the derivation we present allowing impulse response description in terms of the scaling functions is new, as are the results which follow from this fundamental equation (equation (9)).

Section II very briefly reviews wavelet concepts that are important to our presentation and introduces relevant notation. Section III describes our approach in which only the reference signal at the lowest resolution level is retained, allowing the entire analysis/synthesis system to be viewed as a linear, shift-variant system as discussed above. We show that the impulse responses of such a system satisfy difference equations involving both the analysis and synthesis scaling functions. In Section IV we present results and discussion and include a table giving some of the best biorthogonal filters for image compression applications.

II. Scaling functions, wavelets, and their relation to filter banks

IIA. Discrete wavelet transforms

One dimensional discrete wavelet transforms (the separable 2D case is a straightforward extension) can be described in terms of a filter bank as shown in Figure 1a. An input signal $x(n)$ is input to the analysis low pass filter $h_0(n)$ and the analysis high-pass filter $h_1(n)$. The odd samples of the outputs of these filters are then discarded, corresponding to decimation by a factor of two. The decimated outputs of these filters constitute the reference signal $r_1(n)$ and detail signal $d_1(n)$ for a one-level decomposition. For reconstruction, interpolation by a factor of two is performed, followed by filtering using the low-pass and high-pass synthesis filters $g_0(n)$ and $g_1(n)$ as shown. Provided that the system satisfies the perfect reconstruction property, the sum of the outputs of synthesis filters will give $y(n) = Ax(n - n_d)$ where A is a gain factor and n_d is an odd delay.

For a multilevel decomposition, the reference signal $r_1(n)$ serves as the input to a filter bank whose analysis stage is identical to that of Figure 1a. This process, repeated iteratively as shown in Figure 1b, provides after L levels a reference signal $r_L(n)$ with resolution reduced by factor 2^L with respect to the original input $x(n)$, as well as the detail signals $d_L(n)$ $d_{L-1}(n)$, ..., $d_1(n)$. Each detail signal $d_i(n)$ contains precisely the information which, together with the reference signal $r_i(n)$, enables reconstruction of $r_{i-1}(n)$, the reference signal at the next higher resolution. One can associate with a multilevel analysis filter bank (similar to Figure 1b but with an arbitrary number of levels in the low-pass branch) a continuous scaling function and wavelet. A generally different scaling function and wavelet are associated with the synthesis stage. References [8] and [7] contain a thorough treatment of the relationship between the filter coefficients and scaling functions; here we include enough discussion to make the notation clear.

The equivalent filter corresponding to L levels of passage through the reference signal subtree can be expressed using the Noble identities as

$$h^{(L)}(n) = h(n) * h(n/2) * h(n/4) * \ldots * h(n/2^L) \tag{1}$$

where we follow the usual convention that $h(n/K) = 0$ whenever n is not a multiple of K. $H^{(L)}(n)$ is called the Lth iteration of the filter $h(n)$ and will have length $(2^L - 1)(N-1)+1$. In examining the convergence of the iterated filter to a continuous function, it is convenient to denote (after [7]) a piecewise constant function $f_h(x)$ associated with the ith iteration of $h(n)$ through:

$$f_h^{(i)}(x) = 2^{i/2} h^{(i)}(n) \qquad n/2^i \leq x < (n+1)/2^i \tag{2}$$

A filter $h(n)$ is said to be regular if $f_h^{(i)}(x)$ converges in the limit as $i \to \infty$ to a continuous function. In wavelet transforms, the infinite iteration of the analysis filter $h_0(n)$ is the analysis scaling function; i.e. $f_{h0}^{(\infty)}(x) = \phi_A(x)$, and the infinite iteration of the synthesis filter $g_0(n)$ gives the synthesis scaling function $f_{g0}^{(\infty)}(x) = \phi_S(x)$.

IIB. Filter Design

Constraints on filter design include perfect reconstruction, finite-length, and the regularity requirement that the iterated low-pass filters involved converge to continuous functions. The regularity constraint is the crucial distinction between wavelet transforms and perfect reconstruction filter banks and can be related to the number of zeros of the z-transform of the low-pass filters at $z = -1$. Another important characteristic that is often sought is linear phase in all of the filters in Figure 1a. This precludes the use of nontrivial orthogonal filters, but permits a class of filters known as biorthogonal. Biorthogonal filters differ from orthogonal filters in that the subspace spanned by the low-pass synthesis filter response and its even shifts $g_0(n-2k)$ is not orthogonal to that spanned by $g_1(n-2k)$. Completeness, however, is still maintained and any signal in $l^2(Z)$ has a non-zero projection in at least one of these subspaces.

Design techniques for both orthogonal and biorthogonal wavelet filter banks draw heavily on the theory of perfect reconstruction filter banks. Even when all of the above constraints are applied, there remains significant flexibility in filter choice. It has been demonstrated in [7], [8] that maximizing the number of zeros at $z = -1$ for both the analysis and synthesis filters, within reasonable constraints on the filter lengths, results in most cases in regular filters corresponding to smooth scaling functions and wavelets. It is shown in [8] that if the filter $H_0(z)$ is taken to be the length $2N+1$ binomial filter $B(z) = ((1+z^{-1})/2)^{2N}$ then the minimum order $G_0(z)$ for a perfect reconstruction system is the length $2N-1$ remainder filter

$$R(z) = 2\sum_{k=0}^{N-1} \begin{pmatrix} N-1+k \\ k \end{pmatrix} (-1)^k z^{-(N-1-k)} \left(\frac{1-z^{-1}}{2}\right)^{2k}.$$

Since $R(z)$ is linear phase it can be factored into linear phase polynomials with real coefficients by appropriate grouping of the zeros of $R(z)$, which appear in complex quads or real reciprocal pairs (unless they happen to fall on the unit circle). Thus for a given N many different linear phase filter designs are enabled by factoring $R(z)$ into linear phase factors and allocating the factors of $B(z)$ and $R(z)$ to either $H_0(z)$ or $G_0(z)$. In particular, if we fix the number of zeros N_h and N_g at $z = -1$ allocated to $H_0(z)$ and $G_0(z)$ such that $N_h + N_g = 2N$, then the number of possible linear phase filter designs based on the minimal order remainder filter $R(z)$ is 2^{N_r}, where $N_r = (2N-2)/4$ if $2N-2$ is a multiple of 4 and $N_r = (2N-4)/4+1$ otherwise. Here we assume that $R(z)$ has no zeros on the unit circle, which is true for all reasonably short filters ($N \leq 20$).

III. Filter bank selection

IIIA. The wavelet analysis/synthesis bank as a linear system

Our goal is to establish an approximate linear system model that can be used to evaluate the suitability of candidate filter banks for compression. In general, common coding techniques such as scalar and vector quantization and run-length coding preclude linear system description. However, if the number of levels L is small (two or three) the performance of wavelet compression schemes is approximated by the linear system in which the information in the lowest resolution reference signal $r_L(n)$ is perfectly preserved, and the information in the detail signals is discarded. This is similar to actual compression algorithms, where the reference signal is coded extremely accurately (up to 8 bits/pixel), and the detail signals are coded coarsely or discarded. Since the reference signal is finely quantized while the detail signals must be coarsely quantized, it is better to use a filter bank which packs the maximum amount of information about the original image into the reference signal. In addition, the filter bank should not result in a decomposition which leads to artifacts in the image reconstructed from the reference signal alone. This is because these artifacts, which would be canceled by the information in the detail signals if lossless coding were used, can only be partially canceled when the detail signals undergo the severe compression necessary to achieve reasonable overall coding rates. By seeking a filter bank which leads to the highest fidelity reconstruction based on the reference signal, we are distributing the information in the wavelet transform domain in a manner consistent with priority it will given in the coding. We have found that selecting filters in this manner does in fact result in superior image quality when a full coding scheme (i.e. one in which reference and detail signals are coded) is utilized.

For a given filter bank, we can characterize the performance of a wavelet compression system in terms of a shift-variant impulse response relating an impulse $\delta(n - n_i)$ at the input to its reconstruction $h_{AS}^{(L)}(n, n_i)$ obtained using an L-level decomposition when only the reference signal is retained. The shift variance of the system is reflected by the parameter n_i. For a general shift-variant system with a length-N input signal, there are N different impulse responses as n_i varies between 0 and $N-1$.

Since an input image and its reconstruction based on the reference signal are related by a linear shift-variant system, our approach is to identify filter banks whose associated impulse and step responses are well-behaved according to classical criteria of minimum shift variance and sidelobe strength. The shift variance of wavelet transforms has been observed by Strang [4] and Mallat [3] and is viewed as one of the principle disadvantages of applying wavelet techniques to signal and image processing tasks. Given a coding scheme in which an input signal $x(n)$ is decomposed and then reconstructed to furnish $y(n)$, we wish to minimize the sensitivity of the reconstruction to shifts of the input. While strict shift invariance is not achievable, there is an enormous variety in the degree of shift variance associated with different biorthogonal filters. A simple example will suffice to illustrate this point. Figure 2a shows, all of the possible (excluding symmetries) impulse responses associated with a three-level 1D transform using filter 1 from Table 1. Although the impulse response is a function of input location modulo 8, symmetries reduce the number of distinct curves to five. We have plotted all five of these responses on the same graph to emphasize the variation that occurs as the input location is changed. Figure 2b shows the corresponding curves associated with filter 3 from Table 1. While both filter banks display shift-variance, the extent of shift-variance, is clearly larger in figure 2a.

An additional goal is to minimize oscillatory behavior, or ringing, in the system response, as this leads to highly objectionable artifacts in the reconstructed image. To achieve this, we select filters resulting in impulse responses having a favorable peak to sidelobe ratio. In addition, we examine the step responses and identify filters with low "undershoots" (the second oscillation, which occurs immediately after the initial overshoot). As with shift invariance, substantial variation exists in oscillatory behavior among valid biorthogonal filter banks. A further complication arises because impulse and step responses are of course shift-variant themselves, and must be somehow combined into a single measure. Simultaneous minimization of shift-variance, impulse response peak to sidelobe ratio, and step response oscillations is not possible, and the relative importance of these characteristics clearly depends on the application in question. For the work discussed here, we searched the space of valid biorthogonal filter solutions for filters achieving a reasonable compromise.

IIIB. Impulse Response derivation

Consider the input sequence $x(n) = \delta(n - n_i)$, where n_i is located sufficiently far from the boundaries so that edge effects do not occur. After 1 level of decomposition, the reference signal $r_1(n)$ will be the result of convolving $x(n) = \delta(n - n_i)$ with the low-pass synthesis filter $h_0(n)$, followed by decimation by a factor of two. Depending on whether n_i is even or odd, $r_1(n)$ will contain either the even or odd coefficients of the filter $h_0(n)$. The reference signal $r_2(n)$ is obtained by convolving $r_1(n)$ with $h_0(n)$ and decimating the result. and the general case of L levels entails L filter/decimate operations. The analysis impulse response $h_A^{(L)}(n, n_i)$ at the output of the final decimator is obtained by retaining one out of every 2^L samples, and can be expressed as samples of the piecewise constant function $f_{h0}^{(L)}$ associated with the Lth iteration of $h_0(n)$:

$$h_A^{(L)}(n, n_i) = f_{h0}^{(L)}(n - \frac{n_i}{2^L}) \tag{3}$$

Note that the analysis impulse response is finite duration because it consists of samples of a compactly supported function $f_{h0}^{(L)}(x)$. Let the lengths of the analysis and synthesis low pass filters be N_A and N_S respectively. Depending on the location n_i of the delta function and on whether N_A is even or odd, $h_A^{(L)}(n, n_i)$ will contain up to $N_A - 1$ non-zero values. Furthermore, since $h_A^{(L)}(n, n_i)$ is composed of unit-interval samples of $f_{h0}^{(L)}(x)$ offset by $n_i/2^L$, there are in general 2^L different impulse responses that can occur. When symmetry is considered the number of distinct impulse responses will reduce to 2^{L-1} when N_A is even and $2^{L-1} + 1$ when N_A is odd. The particular impulse response that will be expressed for a given n_i depends on $n_i \bmod 2^L$.

Now consider a reference signal of the form $r_L(n) = \delta(n - n_j)$, where $0 \le n \le N/2^L$. Provided as discussed above that the detail signals $d_i(n)$ are equal to zero for $1 \le i \le L$, the reference signal at level $L - 1$, found by interpolating $r_L(n)$ and filtering it with $g_0(n)$, will be $r_{L-1}(n) = g_0(n - 2n_j)$. To generate the reference signal at level $L - 2$, interpolation followed by filtering with $g_0(n)$ is performed again. This procedure, repeated a total of L times, generates a shifted version of the Lth iteration of the filter $g_0(n)$. The synthesis impulse response relating the reference signal $r_L(n) = \delta(n - n_j)$ and the reconstructed sequence it generates is therefore

$$h_S^{(L)}(n, n_j) = f_{g0}^{(L)}(\frac{n}{2^L} - n_j) \tag{4}$$

Note that in contrast with the analysis impulse response (equation (3)) which has approximately constant length regardless of the number of levels L, the synthesis impulse response $h_S^{(L)}(n, n_j)$ has a length that grows with L according to $(2^L - 1)(N_S - 1) + 1$. In addition, because the reconstruction involves interpolation rather than decimation, the numerical values contained in the response $h_S^{(L)}(n, n_j)$ are independent, to within a shift, of n_j.

Combining the synthesis impulse response $h_S^{(L)}(n, n_j)$ with the analysis impulse response $h_A^{(L)}(n, n_i)$ gives the impulse response $h_{AS}^{(L)}(n, n_i)$ of the combined L-level analysis/synthesis system. Noting that reconstruction from a general reference signal is the linear combination:

$$\sum_k r_L(k) \; f_{g0}^{(L)}(\frac{n}{2^L} - k) \tag{5}$$

and that when the input is $x(n) = \delta(n - n_i)$, the reference signal will be

$$r_L(n) = h_A^{(L)}(n, n_i) = f_{h0}^{(L)}(n - \frac{n_i}{2^L}). \tag{6}$$

Substituting (6) into (5) gives:

$$h_{AS}^{(L)}(n, n_i) = \sum_k f_{h0}^{(L)}(k - \frac{n_i}{2^L}) \; f_{g0}^{(L)}(\frac{n}{2^L} - k) \; . \tag{7}$$

We can associate the impulse response with a piecewise continuous function in the manner of equation (3):

$$f_{AS}^{(L)}(x, \Delta x) = 2^{L/2} h_{AS}^{(L)}(n, n_i) \qquad n/2^L \leq x < (n+1)/2^L \tag{8}$$

where $\Delta x = n_i/2^L$ and expresses the offset of the input delta function as a fraction of 2^L. When the number of levels L becomes infinite, we have $f_{h0}^{(\infty)}(x) = \phi_A(x)$ and $f_{g0}^{(\infty)}(x) = \phi_S(x)$, and the impulse response converges to a family of continuous functions given by

$$\lim_{L \to \infty} f_{AS}^{(L)}(x, \Delta x) = f_{AS}^{(\infty)}(x, \Delta x) = \sum_i \phi_A(i - \Delta x) \;\; \phi_S(x - i) \tag{9}$$

IV. Results and Discussion

Equation (7) shows that in general the impulse response of a wavelet filter bank is a linear combination of the iterated synthesis low-pass filter response using weights that are samples of the iterated analysis low-pass filter response. In the limit of large L, the impulse response becomes a combination of the synthesis scaling function and its unit shifts, with weights that are samples of the analysis scaling function. Several important practical properties of wavelet transforms follow directly from the limiting case expressed in equation (9).

First, the impulse response will be a linear combination of approximately N_A shifted versions of $\phi_S(x)$. As a result, the smoothness of $f_{AS}^{(\infty)}(x)$ is essentially the same as that of $\phi_S(x)$. This explains the greater importance of the synthesis scaling function (relative to the analysis scaling function) in determining the quality of a reconstructed image. If in a given filter bank, one of the scaling functions has sharp edges while the other is smooth, it is better to choose the smooth function for the synthesis filter. If the analysis filter is short, $\phi_A(i)$ will contain only a few non-zero values and the undesirable properties of the analysis filter will not generally be passed on to the impulse response.

Although longer analysis filters will cause a greater number of shifted versions of $\phi_S(x)$ to be summed to give the impulse response, the width of the main lobe of $\phi_A(x)$ will be approximately constant regardless of N_A in accordance with the half-band low-pass nature of $h_0(n)$. As a result, many of the samples of $\phi_A(x)$ will have very small magnitudes and will not contribute significantly to the impulse response. What does change as N_A increases is the potential for oscillatory behavior ("ringing") of $\phi_A(x)$, which can increase the number of significant samples used in equations (7) and (9).

Once the impulse response and step response are obtained for a given filter bank, they can be evaluated using any number of criteria. We have found that the most common and objectionable artifacts in reconstructed images are ringing near sharply defined feature boundaries. To select filters less likely to introduce ringing, we chose as our measures the peak to first sidelobe ratio of the impulse response (minimized over all shifts), and the average second sidelobe of the step response.

We evaluated and ranked all (total of over 4300) of the minimum order biorthogonal filter banks with combined analysis/synthesis filter lengths of ≤ 34 according to the impulse and step response criteria given above, and calculated the Holder regularity [11] of the analysis and synthesis filters. To empirically evaluate the performance of each filter and to allow comparison with the rankings obtained using the impulse and step responses, we also performed 16:1 compression on actual images using an algorithm with three levels of decomposition followed by scalar quantization of the subbands. The quantization step sizes were chosen adaptively on an image-specific basis using an approach similar to that proposed by the FBI for compression of grayscale fingerprint images [15].

We present in Table 1 the results of our evaluation. For each filter bank, we give the the analysis (H_0) and synthesis (G_0) low-pass filter length, filter coefficients, and regularity. The impulse response peak to sidelobe ratio and step response 2nd sidelobe strength are also given. We also give the average PSNR over 8 test images using the compression algorithm mentioned above. The final column of the table gives the references (where applicable) to other publications where the filter is discussed, as well as comments. In addition to listing the best filter banks, we have also included two other filter banks that are of interest despite their poorer performance. Filter 8 is included to illustrate that regularity alone is not a sufficient criterion. For this filter, the synthesis filter regularity is quite high, but the compression performance is extremely poor. We also include (filter 7) the results for the Haar basis. The Haar basis shows that a filter with poor regularity can still achieve reasonably good compression if it has good impulse and step response properties. Note that gain may be arbitrarily distributed between H_0 and G_0 as long as product of their DC gains is 2. Filters 4 through 7 may be renormalized by a factor of $\sqrt{2}$ to have shifted integer coefficients, thus greatly simplifying hardware implementation.

We found that even length filters have significantly less shift variance than odd length filters, suggesting that they may be better for many applications. For example it has been noted in [13] that even length filters reduce flicker noise in coded video images.

V. Conclusions

A multilevel analysis/synthesis wavelet filter bank can be evaluated by considering the reconstruction obtained from only the lowest level reference signal. This allows a description in terms of a linear, shift-variant system which can then be evaluated using criteria such as impulse and step response that are important in governing image quality. Although filter evaluation is made based only on the information preserved in the reference signal, the results remain valid when a full compression system employing quantization of both the reference and detail signals is used. Analysis of all reasonable length minimum order biorthogonal perfect reconstruction filters using these metrics identified filter banks that are well suited to image compression, including several that have not previously been published. While our interest was primarily in biorthogonal filters because of the greater analytical difficulty they present, the evaluation techniques we presented here could easily be applied to orthogonal filters or even to non-perfect reconstruction systems.

VI. Acknowledgement and References

This work was supported by the U.S. Department of Justice/Federal Bureau of Investigation, ARPA/CSTO under Contract J-FBI-93-112, Computer Aided Design of High Performance Wireless Networked Systems.

[1] A. Grossmann and J. Morlet, "Decomposition of Hardy functions into square integrable wavelets of constant shape," *SIAM J. Math. Anal.*, vol. 15, pp. 723-736, 1984.

[2] I. Daubechies, "Orthonormal bases of compactly supported wavelets," *Commun. Pure Appl. Match.*, vol. XLI, pp. 909-996, 1988.

[3] S. Mallat, "A theory for multiresolution signal decomposition: The wavelet representation," *IEEE Trans. Patt. Anal. Machine Intell.*, vol. 7, pp. 674-693, 1989.

[4] G.T. Strang, "Wavelets and dilation equations: A brief introduction," *SIAM Rev.*, vol. 31, pp. 614-627, 1989.

[5] M. Antonini, M. Barlaud, P. Mathieu, and I. Daubechies, "Image coding using wavelet transform," *IEEE Trans. on Image Proc.*, vol. 1, pp. 205-220, 1992.

[6] P. Desarte, B. Macq, and D. Slock, "Signal-adapted multiresolution transform for image coding," *IEEE Trans. Information Theory*, vol. 38, pp. 897-903, 1992.

[7] M. Vetterli and C. Herley, "Wavelets and filter banks: Theory and design," *IEEE Trans. on Signal Proc.*, vol. 40, pp. 2207-2232, 1992.

[8] A. Cohen, I. Daubechies, and J. C. Feauveau, "Biorthogonal bases of compactly supported wavelets," AT&T Bell Lab., Tech. Rep., TM 11217- 900529-07, 1990.

[9] E.P. Simoncelli, W.T. Freeman, E.H. Adelson, and D.J. Heeger, "Shiftable multiscale transforms," *IEEE Trans. on Information Theory*, vol. 38, pp. 587-607, 1992.

[10] A.H. Tewfik, D. Sinha, and P. Jorgensen, "On the Optimal Choice of a Wavelet for Signal Representation," *IEEE Trans. on Information Theory*, vol. 38, pp. 747-765, 1992

[11] O. Rioul, "Simple regularity criteria for subdivision schemes," *SIAM J. Math Anal.*, vol. 23, pp. 1544-76, 1992.

[12] R.R. Coifman and M.V. Wickerhauser, "Entropy-based algorithms for best basis selection," *IEEE Trans. on Inf. Theory*, vol. 38, pp. 713-718, 1992.

[13] T. Kronander, "New criteria for optimization of QMF banks to be used in an image coding system," *Proc. ISCAS '89*, pp. 1354-7, 1989.

[14] D. Le Gall and A. Tabatabai, "Subband coding of digital images using symmetric short kernel filters and arithmetic coding techniques," *Proc. ICASSP '88*, pp. 761-5, 1988.
[15] T. Hopper, C. Brislawn, and J. Bradley, "WSQ Gray-Scale Fingerprint Image Compression Specification, Version 2.0," Criminal Justice Information Services, Federal Bureau of Investigation, Washington D.C., February, 1993.

Figure 1a: Basic filter bank for wavelet transformation

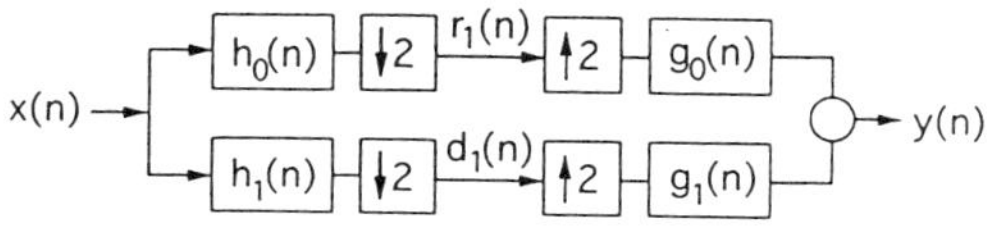

Figure 1b: Tree structure showing three-level transform

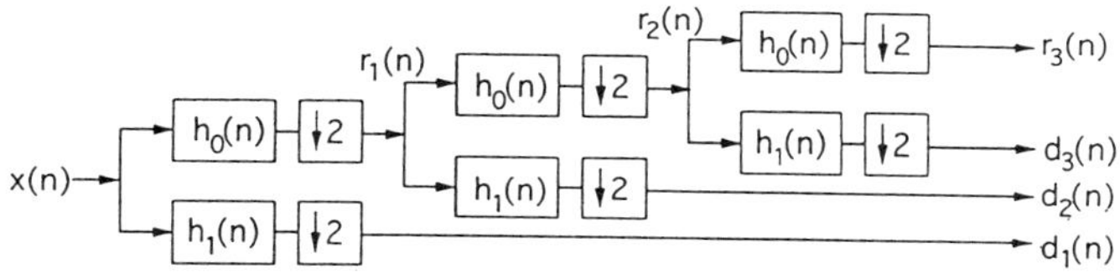

Fig. 2A: Imp. Resp. for Filter #1, Table 1 Fig. 2B: Imp. Resp. for Filter #3

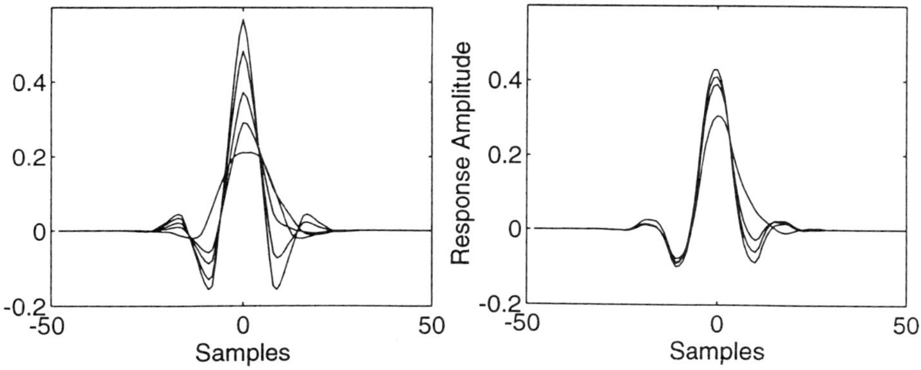

Figure 2: Comparison of shift variance for filters 1 (Fig 2a) and 3 (Fig 2b) from Table 1. In each case, all of the impulse responses (excluding symmetries) occurring when a three-level transform is used are shown. In a shift-invariant system, all impulse responses would be identical. The filter used in Fig. 2b clearly exhibits a lower degree of shift-variance than the filter used in Fig. 2a.

Table 1: Best Biorthogonal Filter Banks for Wavelet Image Compression

		Length	Filter coefficients (origin is leftmost coefficient, coefs for negative indices follow by symmetry)	Regu-larity	Imp. Resp.[1]	Step Resp[2]	PSNR[3]	Reference/ Comments
1	H_0	9	.852699, .377402, -.110624, -.023849, .037828	1.068	11.224	0.02707	29.67	[5]
	G_0	7	.788486, .418092, -.040689, -.064539	1.701				Good overall.
2	H_0	13	.767245, .383269, -.068878, -.033475, .047282, .003759, -.008473	1.899	10.901	0.03629	29.57	
	G_0	11	.832848, .448109, -.069163, -.108737, .006292, .014182	2.324				
3	H_0	6	.788486, .047699, -.129078	0.701	11.941	0.02431	29.53	Good IR, low
	G_0	10	.615051, .133389, -.067237, .006989, .018914	2.068				shift variance.
4	H_0	5	1.060660, .353553, -.176777	Diverg	10.458	0.00244	29.13	[14]
	G_0	3	.707107, .353553	1.000				Integer coeffs.[4]
5	H_0	2	.707107, .707107	0.000	17.457	0.01248	29.28	
	G_0	6	.707107, .088388, -.088388	1.000				Integer coeffs.[4]
6	H_0	9	.994369, .419845, -.176777, -.066291, .033145	0.830	11.080	0.01523	29.13	[5]
	G_0	3	.707107, .353553	1.000				Integer coeffs.[4]
7*	H_0	2	.707107, .707107	0.000	Inf	0.00000	27.48	Haar basis.
	G_0	2	.707107, .707107	0.000				Integer coeffs.[4]
8*	H_0	9	.544089, .296844, .041409, .056710, .040100	1.919	10.762	.04008	22.66	High reg, poor
	G_0	23	1.2680, .6337, -.2967, -.3712, .0072, .1098, .0116, -.0212, -.0027, etc.	3.437				performance.

1. Minimum peak to sidelobe ratio in dB among the eight possible impulse responses in a three-level decomposition.
2. Average fractional overshoot of second sidelobe of step response. A strong overshoot will lead to significant ringing in the reconstructed image.
3. Average PSNR in dB for 8 test images using a three level transform with adaptive scalar quantization of detail signals.
4. A single normalizing factor can be chosen to make all coefficients integers.

* Filters 7 and 8 give poorer performance but are included to illustrate points made in text. Filter 7 is the Haar basis and has zero regularity and good impulse and step responses. Filter 8 is a filter with high regularity but poor compression performance, and illustrates that regularity alone is not a sufficient criterion for filter choice.

Visibility of DCT basis functions: Effects of contrast masking

Joshua A. Solomon Andrew B. Watson Albert Ahumada

NASA Ames Research Center
Moffett Field, CA 94035-1000
jsolomon@vision.arc.nasa.gov

INTRODUCTION

DCT image compression. The discrete cosine transform (DCT) is a standard method by which images may be compressed. Initially, the image is divided into 8x8-pixel blocks, each of which is then transformed into its DCT, which is an 8x8 matrix of coefficients. Each coefficient c_{ij}, specifies the magnitude of a DCT frequency (or basis function), indexed by i,j. For brevity, we adopt a vector notation for the frequencies, so $\mathbf{U} = \{i, j\}$ and $c_{\mathbf{U}} = c_{ij}$. Image compression occurs when each coefficeint block is quantized by dividing it, coefficient by coefficient, by a quantization matrix (QM), and rounding to the nearest integer. For any given block of any image, there will be an 8x8 matrix of remainders produced by this division. The distortion introduced by this method of image compression can be expressed as an error image, which is the inverse transform of each of these remainder matrices. The magnitude of the entries in the QM determine the image quality and bit-rate. Small entries yield little compression and little distortion; large entries yield much compression and much distortion. To effectively compress an image, one must determine the QM which yields the desired bit-rate/distortion trade-off.

The contrast sensitivity function. The human visual system has different sensitivities to different DCT basis functions. Peterson, Peng, Morgan and Pennebaker[1] displayed images of replicated DCT basis functions. For a given ambient luminance, Peterson *et al.* determined the magnitude of the basis function required for human detection. Iteration of this technique with different coefficients yielded a contrast sensitivity function over the range of DCT basis functions. This contrast sensitivity function suggests a QM which is, to some extent, consistent with the human visual system.

Display parameters. Recognizing that the human DCT contrast sensitivity function is itself a function of display parameters such as display luminance and pixel size, Ahumada *et al.* [2,3] performed the measurements required to specify the contrast sensitivity function–and consequently, a more efficient QM–for any combination of these parameters.

Contrast masking. Watson[4] noted several image-dependent factors influencing the detectability of DCT basis functions and showed how to compute custom QMs for given images, in accord with these factors. One image-dependent factor influencing the detectability of DCT basis functions is contrast masking. Typically, sensitivity to quantization error, in a particular DCT coefficient, decreases with the magnitude of that coefficient. Watson's quantization scheme relies on the following model (based on seminal work by Legge and Foley[5,6]) for contrast masking: Given a DCT coefficient c_T and a corresponding absolute threshold t_T, the masked threshold m_T will be

$$m_T = t_T \,\mathrm{Max}\left[1, \left| c_T / t_T \right|^{w_T} \right], \tag{1}$$

where w_T is an exponent that lies between 0 and 1. In the sequel, we will refer to this model as Model 0. In Model 0, sensitivity to a particular coefficient's quantization error is independent of the magnitudes of all the other coefficients (except the DC). Here we present data which indicate that sensitivity to a particular coefficient's quantization error is affected by the magnitudes of other coefficients. We propose a revision of Model 0 to account for between-coefficient contrast masking.

METHOD

Apparatus. Stimuli were displayed on a monochrome CRT with a background luminance of 40 cd m^{-2}. The (binocular) viewing distance was 97.4 cm. At this distance, the spatial extent of the screen was 16° by 16° of visual angle. There was no other source of illumination.

Stimuli. Each stimulus was the sum of a test basis function and a mask basis function. Every pixel of the resultant image was magnified by a factor of 2, both vertically and horizontally, and added to the background luminance of the monitor. Each stimulus subtended 0.25 degrees by 0.25 degrees.

Procedure. Psychophysical threshold estimates were obtained with a version of the Quest procedure[7]. Each trial consisted of two stimulus presentations, each marked by an auditory tone and modulated by a temporal Gaussian with 0.53 seconds between $e^{-\pi}$ points, and separated by 0.5 seconds. The observer identified the test interval by pressing one of two keys. A correct choice was identified by a low frequency tone; an incorrect choice by a high frequency tone. Each plotted symbol in the following figures represents a maximum likelihood estimate of threshold based on a session of 64 trials.

Masked thresholds $m_{\mathbf{T}}$ for four test basis functions were measured as a function of masking contrast for three different masks. The tests, as identified by their DCT frequencies $\mathbf{T}$ were {0,0}, {0,1}, {0,3} and {0,7}. These last three also served as the masks. Additionally, {1,1} and {1,0} were used to mask {0,1}; and {2,2} was used to mask {0,3}. Absolute threshold $t_{\mathbf{T}}$ was also determined for each test. Theoretically, DCT coefficients can assume any real value. In the current study we use coefficients $c_{\mathbf{U}}$, such that $0 \le c_{\mathbf{U}} \le 1$. A coefficient with value 1 fully utilizes the dynamic range of the display. For nearly every test/mask combination, six masking contrasts were used. Here we express these contrasts in decibels ($\mathrm{dB}[c_{\mathbf{U}}] = 20 \ \mathrm{Log}_{10}[c_{\mathbf{U}}]$): -36, -30, -24, -18, -12 and -6. Because t_{07} is so high, when this basis function served to mask others, only the four greatest masking contrasts were used.

An experimental run, lasting about 10 minutes, was devoted to a single test/mask combination and a single masking contrast. Test/mask/masking-contrast combinations were run in a randomized fashion. The first author was the only observer in these experiments.

RESULTS AND DISCUSSION

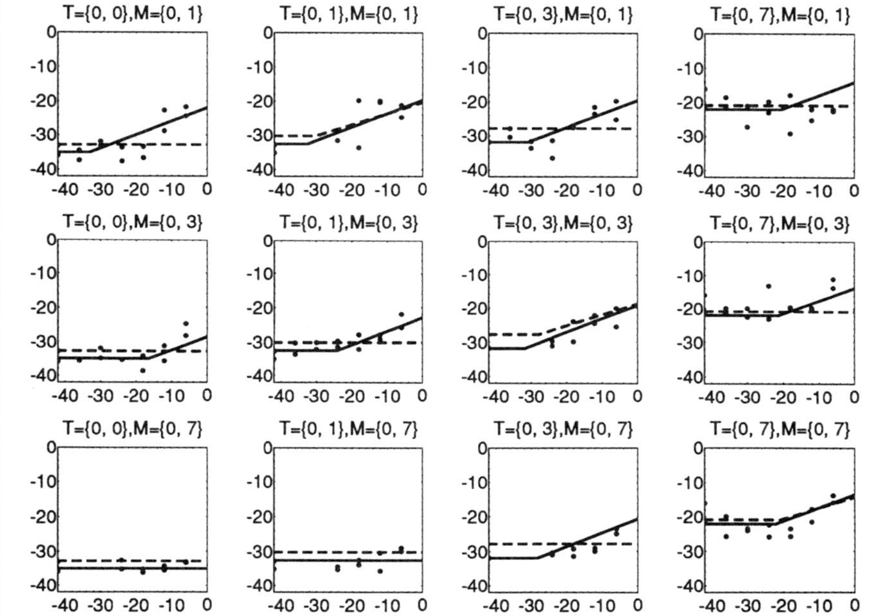

Fig. 1. Masked thresholds ($\mathrm{dB}[m_{\mathrm{T}}]$) for four test basis functions are plotted as a function of masking contrast ($\mathrm{dB}[c_{\mathrm{M}}]$) for three different masks. Unmasked thresholds ($\mathrm{dB}[t_{\mathrm{T}}]$) for the test basis functions are plotted on the ordinates. The dashed and solid lines are the predictions of Models 0 and 1, respectively, as described in the text.

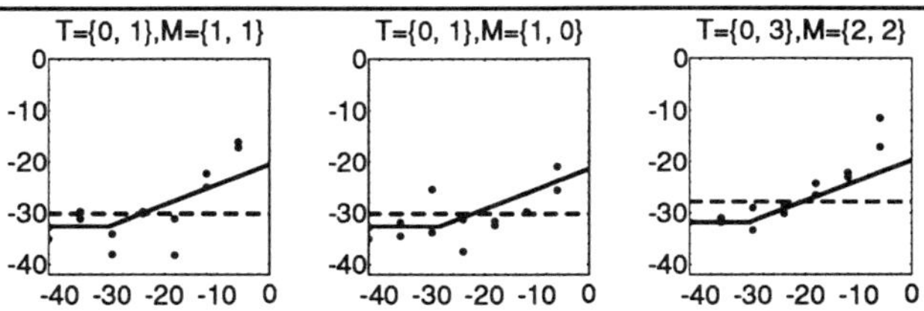

Fig. 2. Masked thresholds for test {0,1} as a function of masking contrast for the masks {1,1} and {1,0}, and for test {0,3} as a function of masking contrast for the mask {2,2}.

The dipper effect. The results are plotted in Figs. 1 and 2. Data gathered with the {0,1}/{0,1} test/mask combination at masking contrasts of -36 and -30 dB have been omitted from the graphs and further analysis. Similarly, we have omitted the {0,3}/{0,3} data at -36 and -30 dB. Measured thresholds for these four viewing conditions fall well below their corresponding unmasked thresholds. These data demonstrate the "dipper effect," a well-documented phenomenon wherein a low contrast grating increases the detectability of a grating of the same frequency and phase[5,8,9]. These data have been omitted because it is not clear that the dipper effect comes into play for natural images. For images composed of more than one 8x8 pixel block, DCT basis functions can appear as gratings (uniform values) or noise (random values; with a quantifiable variance) or anything in between. The dipper effect would appear if both test and mask were gratings. However, there is no indication that it would appear otherwise. The influence of a particular DCT coefficient on the dectability of quantization errors in natural images is similar in concept to the influence of a grating on the detectability of random visual noise. No dipper effect is expected in such a paradigm. Since we ultimately wish to model the detectability of quantization error in natural images, exclusion of the "dipper data" will benefit our initial approximations.

Model 0. Model 0 was fit to the data. Model 0 does not predict between-coefficient contrast masking. Consequently, for any given test basis function, its prediction for masked threshold is the same constant function of masking contrast for every mask having a non-zero coefficient at a different DCT index than the test. By setting all of the w_Ts in Eq. 1. equal to a single parameter w, the total variance (on a log scale) from the model increased by less than 0.3%. Hereafter, when we refer to Model 0, we mean specifically: Given a test DCT basis function c_T, its corresponding absolute threshold t_T and a mask DCT basis function $c_{\mathbf{M}}$ the masked threshold $m_{\mathbf{T}}$ will be

$$m_{\mathrm{T}} = \begin{cases} t_{\mathrm{T}}\ \mathrm{Max}\left[1, \left({c_{\mathrm{M}}}/{t_{\mathrm{T}}} \right)^{w}\right] & \text{for } \mathrm{T} = \mathrm{M} \\ t_{\mathrm{T}} & \text{otherwise} \end{cases} \quad (2)$$

where w is an exponent that lies between 0 and 1. Best fitting (method of least squares) values for w and the $t_{\mathbf{T}}$s, as determined for Model 0, are given in Table 1. Model 0 adequately reflects the data for the viewing conditions in which the mask and target were identical. However, it cannot reflect the between-coefficient masking evident by the increase in measured threshold with masking contrast for the other test/mask combinations.

Model 1. In order to reflect the between-coefficient masking, we propose the following revision of Watson's original model for contrast masking. It will be referred to hereafter as Model 1. Given a test DCT basis function $c_{\mathbf{T}}$, its corresponding absolute threshold $t_{\mathbf{T}}$ and a mask DCT basis function $c_{\mathbf{M}}$ the masked threshold $m_{\mathbf{T}}$ will be

$$m_{\mathrm{T}} = t_{\mathrm{T}}\,\mathrm{Max}\left[1, \left(f[\mathrm{T},\mathrm{M}] \frac{c_{\mathrm{M}}}{t_{\mathrm{T}}} \right)^{w}\right], \quad (3)$$

where w is an exponent that lies between 0 and 1 and $f(\mathrm{T},\mathrm{M})$ is a positive, frequency-dependent scaling factor, that assumes a maximum value of 1 when $\mathbf{T} = \mathbf{M}$. $f(\mathrm{T},\mathrm{M})$ may be described as a family of sensitivity functions. That is, for any test basis function $c_{\mathbf{T}}$, $f(\mathrm{T},\mathrm{M})$ reflects the sensitivity of $c_{\mathbf{T}}$ detection to masks at different frequencies. We have chosen to specify these sensitivity functions with the following one-parameter rule:

$$f(\mathrm{T},\mathrm{M}) = e^{-\pi\|\mathrm{T}-\mathrm{M}\|^2 / \sigma_{\mathrm{T}}^2}, \quad (4)$$

where $\sigma_{\mathrm{T}} = \sigma\,\mathrm{Max}[1, \|\mathrm{T}\|]$. Best fitting (method of least squares) values for σ, w and the $t_{\mathbf{T}}$s, as determined for Model 1, are also given in Table 1.

Model 0 vs Model 1. The average variance (squared rms error on a decibel scale) from Models 0 and 1 is also provided in Table 1.

Table 1

Parameter	Model 0	Model 1
$dB[t_{00}]$	-32.9	-35.1
$dB[t_{01}]$	-30.2	-32.6
$dB[t_{03}]$	-27.8	-31.9
$dB[t_{07}]$	-20.9	-22.1
w	0.324	0.396
σ	n/a	5.50
Average variance from model	16.5	8.95

CONCLUSION

With the addition of a single parameter (σ), our model for contrast masking captures 46% more of the variance in our data than Watson's original model. Incorporating this modification into the current method for computing DCT quantization matrices will yield more efficient image compression.

ACKNOWLEDGEMENTS

We thank Alan Gale and Mark Young for extensive assistance and Heidi Peterson for useful discussions. This work supported by NASA RTOPs 506-59-65 and 505-64-53.

REFERENCES

[1] H. A. Peterson, H. Peng, J. H. Morgan and W. B. Pennebaker. "Quantization of color image components in the DCT domain," in Human Vision, Visual

Processing, and Digital Display II, B. E. Rogowitz, ed. (Proceedings of the SPIE, 1991).

[2]A. J. Ahumada Jr. and H. A. Peterson. "Luminance-Model-Based DCT Quantization for Color Image Compression," in Human Vision, Visual Processing, and Digital Display III, B. E. Rogowitz, ed. (Proceedings of the SPIE, 1992).

[3]H. A. Peterson, A. J. Ahumada Jr. and A. B. Watson. "An improved detection model for DCT coefficient quantization," (Proceedings of the SPIE, 1993).

[4]A. B. Watson. "DCT quantization matrices visually optimized for individual images," in Human Vision, Visual Processing, and Digital Display IV, B. E. Rogowitz, ed. (SPIE, Bellingham, WA, 1993).

[5]G. E. Legge and J. M. Foley. "Contrast masking in human vision," Journal of the Optical Society of America, 70, 1458-1471 (1980).

[6]G. E. Legge. "A power law for contrast discrimination," Vision Research, 21 457-467 (1981).

[7]A. B. Watson and D. G. Pelli. "QUEST: A Bayesian adaptive psychometric method," Perception and Psychophysics, 33, 113-120 (1983).

[8]J. Nachmias and R. V. Sansbury. "Grating contrast: discrimination may be better than detection," Vision Research, 14, 1039-1042 (1974).

[9]C. F. Stromeyer, III and S. Klein. "Spatial frequency channels in human vision as asymmetric (edge) mechanisms," Vision Research, 14, 1409- 1420 (1974).

Visibility of DCT basis functions: Effects of display resolution

Andrew B. Watson Joshua A. Solomon Albert J. Ahumada, Jr.

NASA Ames Research Center
Moffett Field, CA 94035-1000
beau@vision.arc.nasa.gov

Introduction

The JPEG, MPEG, and CCITT H.261 image compression standards, and several proposed HDTV schemes, employ the Discrete Cosine Transform (DCT) as a basic mechanism [1, 2]. Typically the DCT is applied to 8 by 8 pixel blocks, followed by uniform quantization of the DCT coefficient matrix. The quantization bin-widths for the various coefficients are specified by a quantization matrix (QM). The QM is not defined by the standards, but is supplied by the user and stored or transmitted with the compressed images.

The principle that should guide the design of a QM is that it provide optimum visual quality for a given bit rate. QM design thus depends upon the visibility of quantization errors at the various DCT frequencies. In recent papers, Peterson *et al.* [3, 4] have provided measurements of threshold amplitudes for DCT basis functions at one viewing distance and several mean luminances. Ahumada and Peterson [5] have devised a model that generalizes these measurements to other luminances and viewing distances, and Peterson et al. [6] have extended this model to deal with color images. From this model, a matrix can be computed which will insure that all quantization errors are below threshold. Watson [7] has shown how this model may be used to optimize the quantization matrix for an individual image.

Visual resolution of the display (in pixels/degree of visual angle) may be expected to have a strong effect upon the visibility of DCT basis functions, and we therefore collected data to document this effect and to validate and enhance the model.

Plausible Pixel Sizes

Visual resolution of the display (in pixels/degree of visual angle) is determined by display resolution (in pixels/cm) and viewing distance (in cm), according to the formula

$$(\text{pixels/degree}) = (\text{pixels/cm}) \,/\, \cot^{-1}[\text{distance}]$$

In the viewing situations for which block-DCT compression is contemplated, there are limits to the practical range of visual resolutions. At the high end, display resolution will be wasted on spatial frequencies which are not visible to the human eye. The limit of human spatial resolution is about 60 cycles/degree. Nyquist sampling of this frequency would require 120 pixels/degree. This corresponds to 300 dpi printing viewed at a distance of about 23 inches. At the low end, the pixel raster becomes visible. In these experiments, we have examined three viewing distances, 16, 32, and 64 pixels/degree, that span a large part of the range of useful viewing distances.

Methods

Detection thresholds for single basis functions were measured by a two-alternative, forced-choice method. Each trial consisted of two time intervals of 0.5 second, within one of which the stimulus appeared. The stimulus was a single DCT basis function, added to the uniform gray background that remained throughout the experiment. Background luminance was 40 cd m^{-2}, and frame rate was 60 Hz. Observers viewed the display screen from distances of 48.7, 97.4, 194.8 cm. Display resolution was 37.65 pixels/cm. Images were magnified by two in each dimension, by pixel replication, to reduce monitor bandwidth limitations, resulting in magnified pixel sizes of 1/16, 1/32, and 1/64 of a degree, respectively at the three viewing distances (basis functions were 1/2, 1/4, and 1/8 degree in width). We describe these three viewing distances as yielding effective visual resolutions of 16, 32, and 64 (magnified) pixels/degree.

During presentation, the luminance contrast of the stimulus was a Gaussian function of time, with a duration of 32 frames (0.53 sec) between $e^{-\pi}$ points. The peak contrast on each trial was determined by an adaptive QUEST procedure [8], which converged to the contrast yielding 82% correct. After completion of 64 trials, thresholds were estimated by fitting a Weibull psychometric function [9]. Thresholds are expressed as contrast (peak luminance, less mean luminance, divided by mean luminance), converted to decibel sensitivities ($-20 \log_{10}$[threshold])

To reduce the burden of data collection, we measured thresholds for only 30 of the possible 64 basis functions, as indicated in Fig. 1. We felt that thresholds would change sufficiently slowly as a function of DCT frequency that this sampling would constrain our model sufficiently.

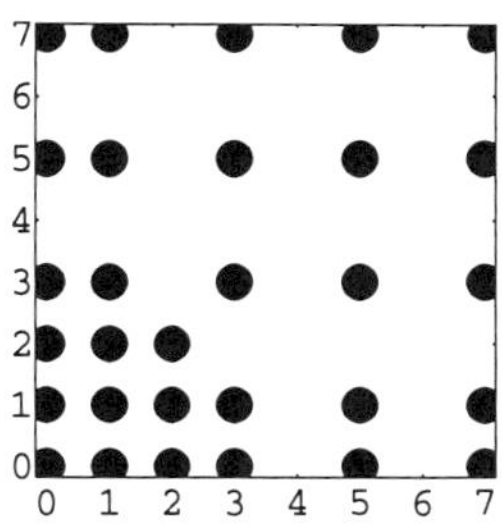

Figure 1. Subset of DCT frequencies used in the experiment.

To date, two data sets have been collected at the low resolution, five at the middle resolution, and one at the highest resolution, as shown in Table 1.

resolution (pixels/degree)	observer				
	abw	mjy	aig	sj	jas
16	0	30	0	30	0
32	7	30	60	30	30
64	0	30	0	2	0

Table 1. Thresholds collected for each observer and viewing distance.

Model of DCT Contrast Sensitivity

The model of DCT contrast sensitivity that we consider here is essentially that described by Peterson et al. [6] In that model, log sensitivity versus log frequency is a parabola, whose peak value, peak location, and width vary with mean luminance. In addition, sensitivity at oblique frequencies ({u≠0,v≠0}) is reduced by a factor that is attributed to the orientation tuning of visual channels. The parameters of significance here are *s0* (peak sensitivity), *f0* (peak DCT frequency at high luminances), and *k0* (inverse of the *latus rectum* of the parabola), and *r* (the orientation effect).

Results

Figures 2, 3, and 4 show decibel contrast sensitivities for the three viewing distances, along with curves showing the predictions of the best fitting version of the model. Within each figure, the three panels show data for horizontal frequencies {u, 0}, vertical frequencies {0, v}, 45 degree orientations {u, v=u}, and the remaining obliques {u>0, 0<v≠u}, all plotted against the radial frequency $f = \sqrt{u^2 + v^2}$. In the case of the obliques, because there is no simple one-dimensional prediction to plot, we plot instead the deviations of the data from the model. These plots, and the fits, do not include the thresholds at {0,0} (DC), which are reserved for a separate discussion. The data at 64 pixels/degree also omit 3 thresholds at very high frequencies which we suspect to be artifactual.

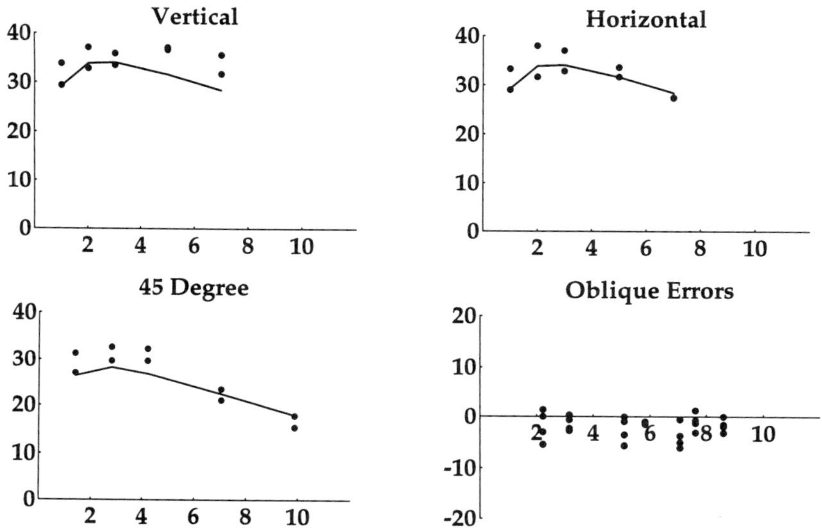

Figure 2. DCT basis function sensitivities at 16 pixels/degree.

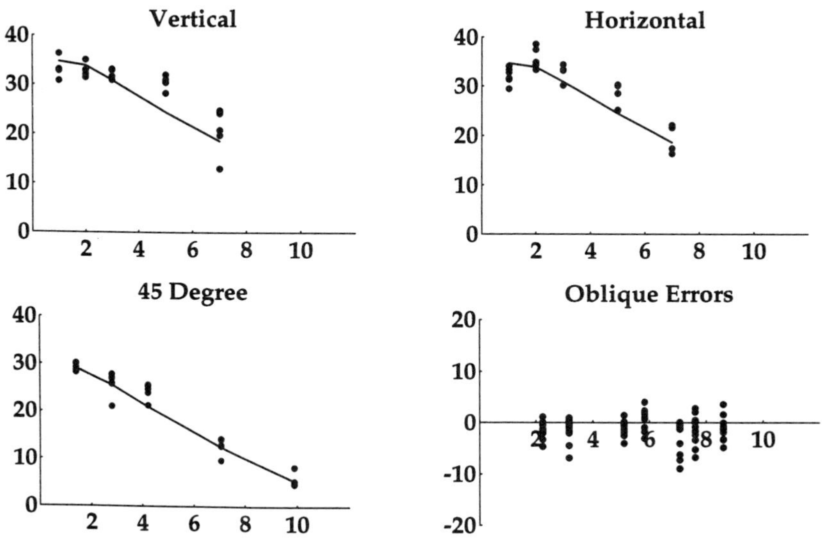

Figure 3. DCT basis function sensitivities at 32 pixels/degree.

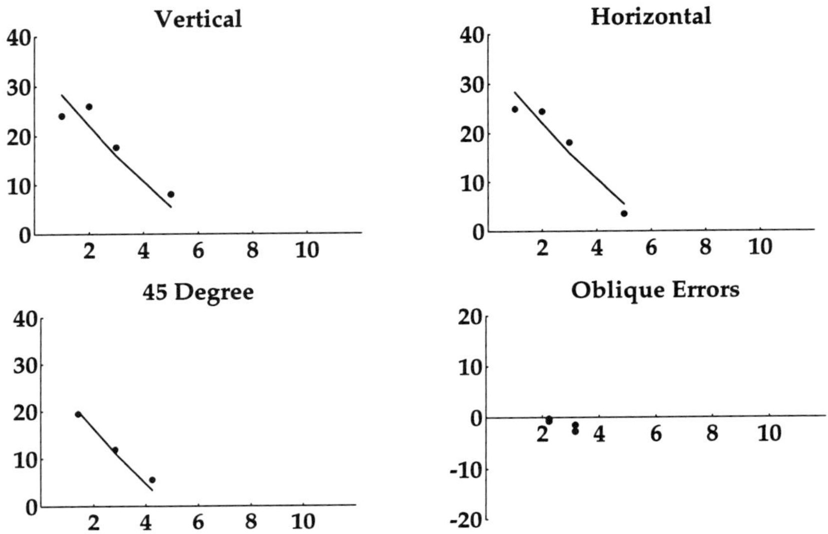

Figure 4. DCT basis function sensitivities at 64 pixels/degree.

The fits are reasonable, though there appear to be some systematic departures from the model. For reference, the RMS error of the raw data at the middle distance is 2.03 decibels, while the RMS error of the fit in Fig.s 2-4 is 2.94 decibels. The estimated parameters are shown in Table 2.

	pixels/degree		
	16	32	64
s0	51.1	56.17	29.84
f0	1.728		
k0	3.68		
r	0.5115		

Table 2. Estimated model parameters.

The parameters *f0, k0, and r* (related to peak frequency, bandwidth, and orientation effects) are equated for all resolutions, while a separate value of *s0* (peak contrast sensitivity) is estimated for each of the three resolutions. The behavior of this parameter is worth considering. Between 64 and 32 pixels/degree, it increases by a factor of 1.88. Between these two resolutions, the basis functions increase in size by a factor of two in each dimension. Thus if sensitivity increased linearly with area (as it should for very small targets [10, 11, 12]) we would expect an increase of a factor of 4. If sensitivity increased due only to spatial probability summation [13, 14], we would expect a factor of about $4^{1/4}$ = 1.414. Thus the obtained effect is nearer to that expected of probability summation. At the closest viewing distance, despite a further magnification by 2, the parameter *s0* actual declines. While we would expect a smaller effect of size at the largest sizes, this decline is unexpected and may be due to 1) the relatively poor fit at this resolution, and 2) aspects of visual sensitivity which are not yet captured by the model.

DC Sensitivities

Figure 5 shows the sensitivities for DC basis functions at the three visual resolutions. Ahumada et al. [5, 6]proposed as a working hypothesis that DC sensitivity is given by the peak sensitivity s0. This prediction is given by the line drawn in Fig. 5. It captures some of the variation in the DC sensitivities, but further data will be needed to adequately test this model.

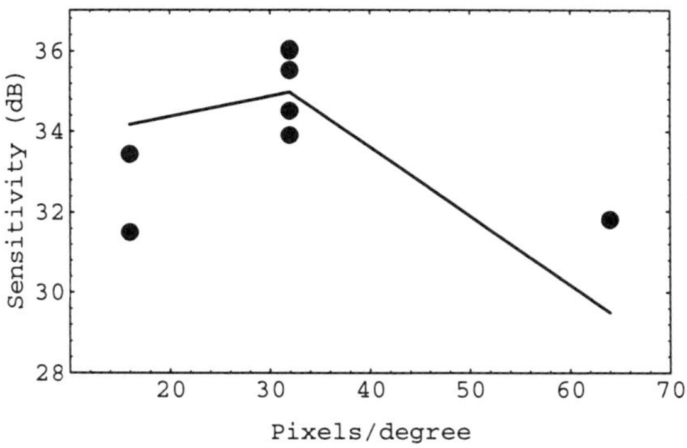

Figure 5. DC basis function sensitivities as a function of display visual resolution.

Discussion

We have examined the variation in visibility of single DCT basis functions as a function of display visual resolution. We have shown that the existing model [5, 6] accommodates resolutions of 16, 32, and 64 pixels/degree, provided that one parameter, the peak sensitivity s0, is allowed to vary. Variations in this parameter are to some extent consistent with spatial summation, although sensitivity is lower at the lowest resolution than summation would predict.

Practical DCT quantization matrices must take into account both the visibility of single basis functions, and the spatial pooling of artifacts from block to block. Elsewhere we have shown that to a first approximation this pooling is consistent with probability summation[15]. If we consider two images of equivalent size in degrees, but visual resolutions differing by a factor of two, then the sensitivity to individual artifacts would be lower by $4^{1/4}$ in the higher resolution image due to the smaller block size in degrees, but higher by $4^{1/4}$ in the same image due to the greater number of blocks. Thus the same matrix should be used with both. The point of this illustration is that the overall gain of the best quantization matrix must take into account both display resolution and image size.

Acknowledgements

We thank Alan Gale and Mark Young for extensive assistance and Heidi Peterson for useful discussions. This work supported by NASA RTOPs 506-59-65 and 505-64-53.

References

1. Pennebaker, W. B. and J. L. Mitchell. "JPEG Still image data compression standard." 1993 Van Nostrand Reinhold. New York.

2. Wallace, G. The JPEG still picture compression standard. Communications of the ACM. **34**(4): 30-44, 1991.

3. Peterson, H. A. "DCT basis function visibility in RGB space." Society for Information Display Digest of Technical Papers. Morreale ed. 1992 Society for Information Display. Playa del Rey, CA.

4. Peterson, H. A., H. Peng, J. H. Morgan and W. B. Pennebaker. Quantization of color image components in the DCT domain. Human Vision, Visual Processing, and Digital Display. Proc. SPIE. **1453**: 210-222, 1991.

5. Ahumada, A. J., Jr. and H. A. Peterson. "Luminance-Model-Based DCT Quantization for Color Image Compression." Human Vision, Visual Processing, and Digital Display III. Rogowitz ed. 1992 Proceedings of the SPIE.

6. Peterson, H., A. Ahumada and A. Watson. "An Improved Detection Model for DCT Coefficient Quantization." Human Vision, Visual Processing, and Digital Display IV. Allebach ed. 1993 SPIE. Bellingham, WA.

7. Watson, A. B. "DCT quantization matrices visually optimized for individual images." Human Vision, Visual Processing, and Digital Display IV. Rogowitz ed. 1993 SPIE. Bellingham, WA.

8. Watson, A. B. and D. G. Pelli. QUEST: A Bayesian adaptive psychometric method. Perception and Psychophysics. **33**(2): 113-120, 1983.

9. Watson, A. B. Probability summation over time. Vision Research. **19**: 515-522, 1979.

10. Noorlander, C., M. J. G. Heuts and J. J. Koenderink. Influence of the target size on the detection threshold for luminance and chromaticity contrast. Journal of the Optical Society of America. **70**(9): 1116-1121, 1980 .

11. Graham, C. H., R. H. Brown and F. A. Mote. The relation of size of stimulus and intensity in the human eye: I. Intensity thresholds for white light. J. Exp. Psychol. **24**: 555-573, 1939.

12. Barlow, H. B. Temporal and spatial summation in human vision at different background intensities. Journal of Physiology. **141** : 337-350 , 1958 .

13. Graham, N., J. G. Robson and J. Nachmias. Grating summation in fovea and periphery. Vision Research. **18** : 815-825 , 1978 .

14. Robson, J. G. and N. Graham. Probability summation and regional variation in contrast sensitivity across the visual field. Vision Research. **21**: 409-418, 1981.

15. Peterson, H. A., A. J. Ahumada Jr. and A. B. Watson. The Visibility of DCT Quantization Noise. SID Digest of Technical Papers. **XXIV**: 942-945, 1993.

On Lattice Quantization Noise

Ram Zamir and Meir Feder

Dept. of Electrical Engineering - Systems
Faculty of Engineering
Tel-Aviv University
Tel-Aviv, 69978, ISRAEL
(e-mail: zamir@eng.tau.ac.il or meir@eng.tau.ac.il)

Abstract

We present several results regarding the properties of a random vector, uniformly distributed over a lattice cell. This random vector is the quantization noise associated with dithered lattice quantization, and at high resolution it is the noise generated in regular lattice quantization of "smooth" sources. We find that the noise associated with the optimal lattice quantizers is wide-sense stationary and *white*. Any desirable noise spectra may be realized by an appropriate linear transformation ("shaping") of a lattice quantizer. As the dimension increases, the normalized second moment of the optimal lattice quantizer goes to $1/2\pi e$, and consequently the quantization noise approaches a white Gaussian process. Actually, in entropy coded dithered quantization where the quantization procedure can be modeled as an additive noise channel, this limit behavior implies that both the asymptotic MSE distortion and the mutual-information between input and output of the quantization channel, approaches the MSE and the mutual-information between input and output of an Additive White Gaussian Noise (AWGN) channel.

I. Lattice Quantization Noise Spectra

Before we present the results regarding lattice quantization noise, let us recall the definition of the lattice quantizer. The code points and the quantization cells of a K-dimensional lattice quantizer form a lattice $\mathcal{L} = \{l_i\}$ and an associated partition $\mathcal{P} = \{P_i\}$ of $\mathcal{R}^K$, respectively, such that

$$P_i = l_i + P_0 = \{\underline{x} : \ \underline{x} - l_i \in P_0\} \ . \tag{1}$$

 1068-0314/94 $3.00

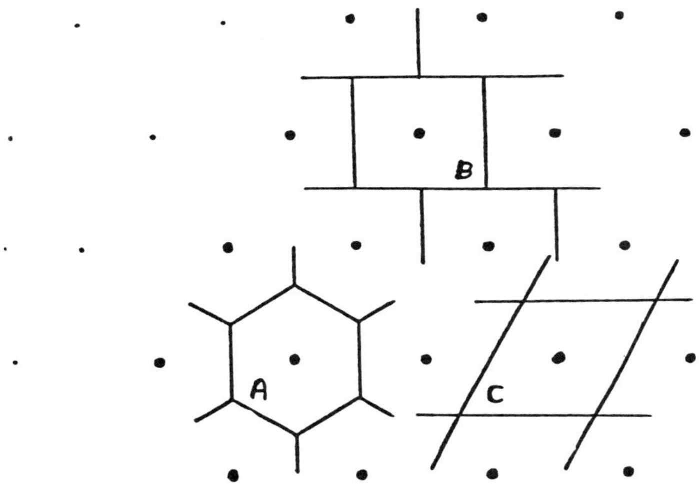

Figure 1: The Hexagonal lattice and three possible associated partitions: (A) Voronoi partition (hexagons), (B) rectangles, (C) rhombuses generated via shaping of the Z lattice and its Voronoi partition.

The *lattice quantizer* $Q_K = \{\mathcal{L}, \mathcal{P}\}$ maps every source vector $\underline{x} \in \mathcal{R}^K$ into the lattice point that is associated with the cell containing $\underline{x}$, i.e.,

$$Q_K(\underline{x}) = l_i, \quad \text{if} \quad \underline{x} \in P_i \; . \tag{2}$$

In general there are many possible partitions with respect to a given lattice, all have the same cells volume $V = \mu(P_0)$, given by the reciprocal of the lattice points density. When every source vector is mapped into the *nearest* code point, the quantization cell becomes a *Voronoi region*

$$V_i = \{\underline{x} : \; ||\underline{x} - l_i|| \leq ||\underline{x} - l_j||, \; \forall j \neq i\} \;\; , \tag{3}$$

where $||\cdot||$ denotes Euklidean norm. Figure 1 shows three possible partitions with respect to the hexagonal lattice, where partition A is into Voronoi regions.

In this paper we focus on the statistical properties of the vector $\underline{Z} \sim \mathcal{U}(P_0)$, uniformly distributed over the basic cell of Q_K. Following [1], [2] and [3], the noise generated in fine or in dithered quantization by the lattice quantizer Q_K is uniformly distributed over the mirror image of P_0, i.e., as $-\underline{Z}$. Hence, $R_z \triangleq E\{\underline{Z}\underline{Z}^t\}$ is the auto correlation matrix of the quantization noise, whose properties are the subject of this section. Note that since the lattice is not degenerated, i.e., it is not contained in any sub-space of $\mathcal{R}^K$, R_z is not singular.

Definition 1: *A lattice quantizer is "white" if its quantization noise samples are uncorrelated and have equal power, i.e.,*

$$R_z = \epsilon \cdot I \tag{4}$$

where $\epsilon = trace\{R_z\}/K$ is the mean square error per dimension of the lattice quantizer, and I is the identity matrix.

Following [4],

$$G(Q_K) \triangleq \frac{1}{K}\frac{\int_{P_0}||\underline{x}||^2 d\underline{x}}{V^{1+2/K}} = \frac{1}{K}\cdot\frac{E||\underline{Z}||^2}{V^{2/K}} = \frac{1}{V^{2/K}}\cdot\frac{\text{trace}\{R_z\}}{K}\,, \tag{5}$$

is the normalized second moment of Q_K. By the arithmetic-geometric means inequality,

$$G(Q_K) \geq \frac{1}{V^{2/K}}\cdot|R_z|^{1/K}\,, \tag{6}$$

where $|\cdot|$ denotes determinant, with equality iff R_z is a diagonal matrix with identical elements on the diagonal, i.e., iff Q_K is a *white lattice quantizer.* The *optimal* lattice quantizer in $\mathcal{R}^K$, denoted Q_K^{opt}, is the lattice quantizer having the minimal possible normalized second moment G_K^{opt}, where the minimization is over all lattice/partition pairs.

Theorem 1 *Q_K^{opt} is "white", and the auto-correlation matrix of its quantization noise is*

$$R_z = G_K^{opt} V^{2/K}\cdot I\;. \tag{7}$$

For example, the hexagonal lattice (A_2) and the body-centered cubic lattice (A_3), together with their Voronoi partitions, form *white* lattice quantizers. Before proving this theorem, we have to introduce the notion of "shaping" a lattice quantizer.

Definition 2: *$Q'_K(\underline{x}) = A\cdot Q_K(A^{-1}\underline{x})$ is the* shaping *of Q_K by A, where A is a $K\times K$ non singular matrix.*

It is easy to verify that $Q'_K = \{\mathcal{L}', \mathcal{P}'\}$ is a lattice quantizer, whose code points and quantization cells are

$$l'_i = Al_i \quad \text{and} \quad P'_i = \{\underline{x} :\; A^{-1}\underline{x}\in P_i\}\,, \tag{8}$$

respectively. For example, Partition C (the rhombuses) in Figure 1 was generated via shaping of the $\mathcal{Z}$ lattice and its associated Voronoi regions (which are squares), by the transformation

$$A = \begin{pmatrix} 1 & 1/2 \\ 0 & \sqrt{3}/2 \end{pmatrix}\;.$$

We observe the interesting fact that the transformed partition *$\mathcal{P}'$ is not the Voronoi partition* associated with the transformed lattice $\mathcal{L}'$! The Voronoi regions associated with the lattice in the example of Figure 1 are, of course, hexagons (Partition-A). The reason is that, in general, $||\underline{x}-l_i|| \leq ||\underline{x}-l_j||$ does not imply $||A(\underline{x}-l_i)|| \leq ||A(\underline{x}-l_j)||$, unless A is proportional to some measure preserving transformation (i.e., iff $AA^t \propto I$), and thus l_i is not necessarily the nearest code point after the transformation.

Figure 2 illustrates various shapings of the hexagonal-lattice/hexagonal-cells quantizer. The dashed line in Figure 2(b) shows the Voronoi cell of the transformed lattice.

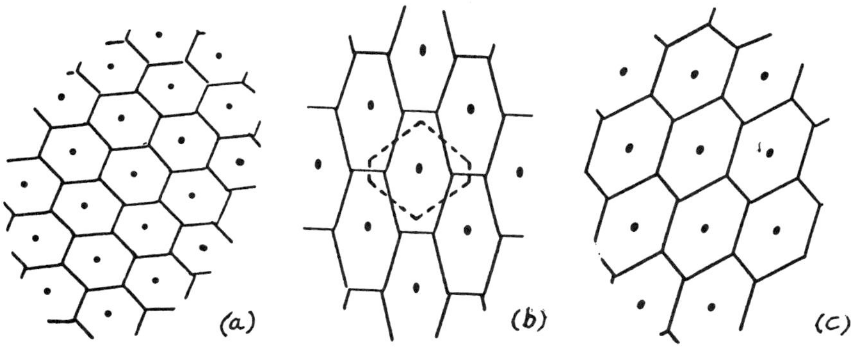

Figure 2: Various shapings of the hexagonal-lattice/hexagonal-cells quantizer: (a) rotation, (b) scaling to the north direction, (c) scaling to the north-east direction.

Following well known formulas from vector analysis, the volume of the shaped quantizer cells is $V' = \int_{P_0'} d\underline{x} = |A| \cdot \int_{P_0} d\underline{x} = |A| \cdot V$, and the noise vector of the shaped quantizer, $\underline{Z}' \sim \mathcal{U}(P_0')$, equals in distribution to $A\underline{Z}$. This implies

$$R_z' = AR_zA^t , \tag{9}$$

i.e., the transformation A "shapes" the spectrum of the quantization noise. We are now ready to prove Theorem 1.

Proof: Choose the *whitening* transformation

$$A = \sqrt{\epsilon} \cdot R_z^{-1/2} , \tag{10}$$

where $R_z^{-1/2}$ is the inverse of a square root of R_z and ϵ is a positive scalar, i.e., $AA^t = \epsilon \cdot R_z^{-1}$. Substituting into (9) we get that the auto-correlation matrix of the shaped noise is $R_z' = \epsilon I$, (i.e., Q_K' is a *white lattice quantizer*), and $V' = |A| \cdot V = \sqrt{\epsilon^K / |R_z|} \cdot V$. Using (5) and (6), we get

$$G(Q_K') = \frac{1}{(V')^{2/K}} \cdot \frac{\text{trace}\{\epsilon I\}}{K} = \frac{|R_z|^{1/K}}{V^{2/K}} \leq G(Q_K) , \tag{11}$$

with equality iff Q_K is white. Since, by definition, Q_K^{opt} must satisfy (11) with equality, the theorem is proved. □

Let us discuss some consequences of the derivation above. First, the "shaping" procedure implies that by appropriate linear transformation of a (non-degenerated) lattice quantizer one may get any desired quantization noise spectra. This is required, for instance, in coding under a *weighted squares* criterion $(\hat{\underline{x}} - \underline{x})^t W(\hat{\underline{x}} - \underline{x})$, where then we use a transformation A which satisfies $AA^t = W^{-1}$. Another case in which lattice quantizers with a non-Voronoi or non-white partition are used is in source coding schemes that incorporates pre- and post-filters or transforms (see e.g. [5]), which is a common procedure, for example, in the recent CELP techniques for speech coding.

Second, it follows from (10) and (11) and the optimality of the Voronoi partition, that the iteration between *whitening* and *Voronoi partitioning* monotonically reduce (i.e., improve) the normalized second moment of a given lattice quantizer. Note also that Theorem 1 adds another necessary condition to the well known Lloyd conditions [6], [7] for the optimal quantizer.

Finally, this theory may also be extended to infinite dimensional lattice quantizers, e.g., trellis quantizers. For this purpose, we replace the matrix A by the discrete time invariant shaping filter whose impulse response is $\{a_n\}$, $n = 0, \pm1, \pm2, \ldots$, and whose frequency response is $A(f) = \sum_n a_n \cdot e^{-jn2\pi f}$, $-1/2 \leq f \leq 1/2$. The shaped infinite lattice quantizer is now $Q'_\infty(x_n) = a_n * Q_\infty(a_n^{(-1)} * x_n)$, where x_n is a source sequence, $\{a_n^{(-1)}\}$ are the coefficients of the inverse filter (i.e., the inverse Fourier transform of $1/A(f)$), and $*$ denotes the convolution operator. Clearly, if the quantization noise spectrum is $S_z(f)$, then after shaping it becomes $|A(f)|^2 S_z(f)$. The normalized second moment of Q_∞ is defined as $G(Q_\infty) \triangleq (2\pi e)^{-1}\epsilon/P(Z)$, where ϵ is the power of Z, and $P(Z)$ is the entropy rate power of Z. This definition coincides with (5) in the finite dimensional case. Hence, if we shape a white quantizer we get $\epsilon' = \epsilon \cdot \int |A(f)|^2 df$, $P(Z') = P(Z) \cdot \exp\left(\int \ln |A(f)|^2 df\right)$ (see [8]), and thus

$$G(Q'_\infty) = G(Q_\infty) \cdot \frac{\int |A(f)|^2 df}{\exp\left(\int \ln |A(f)|^2 df\right)}$$

which, by Jensen's inequality, is greater than $G(Q_\infty)$ with equality if and only if $|A(f)|$ is white.

II. The Gaussian Limit Distribution of Lattice Quantizers Noise

In the previous section we investigated the spectral properties of the lattice quantization noise. This section addresses the *distribution* of the lattice quantization noise, and specifically it focuses on its distance from a Gaussian distribution. A Gaussian quantization noise is desirable, at least for Gaussian sources and MSE criterion, since it resembles the form of the noise in the forward-channel realization of the rate-distortion function (see [8]).

In our context, the natural measure for the distance of the quantization noise from a Gaussian distribution is the (information-) divergence (or "relative entropy" or "Kullback Leibler distance"). We define the *divergence from Gaussianity*, in bits, of a vector $\underline{U} \in \mathcal{R}^n$ with a density $f_{\underline{U}}$, as the divergence

$$\mathcal{D}(\underline{U};\underline{U}^*) = \mathcal{D}(f_{\underline{U}}||f_{\underline{U}^*}) = \int_{\mathcal{R}^n} f_{\underline{U}} \log \frac{f_{\underline{U}}}{f_{\underline{U}^*}} = h(\underline{U}^*) - h(\underline{U}) \tag{12}$$

between $\underline{U}$ and the Gaussian vector $\underline{U}^*$, having the same mean and covariance as $\underline{U}$, i.e., $E\{\underline{U}^*\} = E\{\underline{U}\}$ and $E\{\underline{U}^*\underline{U}^{*t}\} = E\{\underline{U}\underline{U}^t\}$. The decomposition into the difference between entropies in the RHS of (12) follows since $h(\underline{U}^*) \triangleq -\int f_{\underline{U}^*} \log f_{\underline{U}^*} = -\int f_{\underline{U}} \log f_{\underline{U}^*}$ (see [9] p. 234). Similarly, we may define the *divergence from white Gaussianity* as the divergence from a white Gaussian vector having the same power.

We now turn to examine the distance from Gaussianity, measured by the divergence, of the lattice quantization noise. The entropy per dimension of $\underline{Z}$ may be written as

$$\frac{1}{K}h(\underline{Z}) = \frac{1}{K}\log V = \frac{1}{2}\log(\epsilon/G(Q_K)) \,, \tag{13}$$

where $\epsilon = \frac{1}{K}E\|\underline{Z}\|^2$ is the second moment of Q_K, and V is the volume of its basic cell. Now, let $\underline{W}^* \sim \mathcal{N}(\underline{0}, \epsilon I)$ be a white Gaussian vector with power ϵ. The divergence of $\underline{Z}$ from white Gaussianity is given by

$$\frac{1}{K}\mathcal{D}(\underline{Z};\underline{W}^*) = \frac{1}{K}h(\underline{W}^*) - \frac{1}{K}h(\underline{Z}) = \frac{1}{2}\log 2\pi e\epsilon - \frac{1}{2}\log(\epsilon/G(Q_K)) = \frac{1}{2}\log 2\pi e G(Q_K) \tag{14}$$

bits per sample, where like in (12) the divergence was written as a difference between entropies. If the lattice quantizer is "white" (i.e., if $E\{\underline{Z}\underline{Z}^t\} = \epsilon \cdot I$), then $\underline{Z}^* = \underline{W}^*$ and the expression above equals to the divergence of $\underline{Z}$ from Gaussianity, $\frac{1}{K}\mathcal{D}(\underline{Z};\underline{Z}^*)$. Note that shaping the lattice quantizer does not affect $\mathcal{D}(\underline{Z};\underline{Z}^*)$, since the divergence is invariant to invertible transformation of its arguments. But, from the properties of $G(Q_K)$ shown in the previous section, $\mathcal{D}(\underline{Z};\underline{W}^*)$ does vary with shaping, and attains a minimum by whitening the lattice quantizer (i.e., by applying the transformation A of (10)).

The figure $\frac{1}{2}\log 2\pi e G(Q_K)$ is about 0.254 bits for uniform scalar quantizer, where $G(Q_1) = 1/12$, and about 0.227 bits for the 2-dimensional hexagonal quantizer. We show below that for the optimal lattice quantizers $G_K^{opt} \to \frac{1}{2\pi e}$, as $K \to \infty$, and thus, for these quantizers,

$$\frac{1}{K}\mathcal{D}(\underline{Z};\underline{W}^*) \to 0 \,, \quad \text{as } K \to \infty. \tag{15}$$

The interpretation of this result is that the distribution of the quantization noise converges to a Gaussian distribution in the *divergence rate sense.*

Before proving (15), we recall the well known fact that a ball has the minimal moment of inertia among all shapes of equal volume. A simple application of this property provides a lower bound on $G(Q_K)$, (5),

$$G(Q_K) \geq G_K^* \triangleq \frac{1}{K}\frac{\int_{S_K}\|\underline{x}\|^2 d\underline{x}}{V^{1+2/K}} = \frac{1}{\pi(K+2)} \cdot \Gamma^{\frac{2}{K}}(K/2+1) = \frac{1}{(K+2)\cdot V_K^{2/K}} \,, \tag{16}$$

where G_K^* denotes the normalized second moment of a K-dimensional ball S_K (see [4] p. 452), $\Gamma(\cdot)$ is the Gamma function, and $V_K = \frac{\pi^{K/2}}{\Gamma(K/2+1)}$ is the volume of a ball with a unit radius. From (16) we can compute $G_1^* = \frac{1}{12}$, and realize that, as $K \to \infty$, G_K^* decreases monotonically to the limit $\frac{1}{2\pi e} \approx \frac{1}{17}$ with a convergence rate given by $\log 2\pi e G_K^* = O\left(\frac{\log K}{K}\right)$. Now, the quantizer cell is never a ball. Nevertheless, we claim that $\frac{1}{2\pi e}$ can also be attained as the limit of G_K^{opt}:

Lemma 1

$$G_K^{opt} \to \frac{1}{2\pi e}\ , \quad as\ K \to \infty\ , \tag{17}$$

with a convergence rate given by

$$\log 2\pi e G_K^{opt} = O\left(\frac{\log K}{K}\right) . \tag{18}$$

Lemma 1 was originally inferred from [10] and a conjecture made by Gersho in [2] regarding the optimality of tessellating quantizers. The proof below is due to G. Poltyrev [11]:

Proof: Let R_u denotes the covering radius of P_0, and R_l denotes the radius of a ball having the same volume as P_0, i.e., $V = V_K \cdot R_l^K$. For any lattice quantizer Q_K, we can write

$$G_K^* \le G(Q_K) \le \left(\frac{R_u}{R_l}\right)^2 \frac{1}{K \cdot V_K^{2/K}} = \frac{\Theta^{2/K}}{K \cdot V_K^{2/K}}\ , \tag{19}$$

where $\Theta = \frac{V_K \cdot R_u^K}{V} \ge 1$ is the *density of the covering* of $\mathcal{R}^K$ by the lattice quantizer (see [4] p. 31). To see the right inequality in (19), note that, from (5), $G(Q_K) = \frac{1}{K}E||\underline{Z}||^2/V^{2/K}$ where $\underline{Z}$ is uniformly distributed over P_0, and, since $||\underline{z}|| \le R_u$ for every $\underline{z} \in P_0$, we have immediately $E||\underline{Z}||^2 \le R_u^2$.

Now, following a result by Rogers [4] p. 39, there exist lattices whose covering density (with respect to their Voronoi partition) satisfies

$$\Theta \le cK(\log K)^a\ , \tag{20}$$

for some constants c and a, implying that for these lattices $\Theta^{1/K} \to 1$ as $K \to \infty$, and $\frac{1}{K}\log\Theta = O\left(\frac{\log K}{K}\right)$. Substituting into (19), and noting that $\log(K \cdot V_K^{2/K}/2\pi e)$ goes to zero as $O\left(\frac{\log K}{K}\right)$, yield the desired result. □

The proof of Lemma 1 shows that in some sense the Voronoi regions of the optimal lattice quantizers becomes *balls*. This observation provides a simple geometric explanation to the Gaussian limit behavior of the quantization noise, since, by Poincaré theorem (see e.g. [12]), the projection on any finite dimensional hyperspace of a uniform distribution over a ball, becomes, in the limit as the ball dimension increases, a distribution of an i.i.d. Gaussian vector.

By utilizing (15) we can provide a statistical characterization of this limit behavior. Let $\underline{Z}_\theta^{(K)} = Z_{\theta+1}^{(K)} \ldots Z_{\theta+m}^{(K)}$ be a sub-block of size m, starting at θ, of the quantization noise of a K-dimensional lattice quantizer, and let $f_{\underline{Z}_\theta}^{(K)}(\cdot)$ denotes its density. We assume that the noise process is a concatenation of i.i.d. K-blocks, where each one is distributed as $\underline{Z}^{(K)}$, i.e., uniformly over the quantizer cell. Let

$$\phi(\underline{z}) = \frac{1}{(2\pi\epsilon)^{m/2}} e^{-\|\underline{z}\|^2/2\epsilon}$$

denotes the density of a zero mean m-dimensional Gaussian vector with correlation matrix ϵI, where $\epsilon = \frac{1}{K}E\{\|\underline{Z}^{(K)}\|^2\}$ is the MSE per sample of the lattice quantizer. Finally, let

$$\|f - \phi\|_1 \triangleq \int_{\mathcal{R}^m} |f(\underline{z}) - \phi(\underline{z})|\, d\underline{z}$$

denotes the $\mathcal{L}_1$ distance between the densities f and ϕ. Now, if we could assume that $\underline{Z}^{(K)}$ is stationary, then (15) would imply that, for *every* sub-block of size m starting at θ, $\|f_{\underline{Z}_\theta}^{(K)} - \phi\|_1 \to 0$, as $K \to \infty$. However, since this assumption is not true, we show this claim only on the average over all starting points θ:

Theorem 2 *For a fix m and the optimal lattice quantizers*

$$\frac{1}{K}\sum_{\theta=0}^{K-1} \|f_{\underline{Z}_\theta}^{(K)} - \phi\|_1^2 \to 0\,, \quad as\ K \to \infty\,, \tag{21}$$

i.e., $\|f_{\underline{Z}_\Theta}^{(K)} - \phi\|_1 \to 0$ as $K \to \infty$ in Mean Square (MS) sense over $\Theta \sim \mathcal{U}(0\ldots K-1)$.

Since convergence in the MS sense implies convergence in probability, most of the dither sub-blocks tend to have a white Gaussian density in $\mathcal{L}_1$ sense, i.e., Prob$\{\Theta : \|f_{\underline{Z}_\Theta}^{(K)} - \phi\|_1 > \delta\} \to 0$, as $K \to \infty$, $\forall\delta > 0$.

Proof: Let $\underline{\tilde{Z}}^{(K)} = \underline{Z}_0^{(K)}, \underline{Z}_1^{(K)} \ldots \underline{Z}_{K-1}^{(K)}$ denotes a vector of size mK, constructed by concatenating independent vectors taken from $\underline{Z}_\theta^{(K)}$, $\theta = 0\ldots K-1$, and let $W_i^* \sim \mathcal{N}(0,\epsilon)$, $i = 1,2,\ldots$ be i.i.d. Gaussian variables. For any lattice quantizer Q_K we can write

$$\begin{aligned}
\mathcal{D}(\underline{Z}_\Theta^{(K)}; W_1^*\ldots W_m^* |\, \Theta) &\triangleq \frac{1}{K}\sum_{\theta=0}^{K-1} \mathcal{D}(\underline{Z}_\theta^{(K)}; W_1^*\ldots W_m^*)\\
&\overset{(a)}{=} \frac{1}{K}\mathcal{D}(\underline{\tilde{Z}}^{(K)}; W_1^*\ldots W_{mK}^*)\\
&\overset{(b)}{=} \frac{1}{K}\left(\frac{mK}{2}\log 2\pi e\epsilon - \sum_{\theta=0}^{K-1} h(\underline{Z}_\theta^{(K)})\right)\\
&\overset{(c)}{\le} \frac{m}{K}\left(\frac{K}{2}\log 2\pi e\epsilon - h(\underline{Z}^{(K)})\right)\\
&\overset{(d)}{=} \frac{m}{K}\mathcal{D}(\underline{Z}^{(K)}; W_1^*\ldots W_K^*) \overset{(e)}{=} \frac{m}{2}\log 2\pi e G(Q_K)\,,
\end{aligned} \tag{22}$$

where
(a) follows since the divergence of independent variables is given by the sum of their

divergences,
(b) follows from the decomposition in (14), since $E\{\|\underline{\tilde{Z}}^{(K)}\|^2\} = \sum_{\theta=0}^{K-1} E\{\|\underline{Z}_\theta^{(K)}\|^2\}$ $= m\sum_{\theta=0}^{K-1} E\{(Z_\theta^{(K)})^2\} = mK\epsilon$,
(c) follows since, similarly to Theorem 16.5.1 (p. 491) in [9], $h(\underline{Z}^{(K)}) \leq \sum_{\theta=0}^{K-1} \frac{1}{m} h(\underline{Z}_\theta^{(K)})$, and
(d) and (e) follow again from (14).
By Pinsker inequality (see [9] Lemma 16.3.1), we use the divergence to upperbound the $\mathcal{L}_1$ distance, i.e., $\mathcal{D}(f_{\underline{Z}_\theta}^{(K)}\|\phi) \geq \frac{1}{2\ln 2}\|f_{\underline{Z}_\theta}^{(K)} - \phi\|_1^2$. Then, we average over Θ and use (22) to obtain

$$E_\Theta\left\{\|f_{\underline{Z}_\theta}^{(K)} - \phi\|_1^2\right\} \leq m \cdot \ln 2\pi e G(Q_K)\ , \tag{23}$$

which for the optimal lattice quantizers implies (21). □

We recall that the coding rate of Entropy Coded Dithered Quantization (ECDQ) ([3], [13] [5]) is given by the mutual information in an additive noise channel, whose input is the quantized source, and where the noise is independent of the source and is uniformly distributed over the mirror image of the lattice quantizer basic cell. Using Theorem 2 it can be shown that the coding rate of ECDQ tends, in the limit of large (optimal) lattice dimension, to the mutual information in an Additive White Gaussian Noise (AWGN) channel. As shown in [13], this limit behavior results in a simple trade-off between sampling rate and quantization resolution in ECDQ of band limited sources.

Acknowledgment

We wish to thank G. Poltyrev and S. Litsyn for helpful discussions and suggestions, and to Z. Hirst for his help with the figures.

References

[1] W. R. Bennett. Spectra of quantized signals. *Bell Sys. Tech. Jour.*, 27:446–472, July, 1948.

[2] A. Gersho. Asymptotically optimal block quantization. *IEEE Trans. Information Theory*, IT-25:373–380, July 1979.

[3] R. Zamir and M. Feder. On universal quantization by randomized uniform lattice quantizer. *IEEE Trans. Information Theory*, pages 428–436, March 1992.

[4] J. H. Conway and N. J. A. Sloane. *Sphere Packings, Lattices and Groups.* Springer-Verlag, New York, N.Y., 1988.

[5] R. Zamir and M. Feder. Information rates of pre/post filtered dithered quantizers. *IEEE Trans. Information Theory*, submitted, 1993.

[6] S. P. Lloyd. Least squares quantization in PCM. *IEEE Trans. Information Theory*, pages 129–137, March 1982 (originally presented at the Ins. of Math. Stat. Meeting 1957).

[7] Y. Linde, A. Buzo, and R. M. Gray. An algorithm for vector quantizer design. *IEEE Trans. Communications*, COM-28:84–95, Jan. 1980.

[8] T. Berger. *Rate Distortion Theory: A Mathematical Basis fot Data Compression*. Prentice-Hall, Englewood Cliffs, NJ, 1971.

[9] T. M. Cover and J. A. Thomas. *Elements of Information Theory*. Wiley, New York, 1991.

[10] P. Zador. Asymptotic quantization error of continuous signals and their quantization dimension. *IEEE Trans. Information Theory*, IT-28:139–149, Mar. 1982 (previously an unpublished Bell Lab. memo, 1966).

[11] G. Poltyrev. Private communications.

[12] P. Diaconis and D. Freedman. A Dozen de-Finetti-Style Results in Search for a Theory. *Ann. Inst. H. Poincaré, Prob. Stat.*, 23, Suppl. 2:397–423, 1987.

[13] R. Zamir and M. Feder. Rate distortion performance in coding band-limited sources by sampling and dithered quantization. *IEEE Trans. Information Theory*, accepted (pending revision), 1993.

VECTOR QUANTIZATION OF CONTEXTUAL INFORMATION FOR LOSSLESS IMAGE COMPRESSION

Xavier Ginesta and Seung P. Kim
School of Electrical Engineering and Computer Science
Polytechnic University, Brooklyn, NY 11201
email: ginesta@signal.poly.edu, skim@signal.poly.edu

Abstract: In the companion paper [12], we presented a context-tree based lossless image compression approach. The most important step in the implementation of the proposed algorithm is the construction of a context-tree from a given (set of) training image(s). It has been shown that the design process of a context-tree parallels the idea of non-binary Pruned Tree Structured Vector Quantization (PTSVQ). Vectors are represented by the conditional probability tables of the contexts identified by the tree and their respective distances are measured in terms of the overall entropy increase after two tables (vectors) are merged. The PTSVQ requires a fully grown initial context-tree which, in practice, is impossible to achieve due to enormous associated memory requirements. Additionally, even in the case of being able to grow a full context tree, the huge number of contexts that could potentially appear would make the optimal pruning procedure computationally impractical. Therefore, the conventional approach of optimally pruning the *worst* branches off from the initial tree until some performance constraint is satisfied is not applicable. In this paper we present a new TSVQ algorithm, called Incremental Tree Growing (ITG), which incrementally grows and quantizes the context tree locally on a level by level basis, thus drastically reducing both the memory requirements and the computational complexity. After the Incremental Tree Growing is completed, terminal branches are globally vector quaqntized again, which is possible due to significant reduction of the number of initial branches. Using a technique similar in spirit to the Mean Removed VQ (MRVQ) [11], significant reduction in the number of probability tables is achieved. In one of our simulations, for example (see [12]), we reduced the number of probability tables from 262K($=2^{18}$) to 108 by using ITG algorithm, and from 108 to 10 using the modified MRVQ at the conditional entropy increase of only 1.26%. In summary, the proposed ITG algorithm combined with a modified MRVQ provides an efficient framework for the design of context-trees with reduced memory and computational requirements.

1 Introduction

In the companion paper [12] we pointed out the advantages of using high order models of an input source applied to lossless image compression. As discussed there, the design of feasible high order models involves a sequence of three steps: i)context definition, ii)identification (selection) of the most representative contexts in the source

1068-0314/94 $3.00 © 1994 IEEE

and iii) reduction, both in size and number, of the conditional probability tables associated with each context.

In this paper, we address the two latter issues mentioned above. In image coding, symbols are pixel values identified by their (row,col) coordinates, whereas conditioning states are represented by (linear combinations of) pixels in the neighborhood of the pixel being coded. Since high order models can be characterized by a set of contexts and their associated conditional probability tables [12], an efficient conditioning state representation is vital in the design of a good high order model. In the following, we describe the basic context representation adopted in the development of our work.

Let us assume that the sequence of LC's which describes ac conditioning state $CS = \{LC_1, LC_2, \cdots, LC_N\}$ has been defined. Let R_i be the range of values that LC_i can take on. The most straightforward representation that fully specifies any context in the context space is an N-dimensional vector in which the range of the ith dimension equals R_i. The memory requirement to store such a vector is *Conditional-Probability-Table-Size*$\times \prod_{i=1}^{N} R_i$. Clearly, the size of this vector grows rapidly as N increases and it becomes impractical to work with.

On the other hand, a large number of the states (in fact most of them) identified by the vector are very uncommon in typical images and will nearly never be encountered. Therefore, it seems reasonable to find an alternative representation which only allocates memory for meaningful states. An N-level tree meets the specifications of such a representation. The idea is to associate every level of the tree with one of the LC's that defines a context. An example of such a tree is depicted in Fig. 1. The path from the root to a leaf node describes the sequence of LC's that identify a given context. For example, in Fig. 1 state C_i is identified by the LC sequence $\{LC_1 = 0, LC_2 = 20, LC_3 = 2\}$. The advantage of using a tree over the N-D vector approach is that new nodes of the tree can be dynamically allocated as the training set is being scanned and new states are encountered. States that never occur will not use up available memory.

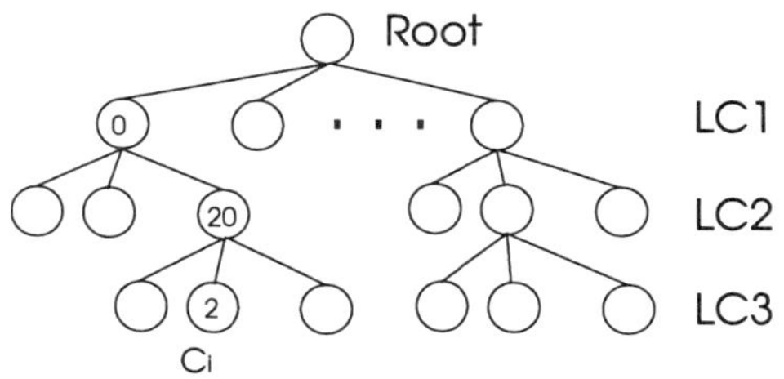

Figure 1: Representation of conditioning states on a tree.

Still, although the savings are quite significant, the overall number of contexts may become quite large as N grows. Sections 2 and 3 study complexity reduction techniques. Section 2 explores heuristics to achieve a reduced-size tree structure and

Section 3 proposes an application of secondary VQ on the overall tree for the reduction of the number of conditional probability tables. This is based on the fact that most probability tables have a very similar Laplacian-like shape, so they can be vector quantized with little degradation in performance. Simulation results reported in [12] show reduction factors of 10 to 1 and higher with performance penalties ranging between 1 to 3% only. In section 4 discussions of the algorithm and the conclusions are presented.

2 Reduction of Conditioning States

Given a context tree, it is obvious that not all the contexts contribute in the same measure to the reduction of the overall entropy. Consequently, we could selectively remove all those branches which contribute the least to reduce the entropy until the *desired number* of contexts is achieved. Alternatively, we continue the branch removal until the resulting *entropy increase* is higher than a given threshold. The concept of trading off performance (entropy) for complexity (number of contexts) parallels the idea of pruned tree structured vector quantization (PTSVQ) [8]. Given a tree structured vector quantizer, the goal of PTSVQ is to optimally minimize a cost function $C(S)$ (e.g.,the number of leaves in the tree) given a distortion constraint $D(S)$, or vice versa. The algorithm is based on the minimization of the Lagrangian $J(S) = D(S) + \lambda C(S)$ over all pruned subtrees of the initial tree. The parameter λ is a Lagrange multiplier and can be interpreted as the slope of the distortion-cost curve. By iteratively pruning off the branches of the tree whose associated λ is the smallest, it can be shown [7] that all distortion-cost pairs of points lying on the convex hull are found.

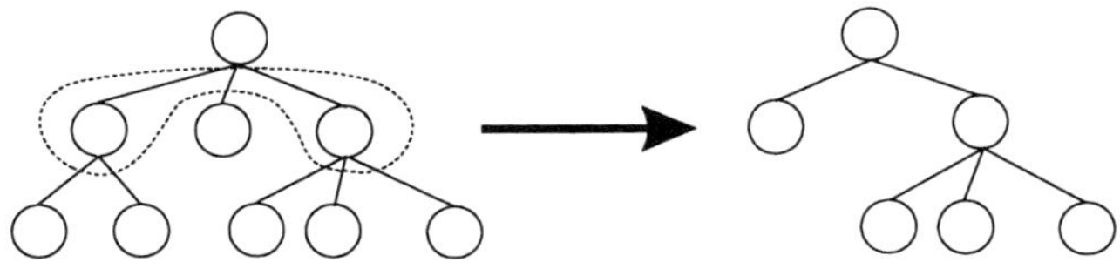

Figure 2: Branch elimination by branch merging.

Conceptually, we could apply the same principle to our problem. The distortion can be measured in terms of the entropy of the tree and the cost can be associated with the number of contexts (leaf nodes). However, there are two facts that prevent us from directly applying the PTSVQ algorithm to context tree pruning. Firstly, PTSVQ assumes that the whole initial tree is available. Secondly, the PTSVQ algorithm was initially developed for binary trees. Although it has been claimed that its extension to non-binary trees is straightforward, this is so only if the number of children of any node in the tree is fixed. However, for non-binary trees with a non-fixed number of children per node, there is another alternative, namely *branch merging* (see Fig. 2), which achieves better results than branch pruning. Application of the PTSVQ algorithm to non-binary trees should involve computing λ for all possible combinations of branch merges, but this, unfortunately, can be shown to be an NP hard problem. Therefore, our goal is the design of a heuristic algorithm which provides a suboptimal solution in a polynomial computation time.

2.1 Estimate of the Source Statistics and a Distance Measure

The necessary statistical information for building a tree structure is estimated using a (set of) training imge(s). Let C_i^k be a terminal state at the tree level k represented by an index i, and $CD_i^k(x)$ its conditional count distribution function. Define

$$N(C_i^k) = \sum_x CD_i^k(x)$$

as the cumulative count of the number of appearance of the terminal state C_i^k, then the total pixel count is

$$M = \sum_{C_i^k \in T} N(C_i^k)$$

where T is the total set of terminal states in the tree. Then, the probability of the context is $P\{C_i^k\} = \frac{N(C_i^k)}{M}$ and the conditional probability of a current pixel x under the conditioning state C_i^k is $P\{x/C_i^k\} = \frac{CD_i^k(x)}{N(C_i^k)}$. From the definition of conditional entropy,

$$H(S/C) = -\sum_{C_j^k \in T} \sum_x P\{C_j^k\} P\{x/C_j^k\} \log_2 P\{x/C_j^k\} \tag{1}$$

the high-order conditional entropy in terms of symbol counts is

$$H(S/C) = -\sum_{C_i^k \in T} \sum_x \frac{CD_i^k(x)}{M} \log_2 \frac{CD_i^k(x)}{N(C_i^k)}. \tag{2}$$

If nodes C_i^{k+1} and C_j^{k+1} are merged to produce context $C_{\Omega_0}^{k+1}$, the entropy increase will be given by

$$\Delta H(C_i^{k+1} \cup C_j^{k+1}) = \frac{N(C_{\Omega_0}^{k+1})}{M} H(S/C_{\Omega_0}^{k+1}) - \frac{N(C_i^{k+1})}{M} H(S/C_i^{k+1}) - \frac{N(C_j^{k+1})}{M} H(S/C_j^{k+1}) \tag{3}$$

where

$$H(S/C_m^n) = -\sum_x \frac{CD_m^n(x)}{N(C_m^n)} \cdot \log_2 \frac{CD_m^n(x)}{N(C_m^n)}.$$

The smaller the entropy increase, the closer the distance between the two nodes.

2.2 Context Quantization by Incremental Tree Growing

The tree structured representation of conditioning states suggests the possibility of trying to reduce their number using a pruned tree structured vector quantization (PTSVQ) approach. However, traditional PTSVQ algorithms operate on a full initial tree and iteratively remove the *worst* branches until a given constraint is satisfied. It has been observed that growing context trees of more than three levels is generally impractical. Additionally, even in the case of being able to grow an arbitrary order tree (understanding by order the number of tree levels), the non-binary nature of context trees together with the freedom to have any number of children per node, would make the optimal pruning procedure an NP hard problem. Therefore, we propose to combine the tree extension and quantization processes in one single step, which we call Incremental Tree Growing (ITG). The idea is to extend the tree on a level by level basis and successively quantize the sibling nodes of the last level before extending on the next level. This extension plus quantization process repeats iteratively until some constraint is satisfied. A more detailed description of the algorithm follows.

2.2.1 Incremental Tree Growing Algorithm

Incremental tree growing starts with a tree which has one single node (the root) and one conditional count table (the zero order histogram of the training set). In the first iteration, the first level of the tree is extended according to a chosen conditioning state parameter, say, LC_1. Fig. 3 shows hypothetical conditional entropy versus number of states (nodes) curves $h_i(n)$ for the first level of the tree where each curve represents sucessive partitioning of LC_1 on different routes. The optimal tree expansion will be described by a (branch growing) point on the optimal line defined by $h(n) = \min_i h_i(n)$. However, it is not practical to find the optimal curve as discussed before and even if the optimal curve is found the prediction of the optimal point before fully expanding the tree is impossible. Therefore, we first try to choose a curve $h'(n)$ close to the optimal one and estimate a branch growing point heuristically considering the increase of the entropy as well as the number of nodes. Alternatively, in a simpler way, we can use only either entropy increase or the number of nodes as a decision parameter. We impose the restriction that only sibling states may be merged. The choice of the branch growing point will affect the structure following the branch. The procedure can be repeated as tree grows.

If only the entropy increase is used as a branch growing parameter, further simplification of the algorithm is possible. Assuming that we recorded a maximum entropy increase at the last merge on the first level of the tree, we can use this value for finding the branch growing points on the following levels of the tree. Since the conditional entropies associated with mutually exclusive conditioning states are independent of each other, the branch growing can be done each branch independently, thus computation and memory requirements are significantly reduced.

Notice that we would not be able to do this if the criterion was minimizing the overall entropy increase, because in that case the order in which nodes are merged is important. The disadvantage of using a entropy increase as the decision parameter is that we have no precise control over the final number of nodes and the entropy. The number of final nodes will be smaller if the tree growing is applied several times with smaller entropy increases. In the next, we present an efficient method for achieving a curve close the optimal one.

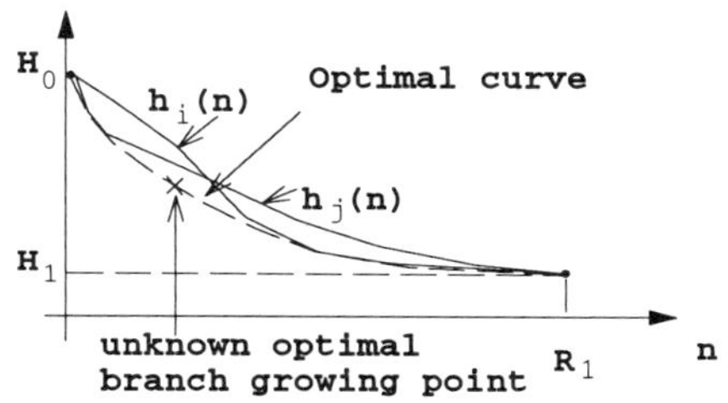

Figure 3: Entropy versus number of states curves. H_0: Zero-order Entropy, H_1: First-order Entropy

2.2.2 Design of a Good yet Fast Node Merging Algorithm

The context merging process is essentially a vector clustering problem, with vectors being represented by the conditional count tables of contexts. We assumed that, for simplicity, only sibling contexts would be considered for merge. Thus, for every set of sibling contexts, the distances from all count tables in the set to each other are computed and the closest ones are successively merged until either the desired number of clusters is reached or the entropy increase matches a given threshold. If we are quantizing the Lth level of the tree, assuming that there are K nodes at level $L-1$ and each of them spawns an average of N children (leaves of the tree), computation of the initial distance tables will be $\theta(KN^2)$ complex. However, depending on the nature of the LC considered, neighbor nodes will have very similar conditional count tables, whereas far away nodes will have quite different tables. One such case arises, for instance, when the LC is defined by a single pixel, a neighbor of the pixel being coded. In that event, the count tables of neighbor sibling nodes have a very similar shape and mean, so that the distance between them is very small. Thus, since the count tables of neighboring sibling nodes are already naturally arranged in a linear fashion according to their respective proximities, we do not need to compute all the entries in the distance table. Given the i-th node and a predefined window size $W \ll N$, only the distances from the i-th node to its W immediate left and right neighbors will be computed. Since this algorithm is similar in spirit to the Fast PNN algorithm described in [10], we shall refer to it as the Modified FPNN (MFPNN) algorithm. Additionally, after a set of sibling nodes has been quantized (or even between every node merge) using the MFPNN algorithm, the LBG algorithm [6] is optionally run in order to reduce the distortion by reassigning nodes to their closest clusters. Notice that even in this case, the algorithm is not guaranteed to perform optimally. However, due to the inherent closeness between the tables of neighboring nodes, it does a very good job even for small values of W.

Here we address some issues regarding the performance of the ITG algorithm. First, due to the incremental fashion in which we extend and simultaneously quantize every tree level, the tree is suboptimal. Therefore, it is important to use the LC's in a decreasing order of significances, i.e., LC_1 should represent the most significant context, LC_2 the second best and so on. Second, it may sometimes be interesting to code error signals from a predicted value such as the DPCM error signals. But using the error signals for conditioning states will not allow capturing meaningful contextual information even though the tree structure will be simpler due to smaller variances of the error signals [1]. In the experimental results reported in [12], various LC sequences were used for several image sets resulting varing performances. Those are; i) *(i,j) Neighbor Pixels:* $p(m-i, n-j)$, ii) *Horizontal Gradient:* $p(m-1, n) - p(m-1, n-1)$, iii) *Vertical Gradient:* $p(m, n-1) - p(m-1, n-1)$, and iv) *Predicted Value:* $p(m, n-1) + p(m-1, n) - p(m-1, n-1)$.

3 Vector Quantization of Conditional Count Tables

In Section 1 we saw that an efficient context representation could reduce the memory requirements of our high order statistical model by several orders of magnitude. Section 2 showed that the number of contexts could be further reduced from several hundred thousands to a few hundreds paying a reasonable performance penalty. These simplifications were based on the quantization of contextual information. In this section we introduce a further simplification exploiting the shapes of conditional probability information. This can reduce the number of tables by one order of magnitude with typical performance degradations ranging between 1 and 3%.

3.1 Count Table Normalization

Given a context tree, the expression for the high order entropy of a source is given by (2). The value that this expression evaluates to is directly related to the shapes of the conditional count tables of every terminal context C_i^j in the tree. In general, a good context selection will result in very narrow, Laplacian-like shaped count tables, which have an associated low conditional entropy. Since the shape is the main attribute of a count table and most tables have a very similar shape, it should be possible to vector quantize them in order to reduce their number without introducing a significant entropy increase. Notice however that, although two count tables may have similar shapes, their mean may be significantly different. Because of this, two count tables identical in shape might never be assigned to the same cluster because the resulting entropy increase after the merge would be intolerable (see Fig. 4). This problem can be easily circumvented by normalizing all count tables with respect to their mean or, for simplicity, their most popular value. By doing so, the merge of two tables with identical shape will result in a zero entropy increase. In fact, the concept of normalizing vectors with respect to their mean prior to quantizing them is not new, and it was introduced in [11] under the name of Mean Removed VQ (MRVQ). This method offers some advantages over the conventional VQ approach but, due to the nature of the vectors that we are trying to quantize, it really shines in our application. After table normalization we are ready to quantize the conditional count tables into clusters in a similar manner as the one used to merge sibling contexts in the context tree. Since the VQ at this time is globally performed, two separated similar tables due to their distinct parent nodes can be merged.

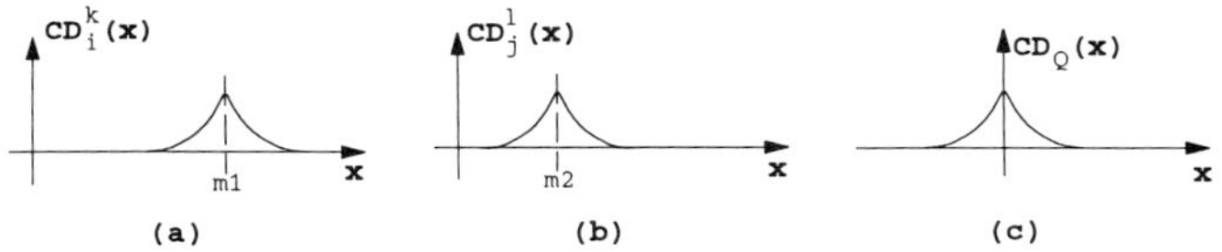

Figure 4: (a) and (b); Examples of two identically shaped count tables with different means. Their respective distance is too high to merge them with a negligible H increase. (c): After Mean-normalization the two distributions are identical

3.2 The Algorithm

In order to speed up the quantization process, we would like to use the MFPNN algorithm introduced in Section 2. However, the situation now is not quite the same as before, for we no longer have the count tables linearly arranged according to their proximity. Nonetheless, we can try to arrange them in such a manner by sorting them according to their conditional entropy, $H(x/C_i^j)$. This is a reasonable criterion because all tables have a 0-mean[1] and, under the assumption that they all have a Laplacian-like shape, their difference in conditional entropy will be a good measure of their proximity as well. Bearing this in mind, the algorithm for conditional count table quantization will consist of the following steps:

1. Normalize all count tables respect to their mean or their most popular value. All terminal states in the tree will have to be updated with the value of either the mean or the most popular value of their count table.

[1]Or nearly 0-mean if the normalization criterion was the most popular value and the Laplacian-like shape assumption holds.

2. Compute $H(x/C_i^j)$ for all tables and sort them according to this value.
3. Use the MFPNN algorithm to vector quantize the normalized tables.
4. Optionally run the LBG algorithm to optimize cluster assignment.
5. Copy to each terminal state in the tree the index of the cluster that it has been assigned to.

4 Discussions and Conclusions

The order in which the LC's are placed in the LC sequence that defines a context tree is crucial in obtaining a good tree. Additionally, the selection of the LC's themselves is also fundamental. Therefore, efficient algorithms that address these two important issues need to be developed. Based on the simulation results, the performance of the ITG algorithm can be deemed as rather acceptable, specially considering that the full set of contexts is not known at each quantization step. However, we do not have a systematic way to decide a good threshold for the entropy increase when quantizing a level, although it seems that values smaller than 1% should be used in general. This threshold is image dependent and must be determined on a trial and error basis. New techniques that automatically determine when to stop merging nodes in a level should be studied to circumvent this problem. On the other hand, a system based on the minimization of the entropy increase while keeping a certain number of nodes at a given level can control the number of terminal nodes more explicitly even though less explicit in entropy increase. Ideally, we want to control both the number of nodes and entropy increase such that near optimal branch growing points are found.

One of the biggest obstacles in designing high order models of a source is the appalling number of contexts that, a priori, can appear in an arbitrary source. We have shown that the reduction of the number of contexts can be treated as a Vector Quantization problem, considering the conditional count/probability tables of a context as the vectors to quantize. We borrowed some of the tools developed in the V.Q. field and adapted them to our needs. We saw that context representation on a context tree naturally mapped to a non-binary Tree Structured Vector Quantizer (TSVQ). In general, however, we were not able to build the whole tree ahead of time, which prevented us from performing an optimal quantization procedure. To overcome this problem, we proposed a heuristic Incremental Tree Growing (ITG) algorithm, that quantizes the tree on a level by level basis without considering the other levels. Additionally, we saw that we could further reduce the overall number of conditioning states by one order of magnitude by vector quantizing conditional count tables using a variation of the MRVQ algorithm [11]. Simulation results reported in [12] show that the techniques described in this paper can reduce the number of different contexts in the context-tree from several thousands (and even hundred thousands in some cases) to a few tens, while preserving the outstanding performance characteristic of high order statistical models.

References

[1] Shaw-Min Lei, Ming-Ting Sun and Kou-Hu Tzou, "Design and Hardware Architecture of High Order Conditional Entropy Coding For Images ", *IEEE Trans. on Circuits and Systems for Video Technology*", Vol. 2, pp. 176-186, June 1992.

[2] S.E. Elnahas, K.H.Tzou and J.G.Dunham, "Low-Rate Entropy Coding of Transformed Images", *Proc. of Applications of Digital Image Processsing IX*, A.G. Tescher, Editor, SPIE Vol. 697, pp.10-13, Aug. 1986.

[3] K.H. Tzou, "A High Order Entropy Coding for Video Applications", *Proc. of IEEE Workshop on Visual Signal Processing and Communication*", Taiwan, July 6-7, 1991.

[4] Tenkasi V. Ramabadran and Keshi Chen, "The Use of Contextual Information in the Reversible Compression of Medical Images", *IEEE Trans. Medical Imaging,* Vol. 11, pp.185-195, June 1992

[5] R.G. Gallager, *Information Theory and Reliable Communication,* Wiley, New York, 1968.

[6] Y. Linde, A. Buzo and R.M. Gray, "An Algorithm for Vector Quantizer Design", *IEEE Trans on Comm.*, Vol. COM-28, pp. 84-95, Jan. 1980.

[7] P. A. Chou, T. Lookabaugh and R. M. Gray, "Optimal Prunning with Applications to Tree-Structutred Source Coding and Modeling", *IEEE Trans. on Information Theory*, Vol 35, pp. 299-315, March 1989.

[8] Allen Gersho and Robert M. Gray, *Vector Quantization And Signal Compression*, KAP, Boston, 1992.

[9] C. E. Shanon, "A Mathematical Theory of Communication", *Bell Syst. Tech. J.*, 27:379-423, 623-656, 1948.

[10] W. H. Equitz, "A New Vector Quantization Clustering Algorithm ", *IEEE Trans. on Acoust., Speech & Signal Proc.*, pp. 1568-1575, Oct. 1989.

[11] R. L. Baker, and R. M. Gray, "Differential Vector Quantization of Achromatic Imagery, *Proc. of the International Picture Coding Symposium*, March 1983.

[12] X. Ginesta, S. P. Kim and M. T. Sun, "Context Tree Based Lossless Image Compression", submitted to the *IEEE Data Compression Conference*, March 1994.

Bayes Risk Weighted VQ and Learning VQ

Richard D. Wesel*and Robert M. Gray

Department of Electrical Engineering, Stanford University

Abstract

This paper examines two vector quantization algorithms which can combine the tasks of compression and classification: Bayes risk weighted vector quantization (BRVQ) proposed by Oehler et al., and Optimized Learning Vector Quantization 1 (OLVQ1) proposed by Kohonen et al.

BRVQ uses a parameter λ to control the tradeoff between compression and classification. BRVQ performance is studied for a range of λ values for four classification problems. Increasing the λ parameter in BRVQ is intended to improve classification performance. However, for two of the problems studied, increasing λ *degraded* classification performance. A majority rule reclassification of the final codebook (using only the training set) greatly improves high-λ BRVQ performance for these cases.

Finally, we compare the classification performance and mean Square error (MSE) performance of BRVQ to that of OLVQ1 for four classification problems. BRVQ with codebook reclassification is found to have a lower MSE than OLVQ1 while maintaining comparable, but slightly inferior, classification performance.

1 Introduction

The methods for obtaining vector quantization codebooks simply to provide the lowest possible squared error distortion for a given codebook size [1] or entropy [2] are well understood and grounded solidly in theory. However, when the objective is classification or a combination of classification and low-distortion compression, there are questions that remain about which algorithms are best and why algorithms behave as they do. In particular, to what extent are compression and classification conflicting goals? Also, which problems are "easy" for classification by vector quantization and which are "hard"?

Kohonen et al. [3, 4] describe an approach to classification based on vector quantization. This method can also be used to simultaneously compress and classify, although the codebook is not explicitly designed to provide good lossy compression. Oehler et al. [5, 6] provide a method for codebook design which explicitly tries to do a good job both at classification and at lossy compression.

*email *wesel@isl.stanford.edu*

In this paper we examine the Bayes risk weighted vector quantization (BRVQ) algorithm of [5] in detail, examining how it controls the trade-off between classification and compression. Then we compare its performance both in terms of classification error probability (P_e) and mean Square error (MSE) distortion to the Optimized Learning Vector Quantization 1 (OLVQ1) algorithm of [3].

Our investigation of the trade-off between classification and compression seems to indicate that these two goals do not conflict to a large extent. This comparison of BRVQ to OLVQ1 provides insight into the types of problems that are "easy" or "hard" for classification by VQ.

2 Bayes Risk Weighted Vector Quantization

A vector quantizer (VQ) maps each input vector X onto a codebook of N codewords $\{Y_k : k = 1, 2, ..., N\}$. Let $\alpha(X)$ be the mapping from the inputs to the integer indices of the codewords, and let $\beta(k)$ be the mapping from the codeword indices k to the codewords Y_k. $\alpha(X)$ is the *encoder* and $\beta(k)$ is the *decoder* of the VQ.

Let $d(X, \beta(\alpha(X)))$ be the distortion between the input vector X and its associated codeword $\beta(\alpha(X))$. A common distortion measure is squared error $||X - \beta(\alpha(X))||^2$. The average distortion of a codebook for a given input vector distribution is $D(\alpha, \beta) = E[d(X, \beta(\alpha(X)))]$. If squared error distortion is being used, then $D(\alpha, \beta)$ is the mean squared error (MSE). Traditional VQ seeks to minimize $D(\alpha, \beta)$. For MSE distortion, this can be accomplished with the Lloyd algorithm [1].

Classification by VQ is performed by assigning a class to each input vector based on which codeword index was assigned to the input vector by the encoder. Let $\delta(k)$, or equivalently $\delta(\alpha(X))$, be this mapping between the codeword indices and the possible classes. Let c_X be the random variable which assigns class membership to X according to a probability mass function which depends on X. A classification error occurs when $c_X \neq \delta(\alpha(X))$. A cost C_{ij} is assigned for classifying a vector actually in class i as being in class j. Typically if $i = j$, $C_{ij} = 0$. Let e_{ij} be the event where X is in class i but $\delta(\alpha(X)) = j$. The risk [5] is given by

$$R(\alpha, \delta) = \sum_{i=1}^{M} \sum_{j=1}^{M} P\{e_{ij}\} C_{ij} \tag{1}$$

where M is the number of possible classes. If $C_{ij} = 1$ when $i \neq j$ and $C_{ij} = 0$ when $i = j$ then the risk is exactly the probability of classification error.

As described in [5], BRVQ seeks a codebook which minimizes $J_\lambda(\alpha, \beta, \delta) = D(\alpha, \beta) + \lambda R(\alpha, \delta)$. BRVQ employs the following three step procedure to minimize $J_\lambda(\alpha, \beta, \delta)$

1 Choose $\delta^{(t+1)}$ to minimize $J_\lambda(\alpha^t, \beta^t, \delta^{(t+1)})$
2 Choose $\beta^{(t+1)}$ to minimize $J_\lambda(\alpha^t, \beta^{(t+1)}, \delta^{(t+1)})$
3 Choose $\alpha^{(t+1)}$ to minimize $J_\lambda(\alpha^{(t+1)}, \beta^{(t+1)}, \delta^{(t+1)})$

For the rest of the paper, we assume that the distortion d is squared error and that the costs C_{ij} have been chosen so that the Bayes risk is exactly the probability of classification error. With these assumptions we have the following interpretation of BRVQ. Step 1 classifies each codebook index by the majority rule of its associated vectors. Step 2 changes each reproduction vector to be the centroid of its associated vectors. Step 3 assigns each input vector in the training set to the codebook index that satisfies

$$\alpha(X) = \arg\min_k\{||X - Y_k||^2 + \lambda I[c_X \neq \delta(k)]\}. \tag{2}$$

where $I[\cdot]$ is the indicator function.

Because class membership is not known for vectors outside of the training set, (2) is replaced by the nearest neighbor (Euclidean distance) rule for encoding and classifying the test data. In the next section, we observe poor performance because the codebook designed for the $\alpha(\cdot)$ of (2) is applied to the test data with the nearest neighbor $\alpha(\cdot)$.

3 BRVQ performance vs. λ

Four Classification Problems

We will examine BRVQ performance vs. λ for four classification problems. Each problem consists of the mixture of two equally likely distributions. Table 1 gives the distributions of each problem's two classes. When examining Table 1, recall that the bivariate normal has the density given in (3). For all the bivariate normal (BN) distributions in Table 1, $\mu_x = \mu_y = 0$ and $\sigma_x = \sigma_y = \sigma$. For the uniform (U) distributions, Table 1 gives the region of support.

$$f(x,y) = \frac{1}{2\pi\sigma_1\sigma_2} e^{\left[\frac{-1}{2(1-\rho^2)}\left(\left(\frac{x-\mu_x}{\sigma_x}\right)^2 - 2\rho\frac{(x-\mu_x)(y-\mu_y)}{\sigma_x\sigma_y} + \left(\frac{y-\mu_y}{\sigma_y}\right)^2\right)\right]} \tag{3}$$

Problem Name	Class 0 Distribution	Class 1 Distribution
different ρ's	BN with $\sigma = 1, \quad \rho = 0$	BN with $\sigma = 1, \quad \rho = \frac{1}{\sqrt{2}}$
different σ's	BN with $\sigma = 1, \quad \rho = 0$	BN with $\sigma = 2, \quad \rho = 0$
Diamond	U $(x,y) \in A = \{x,y : \lvert x\rvert + \lvert y\rvert \leq 1\}$	U $(x,y) \notin A, \ \lvert x\rvert, \lvert y\rvert \leq 1$
Square	U $(x,y) \in B = \{x,y : \lvert x\rvert, \lvert y\rvert \leq \frac{1}{\sqrt{2}}\}$	U $(x,y) \notin B, \ \lvert x\rvert, \lvert y\rvert \leq 1$

Table 1: Distributions used for classification problems.

The Different σ's problem was studied in [4] where it was referred to as the "hard" problem. The Diamond problem is essentially the one studied in [5].

Extreme points of λ

When $\lambda = 0$, step 3 simplifies to the nearest neighbor rule. Thus the BRVQ algorithm simplifies to finding a codebook via the Lloyd algorithm and then classifying each codebook vector to the class most prevalent in its partition.

When $\lambda = \infty$, the encoder and the resulting codebook design algorithm are still well defined. Each vector is forced to be assigned to a codeword which will classify it correctly to avoid infinite cost. This, in turn, prevents a codeword from ever changing from its initial class. Thus, for $\lambda = \infty$ the BRVQ algorithm reduces to designing a separate codebook for each class. This is essentially classified VQ [7]. However, unlike traditional classified VQ, the class information is not available to the encoder for selection of the appropriate codebook. Instead, the final codebook is simply the union of the separate codebooks.

Empirical Study of Performance vs. λ

Every point plotted in this paper represents the average of five runs. Each run used a 100,000 point training set and a 10,000 point test set. Thus each point involved 10 different data sets. For this section, the codebook size was fixed at 32.

Figures 1 and 2 show MSE vs. λ and P_e vs. λ for the Diamond problem and the Different ρ's problem. In each graph there is a clear phase transition from the $\lambda = 0$ dashed line to the $\lambda = \infty$ dashed line.

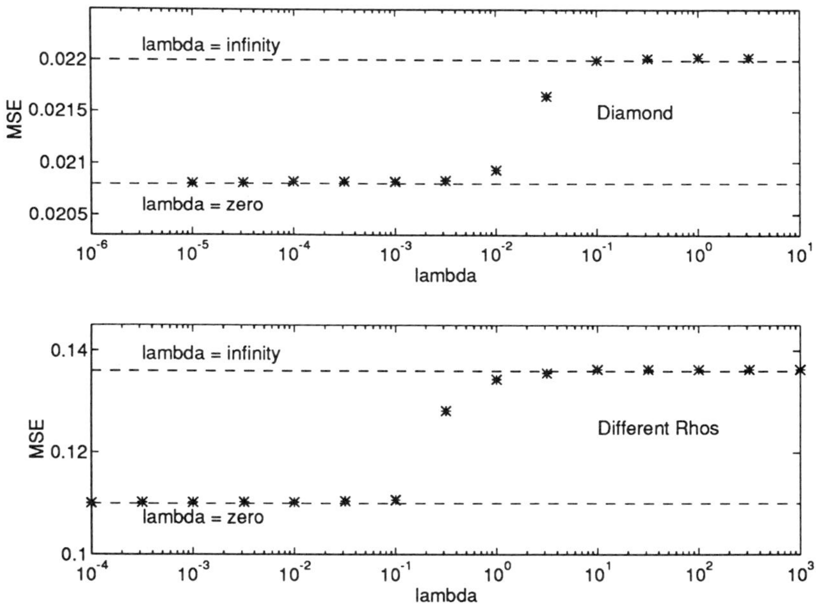

Figure 1: MSE vs. λ for the Diamond problem and the Different ρ's problem.

Figure 1 shows MSE performance vs. λ. As expected, MSE increases with increasing λ as in [5]. For the Diamond problem, there is only a 5% variation in MSE for the whole range of λ. For the Different ρ's problem there is a 19% variation in MSE. However, the best classification is achieved for the lowest MSE values.

The Square and Different σ's problems (not shown) had P_e vs. λ curves similar to the Diamond and Different ρ's problems respectively. For the square problem, there was only a 3% variation in MSE. For the Different σ's problem, there was a 21% variation in MSE, but the best classification was achieved for the lowest MSE values.

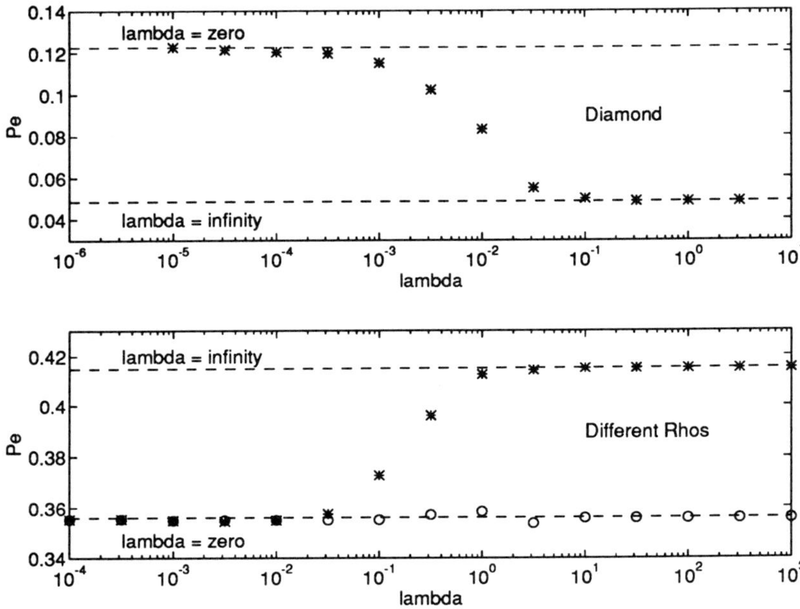

Figure 2: P_e vs. λ for the Diamond problem and the Different ρ's problem. The classification error probability after reclassification for the Different ρ's problem is indicated by o's.

Figure 2 shows P_e vs. λ. Again, the Square and Different σ's problems (not shown) had P_e vs. λ curves similar to the Diamond and Different ρ's problems respectively. For the Diamond problem, P_e decreases with increasing λ as in [5]. For the Different ρ's problem, P_e (before reclassification) *increased* with increasing λ. This result seems counterintuitive at first since higher values of λ give more weight to classification.

Majority rule reclassification

As mentioned at the end of section 2, there is a mismatch between the actual encoding rule and the encoding rule used for codebook design. With regard to the actual encoding rule, some of the codebook vectors may be misclassified. Thus, improved P_e performance can be obtained by reclassifying the final codebook according to the actual encoding rule (i.e., nearest neighbor). This can be accomplished by performing a final iteration of step 1 of the algorithm with $\alpha(\cdot)$ changed to the nearest neighbor encoder. This reclassification does not affect MSE.

Figure 2 shows the effect reclassification had on P_e for the different ρ's problem. Reclassification dramatically lowered classification error for high values of lambda. A similar improvement was observed for the different σ's problem. Misclassification of the type discussed above will be rare in cases where the two classes occupy disjoint regions. Thus for the Diamond and Square problems, reclassification should not have much affect. In fact, only negligible performance differences were observed for these two problems.

4 Learning Vector Quantization

As with BRVQ, the LVQ algorithms each produce a codebook of classified vectors. Test vectors are then assigned to the class of the nearest codebook vector.

BRVQ uses the entire training data set to compute its update for each iteration. However, the LVQ algorithms use only one sample from the training set for each iteration. In all of the LVQ algorithms, the class of each codebook vector remains fixed throughout training. Only the position of the codebook vectors can be adapted. Thus it is possible that performance can be improved by reclassification of the final codebook vectors according to the majority rule of the vectors in the partition. Each LVQ algorithm starts with an initial codebook $\{Y_k(1) : k = 1, 2, \ldots, N\}$, and sequentially updates the codebook using one vector from the training set for each update. Thus on iteration t, the training vector $X(t)$ is processed to produce the new codebook $\{Y_k(t+1) : k = 1, 2, \ldots, N\}$. The algorithms differ in how the vector from the training set is used to update the codebook.

There are four LVQ algorithms which are implemented in the LVQ-PAK [3] software package: LVQ1, LVQ2.1, LVQ3, and OLVQ1. We will restrict our attention to LVQ1 and OLVQ1.

On each iteration t, LVQ1 adapts only the codebook vector nearest to $X(t)$. Let

$$c = \arg\min_k\{||X(t) - Y_k(t)||\}. \tag{4}$$

$Y_k(t+1)$ is computed as shown in (5) where $s(t)$ is $+1$ if $X(t)$ and $Y_c(t)$ are in the same class and -1 otherwise.

$$Y_k(t+1) = \begin{cases} Y_k(t) & k \neq c \\ Y_k(t) + s(t)\gamma(t)[X(t) - Y_k(t)] & k = c \end{cases} \tag{5}$$

The time varying parameter $\gamma(t)$ should only take on values between 0 and 1. In the LVQ-PAK software package, $\gamma(t)$ is initialized to 0.1 and decreases linearly.

OLVQ1 is so named because it is an optimization of LVQ1. The parameter $\gamma(t)$ from LVQ1 is allowed to be different for each codebook vector, and its value is changed in a more complex way than the linear decrease of LVQ1. The update is essentially the one shown in (5). However, now $\gamma(t)$ is replaced by $\gamma_c(t)$, the correct parameter for this codebook vector. The parameter $\gamma_c(t)$ is updated as shown in (6).

$$\gamma_c(t) = \frac{\gamma_c(t-1)}{1 + s(t)\gamma_c(t-1)} \tag{6}$$

The idea behind the adaptation of $\gamma_c(t)$ in (6) is that each input vector from the training set should be given the same weight in affecting the position of the codebook vector. At iteration t, $X(t-1)$ is scaled by $[1 - s(t)\gamma_c(t)]\gamma_c(t-1)$. Equation (6) is simply the solution of the equation that results from setting $\gamma_c(t)$ equal to $[1 - s(t)\gamma_c(t)]\gamma_c(t-1)$.

5 Comparison of BRVQ to OLVQ1

OLVQ1 appears to be the newest routine in the LVQ-PAK software package. The LVQ-PAK manual does not give information about the relative performance of the four algorithms, but it recommends that learning always be started with the OLVQ1 algorithm. Furthermore, the manual implies that all four algorithms have similar accuracies. For these reasons, the studies in this paper use OLVQ1 to represent the LVQ family.

Based on a study of performance vs. number of iterations, it was decided to run the OLVQ1 algorithm for 100,000 iterations. From section 3, BRVQ performance was consistently good for $\lambda = \infty$ as long as the codebook was reclassified by majority rule after training. We use this version of BRVQ in our studies below. To provide a reference point for MSE, we also apply the Lloyd algorithm (BRVQ with $\lambda = 0$) to the four classification problems. Thus, the three algorithms we compared are OLVQ1 with 100,000 iterations, BRVQ with $\lambda = \infty$ and codebook reclassification, and the Lloyd algorithm.

Classification Performance

The top plot in Figure 3 shows the classification performance for the Diamond problem. BRVQ and OLVQ1 perform similarly with neither algorithm having consistently lower P_e. The Lloyd algorithm had noticeably larger P_e's than those of BRVQ and OLVQ1. This is not surprising. Lloyd was not designed as a classification algorithm. Similar classification performance was observed for the Square problem

Codebooks of size 100 or more are required for these two problems to achieve P_e's approaching the Bayes rule P_e of zero. Thus these problems would appear to be "hard" problems for classification by VQ. However, VQ codebooks of size 8 exist, although not found by the algorithms studied, which would give $P_e = 0$.

The bottom plot in Figure 3 shows classification performance for the different ρ's problem. BRVQ consistently had a larger P_e than OLVQ1. The Lloyd algorithm performed comparably to BRVQ and OLVQ1. As codebook size increased, the P_e's of the three algorithms became similar. Similar classification performance was observed for the different σ's problem.

With size 8 codebooks all three algorithms are *already* quite close to the Bayes rule P_e for these problems. This includes the Lloyd algorithm which is doing classification only as an afterthought. These appear to be "easy" classification problems for VQ classifiers.

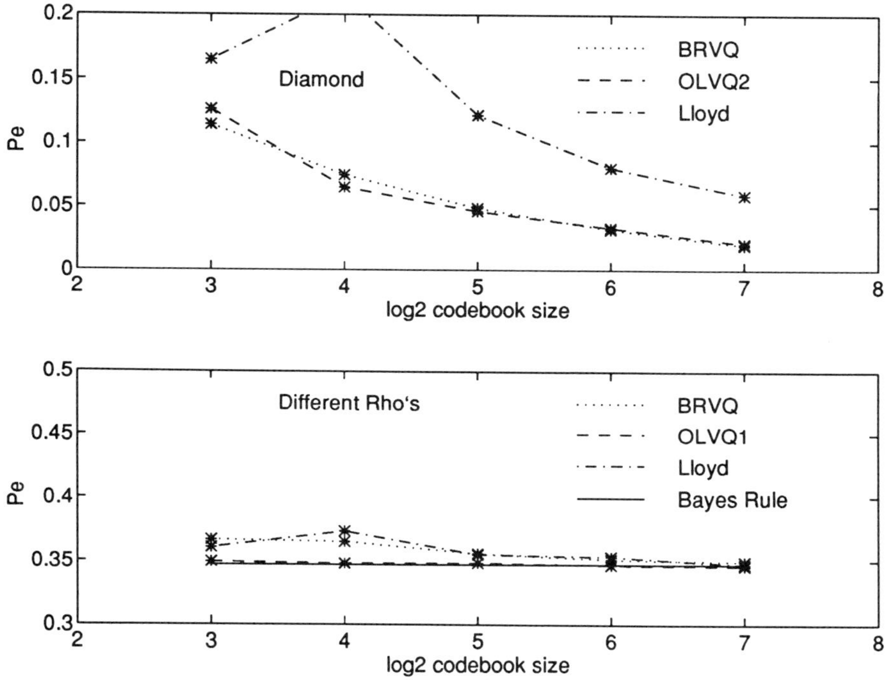

Figure 3: P_e vs. codebook size for the Diamond problem and the Different ρ's problem.

Mean Square Error Performance

Figure 4 shows the MSE performance vs. codebook size for the Diamond problem and the Different ρ's problem. MSE performance was similar for all four problems studied. The three algorithms always had the same ordering at all the codebook sizes considered. As illustrated in Figure 4, the Lloyd algorithm always had the best MSE performance. The BRVQ algorithm was always next, and the OLVQ1 always had the worst MSE performance. As the codebook size increased, the performance of all three algorithms became similar.

It should be noted that OLVQ1 does not explicitly try to minimize MSE. In fact, MSE performance could be improved with no degradation of classification performance by using the centroid of the training vectors in each partition cell as its reproduction vector.

6 Conclusions

Codebook reclassification was shown to improve the poor BRVQ classification performance resulting from the use of one encoder for training and a different encoder

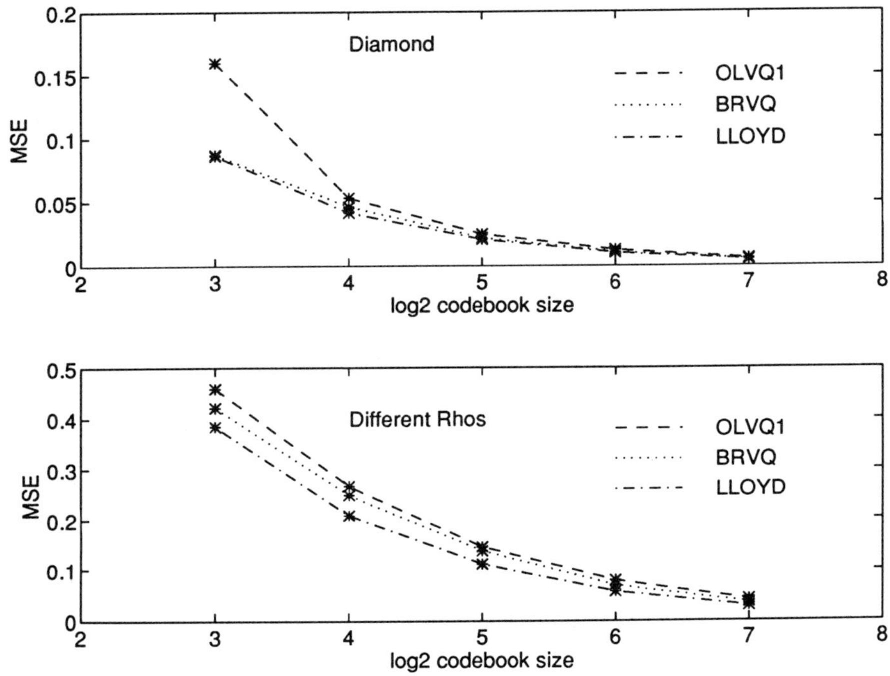

Figure 4: MSE vs. codebook size for the Diamond problem and the Different ρ's problem.

for the test data. Better performance can be obtained by using one encoder for both training and test, as is always done in standard VQ for lossy compression. Some work has recently been done in this direction [8, 9, 10]. If $\Pr[C_X \neq \delta(k)]$ is known or can be estimated from the training set, then $I[c_X \neq \delta(k)]$ can be replaced with $\Pr[C_X \neq \delta(k)]$ or its estimate in (2). This produces one encoder which can be used both for training and test. For this new encoder, BRVQ with $\lambda = \infty$ is exactly classified VQ as in [7]. As a result, at $\lambda = \infty$ it will provide a P_e which is exactly the Bayes rule P_e if the estimate of $\Pr[C_X \neq \delta(k)]$ is perfect (assuming there are at least as many codewords as classes).

For the Diamond and Square problems we saw that BRVQ and OLVQ1 only began to approach the Bayes rule P_e for large codebook sizes. These two problems had likelihood ratios that changed from zero to ∞ at the decision boundaries. Thus, if the decision boundary is not exactly as prescribed by Bayes rule, the P_e will increase dramatically. Perhaps this extreme sensitivity explains the poor small codebook performance of the algorithms on these two problems.

The two problems we studied with a large Bayes rule P_e had slowly changing likelihood ratios making it less critical that the decision boundaries be precisely in the correct place. For these problems the algorithms studied achieved a P_e close to Bayes rule even for codebooks of size 8.

A problem should not be considered "hard" or "easy" for classification by VQ based on its Bayes rule P_e, but rather by how difficult it is to achieve the Bayes rule P_e. An important factor affecting this is the rate of change of the likelihood ratio.

Acknowlegements

The authors would like to thank Karen Oehler for providing the first author with an excellent introduction to the BRVQ algorithm and for helpful comments as the work progressed.

References

[1] Allen Gersho and Robert M. Gray. *Vector Quantization and Signal Compression.* Kluwer Academic Publishers, 1992.

[2] P. A. Chou, T. Lookabaugh, and R. M. Gray. Entropy-constrained vector quantization. *IEEE Transactions on Acoustics, Speech, and Signal Processing*, 37, January 1989.

[3] Teuvo Kohonen, Jari Kangas, Jorma Laaksonen, and Kari Torkkola. *LVQ-PAK: The Learning Vector Quantization Program Package.* Helsinki University of Technology, Laboratory of Computer and Information Science, 1992. available via anonymous ftp to cochlea.hut.fi (130.233.168.48).

[4] Teuvo Kohonen, Gyorgy Barna, and Ronald Chrisley. Statistical pattern recognition with neural networks: Benchmarking studies. In *IEEE International Conference on Neural Networks*, 1988.

[5] Karen L. Oehler and Robert M. Gray. Combining image classification and image compression using vector quantization. In *Data Compression Conference, Snowbird, Utah*, 1993.

[6] Karen L. Oehler, Pamela C. Cosman, Robert M. Gray, and J. May. Classification using vector quantization. In *Twenty-Fifth Annual Asilomar Conference on Signal Systems, and Computers*, 1991.

[7] B. Ramamurthi and A. Gersho. Classified vector quantization of images. *IEEE Transactions on Communications*, COM-34(11):1105–1115, November 1986.

[8] K.L. Oehler and R.M. Gray. Combining image compression and classification using vector quantization. 1993. submitted for possible publication.

[9] R.M. Gray, K.L.Oehler, K.O. Perlmutter, and R. A. Olshen. Combining tree-structured vector quantization with classification and regression trees. In R. Madon, editor, *Proceedings of the Twenty-Seventh Annual Asilomar Conference on Signals, Systems and Computers*, Pacific Grove, CA, November 1993.

[10] K.O. Perlmutter, R.M.Gray, K.L. Oehler, and R.A. Olshen. Bayes risk weighted tree-structured vector quantization with posterior estimation. In *Data Compression Conference, Snowbird, Utah*, 1994.

Improved Techniques for Single-Pass Adaptive VQ

Cornel Constantinescu and James A. Storer
Department of Computer Science, Brandeis University

Abstract: Constantinescu and Storer [CS93, CS94] present a new single-pass adaptive vector quantization algorithm that learns a codebook of variable size and shape entries; they present experiments on a set of test images showing that with no training or prior knowledge of the data, for a given fidelity, the compression achieved typically equals or exceeds that of the JPEG standard. This paper presents improvements in speed (by employing K-D trees), simplicity of codebook entries, and visual quality with no loss in either the amount of compression or the SNR as compared to the original full–search version.

1 Introduction

Constantinescu and Storer [CS93, CS94] show how to combine the ability of lossless adaptive dictionary methods to process data in a single pass with the ability of vector quantization accurately to approximate data. For a given overall fidelity of the decompressed image, the compression achieved by this new approach typically equals or exceeds the JPEG standard. In addition, it often out-performs traditional trained VQ (even in the best case, where the codebook is specifically trained for the type of data being compressed) while at the same time having a number of additional advantages: First, it is a single-pass adaptive algorithm (requiring no codebook to be provided in advance). Second, one can provide precise guarantees in advance on the distortion of any $l \times l$ sub-block of the image (whereas trained VQ simply finds the best match to an available codebook). Third, with a fixed codebook size, one can continuously vary the fidelity / compression tradeoff (whereas trained VQ typically achieves different tradeoffs by employing multiple codebooks). Our algorithm also enjoys some of the advantages of trained VQ, such as fast table-lookup decoding.

This paper presents improvements in speed, simplicity of codebook entries, and visual quality with no loss in either the amount of compression or the SNR as compared to the original full search version. Section 2 reviews the basic single pass adaptive VQ algorithm presented in Constantinescu and Storer [CS93, CS94]. Section 3 presents a k-d tree implementation of the dictionary that greatly improves the speed of serial implementations with no loss in either the amount of compression or the SNR as compared to the original full search version. In fact, due to a minor improvement in the basic algorithm (see the end of Section 2), the experiments reported here improve upon what is reported in Constantinescu and Storer [CS93, CS94]. Section 4 presents a new learning heuristic that employs only square shaped entries. Section 5 presents a new method for distortion computation that improves visual quality without any significant sacrifice in signal to noise ratio (SNR). Section 6 mentions some current areas of research.

2 The Basic Single-Pass Adaptive VQ Algorithm

The basic single-pass adaptive VQ algorithm presented in Constantinescu and Storer [CS93, CS94] is depicted in Figure 2, which is followed by Algorithms 1a and 1b, the Lossy Generic Encoding and Decoding Algorithms for on-line adaptive vector quantization. Figure 1 illustrates the workings of the algorithms by showing on the left a cat-scan chest image, in

 1068-0314/94 $3.00

the center a map of how the compressor covers the image with rectangles, and on the right a portion of the dictionary about half way through the compression process. The operation of the generic algorithms is guided by the following heuristics:

Figure 1: ChestCAT original, map and dictionary

The growing heuristic: Selects one growing point $GP(x, y, q)$ from the available pool GPP. All experiments reported here use the *wave* heuristic (a "wave front" that goes from the upper-left corner down to the lower right corner). Other examples of growing heuristics include *circular* (a "ball" that expands outward from the center), *diagonal* (a successive "thickening" of the main diagonal), and *FIFO* (first-in first-out).

The match heuristic: Decides what block b from the dictionary D best matches $imageGP$ (the portion of the image of the same shape as b defined by the currently selected growing point GP). All experimental results reported here use the *greedy* heuristic (choose the largest match possible of acceptable quality, and among two matches of equal size, choose the one of best quality). The parameters that guide the matching process are: The *distance measure*; we use the standard mean-square measure in all experiments. The *elementary subblock size* l; large matches can be divided into subblocks of constant size $l \times l$, and then distance is computed as the maximum distance among the subblocks; this prevents distortion from being unacceptable in a small portion of a match because it is better than needed in other areas (all experiments reported here use $l \times l = 4 \times 4$). The *type of coverage*; examples of image covering strategies include *first* coverage where the distance is computed only on the uncovered part of $imageGP$, *last* coverage where the match is computed for the entire block (except if it falls outside the image borders), and *average* coverage (used in all experiments reported here) where the match is computed for the entire block as for last, but on overlapped areas the resulting value is the average value between all the values of matches that happen to cover that pixel. The *threshold* t; a real number that defines the maximum allowed distance (distortion) between $imageGP$ and b.

The growing points update heuristic: The growing points update heuristic is responsible for generating new growing points after each new match is made. For all experiments reported here, the concave corners of the partially encoded/decoded image are chosen.

The dictionary update heuristic: The dictionary update heuristic adapts the contents of the dictionary D to the part of the image that is currently encoded/decoded. All experiments reported here use the *OneRow+OneColumn* dictionary update heuristic, depicted in Figure 3, that adds (if possible) two new blocks to the dictionary, constructed by extending the previously matched block (or part of it) vertically and horizontally by one row.

The deletion heuristic: Maintains the dictionary D so it can have a predefined (constant) size D_{max}. All experiments reported here use the *LRU* heuristic (delete the entry that has been least recently used).

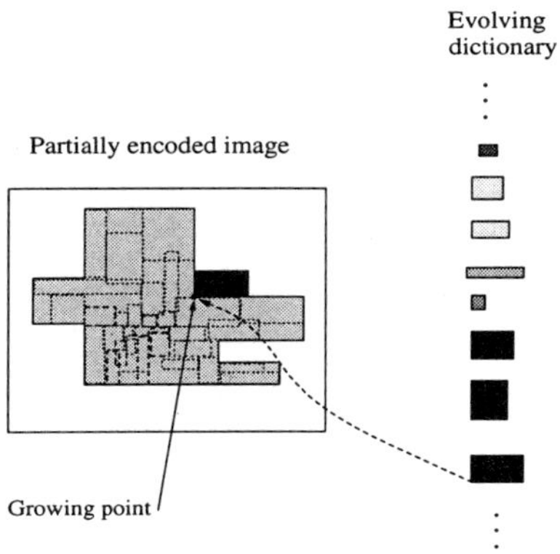

Figure 2: On-Line Adaptive VQ

1. Initialize the *local dictionary* D to have one entry for each pixel of the input alphabet and the *growing points pool* (GPP) with one (or more) growing points.

2. **Repeat** until there are no more growing points in GPP:

   (a) {*Select the next growing point from GPP:*}
   Use a *growing heuristic* to choose a growing point GP from GPP.

   (b) {*Get the best match block b:*}
   Use a *match heuristic* to find a block b in D that matches with acceptable fidelity $image(GP, b)$ (the portion of image determined by GP having the same size as b). Transmit $\lceil log_2|D| \rceil$ bits for the index of b.

   (c) {*Update D and GPP:*}
   Add each of the blocks specified by a *dictionary update heuristic* to D (if D is full, first use a *deletion heuristic* to make space).

Algorithm 1a: Lossy Generic Encoding Algorithm

1. {Initialize D and GPP by performing Step 1 of the encoding algorithm.}

2. **Repeat** until there are no more growing points in GPP:

   (a) {Select the next growing point from GPP:}
   Perform Step 2a of the encoding algorithm to obtain GP.

   (b) {Get the best match block b:}
   Receive $\lceil log_2|D| \rceil$ bits for the index of b. Retrieve b from D and output b at the position determined by GP.

   (c) {Update D and GPP:} Perform Step 2c of the encoding algorithm.

Algorithm 1b: Lossy Generic Decoding Algorithm

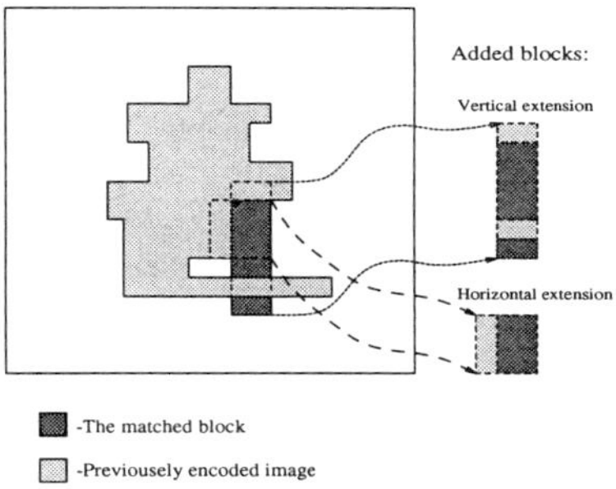

Figure 3: "OneRow+OneColumn" Learning Heuristic

Before closing this section, we should report an experimental finding made after the writing of Constantinescu and Storer [CS93]. Although experiments have shown that the basic algorithm is robust over a wide choice of heuristics, allowing growth in only one quadrant (as long as possible) typically improves compression (by about 10 percent on average) for the same SNR. Because *wave* growing can "fill" the entire image and still satisfy the above restriction, this paper has switched from *circular* (used in Constantinescu and Storer [CS93]) to *wave*.

3 K-D tree dictionary data structure

The basic algorithm presented in Constantinescu and Storer [CS93, CS94] encodes with simple linear search to find matches, and is very slow if implemented on a standard serial architecture (decompression is essentially table lookup, and is quite fast). In this section we present a new algorithm based on k-d trees that reduces the search time from minutes or even hours to a few seconds on a UNIX workstation.

If we consider each dictionary block b with $k_b = m_b \times n_b$ pixels as a point in a k_b-dimensional space, the problem is to find the closest point (best block) to a given point (image area $imageGP$) from a set of points (dictionary of blocks); that is, a nearest-neighbor search problem (e.g., Preparata [PS85], Dasarathy [Das91]). However, the problem has several non-trivial peculiarities: First, the dictionary blocks have *variable dimension* (k_b) and *variable shape* (m_b and n_b can have arbitrary values). Second, the dictionary maintains a *dynamic* set of blocks: in addition to search we need *insertions* and *deletions*. And third, the "best" block is defined by a match heuristic that may use a variety of distortion measures that work over a variety of rectangle sizes (and there is always a perfect match to the unit size). Typically, nearest-neighbor algorithms perform time consuming preprocessing in order to have fast processing time. This works well if the set of points is *static* (doesn't change during processing). However, in our case the set of points (dictionary) consists of the alphabet at the beginning of encoding, and changes during encoding, on average with two insertions and eventually two deletions for each search.

We have employed a data structure based on *k-d trees* (e.g., Bentley [Ben75], Bentley and Friedman [BF79], Overmars and van Leeuven [OvL82]). Each branch in the tree relies on some *discriminating dimension* and a *partition value*. The non-terminal nodes contains the (two) pointers to the sons, the partition value, and the discriminating dimension (which can be data dependent); terminal nodes (named *buckets*) contains data (dictionary blocks). Because we are using the wave growing heuristic, we can assume that a region that is being matched is always "attached" to the already compressed portion of the image at its upper left corner, and we use the upper left 4×4 sub-block of the region to provide the keys for the search. To find matches that are less than 4 pixels in either dimension, we employ a few additional trees, as to be discussed shortly.

A significant difference between our algorithm and Friedman, Bentley and Finkel [FBF77] algorithm, is that we have a bound on the allowable distortion (the distortion threshold d) before starting the search. So, we can start a range search for the "best" block using the distortion threshold to define the range (instead of going first for some nearest neighbor block, compute the distance r between this block and the query block, and then do a range search backward – the so called "bounds-overlap-ball" test). If we use the range $[x_i - d, x_i + d]$ for each dimension i of the query block x (key area), deciding to go left, right or both ways in the k-d tree depending on how this range compares with the partition value v_i associated with the currently visited non-terminal node, we end up by selecting *all* potential best matches (all blocks which meet the distortion threshold on the key area), no matter what distortion measure we use as long as it is monotonic in dimension values as well as in the number of dimensions (conditions required also by Friedman, Bentley and Finkel algorithm). An example of such a measure is the standard L2 (Euclidean) metric. Although mean-square error does not satisfy this condition, it is a bit faster to compute (because there is no square root to compute) and works equally well in practice.

Let us now consider the complexity of our algorithm when the k-d tree data structure is employed. Encoding time is bounded by $O(N + \frac{N(S(D_{max},m)+Q(N)+m)}{r})$, where N is the number of pixels in the image, $S(D_{max}, m)$ is the maximum time to search a dictionary with a maximum of D_{max} entries each with at most m pixels, $Q(N)$ is the time to insert and delete for the growing points queue, and r is the amount of compression (original size / compressed size). Straightforward implementation of the growing heuristics we have considered uses $O(log(N))$ time by employing a heap data structure; however, this time can be reduced to $O(1)$ by implementing all heuristics in a manner similar to FIFO. Under ideal assumptions, it can be shown that the expected time for range search in k-d trees is $O(\log n + B)$, where B is the number of blocks found (Bentley and Stanat [BS75], Friedman, Bentley, and Finkel [FBF77]). If we take $S(D_{max}, m)$ to be $O(log(D_{max}))$ (which from our experiments appears to be a reasonable assumption), the improved encoding time is $O(N + \frac{Nlog(D_{max})}{r})$, under the reasonable assumption that $m = O(log(D_{max}))$. In many applications, it may be reasonable to assume that r is $log(D_{max})$, which brings the encoding time down to $O(N)$ time. As before, decoding is essentially table lookup, and can be done in $O(N)$ time. The following settings were used for all experiments reported here:

bucket size: Maximum 8 blocks per bucket.

discriminating dimension: The dimension with the largest spread of values.

partition value: Mean value between discriminating dimensions in the bucket.

range: $1.25 * d$. (Even though mean-square error is not monotone, by extending the range just a little to $[x_i - 1.25 * d, x_i + 1.25 * d]$, the retrieval quality is as good as for full search with an insignificant increase in search time.)

number of k-d trees: Four trees with the following key sizes and block assignment:

- **t1** has 1×1 key and contains blocks of size $1 \times n$ or $n \times 1$, with $n \geq 2$. ($t1$ is simply a binary search tree).
- **t2** has 2×2 key and contains blocks of size $2 \times n$ or $n \times 2$, with $n \geq 2$.
- **t3** has 3×3 key and contains blocks of size $3 \times n$ or $n \times 3$, with $n \geq 3$ and

t4 has 4×4 key and contains blocks of size $m \times n$, with $m, n \geq 4$.

For each test image of Figure 4, we adjusted the threshold to get three compressed files, one of very good quality, one of good quality, and one of fair quality; the results are shown in Table 1. Although the compression obtained is nearly identical with the basic full search algorithm, the execution time for a 4K dictionary was about 60 times faster (roughly speaking, we now use seconds rather than minutes to encode on a UNIX workstation). Moreover, using a larger dictionary (8K or 16K) to get better compression, the increase in tree search time is only 15% - 30% while the full search time will increase 2 - 4 times.

4 Square shapes

One important question regarding our compression algorithm is how sensitive it is to the shapes of the blocks, and whether it is possible to use only few different shapes and still achieve the same performance. To check this, we introduced a "shape filter" in the compressor that "cut" all the blocks added to the dictionary to a given set of allowable (rectangular) shapes. To make this filter work for a variety of shapes while the learned blocks become bigger and bigger, we extended the *OneRow+OneColumn* learning heuristic to a *ThreeBlock* learning heuristic that learns in addition (if possible) a third rectangular block that extends the current match both vertically and horizontally by one unit. With *ThreeBlock* learning we can restrict the shapes of the blocks to squares, and still obtain similar or better compression/quality as with arbitrary shapes. Figure 5 shows part of the original HandWriting image together with the JPEG result for 70-to-1 compression. Figure 6 compares results of our compression algorithm on the HandWriting image at 70-to-1 compression using unrestricted rectangular shaped blocks on the left and only square shapes on the right. Figure 7 shows a portion of the contents of the dictionary at about 2/3 the way through the compresion process.

5 Visual quality

As discussed in Constantinescu and Storer [CS93], it is sometimes the case (especially with magazine images at high compression ratios) that our algorithm seems to be too good on edges and active areas (compared with JPEG) while on smooth areas there can be more visible distortions. A likely explanation is that SNR, which is not the best measure of visual quality, becomes a progressively worse measure of visual quality as the match size becomes large. Error images (the difference between the original and decompressed image) seem to support this explanation, where for our algorithm the error is uniformly distributed, while for JPEG it is more intense in active areas. Here we describe a method that improves the visual appearance of the decoded images produced by our compression algorithm by enforcing lower distortion on smooth areas while accepting slightly larger errors on active areas. We use the method described in Manikopoulos and Sun [MS88] to estimate the "activity" in a region of the image as the ratio between the variance (to the mean) V and the mean M on this region. From experimentation, we can say that if the ratio A is smaller than 4% - 5%, then the area is smooth and we use a smaller distortion threshold of $0.4 * d$ for this area; if $5\% < A \leq 10\%$ we use an intermediary threshold of $0.6 * d$, and if $A > 10\%$ than the area is active and we use the entire threshold d. Figure 8 shows our algorithm on ChestCAT and WomanHat images, using a constant distortion threshold at

ChestCAT: Cat-scan chest image, 512 by 512 pixels, 8 bits per pixel.

BrainMrSide: Magnetic resonance medical image that shows a side cross-section of a head, 256 by 256 pixels, 8 bits per pixel; this is the medical image used by Gray, Cosman, and Riskin [GCR91].

BrainMrTop: Magnetic resonance medical image that shows a top cross-section of a head, 256 by 256 pixels, 8 bits per pixel.

NASA5: Band 5 of a 7-band image of Donaldsonville, LA; the least compressible of the 7 bands by UNIX compress.

NASA6: Band 6 of a 7-band image of Donaldsonville, LA; the most compressible of the 7 bands by UNIX compress.

WomanHat: The standard woman in the hat photo, 512 by 512 pixels, 8 bits per pixel.

LivingRoom: Two people in the living room of an old house with light coming in the window, 512 by 512 pixels, 8 bits per pixel.

FingerPrint: An FBI finger print image, 768 by 768 pixels, 8 bits per pixel; includes some text at the top.

HandWriting: The first two paragraphs and part of the figure of page 165 of *Image and Text Compression* (Kluwer Academic Press, Norwell, MA) written by hand on a 10 inch high by 7.5 inch wide piece of gray stationary scanned at 128 pixels per inch, 8 bits per pixel; approximately 1.2 million bytes.

Figure 4: Description of the images

	"Very Good "		"Good "		"Fair"	
	Quality	Compression	Quality	Compression	Quality	Compression
	SNR (PSNR)	TREE / FULL / JPEG	SNR (PSNR)	TREE / FULL / JPEG	SNR (PSNR)	TREE / FULL / JPEG
BrainCAT	29 (36)	4.3 / 4.3 / 3.0	22 (29)	8.9 / 8.9 / 4.8	18 (25)	12.8 / 12.7 / 6.7
BrainMR_Side	28.5 (39)	4.1 / 4.1 / 4.6	26.5 (37)	4.8 / 4.9 / 6.1	20.5 (31)	10.4 / 10.3 / 15.8
BrainMR_Top	27 (35)	2.8 / 2.9 / 2.4	20.5 (28.5)	5.7 / 5.7 / 3.9	15.5 (23.5)	10.4 / 10.8 / 6.6
NASA5	30.5 (41)	4.1 / 4.2 / 4.1	28 (38.5)	5.6 / 5.6 / 5.9	26 (36.5)	7.4 / 7.5 / 8.5
NASA6	46 (51.5)	22.6 / 22.8 / 8.4	40.5 (46.5)	74.4 / 80.1 / 64.7	39 (45)	107.8 / 106.5 / 65.1
WomanHat	35 (40.5)	4.0 / 4.1 / 4.4	30 (35)	8.6 / 8.8 / 13.7	27 (32.5)	14.4 / 14.5 / 23.5
LivingRoom	32 (38)	3.9 / 4.0 / 4.3	27 (33)	7.4 / 7.5 / 9.1	24.5 (30.5)	10.8 / 11.0 / 14.3
FingerPrint	32 (35)	6.2 / 6.3 / 6.5	24 (27)	26.5 / 26.5 / 27.3	22 (25)	37.6 / 38.9 / 35.0
HandWriting	32 (33)	17.3 / 17.0 / 9.5	24.5 (25.5)	61.0 / 60.1 / 32.0	17.5 (18.5)	172.0 / 177.0 / 67.3

Table 1: Comparison of compression ratios for the same SNR (PSNR)
Each of the three columns shows for the same SNR (the corresponding PSNR is shown in parentheses) the compression achieved by our algorithm with the new tree search data structure, our basic full-search algorithm, and by JPEG.

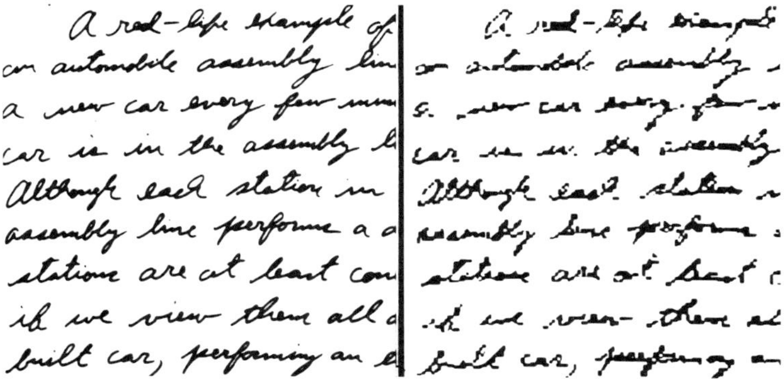

Figure 5: HandWriting original (left) and JPEG at 70-to-1 (right)

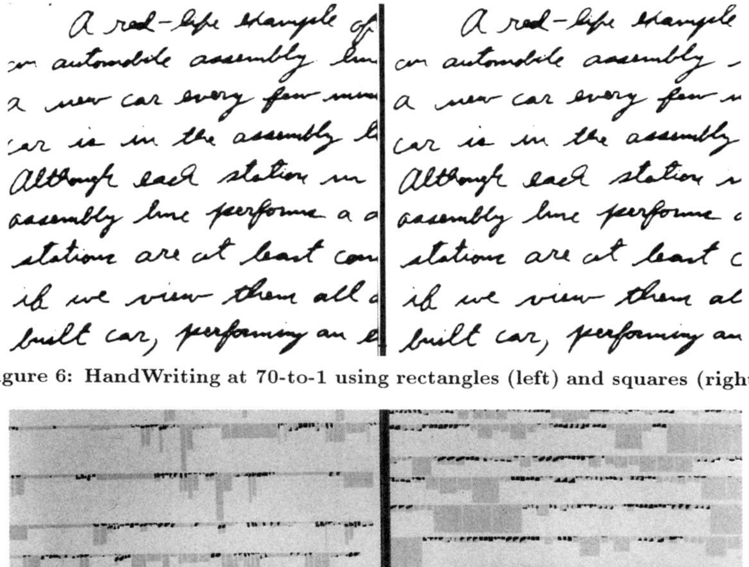

Figure 6: HandWriting at 70-to-1 using rectangles (left) and squares (right)

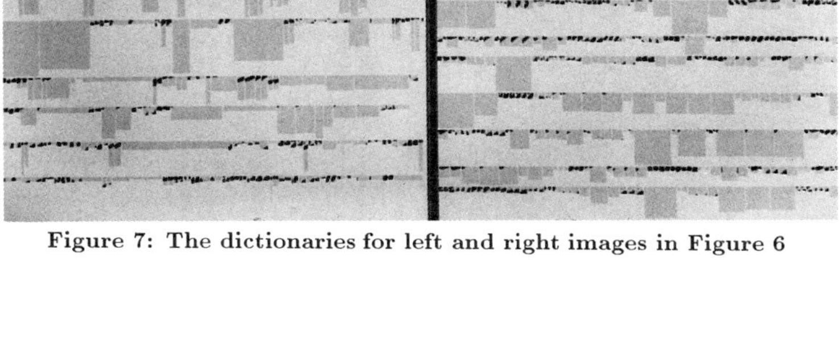

Figure 7: The dictionaries for left and right images in Figure 6

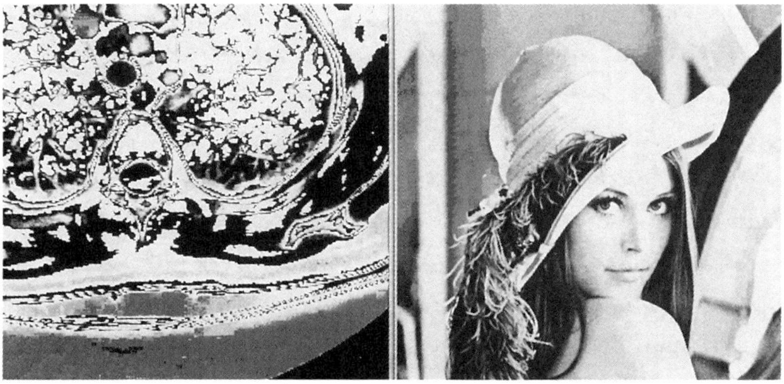

Figure 8: ChestCAT and WomanHat images at 10 to 1 using constant threshold

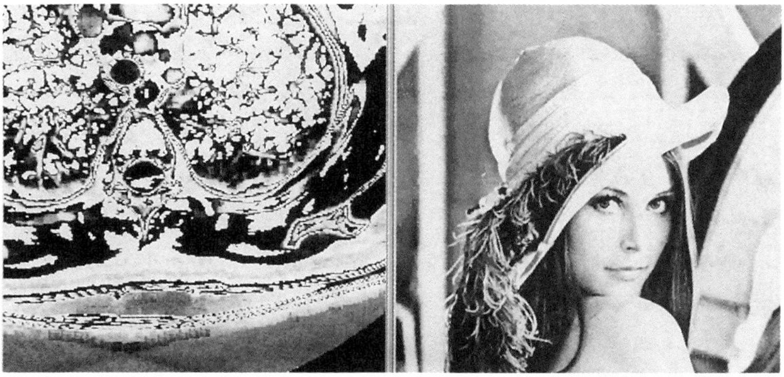

Figure 9: ChestCAT and WomanHat images at 10 to 1 using variable threshold

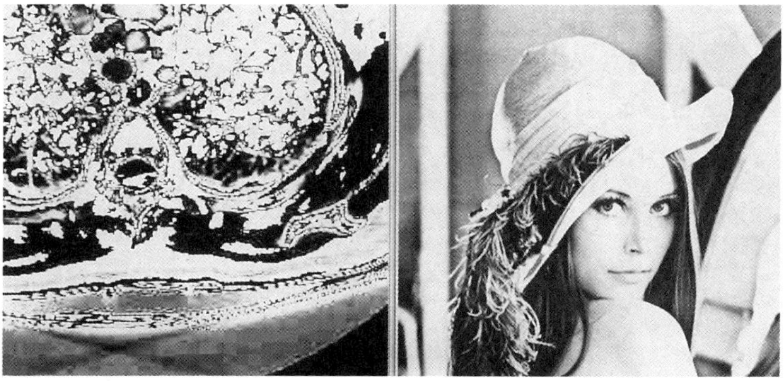

Figure 10: ChestCAT and WomanHat images at 10 to 1 using JPEG

10 to 1 compression. Figure 9 shows the results of the method described above on the same images at 10 to 1 compression. The visual quality is much improved (especially on smooth areas such as the shoulder in the WomanHat image and the smooth part with the "X" in the ChestCAT image). For comparison, Figure 10 shows JPEG at 10 to 1 compression on the same images; the ChestCAT is blocky and the edges are not preserved, however the WomanHat is about as good as that in Figure 9.

6 Current research

We are currently working on a number of extensions to the basic approach presented in this paper. First we are continuing experiments to better understand how different heuristics affect performance in terms of both speed and quality. Second, parallel algorithms that run in nearly $O(\sqrt{N})$ time with $O(\sqrt{N})$ processors are possible. Third, of interest are formal proofs addressing compression - fidelity tradeoffs.

References

[Ben75] J.L. Bentley. Multidimensional binary search trees used for associative searching. *Communications of the ACM*, 18:509 – 517, 1975.

[BF79] J. L. Bentley and J. H. Friedman. Data structures for range searching. *ACM Computing Surveys*, 11:4:397–409, 1979.

[BS75] J. L. Bentley and D. F. Stanat. Analysis of range searching in quad trees. *Information Processing Lett.*, 3:6:170–173, 1975.

[CS93] C. Constantinescu and J. A. Storer. On-Line Adaptive Vector Quantization with Variable Size Codebook Entries. In *Proceedings IEEE Data Compression Conference*, Snowbird, Utah, 1993. IEEE Computer Society Press.

[CS94] C. Constantinescu and J. A. Storer. On-Line Adaptive Vector Quantization with Variable Size Codebook Entries. *Journal of Information Processing and Management*, To appear, 1994.

[Das91] B. V. Dasarathy, editor. *Nearest Neighbor (NN) Norms: NN Pattern Classification Techniques.* IEEE Computer Society Press, 1991.

[FBF77] J. H. Friedman, J. L. Bentley, and R. A. Finkel. An algorithm for finding best matches in logarithmic expected time. *ACM Trans. Math. Softw.*, 3:3:209–226, 1977.

[GCR91] R. M. Gray, P. C. Cosman, and E. A. Riskin. Combining Vector Quantization and Histogram Equalization. In *Proceedings IEEE Data Compression Conference*, pages 113–118, Snowbird, Utah, 1991. IEEE Computer Society Press.

[GG91] A. Gersho and R. M. Gray. *Vector Quantization and Signal Compression.* Kluwer Academic Publishers, Norwell MA, 1991.

[Lin92] J. Lin. *Vector Quantization for Image Compression: Algorithms and Performance.* PhD thesis, Computer Science Dept., Brandeis University, Waltham, MA., 1992.

[MS88] C. N. Manikopoulos and H. Sun. Activity index threshold classification in adaptive vector quantization. In *Conf. Proc. 1988 Int. Conf. Acoustics, Speech, Signal Processing*, pages 1235–1239. IEEE, 1988.

[OvL82] M. H. Overmars and J. van Leeuven. Dynamic multi-dimensional data structures based om quad- and K-D trees. *Acta Informatica*, 17:267–285, 1982.

[PS85] F. P. Preparata and M. I. Shamos. *Computational Geometry: An Introduction.* Springer-Verlag, 1985.

[Sto88] J. A. Storer. *Data Compression: Methods and Theory.* Computer Science Press, Rockville, MD, 1988.

Variable-Dimension Vector Quantization of Speech Spectra for Low-Rate Vocoders

Amitava Das, Ajit V. Rao, and Allen Gersho

Center for Information Processing Research
Department of Electrical and Computer Engineering
University of California
Santa Barbara, CA 93106.

Abstract

Optimal vector quantization of variable-dimension vectors in principle is feasible by using a set of fixed dimension VQ codebooks. However, for typical applications, such a multi-codebook approach demands a grossly excessive and impractical storage and computational complexity. Efficient quantization of such variable-dimension spectral shape vectors is the most challenging and difficult encoding task required in an important family of low bit-rate vocoders. We introduce a simple and effective formulation of *variable-dimension vector quantization* (VDVQ) which quantizes variable-dimension vectors using a single universal codebook having fixed dimension yet covering the entire range of input vector dimensions under consideration. This VDVQ technique is applied to quantize variable-dimension spectral shape vectors leading to a high quality speech coder at the low bit-rate of 2.5 kb/s. The combination of a universal spectral codebook and structured VQ reduces storage and computational complexity, yet delivers a high quantization efficiency and enhanced perceptual quality of the coded speech.

1. INTRODUCTION

In various signal compression applications, a sequence of random vectors with varying dimension represents the signal as it evolves in time. The dimension L of such a variable-dimension vector **S** can be modeled as a random variable and the observed value taken on by such a vector is characterized by both a dimension d and an ordered set of d real numbers. We first introduce the concept of *variable-dimension vector quantization* (VDVQ) in its simplest form and then later describe a modified formulation that is particularly suited to the quantization of spectra in parametric vocoders.

A variable-dimension vector quantizer for the random pair $(L, \mathbf{S})$ is a mapping of the pair into a reproduction $(L, \hat{\mathbf{S}})$ where $\hat{\mathbf{S}}$ takes on one of a finite set of possible reproduction values. It is assumed that the set of allowed dimensions is finite. The resulting quantizer consists of a finite set of codebooks, one for each possible input dimension. The optimal quantizer simply observes the particular input dimension d of an input vector **s** and finds the best matching code vector in the codebook for that particular dimension. Each optimal VDVQ codebook CB_j having codevectors of dimension d_j is designed from a sufficiently large training set T_j of pairs $\{d_j, \mathbf{s}_j\}$. The overall training

This work was supported by Fujitsu Laboratories, Ltd. and the National Science Foundation.

set **T** needed to train all of these optimal codebooks will include all such T_j's and therefore can be excessively large. The earliest published formulation of VDVQ was apparently given by Adoul and Delprat who viewed the input vector as a semi-infinite sequence and coded a truncated version of this sequence by searching a single codebook containing code vectors of various dimensions [1]. Our VDVQ formulation above is slightly more general but in most respects is equivalent to the formulation of [1].

In certain applications, a substantially different (and in some respects more general) formulation of VDVQ is needed. We focus in this paper on this alternative formulation. Each input vector to be quantized consists of a random subset of the components (or *samples*) of a higher dimensional (but possibly not observable) random vector **Z** of fixed dimension K. The input to the VDVQ encoder consists of a signal vector **S** of dimension L and a vector **Q** of dimension K with binary-valued components, called the *selector* vector, which has L nonzero components to identify the particular ordered subset of samples of **Z**. Thus, given **Z** and **Q**, a variable dimension vector **S** of dimension L is implicitly specified where L is the number of nonzero elements in **Q** and **S** consists of those components of **Z** corresponding to the nonzero elements of **Q** while retaining the ordering of the components of **Z**. Thus, if $\mathbf{Z} = (z_1, z_2, z_3, z_4)$ and $\mathbf{Q} = (1, 0, 1, 1)$, then $\mathbf{S} = (z_1, z_3, z_4)$. In effect, what is being quantized is a subsampled version of a fixed dimension random vector where the location and number of the selected subsamples are also random. This version of VDVQ tends to requires an astronomical amount of storage and computational complexity except in the most trivial of applications.

In our formulation of VDVQ, not only is the dimension L random, but there may also be a large number of distinct selector vectors for each dimension and for each distinct selector vector having a particular dimension d, the physical meaning of the d components changes. In general, a separate codebook is needed for each distinct selector vector for an optimal VDVQ. If there are no restrictions on the possible selector vectors that can arise and the dimension can vary from 1 to K, the number of distinct codebooks needed is $2^K - 1$. Consequently, the training set must be extraordinarily large to have an adequate representation of vectors for the design of each codebook with an adequate training ratio. The storage requirement for such a set of codebooks can be grossly impractical to realize. Constructing such a large training set can itself be excessively burdensome.

An interesting and significant application of VDVQ arises in an important new direction in parametric speech coding with frequency domain vocoders, such as *sinusoidal transform coding* (STC) [2] and the *multiband excitation* (MBE) coder [3-7]. The most challenging task in such coders is efficient quantization of the speech spectral magnitude. Since the short-term speech spectrum changes in character with time and the number of spectral attributes that need to be reproduced are related to the pitch, which also varies with time, the number of needed samples of each spectrum is variable. Thus, optimal quantization calls for VDVQ.

Several indirect methods have been attempted [2-7] to circumvent the hurdle of variable dimensionality. A few approaches [2,4] convert the variable-dimension VQ problem to a fixed dimension VQ problem by approximating the spectral shape with an all-pole model and then vector quantizing the fixed-dimension model parameters. These methods clearly pay the extra penalty of modeling error, which often is quite significant.

One approach [5] uses the DCT for data compaction and then scalar quantize the DCT coefficients allocating bits and step sizes according to the dimension. This requires a large number of bits and a complex scheme and does not offer the efficiency of vector quantization over scalar quantization. Two other approaches [6, 7] convert the variable-dimension vectors to fixed dimension vectors using sample rate conversion and then vector quantize the fixed dimension vector. The error due to such dimension conversion is also quite significant. For frequency domain vocoders, the quality of the coded speech depends heavily on the quality of spectral quantization. Particularly at low bit rates, when "bit-starvation" itself causes high quantization noise, there is simply no room to tolerate any added distortion due to further modeling or dimension-altering techniques.

We propose a simple and effective VDVQ technique which provides a fitting solution to the variable-dimension spectral quantization problem of frequency domain vocoders mentioned above. In our VDVQ method, a single universal codebook is used to represent variable-dimension vectors of all dimensions under consideration. A simple training algorithm captures the source statistics in a single codebook, keeping both the storage and training complexity well within practical limits. A structured vector quantization technique leads to further reduction of storage and training complexity. Since each training vector contributes to the design of the entire codebook, a much reduced training set is required while maintaining near-optimal VDVQ performance. In one practical example, to quantize vectors of dimensions ranging from 10 to 50 using 20 bits, our method needs only 2^{17} words of memory, performs well with 80,000 training vectors, and needs only $2^{17} N_T$ multiplications for each training iteration, where N_T is the training set size. In comparison, an optimal multi-codebook VDVQ scheme would need 2^{30} words of memory, 2^{30} training vectors, and $2^{30} N_T$ multiplications per iteration.

Using this VDVQ technique, we designed an MBE-type vocoder operating at 2.5 kb/s. Direct quantization of the spectral shape vectors using VDVQ led to a high speech quality with performance better than/comparable to a higher rate (4.15 kb/s) IMBE coder that was adopted as the INMARSAT-M standard [5] for satellite voice communications.

2. EXTRACTION OF SPECTRAL PARAMETERS

As in other frequency domain vocoders, the operating principle of our vocoder is to model and quantize the short-term spectrum of speech so that the receiver can synthesize a new speech signal with nearly the same time-varying spectral character. We focus on a pitch dependent method of sampling to represent the spectrum. The spectrum of each 20 ms frame, computed with a Hamming window and a 256-point discrete Fourier transform (DFT), is divided into L bands. Each band of width F_o is centered at a harmonic of F_o, where F_o is the *pitch*, i.e., the fundamental frequency of the periodicity, as estimated for the speech segment.

Since the pitch F_o varies with time, the number of pitch-dependent spectral bands L is variable too. For each band, a *voicing probability* is estimated, a value of 1 indicating that the band is voiced (resembling a pitch harmonic peak), a value of 0 indicating unvoiced (resembles noise). For coding convenience, the L-bit voicing vector is replaced with a 12-bit vector **V**, each component representing 3 contiguous bands and the last component representing the high end of the spectra. For each of the L bands, one spectral magnitude sample corresponding to the spectral energy of that band is also computed, thereby forming an L-dimensional *spectral shape vector* (SSV) denoted by **S**.

In this way, the spectrum is represented by a set of spectral parameters: the pitch F_o, the voicing vector **V**, and the variable-dimension spectral shape vector **S** (Figure 1). The pitch is estimated using a joint time and frequency domain method. The vectors **V** and **S** are estimated by minimizing a perceptually weighted spectral distance between the original and the model spectrum in a manner similar to [5].

3. VDVQ OF SPEECH SPECTRA

The challenge, as mentioned before, is to quantize this variable-dimension spectral shape vector **S** for each frame of speech in a direct and near-optimal way without introducing any intermediate approximations by further modeling or dimension conversion. Thus our task is to quantize the vector **S** which contains a selected set of samples of the spectral shape corresponding to frequency locations dictated by harmonics of the pitch F_o. Due to the changing pitch, each frame has a different number of harmonics in the fixed voice bandwidth. Therefore, we are actually dealing with spectral shapes specified by these variable-dimensionality vectors. (The vocal tract "shape" determines the shape of the spectral envelope of a short-term speech spectrum, while the pitch determines the "fine structure" visible as local peaks in the spectrum corresponding to pitch harmonics).

We assume statistical independence of the pitch and the vocal tract shape (which is a reasonable approximation justified by the physiology of human speech production and by phonetics). Thus, for example, any particular phoneme will exhibit the same spectral shape irrespective of whether it is uttered by a male or a female speaker. However, the SSV representing the spectral shape of the phoneme will have different dimensions for typical male and female speakers. For female speech, the SSV will have a lower dimension since F_o will be higher and hence the number of harmonics will be smaller. For male speech, a lower F_o will generate a higher dimensional SSV. Therefore, even though SSVs of varying dimension will be generated due to varying pitch, the key problem essentially is how to quantize the spectral shape inherent to the phoneme being processed.

In our approach, we construct a universal spectral shape codebook containing a rich collection of K dimensional code vectors representing various spectral shapes over the full spectral range. Now, any SSV **S** representing a particular spectral shape can be well approximated by a code vector with a matching shape -- regardless of the dimensionality of **S**. The quantized version of the SSV will then be a properly sub-sampled version of the higher dimensional matching universal code vector. To find the best matching code vector, we simply need to compare the SSV components to the appropriate corresponding components of all the universal code vectors. In other words, before comparison with SSV, each universal shape code vector will be sub-sampled in exactly same way the SSV was originally sampled from the full-band spectrum. For mathematical convenience, we describe the VDVQ in a somewhat different but entirely equivalent way.

3.1 VDVQ Formulation

The VDVQ receives as input the pair $\{F_o, \mathbf{S}\}$, where the value of F_o determines both the dimension L of the SSV, **S**, and the selector vector **Q**. With the aid of the selector vector, the encoder first maps **S** into a K dimensional *extended* spectral vector **X** by assigning the components of **S** to the component positions of **X** corresponding to the correct frequency locations of the input spectrum and assigning zeros to all missing component positions where no spectral sample values are available. The kth component of the selector vector **Q** corresponds to the frequency $\frac{k \cdot \pi}{K}$. The frequency scale is normalized so that 2π radians is the sampling frequency of the speech signal.

Given the input pair $\{F_o, \mathbf{S}\}$, **Q** is generated according to:

$$Q[k] = \begin{cases} 1 & \text{if } k = \left\lceil \frac{j \cdot KF_o}{\pi} \right\rceil; \ j \textit{ any positive integer} \\ 0 & \textit{otherwise} \end{cases} \tag{1}$$

for $1 \le k \le K$.

In a similar way, the SSV is converted into an extended spectral vector as follows:

$$\mathbf{X}[k] = \begin{cases} \mathbf{S}[j], & \text{if } k = \left\lceil \frac{j \cdot KF_o}{\pi} \right\rceil; \ j \textit{ any positive integer} \\ 0, & \textit{otherwise} \end{cases} \tag{2}$$

for $1 \le k \le K$.

To complete the formulation, we define the distortion measure between an input SSV **S** with its associated selector vector **Q** and a spectral shape code vector $\mathbf{Y}_j$ in the universal codebook. This measure is based on matching the input SSV samples to the corresponding subset of components of the spectral shape code vector $\mathbf{Y}_j$. Thus,

$$d(\mathbf{X}, Y_j) = \frac{1}{L_Q} \sum_{k=1}^{K} \mathbf{Q}[k] \cdot d_1(\mathbf{X}[k], \mathbf{Y}_j[k]) \tag{3}$$

where L_Q denotes the number of nonzero components of **Q** and $d_1(s, y)$ is a specified distortion measure between two scalars s and y. Note that, the selector vector $\mathbf{Q}[k]$ has exactly L_Q 1's and $(K - L_Q)$ 0's. The role of **Q** is to select the proper L_Q components of $\mathbf{Y}_j$s for comparison with **S**.

3.2 VDVQ Encoding Algorithm

Suppose a universal spectral codebook is given with N code vectors $\mathbf{Y}_j$ of dimension K and the VDVQ receives the input pair $\{F_o, \mathbf{S}\}$. The encoding then proceeds as follows:

1. *Compute the selector vector* $\mathbf{Q}[k]$, *of dimension* K, *according to (1).*
2. *Convert the* L *-dimension* $\mathbf{S}$ *to an extended* K*-dimension* $\mathbf{X}$ *according to (2).*
3. *Search through the spectral code vectors* $\mathbf{Y}_1$ *to* $\mathbf{Y}_N$ *in the universal codebook to find the index* j^* *for which* $d(\mathbf{X}, \mathbf{Y}_j)$ *is minimum over all* $j = 1, 2, \cdots, N$. *(An arbitrary tie-breaker rule can be used.) The spectral shape is thus quantized with* $\log_2 N$ *bits to specify the index.*

3.3 VDVQ Decoding Algorithm

The decoder receives the exact pitch F_o and the optimal index j^* and it has a copy of the universal spectral codebook. Thus, the decoder can immediately extract the optimal spectral vector Y_{j^*} from the codebook and use it as a reproduction of the full spectral shape. However, if the application needs a reproduction of the SSV, then the decoder performs the following operation:

1. Compute the selector vector $\mathbf{Q}$[k], of dimension K, according to (1) using given F_o.
2. Recover an L dimensional SSV $\hat{\mathbf{S}}$ as the reproduced approximation to the original SSV $\mathbf{S}$ by extracting those components of Y_{j^*} for which the corresponding components of $\mathbf{Q}$ are nonzero, proceeding in order of increasing component index values and then concatenating these samples to form $\hat{\mathbf{S}}$.

3.4 VDVQ Training Algorithm

Given a training set and an initial codebook of size N and dimension K, the codebook is iteratively designed in a manner similar to the usual generalized Lloyd algorithm (GLA). Each training iteration has the following two key steps: 1) clustering of training vectors around the code vectors using a nearest neighbor rule, and 2) replacing the old code vectors by the centroid of such clusters (Centroid Rule) [8]. At the end of training, the code vectors will be given by the centroids of the final clusters.

The training set consists of a large set of pairs $(F_{oi}, \mathbf{S}_i)$, where F_{oi} is the pitch period and $\mathbf{S}_i$ is the SSV. Denote the code vectors of the codebook prior to the current iteration as $Y_j, j = 1, 2, \cdots, N$. The two key steps of each training iteration are:

1. NEAREST NEIGHBOR RULE

a. *For each training element* $(F_{oi}, \mathbf{S}_i)$*, form the selector vector* $\mathbf{Q}_i$ *and the extended vector* $\mathbf{X}_i$.

b. *Assign* $\mathbf{X}_i$ *to cluster* C_m *if* $d(\mathbf{X}_i, Y_m) \leq d(\mathbf{X}_i, Y_j)$ *for* $j = 1, 2, \cdots, N$, *with a suitable tie-breaking rule.*

2. CENTROID RULE

For each cluster, C_m, $m = 1, 2, \cdots, N$, *find a new code vector* $\mathbf{Y}'_m$ *such that over all vectors* **y** *it minimizes the cluster distortion given by* $D_m = \sum_{j \varepsilon C_m} d_1(\mathbf{X}_j, \mathbf{y})$.

For the mean squared error distortion, where $d_1(s, y) = (s - y)^2$, *the centroid rule gives*

$$\mathbf{Y}'_m[k] = \frac{\sum_{j \varepsilon C_m} \frac{1}{L_j} \cdot Q_j[k] \cdot \mathbf{X}_j[k]}{\sum_{j \varepsilon C_m} \frac{1}{L_j} \cdot Q_j[k]} \quad \text{for } k = 1, 2, \cdots, K. \tag{4}$$

4. QUANTIZATION OF SPECTRAL PARAMETERS

The variable-dimension spectral shape vector is quantized using a combination of *split VQ* and *shape-gain VQ* (Figure 2). The SSV is first converted to the log domain and then split into two sub-vectors $\mathbf{S_L}$ and $\mathbf{S_H}$. Components of $\mathbf{S_L}$ belong to the lower end of the spectrum (DFT indices 2 to 48) and those of $\mathbf{S_H}$ belong to the upper end of the spectrum (DFT indices 48 to 115). For our application, the remaining DFT indices (0-1 and 116-127) are not used. A gain component (actually the log-gain) is extracted from each sub-vector to form a log-gain vector $\mathbf{G} = \{G_L, G_H\}$. which is quantized using 2 dimensional VQ with a 10 bit codebook. (Actually, G_L is the average of the elements of $\mathbf{S_L}$ and G_H is the average of $\mathbf{S_H}$.) The shape sub-vectors are normalized by subtracting the quantized log gains $\hat{\mathbf{G}} = \{\hat{G}_L, \hat{G}_H\}$, producing the normalized shape sub-vectors $\mathbf{S_{Ln}}$ and $\mathbf{S_{Hn}}$ which are then quantized with VDVQ using 20 bits (10 bits/sub-vector) producing quantized sub-vectors $\hat{\mathbf{S}}_{\mathbf{Ln}}$ and $\hat{\mathbf{S}}_{\mathbf{Hn}}$. By providing a larger bit allocation to the first sub-vector, a higher quantization resolution is given to the perceptually important low-frequency part of the spectrum. Thus the variable-dimension spectral shape vector $\mathbf{S}$ is represented by a 10-bit gain index I_{sg} and two 10-bit shape indexes I_{ssH} and I_{ssL}.

At the decoder, the quantized shape vector $\hat{\mathbf{S}}$ is formed by extracting the quantized gain and shape subvectors given by $\hat{\mathbf{S}}_{\mathbf{H}} = \hat{\mathbf{S}}_{\mathbf{Hn}} + \hat{G}_H$ and $\hat{\mathbf{S}}_{\mathbf{L}} = \hat{\mathbf{S}}_{\mathbf{Ln}} + \hat{G}_L$, concatenating them and returning to the spectral amplitude domain by exponentiation. The pitch F_o is quantized using 8 bits and the voicing vector $\mathbf{V}$ is represented with 12 bits. Therefore, for each 20 ms frame, a total of 50 (8+12+10+20) bits are used giving a rate of 2.5 kb/s.

5. SYNTHESIS OF SPEECH FROM THE SPECTRAL PARAMETERS

During synthesis, the spectral parameters generate a voiced frame S_v and an unvoiced frame S_{uv} which when added together deliver the output speech frame.

The unvoiced frame S_{uv} is generated by coloring a white noise spectrum band by band using the decoded spectral shape vector $\hat{\mathbf{S}}$ and the multiband voicing probability information $\mathbf{V}$. If the i-th band is declared voiced, then the spectrum in that region is set to zero. If the i-th band is declared unvoiced, then the spectrum in that region is formed by shaping the white noise spectrum with the i-th spectral sample $\hat{\mathbf{S}}[i]$. The fullband spectrum composed in this fashion is then transformed using IDFT to the time domain to form the output unvoiced frame S_u. An overlap-add interpolation of S_u with the S_u of the previous frame generates the final synthesized unvoiced frame S_{uv}. Such interpolation ensures a smooth transition from one frame to the next.

The voiced frame S_v is formed as a sum of sinusoids with frequencies equal to F_o and its multiples having amplitudes equal to the components of an interpolated version of $\hat{\mathbf{S}}$. Based on the voicing probability vector **V** of the previous frame and the current frame, a simple linear interpolation between the spectral shapes of the current frame and the previous frame is performed. This ensures a smooth spectral transition from frame to frame. If a frequency band is declared unvoiced, then the amplitudes of sinusoids with frequencies belonging to that band are set to zero. An artificial phase term for each harmonic is generated in a manner similar to [5] in order to avoid any artifacts due to phase discontinuity at frame boundaries.

6. PERFORMANCE

We have compared the performance of our VDVQ technique with two other spectral quantization techniques applied to frequency domain vocoders in the past [4, 5]. The spectral distortion (SD) measure used for the comparison is given below:

$$SD(\mathbf{S}, \hat{\mathbf{S}}) = \sqrt{\frac{100}{L-1} \sum_{k=1}^{L-1} (\log_{10} \mathbf{S}[k] - \log_{10} \hat{\mathbf{S}}[k])^2} \qquad (4)$$

where **S** is the original SSV of dimension L and $\hat{\mathbf{S}}$ is the quantized version of **S**.

Table 1 presents the average spectral distortion for different spectral coding techniques applied to a multi-speaker speech database. LP-10 refers to a tenth order all-pole modeling of SSVs similar to the technique used in [4] and subsequent split vector quantization of the 10 LSP parameters and scalar gain quantization using a total of 30 bits. IMBE refers to the INMARSAT-M IMBE coder [5] which uses 63 bits for spectral coding. VDVQ refers to our coder which uses 30 bits for spectral coding.

	Spectral Distortion in dB		
	IMBE (63 bits)	LP-10 (30 bits)	VDVQ (30 bits)
Male Speech	3.00	2.75	1.45
Female Speech	3.03	2.28	1.18
Overall	3.02	2.52	1.31

Table 1. Average Spectral Distortion for Various Quantization Techniques

The superiority of the VDVQ compared to these two other techniques is quite evident.

Informal listening and a subjective test using a multi-speaker speech database (both male and female) have shown that the speech quality of the VDVQ-based 2.5 kb/s coder is better than the U.S. Federal Standard 1016 CELP algorithm at 4.8 kb/s [9] and comparable to or better than the quality of the INMARSAT-M IMBE 4.15 kb/s standard coder [5]. Specifically, we conducted an A-B subjective comparison test where 10 listeners each compared 32 sentence pairs, 16 VDVQ vs. IMBE pairs and 16 VDVQ vs. CELP pairs. When compared with IMBE, our coder was preferred 35% of the time, 39%

of the time they were judged indistinguishable (in quality), and 26% of the time IMBE was preferred. When compared with FS 1016 CELP, our coder was preferred 56% of the time, 27% of the time they were indistinguishable, and 17% of the time CELP was preferred. Considering the much higher bit rate of the CELP and IMBE coders, this clearly shows a significant improvement in rate-distortion trade-off offered by the VDVQ coder.

7. CONCLUSION

A novel and direct variable-dimension vector quantization (VDVQ) scheme is presented which provides an effective solution to the challenging task of spectral quantization in frequency domain vocoders. Our VDVQ method offers the advantage of direct quantization of the variable-dimension vectors without the onerous computation and storage complexity of a separate codebook for each dimension by capturing the source statistics in a universal spectral shape codebook. Direct quantization of spectral samples avoids any additional penalty due to all-pole modeling or dimension altering techniques used in earlier works. The concept of a universal spectral codebook implemented with structured vector quantization reduces complexity, yet delivers a higher quantization efficiency and enhanced perceptual quality at lower bit rates than prior spectral quantization methods for frequency domain vocoders. Our approach to VDVQ can be readily modified for application to other signal compression problems.

8. REFERENCES

[1] J-P. Adoul and M. Delprat, ''Design algorithm for variable-length vector quantizers,'' *Proc. Allerton Conf. Circuits, Systems, Computers*, pp. 1004-1011, October 1986.

[2] R. J. McAulay and T. F. Quatieri, ''Speech analysis/synthesis based on a sinusoidal representation'', *IEEE Trans. Acoust., Speech, Signal Processing*, vol. 34, pp. 744-754, August 1986.

[3] D. W. Griffin and J. S. Lim, ''Multiband excitation vocoder'', *IEEE Trans. Acoust., Speech, Signal Processing*, vol. 36, pp. 1223-1235, August 1988.

[4] M. S. Brandstein, ''A 1.5 Kbps multi-band excitation speech coder'', *S.M. Thesis*, EECS Department, MIT, 1990.

[5] Digital Voice Systems, ''Inmarsat-M Voice Codec, Version 2'', *Inmarsat-M specification*, Inmarsat, February 1991.

[6] P. C. Meuse, ''A 2400 bps Multi-Band Excitation Vocoder'', *Proc. IEEE Int. Conf. Acoust., Speech, Signal Processing*, pp. 9-12, April 1990.

[7] M. Nishiguchi, J. Matsumoto, R. Wakatsuki, and S. Ono, ''Vector quantized MBE with simplified V/UV decision at 3.0 kbps'', *Proc. IEEE Int. Conf. Acoust., Speech, Signal Processing*, pp. 151-154, April 1993.

[8] A. Gersho and R.M. Gray, *Vector Quantization and Signal Compression*, Kluwer Academic Publishers, 1991.

[9] J.P. Campbell, Jr., T.E. Tremain, and V.C. Welch, ''The DOD 4.8 KBPS Standard (Proposed Federal Standard 1016),'' in *Advances in Speech Coding*, B.S. Atal, V. Cuperman, and A. Gersho, editors, pp. 121-133, Kluwer Academic Publishers, 1991.

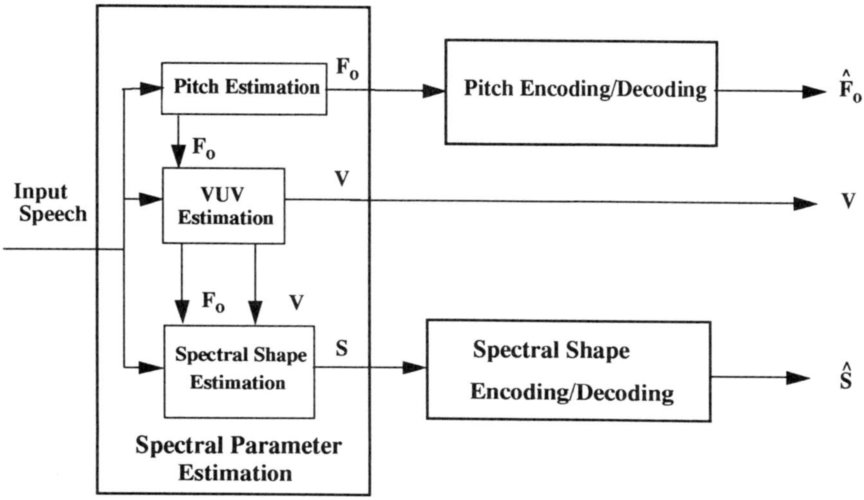

Figure 1: Estimation and Quantization of Spectral Parameters

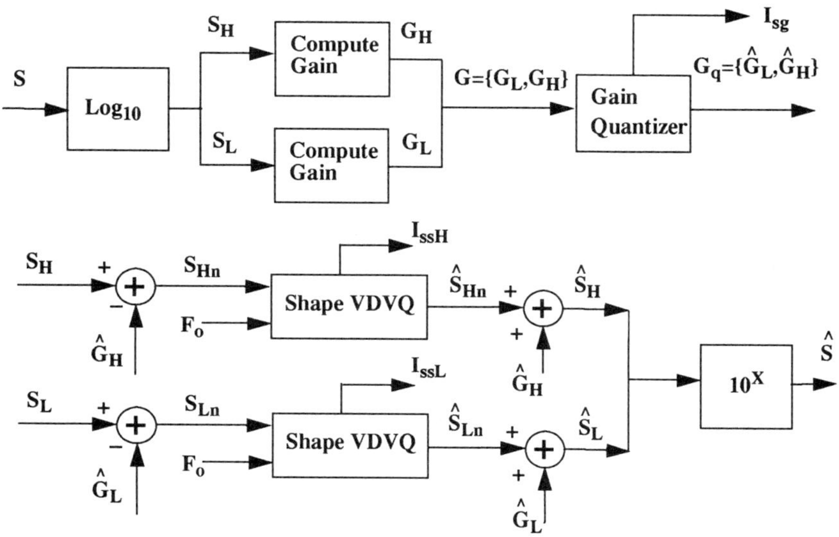

Figure 2: Spectral Shape Encoding/Decoding using VDVQ

A Rapidly Adaptive Lossless Compression Algorithm for High Fidelity Audio Coding

Talal Shamoon and Chris Heegard
School of Electrical Engineering, Cornell University, Ithaca, NY 14853
talal@ee.cornell.edu, heegard@ee.cornell.edu

§ 1 Abstract

A new adaptive algorithm for lossless compression of digital audio is presented. The algorithm is derived from ideas from both dictionary coding and source-modeling. An adaptive Lempel-Ziv style fixed dictionary coder is used to build a source model that fuels an arithmetic coder. As a result, variable length strings drawn from the source alphabet are mapped onto variable length strings that are on average shorter. We show that this algorithm outperforms arithmetic coding or Lempel-Ziv coding working alone on the same source (in our experiments our source is an ADPCM quantizer). Adaptation heuristics for the Lempel-Ziv coder, relevant data structures, and a discussion of audio source modeling (entropy estimation) experiments are described. While the algorithm presented herein is designed to be used as a post-compressor in a lossy audio transform coding system, it is well suited for any instance where non-stationary source outputs must be compressed.

§ 2 Introduction

Real-time algorithms for the compression of high-fidelity audio are under study [1,2,3]. The objective is to provide a compact, high fidelity, digital representation for an input stream of audio samples. Our goal is to derive fast algorithms that achieve low bit rate (on the order of 2-3 bits per sample at 44.1KHz sample rates) with CD quality fidelity. A specific interest is to obtain bit rates that permit digital radio broadcasting of high fidelity audio. In this vein, we are developing an adaptive transform coding system that consists of five specialized functional blocks:

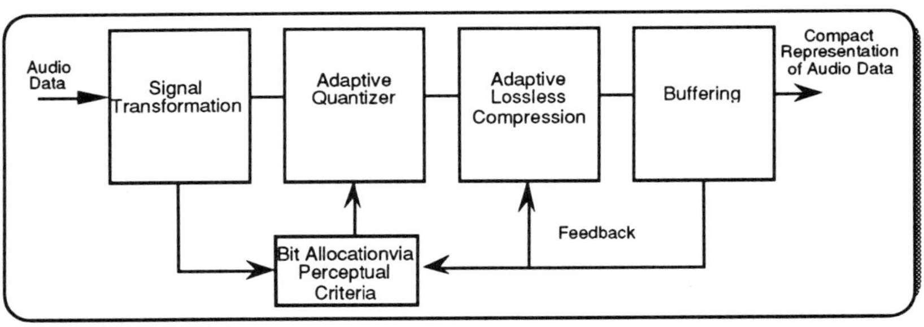

Figure 1. High-Fidelity Audio Compression System

The first block partitions the frequency band into non-uniform sub-bands. In [1] we presented a scheme that partitions the frequency band based on an octave scale. This was extended in [2] into a tree that produced a fractional-octave decomposition of the input band. Both schemes use a bank of perfect reconstruction filters arranged in binary-tree structures. The leaves of the binary tree represent the respective sub-bands. The second module quantizes the octave bands via a bank of variable-level ADPCM scalar quantizers. Perceptual criteria (psychoacoustic masking) provide side-information to the quantizers in order to assist in adaptive bit-allocation. This allows the quantizer structure to concentrate bits on the sub-bands that the listener is most likely to perceive. The output of these quantizers is fed into lossless compression and buffering modules that are designed to eliminate redundancy in the quantizer bank's output, and assure fixed-rate output from the entire encoder.

This paper concerns a new adaptive algorithm for the lossless compression stage. We demonstrate that significant data reduction can be wrought from our lossless compressor. While existing audio compression systems such as MUSICAM [4] include lossless compressors, they tend to use fixed-codebook Huffman coders. While computational efficient, these techniques do not attain optimal compression. Even if the source were stationary, Huffman coding would only achieve entropy if the source is i.i.d (and the relative frequencies of the symbols were powers of two.) A complaint frequently voiced in audio compression circles is that existing adaptive compressors tend not to adapt quickly enough to changes in digital audio. Our study of the audio source shows that it is at best locally stationary. In [3], we presented results from entropy estimation experiments that we conducted on audio data that illuminate the statistical nature of the source. These experiments analyzed compact-disc digital audio (44.1KHz, 16 bits/sample, 2 channels) that had been requantized to a lower bit rate via ADPCM. Algorithms that rely on fixed statistical source models, such as non-adaptive Huffman coding, or algorithms that build a source model based on a small observation period at the beginning of a compression run, such as Lempel-Ziv-Welch [5], fail to track the statistical nuances of audio. We concluded that in order to obtain good compression performance, a lossless compressor for this type of source must aggressively adapt to these nuances. A brief review of the entropy estimation experiments in [3] is given below. Subsequently, we present a new *adaptive* variable-length-input to variable-length-output algorithm that efficiently adapts to the time varying statistics of the audio source. While the results presented herein were developed in the context of audio compression, they can effectively be applied to a wide variety of lossless compression applications, especially those where the source exhibits time varying, locally stationary, behavior.

§ 3 The Digital Audio Source

In order to better understand the information theoretic limits on the performance of a lossless compressor attacking audio, we conducted a series of source modeling experiments. These results were presented in [3], and are reviewed here for completeness. We chose to study the output of an ADPCM quantizer. We took audio captured from compact disc (44.1KHz at 16 bits/sample), and requantized it to different bit rates using ADPCM. We concentrated on bit rates around 5 bits per sample; this region we found, through subjective listening experiments [6], is the threshold where listeners begin to perceive a departure in fidelity from the compact disc *.

Let $Q = \{0 \ldots N-1\}$ be the set of symbols output by an $n-bit$, $N = 2^n$ ADPCM quantizer Q. The entropy of this source with i.i.d. statistics is defined as:

$$H(Q) = -\sum_{i=0}^{N-1} p_i \log_2 p_i \quad \text{bits}$$

Here, p_i is the probability of symbol i, $i \in Q$. From Shannon's First Source Coding Theorem [7], we know that, in the compressibility of a source's output is lower-bounded by the entropy. If the probability distribution of an i.i.d. source is known, the entropy can be computed via the above, and this bound becomes clear. However, when dealing with real data, the source statistics can be quite elusive. For example, the entropy of the English language changes over time as certain words come into vogue. Further, these statistics vary within different classes of documents (a C program has a much higher incidence of semi-colons than a Shakesperean comedy).

Hence, statistical experiments must be conducted to arrive at estimates of the entropy of the source at hand. Measuring the relative frequency of occurrence of each symbol in Q is the most obvious way to obtain an idea of the marginal probability distribution of a source. This method provides an upper bound on the entropy as it ignores higher-order dependencies between source characters. In order to track these dependencies, we adapt an entropy estimation technique from Jelinek and Schneider [8]. In this paper, it is shown that for an i.i.d source S, the entropy is inversely proportional to the average length of strings $w \in T \subset S^*$ parsed (as shown below) from the source alphabet. In particular, if $L(w)$ is the length of w, then

$$\frac{log|T|}{E[L(w)]} \rightarrow H(Q)$$

as $|T| \rightarrow \infty$. Sindhushayana and Heegard extended this result to cover a larger class of non-i.i.d stationary sources [10].

Strings are parsed into a dictionary from the stream of characters emanating from the source output using a trie abstract data type (ADT) [9]. An example of such a trie that encodes the English strings (the, then and this) is given in figure 2 below.

* Note that through effective use of psychoacoustic masking, fidelity preserving bit rates of about 2-3 bits per sample can derived. In studying lossless compression, we opted to work with raw ADPCM output.

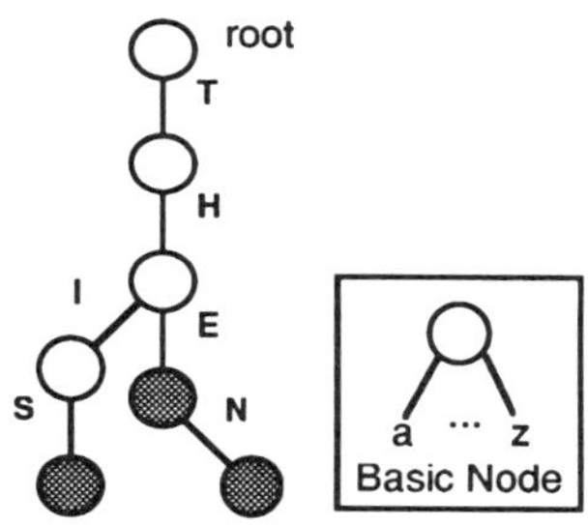

Figure 2. Example of a Trie Dictionary

Our implementation of the trie abstract data type uses a tree structure where each node can be have up to N children. This trie ADT supports a CHILD(node, i) operation. The root node is initialized with N children, each representing a letter in the source alphabet. Strings of source outputs are thus represented by paths from the root to any leaf or any inner node that still has unused children. Starting at the root, we traverse the trie by using each successive source character to chose the next node to visit. If the current node does not have a child at the location pointed to by the current character, a new child is created there, and we return to the root. The trie is grown to a predetermined number of words, T. Once the dictionary is full, stop, compute the average word length, $\bar{L}$ and obtain an estimate of the entropy $log|T| \,/\, \bar{L}$. At this point, erase the current dictionary and start again. Repeat this process over the course of a long audio sample, and maintain a running average of the entropy estimates.

We applied this algorithm to a series of data files to obtain entropy estimates. The audio data is taken from a CD and requantized via ADPCM down to 5bits per sample from the original 16bits per sample at 44.1KHz. A set of estimates for a 2 min, 30 sec. BB King segment is given in the appendix. We estimate that for 5 bit ADPCM, the entropy of is typically on the order of 3.8 bits per sample with a standard deviation of 0.1 bits. We compared these estimate with entropy estimates made by calculation of marginal probabilities drawn from counting relative frequencies of individual source symbols. This method provided estimates on the order of 4.6 bits per sample. Interestingly enough, we found nominal variation between estimates of different types of music quantized to the same bit rate.

§ 4 Motivation for a new Lossless Compression Algorithm

Subsequent analysis of the source data showed that strings of audio samples exhibited locality of reference. We attempted to compress audio files using a variety of standard compression techniques. We implemented a Bell-Cleary-Witten (BCW) [11] fixed-point Arithmetic coder using a source model that maintained a table with counts of the relative frequency of each source symbol. This coder consistently compressed audio files down to the entropy estimates based on marginal probabilities given above. We also applied a Lempel-Ziv-Welsh [5] coder to audio. Recall that this type of coder builds a dictionary of commonly occurring source words at the outset of the compression run. Once the dictionary fills, the coder proceeds to use it for the rest of the run without further adaptation. In our implementation, the first N words of the dictionary were the letters of the source alphabet. When applied to a 5 bit source ($N = 32$ letters in the source alphabet), a version of this coder with an 11 bit (2048 words) dictionary actually *expanded* most audio files. This can be explained by the fact that the source statistics shift so much beyond those captured by the dictionary that very few words longer than one letter are actually generated by the coder.

Hence a highly adaptive compressor that is computational efficient is called for. Lossless data compression algorithms fall into two classes: *Statistical Coders* and *Dictionary Coders*. The former, like Arithmetic or Huffman coding, rely on a source model that provides them with the source statistics. Each source symbol is mapped onto a variable length encoding whose length is proportional to the symbol probability. Less frequently occurring symbols are mapped onto longer sequences. Due to this property, these compressors are sometimes dubbed: *fixed-to-variable length* coders. Compressors in the latter class (the Lempel-Ziv family of algorithms for example) parse source symbols onto frequently occurring strings thereby obviating the need to build a explicit statistical model. A fixed number of frequently occurring strings is kept in a dictionary, and these coders are sometimes referred to as *variable-to-fixed length* compressors.

The performance of a statistical coder is limited by the entropy of its source model. Our assessment of the options revealed that advanced techniques for statistical source modeling were limited. Counting relative frequencies for an arithmetic coder proved quite inefficient with respect to the entropy estimates as shown above. *Dynamic Markov Modeling* is a promising technique [12] that can be used in conjunction with arithmetic coding. Here, a directed graph representing the state transition diagram of the Markov chain that underlies the source data is grown from a kernel graph. Nodes in the kernel are split based on the number of times they are visited. Details of this technique, know as *cloning* are given on [12] and [11]. Unfortunately, while these techniques grow the Markov chain effectively, they fail to keep its size in check, as there is a dearth of effective state-merging techniques.

The primary limiting factors on the performance of Dictionary coders are fixed size dictionaries and the adaptation strategy used for dictionary update. By placing a limit on the number of strings that a dictionary can encode, we place a lower bound on the compression ability of the algorithm that is higher than source entropy. Lempel and Ziv [13] show that source entropy is achieved as the size of the dictionary is allowed to go to infinity. By using a fixed length dictionary, we are in effect forcing a certain amount of redundancy to remain in the encoding. A clever adaptation strategy can boost compression performance given the fixed dictionary constraint. In [14], we will present results of a study of the effectiveness of different adaptation techniques on the compression-ability of different Lempel-Ziv algorithms. The adaptation heuristic used must keep abreast of the subset of strings, or *Dialect*, $D \subset Q^*$ that is currently in vogue. For a non-stationary source, the dialect will change over time.

§ 5 A New Lossless Compression Algorithm

5.1 *Overview*

In order to bypass these limitations, we have developed a hybrid algorithm that seeks to incorporate the best aspects of both classes of compressors. Our algorithm maps a variable length strings of input symbols onto a variable length output string that is on average shorter. Given the hybrid nature of the algorithm it must be analyzed both as a dictionary coder and a statistical coder. A block diagram of the system is given in figure 3.

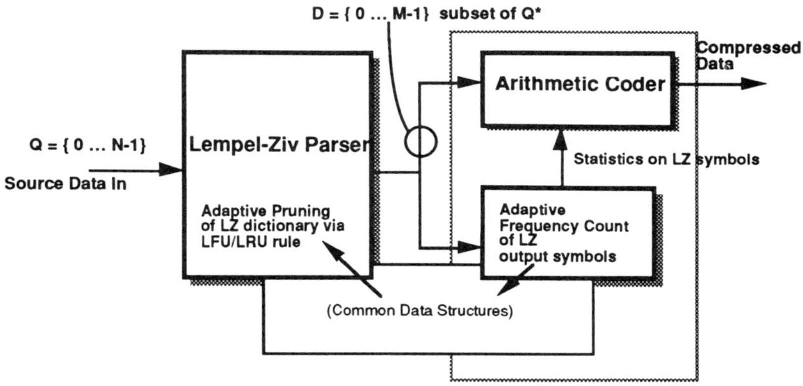

Figure 3. Variable-Variable Length Algorithm

The algorithm consists of a front end Lempel-Ziv style parser that maps source symbols onto variable length strings. A fixed size dictionary is used, along with an adaptation heuristic that responds to the locally stationary nature of the audio source. This part of the algorithm is variable-to-fixed length, mapping strings from Q^* onto the dictionary set $D = \{0 \ldots M - 1\}$ where, $(M = 2^m) > N$. The output of the Lempel-Ziv coder is fed into an arithmetic coder. This device adaptively updates a list of occurrence frequencies of the Lempel-Ziv output alphabet, D, feeding them to the interval update component of the arithmetic coder as needed. The arithmetic coder proceeds to map the fixed length output of the Lempel-Ziv coder onto variable-length strings that are proportional to the relative frequency of their occurrence. In the context of statistical coding, we can view the adaptive Lempel-Ziv coder as a source modeler. Intersymbol correlations are implicitly represented by the string themselves. The probability distribution of the strings is closer to i.i.d than that of the individual symbols. The advantage of this type of modeler over such schemes as Dynamic Markov Modeling is speed (parsing is a fast procedure) and data structure complexity. The structure does not grow beyond the maximum dictionary size. Growth and pruning of the dictionary is performed via a concise LFU/LRU scheme that is discussed below.

In the context of dictionary coding, this arithmetic coder can be viewed as a device that attempts to eliminate the redundancy left over from the fixed-dictionary size constraint. The presence of the arithmetic coder allows better compression at smaller dictionary sizes thereby boosting the performance of the algorithm by reducing search times.

5.2 *The Lempel-Ziv Parser*

Dictionary encoding is done via a modified Lempel-Ziv-Welsh algorithm. We use a trie data structure to represent the dictionary. As in the experiment in section 3, The trie abstract data type supports a CHILD(node, i) operation. This operation returns the node located at the i-th child of the node. As in the example of figure 2, each node has N possible children. The root always has N children, one for each letter in the alphabet. At the outset of the compression run, we start with a trie that consists of a root node and its N children. As each source symbol comes in, we traverse the tree initially starting at the root. We use the current source symbol to choose the next node down the trie, ie:

nextnode = CHILD(currentnode,currentsymbol)

If we reach a point where the trie ends, we stop, encode the current node and update the trie by adding a node at CHILD(current node, current symbol). This is called the *innovation phase.* Once the dictionary is full we move from the innovation phase of the LZ algorithm to the adaptation phase.

5.3 *The Arithmetic Coder and the LZ Adaptation Phase*

The arithmetic coder source model maintains a count of the frequency of occurrence of each of the parser's outputs. These are kept in a sorted list. The arithmetic coder uses this list to allocate portions of each successively refined interval in proportion to the frequency of each symbol. In our implementation, we use the Bell-Cleary-Witten fixed point arithmetic coding algorithm with an expanded source model [11]. The list of symbol frequencies clusters into regions of symbols with the same frequency. We call these regions *frequency classes*. Symbols within the *least frequently used* (LFU) frequency class are further sorted by our update algorithm in recency rank. The frequency tables are updated after each LZ parser output is arithmetic encoded. When the Lempel-Ziv parser reaches full dictionary size, we scan the LFU class, choosing the least frequently used, least recently used (LRU) symbol that corresponds to a leaf (and is more than one level from the root). The trie node corresponding to this symbol is pruned from the tree (and eliminated from the frequency table.) As the arithmetic coder is fixed point, we normalize the frequency table as in [11] by halving the all frequency values when the sum of all the entries exceeds a predetermined threshold. Pruned nodes are placed on a queue and the LZ parser now returns to innovation phase. Pruned symbols are removed from the frequency list and the arithmetic coder's input alphabet size changes appropriately. Pruning is performed whenever the free node queue is empty. Results of this algorithm operating on three representative data files are presented in appendix two.

Sometimes a recording contains a sequence of repetitive samples that does not recur in the short term. An example of this would be a brief pause in a song. Such sequences cause trie nodes to be parsed into a path of single nodes. In order to liberate nodes in such a path after their utility has decreased, we are experimenting with a table management heuristic known as *Ancestor Pruning*. In ancestor pruning, if the least frequently used node has no siblings, and its parent's frequency count differs from it by 1, the parent is also pruned (provided it is more than one level from the root). Upon pruning the parent, we check it for siblings, and check its parent's frequency. If it meets the aforementioned criteria, it too is pruned. We continue this procedure up the ancestor path until the pruning rule is violated. Again, pruned nodes are placed on the free node queue.

5.4 *Conclusions*

The aforementioned algorithm has been used on a variety of audio files. It consistently outperforms standard arithmetic coding, and achieves compression results that are closer to the entropy estimates discussed above. Complexity is minimized by sharing data structures between the two coders, and the result is an algorithm that bypasses the limitations of its two components.

§ 6 Appendix 1: Sample Entropy Estimation Experimental Results

The following are estimation results mentioned in section 3. Data on the trie are also provided. The audio data is captured digitally from CD (44.1KHz sample rate, 16bits/sample) using a Macintosh IIFX equipped with a DARE DSP card. Data are requantized to 5 bits using the ADPCM algorithm from Jayant and Knoll [15], adaptation parameters are those from [15] p206. The audio sample is the entire piece (2 mins, 27 secs) *Every Day I Have the Blues* by B.B. King. Captured from track 1 of the CD *B.B. King Live at the Cook County Jail*, MCA Records.

Entropy Estimates via Tree Algorithm	Channel 1	Channel 2
Average Entropy Estimate (Bits)	3.87	3.87
SDEV Entropy Estimate (Bits)	0.11	0.11
Average Longest Path (Levels)	4.37	4.38
Average Leaves/Tree	716.34	713.60
Average Children/Node	2.56	2.56
Entropy Est. via Marginal Probs (Bits)	4.58	4.58

Table 1: Entropy Estimation Experiment

§ 7 Appendix 2: Compression Results

The following are experimental results comparing the variable-to-variable length algorithm (referred to as VV in the table below) to arithmetic coding. Information on the source material is presented below. The files were digitally transferred from CD to a Macintosh equipped with a DARE DSP card. They were subsequently requantized from 16bits to 5bits via an ADPCM quantizer (see appendix 1). Thus the source data used is 5bits ADPCM at 44.1 samples/second. The percentages following the compressed file sizes below refer to percent reduction from the 5 bits ADPCM original. In addition to the audio samples, each file contains a 92 byte information header. The arithmetic coder used is the adaptive arithmetic coder from [11]. The VV implementation below uses a 2048 word dictionary in the Lempel-Ziv source modeler. Ancestor pruning was not applied to this data.

	U2	Paul Simon	Copland
ADPCM 5 Bits (bytes)	275,720	826,968	1,653,844
Arith Coder (bytes)	253,604 (8.0%)	762,192 (7.8%)	1,518,044 (8.2%)
VV Coder (bytes)	236,604 (14.2%)	738,440 (10.7%)	1,385,276 (16.2%)

Table 2: Comparison of Compression Results

Details on each piece:

U2: *Love is Blindness* first 5 seconds from *Achtung Baby* Track 12, Island Records

Paul Simon: *Graceland* first 15 seconds from *Graceland* Track 2, Warner Bros.

Copland: *Rodeo* first 30 seconds from *Aaron Copland.* Track 2, Telarc CD80078.

§ 8 References

[1] Talal Shamoon and Chris Heegard, "Audio Compression via Wavelets and Multiresolution Analysis," *Proceedings of the 25th Annual Conference on Information Sciences and Systems*, pp. 902-906, March 1991.

[2] Chris Heegard and Talal Shamoon, "High Fidelity Audio Compression: Fractional Band Wavelets," *Proceedings of 1992 International Conference on Acoustics, Speech and Signal Processing*, pp. II-201 - II-203, March 1992.

[3] Talal Shamoon and Chris Heegard, "Lossless Compression Algorithms for High Fidelity Audio Compression" *1993 International Symposium on Information Theory, San Antonio, TX*, January 1993.

[4] *Committee Draft for MPEG Audio Coding Standard*, International Organization for Standardization, 1990.

[5] T.A. Welch "A Technique for High Performance Data Compression," *Computer*, 17:8-19, 1984.

[6] Scott Satterthwaite "The Audibility of Audio Compression Techniques" *Cornell University Laboratory for Communications, Data Storage and Signal Processing Internal Report*, December 1992.

[7] Thomas Cover and Joy Thomas, *Elements of Information Theory*, J. Wiley & Sons, 1991.

[8] Frederick Jelinek and Kenneth Schneider "On Variable-to-Block Length Coding," *IEEE Transactions on Information Theory*, IT-18:6 pp765-774, 1972.

[9] Alfred Aho, John Hopcroft, Jeffrey Ullman, *Data Structures and Algorithms*, Addison-Wesley, 1983.

[10] Nagabhushana T. Sindhushay and Chris Heegard, "A Source Coding Theorem for Stationary Sources Parsed with Trees," submitted *IEEE Transactions on Information Theory*.

[11] Timothy Bell, John Cleary, and Ian Whitten, *Text Compression* Englewood Cliffs, NJ, Prentice-Hall, 1990.

[12] G.V. Cormack & R.N.S Horspool "Data Compression Using Dynamic Markov Modeling," *Computer Journal*, 30 (6), pp541-550, December.

[13] Jacob Ziv and Abraham Lempel "A Universal Algorithm for Sequential Data Compression," *IEEE Transactions on Information Theory*, IT-23: 337-343, 1977.

[14] Talal Shamoon and Chris Heegard, "Adaptive Update Algorithms for Fixed Dictionary Lossless Data Compressors" *1994 International Symposium on Information Theory, Trondheim, Norway*, June 1994.

[15] N.S Jayant and Peter Knoll, *Digital Coding of Waveforms* Englewood Cliffs, NJ, Prentice-Hall, 1984.

SHARPER BOUNDS ON OCCAM FILTERS AND APPLICATION TO DIGITAL VIDEO

B. K. Natarajan
Hewlett-Packard Laboratories
1501 Page Mill Road
Palo Alto, CA 94304

1. Abstract

Occam filters are a general technique for filtering random noise via data compression. Previously it was established that these filters converge in a learning theoretic sense, with convergence bounds that depended on the probability distribution of the noise variable. In this paper, we present a convergence bound for uniformly sampled signals that is independent of the probability distribution of the noise variable, barring some minimal assumptions. We also examine an application of Occam filters to remove random noise from digital video, thereby enabling improved nearly lossless compression.

2. Introduction

Let f denote the noise-free function of interest to us. For simplicity, we assume that f is a function from the unit interval $[0,1]$ to the unit interval $[0,1]$. We are allowed to sample f at discrete points. These samples are corrupted by random noise denoted by the random variable ν. Assume that we have at our disposal a lossy data compression routine whose allowed loss can be controlled in some metric $\|\cdot\|$. Set the allowed loss to be $\|\nu\|$. Take n noisy samples of f and compress it with the compression routine, then decompress to obtain a function g. Will the noise and the compression loss add so that $\|f-g\| \sim 2\|\nu\|$, or will the noise and the loss cancel $\|f-g\| \sim 0$? Natarajan (1993a,b) showed that the noise and the loss cancel and gave a convergence bound on the rate at which the residual noise goes to zero as n goes to infinity, subject to the following three restrictions. (1) the bound holds only when $\|\cdot\|$ is the L_∞ metric, and hence is limited to the few compression algorithms that allow control of the loss in the L_∞ metric, (2) the bound holds for random sampling, rather than uniformly spaced samples as is common in the practical signal processing setting, and (3) the bound has the undesirable property that it is not independent of the probability distribution governing the noise. In this paper, we address these limitations by (1) choosing $\|\cdot\|$ to be the sum-of-squares metric, (2) assuming that the samples are uniformly spaced, and (3) establishing a convergence bound that is independent of the distribution of the noise, barring the minimal assumptions that the noise has zero mean and bounded amplitude. Of related interest are the papers by Donoho (1992) and Devore and Lucier (1992), that examine the filtering of random Gaussian noise using wavelets, by shifting the transform coefficients by an amount proportional to the noise strength, and then inverting to obtain the filtered signal.

We also examine an application of Occam filters in the context of digital video compression. Lossless or nearly lossless compression is desirable for studio quality storage of digital video. It is difficult to achieve such at compression ratios better than 2:1 using standard techniques such as linear prediction, Lempel-Ziv or Huffman coding. The primary reason behind this difficulty is the presence of random noise in the data, which resists lossless compression. One way to improve the compression is to filter out the random noise in a preprocessing step. A number of papers in the literature consider motion-compensated filtering of noise from video sequences Dennis (1980), Martinez and Lim (1985), Dubois and Sabri, (1984), Sezan, Ozkan and Fogel (1991), amongst others. Broadly speaking, these papers suggest a weighted averaging of several frames, with the weights depending on motion estimates between the frames. In this paper, we discuss the use of Occam filtering, where the compression algorithm is directly used to filter out the random noise, simultaneously resulting in improved compression *and* reduced noise.

3. Theoretical Results

Let **R** be the reals and **N** the natural numbers. For a probabilistic event A, $\mathbf{Pr}\{A\}$ denotes the probability of the event occurring. We consider functions f from **R** to **R**, and in the interest of technical convenience limit the discussion to Baire functions, Feller (1957), on the unit interval, i.e., $f:[0,1]\rightarrow[0,1]$. A *class* of functions is simply a set of functions. For a function f and natural number n, f_n refers to the sequence of uniform samples of f spaced $1/n$ apart. Specifically, f_n is the sequence of $n+1$ samples $\{f(0), f(1/n), f(2/n),\ldots,f(1)\}$. We call f_n a *sample sequence*. Our discussion will involve the *sum-of-squares* metric on sample sequences. For sequences f_n and g_n,

$$\|f_n,g_n\| = \frac{1}{n}\sum_{i=0}^{n}\Big(f(i/n)-g(i/n)\Big)^2 .$$

Note that the metric defined above is the square of the standard Euclidean metric, and is defined so in the interest of technical convenience.

A *lossy compression* algorithm C is a program that takes as input a sequence of samples f_n and a loss tolerance $\epsilon \geq 0$, and produces as output a binary string s that represents the sample g_n of a function g, such that $\|f_n,g_n\| \leq \epsilon$. A *decompression* algorithm D takes as input a binary string and produces as output a sample sequence. In particular, the decompression algorithm D corresponding to C would output g_n on input s. We use $C(f_n,\epsilon)$ to denote the string s obtained by running C on input f_n and ϵ, and we use $D(s)$ to denote the sequence g_n obtained by running D on string s. We assume that the noise ν is a random variable distributed between [-1, + 1], with variance σ^2. We use $\hat{f}_n$ to denote the sequence of n noisy samples of f, i.e., $\{f(0)+\nu, f(1/n)+\nu,\ldots,f(1)+\nu\}$. The *length* of a binary string s is the number of bits in the string. We use $\chi(f_n,\epsilon)$ to denote the length of the shortest string s such that $\|f_n,D(s)\| \leq \epsilon$. We have to be careful about the class of algorithms we will accept as compression algorithms. Surely, we must admit optimal algorithms, i.e., algorithms that on input f_n and ϵ, output a string of length $\chi(f_n,\epsilon)$. But we would like to allow a much broader class of compression algorithms, those that are not optimal, but within a weak function of the optimal. We characterize these below. We say that a compression algorithm C is *admissible* for a class of functions F if for each $f \in F$ and $\epsilon > 0$, on input f_n, and ϵ, C outputs a string of length at most $n^{\alpha}\epsilon^{-\beta}p(\chi(f_n, q(\epsilon)))$, where $0 \le \alpha < 1$ and $\beta \ge 0$ are fixed constants, and $p : N \to N$ and $q : \mathbf{R} \to \mathbf{R}$. By default, we assume that F is the Baire functions.

We are concerned with the classical filtering problem: given n noisy samples $\hat{f}_n$ of an unknown function f, estimate f_n. Our main theorem says the following: Take n noisy samples $\hat{f}_n$ of f, compress them with allowed loss $\sigma^2 + \epsilon$, then decompress to obtain g_n. The confidence that the residual noise $\|g_n, f_n\|$ is at most ϵ increases as n increases. That is $\lim_{n \to \infty} \mathbf{Pr}\{\|g_n, f_n\| \le \epsilon\} \to 1$. In other words, at a fixed confidence level, the residual noise decreases as n increases.

Theorem 1: Let C be an admissible compression algorithm and D the corresponding decompression algorithm. Let σ^2 be the variance of the noise variable ν. For $\epsilon > 0$ and $n \in \mathbf{N}$, let $g_n = D(C(\hat{f}_n, \sigma^2 + \epsilon))$. Then $\|g_n, f_n\| \le \epsilon$, with probability at least

$$1 - 2^{n^{\alpha}\epsilon^{-\beta}p(\chi(f_n, q(\epsilon/4))) + 3} e^{-\frac{n\epsilon^2}{288}} .$$

Proof: Let h be a function from $[0,1]$ to $[0,1]$.

$$\begin{aligned} \|h_n, \hat{f}_n\| &= 1/n\sum_0^n \left(f(i/n) + \nu - h(i/n)\right)^2 \\ &= \frac{1}{n}\sum_0^n \left(f(i/n) - h(i/n)\right)^2 + \frac{1}{n}\sum_0^n \nu^2 + \frac{1}{n}\sum_0^n 2\nu \left(f(i/n) - h(i/n)\right) . \\ &= \|h_n, f_n\| + \frac{1}{n}\sum_0^n \nu^2 + \frac{1}{n}\sum_0^n 2\nu \left(f(i/n) - h(i/n)\right) . \end{aligned} \tag{1}$$

Subtracting σ^2 from both sides of the above and rearranging, we get

$$\|h_n, \hat{f}_n\| - \|h_n, f_n\| - \sigma^2 = \left(\frac{1}{n}\sum_0^n \nu^2 - \sigma^2\right) + \frac{1}{n}\sum_0^n 2\nu f(i/n) - \frac{1}{n}\sum_0^n 2\nu h(i/n) . \tag{2}$$

From (2), we can write

$$\begin{aligned} \mathbf{Pr}\left\{\left| \|h_n, \hat{f}_n\| - \|h_n, f_n\| - \sigma^2 \right| > \eta\right\} &\le \mathbf{Pr}\left\{\left|\sigma^2 - \frac{1}{n}\sum_0^n \nu^2\right| > \eta/3\right\} + \\ &\mathbf{Pr}\left\{\left|\frac{1}{n}\sum_0^n 2\nu f(i/n)\right| > \eta/3\right\} + \mathbf{Pr}\left\{\left|\frac{1}{n}\sum_0^n 2\nu h(i/n)\right| > \eta/3\right\} . \end{aligned} \tag{3}$$

Since $0 \le f(i/n) \le 1$,

$$\left|\frac{1}{n}\sum_0^n 2\nu f(i/n)\right| \le \left|\frac{1}{n}\sum_0^n 2\nu\right|$$

and hence

$$\mathbf{Pr}\left\{\left|\frac{1}{n}\sum_{0}^{n}2\nu f(i/n)\right| > \eta/3\right\} \le \mathbf{Pr}\left\{\left|\frac{1}{n}\sum_{0}^{n}2\nu\right| > \eta/3\right\}.$$

Similarly

$$\mathbf{Pr}\left\{\left|\frac{1}{n}\sum_{0}^{n}2\nu h(i/n)\right| > \eta/3\right\} \le \mathbf{Pr}\left\{\left|\frac{1}{n}\sum_{0}^{n}2\nu\right| > \eta/3\right\}.$$

Hence, we can write (3) as

$$\mathbf{Pr}\left\{\left|\,\|h_n,\hat{f}_n\| - \|h_n,f_n\| - \sigma^2\right| > \eta\right\} \le \mathbf{Pr}\left\{\left|\sigma^2 - \frac{1}{n}\sum_{0}^{n}\nu^2\right| > \eta/3\right\} + 2\mathbf{Pr}\left\{\left|\frac{1}{n}\sum_{0}^{n}2\nu\right| > \eta/3\right\}. \tag{4}$$

We now estimate the terms on the right-hand side of (4). Since $|\nu| \le 1$ and $\mathbf{E}(\nu^2) = \sigma^2$, by Hoeffding's inequality, Pollard (1984),

$$\mathbf{Pr}\left\{\left|\frac{1}{n}\sum_{0}^{n}\nu^2 - \sigma^2\right| > \eta/3\right\} \le 2e^{-\frac{2n\eta^2}{9}}. \tag{5}$$

Since $|2\nu| \le 2$ and $\mathbf{E}(2\nu) = 0$, again by Hoeffding's inequality,

$$\mathbf{Pr}\left\{\left|\frac{1}{n}\sum_{0}^{n}2\nu\right| > \eta/3\right\} \le 2e^{-\frac{n\eta^2}{18}}. \tag{6}$$

Substituting (5) and (6) in (4), we get

$$\mathbf{Pr}\left\{\left|\,\|h_n,\hat{f}_n\| - \|h_n,f_n\|^2 - \sigma^2\right| > \eta\right\} \le 2e^{-\frac{2n\eta^2}{9}} + 2e^{-\frac{n\eta^2}{18}} \le 4e^{-\frac{n\eta^2}{18}}. \tag{7}$$

Let h be such that $\chi(f_n,\epsilon/4) = \chi(h_n,0)$ and $\|h_n,f_n\| \le \epsilon/4$. For such h,

$$\mathbf{Pr}\left\{\|h_n,\hat{f}_n\| > \sigma^2 + \epsilon/2\right\} \le \mathbf{Pr}\left\{\|h_n,\hat{f}_n\| > \sigma^2 + \|h_n,f_n\| + \epsilon/4\right\}$$

$$\le \mathbf{Pr}\left\{\left|\,\|h_n,\hat{f}_n\| - \sigma^2 - \|h_n,f_n\|\right| > \epsilon/4\right\}.$$

Invoking (7) on the above inequality we get

$$\mathbf{Pr}\left\{\|h_n,\hat{f}_n\| > \sigma^2+\epsilon/2\right\} \leq 4e^{-\frac{n\epsilon^2}{288}}.$$

If $\|h_n,\hat{f}_n\| \leq \sigma^2+\epsilon/2$, then $\chi(\hat{f}_n,\sigma^2+\epsilon/2) \leq \chi(h_n,0) \leq \chi(f_n,\epsilon/4)$. Combining this with the above inequality, we get

$$\mathbf{Pr}\left\{\chi(\hat{f}_n,\sigma^2+\epsilon/2) > \chi(f_n,\epsilon/4)\right\} \leq 4e^{-\frac{n\epsilon^2}{288}}. \tag{8}$$

Call a particular function h to be "bad" if $\|h_n,f_n\| > \epsilon$. For such h,

$$\mathbf{Pr}\left\{\|h_n,\hat{f}_n\| \leq \sigma^2+\epsilon/2\right\} \leq \mathbf{Pr}\left\{\|h_n,\hat{f}_n\| < \sigma^2+\|h_n,f_n\| - \epsilon/2\right\}$$
$$\leq \mathbf{Pr}\left\{\left|\,\|h_n,\hat{f}_n\| - \|h_n,f_n\| - \sigma^2\right| > \epsilon/2\right\} \leq 4e^{-\frac{n\epsilon^2}{72}}, \tag{9}$$

where the last inequality follows from (7). Thus, the probability that C will identify h_n in its output when given $\hat{f}_n$ and $\sigma^2+\epsilon/2$ as input is at most $4e^{-\frac{n\epsilon^2}{72}}$. If $\chi(\hat{f}_n,\sigma^2+\epsilon/2) \leq \chi(f_n,\epsilon/4)$, since C is admissible the output of C is a string of length at most $n^{\alpha}\epsilon^{-\beta}p(\chi(f_n,q(\epsilon/4)))$. Hence, C can identify at most $2^{n^{\alpha}\epsilon^{-\beta}p(\chi(f_n,q(\epsilon/4)))}$ sequences. By (9), the probability that C can identify any bad one from amongst these is at most

$$2^{n^{\alpha}\epsilon^{-\beta}p(\chi(f_n,q(\epsilon/4)))}4e^{-\frac{n\epsilon^2}{72}}. \tag{10}$$

Since (10) is conditional on $\chi(\hat{f}_n,\sigma^2+\epsilon/2) \leq \chi(f_n,\epsilon/4)$, we can combine (10) and (8) to say that the probability that C identifies g_n such that $\|g_n,f_n\| > \epsilon$ is at most

$$2^{n^{\alpha}\epsilon^{-\beta}p(\chi(f_n,q(\epsilon/4)))}4e^{-\frac{n\epsilon^2}{72}} + 4e^{-\frac{n\epsilon^2}{288}} \leq 2^{n^{\alpha}\epsilon^{-\beta}p(\chi(f_n,q(\epsilon/4)))+3}e^{-\frac{n\epsilon^2}{288}}.$$

In other words, the probability that C identifies g_n such that $\|g_n,f_n\| \leq \epsilon$ is at least

$$1 - 2^{n^{\alpha}\epsilon^{-\beta}p(\chi(f_n,q(\epsilon/4)))+3}e^{-\frac{n\epsilon^2}{288}}.$$

3.1 Theorem 1 Simplified

We now give an intuitive form of Theorem 1. The discussion is not meant to be rigorous, but in the interest of clarity. Consider (10) in the proof of Thereom 1. Notice that the term $2^{n^{\alpha}\epsilon^{-\beta}p(\chi(f_n,q(\epsilon/4)))}$ stands for the length of the strings C

outputs. As a simplification, let us replace the term with L, standing for the compressed length. Thus when we combine (10) and (8), we get that the probability that C identifies g_n such that $\|g_n, f_n\| > \epsilon$ is at most

$$2^L 4e^{-\frac{n\epsilon^2}{72}} + 4e^{-\frac{n\epsilon^2}{288}} \leq 2^{L+3}e^{-\frac{n\epsilon^2}{288}}$$

Suppose we want the filter to work with 99% confidence, then we need

$$2^{L+3}e^{-\frac{n\epsilon^2}{288}} \leq .01$$

Solving we have that it suffices if $\epsilon^2 \geq \frac{288}{n}(L+8)$, therefore implying that with 99% confidence, the residual noise $\|g_n f_n\|$ satisfies

$$\|g_n, f_n\|^2 \leq \frac{288}{n}(L+8)\,. \tag{11}$$

Intuitively, (11) tells us that the residual noise decreases as L decreases, i.e., with improved compression, and as n increases, i.e., with increased sampling of the signal.

4. Application to Digital Video

We now consider an application of Occam filtering in the context of digital video sequences. Our aim is to filter random noise from the sequences, in order to permit improved nearly lossless compression.

An obstacle to the practical realization of an Occam filter is that the strength of the noise must be known. Natarajan (1993a), suggests the following heuristic for determining the noise strength:
Run the lossy compression algorithm on a representative sample of the noisy signal with various values of allowed loss, and construct a rate-distortion plot. The knee point of this plot, i.e., the value of the distortion at which the rate rises sharply, is the noise strength. If the plot does not display a knee point, increase the sampling rate, or employ a more effective compression algorithm.
In the above, one method for a more precise identification of the knee point is to plot the second derivative of the rate-distortion curve, and select its maximum as the knee point.

We consider sequences of digitized video. We select the following lossy compression algorithm which operates on batches of three frames. (1) The second frame is the anchor frame and is processed using the linear prediction scheme described in Appendix A, setting to zero prediction errors that are no greater than ϵ in magnitude, where ϵ is the loss parameter. (2) Compute the motion compensated difference between frame 1 and the decompressed version of frame 2.

Motion vectors are calculated using 8×8 blocks, +/-8 pixels search region, half-pixel accuracy. Set to zero all pixels in the difference frame that are no greater han ϵ in magnitude. (3) Compute the motion compensated difference between frame 3 and the decompressed version of frame 2. Set to zero all pixels in the difference frame that are no greater than ϵ in magnitude. (4) Compress the prediction errors of frame 2, and the motion compensated differences of frames 1 and 3 using context Huffman coding, Todd et al (1985). (5) Compress the block motion vectors of frames 1 and 3 using context Huffman coding.

Decompression is achieved as follows. (1) Decode the Huffman encodings. (2) Reverse the linear prediction scheme to obtain frame 2. (3) Using the motion vectors, recover frames 1 and 3.

In our computational experiments, we used grey-scale CCIR601 sequences, comprising 480×720 pixels per frame. We used three sequences, the first of a football game that we refer to as the *football* sequence, the second of table-tennis game that we refer to as the *tennis* sequence. and the third of a statue that we refer to as the *statue* sequence. Figure 1 is the rate-distortion plot for a batch of frames from the *football* sequence. The vertical axis is the reciprocal of the compression ratio achieved. The horizontal axis is the loss tolerance ϵ. Also shown is the second derivative of the rate-distortion curve. Since the second derivative is maximum at $\epsilon = 5$, we select it to be the knee point. Figure 2 is the rate-distortion plot for the same batch of frames, except that the horizontal axis expresses the average power of the distortion in decibels. Specifically, the horizontal axis is $10\log_{10}(V/255^2)$, where V is the variance of the difference between the reconstructed frames and the original frames. Figure 2 also shows the second derivative of the rate-distortion plot. Figure 3 is the rate-distortion plot for a batch of frames from *tennis*, and corresponds to Figure 1. Notice that the knee point occurs at $\epsilon = 6$. Figure 4 is the corresponding plot for a batch of frames from the *statue* sequence. Notice that the knee point occurs at $\epsilon = 5$. Assuming that the noise source is the same for all the three sequences, and bearing in mind that the knee-point method is a heuristic rather than an exact calculation, we can conclude that $\epsilon = 5$ is a good estimate for the noise strength over the three sequences. If the actual noise strength is $\|\nu\| \neq 5$, the residual noise will converge to the absolute value of $\|\nu\| - 5$ rather than to zero, and hence inaccuracies in the estimate are not catastrophic.

For the *football* sequence, lossless compression at $\epsilon = 0$ gives a compression ratio of $1/.5 = 2$. From Figure 1, lossy compression at $\epsilon = 5$ yields a compression ratio of $1/.225 = 4.4$. From Figure 2, although the knee point corresponds to a distortion of roughly $-40dB$, this distortion is the noise that has been removed. The decompressed sequence should actually be closer to the noise free sequence, and in that sense, we have simultaneously improved compression and reduced noise. For the *tennis* sequence, lossless compression at $\epsilon = 0$ gives a compression ratio of $1/.67 = 1.5$. From Figure 3, lossy compression at $\epsilon = 5$ yields a compression ratio of $1/.45 = 2.2$. For the *statue* sequence, lossless compression at $\epsilon = 0$ gives a compression ratio of 1/.53 = 1.9. From Figure 4, lossy compression at $\epsilon = 5$ yields a compression ratio of 1/.28 = 3.6. Thus, operating at the knee point improves the compression achieved, while reducing random noise.

5. Conclusion

We presented a convergence bound on Occam filters independent of the distribution of the noise variable beyond some minimal assumptions. We then considered an application of Occam filters to digital video sequences, and showed how they can be used to operate a lossy compression algorithm at the "optimal" loss, so as to enable improved nearly lossless compression, while reducing noise.

6. Appendix A

We describe a linear predictive scheme for compressing single frames. $I[i][j]$ denotes pixel (i,j) in the input frame, ϵ denotes the loss tolerance. The prediction error frame $B[i][j]$ is constructed as follows, using fixed constants a,b and c.

```
for j=0 to M do B[0][j] = I[0][j]; end
for j=0 to M do  B[i][0] = I[i][0]; end
for i=0 to N for j=0 to M do
    x = aB[i][j-1]+bB[i-1][j]+cB[i-1][j-1]- I[i][j];
    if (x ≤ ε)x = 0
    B[i][j] = x;
    I[i][j] = aB[i][j-1]+bB[i-1][j]+cB[i-1][j-1]- x;
    end
```

7. References

Dennis, T.J., (1980). Non-linear temporal filter for television picture noise reduction, IEEE Proceedings, Vol.127, part G., pp. 52-56.

DeVore, R.A., and Lucier, B. J., (1992) Fast wavelet techniques for near-optimal image processing, IEEE Military Comm. Conf., IEEE Comm. Society, 1992.

Donoho, D. L., (1992). De-noising by soft thresholding, Tech. Rep 409, Dept. of Statistics, Stanford University.

Dubois, E., and Sabri, S., (1984). Noise reduction in image sequences using motion compensated temporal filtering. IEEE Trans. Comm. vol. COM-32, pp. 826-831.

Feller, W., (1957). Intro. to Prob. Theory and its Applications, John Wiley, N.Y.

Martinez, D., and Lim, J.S., (1985). Implicit motion compensated enhancement of noisy image sequences, Proc. ICASSP, pp. 375-378.

Natarajan, B.K., (1993a). Filtering random noise via data compression, Proc. IEEE Data Compression Conference, Snowbird, Utah, pp.60-69.

Natarajan, B.K., (1993b). Occam's Razor for functions, Proc. ACM Conf. on Comp. Learning Theory, Santa Cruz, CA.

Pollard, D., (1984). Convergence of stochastic processes. Springer Verlag, N.Y.

Sezan, M.I., Ozkan, M.K., and Fogel, S.V., (1991). Proc. ICASSP, pp. 2429-2432.

Todd, S., Rissanen, J., and Langdon, G., (1985). Parameter reduction and context selection for compression of gray-scale images. IBM J. of R&D, V. 29, pp. 188-193.

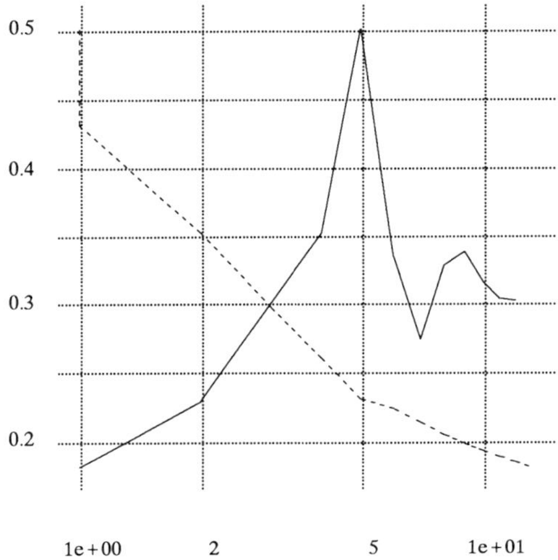

Figure 1: Rate distortion plot for a batch of frames from the *football* sequence, dotted line. Vertical axis is the reciprocal of the compression ratio, horizontal axis is the loss tolerance ϵ. Also shown is the second derivative, solid line, scaled to fit along the vertical axis.

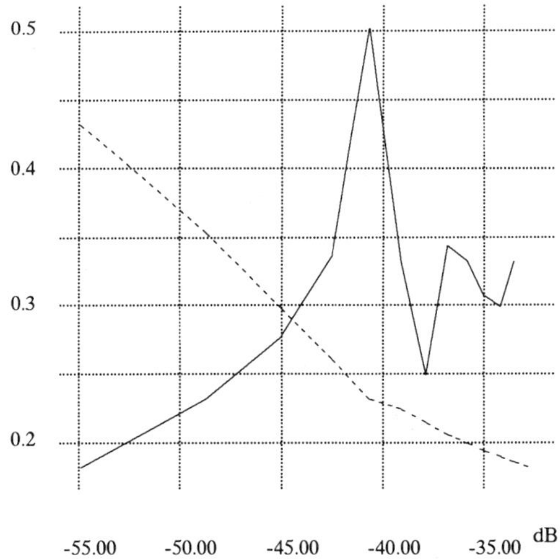

Figure 2: Rate distortion plot for a batch of frames from the *football* sequence, dotted line. Vertical axis is the reciprocal of the compression ratio, horizontal axis is the variance of the distortion expressed in dB. Also shown is the second derivative, solid line, scaled to fit along the vertical axis.

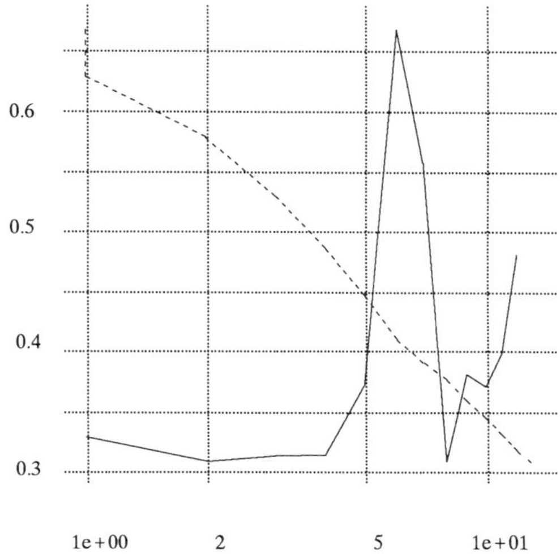

Figure 3: Rate distortion plot for a batch of frames from the *tennis* sequence, dotted line. Vertical axis is the reciprocal of the compression ratio, horizontal axis is the loss tolerance ϵ. Also shown is the second derivative, solid line, scaled to fit along the vertical axis.

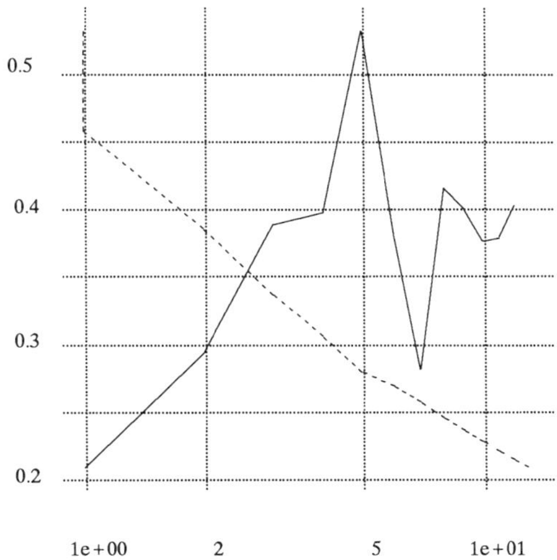

Figure 4: Rate distortion plot for a batch of frames from the *statue* sequence, dotted line. Vertical axis is the reciprocal of the compression ratio, horizontal axis is the loss tolerance ϵ. Also shown is the second derivative, solid line, scaled to fit along the vertical axis.

POSTER SESSION

Adaptive Intraframe Coding for Very Low Bit-Rate Image Sequence Compression using Classifier Constrained DCT-VQ

Mustafa Ali TÜRKER and **Mete SEVERCAN**
The Scientific and Technical Research Council of Turkey,
Ankara Electronics Research and Development Institute ODTÜ,06531,Ankara,TURKEY.
E-mails : c55261@vm.cc.metu.edu.tr, severcan@vm.cc.metu.edu.tr

An adaptive method for intraframe coding of image sequence frames at very low bit rates is proposed. Adaptivity is achieved by constructing a so called *classifier constrained vector quantizer* (CCVQ) codebook using the first frame of the sequence. 8×8 DCT-II of each frame sub-block is taken. 14 zig-zag scanned non-DC coefficents are used as input vectors, and two DCT coefficients, $V1$ and $H1$, are used as the edge-oriented classifier feature vector of the sub-block. DC coefficents are scalar quantized using a 256-level, nonuniform Lloyd-Max quantizer for Gaussian sources. Both the codebook and the classifier are obtained in the DCT domain simultaneously, using Lagrangian methods, so that a part of the overall VQ codebook, $C = \cup_{i=1}^{M} C_i$, would be assigned to each of M classes and subcodebook sizes would be optimized to yield minimum total average distortion (the major problem of Classified VQ). Then the algorithm offers a kind of entropy coding via varying subcodebook sizes. Overall PSNR performance of the system is quite high, while subjective edge degradation and coding complexity is reduced due to edge-oriented classification.

CCVQ maps each source vector $\mathbf{X} \in \Re^n$ onto a set of codewords, $Q(\mathbf{X}) = \mathbf{Y}_{i,k}$ where $\mathbf{Y}_{i,k} \in C_i$ and $C_i \subset C \subset \Re^n$, subject to the constraint that all codewords in C_i are of the same class as the input vector. Given a vector $\mathbf{Z} \in \Re^n$, let $\mathbf{Z}_f \in \Re^m$ be the class feature vector of dimension $m \leq n$, extracted from $\mathbf{Z}$ by choosing certain elements of $\mathbf{Z}$. Assume that the classifier partitions the feature vector space into M regions, $\mathcal{P} = \{P_1, P_2, ..., P_M\}$, and that the quantizer partitions the source vector space into N regions, $\mathcal{R} = \{R_{1,1}, .., R_{1,N_1}, R_{2,1}, .., R_{2,N_2}, ..., R_{M,1}, .., R_{M,N_M}\}$, so that $\mathbf{V}_i$ is the representative feature vector of the region P_i, and $\mathbf{Y}_{i,k}$ is the representative vector of the region $R_{i,k}$. Then $\gamma(\mathbf{Z}) = i$ if $\mathbf{Z}_f \in P_i$ is the classifier, $\alpha(\mathbf{X}, \gamma(\mathbf{X})) = k$ if $\mathbf{X} \in R_{\gamma(\mathbf{X}),k}$ is the encoder and $\beta(k, \gamma(\mathbf{X})) = \mathbf{Y}_{\gamma(\mathbf{X}),k}$ is the decoder. For generating optimum quantizer and classifier partitions, the average distortions, $D_Q(\alpha, \beta, \gamma) = E[d_n(\mathbf{X}, \beta(\alpha(\mathbf{X}, \gamma(\mathbf{X})), \gamma(\mathbf{X})))]$ and $D_{Cl}(\alpha, \beta, \gamma) = E[d_m(\beta(\alpha(\mathbf{X}, \gamma(\mathbf{X})), \gamma(\mathbf{X}))_f, \mathbf{V}_{\gamma(\mathbf{X})})]$ where $d_r(\mathbf{A}, \mathbf{B}) = \frac{1}{r} \sum_{i=1}^{r} (a_i - b_i)^2$ must be jointly minimized. To solve the minimization problem, methods from entropy-constrained VQ can be applied and a Lagrangian modified distortion expression $J_\lambda = D_Q(\alpha, \beta, \gamma) + \lambda D_{Cl}(\alpha, \beta, \gamma)$, can be minimized by alternately improving α, β and γ using, basically, generalized Lloyd algorithm.

Simulations made on Miss America test sequence showed that, if each frame of the sequence is compressed into 0.25 bpp (without interframe coding) using the same codebook and classifier generated from the first frame, the overall PSNR performance of the sequence would be about 34 dB. This performance is almost the same as the sytems which use PNN-LBG, Stochastic Methods, or Kohonen Learning for codebook generation, but convergence time (codebook and classifier generation time) and codebook search time of the algorithm is much less than those of others permitting real-time applications. The system is especially suitable for videophone applications as the initial codebook and classifier can be obtained using many head and shoulder views of human speakers, making the result closer to optimal, and shortening execution time of the minimization algorithm.

 1068-0314/94 $3.00

ADAPTIVE LOSSLESS DATA COMPRESSION

Author: David J. Craft (IBM Microelectronics)

Adaptive Lossless Data Compression (ALDC) is IBM's general purpose data compression technology. ALDC is an LZ_1 (a.k.a. Lempel-Ziv) based algorithm realized in IBM's advance VLSI technology to produce general purpose data compression hardware at speeds over 40MB/sec.

ALDC achieves these speeds without affecting compression ratio performance. Benchmark tests show equivalent or better compression ratios compared to other leading LZ_1 and LZ_2 (a.k.a Ziv-Lempel) compression solutions. This is done while maintaining history buffers substantially smaller than those used by the competition. A smaller history buffer coupled with IBM's custom circuit technology has allowed ALDC compression engines to be produced in small single chip solutions.

This paper reports on the development of IBM's general purpose data LZ_1 compression algorithm. A brief description is given, partly to introduce terminology, of the main data categories and their corresponding compression options. A discussion follows on some of the likely economic consequences of widespread use of compression, showing why the initial focus is on algorithms of a more general type suitable especially for DASD capacity enhancement. Some early work on algorithm evaluation is presented, and arguments leading to a preference for the adaptive LZ_1 class of algorithm are given.

IBM's ALDC hardware implementation of LZ_1 is described from evolution to development and implementation. Derivation of ALDC's CAM (Content Addressable Memory) is reviewed showing the effectiveness and efficiency of such custom circuitry in respect to history buffer utilization. This follows with explanation of reduced history buffer size and effective compression ratios affects. Coupled together, the CAM and reduced history buffer size have direct impact on the hardware implementation (Silicon size, costs and effective compression speeds). ALDC's compression performance is considered, using the standard Calgary corpus of data files, and other data. Superiority of ALDC is seen with respect to other general purpose software and hardware implementations.

The ALDC compression technology is able to cover a very wide of range applications. The very small Silicon area needed allows integration within the smallest portable, handheld or wireless devices where it consumes far less power at greater speed than software. It is even viable for integration within credit-card sized removable storage devices themselves. At the other end of the spectrum, this same design and algorithm is already capable of providing more than enough thruput for our most powerful mainframes and network file servers. Using IBM's .5 micron technologies, we can easily fit multiple engines on to a single chip. In turn, this allows us to design ALDC compression systems which have sustained thruput in the Gigabyte/second range. This is a significant enough range of cost and performance to merit consideration as an industry-wide compression standard, not only for system storage, but also for system networking applications.

Adaptive quantization without side information

A. Ortega* and M. Vetterli‡

* Dept. of EE and Center for Telecomm. Research
Columbia University, New York, NY 10027

‡ Dept. of EECS, University of California,
Berkeley, CA 94720

We propose to extend some of the ideas of adaptive lossless compression to design an adaptive quantization algorithm. Noting that the performance of an arithmetic coder is as good as its estimation of the statistics of the input, we split our quantizer into two building blocks: *model estimation* and *quantizer design*. The main idea is that, as long as the model estimation manages to track down the changes in source statistics, a standard quantizer design technique *which assumes that the source follows the estimated model* can be used. As an example of this type of design we study an adaptive quantizer for a memoryless non-stationary source and we impose the restriction that no side information can be sent, i.e. encoder and decoder must perform their adaptation based on the quantized information.

The goal of the *model estimation* is to track the (changing) source statistics by providing an approximation to the true pdf of the source. The main difficulty involved stems from the fact that the estimation has to be performed based on the quantized data, i.e. the only available information are the counts of how many samples fell into each of the quantizer bins. We split the estimation into three main tasks, namely, (i) estimation of the dynamic range of the source, (ii) matching the observed quantized sample counts to an approximate pdf, and (iii) varying the speed of adaptation, i.e. determining how fast the accumulated information should be "forgotten". As an example of this approach to adaptive quantization, we adopt a piecewise linear model for the estimated pdf and devise simple techniques to update the dynamic range and change the speed of adaptation.

For the given estimated model, we show as an example a *quantizer design* based on a constant rate Lloyd-Max algorithm. Both encoder and decoder estimate the distribution and use the Lloyd-Max algorithm to determine the optimal quantizer for the estimated distribution. Note that if our estimate of the pdf were exact the performance of the quantizer would be optimal.

The results for our example show that the input distribution can be estimated and the quantizer "learned" starting with no prior knowledge. For a stationary input adaptivity produces a very slight performance degradation with respect to the optimal Lloyd-Max quantizer (less than 0.05 dB), while being adaptive is clearly advantageous when quantizing a non-stationary input (over 1.5 dB gain over a Lloyd-Max quantizer designed for the entire input sequence). A further advantage of adaptivity is that, as the distribution is learned without prior information, there are no losses in performance due to mismatches between the distribution assumed in the design and the actual observed input distribution. Future work will be focused on extending our techniques to entropy-constrained variable rate adaptive quantization.

Adaptive Source Coding Schemes for Geometrically Distributed Integer Alphabets *

Kar-Ming Cheung and Padhraic Smyth
Communications Systems Research Section
Jet Propulsion Laboratory, 4800 Oak Grove Dr., Pasadena, CA 91109

It is well-known for image coding that the error samples in lossless and lossy predictive coding and the transform coefficients in transform coding before quantization can be modelled with a Laplacian distribution. In previous work [1] we introduced a modified Laplacian distribution for unquantized outputs and showed that the probability distribution of the quantized output integers derived from the modified Laplacian distribution is geometric for all integers except zero. This discrepancy can be shown to be small and the quantized output integers can be modelled using a simple single-parameter discrete 2-sided geometrical probability distribution.

In this paper we revisit the Gallager and van Voorhis (GVH) optimal source coding scheme for geometrically distributed non-negative integer alphabets

$$p_{G1}(i) = (1-\theta)\theta^i \quad \forall\, \theta \geq 0, \tag{1}$$

where $\theta = 1 - r(0)$, and $r(0)$ is the fraction of zeros in the sample set. $r(0)$ can be directly estimated from the data. We show that the various subcodes in the popular Rice algorithm [2] can be derived from the GVH code. In fact the Rice subcodes are also a subset of the class of optimal codes for runlength encodings proposed by Golomb. We modify and generalize the GVH code for 2-sided geometrically distributed integer alphabets (positive and negative), which have the following distribution

$$p_{G2}(i) = \frac{1-\theta}{1+\theta}\theta^{|i|} \quad \forall\, i, \tag{2}$$

where $\theta = \frac{1-r(0)}{1+r(0)}$, and $r(0)$ is the fraction of zeros in the sample set. The 2-sided geometrically distributed integer alphabets are typical inputs to the back-end entropy coding stage of lossless predictive coding schemes and lossy transform coding schemes. We presented some theoretical and experimental results for this scheme. We develop an adaptive coding scheme which has low implementation complexity and is similar to the Rice coding scheme. This scheme consists of three subcodes which account for low, medium, and high activity data and an escape code that prevents data expansion.

References:

[1] K. Cheung, P. Smyth and H. Wang, "A High-Speed Distortionless Predictive Image Compression Scheme," TDA Progress Report 42-102 Jet Propulsion Laboratory, Pasadena, CA, pp.73–90, August 15th 1990.

[2] R. Rice, "Some Practical Universal Noiseless Coding Techniques," Part I and II, JPL Publications 79-22 and 83-17, March 1979.

---

* The research described in this paper was carried out by the Jet Propulsion Laboratory, California Institute of Technology, under a contract with National Aeronautics and Space Administration

ADVANCED END-TO-END SIMULATION FOR ON-BOARD PROCESSING (AESOP)

Alan S. Mazer

Jet Propulsion Laboratory, California Institute of Technology
4800 Oak Grove Drive, Pasadena, California 91109

Developers of data compression algorithms typically use their own software together with commercial packages to implement, evaluate and demonstrate their work. While convenient for an individual developer, this approach makes it difficult to build on or use another's work without intimate knowledge of each component. When several people or groups work on different parts of the same problem, the larger view can be lost. What's needed is a simple piece of software to stand in the gap and link together the efforts of different people, enabling them to build on each other's work, and providing a base for engineers and scientists to evaluate the parts as a cohesive whole and make design decisions.

AESOP (Advanced End-to-end Simulation for On-board Processing) attempts to meet this need by providing a graphical interface to a developer-selected set of algorithms, interfacing with compiled code and standalone programs, as well as procedures written in the PV-Wave command language. As a proof of concept, AESOP is outfitted with several data compression algorithms integrating previous work on different processors (AT&T DSP32C, TI TMS320C30, SPARC). The user can specify at run-time the processor on which individual parts of the compression should run. Compressed data is then fed through simulated transmission and uncompression to evaluate the effects of compression parameters, noise and error correction algorithms.

Implementation is straightforward, with available functions and executables (*modules*) listed in ASCII *dictionaries*. Dictionaries also define complete applications, made up of individual modules, including their graphical layout in a dataflow diagram. Most user interactions can be done with the mouse. Each module has an associated list of parameters which the user can specify using popup windows; AESOP provides this GUI automatically based on information in the dictionaries. The user monitors module inputs and outputs using a variety of display types, from a list based on data dimensionality and type. A basic set of input and output methods is in place; others may be locally defined.

AESOP currently runs on Sun SPARCstations using SunOS 4.1.3 and Motif. While PV-Wave is not required, support for it is built in and the current dictionaries use it for image display. Operating system dependencies are minimal. AESOP is written in ANSI C. AESOP uses dynamic loading to execute compiled modules, which is available on AIX 3.2, HPUX 8.0 and VMS 5.0 in addition to SunOS.

Algorithmic significance, mutual information, and DNA sequence comparisons

Aleksandar Milosavljević
Genome Structure Group
Center for Mechanistic Biology and Biotechnology
Argonne National Laboratory
Argonne, Illinois 60439-4833
e-mail: milosav@anl.gov

The newly proposed *algorithmic significance method* (Milosavljevic, A. and Jurka, J., "Discovering Simple DNA Sequences by the Algorithmic Significance Method", Computer Applications in Biosciences, 9(4), 1993.) enables recognition of patterns in DNA sequences at prespecified significance levels via minimal length encoding. The method is now extended to provide a formal framework for DNA sequence comparisons via algorithmic mutual information, which is defined as the encoding length of a sequence by itself minus its encoding length using the other sequence as a source dictionary. Under a few simplifying assumptions, it is shown that the significance of sequence similarity depends exponentially on algorithmic mutual information. The concept of mutual information provides solutions to the following two open problems in DNA sequence comparisons: [1] Factoring out similarity due to shared repetitive patterns (mutual information depends on both the complexity of compared sequences and their mutual similarity); [2] Factoring out bias due to partial sequencing by hybridization (the bias due to the *a priori* choice of words for partial sequencing by hybridization is factored out by conditioning mutual information). DNA sequence comparison is only one of the many possible applications of algorithmic significance and mutual information. Many other pattern recognition and machine discovery tasks can be approached in a similar way.

This work was supported in part by U.S. Department of Energy, Office of Health and Environmental Research, under Contract W-31-109-Eng-38.

Applications of Run-Length Lists (RLL)

by Lester A. Potter
PRC, Inc.
1500 PRC Drive
McLean, VA 22102

Abstract

Bitmap information in its raw form consumes a great deal of space; thus there exist many compression schemes aimed at reducing bitmap disk storage requirements. Currently, most software engineers are compelled to design and implement bitmap manipulation operations on raw data. When working with raw bitmap data, in-core memory requirements grow dramatically as bitmap sizes and pixel densities increase. As in-core memory requirements have increased, several strategies have emerged for making effective use of limited memory resources (such as, tiling and striping). This presentation explores how Run-Length Lists (RLL) can be used to cope with bitmap manipulation on memory-starved machines. RLL, a simple data compression scheme for encoding bitmap information, represents a scan-line as an increasing sequence of integral values. These values identify transition points within a scan-line, from runs of black pixels to runs of white and vice versa. A bitmap is made up of a series of such scan-lines. Therefore, a series of RLL encoded scan-lines comprise an RLL bitmap. RLL reduces image storage requirements by maintaining only transition point information, instead of each black and white pixel. Compression schemes exist that achieve greater compression with better worst case storage requirements but RLL is a more useful compressed form because of the diversity of operations that may be performed upon it. Operations such as scaling, image smearing, shifting and stretching, as well as detecting connected pixels, constructing bounding rectangles, and cutting and pasting arbitrary polygonal regions are easily and efficiently implemented on RLL; these same operations on Group 4 data are extremely difficult to implement. This presentation discusses several algorithms for operations on RLL data. It begins with basic building blocks, progresses to advanced operations, and concludes with implementation considerations.

 1068-0314/94 $3.00 © 1994 IEEE

An Approach to Achieving Maximum Lossless Compression of Medical Images[1]

Robert J. Stewart, Y. M. Fleming Lure, C. S. Joe Liou

Dr.'s Stewart & Lure are with Caelum Research Corp., Silver Spring, MD 20901
Phone: (301) 593-1748.
Dr Liou is at the University of Pennsylvania, University Park, Pa 16802.

Abstract

Image compression without loss of fidelity and with an acceptable degree of compression is difficult to achieve in a cost/effective practical manner. The need for a lossless compression subsystem within medical systems that can perform its function at system throughput rates and provide compression ratios better than the 1.5 to 2.5 typically achieved today, is clear with today's focus on health costs. In this paper we analyze several lossless compression techniques applied to medical images and determine the best combination of source modelling and coding to give maximum compression. We analyze the effect of separating the pixel intensity bits contaminated with noise from the true data bits and compressing the resulting components independently using different coding techniques. Our analysis shows that separating noise from signal is not the optimum approach and that best results are obtained by performing bilinear interpolation to re-map the original image, including the noise, and then performing arithmetic coding with high-order adaptive modeling of the re-mapped image. Various approaches to image re-mapping were considered and the results of applying them to different classes of medical image are discussed. It is shown that arithmetic coding performs better than other compression techniques for all medical images and we show that, depending on the type of image, higher-order statistical models may or may not be beneficial in achieving good compression ratios.

To be useful to the medical systems community, lossless compression approaches must have acceptable performance and give as high a compression ratio as can be achieved. Acceptable performance is a function of hardware platform complexity and cost, with the platforms designed to operate at throughput rates determined by the systems into which they are imbedded. We analyze different hardware architectures for performing our preferred re-mapping , source modelling, and arithmetic coding techniques and show performance results. The architectures discussed include RISC architectures with large data caches, DSP arrays, and parallel processing with low cost RISC processors.

[1]This work was partially funded under NIH SBIR contract RR07735-01. The opinions expressed are solely those of the authors and not NIH.

An Asymmetric, Semi-adaptive Text Compression Algorithm

Harry Plantinga
Department of Computer Science
University of Pittsburgh
Pittsburgh, PA 15260
planting@cs.pitt.edu

Abstract

Applications involving the distribution of large text files such as electronic books or reference material may benefit from a text compression algorithm that compresses slowly but decompresses very quickly, if good compression ratios can be achieved. Such an algorithm is said to be asymmetric. In addition, such applications may benefit from or even require the ability to access and decompress small parts of a large compressed file without decompressing the whole file. This random access is extremely inefficient with adaptive compression algorithms, since the encoding of a part of a file depends on the earlier part of the file, but it is possible with semi-adaptive compression algorithms, which adapt for a particular file but do not adapt across the file.

The assymetric, semi-adaptive text compression algorithm presented here is well suited to such applications. It involves a new heuristic for digram-replacement text compression, in which common pairs of tokens in the text are replaced with a new token. This process is iterated until compression is no longer possible. There results a dictionary with two token entries or a literal byte for each token.

Finding the optimal dictionary is NP-hard, and several heuristics have been proposed. We propose a heuristic that is computationally expensive but very effective. The heuristic is an estimate of the change in the entropy-coded size of the file and dictionary that would result from a particular digram replacement. Suppose that tokens j and k are replaced with a new token m. Let c_t be the number of occurrences in the text of token t. If the length of the text + dictionary is n tokens, the new length will be $n' = n - c_m + 2$, since two tokens will be added to the dictionary. The new number of occurrences of tokens j and k will be $c_j' = c_j - c_m + 1$ and $c_k' = c_k - c_m + 1$. The number of bits saved is estimated as the decrease in the number of bits required to represent the text and dictionary according to the entropy estimate, namely

$$n \log n - n' \log n' - c_j \log c_j + c_j' \log c_j' - c_k \log c_k + c_k' \log c_k' + c_m \log c_m$$

The resulting tokens and dictionary are then entropy coded. The results below reflect the use of a new, non-optimal entropy coding scheme that can be decoded faster than Huffman coding.

This algorithm compresses slowly (e.g. five hours on a RISC workstation for a megabyte file), but decompression is extremely fast, requiring less than two dictionary look-ups per output character in addition to entropy decoding. Compression ratios are better than those for the best dictionary-based methods (such as gzip) for many large text files such as electronic books. A standard corpus of texts [Bell, *et al. ACM Computing Surveys* **21**(4), 1989] was compressed from a total of 3,141,622 bytes to 965,620 bytes with this algorithm, compared to 1,061,830 for gzip. On a DECstation 5000/200, the total compression time was 15:53:10, compared to 0:01:01 for gzip, and the total decompression time was 30 seconds, compared to 35 for gzip.

Attribute Enumerative Coding: A Compression Technique for Tuple Data Structures *

WEE K. NG   CHINYA V. RAVISHANKAR

Department of Electrical Engineering and Computer Science
The University of Michigan, Ann Arbor, MI 48109-2122
E-mail: {wkn,ravi}@eecs.umich.edu

Technological progress in the computing arena has produced dramatic improvements in all aspects except I/O. Thus, I/O-bound applications suffer from the I/O bottleneck problem. Examples of which are relational databases, and databases constructed from social, economic, technological, inventory, environmental, medical or demographic surveys. The importance of the problem is demonstrated by the fact that database sizes are growing rapidly and future databases are expected to be several orders of magnitude larger than the largest database in operation today. Databases of terabyte (10^{12} bytes) size will soon be in active use. In addition, database queries generate a lot of I/O. Queries that compute aggregates such as averages require the access of large portions of the database. Table concatenation (*joins* in relational database terminology), a frequent operation in queries, involves the access of several tables simultaneously. Such queries are data intensive.

One of the solution approaches is to reduce the amount of I/O through database compression. Due to the operational characteristics of databases, the majority of the data compression techniques, other than the ad hoc techniques, are *fundamentally inappropriate* for database compression. We propose a new compression technique, called *Attribute Enumerative Coding* (AEC), for data that are stored in *tuple* data structures. A tuple is a sequence of symbols, each of which belongs to an alphabet. The technique has wide applicability as a feature among most databases is that data are often organized as tuples.

In a relational database, a relation consists of a collection of ordered tuples. Often, consecutive tuples share several commmon attributes. The conventional approach stores the tuples on disk without modification. AEC exploits the redundancy among the common attributes between ordered consecutive tuples. The elimination of these redundancies reduces the average size of a tuple, thus achieving compression. The essence of AEC is differential coding on pairwise consecutive tuples.

We have performed a detailed analysis of AEC and showed that it is perfectly lossless and that it always achieve positive compression efficiency. In addition, we have derived upper and lower bounds on its efficiency. We have also optimized the process of encoding/decoding a tuple so that no arithmetic operations are required. As an illustration of its efficiency and practicality, we apply AEC to the compression of the 1990 U.S. Census of Bureau Population and Housing data. It achieves a compression ratio of around 80% (5:1) and reduces the size of the data from approximately 4 gigabytes to around 800 megabytes.

*This work was supported in part by the Consortium for International Earth Science Information Networking.

1068-0314/94 $3.00 © 1994 IEEE

Biorthogonal Wavelets for Data Compression

Eric E. Majani
Jet Propulsion Laboratory (MS 168-522)
4800 Oak Grove Drive
Pasadena, CA 91109
email: eric@elroy.jpl.nasa.gov

Michael Lightstone
Department of Electrical and Computer Engineering
University of California at Santa Barbara
Santa Barbara, CA 93106

Abstract

While the family of Daubechies orthogonal filters is derived from an orthogonal factorization of *binomial product filters*, a family of biorthogonal filters can be derived from the symmetric factorization of the same binomial product filters. At least two well-known biorthogonal filters belong to this family [1][2], and yield good performance when used in wavelet-based lossy data compression.

We propose to identify members of this family (for product filters of order up to 62) with high lossy compression performance. To help narrow the large number of candidate filters, a number of filter characteristics based on stopband attenuation and orthogonality are introduced with final selection being determined by the experimental rate-distortion performance of seismic and image data. Our results clearly show the superiority of the biorthogonal filters obtained over the Daubechies orthogonal filters.

[1] D. Le Gall and A. Tabatabai, "Subband coding of digital images using symmetric short kernal filters and arithmetic coding techniques," *Proc. of the IEEE Int. Conf. on Acous. Speech and Sig. Proc. 1988*, vol. M2, pp. 761-764.

[2] I. Daubechies, *Ten Lectures on Wavelets,* SIAM, Philadelphia, Pennsylvania, 1992

Codebook Organization for MAP Detection of Weighted Universal Vector Quantized Image Transmission over Noisy Channels *

Ren-Yuh Wang Eve A. Riskin Richard Ladner

University of Washington

One of the more sophisticated forms of VQ is the new Weighted Universal VQ (WUVQ) by Chou and Effros [1], which is a locally optimal multi-codebook vector quantizer. In WUVQ, the encoder encodes a *supervector* with each subcodebook and transmits the index of the subcodebook that measures the lowest distortion on the supervector to the decoder. The encoder then encodes each vector in the supervector with the selected codebook and sends the codeword index for each vector. In this paper, we use some recently developed techniques for *codebook organization* [2] to organize a fixed rate WUVQ codebook for protection against channel errors.

In our previous work [2], we used PCP and a Switching algorithm to organize a full search VQ codebook for transmission over noisy channels. We found that the organized codebook has the property that the MSB's of the codeword indices are much more important to the image quality than the LSB's. The MSB's are also highly correlated and can be corrected by the MAP detector. In this paper, we use these algorithms to organize WUVQ for transmission over noisy channels.

For WUVQ, most of the increased distortion D_{inc} between the transmitted and received data caused by channel errors consists of two parts: one is due to channel errors occurring on the codeword index and the other on the codebook index. We develop three steps to sequentially reduce D_{inc}. First, we organize the codewords in each codebook independently but according to the same partition rule. We then organize the codebooks themselves. Finally, we remap the received codebook and codeword indices to a new index to enhance MAP detection on the MSB's of the remapped indices.

Our simulation showed that our codebook organization techniques led to an increase in the SNR of 7.26 dB for image transmission over a noisy channel with channel bit error rate (BER) of 10% over unorganized WUVQ, and led to similar increases over a wide range of BERs.

[1] P. A. Chou and M. Effros. Rate and distortion redundancies for source coding with rspect to a fidelity criterion. In *IEEE ISIT*, page 53, January 1993.

[2] R. Wang, E. Riskin, and R. Ladner. Codebook organization to enhance maximum a posteriori detection of progressive transmission of vector quantized images over noisy channels. UWCSE Technical Report #93-12-07. Preliminary version appears in ICASSP 1993, Volume 5, pp.233–236.

*This work was supported by an NSF Young Investigator Award, NSF Grant No. CCR-9108314, and the Washington Technology Center.

Combining Data Compression with Channel Modulation and/or Error Correction

Michael J. Gormish

Information Systems Lab, Department of Electrical Engineering
Stanford University, Stanford, CA 94305-4055

Ricoh California Research Center
Menlo Park, CA 94025-7022

email: gormish@crc.ricoh.com

Lossless data compression systems should provide a efficient sequence of channel symbols which allow the original data to be recreated exactly. Proceeding primarily from these two postulates, i.e. efficiency and finite delay, a generalized arithmetic coding algorithm is presented. This algorithm considers short sets of sequences of allowable channel symbols instead of the 'subinterval of the real line' used by arithmetic coders. Sets of sequences are partitioned to match input probabilities in an equivalent manner by both the encoder and the decoder.

As with arithmetic coding the algorithm operates using only finite precision arithmetic operations, and as the precision is increased, the compression efficiency rapidly approaches the "entropy limit." Unlike typical implementations of arithmetic coding the algorithm has a guaranteed maximum delay between the coding of a symbol by the encoder and the production of an output.

The algorithm also provides a guaranteed maximum number of channel symbols that must be examined by the decoder to decode any symbol. The length of these delays is a design choice and can be traded off with coder efficiency. The main generalization is the ability to directly generate compressed data streams satisfying a constraints. Essentially, any channel that can be represented by a finite state transition diagram can be used. This class of channels includes run length limited channels, DC-balanced or charge constrained channels, the telegraph or "Morse code" channel, and even trellis error corrected channels. Thus the input to a generalized coder is a sequence of probabilities and outcomes and the output is a stream of channel symbols which could meet a run length limited constraint and have forward error correction information included.

In the case of encoding binary decisions, generalized arithmetic coding can be implemented without any arithmetic operations. A finite state machine can be designed using the coding algorithm which provides exactly the same outputs. Instead of using a numeric representation of the probability estimates, the finite state machine inputs only a probability class identifier. This can simplify both the finite state machine and the probability estimation stages in a data compression system.

Extensive comparison has been done with finite state machines and the QM-coder. The finite state machines provide better performance at probabilities closer to one half, while the QM-coder provides better performance at probabilities very close to one. When tested inside the JPEG standard, a 62 state finite state machine performed consistently better than the QM-coder. Comparison has also been done with fixed rate coders used to generate run length limited codes. State machines have been designed which obtain a higher channel utilization than the fixed rate codes for the run length limited (1,3), (1,7) and (2,7) channels used in magnetic disk drives.

 1068-0314/94 $3.00 © 1994 IEEE

A Comparison Of Spectral Decorrelation And Rate Allocation Techniques For A Wavelet Transform-Based, Multispectral Data Compression Algorithm

Roy M. Matic
Hughes Research Laboratories
Malibu, CA

Judith I. Mosley
Santa Barbara Research Center
Goleta, CA

Future space-based, remote sensing systems will have data transmission requirements that exceed available downlinks, necessitating the use of lossy compression techniques for multispectral data. In this work, we describe several algorithms for lossy compression of multispectral data which combine spectral decorrelation techniques with an adaptive, wavelet-based, image compression algorithm to exploit both spectral and two-dimensional spatial correlation.

To remove spectral redundancy, we study the performance of several spectral decorrelation techniques including the Karhunen-Loeuve transform (KLT), prediction schemes, and the use of the wavelet transform. The non-KLT techniques are amenable to real-time implementation. Another issue we address is the allocation of bit rate among the spectrally decorrelated images. We evaluate the performance of several different rate allocation schemes: schemes based on the variance or entropy of the decorrelated images and on the variance of the wavelet transform coefficients of the decorrelated bands.

Of greatest importance for multispectral remote sensing systems is the requirement that the compression process minimize the degradation of spatial and spectral fidelity to ensure that data exploitation is not compromised. Therefore, we use the results of Maximum Likelihood multispectral classification as part of our algorithm evaluation procedure. We have also developed and evaluated a set of metrics designed to predict the effect of lossy compression on multispectral classification algorithms. These metrics, called Spectral Covariance Measures, are derived from the covariance matrix of the original, decompressed, and/or residual multispectral images. The most promising of these measures is called the Sum Delta Covariance measure.

We simulated the performance of each compression algorithm on four multispectral images at compression ratios ranging from 4:1 to 16:1. Each multispectral image consists of 8 co-registered 512x512 images, each representing a spectral band ranging from the Visible to the Near IR. Performance measures used to evaluate the decompressed imagery are visual examination, Mean Square Error (MSE), the Spectral Covariance Measures, and multispectral classification accuracy. We use these measures to determine the best spectral decorrelation and rate allocation technique, and to evaluate how well the Spectral Covariance Measures predict multispectral classification performance.

From our results, we conclude that the best spectral decorrelation technique is the KLT, followed by either a prediction scheme that uses two of the spectral bands as reference bands, or a one dimensional wavelet transform. The best rate allocation technique allocates rate based on the variance of the wavelet subbands, with the subbands from the decorrelated spectral bands all combined together in the allocation procedure. For any given image the linear correlation between Sum Delta Covariance and classification accuracy is slightly better than that of MSE and classification accuracy. However over several images, Sum Delta Covariance correlates much more strongly than MSE to classification accuracy. Thus the Sum Delta Covariance measure appears to be less sensitive than MSE to scene, sensor, or spectral variations when used as a predictive measure of classification accuracy. Further refinement of the Sum Delta Covariance measure is required for it to become the basis of a useful predictive measure of classification accuracy.

A Comparison of Wavelet Coding Sequences for Noisy Channels

Michael L. Hilton Prasanjit Panda
Department of Computer Science
University of South Carolina, Columbia SC, 29208

A number of wavelet-based coding schemes have been proposed recently. Most of these methods were designed to operate under noiseless channel conditions, and as a consequence are extremely vulnerable to transmission noise. When variable length coding is used, for example, flipping a single bit in a compressed image can result in catastrophic loss of synchronization during decoding. We have developed a combined source/channel coding scheme that uses error detection and recovery, rather than forward error correction coding, to abate the deterioration of image quality caused by channel errors. In addition, we investigate the effect of the *coding sequence* — the particular sequence in which wavelet coefficients are chosen for coding — on image quality.

The image coder used in this study is very simple, designed to require no side information that must be transmitted to the decoder. Images are compressed by applying the forward wavelet transform and then thresholding, quantizing, and runlength encoding the resulting coefficients. A Huffman coder is used to entropy encode the image data. Decompression is accomplished by inverting the compression procedure.

The bitstream produced by the compressor is extremely fragile when subjected to bit errors. To provide some robustness to bit errors, we divide the compressed data into independent fixed-length segments, called *frames*, which contain header information that allows the decoder to resynchronize at the start of decoding each frame. In this way, the effects of each bit error are confined to within one frame. If the frame size is kept well below 1/BER then most of the image data will be decoded correctly. We have investigated two decoding strategies for dealing with bit errors: a naive method, in which the decoder resynchronizes at the beginning of every frame without bothering to test for the possibility of transmission errors; and a zeroing method, in which the frame header is protected by an error correcting code. In the zeroing method, when a codeword error is detected in frame i, all of the coefficients in the coding sequence encoded in frame i are set to zero. The bandwidth cost of framing depends on the frame size chosen. When coding at 0.25 bpp (32:1 compression), the cost of header and padding bits for the naive method is 3% for a frame size of 1024 bits, up to 18% for a frame size of 128 bits. The zeroing method outperforms the naive method, and provides good image quality at BERs below 10^{-3}.

We have investigated the effects of channel errors on four different coding sequences. The choice of coding sequence does not appear to have a significant effect on the objective and subjective performance of the image compressor under noisy conditions. This result is important, because it indicates that compression system designers can chose the sequence which compresses best and not worry much about compromising channel error performance.

 1068-0314/94 $3.00 © 1994 IEEE

A Comparative Study of SAR Data Compression Schemes

Dr. C.Lambert-Nebout
CNES, CT/AE/SEA/TB
18 av Edouard Belin
31055 Toulouse
e_mail : lambert@hathor.cnes.fr
phone : 33.61.27.33.08
fax : 33.61.28.19.96

Dr. O.Besson
ENSICA
49 av Leon Blum
31000 Toulouse

Dr D.Massonnet, Dr B. Rogron
CNES, CT/IA/QTIS/PR
18 av Edouard Belin
31055 Toulouse

In spaceborne remote sensing, the amount of data collected has substantially increased in the last years. In the same time, the ability to store or transmit it has not increased as fast, so that there is a growing interest in developing compression schemes that could provide both higher compression ratios and lower encoding/decoding errors. In the case of the spaceborne **S**ynthetic **A**perture **R**adar (SAR) earth observation system developped by the French Space Agency (CNES), the volume of data to be processed is planned to exceed on-board storage capacities or telecommunication link. The objectives of this paper are :

- to present various compression schemes adapted to SAR data
- to define a set of quality evaluation criteria on images and on raw SAR data
- and to compare the compression schemes on ERS1 SAR data with such quality criteria and also complexity criteria.

We review first two classical methods of SAR data compression : Block Floating Point Quantizer (**BAQ**) and Block Floating Point Quantizer (**BFPQ**) and propose then novel approaches based on Fourier Transforms and spectrum coding.
The first novel approach is a generalisation of the popular Discrete Cosine Transform method of image compression to the case of SAR data. As a matter of fact, DCT concerns real data and can not be applied directly to SAR data, which, by definition, is complex. We then propose to replace the Discrete Cosine Transform by a 2D Fast Fourier Transform (**FFT**).
The second one is named **Presumming**.The knowledge of some features of the radar signal suggests a more sensitive way to reduce the data flow in the spectral domain. The idea of presumming is to have a supervised coding of the 2D Fourier transform of the image. There would be no coding of the range region outside the useful signal (which results in a moderate saving of 20%). The coding in the azimuth spectrum would apply only to the central part where the signal to noise ratio is the highest. Presumming could easily achieve a factor of two in data compression with a minimal signal loss and an improvment of the quality due to the elimination of most of the ambiguous signal. This is true regardless of any further encoding of the conserved data.

These four algorithms have been developped in C language on a SUN station. Their performances have been studied and compared through image quality criteria and data criteria on data supplied from ERS-1. The choice of the best algorithm (specially for space on-board application) is indeed a trade-off between performance and complexity. Compression by presumming seems to be a very attractive method but we have to further study its on-board implementation.

Compressed Pattern Matching

Amar Mukherjee
amar@cs.ucf.edu

Tinku Acharya
acharya@cs.ucf.edu

Department of Computer Science
University of Central Florida
Orlando, Florida 32816

Abstract

Data compression methods are used to reduce the redundancy in data representation in order to decrease the storage requirements and communication costs. In order to exploit the benefits of data compression to conserve internal processor storage and computation resources, it is desirable to perform operations on compressed data without decompressing it and we believe that this will have an impact on future computer and communication systems. In this paper we present hardware algorithms and their software implementation to search a compressed text with respect to keys or patterns in compressed form using tree-based codes such as Huffman code. The algorithm handles fixed and variable length don't care characters in the pattern [1]. As the tree-based codes are variable length codes, we keep track of the boundary of two valid codes for proper matching of the compressed pattern into the compressed text using a binary vector called the **"CRBS (Character Boundary Signal) vector"** which is a direct mapping of the nodes of the Huffman tree into the bit vector which is generated during the compression of the text [2]. The pattern matching is done on-the-fly requiring only one pass of the compressed text file which is useful for on-line applications and in situations where the amount of main memory is limited. The software simulation of the hardware compressed pattern matching algorithm with don't care characters based on the Huffman code has been implemented by C programming language. It has been tested with different random text files and patterns[1]. A total hardware VLSI architecture for this compressed pattern matching scheme is being developed and it will be reported in future papers. The idea of compressed pattern matching scheme has been utilized to perform the join operation of two big compressed database files without decoding it. The issues of this implementation will be subject matter of future papers. We also proposed a compressed pattern matching algorithm for adaptive Huffman type tree based codes using a simple modification of the said scheme. We proved that compressed pattern matching using arithmetic codes is not possible. We also discussed the issues related to complex compressed pattern search using LZ-codes and arithmetic codes.

References

[1] Mukhopadhyay, A., "Hardware Algorithms for Nonnumeric Computation", IEEE Tran. on Computers, June 1979.

[2] Mukherjee A., Flieder J., Ranganathan N. and Acharya T., "MARVLE : A VLSI chip of a Memory Based Architecture for Variable Length Encoding & Decoding", IEEE Trans. on VLSI Systems, Vol. 1, No. 2, June 1993, pp. 203-214.

[1]Interested readers may contact the authors to retrive the "C" codes of implementation of the algorithms

Compressing Computer Programs

Rod M. Davies
Computer Science, University of Waikato, Hamilton, New Zealand

Ian H. Witten
Computer Science, University of Waikato, Hamilton, New Zealand

Computer programs offer great potential for compression. The small literature that exists on program compression invariably describes compression methods that are lossy in that all whitespace is discarded, and, in most cases, comments also [1, 2, 3].

This paper describes a scheme for compressing programs written in a particular programming language - which can be any language that has a formal lexical and syntactic description - in such a way that they can be reproduced exactly.

The compression scheme works as follows. A syntactically correct program is parsed into a parse tree. The parser interacts with a lexical analyser that produces a stream of language tokens. Nodes of the tree are labelled with token types - such as "identifier" - rather that actual instances of the tokens. Some language tokens require no more knowledge than the token type to reproduce the original text - for example operators, keywords and punctuation - others - for example numbers, strings and identifiers - require the actual instance of the token to be preserved separately. The lexical analyser must provide enough extra information to allow the original tokens to be reproduced, and to permit whitespace and comments to be preserved.

Once parsing is complete, the program is represented by a parse tree, a whitespace and comments stream, and several token streams. Taken together, these provide enough information to allow the original program to be reconstructed exactly.

The parse tree, each of the token streams and the whitespace and comments are each compressed separately using specialised compressors. The parse tree is adaptively encoded using the current non-terminal being parsed as the context. The identifier stream is converted into a symbol table with counts and a stream of symbol table indices. The symbol table and counts are encoded using PPMC while the index stream is encoded adaptively using the symbol counts and the order of symbols in the symbol table to predict the next identifier. Whitespace is encoded by assuming each token has a string of whitespace symbols following (this may be null). Each whitespace string is treated as a horizontal and vertical offset from the last piece of text and encoded. Strings, numbers and comments are encoded using PPMC.

The compression rate of the new method averaged about 1.8 bits per character over a corpus of twenty PASCAL programs. Comparing it with PPMC, very similar results are achieved, with an average improvement of only about 4%. Priming improves the overall compression figure by about 10%, with 9% improvement over primed PPMC.

[1] Cameron, R.D. (1988) "Source encoding using syntactic information source models." *IEEE Trans Information Theory IT-34(4)*: 843–850.

[2] Katajainen, J. and Mäkinen, E. (1990) "Tree compression and optimization with applications." *Int J Foundations of Computer Science 1*(4): 425–447.

[3] Stone, R.G. (1986) "On the choice of grammar and parser for the compact analytical encoding of programs." *Computer Journal* 29(4): 307–314.

Compression of Binary Images by Composite Methods Based on the Block Coding

Pasi Fränti and Olli Nevalainen
Dept. of Computer Science, Univ. of Turku
Lemminkäisenkatu 14 A, SF-20520 Turku, FINLAND
email: franti@utu.fi

Composite methods for compressing binary images are studied. *Block coding* [1] is the main component in all of them. It is an attractive compression technique due to its relatively simple implementation, speed, and reasonable compression ratio. In the present study an attempt is made to increase the power of block coding by augmenting it by *predictive coding* and *bit row reordering*. The purpose of predictive coding and reordering is here to increase the global dependencies by reducing the local ones. This is achieved by calculating a difference between the predicted values and the original ones. An *error image* is constructed from these differences and then coded by block coding, which takes advantage of the global level dependencies. The local dependencies are exploited by Huffman coding.

In the paper we consider 1-, 4- and 8-pixel templates for the prediction function. Large template improves the prediction, however this is achieved at the cost of time. The 4-pixel predictive coding gives much better compression results than the 1-pixel predictive coding. On the other hand, the 8-pixel context is excessive to gain any remarkable improvement so the 4-pixel predictive coding is preferred. In typical facsimile images the local level dependencies are quite constant from image to image and thus a static prediction function is sufficient. However, this is not the case for all images. The prediction function can also be constructed adaptively from the image to be compressed, but the increase in the running time is remarkable.

The results of the composite methods (*PB4* and *OB4*) are compared to the *CCITT Group 3* (*G3*) and *Group 4* (*G4*) compression algorithms, and to the QM-coder with an 8-pixel context model (*QM8*). The simple block coding (*B*) is clearly the fastest but the compression ratio is much lower than that of the others. The performance of the composite block coding gets closer to the CCITT Croup 4 algorithm, but so does the running time. The compression ratios and running times for a set of test images were (ratio, time): *B*=(9.8, 4 s), *PB4*=(12.6, 16 s), *OB4*=(13.0, 19 s), *G4*=(13.9, 24 s), *QM8*=(18.7, 36 s). Thus the performance of the QM-coder with a local context model is yet superior of the all. This leads to another interesting hybrid method which is got by combining block coding and arithmetic coding [2].

[1] M. Kunt and O. Johnsen, "Block Coding: A Tutorial Review", *Proc. IEEE*, vol. 68, no. 7, pp. 770-786, July 1980.
[2] P. Fränti, O. Nevalainen, "A Two-Stage Modelling Method for Compressing Binary Images by Arithmetic Coding", *The Computer Journal*, vol. 36, no. 7, pp. 615-622, October 1993.

On Compression of Data from a Meteorological Station

Glen Langdon† Rob Antonucci†
William Macy† Dean Long‡

†Computer Engineering Dept ‡Computer Science Dept
University of California, Santa Cruz CA 95064

ABSTRACT

This project is a part of REINAS, a real-time environmental project sponsored by the Office of Naval Research. The site is the Monterey Bay, recently declared a national marine sanctuary. REINAS involves a cooperative effort headquartered at the Baskin Center for Computer Engineering and Information Science at the University of California, Santa Cruz. Co-operating entities include the Monterey Bay Aquarium Research Institute (MBARI), the National Atmospheric and Oceanographic Administration, the Naval Postgraduate School, and the Naval Research Lab, all located in Monterey, California. The objective is to apply computer science and engineering technology to aid meteorologists and oceanographers in their use of measured quantities to model and visualize phenomena in real-time. The real-time aspect is pushing the compression, communications, and database technologies into the new application area.

A related objective of the REINAS project is to apply data compression techniques in a real-time scientific data collection and storage system. This work describes some results from the study of compressing data acquired from meteorological stations. The quantities are temperature, pressure, humidity, wind speed and wind direction. A recommendation to use one- or two-minute averages and maintain archives on a daily basis resulted from discussions with meteorologists.

The general approach is to encode prediction errors, and to judiciously use contexts while reducing the number of coding parameters [1], and avoiding the sparse context problem [2]. Several ways of binarizing the error (via binary decision trees) are studied and compared. Different approaches to coding the binarized error sequence are also compared.

References

1. S. Todd, G. Langdon, and J. Rissanen, "Parameter Reduction and Context Selection for Compression of Gray-scale Images", *IBM Journal of Research and Development*, vol. 29, No. 2, 1985, 188-193.
2. G. Langdon, A. Gulati, and E. Seiler, "On the JPEG Model for Lossless Image Compression", *IEEE Data Compression Conference*, Snowbird UT, 1992, 172-180.

W. Macy and R. Antonucci were supported by a URI research grant at UCSC from the Office of Naval Research. G. Langdon has been supported as an Associate of CESDIS, and by an Erskine Fellowship of the University of Canterbury, Christchurch, N.Z.

Compression of Multispectral Landsat Imagery Using the Embedded Zerotree Wavelet (EZW) Algorithm

Jerome M. Shapiro, Stephen A. Martucci and Martin Czigler
David Sarnoff Research Center, Princeton, NJ 08543-5300

Multispectral image compression presents a set of new challenges in the area of image compression. In their raw form, multispectral images constitute a tremendous amount of data, and compression is essential for efficient data access, storage, and transmission of this class of imagery. Because there is also a large degree of interband correlation, there is potential for extremely high data compression without a large sacrifice in image quality, both subjectively and numerically.

In prior work described in [1], an image dependent Karhunen-Loeve Transform (KLT) was used to decorrelate a set of seven-band Landsat Thematic Mapper (TM) images prior to compression using a wavelet/subband coder. In the current work, the same image dependent KLT is used, but the compression engine that follows the KLT is replaced by a multiband implementation of the Embedded Zerotree Wavelet (EZW) algorithm, which attempts to order the bits in numerical importance so that a given EZW code contains all lower rate EZW encodings embedded in the bit stream [2]-[4]. Because of the coarse to fine nature of the EZW algorithm, jointly encoding multiband images such as color or multispectral imagery involves simply including the additional wavelet coefficients for each band in the scanning used in EZW. In contrast to the independent coding of the principal component images that was used in [1], the EZW algorithm jointly optimizes the bit allocation uniformly across all of the bands. Furthermore, the embedding and adaptivity features inherent in EZW allow precise rate control and eliminates the need to train the coder for a particular class of imagery.

Experiments show that combining an image dependent KLT for spectral decorrelation and the multiband EZW algorithm for compression is an effective way to jointly encode the spectral bands of multispectral images. This new coder significantly outperforms the earlier one, both numerically and subjectively.

[1] B. R. Epstein, R. Hingorani, J. M. Shapiro, and M. Czigler, "Multispectral KLT-Wavelet Data Compression for Landsat Thematic Mapper Images", *Data Compression Conf.*, Snowbird, UT, IEEE Comp. Society Press, 1992.

[2] J. M. Shapiro, "An Embedded Wavelet Hierarchical Image Coder", *Proc. IEEE Int. Conf. Acoust., Speech, Signal Proc.*, San Francisco, CA, March 1992.

[3] J. M. Shapiro, "An embedded hierarchical image coder using zerotrees of wavelet coefficients", *Data Compression Conf.*, IEEE Comp. Society Press, 1993.

[4] J. M. Shapiro, "Embedded Image Coding using Zerotrees of Wavelet Coefficients", *IEEE Trans. Signal Processing*, , Dec. 1993.

Compression Performance of the Xremote Protocol [1]

John Danskin [2] Pat Hanrahan

Department of Computer Science, Princeton University

Window systems provide an abstraction for the display screen, and arbitrate between applications competing for display space. The X Window System version 11 (X) also provides *network transparency*. Network transparency decouples the application's user interface from its computer without application intervention. Usually, remote X connections are made over the ethernet; however, modem performance has improved to the point where it is possible to use X across normal telephone connections using special compressed protocols such as Xremote.

X clients (applications) communicate with the X server using a single reliable byte-stream connection such as a Berkeley socket using the TCP/IP network protocol. To complete an Xremote connection, X clients connect to a local Xremote pseudo-server, which compresses and forwards X messages across a serial line to the Xremote pseudo-client, which uncompresses the X messages and forwards them to the X server. When the X server sends messages to the X client, they are compressed by the pseudo-client, sent across the serial line, decompressed by the pseudo-server, and forwarded to the client. Messages from multiple connections are multiplexed on the serial line.

Xremote uses a two phase compression technique. The first compression stage is a Delta encoder which remembers the last 16 messages of less than 64 bytes. If an incoming message is the same size as one of the remembered messages, and differs by at most 8 bytes from the remembered message, then a delta message is generated. If the delta message is smaller than the original message, the delta message is sent instead. The second compression stage is an LZW coder similar to UNIX *compress*. This coder has a maximum word size of 12 bits and resets on a full dictionary.

We measured Xremote compression by gathering traces, implementing an instrumented Xremote simulator, and feeding the traces through the simulator.

The unweighted average compression ratio across our 11 traces was 2.4:1. Text based traffic compressed well (3:1), geometry and images compressed poorly (nearly 1:1), except for very simple repetitive geometry which was compressed by nearly 5:1. The Delta compression phase performed very well on input events like keystrokes and other very small messages, but didn't compress larger messages at all. The LZW compression phase accounted for most of the overall compression we found; although the higher compression achieved in special cases with Delta compression is important in common cases such as keystroke echo and mouse tracking.

[1] Full paper available from Princeton University Computer Science Department as Technical Report CS-TR-442-94.

[2] Funded by an AT&T PhD fellowship and a generous grant from Apple Computer

1068-0314/94 $3.00 © 1994 IEEE

CONTEXT-TREE BASED LOSSLESS IMAGE COMPRESSION

Seung P. Kim, Xavier Ginesta* and M. T. Sun***
** Department of Electrical Engineering, Polytechnic University*
Brooklyn, NY 11201, email: skim@signal.poly.edu
*** Bellcore, 331 Newman Springs Rd, Red Bank, NJ 07701*

Abstract: As indicated in Shannon's information theory, substantial improvement in coding efficiency can be obtained by considering the high order entropy of a source. In practice, using the high order entropy concept involves building a model of the source which identifies its most representative contexts using a limited amount of memory resources. A well defined high order model allows effective decorrelation which is essential for efficient lossless compression. We propose the use of context-trees as the key element to attaining this goal with reduced complexity. First, we introduce the concept of context-tree model of a source. Then, an efficient algorithm to construct the context-tree is presented. The details of this algorithm are described in the companion paper [1]. We demonstrate the compression capabilities of the proposed algorithm by comparing the conditional entropies of the input data source, based on the context-tree, to the outputs of a conventional 2-D DPCM coder. Compression ratios reported in this paper are presented in terms of conditional entropies since the lower bounds determined by the conditional entropy can be achieved very closely using the arithmetic coding technique.

The proposed context-based lossless image compression system is attractive for compression of multiple frames of images sharing similar characteristics, such as earth/space, medical and other image data where significant contextual redundancies exist within (intra) and among (inter) image frames. Such image frames usually have relatively small differences in their image characteristics due to changes of measurement conditions over time or replacement of specimen, etc. If a certain group of images is well defined in terms of measurement conditions and objects, the context-tree can be precomputed and the information may be shared by many users at different sites for efficient coding/decoding.

Computer simulations show that very simple 2-level trees, constructed using a single training frame from each group of images, achieved coding rate improvements over the conventional DPCM method which ranged from 11.7% to 38.1%. The number of context nodes were around one to two hundreds. However, the number of different conditional probability tables used by the context trees range between 10 and 34 due to additional vector quantization of the probability tables. It was also observed that the compression performance was not very sensitive to the choice of a specific training image in a group to construct the tree. The image groups used in our simulations are 8-bit cardiac X-ray images, ultra-sound medical images and satellite pictures of the surface of Mars.

[1] Vector Quantization of Contextual Information for Lossless Image Compression, DCC'94

Data Compression Using Linear Feedback Shift Registers

G I Davida, L Rodrigues
Department of EE and CS
University of Wisconsin-Milwaukee
Milwaukee, WI 53201

Abstract

An approach to data compression in which a string in $GF(p^m)$ is represented by its minimum length linear feedback shift register(LFSR) description is presented. This description consists of initial contents, a connection polynomial and the LFSR length. If a string of length N is given, the minimum length LFSR that generates this string can be computed using the Berlekamp-Massey shift register synthesis algorithm. The original string can be reconstructed by loading the LFSR with the initial contents and then shifting it by N times. The Berlekamp-Massey algorithm is the basis of our approach to data compression. Since the application of this algorithm directly to a data string does not always result in compression, the original string is manipulated in order to generate a small LFSR description. The manipualtion techniques employed here are *rotate*, *reverse*, *distance*. In the *reverse* technique, the Berlekamp-Massey algorithm is applied on the original and reverse string. In the *rotate* technique, the original string is cyclically shifted one bit at a time and each time the Berlekamp-Massey algorithm is applied to the shifted string. In the *distance* technique, the original string is represented by a distance string and a string that has small LFSR description. The original string is obtained by exclusive oring these two strings. A number of heuristics were employed to generate distance strings.

The above mentioned LFSR techniques were tested for $GF(2^m)$ strings, however, they can be easily extended to $GF(p^m)$ strings. A text file compression program using the LFSR techniques was also implemented. In this implementation, the text file is initially encoded into binary sequences ($GF(2)$) which are then compressed by applying the appropriate LFSR techniques. The results obtained by this implementation are comparable to the other compression algorithms such as Adaptive Huffman, Lempel-Ziv-Welch, etc.

1068-0314/94 $3.00 © 1994 IEEE

Detector-Activated Predictive Wavelet Transform Image Coding

Jonathan N. Bradley and Christopher M. Brislawn

Los Alamos National Laboratory

We describe a system for the storage and transmission of digital imagery acquired by a remote surveillance camera. The research was originally performed for the application of monitoring sensitive nuclear materials at Department of Energy facilities but is applicable to more general surveillance scenarios.

The overall system is based on a CPU that controls one or more charge-coupled device (CCD) cameras operating with frame rates on the order of one frame every 2 or 3 seconds. The system provides a change detection capability through digital image processing that can alert security personnel of a possible incident. The digital image data are to be stored and/or displayed in real time. Relatively high compression ratios are possible for such image data since the scene monitored by the camera changes little from frame to frame except on relatively rare occasions, such as an authorized (or unauthorized) entrance.

The compression algorithm is based on traditional predictive image coding strategies: a prediction of each frame is made from previous frames and the error residual (the difference between the actual and predicted frames) is coded for storage or transmission. Compression of the residuals is achieved by subband coding. The subband coder is based on a two-channel perfect-reconstruction multirate filter bank with linear phase FIR filters corresponding to a family of regular, biorthogonal wavelets. The filters are applied to row and column vectors of an image using symmetric extrapolation at the image boundaries. The resulting two-dimensional transform is then cascaded down five levels to produce a 16-band octave-scaled decomposition. Once the subband decomposition of an image has been formed, a bank of 16 uniform scalar quantizers is used for quantizing the wavelet coefficients in the 16 subbands, based on optimal bit allocation criterion.

The scalar quantizer indices are compressed by zero-run-length and Huffman coding. Low bit rates for the high-frequency subbands produce long runs of zeros in those portions of the subbands corresponding to smooth regions of the image; this is the principal source of additional lossless coding gain over and above the lossy gain produced by wavelet coefficient quantization. This technique makes use of the good space/frequency localization properties of subband image coding with short FIR filters.

One potential refinement under investigation is to use the change detection algorithm to adjust the quality level in the frame-difference coder based on the activity in the scene. Very large compression ratios could be realized by using relatively low quality coding for frames with low activity, while high-resolution coding could be used only when a change is detected in the scene under surveillance.

A DIRECT IMPLEMENTATION OF ARITHMETIC DATA COMPRESSION ALGORITHM

Jianmin Jiang, MIEEE, MIEE, CEng
Bolton Institute of Higher Education
United Kingdom

ABSTRACT: Reference [1] contributed the first practical implementation of arithmetic coding algorithm in C. We simply use the same notation and the same model for the convenience of description of the alternative. Instead of describing the coding range in its two end points, 'low' and 'high', the new alternative uses 'low' and the size of the range to describe the coding process. The output codes are from the value of 'low' updated by the normalization procedure.

The specific coding of any symbol 'x' is divided into two steps. One is to scale down the existing coding range into a new range with its cumulative frequency intervals. The other is to normalize the new coding range to send codes out and make the new coding range ready for the next symbol.

The first advantage of this new alternative is that as long as the coding range is greater than the maximum cumulative frequency, which could be easily incorporated into the normalization procedure, underflow will never occur. The second advantage of the new alternative lies in the easier normalization, which can be achieved by shifting 'range' left until it is no less than one half of the Top_value. In fact, when the 'New_range' is less than half of the Top_value, the first MSB bit must be the same for both the end points of the coding range. Therefore, this bit of 'New_low' can be sent out as output code.

To sort out the carry propagation problem, the technique of staffing bit is adopted.[2]

The correct decoding can be proved as the following:

```
cum1=((value-low+1)*cum[0])/R;
cum2=((value-low)*cum[0])/R;
for(symbol=1; cum[symbol]>cum; symbol++);
if(cum[symbol]>cum2)correct_s=symbol+1;
else correct_s=symbol;
```

A series of experiments are run for the new implementation and proved to be correct.

The work presented will be the main engine for real time implementation of arithmetic coding algorithm, and more powerful real time development such as parallel processing architectures can be built up and further improved.

References

[1] Witten I.H., Neal R., and Cleary J.G. 'Arithmetic coding for data compression', Communications of the ACM, 30(6), 520-540, June 1987.

[2] Langdon G. and Rissanen J. 'Compression of Black-white images with arithmetic coding' IEEE Trans. on Communications, Vol. com-29, No. 6, June 1981, pp 858-867.

1068-0314/94 $3.00 © 1994 IEEE

An Edge-Oriented Image Compression Technique Using Edge Prediction and Classified Vector Quantization

Chiung-Kuang Chou and **Fikret Ercal**
Computer Science Dept., University of Missouri - Rolla, Rolla, MO 65401

Abstract

Vector quantization (VQ) has been extensively employed for image compression. In this paper, a predictive classified vector quantization (PCVQ) algorithm in the discrete cosine transform (DCT) domain is presented. A total of 221 subcodebooks are generated by exploiting the edge information for 8 x 8 blocks which affects the distribution of DCT coefficients. The encoding complexity is reduced significantly since the codebook is divided into subcodebooks with much smaller sizes and dimensions. Simulation results show that a comparable reconstruction quality is obtained for a given bit rate with a significant reduction in complexity.

A simple and efficient classification algorithm is developed by using two DCT coefficients and spatial data. An edge block is classified according to the orientation and location of the edge. Separate subcodebooks are designed for each class using the LBG algorithm. This CVQ scheme not only preserved the edge fidelity but also reduced the computational complexity since only one subcodebook needed to be searched. Moreover, a prediction algorithm is used to predict the class of a block which eliminated the need to transmit the class number and hence reduced the bit rate.

The performance of the proposed DCT-PCVQ coding technique was evaluated using two standard test images (Lena and Pepper). The Kohonen's SOFM algorithm is employed for the design of 221 subcodebooks. 28 different 512 x 512 images were used for the training set. The peak signal-to-noise ratio (PSNR) is used to measure the quality of reconstructed images. PSNR is computed as $PSNR = 10log_{10}(\frac{255^2}{MSE})\ dB$ where MSE is the mean square error given by $MSE = \frac{1}{N^2}\sum_{i=1}^{N^2}(x_i - \hat{x}_i)^2$. The compression performance for the two test images, Lena and Pepper, is summarized in Table 1. For the two images tried, overall prediction accuracy turned out to be around 40%. Even though this is a low prediction accuracy, it is within the acceptable margins and encouraging, for a prediction accuracy of only 17% is needed to break even. Our approach achieves a significant reduction in the computational complexity of the encoding process while maintaining a reasonable compression ratio. The results obtained are comparable to the best results reported so far for the same set of images tested here.

Table 1: DCT-PCVQ results for LENA and PEPPER

Image	PSNR(dB)	Bit Rate (bpp)
Lena	31.86	0.479
Pepper	29.59	0.507

AN EFFICIENT PYRAMID VQ-BASED IMAGE COMPRESSION ALGORITHM

Anna Tatsaki, Thanos Stouraitis, and Costas Goutis
Department of Electrical Engineering, University of Patras
Rio, 26110 Greece, tel: +30 61 997283, fax: +30 61 997321

In image coding systems, transform coding is considered as one of the most effective methods for image data compression. The Discrete Cosine Transform (DCT) is often chosen for de-correlating a signal and it is supplemented with other redundancy reduction methods, such as the highly regular Pyramid Vector Quantization (PVQ) stucture proposed in [1].

In this paper a high-quality and low-computational-complexity compression scheme for still images is presented. The image to be compressed is partitioned into an abstract and a texture image, each of which could be separately processed. The abstract image contains the four most significant bits and the texture one the remaining least significant bits of the original image. Both images are divided into blocks of 12*12 pixels and the zonal sampling technique is used for the computation of only a selected subset of the DCT coefficients. By using the 2-D prime factor DCT algorithm presented in [2], with some modifications, only a few 3-point and 4-point 1-*D* DFTs are required for the computation of the 37 low frequency zonal sampled DCT coefficients. Three PVQs with different radii are used, two for the quantization of the non-DC DCT coefficients of the abstract image, one of dimension 12 and the other of dimension 24, and one PVQ for the quantization of the non-DC DCT coefficients of the texture image of dimension 36. The DPCM coding is used for the DC coefficients.

In the experiments performed, the proposed compression algorithm has been tested on standard images. For a bit-rate of 0.8, 0.5, and 0.25 per pixel, the reconstructed "Lenna" has been obtained with PSNR of 33.8, 32.6, and 30.6 dB, respectively. The PSNR ratio is 31.7 dB for the "F-16" and 30.3 dB for the "Lake" image at 0.5 bit/pixel compression rate.

The separation of the image into two images enables their parallel compression, improves the PSNR, and reduces the blocking effect. The advantages of this algorithm are a) each block is separately vector quantized without a need for the DCT computation of other neighbouring blocks, b) the processing of data with a half of length reduces the complexity and makes the algorithm faster, and c) the algorithm could be implemented in parallel.

References

[1] T. Fischer, "A Pyramid Vector Quantizer," IEEE Trans. Information Theory, vol. IT-32, No.4, July 1986.

[2] C. Dre, A. Tatsaki, T. Stouraitis, and C. Goutis, " A Novel Prime Factor Algorithm for the 1-D and 2-D Discrete Cosine Transform,"in Proc. ECCTD '93, Aug. 1993.

AN EXPERIMENTAL INVESTIGATION INTO TABLE DRIVEN DATA COMPRESSION ALGORITHMS FOR SOLID STATE DISCS

M. Gooch S. R. Jones
Department of Electronic & Electrical Engineering,
Loughborough University of Technology, Loughborough, England.

Solid state discs utilize semiconductor memory as a backing store, which implies a memory-bandwidth speed requirement for any form of data compression directed at this growing market. This often requires special purpose hardware, with table driven algorithms being suitable candidates due to their regular structure and usually simple, repetitive ordering techniques.

For this investigation the BSTW data compression algorithm was considered. This consists of a p location table with each location storing an n byte word (referred to as a tuple) and being represented by a fixed length binary code. The algorithm requires a table search operation to locate incoming data in the table, followed by a table shift operation (referred to as move-to-front) to maintain table order. Both of these functions can be implemented in hardware using a selectively shiftable content addressable memory structure.

A multimedia test data set consisting of 48 files (totalling over 6 Mbyte) has been constructed, with 12 files in each of 4 categories - audio, image, object code and text. The basic algorithm achieves a compression ratio of 0.92, where compression ratio is defined as the ratio of output bits to input bits. By using a k-bit counter for each location, as opposed to a move-to-front strategy, a count-ordered table structure can be maintained. This was seen to give a small improvement in compression ratio to 0.90 at best.

The use of fixed data block sizes is necessary for any solid state disc to allow it to utilise current disc interface technology for compatibility. Data block sizes of 512, 1024, 2048 and 4096 bytes were examined, and results showed that the block size needs to be approximately 16 times greater than the table size to ensure that no deterioration in compression ratio occurs.

Observation of the distribution of incoming data hits within the table reveals a variation of typically four orders of magnitude from the start to the end of the table, which suggests a coding scheme other than straight binary. Static Huffman coding was investigated using both exact probabilities (from the test data) and an approximate reciprocal probability distribution. The difference in compression ratios achieved by the two methods was less than 0.01, with the approximate method generating smaller codes and hence a smaller hardware realisation. Overall a compression ratio of 0.83 was achieved using a 128 location table, 2 byte tuples and a 512 byte block size. A hardware requirement of 60K gates will achieve this using a structure based around content addressable memory for both the table searching and reordering operations as well as the Huffman coding section. Due to the single clock cycle compression or decompression operation an output data rate of up to 320 Mbit/second can be achieved using a basic clock frequency of only 20 MHz.

A Fast Algorithm for the 2-D Discrete Cosine Transform[1] (Abstract)

PeiZong Lee, Gau-Shin Liu, Fang-Yu Huang, Jyh-Horng Wen[2]

We present a new algorithm for computing the 2-D discrete cosine transform (DCT):

$$y_{m,n} = \sum_{i=0}^{N-1} \sum_{j=0}^{N-1} x_{i,j} \cos(\frac{(2i+1)m}{2N}\pi) \cos(\frac{(2j+1)n}{2N}\pi).$$

First, we arrange the input data matrix $\{x_{i,j} \mid i = 0, \cdots N-1,\ j = 0, \cdots N-1\}$ in a certain order which is defined in [1]. Let $\{A_{p,i}\}_{i=0}^{N-1}$ and $\{B_{p,i}\}_{i=0}^{N-1}$ be the $(\frac{p-1}{2})$-th and $(N-1-\frac{p-1}{2})$-th columns of the rearranged input data matrix and whose 1-D DCT output vectors are $\underline{\mathbf{f}}_{\frac{p-1}{2}}$ and $\underline{\mathbf{f}}_{N-1-\frac{p-1}{2}}$, respectively. Second, we formulate the output data matrix to a block-structure matrix multiplication: $\mathbf{Y}_{N^2\times 1} = (\mathbf{E}_N)_{N^2}\mathbf{F}_{N^2\times 1}$, where $\mathbf{Y}_{N^2\times 1} = (\underline{\mathbf{y}}_0, \underline{\mathbf{y}}_1, \cdots, \underline{\mathbf{y}}_{N-1})^t$ and $\underline{\mathbf{y}}_n = (y_{0,n}, y_{1,n}, \cdots, y_{N-1,n})^t$; $\mathbf{F}_{N^2\times 1} = (\underline{\mathbf{f}}_0, \cdots, \underline{\mathbf{f}}_{N-1})^t$ and $\underline{\mathbf{f}}_i$ is the i-th 1-D DCT output vector. Then, we show that the block-structure matrix $(\mathbf{E}_N)_{N^2}$ has the same properties as the 1-D DCT kernel matrix. Therefore, the 2-D DCT problem is reduced to the 1-D DCT problem. We thus can provide a procedure for computing the 2-D DCT which is similar to that of the 1-D DCT. The proposed algorithm, which has regular structure, only requires $\frac{1}{2}N^2 \log N$ scalar multiplications for computing an $(N \times N)$-point 2-D DCT.

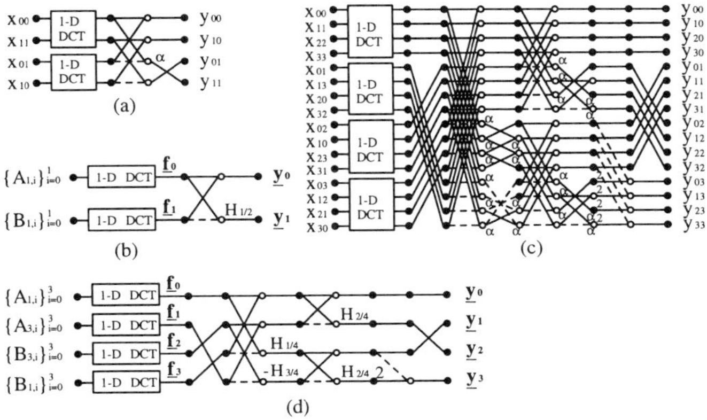

Figure 1: The 2-D DCT signal-flow graphs and abstract signal-flow graphs for (a) (b) $N = 2$ and (c) (d) $N = 4$. Solid lines represent transfer factor 1, while dashed lines represent transfer factor -1. Circles ∘ represent adders. $H_{i/N}$ is the $(n, \frac{p-1}{2})$-th block entry in $(\mathbf{E}_N)_{N^2}$ with $i = np$. $\alpha = 1/2$.

Reference: [1] P.-Z. Lee and G. S. Liu. "An Efficient Algorithm for the 2-D Discrete Cosine Transform." Technical Report TR-94-001, Institute of Information Science, Academia Sinica, Taipei, Taiwan, R.O.C., 1994.

[1]This work was partially supported by the NSC under Grant NSC 82-0408-E-001-016.

[2]PeiZong Lee: Inst. of Information Science, Academia Sinica. Gau-Shin Liu and Jyh-Horng Wen: Dept. of EE, Chung-Cheng Univ.. Fang-Yu Huang: National Bureau of Standard, Taipei, Taiwan.

Fast Image Compression Using Direct Quantisation of Colour Components

Michael Semenov
Canterbury Christ Church College
North Holmes Road,
Canterbury, Kent CT1 1QU, England
Tel.: +44-227-767700, ex. 282
Fax.: +44-227-470442
E-mail: semenov@c71.canterbury.ac.uk

A fast 24-bit colour-image compression algorithm based on direct quantisation of colour components (DQCC) has been developed that produces a compression ratio of 5:1 with SNR≈31 and PSNR≈35. Decompression can be performed in real time on IBM compatible computers with Intel-80386 or Intel-80486 processors. The compression speed is also high. The algorithm uses only integer arithmetic and can be applied in any fields where 24-bit colour images of high-quality are needed: presentations of Art Gallery Paintings, Museum Artefacts, Multimedia etc.

The first step of the DQCC algorithm is conversion of the RGB representation to a luminance and chrominance model. In order to avoid floating-point arithmetic, which may slow down the speed of the algorithm, the following integer model was used (L represents luminance, and D_1 and D_2 chrominance):

$$L=\frac{R+2\cdot G+B+2}{4};\quad D_1=\frac{G-R+255}{2};\quad D_2=\frac{G-B+255}{2}$$

The next step of the compression process is for each 8x8 pixel square to calculate the maximum and minimum of L, D_1 and D_2, these are denoted by L_{min}, L_{max}, D_{1min}, D_{1max}, D_{2min}, D_{2max}. Then new *reduced* values $\boldsymbol{l}$ for luminance and $\boldsymbol{d_1}$ and $\boldsymbol{d_2}$ for chrominance components are produced using the following formulae:

$$l=\frac{16\cdot(L-L_{min})+L_{max}-L_{min}}{2\cdot(L_{max}-L_{min})};\quad d_1=\frac{8\cdot(D_1-D_{1min})+D_{1max}-D_{1min}}{2\cdot(D_{1max}-D_{1min})}$$

$$d_2=\frac{8\cdot(D_2-D_{2min})+D_{2max}-D_{2min}}{2\cdot(D_{2max}-D_{2min})}$$

The accumulated error resulting from the sequential compression and decompression is rather low. The experiments with the above images showed that after six sequential compressions and decompressions the number of colours does not drop by greater than 25%, the entropy does not change by more than 5%. The algorithm was tested on 24-bit original KODAK images 'Face', 'Balloons' and 'Bikes'. The compression did not show any visual distortion on all images, except 'Balloons', where the distortion was hardly noticeable.

 1068-0314/94 $3.00

Fourier Based Tools for Compression and Vector Quantization

Seetamraju Uday Bhaskar Sarma, Dr. Pepe Siy
ECE Dept., College of Engg, Wayne State U.
email : psiy@ece.eng.wayne.edu

The tessellation tool is based on utilizing frequency domain information to partition (tessellation) the time-domain objective function envelope, by creating a data structure of partitions, that retain both frequency and time domain information. The frequency domain information used is the zero-slope coordinates of the various harmonics obtained from the Discrete Cosine Transform. A partition boundary is created at each zero-slope coordinate resulting in many small partitions. But theoretical results have been achieved, wherein, its shown that almost all local optima occur in concave or convex partitions only, while the remaining monotonic partitions are collapsed into larger partitions.

This rearranged partitioning, wherein partitions are collapsed and merged, is quite rich in informational structure. In addition, the partitioning is more perceptive to humans - viz., the partitions (termed Tessels) are either convex, concave or monotonic **only**, such that concave and convex tessels are separated by one of more monotonic tessels. The end result is a tessellation which is very simple and intuitively comprehensible partitioning of the function envelope.

The number of such partitions is a low theoretical upper bound, but, in practice is even lower. This result is detailed for the one-dimensional case, using *Fourier Transform*, and is extended successfully to multiple dimensions using *multiple-dimensional Discrete Cosine Transform*. This is the first known serious application of *n-Dim* DCT, for signal processing or otherwise. The tessellation structure is used for detailed, but surprisingly simple and easy study of the various local optima (maximuma and minima) as well as the information present in "monotonic tessels". The result described uses a combination of new techniques and tools, not observed in literature.

The discussion in this result is restricted to "lossy" (coding oriented) data compression. Signal encoding pursued here, is about richer and more accurate signal characterization, availing richer information about the whole signal. But, whether or not, transforms compress all signals, the issue of, whether the data compressed using transforms, is in an "useable" format, is often ignored. There are some time-domain features, which characterize that signal pretty well, while the rest of the time-domain features are relatively unimportant. This latter notion is useful in applying the tessellation technique, introduced here, for lossy signal compression.

VQ acts like a complexity reducing technique, which thereby simplifies and speeds up the subsequent computations. Codebooks are becoming a very cumbersome and inaccurate way to code signals of a general nature. Hence ideally one would like that the codebooks store the *most prominent* features - "prominence" is very much human and intuitive by definition. This is something that the tessellation tool is well suited for, since, the time-domain envelope of the signal is split up into "peaks, troughs and monotonic segments", which mirror human thought process. Hence, using the tessellation technique, one can obtain reduction of complexity in encoding (for codebooks etc...)

1068-0314/94 $3.00 © 1994 IEEE

Fractal Interpolation Functions For Image Compression

Said Abdallah
Nazif Tepedelenlioglu
Department of Electrical and Computer Engineering
Florida Institute of Technology

Extended Abstract

Visual complexity of an image does not necessarily imply high information content, this is most evident in images that are fractal objects. Fractals have the property of being highly self-similar with detail at all levels of magnification, in addition they can be generated from a small set of transformations, this has the potential of translating into high compression ratios if we are able to use these objects to approximate general images. The degree and quality of compression is dependent on the degree of self-similarity of the image.

This leads to the question of whether fractals are an acceptable model for the type of images to be compressed. Assuming an acceptable fractal approximation exists that achieves some compression, is it possible to find this approximation in a reasonable amount of time. This paper discusses a fractal compression scheme that answers the above questions positively by employing a combination of image pre-processing, fractal interpolation functions and adaptive basis functions.

Fractal images generated by a small number of transformations have the properties of extremely high compression ratios and redundancy. The aim of fractal compression is to maintain similar compression ratios for a more general class of images.

In many cases this is not possible because the images to be compressed are not good candidates for approximation by fractal objects, instead of forcing a good approximation by sacrificing high compression we employ a different strategy. In the first step the image is pre-processed in an attempt to make it more fractal in nature, we then present the result to the fractal compressor, where the compressor is limited to a certain minimum compression ratio. If the first two steps are not sufficient the fractal approximation is used to adaptively generate a set of orthonormal functions that augment the fractal approximation.

Fractal image compression has great potential when the function to be compressed has some fractal properties. The scanning part of the proposed algorithm attempts to make use of this potential by presenting the fractal algorithm with functions that are closest to being fractal in nature. If this is not sufficient to achieve the desired result we found it better to make use of orthogonal functions instead of attempting to force the fractal compressor to do a better job modelling the function.

1068-0314/94 $3.00 © 1994 IEEE

A Gambling Estimate of The Rate Distortion Function for Images

Thomas M. Cover and **Richard D. Wesel**
cover@isl.stanford.edu *wesel@isl.stanford.edu*

Department of Electrical Engineering, Stanford University

Abstract

We describe an experiment which shows that lossy data compression of images can be improved over existing standards by at least an order of magnitude. The idea is that human beings have a greater ability to see images, to quantify the distortion between images, to predict the next pixel in images, and in general, to describe images than do existing computer algorithms.

The lossy data compression that we describe takes place in two steps. First, we predistort the image to one that is simultaneously close (in some subjective distortion sense) to the original image and is easy to predict for use in arithmetic coding. We then noiselessly compress the predistorted image and reconstruct it using an arithmetic decoder.

We first argue that predistortion followed by noiseless compression is asymptotically optimal. For the predistortion phase we use an artist who attempts to achieve two goals simultaneously — an image that is close aesthetically to the original image and is easy to predict, pixel by pixel, given the past. For the noiseless data compression using arithmetic coding, we use a human gambler to estimate the data compression achievable by arithmetic coding. Here we use the technique used by Cover and King to compress English text. We expect the same sort of improvement for images. In fact, we found that humans were able to achieve 30% better noiseless compression than the best of 10 arithmetic coding algorithms.

The overall data compression achievable on images for reasonable distortions turns out to be an order of magnitude better than JPEG. For example, on one run of the experiment we achieved a descriptive complexity of .04 bits per pixel on a 256 gray level image. The resulting image can be seen by eye to be reasonably similar to the original image. This represents a data compression of 200 to 1. Even at 70 to 1, JPEG reconstructs an image which is aesthetically much farther away than the one achieved by our experiment.

In summary, we found that the more an image was simplified, the more our human predictors outperformed the computer predictors. Furthermore, for large compression ratios we found that human simplification followed by human prediction provides performance significantly beyond current algorithms.

1068-0314/94 $3.00 © 1994 IEEE

Heuristic Algorithms for Quadtree Compression using a Content Addressable Memory

George Betzos
School of Computer and Information Science
College of Engineering and Computer Science
Syracuse University

Abstract

The quadtree is a widely used hierarchical spatial data structure for encoding two-dimensional data. The most well known quadtree representations are the pointer-based quadtrees and those that use a linear list of locational codes. A variation of the later that uses a ternary representation of locational codes is suitable for processing by Content Addressable Memory (CAM), and results in more efficient algorithms. Compression of such a representation can be achieved by replacing pairs of locational codes that differ in one trit position, by a new code that has a "don't care" trit at that position. The process can be repeated recursively. A minimum quadtree representation can be obtained in this way but in general this is an NP-complete problem. A basic, simple and fast, CAM-based, heuristic algorithm is described which produces good results. Extensions of this algorithm are presented which deal with the problems of fixed size and fixed word length of the CAM and with grayscale data. Finally compression results are provided for a number of sample images.

A high bit rates MPEG video coding scheme

Wen Gao, Debin Zhao and Weiyi Yang
Department of Computer Science
Harbin Institute of Technology
Harbin, 150001, P.R. China

MPEG I standard is aimed at compressing the source input format (SIF: source input format, 1/4 size of CCIR Rec.601) video at about 1.5 Mbits/sec bit rates [1, 2]. The next version is to increase the resolution of the video information and keep the compatibility with MPEG I. MPEG's current work has been aimed at compressing full CCIR Rec.601 resolution pictures at bit-rates in 4 up to 10 Mbits/sec.

In this paper, we proposed an extended MPEG video coding scheme for the motion image coding application in a higher bit-rates situation up to 10 Mbits/sec. The key point of proposed scheme is to resample the high resolution picture (CCIR Rec.601 picture) into 4 lower resolution pictures (SIF picture) firstly, then do the difference between resized pictures. In other words, the scheme devides the input picture into multiple sub-pictures and represents it by a parameter set of models and a predictive error matrix. Only 1/4 of the original frame data is coded directly, and the rest are coded in the difference form. By this, we divide the CCIR Rec.601 format video signals into one 1/4 sized source signal part (frame part) and three 1/4 sized difference signal parts (detail enhancement parts). It is then possible to introduce the parallel processing into the coding process. Because of the comparability between the original four parts of the frame, the difference signals contain large part of little values like 0 and 1. A parallelism can be leaded by multiple channels MPEG I flows in which each is a standard MPEG I processing channel. Since the difference part has much better compression benefit in both motion compensation and DCT transform than the source, this gains the major profit and makes the main difference with MPEG I.

The other parts of the scheme have little difference with MPEG I(2). We convert the CCIR 601 format into a sequence of 4:2:0 subsampled fields through pre-processing and do the reverse through post-processing. We use the same DCT, Zigzag, Quantization, Run-length, and Huffman method through source coding. When doing the motion compensation, we use four motion compensaters, dealing with the four parts we mentioned before. The scheme is also downward-compatible with the MPEG I standard. The decoder of this scheme can process the standard MPEG I coded video, but the original decoder may not accept which coded by this encoder. It is also robustic against random errors at the decoding process. When there is a cell loss, the loss area will be a 'Calculated area', which means to use a former picture and a later picture to interpolate and calculate and make a pseudo part of the picture.

Reference

[1] D. LeGall, "MPEG: A video compression standard for multimedia", *Comm. ACM*, Vol. 34, 1991.
[2] ISO-IEC JTC1, CD 11172, Information technology - Coding of moving pictures and associated audio for digital storage media up to about 1.5 Mbit/s - Part 2: Coding of moving pictures information, 1991.

An Image Assessment Study of Image Acceptability of the Galileo Low Gain Antenna Mission

S. L. Chuang[(1)] R.F. Haines[(2)] T. Grant[(1)] Yaron Gold[(2)] Kar Ming Cheung[(3)]

(1) Ames Research Center
Spacecraft Data Systems Research
Moffett Field, CA 94035

(2) Recom Technologies
Ames Research Center
Moffett Field, CA 94035

(3) Jet Propulsion Laboratory
Communications Systems Research
Pasadena, California 91109

ABSTRACT

This paper describes a study conducted by NASA Ames Research Center (ARC) in collaboration with the Jet Propulsion Laboratory (JPL), Pasadena, California on the image acceptability of the Galileo Low Gain Antenna mission. The primary objective of the study is to determine the impact of the Integer Cosine Transform (ICT) compression algorithm (Cham, 1989) on Galilean images of atmospheric bodies, moons, asteroids and Jupiter's rings. The approach involved fifteen volunteer subjects representing twelve institutions involved with the Galileo Solid State Imaging (SSI) experiment (Belton et al., 1990). Four different experiment specific quantization tables (q-table) and various compression stepsizes (q-factor) to achieve different compression ratios were used. It then determined the acceptability of the compressed monochromatic astronomical images as evaluated by Galileo SSI mission scientists. Fourteen different images were evaluated. Each observer viewed two versions of the same image side by side on a high resolution monitor; each was compressed using a different quantization stepsize. They were requested to select which image had the highest overall quality to support them in carrying out their visual evaluations of image content. Then they rated both images using a scale from one to five on its judged degree of usefulness. Up to four pre-selected types of images were presented with and without noise to each subject based upon results of a previously administered survey of their image preferences. Fourteen different images in seven image groups were studied. The results showed that: (1) Acceptable compression ratios vary widely with the type of images; (2) Noisy images detract greatly from image acceptability and acceptable compression ratios; (3) Atmospheric images of Jupiter seem to have higher compression ratios of 4 to 5 times that of some clear surface satellite images. Findings included compression acceptability as a function of image type, quantization table, and the influence of radiation noise.

Image Compression via Image Fragmentation and Heuristic Search Techniques

Dan E. Tamir and Kim Phillips
Computer Science Program
Florida Institute of Technology
150 West university Blvd.
Melbourne, FL 32901

This paper reports the results of a set of experiments that apply state-space search methods to explore efficient ways for on-line optimal image segmentation and data compression under a given bit-rate constraint.

Given an original image X and a bit-rate constraint T, any image derived from X through region split and merge operations is called a solution image if it satisfies the bit-rate constraint. The optimal solution is defined to be a solution image that yields a predetermined compression rate and at the same time introduces least distortion to the reconstructed image. The system reported in this paper attempts to obtain the optimal solution image via Adaptive Thresholding and Heuristic Search Techniques.

In the process of compression, arbitrary-size uniform regions of a digital image are extracted via a connected-component labeling algorithm. These regions are created using an adaptive variance thresholding algorithm applied until a reasonable number of regions is reached. The resulting image fragmentation is considered to be the initial state in a state space representation. The successor of a state in this space is any image obtained from the parent state by merging two regions or splitting a region into two.

Under efficient encoding of a fragmented image, each region is represented by 3 bit per pixel for boundary pixels plus the average region gray level and the coordinates of one boundary pixel. Any split/merge operation might therefore increase or decrease the bit rate and at the same time increase or decrease the distortion of the reconstructed image. Hence, a weighted search space can be constructed by labeling each transition from a parent state to any of its successors by the amount of introduced distortion and bit-rate.

Search procedures are applied to this state space to obtain the optimal solution image. However, due to the enormous search complexity involved, the optimal solution cannot be practically attained. This precludes the usage of un-informed search methods and limits the utility of informed, heuristic, search procedures such as best first search or A*.

In search of more practical methods, simple heuristic search procedures are developed. This includes: a hybrid strategy called staged hill-climbing with backtracking, an adaptive-threshold method, and splitting hill-climbing method.

The results of our experiments show that these heuristic methods can yield a very good compression rate in a reasonable computation effort. Comparison with the literature proves that in some cases, for a given bit rate constraint, a greedy splitting based hill-climbing search algorithm yields better compression than well known image compression methods such as wavelet-based vector quantization.

IMAGE QUALITY MEASURES AND THEIR PERFORMANCE

Ahmet M. Eskicioglu, Paul S. Fisher and Siyuan Chen

Department of Computer Sciences
University of North Texas
Denton, TX 76203
Email: eskiciog@ponder.csci.unt.edu
fisher@gab.unt.edu

A major problem in evaluating lossy image compression techniques is the extreme difficulty in describing the type and amount of degradation in reconstructed images. Because of the inherent drawbacks associated with the subjective measures of image quality, there has been a great deal of interest in developing a quantitative measure, either in numerical or graphical form, that can consistently be used as a substitute.

We attempt to evaluate the usefulness of some of the objective quality measures listed in a recent extensive survey [1] through a set of experiments. The measures included in our evaluation are all discrete and bivariate, i.e., they provide some measure of closeness between two digital images by exploiting the differences in the statistical distributions of pixel values.

It is demonstrated that although a group of numerical measures correlates well with the observers' response for a given compression technique (The incorporation of a common human visual system model into NMSE gives the strongest correlation.), they are not reliable for an evaluation across different techniques. The two graphical measures (histograms and Hosaka plots), however, can be used to specify not only the amount, but also the type of degradation in reconstructed images. Hosaka plots, in particular, provide a good indication of how images lose their fidelity.

A combination of numerical and graphical measures may prove more useful in judging image quality. There is also a need for the development of new graphical measures with better judgment capabilities. Further research in these areas is now ongoing.

Reference

[1] A. M. Eskicioglu and P. S. Fisher, "A Survey of Quality Measures for Gray Scale Image Compression," Proceedings of 1993 Space and Earth Science Data Compression Workshop (NASA Conference Publication 3191), Snowbird, Utah, USA, April 2, 1993.

Improvement of Sliding-Window Data Compression Using Splay-Tree Coding

Shigeru Yoshida, Yoshiyuki Okada, Yasuhiko Nakano, and Hironori Yahagi
Holography and Color-Imaging Lab., Fujitsu Laboratories Ltd.
Email: {per241, yokada, nakano, yahagi}@flab.fujitsu.co.jp

1. Introduction

Lempel-Ziv coding is the most popular lossless universal compression scheme. It achieves reasonable compression ratios and a practical processing speed, but it is not good for small files. Bailey et al. [1] reported that a pipelining algorithm for LZW coding [2] and splay-tree coding [3] compressed small files well. Splay-tree coding is a fast dynamic fixed-to-variable length coding method. We aimed to improve the Lempel-Ziv sliding-window algorithm by using splay-tree pipelining. To develop our slide-splay scheme, we based on fixed-length LZSS coding [2] with a 2-kilobytes reference buffer.

2. Pipelining Algorithm

LZSS uses two coding modes: raw data (8 bits) and copy. In copy mode, the starting address (11 bits) and the length (5 bits) of the longest matching string in the reference buffer are encoded. We modified the LZSS codes as follows: (1) We made a new symbol source combining 256 kinds of raw data bytes and 32 kinds of matching lengths. (2) Since the starting addresses have nearly random values, we encoded the upper address bits using the splay-tree and output the remaining lower bits as raw data.

3. Experimental Results

We compared the initial compression ratios of slide-splay with conventional schemes (Fig. 1). For slide-splay, SxRy indicates that the upper "x" bits of the starting address are encoded by the splay-tree, and the lower "y" bits output as raw data. Slide-splay is superior to conventional schemes for files less than several kilobytes long. Slide-splay with the starting address bits division (S4R7) compressed all the files as well as or better than slide-splay without divisions (R11 and S11). We compared the compression ratios for files 2 kilobytes long and hundreds of kilobytes long (Fig. 2). Slide-splay compressed all the small files better than LZSS, and it compressed the noncharacter large files about 10% better than LZSS.

4. Conclusion

We improved the sliding-window algorithm for small files. Since splay-tree coding has a low computational load, our algorithm maintains a practical processing speed. It is useful for specific applications such as variable-sized packet transmission or random access of logical records ranging from hundreds of bytes to several kilobytes long.

5. References

[1] R. L. Bailey et al., "Pipelining data compression algorithms," Computer Journal, Vol. 33, No. 4, 1990.
[2] T. C. Bell et al., Text Compression, Prentice-Hall Inc., 1990.
[3] D. W. Jones, "Application of splay trees to data compression," Comm. of the ACM, Vol. 31, No. 8, 1988.

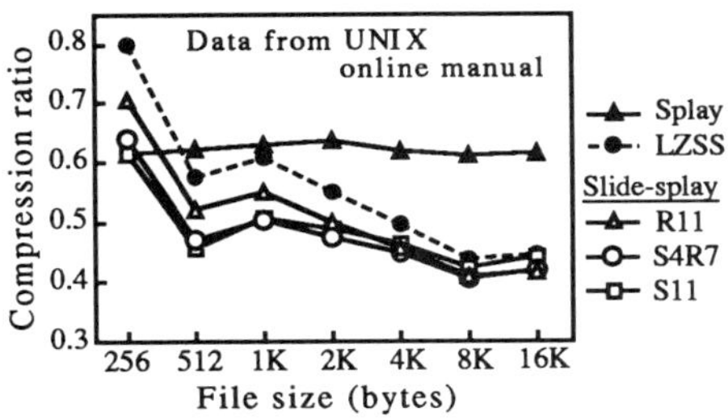

Fig. 1 Compression ratio for small files

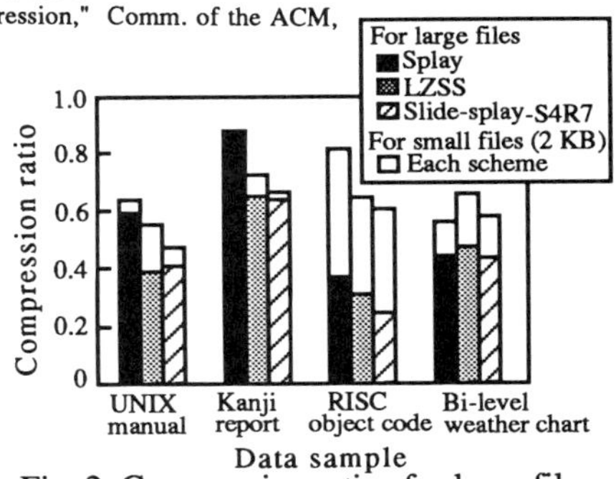

Fig. 2 Compression ratios for large files

Improving the Performance of Tree-Structured Vector Quantizers

Jianhua Lin
Department of Computer Science
Eastern Connecticut State University
Willimantic, CT 06226
E-mail: linj@ecsu.ctstateu.edu

Abstract

Tree-structured vector quantization (TSVQ) can be used to reduce the complexity of vector quantization (VQ). The result is an approximation to optimal VQ which achieves minimum distortion subject to a cost constraint. This approximation can be divided into two separate processes, the approximate tree design and the approximate tree search. Based on the fact that most of the performance loss of existing TSVQ is due to the heuristic tree search, we believe that further performance improvement may have to come from improving the search. We demonstrate, however, that search performance is affected by tree design. Such effect has not been considered in the past in the design of TSVQ. We propose a new design heuristic aimed to improve the accuracy of tree search. Experimental results in image compression show that the new tree-structured vector quantizers obtained perform significantly better than existing ones or even full-search VQ in terms of the distortion versus the entropy rate. The performance improvement is the most significant among what we have seen.

This material is based upon work supported in part by the State of Connecticut under Grant 92H022.

A Learning Vector Quantization Neural Model for Image Data Compression

W. Chang, H. S. Soliman & A. H. Sung
New Mexico Institute of Mining and Technology, Socorro, NM 87801-4682
Email: changw@nmt.edu Tel: (505)835-4069/-5449 Fax: (505) 835-5737

Abstract

The classical vector quantization (VQ) applied to image compression has delineated the issues of complex computation and the blockiness artifacts in the decompressed pictures, and other neural approaches have prolong training time and the same blockiness in the recalled pictures. We address these issues by proposing a single-layer feed-forward self-organizing neural model having a faster centroid adaptation as a VQ method for still image compression. In general, learning vector quantization (LVQ) is a robust clustering technique which requires supervision but our sampling-frequency self-organizing network (SSN) is capable of performing an unsupervised LVQ. The merit of the self-organization is the capability of forming pattern classes through a natural clustering process which requires no supervision and suffers no learning difficulty such as local minima.

In a self-supervision training scheme, SSN learns to classify subimages partitioned from a target picture and adapts a decompression codebook in the synaptic weights. After the training, SSN compresses the picture by coding the subimages into their corresponding class indices. The decompression is done by recalling the subimages using the coded indices and the synaptic codebook. We introduce two techniques to enhance the codebook construction: a centroid adaptation for the winning neurons when the pattern classes are established, and a neuron replenishment method which perturbs the less-used or the idling neurons (the neurons win fewer or no training pattern) to move into the class regions having larger quantization distortions. The centroid adaptation method eliminates the prolong centroid approximation in the LVQ training. The neuron replenishment technique reduces the total quantization error and hence, yields better recalled picture quality.

We also experiment with a signal-to-noise ratio (SNR) weight adaptation and training with overlapping subimages to show their filtering effects in the recalled picture. The SNR weight training produces a lower contrast in the decompressed picture and thus eliminates the high-contrast artifacts produced by the conventional weight training. The overlapping subimages for compression training gives a smoothing effect in the overlapping areas in recalled pictures but the toll is the reduced compression ratio, i.e., the greater the overlapping area, the smoother the recalled picture looks, but since the overlapping partitioning gives a larger number of subimages in the coding (compression) process and a larger number of coded class indices than the non-overlapping partitioning, the compression ratio is relatively reduced.

SSN's compression ratio and recalled picture quality are very competitive comparing with JPEG and a wavelet method recently developed by the joint effort of Los Alamos National Laboratory and FBI as a gray-scale fingerprint image compression standard. SSN achieves higher compression and quality (SNR) than JPEG and the wavelet method in processing the fingerprint images.

Our neural approach is a compression-by-classification technique similar to classical vector quantization but has a lower computation complexity. The SSN model also resolves the issue of the underutilization of neurons in the Kohonen feature map and the counterpropagation network. Our model has robust clustering capability, low training time complexity, high utilization of network neurons, and simple computation. A VLSI implementation is highly feasible for SSN.

Lossless Compression of Vector Quantization Indices

Chai Huat Chong, Chien-Min Huang & Richard W. Harris
Department of Electrical Engineering
Utah State University, Logan UT 84321

This paper investigates the amount of compression that can be achieved from lossless coding of vector quantization (VQ) indices. A new method of configuring the index sequence (prior to the lossless coding) is also proposed which not only allows the efficient use of Rice coder but is also shown to have resulted in faster coding with the multi-alphabet arithmetic coder. The two classes of VQ algorithms implemented were the multistage, tree-structured VQ (MTSVQ) and the multistage, optimal bit-allocation VQ (MBAVQ). The lossless coders implemented were the multi-alphabet arithmetic coder (AC), the Lempel-Ziv-Welch coder (LZWC), and the Rice coder (RC). The test database comprised 120 television and magnetic resonant images.

One major concern with coding indices of large codebook is the large number of alphabets possible (e.g. $N = 2^{12} = 4096$ for a 12-bit codebook). This is definitely a drawback since the AC and LZWC may not be able to adapt fast enough to the possibly large variation of alphabet. Besides adversely affecting their coding efficiency, the large alphabet size also slows down the coding process, particularly the AC. In addition, the implementation of the AC becomes rather cumbersome, both in software and hardware. Another obvious problem arises when the RC is used. It is a well known fact that the RC requires its input data to be both positive, i.e. alphabet $\delta \geq 0$, and Laplacian distributed.

The preprocessing technique, called the segmentation-mapping technique, is carried out in two steps:

1. Sort the codevectors during the codebook generation process such that the vectors in each branch are arranged in descending order in terms of their frequency of reach, and
2. Dynamically map the codevectors during the encoding process such that the more frequently visited codevectors are assigned smaller-value indices.

The experimental results show considerable improvement for the coding efficiency of both the LZWC and RC. The LZWC improves by about 7.4% for the MTSVQ and 6.7% for the MBAVQ, while the RC improves by about 7.1% and 5.6%, respectively. The AC's coding/decoding speed is greatly enhanced at the expense of some degradation in its coding efficiency. The average speedup for the AC encoding and decoding (software implementation) is approximately 40 and 60 times, respectively, while its coding efficiency degradation is about 1.3% for the MTSVQ and 3.9% for the MBAVQ.

1068-0314/94 $3.00

A Lossless Data Compression Method for Chinese Characters

S. Kwong, C.H.Lee and S.H. Tong
Department of Computer Science
City Polytechnic of Hong Kong
83 TatChee Ave.
Kowloon, Hong Kong.
EMail: CSSAMK@CPHKVX.BITNET

ABSTRACT

Chinese characters are almost invariably stored in bit-mapped format. In order to support the bit-mapped storage, a substantial amount of disk space is required. For example, a 24 x 24 bit-mapped Chinese character, one Chinese character requires 72 bytes memory storage. If a bigger font is employed, there will be an exponential increase in the storage requirement[3]. To make the situation even worse, multiple-style fonts characters are required in Chinese information processing. Thus, the great demand in storage provides a barrier for the popularity of Chinese language to be used in the computer industries.

In this paper, different combination of compression techniques based on Huffman Algorithm[1] and Run Length Encoding[2] applied to a set of four thousands of Chinese characters are presented. In the bitmap of the Chinese characters, it is composed of either a '1' or '0' to represent the black and white pixel of the Chinese character. Run-Length Encoding is basically used as the first pass of the compression algorithm to collect the number of different symbols in the four thousands Chinese characters. We use four different approaches to apply the Run Length algorithm to the Chinese characters. They are the Run Length Encoding for the whole character, Run Length Encoding with Row Separation, Run Length Encoding with Row Separation and Repeat Count, Run Length Encoding with Relative Counts. Huffman Technique is then applied on the top of these algorithms. In our sample of four thousands of Chinese characters from the BIG-5 24x24 Chinese characters set. Upto 35% of data storage can be saved by using these compression techniques.

In this paper, a data compression technique based on Run Length Algorithm and Huffman coding for Chinese characters is presented. The common points of these two schemes are the simplification of the coding methods. Unlike other compression techniques, these two schemes are not too computational involved and it can be decompressed very easily with very little CPU time. Another attraction for these coding methods is that they are lossless compression techniques. All compressed Chinese characters can be recovered in the decompression phase without any noise when compared with the original data. It means that the compressed Chinese characters can be reproduced exactly the same as the original characters.

References

[1] Huffman,, D." A Method for the Construction of Minimum Redundancy Codes", Proc. IRE, Vol.40, pp.1098-1101, 1952.

[2] S.W. Golomb, "Run-Length Encodings" IEEE trans. Inform. Theory IT-12, pp. 399- 401, July, 1966.

[3] S. Kwong, H. Wong, and Y.S. Yu, "An Effective Method for Storing and Retrieval of Chinese Characters", Proceedings of the International Conference of Information Engineering, Dec. 2-5, 1991, Singapore, pp. 368-376.

Mapping Algorithms into ASIC: A Multi-resolution Algorithm for Image Compression

M. G. Albanesi, M. Ferretti, S. Leoni
University of Pavia, Dipartimento di Informatica e Sistemistica
Via Abbiategrasso 209, I-27100 Pavia, Italy- e-mail: albanesi@ipvmv1.unipv.it

The algorithm

The paper proposes an adaptive compression technique for still grey-level images (8 bit/pixel); the algorithm has been implemented in a UNIX environment as a machine-independent software (C language) and it has been tested, in a rather exhaustive set of benchmarks, on a general class of data (robotic, naturalistic and astronomic images). The goal is to define a compression-decompression technique which can be easily mapped into a dedicated architecture suitable to be transferred into silicon; therefore the target specifications are *real-time processing*, *high modularity* and *low computational complexity*.
The algorithm is decomposed into a pipeline of *tasks*; the input image undergoes a *digital transformation*, in which data correlation is reduced. More precisely, the algorithm adopts a multi-resolution formulation of the Bidimensional Discrete Haar Transform, in which the coefficients can be considered as a collection of three quaternary trees.The *compression task* is achieved by a *pruning* operation on the trees. A set of adaptive thresholds, superimposed by the operator, are applied on the values of the coefficients of the Haar Transform. The pruning operation is performed independently on each tree and on each level, in order to adapt the compression to the specific spatial distribution of the value of pixels, and to the energy contribution in the frequency domain.The pruned coefficients in the trees are substituted by zero values.The pruned trees are coded in loss-less way, by adopting a run-length encoding with a variable length word in the three lower levels, and a *Delta* coding with a fixed length word for the upper levels of the trees.The decompression-task is quite straightforward and consists of: (a) interpreting the bit streams of the Run-length and Delta coding and (b) applying the Inverse Haar Transform.
The new compression algorithm has been tested on a broad set of indoor and outdoor scenes, natural subjects, robotics and standard images from literature ("Lena"). The achieved compression ratios is in the range 8÷25 (MSE from 35 to 80).

Mapping the algorithm into ASIC

Starting from the complete functional description of the compression algorithm, each task has been implemented in distinct functional blocks of the dedicated architecture.The design has been completed at a gate level, using a standard cell approach, with 1 μm CMOS technology (1.3 x 1.3 cm, 469134 equivalent transistors, operative frequency 32 Mhz) while for the decompression sub-system only a functional description of the architecture has been provided. Future works include, for the hardware, the complete design of the ASIC for the decompression task; for what concerns the software, the extension of the algorithm to other Wavelet Transforms and the automatic choice of the thresholds for the pruning phase.

 1068-0314/94 $3.00

Model Based Vector Quantization

M. Manohar
Hughes STX, Code 930.1,
Goddard Space Flight Center
Greenbelt, MD 20771

Ben Kobler
Code 505.0,
Goddard Space Flight Center
Greenbelt, MD 20771

James C. Tilton
Code 930.1,
Goddard Space Flight Center
Greenbelt, MD 20771

P.C. Hariharan
Systems Engineering & Security, Inc.
7474 Greenway Center Dr., Suite 720
Greenbelt, MD 20770

Vector Quantization (VQ) is limited as a practical compression technique by the need to generate (train) and maintain codebooks. Model based VQ (MVQ) is a variant of VQ that generates the codebook internally using Laplacian error models and source statistics, thereby eliminating the need to train and maintain codebooks. In addition, the computational requirements for generating the model based codebook is much less than that required to generated a conventional codebook. The source dependent parameters are included in the compressed file so that the decoder can generate the codebook that encoder used for coding. Thus, the use of codebook in MVQ is transparent.

In the MVQ algorithm, the input image is normalized with respect to maximum pixel value in the image. Then the image is vectorized by dividing it into rectangular (k = k1xk2) blocks. The mean value of the each vector (μ) is computed and subtracted from the vector (the result is called mean removed vectors). Now the statistics of the mean removed vectors of the source are used to generate a codebook from uniform random number generator. The source statistics are obtained by computing the covariance matrix, Σ, of the mean removed vectors. The diagonal elements of the covariance matrix (Σ_{ii}) are approximately equal and corresponds to the variance of the normalized mean removed pixel values in the image. The square root of Σ_{00} (= λ) is used to generate independent and identically distributed (iid) Laplacian random variables. The consecutive Laplacian iid random numbers are grouped into vectors of size k (= k1xk2). Now these vector elements are filtered in a such a way that the resulting vector will have approximately same covariance matrix as Σ. This can be accomplished by factorizing the positive definite and symmetric matrix, Σ into L, U where L and U are upper and lower triangular matrices respectively. The factorization is normally done by using Cholesky decomposition algorithm. When the Laplacian vectors are mapped onto L, the resulting vectors will have same multivariate distribution as Σ. These vectors are used as the code vectors for the input source (mean removed residual vectors).

The input image now is coded using the codebook generated by the model and source statistics. The codebook is completely specified by λ and the lower triangular matrix, L. The lower triangular matrix will have at most $(k^2 + k)/2$ nonzero real numbers, where k is the size of the vector. Thus by transmitting λ, and L as header of coded file the decoder can generate the codebook to decode the VQ coded image.

The MVQ codebook generation model can be simplified because, the matrix, L is found to have only two or three significant coefficients showing that mean removed vector elements can be modeled by first order Markov process. The iid Laplacian random variables are passed through a filter corresponding to Markov first order Markov process. The optimum filter coefficients can be estimated by minimizing the mean squared error.

The above filter converts the output of the iid Laplacian numbers into correlated numbers forming the codevectors. The parameter λ for Laplacian random number generator and two filter coefficients are included in the compressed image for the decoder to generate the same codebook. The results of MVQ are encouraging.

1068-0314/94 $3.00 © 1994 IEEE

Model Selection in Linear Regression using the MML criterion

Rohan A. Baxter
David L. Dowe
Department of Computer Science
Monash University
Clayton Vic. 3168
Australia
e-mail: {rohan,dld}@bruce.cs.monash.edu.au

We use the minimum message length (MML) criterion for model selection in regression problems. The MML criterion uses an accurate estimate of the length of a code for the parameters of a Bayesian density. The criterion has us choose the parameters θ so as to minimize the message length [1]:

$$MessLen(\theta) = -\log h(\theta) - \log f(x|\theta) + \frac{1}{2}\log|I(\theta)| + \frac{k}{2} + \frac{k}{2}\log\kappa_k \qquad (1)$$

where $h(\theta)$ is the prior distribution on the k parameters θ, $f(x|\theta)$ is the likelihood function, $I(\theta)$ is the empirical Fisher information and κ_k is a constant dependent on optimal k-dimensional quantising lattices.

Existing model selection criteria (AIC,BIC,etc) have the same asymptotic behaviour as the MML criterion for this problem. The motivation for applying another information-theoretic criterion to linear regression model selection is to improve the estimation of the model complexity for small data sets.

The MML criterion is very similar to Bozdogan's CAICF [2] extension of Akaike's information criterion(AIC) in the present problem. CAICF penalizes higher order models slightly more than MML.

We have applied the MML criterion to the classic problem of choosing the degree of a polynomial in least-squares regression. The MML criterion performed well in Monte Carlo experiments with small and/or noisy data sets relative to the other criteria examined.

The authors gratefully acknowledge the support of a Monash Graduate Scholarship and Australian Research Grant No. A49030439.

[1] C.S. Wallace and P.R. Freeman. Estimation and inference by compact coding. *J. R. Statist. Soc B*, 49(3):240–265, 1987.

[2] H. Bozdogan. Model selection and Akaike's information criterion (AIC): The general theory and its analytical extensions. *Psychometrika*, 52(3):345–370, 1987.

Multiresolution Surface Approximation Using Vector Quantization in Image Compression

Lifeng Chen and W.K. Tsai
Department of Electrical and Computer Engineering
University of California, Irvine, CA 92717
wtsai@balboa.ece.uci.edu

Abstract

In this paper first a review and classification of image coding methods is presented from the image modelling viewpoint. Then we apply image modelling and multiresolution concepts to image coding. The basic idea is that we view the original image as a 3-D geometric surface, and image coding problem as a 3D surface approximation and compact representation problem. Multiresolution surface approximation (MSA) algorithm is introduced which combines with recursive vector quantization (RVQ) and modified block quantization coding (MBTC). It provides advantages such as fast decompression (only search and integer additions); semantic representation by using codebook as a dictionary; and flexibility for compression rate control.

In MSA algotithm, the original image is viewed as a 3-D geometric surface and at each stage a vector quantizer approximates the original image at different resolution level, from coarse to fine. MBTC is employed in the process of compacting the codebook and an universal codebook is utilized at the final encoding stage. Decoding phase is pretty quick and easy, the only operations needed are to retrieve the codewords it selected in the encoding phase and add them together. Computer simulations were carried out using MSA algorithms on the Lena image. And we used Truck image as the training image to generate universal codebook for error pattern. Our scheme produces compression ratios up to 40:1 with PSNR equals to 28.11db.

Our goal in this work is try to develop a very efficient decompression algorithm that only required limited computing and power resource with very low hardware complexity. This is usually required by many mission-critical multimedia services such as wireless handhold digital video. MSA algorithms have the advantage that it can decompress image very fast, only search and integer addition involved, while greatly reduces the blocking effect compared to traditional vector quantization algorithm. It is also well suited for different kinds of multimedia services such as portable wireless video communication, interactive image database browsing, content-based image database searching and video-on-demand.

In conclusion, our study indicates that the combination of concepts of multiresolution, image modelling, 3D surface approximation and assymetric architecture may be an effective approach of image compression.

NEURAL NETWORK MINIMIZATION TECHNIQUES FOR MULTISTAGE ORTHOGONAL QMF FILTERS WITH VANISHING MOMENTS

Stuart Schweid, Student Member, IEEE and T.K. Sarkar, Fellow, IEEE

ABSTRACT

Successive multirate filter bank decompositions (especially QMF filters) are used in a variety of applications such as signal and image compression and singularity detection. In many applications, the filters of any stage are chosen to locally minimize/maximize a given cost/performance criteria. In signal and image compression, for example, the minimization is done locally and sequentially; the filter for the first stage is determined, then the second, stage, the third stage, etc until all stages are determined. Each successive stage's choice of filter is dependent on the choice of filter of the previous stages' filters, but does not affect it.

A better global minimization occurs when the minimization technique modifies all filters of the multi-stage decomposition simultaneously. Previous stages are changed in conjunction with future stages to minimize an overall cost function. The approach is analogous to some neural techniques used in solving the familiar "traveling salesman" problem - changes in the path taken minimize the overall distance traveled rather than choosing the next closest city.

In this paper a feedforward neural network is used to address multi-stage decomposition signal compression. The neural network uses back-propagation to update the filter coefficients of all stages simultaneously in each iteration. Back propagation is the vehicle that allows the optimization to proceed in a forward and backward direction, thus achieving a better signal compression than forward only stage by stage compression.

In addition, the paper will address how to use the algorithm when all stages are constrained to be identical: a restriction that results in a wavelet type decomposition.

A New Access Control Schemes Based on Minimal Perfect Hashing Functions

Min Lin Hui
email:u8134539@cc.nctu.edu.tw
Institute of Information Management
National Chiao Tung University
Hsinchu, 300, Taiwan, R.O.C.

Judy C. R. Tseng+
email:judycrt@cc.nctu.edu.tw
Department of Computer Science
Chung-Hua Polytechnic Institute
30 Tung Shiang, Hsinchu, Taiwan, R.O.C.

As the use of computer networks grows, the way to prevent data stored in computers from illegal action, such as duplication, deletion, updation, has become an important issue. To solve this problem, many access control schemes have been proposed, such as the access control matrix, the Capability-list method and various access control schemes that based on Single-Key-Lock (SKL) systems. However, these methods do not effectively resolve the case that most of the elements of the access control matrix are zeros.

In this paper, we apply the idea of minimal perfect hashing function which maps the key set one-to-one and onto the address space to devise a new access control scheme. By using the new proposed scheme, only non-zero access rights and corresponding mapping values to solve collisions are recorded. The address for storing a non-zero access right and mapping value is determined by a minimal perfect hashing function. That is, only one hashing function calculation is needed for checking access privilege. Therefore, the new scheme is efficient in both space and time.

In our method, we do not limit the choice of the minimal perfect hashing function. All the minimal perfect hashing functions for numbers can be used here. To demonstrate the validity of our method, we choose C. C. Chang's ordered minimal perfect hashing function which hashes its key set in ascending order.

To verify the power of our new access control scheme, the access control matrix, the Capability-list method, Wu and Hwang's Single-Key-Lock, Chang's Key-Lock-Pair, Jan's Single-Key, Laith, Harn and Lee's Single-Key-Lock, and our new access control schemes are simulated on IBM PC. Comparisons among them are made in both storage space and execution time. For the access control matrix of size 10*10, the storage space required by each method are also compared under various sparse degrees, the new method needs less memory space than all other methods when the sparse degree is above 75%. With regard to the execution item for determining the access right of an user to a file, access control matrix requires O(1), Capability-list $O(n)$, Wu and Hwang's $O(n)$, Chang's O(1), Jan's $O(log^n)$, Laith, Harn, and Lee$O(n^2)$, and our new method O(1). To sum up, our new access control scheme achieves optimal performance on both storage space and execution item.

With C. C. Chang's ordered minimal perfect hashing function, our new method has to store a large number, C. That makes the result not so promising as expectation. We will find other minimal perfect hashing function to minimize the extra storage space for C. Beside, we will also try to find a dynamic minimal perfect hashing function which can be applied to our access control scheme.

NONLINEAR-PREDICTED VECTOR QUANTIZATION

Daniele D. Giusto
Istituto di Elettrotecnica, Universita' di Cagliari, Italy
myrddin@elettro1.unica.it

This paper proposes a novel predicted-VQ scheme (called Dynamic Codebook Reordering VQ), where the prediction aims to reorder the codebook dynamically, so allowing an efficient Huffman encoding of codevector addresses, as their entropy is notably reduced. The predictor is implemented by a three-layer perceptron neural network trained (by back-propagation) to reconstruct a given codevector $\mathbf{x}_{i,j}$ on the basis of the four neighboring codevectors previously decoded $\mathbf{x}_{i-1,j-1}$, $\mathbf{x}_{i-1,j}$, $\mathbf{x}_{i-1,j+1}$, $\mathbf{x}_{i,j-1}$. To exploit the predictor's output $\mathbf{x'}_{i,j}$, the difference between the predicted vector and the codevector to be transmitted is coded. If the predictor succeeds every time, a sequence of 0's is generated. In real cases, the predictor produces vectors close enough to the correct codevector, so maintaining smaller distances.

A practical way to implement this concept is to reorder the codebook for each codevector to be transmitted, on the basis of the distances from the predicted vector. As a result, a sequence of quite similar addresses is produced, characterized by a low entropy. An example of an address histogram for a memoryless VQ is given in Figure 1.a; Figure 1.b shows the same histogram for DCRVQ.

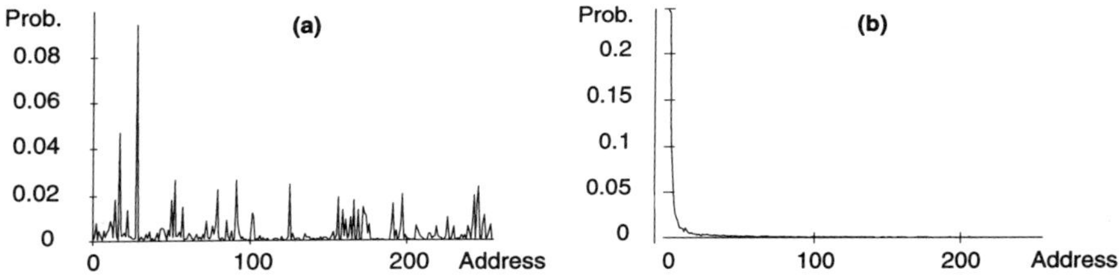

Figure 1. Address histogram for memoryless VQ (a) and for DCRVQ (b).

The neural predictor is identical for the encoder and the decoder; the values of the synaptic weights computed during the training phase are stored and used by both the encoder and the decoder. In order to decrease the bitrate without further losses, the networks work in a synchronous way, in the sense that they receive the same data and produce the same predicted vector. The coder computes both the MSE between each codevector $\mathbf{x}(h)$ and $\mathbf{x}'_{i,j}$ (called E_h) and the MSE between $\mathbf{x}_{i,j}$ and $\mathbf{x}'_{i,j}$ (called E); the address to be transmitted is $a = \dim\{E_\ell; \ell = 1,\dots,N : E_\ell < E\}$.

The decoder is synchronous with the encoder, so it has to compute the predicted vector, E_h and E, and to reorder the codebook on the basis of the $\{E_h\}$'s. Then it has to extract, from the reordered codebook, the codevector corresponding to the transmitted address.

Bitrates ranges from 0.3 to 0.5 bpp, in the case of vectors of dimensions 3*3 pels, 256 gray levels per pel, and a codebook made up of 256 codevectors. It has to be pointed out that the neural prediction has a great flexibility, as its performances are quite similar for images both included or not in the training set.

1068-0314/94 $3.00 © 1994 IEEE

A Novel DCT Implementation Using Bit-Serial Arithmetic

Glen U. Sunada and Tom Chen
Electrical Engineering Department
Colorado State University

With the advent of high resolution digital displays the need for efficient digital storage and transmission of continuous tone images is increasing. The most popular lossy image compression schemes are based on an image transform that removes correlation in the data stream, thereby allowing for efficient entropy coding of the transformed data. The discrete cosine transform (DCT) is widely used for image compression because it approaches the performance of the statistically optimal Kharunen-Love transform for highly correlated signals.

The most common image compression schemes use the 8x8 point 2-D DCT. The 2-D DCT can be implemented as two sequential 1-D DCT. The first DCT transforms each row of the original 2-D signal to a 8-point 1-D DCT. Then the second DCT transforms the columns of the result of the first part to get the final 2-D DCT.

Several VLSI implementations of the 2-D DCT and other decorrelation transforms have recently been reported to achieve real time operation. The problem with these chips is that the real time operation is only valid for images that contain only one map such as grey scale images, not for the three map images found in a color video system. This problem leads to overestimation of the performance of these chips in a full color video system. It is possible to perform the DCT on more than one map using the linearity of the DCT. When applying this property the scaling factors must be chosen large enough that the fractional part of one map will not be added to the integer part of another map.

To implement the 2-D DCT in silicon we chose to use a pipelined hybrid bit-serial/bit-parallel structure because it provides the best compromise of expandability, computation time, and silicon area. Using an internal data format of 23 bits fractional part and 12 bits integer part these scaling factors are $1, 2^{35}, 2^{70}$. Using an input data format of eight bits per map the timing of the three map multiply operation is 8 clock cycles to input the map element, 15 clock cycles to finish filling the pipeline, 23 clock cycles to output the fractional portion, and 12 clock cycles to output the integer portion for a total of 58 clock cycles to perform one multiply. The pipelined nature of the multiplier allows us to start inputting a new value 35 clock cycles before the current value is output. This overlap and timing results in a three map multiplication time of 129 clock cycles. If the three maps were not pipelined it would require the full 58 clock cycles for each map or 174 clock cycles for all three maps, therefore the pipelining saves about 25% of the processing time for three maps.

The COBRA chip presented in this paper includes 128 hybrid multipliers, a 128x128 crossbar switch matrix and I/O interface logic. The die size is 13 by 11 mm in 0.75 μm triple metal CMOS process and is capable of performing a full 8x8 point 2-D DCT with two six map passes through the multipliers and extra adds, giving a computation time of 468 clock cycles for an 8x8 2-D DCT. At 70 MHz we achieve a processing time of 6.7 μsec for a input data rate of about 28 MByte/sec. NTSC TV frame compression requires an input data rate of about 27 MByte/sec if no subsampling is applied, meaning that we can perform real time compression of NTSC frames with one chip. Most current DCT processors require one chip per map to perform real time compression, providing our system with a savings in chip count.

1068-0314/94 $3.00

Optimal Asymptotic Adaptive Text Compression using Markov Chains

Kevin Atteson - University of Pennsylvania

We analyze the asymptotics of the expected coding length of Bayes rules for first order Markov chains. This analysis is the same as [2] except where they analyze the case of independent and identically distributed random processes (for a wide range of distributions), we consider first order Markov chains:

Theorem 1 *For any m-symbol stationary first order Markov chain with non-zero transition probabilities and for a prior (on the transition probabilities) with continuous density g:*

$$\lim_n \sum_{x_{1:n}\in X^n} p(x_{1:n}) \log_m \frac{p(x_{1:n})}{q(x_{1:n})} - \left(\frac{m-1}{2}\log_m \frac{n}{2\pi e^{m+2}} - \log_m g(p) + \frac{m-1}{2}\sum_s \log_m p_s - \frac{1}{2}\sum_{s,t}\log_m p_{t|s}\right) = 0$$

where $x_{1:n}$ is the vector of the first n data samples, $p(x_{1:n})$ is the probability of $x_{1:n}$ in the Markov chain with probabilities p and $q(x_{1:n})$ is the estimated probability of $x_{1:n}$ according to the Bayes rule i.e. $q(x_{1:n}) = \int p(x_{1:n})g(p)dp$.

In order to obtain this result, we use results about the asymptotic independence of Markov chains, in particular, the theory of ϕ-mixing random processes as discussed in [3]. This result allows us to determine the prior for a Bayes equalizer rule $g(p) = c\prod_s p_s^{\frac{m-1}{2}} / \prod_{s,t} p_{s|t}^{\frac{1}{2}}$ where c is chosen to normalize $g(p)$. However, for Markov chains, the decision rules corresponding to Bayes rules typically involve integrals which cannot be solved in closed form (including the prior mentioned above). Hence, the minimax rule is computationally impractical (it would require a multi-dimensional numerical integration for each data point). Hence, we derive the asymptotics of this decision rule, which, not surprisingly corresponds with the minimax decision rule discussed in [2] for the independent case (this is not surprising since, as mentioned, Markov chains are asymptotically independent). For a complete treatment of these results, see [1] where we also plan to include the generalization to fixed but arbitrary order Markov chains and other related results.

[1] Kevin Atteson. *Some Mathematical Analyses of Adaptive Text Data Compression.* PhD thesis, University of Pennsylvania, To appear.

[2] Bertrand Salem Clarke. *Asymptotic Cumulative Risk and Bayes Risk under Entropy Loss, with Applications.* PhD thesis, University of Illinois at Urbanna-Champaign, 1989.

[3] M. Iosifescu and R. Theodorescu. *Random Processes and Learning.* Springer-Verlag, 1969.

OPTIMAL PREDICTORS AND TRANSFORM CODING METHODS FOR THE DATA COMPRESSION OF DIGITAL ELEVATION MODELS

M. Lewis
Department of Mathematics and Computing, The University of Glamorgan, Pontypridd, Mid-Glamorgan, CF37 1DL., U.K.
Tel.U.K. 443 480480 ext. 2712., Fax: U.K. 443 480553.,
Email : MLEWIS@uk.ac.glam

ABSTRACT

Square or rectangular grids are extensively used for digital elevation models (DEM's) because of their simplicity, their implicit topology and their minimal search time for applications. However, their inability to adapt to the variability of the terrain results in data redundancy and excessive storage requirements for large models. One approach to mitigating this is the use of a model that predicts the data values. The method of Lagrange Multipliers for minimisation of the root mean square prediction error has been applied to local geometric predictors and compared with the least-squares fitting of quadratic and bilinear surface patches. Alternative approaches are transform techniques - the two-dimensional discrete cosine transform (2D-DCT) and the wavelet transform. Transform coding allows greater compression but is computationally intensive and with the 2D-DCT gives some error on reconstruction of the data. The 2D-DCT can be combined with either Huffman encoding or Run Length Encoding of the DCT coefficients to achieve greater compression. Further compression can be achieved when using the Huffman DCT method by blocking the transformation coefficients. The best compression achievable for the same data set using the DCT algorithm with blocking is about 35.24:1, i.e. a storage saving of 96.49% for at most an error of 5 metres and an rmse of 0.5. For error-free compression (accurate to the nearest metre), the simple prediction method gives a compression ratio of 13.04:1 with blocking the prediction errors before Huffman encoding. This gives a storage saving of about 92.30%. Similar results for a second more variable data set give a compression ratio of 17.60:1 or a storage saving of 94.12%, again for an equivalent maximum error of about 5 metres and an rmse of about 0.8. In the error-free Huffman method with blocking, equivalent results for the second data set are a compression ratio of about 7.13:1 and a storage saving of 85.93%. The Lagrange Multiplier method will give an improvement of about 7% to the error-free compression ratios quoted. The use of the two dimensional Daubechies Wavelet transform shows similar performances with blocking of the coefficients before Huffman encoding. The best performance for the first data set was a storage saving of 95.31% or a compression ratio of about 23.01:1 with the 12-coefficient ('smooth') transform. For the second data set, a storage saving of 91.47% or a compression ratio of about 11.76:1 with the 4-coefficient ('local') transform.

The Optimal Symbol-Probability Estimate for Lossless Compression[†]

Edward Hatton and George H. Freeman

Department of Electrical and Computer Engineering
University of Waterloo, Waterloo, Ontario, Canada N2L 3G1
(519) 885-1211, Ext. 2876, FAX (519) 746-3077
G.Freeman@EandCE.UWaterloo.CA

Abstract—The general issue of estimating symbol probabilities from counts, and the zero-frequency problem in particular, have received considerable attention for their application to lossless data compression. The philosophical issues surrounding the problems are possibly unresolvable. Here, we consider a specific model for the random process handled by an entropy coder after some good source modelling. It is treated as a stationary, nonergodic process with sample sequences generated in an i.i.d. fashion on a finite alphabet but according to a randomly selected probability distribution p. We only consider the (worst) case of p uniformly distributed over

$$\mathcal{P} = \left\{ p: \; p_i \geq 0; \; i = 0, \cdots, n-1 \text{ and } \sum_{i=0}^{n-1} p_i = 1 \right\} \in \mathcal{R}^n.$$

Suppose symbol i from the alphabet of size n appears a_i times in the message block of length N. A commonly used heuristic

$$q_i = \frac{a_i + 1}{N + n}$$

for estimating the true symbol probability p_i satisfies $q_i \to a_i/N \to p_i$ as $N \to \infty$ while also ensuring that $q_i \neq 0$ to avoid the zero-frequency problem. We show that it is also optimal in the sense of minimizing the encoded message length. Adaptive symbol-at-a-time encoding and updating the probability estimates using this formula gives the same performance (in the limit of ideal code-word lengths) as a semi-adaptive encoding that counts the whole message before sending the first symbol and adapts its encoding symbol-at-a-time to the remaining symbols in the message block. However, the semi-adaptive encoder must be explicitly given the number of symbols in the message. When there is an interleaving of context-dependent subsources, this gives a coding advantage to the adaptive method.

[†]This work has been supported by the Natural Sciences and Engineering Research Council of Canada under Research Grant A6658 and by the Information Technologies Research Centre, an Ontario Centre of Excellence.

A Parallel Algorithm for a Tree Structured Vector Quantizer for Image Compression

Robert G. Palmer, Jr.†, *John K. Antonio*†, *Janet McWaid*††, *Howard Jay Siegel*†

†Parallel Processing Laboratory
School of Electrical Engineering
Purdue University
West Lafayette, IN 47907-1285 USA

††Electrical Engineering Department
California Institute of Technology
Pasadena, CA 91125 USA

Abstract

The work presented here is based on a binary TSVQ (tree structured vector quantizer) image compression algorithm with N code vectors in the final codebook. The goal of our research is to contrast several modes of parallelism with a serial implementation of TSVQ.

To parallelize the codebook generation, the training data are first divided evenly among P PEs (processor/memory pairs). Each PE therefore receives $1/P$-th of the training data. Each PE maintains a local copy of the current codebook tree. The following process is initially performed using one partition to create the root node of the codebook tree. First, the centroid is calculated for each partition. All PEs sum the local training vectors for each partition, and then the global sum for each partition, across all PEs, is calculated using a tree reduction algorithm. Upon completion of the tree reduction, each PE will have the global sum for each partition. The partition sizes are calculated using the same procedure. Each PE divides its local copy of the global sum by the partition size to calculate its own copy of the centroid for each partition. The centroids are the current code vectors.

Splitting the partitions is the next step. Each PE duplicates each current code vector to create a left child and a right child. A perturbation vector is added to each right child. The partition assignments are then calculated, based on minimum squared-error between each training vector and code vector, for each PE's local training data. Because each PE maintains a local copy of the codebook tree, no communication is required during the splitting process. Then, the centroid (code vector) for each new partition is calculated as described above.

In each PE, the squared-error distortion is calculated for each local training vector using the data contained in the local codebook tree. Then, a tree reduction is executed to obtain the global distortion measure. Each PE receives the result and performs a local comparison to determine whether to exit or continue iterating.

For the encoding process, each PE initially receives $1/P$-th of the image to be encoded and a copy of the codebook. All calculations are performed locally, with no communication among PEs. Every PE begins with an image vector and performs a binary-tree search to find the correct code vector. Even though a balanced tree is currently generated, the encoding procedure can be used with unbalanced trees as well. At every level of the tree, all PEs simultaneously make a comparison to determine if a leaf (code vector) has been reached. If a PE determines that a leaf has been reached, it will output the code vector index and immediately retrieve the next image vector for encoding. This algorithm allows all PEs to function independently in terms of the current tree-search level and current image vector even though the code may be executing on a SIMD machine requiring all PEs to function synchronously at the instruction level.

This work demonstrates that TSVQ is a viable compression method for implementation on parallel computers. TSVQ can provide the high compression rates required, while parallel implementations can provide significant speed-up over serial implementations for codebook generation, encoding, and decoding. Implementations on the PASM parallel mixed-mode system prototype and on the SIMD MasPar MP-1 machine are under development.

This research was supported in part by NSF under grant CDA-9015696.

Parallel Data Compression on a Transputer Network

Graham D. Finlayson, Stella Atkins and Michael Zastre
School of Computing Science
Simon Fraser University, B.C. Canada
email: graham@cs.sfu.ca

The speed of compression and decompression is critical for many applications. Existing compression algorithms executing serially on a general purpose CPU are often inadequate for the task. We therefore considered methods for speeding up the compression using a parallel architecture.

In this work our target architecture is a network of Transputers. Each transputer consists of a processing unit with private RAM memory. Data is shared between transputers by explicit transfer along one of four bi-directional data links. As a consequence, inter-processor communication is costly and should be kept to a minimum—each processor should, as far as possible, work autonomously.

We propose that a Master-Slave decomposition is an effective method for parallelizing compression algorithms keeping inter-process communication costs low. Under our Master-Slave scheme, a single Master transputer is responsible for file I/O, and there are many Slaves responsible for data compression. During compression the Master reads data blocks from a file and distributes them to the Slave transputers. On receipt of a file block the Slave performs the compression and returns the compressed block to the Master. The Master outputs compressed blocks to a file. The Slaves communicate only with the Master and this communication is restricted to the initiation and termination of a block compress. Decompression is implemented in an analogous manner.

We implemented the Huffman coding algorithm using the Master-Slave decomposition. We compared the compression/decompression times for for the Master-Slave implementation (with 3 and 9 Slave transputers) with those of serial Huffman coding. Compression and decompression rates increase almost linearly in the number of Slaves. We propose that the Master-Slave paradigm is readily applicable to many other existing compression algorithms, for example the non-adaptive Lempel-Ziv algorithm. Moreover, the Master-Slave scheme can be implemented on any similar Multiple Instruction Multiple Data architecture such as hypercubes and the Motorola C40 architecture family.

Parallel Decoding of Huffman Codes

*Belle W. Y. Wei**
Pei-Jun Lan
Department of Electrical Engineering
San Jose State University
San Jose, CA 95192-0084
(408) 924-3881; wei@ee0.sjsu.edu

Huffman coding is a variable-length entropy coding scheme that assigns shorter encodings to more frequently referenced source symbols. It employs, on average, a fraction of the number of bits used for fixed-length codes, and thus achieves data compression. It has been difficult to implement parallel Huffman decoding. The decoder inputs variable-length codewords whose boundary cannot be determined until preceding codewords have been decoded. The "sequential" property defies a straightforward pipelined parallel implementation essential for delivering video-rate high resolution images and constant decoding rate. Furthermore, standards such as JPEG (the Joint Picture Expert Group) require that Huffman coding tables be programmable. The Huffman coding tables are not fixed, and there is no *a priori* hardwired logic to be optimized.

Our scheme takes advantage of numerical properties of monotonic Huffman codewords used in JPEG, in which codes of the same codeword length are numerically sequential. Each codeword is expressed as an offset with respect to its minimum code of the same length. Decoding operations compare, in parallel, the leading bits of the input string with the minimum codes of all codeword lengths. The codeword length at which the comparison results, i.e., subtraction results, switch signs is the decoded code length. The corresponding magnitude of the comparison difference is the offset for the decoded codeword. To reduce the number of bits used for comparison, we have proved that only a limited number of trailing bits of minimum codes are needed for decoding.

Our decoding operation is arithmetic instead of matching, thus eliminating the need for a large memory. The design of a single JPEG AC table of 256 Huffman codewords of up to 16 bits uses 272-byte memory. Its IC implementation in 1.2 μm CMOS technology is estimated to run at 40 MHz with a chip area of 11 mm^2, decoding one codeword per clock cycle. Most of the chip area is occupied by comparison (subtracter) circuits which can be traded-off for possible slower decoding. For instance, a set of four comparison circuits instead of 16 requires one or two cycles for decoding codewords of up to 8 bits, which occur most of time. In the worst case, it uses four clock cycles. In case of pure Huffman decoding where Huffman codes are not sandwiched between non-Huffman values, our design can be pipelined to increase throughput.

---

* This work was supported in part by National Science Foundation grant MIP 9019862.

Parallel Entropy Coding Using Multiple Coders

Martin Boliek, James D. Allen, Edward L. Schwartz
RICOH California Research Center, Menlo Park, California
boliek@crc.ricoh.com

Presented here is a method that allows for parallel compression and decompression in hardware. This parallelism can result in extremely high rates, often 100 million symbols per second or higher. The system can be generalized to any lossless or lossy system with deterministic decompression or decoding. The focus is on high-speed entropy coding. Efforts to build high-speed hardware versions of many different entropy coders are limited by fundamental feedback loops. Dividing the data into multiple streams that are fed into parallel coders is an design option. For this design to be feasible, however, the problem of efficient transmission of multiple streams of variable-length coded data must be solved.

Imagine image data delivered in raster scan data divided into multiple parallel streams. There are many choices of how this is done. For example, each parallel stream could be the data associated with a context bin or bins or it could have the same or similar predictor value. The data could be divided into probability classes. Or it could be parallelize arbitrarily by regions or tiles or every Nth pixel.

These parallel streams are encoded by separate variable-length entropy encoders in parallel. The codewords are placed in parallel buffers. If a decoder has the same structure (satisfying causality) and access to all the streams simultaneously, it is clear that the parallel codewords could be decoded and the original data stream could be regenerated. Note that the parallel decoders take codewords from the appropriate code stream in some, perhaps complicated, deterministic order, called codeword order. Because of the parallelization, this codeword order is very different than the original raster order.

In a real system it is unrealistic to have several channels for the parallel code streams. If the codewords from the parallel code streams are interleaved in the codeword order then a single channel will suffice. This interleaving can be performed by having a "snooper" decoder at the encoder to determine the proper order. A system such as this has variable-length codewords. Thus, it requires a bit shifter at the decoder to align the codeword and deliver them to the proper parallel decoder. This is the bottleneck of the system and mitigates the virtue of parallelism.

The solution offered here is to group the codewords from each independent code stream into fixed-length words, called interleaved words. The interleaved words can contain many codewords and parts of codewords. These words are interleaved according to the demand at the decoder. Each independent decoder receives an entire interleaved word. The shifting operation is now done locally at each decoder, maintaining the parallelism of the system.

An important feature of this interleaving is that it allows codes that are single context to be used in multi-context system. Experiments with run length codes, such as Golomb or Rice codes, show coding efficiency comparable to the multi-context QM-coder. Experiments with a prototype hardware suggest that a run length code system could run 10 to 20 times faster in a VLSI implementation with the same gate count as the QM-coder.

 1068-0314/94 $3.00

Perceptual Compression of Magnitude-Detected Synthetic Aperture Radar Imagery [1]

John D. Gorman and Susan A. Werness

Environmental Research Institute of Michigan
Box 134001, Ann Arbor, MI, 48113-4001
Email: gorman@erim.org, werness@erim.org

Overview

We present a perceptually-based compression algorithm along with a preliminary evaluation of its performance on fine-resolution synthetic aperture radar (SAR) imagery. Properties of the algorithm are: (i) spatial adaptability to accommodate both the large dynamic ranges and unique image textures seen in SAR imagery, and (ii) the use of perceptually-based design criteria to optimize image quality rather than mean-squared error. Key components of the approach are a multiresolution wavelet transform, a bit allocation method based on an empirical human visual system (HVS) model, and hybrid scalar/vector quantization (VQ). Specifically, wavelet shrinkage techniques are used to segregate wavelet transform coefficients into three components: local means, edges, and texture. Each of these three components is then quantized separately according to a perceptually-based bit allocation scheme. Wavelet coefficients associated with local means and edges are quantized using high-rate scalar quantization while texture information is quantized using low-rate VQ.

A consistent motivation for the multiresolution decomposition is its conceptual similarity to scene decompositions performed by the human visual system, which set the stage for application of simple, effective HVS bit allocation schemes. Two elements that we have found to be particularly useful for SAR imagery are: (i) the use of wavelet shrinkage techniques [1] for spatially-adaptive edge detection and encoding, and (ii) a fixed-weight perceptually-based bit allocation scheme. A minimum rate constraint is set for the local mean and edge components so that essential image content is preserved even at bit rates as low as 1/8 bpp. The perceptually-based bit allocation scheme is implemented by applying a weighting table to the wavelet transform coefficients. Our approach uses a fixed table rather than the weighted mean-squared error approach reported in [2]; in the latter reference, a data-dependent bit allocation table was used, in which each subband weight was scaled by the standard deviation of that subband. Based on empirical evidence collected to date, we find that fixed-weight bit allocation may be more appropriate for SAR imagery.

References

[1] Donoho, D. L. and Johnstone, I. M., "Ideal Spatial Adaption via Wavelet Shrinkage," Preprint, Technical Report No. 400, Department of Statistics, Stanford University, (available via anonymous ftp at stat.stanford.edu), April 1993.

[2] Perkins, M.G. and T. Lookabaugh, "A Psychophysically Justified Bit Allocation Algorithm for Subband Image Coding Systems," *Proc. ICASSP,* pp. 1815-1818, 1989.

---

[1] This research funded in part under ERIM Internal Research and Development Funds.

Pruned tree and bit allocation vector quantization

K. M. Liang, C. M. Huang & R. W. Harris

Department of Electrical Engineering, Utah State Univ. Logan Utah 84321.

For a set of quantizers, if the distortion function and the bit-rate function for those quantizers are known, bit allocation algorithm distributes different bit rate to different quantizer according to those functions for a total fixed amount of bit rate. For tree-structured vector quantization (TSVQ), we can classify the training set, build a codebook for each classified training set, and apply the bit allocation algorithm to those codebooks (quantizers). The bit allocation algorithm uses Lagrangian multiplier method to achieve minimum distortion for a fixed amount of bit rate. In this paper, the Lagrangian multiplier method is applied to a set of distortion functions associated with the codebook. That is, the encoded distortions for each input vector are treated as the output of a quantizer. The Lagrangian multiplier method is then applied among those quantizers.

For pruned tree algorithm, after the tree is pruned, each input vector is encoded to the bottom level of the tree. Although the bottom levels of the tree have different depth for each branch of the tree due to the pruning. For bit allocation, the input vector is encoded to different level of the tree-structured codebook according to the assigned bit rate. The first difference between the pruned tree algorithm and the bit allocation algorithm is that the pruned tree algorithm uses a pruned tree-structured codebook to encode and decode the input vectors. The pruned tree-structured codebook is an unbalanced tree-structured codebook. But the bit allocation use a complete (balanced) tree-structured codebook to encode and decode the input vectors. The second difference is that side information is required to identify the level of the tree for the bit allocation but the pruning algorithm do not require to send such information. The pruned tree encodes each input vector to the bottom node of the pruned tree-structured codebook.

The performance of the pruned tree and bit allocation algorithms are compared. At the given bit rate (0.8125 bpp), the PSNR of using the bit allocation algorithm has 0.3 dB advantage over the PSNR of the pruned tree algorithm for mean-removal TSVQ. An unbalanced tree can be obtained by pruning the balanced tree using a distortion criterion. By treating the unbalanced tree as an equavalent balanced (renumbering the bottom nodes), the bit allocation algorithm is then appied to the equavalent balanced tree. For the bit allocation algorithm, the PSNR for the equavalent balanced tree has 0.57 dB better than the PSNR of the balanced tree in the given bit rate.

Rapid Prototyping of a JPEG Image Compression System using Synthesis Tools*

Chih-Tung Chen, Pravil Gupta, J.C. DeSouza-Batista†, Alice Parker
Dept. of EE - Systems, Univ. of Southern California
Los Angeles, CA 90089-2562, USA

Abstract

In this work we show how synthesis tools can help a designer in rapidly prototyping a real-time system using multiple application-specific integrated circuits while meeting cost and performance constraints. A JPEG still-image compression system was designed using the Unified System Construction (USC) tool set to demonstrate the feasibility of automatic synthesis.

The USC project involves the production of system-level tools for synthesizing multi-chip, heterogeneous application-specific systems. Once a style is selected by the user for the system and a functional specification is produced in VHDL, specialized tools are invoked to complete the design process. Ultimately, any custom VLSI chips which must be synthesized are then processed by the ADAM high-level synthesis system (a subset of USC tools), which produces a cell netlist. From this netlist, a chip layout is produced using Cascade Design Automation's ChipCrafter (now Epoch) Silicon Compiler.

For the synthesis of the JPEG system, the following steps were taken. First, we determined cost and performance parameters of the system's components. The 2D-DCT was decomposed into repeated row-column 1D-DCTs, and a 2D-DCT architecture consisting of two 1D-DCT macros and 8×8 frame buffer was selected. Five datapath architectures of the 1D-DCT macro with varying cost and performance were synthesized from the VHDL description. SMASH (Synthesis of Memory-intensive Application Specific Hardware) was used for datapath scheduling and MABAL (Module And Bus ALlocation) for generating the corresponding register-transfer level netlists. The parameters for quantizer were estimated and for Huffman codec those of an existing implementation were used. Next, ProPart, a process-level chip partitioner, was used to find a cost-effective 3-chip partition for the system. Finally, we generated the layouts of the 1D-DCT macro and 2D-DCT chip. The chip parameters were comparable to those in the literature. We also performed an additional study of the 2D-DCT architecture using SOS (Synthesis Of Systems), a heterogeneous multiprocessor synthesis tool, which produced five alternatives with varying cost and performance.

The entire design exercise took less than a week of time for three graduate students familiar with all the tools, and able to write VHDL descriptions rapidly. The speed with which we were able to generate layouts and the number of tradeoffs which could be examined during that time clearly indicate the value of automatic tools for many application-specific system designs.

*This work was supported by the Advanced Research Projects Agency and monitored by the Federal Bureau of Investigation under Contract No. JFBI90092.

†Supported by Conselho Nacional de Desenvolvimento Cientifico e Tecnologico - CNPQ/Brazil.

A recursive algorithm for image compression with finite automata *

Karel Culik II
Department of Computer Science
University of South Carolina, Columbia, S.C. 29208
Jarkko Kari
Academy of Finland

A Weighted Finite Automaton (WFA) with a 4-letter input alphabet computes a function of two variables on the unit square $[0,1] \times [0,1]$. We interpret it as a grayness function; therefore, a WFA defines a grayscale image. Recently we developed an efficient recursive inference algorithm that, given a grayscale image, constructs a small WFA that generates a good approximation of the image. Our new implementation also includes a sophisticated quantization of the constructed WFA.

We can use our algorithm alone or after a discrete wavelet transformation. In the latter case, instead of applying the inference algorithm directly to the original image, we first execute a discrete wavelet transformation on the original image (a lossless transformation), and then arrange the computed wavelet coefficients in the Mallat form. Finally, we apply our compression algorithm to the Mallat form viewed as an image. Decoding is, of course, done in the opposite order: first we decode the WFA, and then we compute the inverse discrete wavelet transformation. Because the wavelets we use are orthogonal, the L2-error done on the Mallat form by the lossy WFA encoding is equal to the encoding error of the original image.

This wavelet-WFA combined encoding method can be viewed as a sophisticated quantization of wavelet coefficients. Instead of storing approximate values of a subset of the coefficients, we approximately encode all of them by a WFA.

We will demonstrate a number of examples of varied grayscale images and compare the results obtained by WFA alone, the combination of Daubechies W_6 wavelets and WFA, and the biorthogonal closed wavelets. These examples will indicate that our method seems to be the best high-compression method available as far as the quality of the regenerated images is concerned. It is also relatively simple and time efficient; however, it is slower than wavelet-based compression or JPEG.

Compared to wavelet based compression, our compression method is even more advantageous for color images. In WFA-based compression of color images, we use a modified algorithm that creates one WFA for all three components and takes advantage of their similarity, if any.

*Research was supported by the National Science Foundation under Grant No. CCR-9202396

1068-0314/94 $3.00 © 1994 IEEE

A REGION-BASED APPROACH TO IMAGE CODING

Stefano Fioravanti
Dept. of Biophysical and Electronic Engineering, University of Genoa
Via All'Opera Pia 11A, I-16145 Genova, Italy
phone: + 39 10 3532 947, fax: + 39 10 353 2134, e-mail: steve@dibe.unige.it

ABSTRACT

The paper presents an adaptive scheme for image-data compression. In short, it is a region-based approach that integrates, in a suitable way, two approaches to image coding which are characterized by different philosophies, i.e., vector quantization (VQ) and polynomial approximation (PA).

The scheme is adaptive from the point of view of the human observer: the perceptually most significant areas are those near edges or details. In smoothed areas, PA can be used with notable results, but there another technique (i.e., VQ) must be employed to ensure high fidelity. The two techniques exhibit a perfect complementarity in both advantages and drawbacks. PA is not efficient in compressing high-frequency areas, but yields the best results when applied to highly correlated data. VQ is unable to reach high-compression ratios because of its low adaptability, but is quite suitable for compressing uncorrelated data.

The means to achieve the integration of the two techniques is a control image containing information about edge and texture locations.

In the work, other topics are addressed, which are closely related to the proposed hybrid scheme, i.e., edge encoding and restoration. VQ block prediction is also utilized to further reduce the residual redundancy between code blocks.

The exploitation of the best features of both approaches results in high compression factors, and in perceivable good quality. In particular, bit rates range from 0.15 bpp to 0.07 bpp.

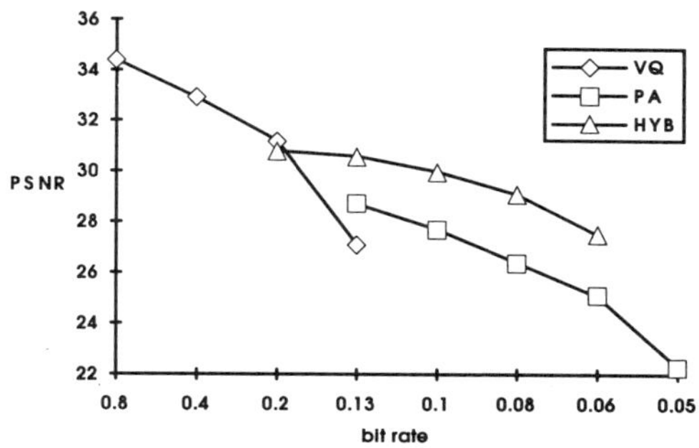

Comparison between VQ, PA, and hybrid approaches.

Main applications of this compression scheme are in the areas of very-low bitrate image transmission and image archiving.

A Segmentation Based Prediction Algorithm

Saif S. Zahir, Shih-Wen Lee, and Morton Kanefsky

Dept. of Electrical Engineering, Univ. of Pittsburgh

A forward-adaptive prediction algorithm for the encoding of images is presented which assumes that the image can be segmented (either intensity or texture based) into homogeneous regions (of any size); the remaining regions are presumed to be nonstationary. A binary *guide* which identifies these regions is generated and encoded using efficient facsimile techniques. For homogeneous regions that exceed some minimum size, statistical measurements (means, covariances) are also encoded. Both the encoder and decoder determine the optimal predictor for pixels inside a homogeneous region (R_{hi}), using a causal region of support $\{R_m \cap R_{hi}\}$, where R_m is an acceptable maximum region of support. Thus for pixels near the boundary of a homogeneous region, both the region of support and hence the prediction coefficients are being optimally adapted. For pixels in nonstationary regions (as well as in very small homogeneous regions), local mean estimators are used for prediction.

This guided prediction algorithm preserves object boundaries and textures in homogeneous regions extremely well. If one can argue that precision in nonstationary regions is often unnecessary, then a near information preserving algorithm is achieved. The degree of compression is comparable to standard prediction techniques since the binary guide is highly compressible. The adapting of the region of support does increase the computation time somewhat. Compression bounds for information preserving coding (which employ coding tables) are determined for our test image. For near information preservation (i.e. everywhere but in the nonstationary regions), these bounds are significantly lower.

1068-0314/94 $3.00 © 1994 IEEE

SET QUANTIZER

Shaolin Bi, Khalid Sayood
Dept. of Electrical Engineering
University of Nebraska-Lincoln
Lincoln, Nebraska 68588-0511
Tel. (402)472-6688, FAX (402)472-4732
ksayood@eecomm.unl.edu

In this paper a new quantizer called the *set quantizer* (SQ) is introduced. In quantization, the input space is partitioned into quantization regions. A single output point in a quantization region is used to represent all of the inputs falling into that region. The SQ presented in this paper uses a collection, or a *set* (hence the name), of output points to represent the input points in a quantization region. This is done with little or no increase in the rate over a scalar quantizer with the same number of quantization *regions*. By using a set of output points in a quantization region and properly choosing the quantizer output for a given input from the set, the average quantization error is reduced and the performance of the quantizer is improved.

The selection of the output point in a given set is the key to the success of the SQ. Two schemes are proposed for this purpose: the first borrows ideas from the *hidden Markov model*, and the second is based on a *random sequence coding* approach.

The proposed quantizer was implemented and tested on Markov sources, memoryless sources and image data. Simulation results show that the SQ quantization algorithm based on the hidden Markov model performs better than minimum mean square error scalar quantizers when there is redundancy in the source data. However, the SQ algorithm based on the random sequence coding approach compares favorably with most existing quantizers for memoryless sources. We also present an application to image compression.

Shell Coding of 3D Image Sets

Martin J. Turner, mjt@uk.ac.cam.cl
University of Cambridge Computer Laboratory, England.

Autostereoscopic Displays are being developed which create and display a three dimensional image without the need for special glasses or headsets. They work by displaying multiple images each viewable over a very narrow field of view. Many viewers can simultaneously see different images in each eye giving them true stereo vision. This also has the advantage of being able to allow observers to look around objects giving motion parallax.

Increasing the number of images per view subsequently increases the bandwidth required. Current displays have been constructed with up to sixteen different horizontally displaced views and larger ones are being designed. Commercially available framestores are at present just fast enough to display the image sets but transmission times over the network has proven to be a bottleneck.

The concept of extending a *Contour Coding* scheme, which codes standard two dimensional images, into the third dimension has been undertaken. The *3D Image Set* is split up into a collection of *Shells* which are grouped into a hierarchical data structure called a *Shell Tree*. The subsequent use of a *Shell Coder* gives a potential direct compression ratio and therefore a transmission rate speed-up.

To aid stereo disparity in the human visual system the important features to retain in stereo sets are subtly different from standard two dimensional images. Edge information and highlights have been shown to be of paramount importance for the human visual system to accurately perceive depth. This means that many common lossy compression techniques which blur or distort edges have unfortunate side effects.

A level of noticeability according to the human visual system can be assigned to each *shell* according to its shape, intensity and surroundings. Repeatedly merging shells whose combined noticeability is sufficiently close, according to some threshold value, to the individual shells results in a simplified *shell tree*. Subsequent *shell coding* results in improved compression ratios which are comparable to using Quantised Discrete Cosine Transformation methods whilst retaining as many of the stereo cues as possible.

References

[Turner 1992] Martin J. Turner. *Entropy Reduction via Simplified Image Contourization* Space and Earth Science Data Compression Workshop, pages 27–43. NASA Conference Publication 3183, March 1992.

[Lang 1992] Stewart R. Lang et al. *A 2nd Generation Autostereoscopic 3-D display* Seventh Workshop on Graphics Hardware, pages 53–63. Eurographics Technical Report Series EG92 HW, September 1992.

Some Fast Search & Partial Search VQ Encoding Algorithms

Anamitra Makur, K V Hari Narayanan
Dept. of ECE, Indian Institute of Science, Bangalore, India

We propose two fast search algorithms for MMSE vector quantizer, based on parameter-based codebook ordering followed by two-phase search, and on largest hypersphere in a cell. Instead of searching through a K-dimensional codebook, C, initial phase of encoding search is done through a projection of the codebook on fewer dimensions, $\hat{C}$. Computing $\hat{X}$, projection of X, is equivalent to finding some parameters for X. The second phase search begins from the first phase match, and proceeds through C, ordered using these parameters (projections). We tried various parameters with $\hat{C}$ having a single dimension as well as two dimensions. Further, if d is the distance between X and the nearest codeword found so far, then any other codeword nearer to X should fall within the hypersphere of radius d around X. The projection of this hypersphere on the parameter line is its diameter (possibly scaled), $2d'$. Therefore any codeword whose projection is outside the projection of this hypersphere need not be considered. This is Alg-I. Secondly, define r_i as the minimum distance of any other codeword from a codeword Y_i. Then any input vector X falling within a hypersphere of radius $r_i/2$ around Y_i is mapped to Y_i. This scheme, Alg-II, may be applied along with any other algorithm. We also propose the parameter-based partial search, which reduces the worst case search time and the rate while slightly increasing distortion. Once a match has been found in initial phase, a region $\hat{B}$ ($\hat{B} \subset \hat{C}$) around it is chosen to be the likely domain of the best match. The region B ($B \subset C$), which is projected as $\hat{B}$, is then searched in the second phase to find the best match.

Assuming multiplication to be α times costlier than addition/comparison, Alg-I with mean as the parameter outperform the existing algorithms (such as Probability Ordering Partial Distance Search of Paliwal & Ramasubramanian and Shrinking Hypercube of Soleymani & Morgera) for any $\alpha<161$. For some data, Alg-II performs best when $\alpha<3.8$. Partial search results show almost no performance degradation while substantially reducing the encoding computation. All our results consider conditional branch statements as comparisons.

Spatial Multi-resolution Algorithm for Image Data Compression

Wei Kang Tsai and Raymond Lim
Department of Electrical and Computer Engineering
University of California
Irvine, CA 92717
wtsai@ece.uci.edu, rlim@ece.uci.edu

Abstract

In this paper, a spatial multi-resolution algorithm for image data compression is proposed. Similar to the common multi-resolution techniques, the algorithm decomposes the image into square sub-images of different resolutions according to the sampled variance. These sub-images are then subsampled at different rates: high variance blocks are subsampled at high rates. The subsampled image will be interpolated into an approximate image which is then subtracted from the original image to get a residual image. The residual image is then vector quantized using a universal codebook. To boost the compression gain, the image is first scalar quantized before the subsampling. Initial results show that the above approach produces compression quality compatible with the quality of the MIT EPIC program.

At a coarse resolution level, the image is similar to a slow-varying texture, and the bulk of the texture can be captured with a few parameters. At the next finer (higher) resolution level, the image has a little more detail. The coarse resolution part of the image can be subtracted from the original image to get a new image. In this new (second) image, the coarse resolution part contains actually some details not captured in the coarse part of the original (first) image. Now the coarse part of the second image can be subtracted from the second image to get a third image. This process can be repeated until most of the interesting details have been extracted. At each stage, only a few parameters are needed to encode the features. The total number of stages (or levels of resolution) is often quite small, thus producing a high compression ratio image.

There are several advantages. First, the coded data have grey-level interpretations, making content-based image database query easy. Second, multi-resolution decomposition is still the corner-stone of this approach and all the advantages of multi-resolution decomposition still apply. Third, from the experience of control system engineering, researchers have discovered that there is little difference between time domain and frequency domain techniques. In fact, there is a time-domain technique corresponding to every frequency domain technique. By working directly in the spatial domain, one can easily incorporate psycho-visual techniques in the compression algorithm. In the transform domain, since the data have been transformed, it is more difficult to translate psycho-visual effects into the transformed domain counterparts. We have not, though, in this paper exploited the benefit of incorporating the psycho-visual interactions in the spatial domain.

1068-0314/94 $3.00 © 1994 IEEE

Study of Image Compression through Wavelet Decomposition and Approximate String Matching

T.L. Yu, CS, CSUSB, CA 92407, USA. tyu@wiley.csusb.edu

K.W. Yu, CUHK, Hong Kong. kwyu@phys.phy.cuhk.hk

Recently, people began to adopt string matching algorithms to lossy image compression and achieve good results; in previous works, raw image data are directly compressed by approximate string-matching algorithms. It is reasonable to expect that we may achieve better results if we first perform a wavelet-transform on the raw data and then apply the string-matching algorithms to compress the transformed data as the transformation separates the high-frequency components from the low-frequency ones and thus clusters the data into blocks which are more easily matched by each other. In this paper, we discuss our study of image compression based on this technique.

In our work, we first decompose an image by the tensor product of the Box function and Haar wavelet; the main reason of choosing this transformation is its simplicity. The transformed values are compressed by an approximate string matching algorithm based on the work of Sadeh[1] who presents two algorithms and proves that their compression rate converges to the theoretical bound of distortion rate R(D) for a large class of processes as the database size and string tend to infinity. Starting from Scheme 2 of Sadeh's algorithms[1], we find an empirical algorithm that compresses the wavelet coefficients best. The algorithm is implemented by the techniques used by Fiala and Greene[2] in which a McCreight suffix tree is constructed to represent the string and a finite size buffer is used to store the portion of the string that is currently processed.

We performed experiments using some popular PC gray scale images such as Lisa, Clown, Cheetah, Mouse and Rose and compare the results with those obtained using the JPEG standard which employs Discrete Fourier Transform (DCT) and entropy coding to compress images. The performances are compared in terms of the peak signal to noise ratios (PSRN). We find that our method achieves performance comparable to (but not better than) that of the JPEG standard; on the other hand, the results are better than that of compressing the raw image directly by the approximate string matching algorithm. However, the performance of our method is not as good as we first expected. We believe that there is still a lot of room for improvement of this technique.

References :

[1] Sadeh, "On Approximate String Matching", IEEE DCC93 Proc. p.148, Snowbird, Utah, March, 1993.

[2] E.R. Fiala and D.H. Greene, "Data Compression with Finite Windows", CACM, 32 (4), p.490, 1989.

This work is supported by Univ. Direct Grant for Research, Project # 220-600-410

Sub-Band Coding of Video using 2-D Adaptive Deltamodulation for Packet Video Applications

K.Hong, D.R.Vaman, C.V.Chakravarthy
EE/CS Department, Stevens Institute of Technology
Hoboken, N.J. 07030

In this paper we describe the performance of a 4 Band Sub-band encoder for video using a 2 - D Adaptive Deltamodulation (ADM) encoder as the main digitizer. The picture signal is split into four Sub-bands using conventional separable 2 -D filters. The four bands obtained are LL, LH, HL and the HH. The first three Sub-bands contain significant correlation in one or both spatial directions and so we use an ADM (one bit /pixel) for encoding these signals after decimation by a factor of 2, while the HH band with little or no correlation in either direction is encoded using a conventional PCM encoder with 2 bits/pixel. Hence the average # of bits/pixel is 1.25. Further reduction of up to 0.5 bits/pixel is possible with straight forward data compression methods. One of our motivations for choosing the ADM as opposed to other techniques which offer better data compression is the ability of the ADM to function better in the presence of channel errors.

The predictor used for the ADM is a 2- D predictor that uses correlation data in the hirizontal, vertical and the two diagonal directions. Correlation data has been measured for a number of standard pictures like LENA, KEIL etc and averaged for the use in the encoder. With pictures having predominantly low frequency content, the reproduced picture quality is excellent. However with a picture having a large amount of high frequency content the quality is not so good. We have compared the quality of the picture with those reproduced using other techniques like Adaptive Block Truncation Coding . In most cases the ADM quality is found to be better.

Our ultimate aim is to use the encoder to transmit data over a lossy high speed network such as an ATM network. To transmit data over an ATM network for example, we formed cells of 53 bytes including data and overheads as recommended for an ATM cell. If the network discards cells occassionally due to congestion or if there are errors in a cell the video quality may suffer. While many techniques exist for masking errors, we opted to use error correction. As long as we know that a cell is corrupted we may as well discard it and use error the correction technique we have implemented. The technique used is a simple extension of the Vertical/Horizontal parity error correction method. This allows us to recover exactly any packet(s) that may be missing, as long as we are willing to accept the modest increase in the data due to parity overheads (about 5 % maximum depending upon the error correction capability). We have been able to recover data with loss rates of up to 1 in 50 cells.

 1068-0314/94 $3.00

Subband Coding of Images Using Finite-State Vector Quantization by Exploiting Inter-band and Intra-band Correlations *

Ruey-Feng Chang and Yu-Len Huang
Department of Computer Science and Informaion Engineering
National Chung Cheng University
Chiayi, Taiwan 62107, R.O.C.

Abstract

Subband coding has been shown to be an effective method for coding images at low bit rates. The basic idea of subband coding is to split up the frequency band of the signal and then to encode each band separately. Reconstruction is performed by decoding and merging the interpolated subband images.

In this paper, a frequency band decomposition of the image is carried out by means of 2-D separable quadrature mirror filters (QMF's), which split the image spectrum into seven subbands (LL_1, LH_1, HL_1, HH_1, LH_0, HL_0, and HH_0 bands). Adaptive vector quantization (AVQ) and finite-state vector quantization (FSVQ) methods are employed in coding the subband images by exploiting inter-band and intra-band correlaions. The difference between the ordinary FSVQ scheme and our new FSVQ scheme is that our FSVQ scheme exploits the information of high frequency signals to select the states of low frequency signals. We combine three kinds of vector quantization (VQ) encoders in our seven-band SBC system to encode the subbands. Firstly, the LH_1-band and the HL_1-band are encoded by the intra-band VQ scheme. The other subbands will be encoded by exploiting the information of the two encoded LH_1 and HL_1 subbands. Then, the AVQ scheme is used to encode the higher bands (HH_1, LH_0, HL_0, and HH_0 bands) in order to reduce the bit rate. In the AVQ scheme, we exploit inter-band correlations to decide whether the block is encoded or not. Finally, a new FSVQ scheme is used to encode the LL_1-band to reduce the bit rate and to improve the image quality. Note that our scheme utilizes the inter-band correlations between subbands, thus the HL_1-band and LH_1-band must be encoded before encoding the other subbands.

Comparisons are made between our scheme and other coding techniques. The new scheme yields a good peak signal-to-noise ratio (PSNR) performance in the region between 0.28 and 0.32 bit per pixel, both for images inside and outside a training set of five 512×512 mono-chrome images. In the experiments, the improvement of our scheme over the ordinary VQ is up to 3.12 dB at nearly the same bit rate for the image Lena. Moreover, our scheme can improve the encoded image quality of the edges and high-frequency areas. The PSNR of the encoded image Lena using the proposed scheme is 31.63 dB at 0.29 bit per pixel.

---

* This work was supported by the Nation Science Council, Taiwan, Republic of China, under grant NSC82-0113-E-194-034-T.

SUBBAND CODING USING OVERCOMPLETE DECOMPOSITIONS WITH APPLICATIONS TO PLANETARY IMAGES*

Sergio D. Cabrera, Sing-Wai Wu, and Gerardo Gonzalez
Electrical Engineering Department / University of Texas at El Paso
El Paso, TX 79968-0523 USA
Email: cabrera@ee.ep.utexas.edu

In this paper we describe and illustrate image Subband Coding (SBC) with redundancy in the form of (arbitrary) *overcomplete* subband decompositions. Such decompositions, which are equivalent to discrete-time *wavelet* transforms, are effected here in a row/column separable manner using N-channel multirate filterbanks, with a decimation/interpolation rate of M, where M<N [1]. Arbitrary decompositions lead to finite reconstruction error in the absence of quantization. However, those that are overcomplete give us the ability to recover lost data due to the redundancy that is guaranteed to be present in the decimated subband data. Defining more than one subband within an important frequency band, without proportionally higher decimation, is an example of a useful overcomplete decomposition.

We develop and use a *constrained-length* optimal Finite Impulse Response (FIR) synthesis filter design procedure to reconstruct the input signal after decomposition with an arbitrary set of stable analysis filters. Therefore, we do not restrict our attention to Perfect Reconstruction (PR) *Analysis/Synthesis* (A/S) systems, but allow instead, some degree of transform inversion error. First, we derive a procedure to recover a *block* of a few samples of the A/S system input signal from a limited amount of subband data, using the theory of linear inversion with *regularization* [2]. Block-by-block use of this estimator can be implemented by interpolation followed by (synthesis) filtering and the polyphase components of the desired FIR filters can be readily identified.

An objective measure of *transform error* for the overall A/S system is defined as the average energy of the M impulse response differences from their ideal PR outputs. Also, a *quantization error* sensitivity measure is defined as the average output quantization noise variance for the whole A/S system when additive, uncorrelated, white noise errors appear on the subbands. The regularization procedure induces a tradeoff whereby, reduced quantization error can only be obtained at the expense of higher transform error.

We illustrate the use of these overcomplete analysis/synthesis systems in image SBC. The motivating application considered is the compression of *planetary images* with significant redundancy in the decomposition to allow for recovery of lost data. Using a standard *bit-allocation* scheme in the quantization of the subbands, we obtain rate-distortion curves for test images and compare the results with those obtained with *maximally-decimated* systems (N=M) that use the same analysis filters.

[1] S-W Wu and S. D. Cabrera, "**FIR Synthesis Filter Banks for Incomplete and Overcomplete Single-Pole Subband Decompositions**," Proc. Conference on Information Sciences and Systems, The Johns Hopkins Univ., pp. 779-784, March 1993.
[2] M Bertero, C DeMol and E. R. Pike, "**Linear Inverse Problems with Discrete Data II: Stability and Regularisation**," Inverse Problems, Vol. 4 (88), pp. 573-594.

---

*This work was supported by NASA Grant NAG 3-1380.

Subband Image Coding Using Pruned Multi-Stage Tree-Structured Vector Quantization

Chun-Chia Huang, Chien-Min Huang, and Richard W. Harris
Department of Electrical Engineering
Utah State University
Logan, Utah 84321

Subband coding of images combined with optimal bit allocation algorithm which is achieved by using pruned multi-stage tree-structured vector quantization (PM-STSVQ) algorithm technology is investigated. This PMSTSVQ algorithm is derived from the work of pruning tree search VQ algorithm (G-BFOS) which is applied to tree-structured vector quantization by Chou et al. and combined with the idea of multi-stage VQ algorithm coding. G-BFOS algorithm is an extension of the algorithm of Breiman et al. for optimal pruning in tree-structured classification and regression to coding. Those fullband and subband multi-stage tree-structured codebooks created for testing are obtained from LBG algorithm. After the input vector is encoded to the bottom level of the codebook, pruning back the subband codebooks of baseband and non-basebands that follows the distortion-rate (D-R) functional which is the convex hull of the codebooks to the desired bit rate will achieve optimal bits allocation, i.e., each input vector is assigned to a different level of the multi-stage tree-structured codebook according to the assigned bit rate.

The technologies of bit allocation algorithm and pruning algorithm in multi-stage tree-structured vector quantization of subband coding are described and simulations evaluate their performance by averaging seven MRI test images in test bit rate from 0.5 to 4 bits per pixel (bpp). Subband PMSTSVQ algorithm coding results are also compared to ad hoc standard DCT-based JPEG algorithm coding.

From the coding results, the subband coding using PMSTSVQ algorithm applied to MRI medical images yields the best performance with the block size combination of baseband and non-basebands codebooks in 22 x 22 when rate is greater than 2 bpp, in 44 x 88 when rate is less than 2 bpp. Subband PMSTSVQ algorithm coding outperformed fullband PMSTSVQ algorithm coding and ranging from 4.91 dB in 4 bpp, 1.92 dB in 0.75 bpp and 2.03 dB in 0.5 bpp in the peak signal-to-noise ratio (PSNR) measure. The performance of subband PMSTSVQ algorithm coding is also superior to JPEG algorithm coding in all test bit rate and ranging from 6.8 dB in 4 bpp, 1.34 dB in 0.75 bpp and 0.79 dB in 0.5 bpp.

A Taxonomy for Lossless Image Compression

Abstract

Nasir D. Memon
Dept. of Computer Science
Arkansas State University

Khalid Sayood
Dept. of Electrical Eng.
University of Nebraska-Lincoln

Researchers have identified two basic components in a lossless image compression technique, *decorrelation* and *coding*. We give a classification scheme for both decorrelation and coding. The two classifications put together give us a framework for discussing, comparing and evaluating lossless image compression schemes. The classifications also enable us to clearly identify areas where not enough work has been done, thus identifying avenues for future research.

We identify three component functions in an image decorrelation scheme, which are induced by a given image. These are: 1) An *Ordering* function, 2) A *Neighborhood* function and 3) A *Replacement* function. These functions can be *static, backward adaptive* or *forward adaptive* Static functions are fixed for all images. Backward adaptive functions are dependent only on the already decorrelated pixels and can be deduced from the data. Forward adaptive functions depend on the entire image under consideration and need to be explicitly transmitted.

The above definitions provide us with a classification scheme for image decorrelation techniques. A decorrelation technique is classified as one of the types $(X/Y/Z)$ where $X, Y, Z \in \{S, A\}$. The symbol S stands for static and A for adaptive. So for example an $(S/A/A)$ scheme has a static ordering function, an adaptive neighborhood function and an adaptive replacement function. We describe some known decorrelation methods under each of the categories identified by our classification scheme. In some cases it will turn out that no scheme is known. This identifies avenues for further research.

We also give a simple classification of residual image encoding techniques, similar to the one for decorrelation schemes. A residual image encoding scheme is said to be of type S/S if it uses a single static model for encoding all images. If this model is adaptive then the scheme is said to be of type S/A. Schemes that use multiple models are classified as MX/Y where X could be either S or A indicating a static or adaptive family of distributions and Y could be F or B to indicate a forward adaptive or backward adaptive activity function respectively. Unlike the decorrelation case, there has been some work in all categories defined by our classification of coding schemes. However, the total activity in the coding area is significantly less than in the decorrelation area. Furthermore except for the MA/B case most areas have not received much attention.

While this is not exhaustive survey, it does point out a few interesting things. One is the relatively small amount of work in error modeling. Another is the paucity of adaptive ordering functions. Finally, the classification reinforces the view that the development of decorrelation techniques is far from being a mature area.

1068-0314/94 $3.00 © 1994 IEEE

Time Domain Evaluation of Compression Algorithms

Mark W. Maier
Assistant Professor
Electrical and Computer Engineering
University of Alabama in Huntsville
Huntsville, AL 35899

Mark S. Moellenhoff
Dynetics, Inc.
Huntsville, AL 35806

Abstract

The two major applications for lossless data compression are file compression and throughput improvement on low speed communication links. For file compression the obvious figures of merit for an algorithm are the compression achieved and the computational resource requirements. For communication applications we are trying to improve application throughput, which depends on the interaction of the communication protocol and the compression algorithm. This interaction is not fully determined by the compression ratio and the computational resource requirements. To understand this relationship we have undertaken a series of experiments to determine the time-domain characteristics of various compression methods. Our experiments use simulated multi-source data of interleaved packets drawn from the compression corpus. Our initial experiments have looked at instantaneous communication rates and buffer backlogs in interfaces between synchronous communication channels. These experiments are being extended to direct simulation of protocol and compression interaction. Some initial conclusions are:

1. Finite window algorithms, like LZSS, exhibit relatively smooth backlog behavior but are very stochastic in their instantaneous rates.
2. Dictionary algorithms with "bump-flush" dictionary management have intermittent large backlogs but smoother instantaneous rate performance. The V.42bis compression algorithm smoothes backlog behavior.
3. The proposed PPP public domain compression standard, predictor type 1, has smooth behavior, but relatively poor overall compression.

Acknowledgment: Dr. Maier's work has been supported by Adtran, Inc.

USING LINEAR FRACTAL INTERPOLATION FUNCTIONS TO COMPRESS VIDEO IMAGES[1]

Maaruf Ali, AMIEE, Student IEEE & Dr. Trevor G Clarkson, MIEE, SMIEEE

Communications Research Group
Department of Electronic & Electrical Engineering
King's College London, Univ. of London
Strand, London WC2R 2LS, U.K.

Phone: +44-71-836-5454 Ext. 3583 Fax: +44-71-836-4781
Email: m.ali@bay.cc.kcl.ac.uk [Internet]

This paper describes the novel application of using linear fractal interpolation functions to model video signals represented as single-valued discrete-time sequences to compress video images. In linear fractal interpolation, a set of interpolation points is interpolated with a continuous, single valued function that passes through the given interpolation points. The interpolation function is constructed using a set of affine maps. These affine maps form the Iterated Function System (IFS) codes. The IFS codes obtained model the video signal. Compression is achieved since the IFS codes are a compact representation of the function. A summary of the inverse algorithm to determine the IFS parameters is given. Decompression is by using the random iteration algorithm applied to the IFS codes.

The viability of using fractal interpolation functions to model video signals is shown by modelling a single line from various test images. Compression of a whole static image frame is described. This is obtained by representing the whole frame as one single video line. If more than one line is represented as a video line waveform, then the self-similarity between adjacent lines may be exploited fully by the fractal interpolation functions. Thus if one line does not show self-similarity, then two or more lines will and this will be easier to represent succinctly using fractal interpolation functions.

Extension of this work to compress motion video is described. By representing whole frames as one single video line waveforms, the changes in the waveform from one frame to the next may be coded using fractal interpolation functions or the error difference sent if the changes are within some tolerance limit. If there is a discontinuity (due to a scene change, for example), then the video line waveform for the new frame must be coded fully and sent as a new fractal interpolation code.

Finally various image data are analysed by calculating and plotting the fractal dimensions of each line in the frame against the line for that image.

The biggest advantage with fractal coding is the resolution independence of the code, thus images may be decoded to higher resolutions and be suitable for high definition television use. Enlarged fractal images do not generate pixellation as common with other codes such as discrete cosine based codes.

---

[1] Research in this area is funded by The British Council under the British-German Academic Research Collaboration Programme, Project 522, *Application orientated fractal image compression for video data transmission with limited bandwidth.*

1068-0314/94 $3.00 © 1994 IEEE

Using Spatial Locality for Trace Compression

B. Gopinath
Electrical Engg Dept., Rutgers University,
gopinath@cs.rutgers.edu

Vidyadhar Phalke
Computer Science Dept., Rutgers Univ.,
phalke@paul.rutgers.edu

Trace driven simulations are used extensively for memory performance analysis. These require long traces — a million references long traces are quite common, resulting in huge space requirements. We present a trace compaction technique, *Page-Mache*, based on *paging*, that produces compression ratios up to 5.2%, an improvement of more than a factor of 4 over compression ratios obtained with the standard UNIX *compress*.

The traces have a general format of (l_1,a_1), (l_2,a_2), (l_3,a_3), ..., a sequence of label, address pairs, the *i*th pair representing the *i*th access from the start of the trace. The label l_i is used to denote whether the reference was a read, write, instruction fetch or some other type of access, depending on the trace, and a_i is the virtual address of the word referred to. There are three phases in our compaction. In the first phase, a page size P (a power of 2) is fixed, and we split the given trace into two levels — a page level and an offset level. This is done by viewing the trace $L = (l_1,a_1), (l_2,a_2), (l_3,a_3), \ldots$ as a sequence of page references and offset references within each of the pages. The page level trace is created by simply dividing each a_i by P, and creating a trace $\Pi = (l_1, a_1/P)$, $(l_2, a_2/P)$, ... The offset level trace is created for each of the pages referred to in Π. If the *i*th reference is to page m, the pair $(l_i, a_i \bmod P)$ is added to page m's offset trace. So if M pages are referred to in the entire trace Π, we get a set of $M+1$ traces. The second and third phases comprise a method of *differencing* followed by UNIX *compress*, which is identical to the *mache* method of Samples (SIGMETRICS 1989). We *mache* the $M+1$ traces generated in the first step above and get $M+1$ compressed streams.

We experimented both with UNIX *compress* and *gzip* and found that our technique improved on the UNIX technique and *mache* for all our traces. The following table shows the compression ratios in % both with *compress* and with *gzip* as backend.

Trace Name	UNIX		Mache		Page-Mache	
	compress	*gzip*	*compress*	*gzip*	*compress*	*gzip*
GNU C Compiler	34%	17.9%	10.7%	5%	9.2%	3.3%
SPICE circuit simulator	21%	10%	6.2%	2%	5.2%	1.3%
Kenbus1 SPEC benchmark	36%	22.8%	16%	8.6%	6.8%	3.3%
DEC Interconnect Verify	32%	18.5%	16.1%	9%	14.6%	6.9%
LISP Boyer Theorem Prover	22%	12.9%	11.1%	6.5%	7.1%	2.4%

Our method (*page-mache*) has three distinct advantages over *mache*. First, it improves compression ratio over *mache* up to a factor of about 2.5. Improvements were observed for all the traces we had. Second, we can easily generate a single page's reference stream without decompressing the rest (sort of a random access). Finally, we observed that *mache* performed very poorly in the absence of the label fields, whereas *page-mache* showed an improvement.

The Visibility of DCT Quantization Noise: Spatial Frequency Summation

H. A. Peterson**, A. J. Ahumada, Jr.*, and A. B. Watson*
IBM Watson Research Center** and NASA Ames Research Center*

In DCT-based compression [1,2] the image is divided into blocks of pixels, the DCT is applied to each block, and the resulting coefficients are quantized and encoded to form the compressed version of the image. Quantization induces distortion in the decompressed image. For small quantizer step size, q, quantization of a particular coefficient in all the blocks of an image induces an error image which can be modeled by replications of the corresponding DCT basis function, with independent random amplitudes uniformly distributed over $[-q/2,\ q/2]$. Quantization of multiple coefficients induces an error image that is the sum of the error images due to quantization of the individual coefficients. Visibility of this error depends on summation of individual errors across blocks,[3] and across DCT frequencies. In this paper we report psychophysical measurements of summation across DCT frequencies, and compare the results to area summation results.[3] These measurements provide useful information for optimal DCT quantization.

All experiments were performed using the same equipment and viewing conditions as in Peterson *et al.* [3] The basis functions are indexed by frequency numbers $(u,\ v)$. Individual basis function error images were generated for $(u,\ v)$ values (0,1), (0,3), (0,5), and (0,7) (These four are the transform components of a vertical edge centered in a block.). The $(u,\ v)$th basis function error image was constructed as a 6×6 array of replications of the $(u,\ v)$th basis function, with each replication assigned a random amplitude uniformly distributed on $[-q_{u,v},\ q_{u,v}]$. The value for $q_{u,v}$ is the threshold for basis function $(u,\ v)$, measured as described in Peterson *et al.* [3]. A full test stimulus was generated by pixel-wise summing the four individual basis function error images, and adding the result to a flat gray background.

In each trial the test stimulus (less the background) was multiplied by a factor A to produce an attenuated or amplified version. The factor A was varied from trial to trial order to establish a visibility threshold. We used a forced-choice procedure with two temporal intervals and feedback. The stimulus duration was 31 frames (approximately 517 milliseconds), the amplitude of the stimulus had a Gaussian shaped envelope in time, and in each test session, 64 trials were performed.

We found a decrease in threshold of approximately 5 dB due to summation of quantization error over spatial frequency. This result lies between that predicted by probability summation and that predicted by linear summation (3 dB < 5 dB < 12 dB).

1. W. B. Pennebaker, J. L. Mitchell, *JPEG Still Image Data Compression Standard*, van Nostrand Reinhold, New York, 1993.
2. D. LeGall, "MPEG: A video compression standard for multimedia applications", *Communications of the ACM*, vol. 34, no. 4, pp. 46-58, 1991.
3. H. A. Peterson A. J. Ahumada, Jr., and A. B. Watson (1993) "The Visibility of DCT Quantization Noise," J. Morreale, ed., *Society for Information Display Digest of Technical Papers,* Society for Information Display, Playa del Rey, CA, pp. 942-945.

VLC Tries

Karl W. Glander
glander@cs.colostate.edu

Karl P. Dürre
durre@cs.colostate.edu

Computer Science Department
Colorado State University
Fort Collins, CO 80523, U.S.A

Tries have the desirable feature of O(| W |) access time to determine if key word W is present, yet they have the undesirable feature of an excessive amount of wasted storage. The storage requirements of tries is re-examined when dealing with large, static data sets by applying a divide and conquer approach to minimize the storage through the efficient storage of the different components of the basic trie structure. The resulting trie variation is called a VLC trie.

A trie is transformed into a VLC trie by partitioning the trie edge set and decomposing the trie node set. In particular, trie T is decomposed into $\{ \tau, t_1, t_2, \cdots, t_n\}$ such that τ contains the top k levels of T and each t_i is a subtrie defined by the edges between the k and (k + 1) levels of the trie. The selection of k is based on which level a storage minimum occurs. The trie nodes in τ are stored as a linked list of chained records while each t_i is stored as a Single-Linked Compressed (SLC) trie. This decomposition of T does not affect the access time of the trie structure. The access time for the VLC trie is proportional to the length of the key word being searched for, i.e. O(| W |), and not to the number of words stored in the VLC trie.

To measure the effectiveness of this approach, storage requirements for the VLC trie, binary tree, and B-tree were calculated for data sets containing between 10,000 and 351,644 key words from two distinct databases: WORDS (English words, names and abbreviations), and NUMBERS (9 digit numbers randomly selected from the range 000,000,000 to 999,999,999). To normalize the storage estimates for each data set, each calculated storage requirement was divided by the size of the original data set to get the *cost* of using the given structure.

The performance of the VLC trie was found to be better than that of both the binary tree and B-tree. The VLC trie costs exhibit a decreasing cost to increasing set size relationship in contrast to the increasing cost to increasing set size relationship exhibited by the binary tree and B-tree structures. Specifically the VLC trie, when dealing with data sets from WORDS, had the upper bound costs decreased from 1.25 to 1.01 and lower bound costs that decreased from 1.24 to 0.78 while the B-tree costs increased from 1.34 to 1.48 and the Binary tree costs increased from 1.58 to 1.78. When dealing with data sets from NUMBERS the VLC trie upper bound costs decreased from 0.67 to 0.50 and lower bound costs decreased from 0.67 to 0.44 while the B-tree costs increased from 1.35 to 1.50 and the Binary tree costs increased from 1.60 to 1.80.

A complete version of this paper can be obtained in Colorado State University technical report cs-94-102.

Wavelet Compression Techniques for Hyperspectral Data

Bruce Evans, Brian Ringer and Mathew Yeates
Data Technologies Division
TRW Systems Integration Group
One Space Park, Bldg. R2/2170
Redondo Beach, CA 90278

Hyperspectral sensors are electro-optic imaging sensors which resolve relatively large numbers (tens to hundreds) of contiguous spectral bands. For each spatial resolution cell, they produce a detailed profile of a segment of the electromagnetic spectrum, typically in visible and/or infrared regions. In contrast, multispectral sensors measure relatively few non-contiguous spectral bands. As the result of fine resolution and broad coverage in both spatial and spectral dimensions, hyperspectral sensors can generate large amounts of data.

We compare three algorithms representing key approaches to extending current lossy compression methods for two-dimensional images to hyperspectral data. The first approach compresses all spectral bands independently, treating the hyperspectral data as an ensemble of independent images. The second approach first uses a Karheunen-Loeve transform (KLT) to decorrelate the spectral bands, then independently compresses each equivalent band of the transformed data. The third approach directly generalizes image transform coding by applying three dimensional analogs of the usual *transform-quantize-entropy code* stages. These algorithms all use discrete wavelet transform image coding. The first two apply it to perform the two dimensional compression steps, and it is the basis for the three dimensional generalization.

Comparing these algorithms requires appropriate distortion metrics. Signal to noise ratio (SNR) and related mean square error metrics are convenient and popular, but interpreting them in terms of the practical utility of the restored data can be problematic. Perceptually ranking derived images (from individual spectral bands or combinations thereof) may not be relevant to applications which primarily rely on spectral characteristics. In addition to SNR measurements and "eyeball" comparisons, we applied example pixel classification (using a form of K-means classifier) and region segmentation algorithms (based on spectral similarity of adjacent spatial resolution cells) to reconstructed data sets to assess the effects of distortion on automatic data exploitation.

Data from the TRW imaging spectrometer (TRWIS) was used for the tests. This sensor measures 90 uniform width spectral bands spanning wavelengths from 400 to 800 nm. Spectra are measured simultaneously across an array of 256 spatial resolution cells; scanning the instantaneous field of view provides resolution in the other spatial dimension. A typical data set contains 90x256x400 eight bit samples.

The spectral decorrelation algorithm performed best in our tests with respect to all distortion measures. Distortion was almost imperceptible even at more than 100:1 compresiion. We attribute this performance to KLT's optimal exploitation of the high degree of inter-band correlation. Three dimensional transform coding clearly out-performed band independent compression, producing 2-3 dB higher signal to noise ratios at the same compression ratios.

1068-0314/94 $3.00 © 1994 IEEE

INDUSTRY WORKSHOP

Industry Workshop
"Image Compression - Applications and Innovations"

Snowbird, Utah, April 1, 1994

(Held in conjunction with the IEEE Data Compression Conference (DCC '93), Snowbird, Utah, March 29-31, 1994

This Workshop focuses on current industrial applications of data compression technology. Emerging compression-related technologies and products are shaping the future of multimedia industries. Papers were invited on all aspects of data compression involving industry hardware and software techniques and applications. Participants include developers, designers and users.

Demonstrations by the majority of the presenters provides an opportunity to interact with the developer and witness the applications.

Papers were selected from submissions to DCC '94 and a limited number of direct submissions to the Workshop. The Multispectral Compression Session is co-sponsored by the Defense LANDSAT Program Office (DLPO).

Full papers (Industry Workshop Proceedings) are being published and will be available after the workshop. Additional copies may be obtained from the workshop organizer.

The Industry Workshop is comprised of three sessions: Multispectral, Multimedia, and Varied Industry Applications.

WORKSHOP ABSTRACTS

One page abstracts of most of the papers at the Industry Workshop appear on the following pages. However, the paper listed below was also presented at the Data Compression Conference:

Compression of HDTV signals for low bit-rate transmission using motion compensated subband transform coding and a self-organization neural network
R. Bhaskaran & S.C. Kwatra

WORKSHOP ORGANIZER

Robert L. Renner, TRW, R7/2214, One Space Park, Redondo Beach, CA 90278; phone: (310) 812-4868; Internet: renner@spf.trw.com

ACKNOWLEDGMENT

The organization of the first Industry Workshop was supported by NASA/CESDIS, Georgia Flanagan, by Jim Storer and Marty Cohn of Brandeis University, and by Jay Tullos, Geodynamics.

An Adaptive Differential Pulse Code Modulation Bandwidth Compression Algorithm for Advanced LANDSAT Downlink Applications

B. V. Brower[+], D. Couwenhoven[*], B. Gandhi[*], C. Smith[*]
[+]Commercial and Government Systems Division
*Image Science Division
Eastman Kodak Company
Rochester, New York 14653-7208

ABSTRACT

Under funding from the Defense LANDSAT Program Office, a method was developed for compressing multispectral data. A rate-controlled Adaptive Differential Pulse Code Modulation technique was developed with minimal complexity for downlink applications. This algorithm uses an adaptive 2-D and 3-D prediction of pixels. The difference between the predicted and original pixel is quantized with a locally adaptive quantizer. This technique has produced compression ratios of up to 2.5:1 losslessly and up to 5:1 with minimal visual image quality loss on LANDSAT and M-7 high resolution multispectral data. The compression algorithm has been tested over a variety of imaging parameters. This paper describes the ADPCM algorithm and its impact on numerical, visual and machine exploitation performance.

ADVANCED END-TO-END SIMULATION FOR ON-BOARD PROCESSING (AESOP)

Alan S. Mazer

Jet Propulsion Laboratory, California Institute of Technology
4800 Oak Grove Drive, Pasadena, California 91109

Developers of data compression algorithms typically use their own software together with commercial packages to implement, evaluate and demonstrate their work. While convenient for an individual developer, this approach makes it difficult to build on or use another's work without intimate knowledge of each component. When several people or groups work on different parts of the same problem, the larger view can be lost. What's needed is a simple piece of software to stand in the gap and link together the efforts of different people, enabling them to build on each other's work, and providing a base for engineers and scientists to evaluate the parts as a cohesive whole and make design decisions.

AESOP (Advanced End-to-end Simulation for On-board Processing) attempts to meet this need by providing a graphical interface to a developer-selected set of algorithms, interfacing with compiled code and standalone programs, as well as procedures written in the IDL and PV-Wave command languages. As a proof of concept, AESOP is outfitted with several data compression algorithms integrating previous work on different processors (AT&T DSP32C, TI TMS320C30, SPARC). The user can specify at run-time the processor on which individual parts of the compression should run. Compressed data is then fed through simulated transmission and uncompression to evaluate the effects of compression parameters, noise and error correction algorithms.

Implementation is straightforward, with available functions and executables (*modules*) listed in ASCII *dictionaries*. Dictionaries also define complete applications, made up of individual modules, including their graphical layout as a dataflow diagram. Most user interactions can be done with the mouse. Each module has an associated list of parameters which the user can specify using popup windows; AESOP provides this GUI automatically based on information in the dictionaries. The user monitors module inputs and outputs using a variety of display types, from a list based on data dimensionality and type. A basic set of input and output methods is in place; others may be locally defined.

AESOP currently runs on Sun SPARCstations using SunOS 4.1.3 and Motif. While PV-Wave is not required, support for it is built in and the current dictionaries use it for image display. Operating system dependencies are minimal. AESOP is written in ANSI C. AESOP uses dynamic loading to execute compiled modules, which is available on AIX 3.2, HPUX 8.0 and VMS 5.0 in addition to SunOS.

An Approach to Achieving Maximum Lossless Compression of Medical Images[1]

Robert J. Stewart, Y. M. Fleming Lure, C. S. Joe Liou

Dr.'s Stewart & Lure are with Caelum Research Corp., Silver Spring, MD 20901
Phone: (301) 593-1748.
Dr Liou is at the University of Pennsylvania, University Park, Pa 16802.

Abstract

Image compression without loss of fidelity and with an acceptable degree of compression is difficult to achieve in a cost/effective practical manner. The need for a lossless compression subsystem within medical systems that can perform its function at system throughput rates and provide compression ratios better than the 1.5 to 2.5 typically achieved today, is clear with today's focus on health costs. In this paper we analyze several lossless compression techniques applied to medical images and determine the best combination of source modelling and coding to give maximum compression. We analyze the effect of separating the pixel intensity bits contaminated with noise from the true data bits and compressing the resulting components independently using different coding techniques. Our analysis shows that separating noise from signal is not the optimum approach and that best results are obtained by performing bilinear interpolation to re-map the original image, including the noise, and then performing arithmetic coding with high-order adaptive modeling of the re-mapped image. Various approaches to image re-mapping were considered and the results of applying them to different classes of medical image are discussed. It is shown that arithmetic coding performs better than other compression techniques for all medical images and we show that, depending on the type of image, higher-order statistical models may or may not be beneficial in achieving good compression ratios.

To be useful to the medical systems community, lossless compression approaches must have acceptable performance and give as high a compression ratio as can be achieved. Acceptable performance is a function of hardware platform complexity and cost, with the platforms designed to operate at throughput rates determined by the systems into which they are imbedded. We analyze different hardware architectures for performing our preferred re-mapping , source modelling, and arithmetic coding techniques and show performance results. The architectures discussed include RISC architectures with large data caches, DSP arrays, and parallel processing with low cost RISC processors.

---

[1]This work was partially funded under NIH SBIR contract RR07735-01. The opinions expressed are solely those of the authors and not NIH.

An Assessment of the Effects of Data Compression on Multispectral Imagery

***Ken Riehl Jr., Carey D. Erdman**
Itek Optical Systems
10 Maguire Rd.
Lexington, MA 02173-3199

Phone: (617) 276-2221
Fax: (617) 276-3306

ABSTRACT

The Defense Landsat Program Office (DLPO) is developing advanced multispectral data compression techniques because future multispectral land remote sensing satellite systems will likely be constrained in terms of cross-link and/or downlink communications bandwidth. In support of this initiative, a study was performed to characterize the effects of data compression on multispectral imagery. The study had two principle objectives: (1) evaluate advanced multispectral data compression algorithms and (2) develop effective data compression analysis measures (metrics) in support of advanced Landsat concepts. Fifteen data compression metrics were used to evaluate three different compression techniques using twenty-three multispectral images. The images consisted of up to 12 bands each and ranged in spatial resolution from 2 to 10 meters.

A set of recommended metrics will be presented that uniquely characterize data compression effects on multispectral imagery. Compression technique performance will be characterized as a function of bit rate for each metric and it will be shown how each technique is affected by image characteristics (e.g., scene dynamic range, band-to-band correlation, entropy). Relationships between statistical and multispectral exploitation of compressed imagery will be derived.

Multispectral Data Compression using Inter-Band Prediction

Ashok K. Rao[*] & Sanjai Bhargava[+]

COMSAT Laboratories
22300 Comsat Drive, Clarksburg, MD 20871

[*] Ph: (301) 428-4079, Fax: (301) 428-9287; e-mail: rao@ctd.comsat.com
[+]Ph: (301) 428-4502, Fax: (301) 482-9287; e-mail: sanjai@ctd.comsat.com

ABSTRACT

The sensors aboard present day and proposed remote sensing spacecraft can produce prodigious amounts of information which have to be transmitted on a limited bandwidth cross-link or down-link channel. This paper describes an inter-band prediction technique which exploits the correlation between the data in different bands to reduce the amount of data required to be transmitted back to the earth. While the low complexity nature of this technique makes it particularly attractive for on-board implementations, the technique can also be used effectively for data compression of multispectral data archives on earth.

The prediction model assumes that the intensities of the pixels in a block in one band are related to those in other bands by a linear regression. A simple least-squares based scheme is used to obtain the regression coefficients for different blocks and bands thereby yielding a compact and easily computed representation for the inter-band dependency. In the proposed scheme, one or more bands are chosen as anchor bands and are compressed using a spatial block-coding algorithm such as the Discrete Cosine Transform or Vector Quantization. The decompressed anchor blocks are then used in the regression to predict the other band blocks. The prediction errors for each block are compressed using the spatial coding technique. In the case of multiple anchors, the anchors themselves can be coded using inter-anchor prediction followed by spatial coding.

The anchor band selection criteria and the specific prediction schemes which have performed well will be discussed in greater detail in the paper. Simulation results will be presented for a variety of multispectral imagery and the performance of the inter-band prediction scheme will be compared to a generic block-adaptive KLT scheme. The effects of compression on multispectral exploitation techniques such as supervised classification will also be discussed.

Multispectral Image Compression for The Advanced Land Remote Sensing System

Capt. David Ehrhard, USAF Defense Landsat Program Office
Val D. Vaughn, The Aerospace Corporation

ABSTRACT

In 1992, Congress passed the Land Remote Sensing Policy Act in order to provide continuing Landsat coverage into the 21st century and to maintain U.S. leadership in remote sensing capabilities. This act mandated that a joint DOD-NASA program be established to insure continuity of Landsat image collection to support national security, governmental and commercial use in programs of scientific, economic and social importance. As part of this law, provisions were made to set up an advanced technology program to identify and develop critical technology areas that will support the follow-on to Landsat 7, known as the Advanced Land Remote Sensing System (ALRSS). The Defense Landsat Program Office has initiated several technology studies to support ALRSS. Multispectral image compression was identified as a critical technology to facilitate the high collection data rates expected from ALRSS. Because of this, several studies were initiated to develop multispectral image compression technology for space application and to better understand the effects of compression artifacts on classical multispectral exploitation.

This presentation will outline the ALRSS technology effort in general, discuss the need for data compression in future multispectral imaging systems and update the status of the current compression technology efforts.

Parallel Entropy Coding Using Multiple Coders

Martin Boliek, James D. Allen, Edward L. Schwartz
RICOH California Research Center, Menlo Park, California
boliek@crc.ricoh.com

Presented here is a method that allows for parallel compression and decompression in hardware. This parallelism can result in extremely high rates, often 100 million symbols per second or higher. The system can be generalized to any lossless or lossy system with deterministic decompression or decoding. The focus is on high-speed entropy coding. Efforts to build high-speed hardware versions of many different entropy coders are limited by fundamental feedback loops. Dividing the data into multiple streams that are fed into parallel coders is an design option. For this design to be feasible, however, the problem of efficient transmission of multiple streams of variable-length coded data must be solved.

Imagine image data delivered in raster scan data divided into multiple parallel streams. There are many choices of how this is done. For example, each parallel stream could be the data associated with a context bin or bins or it could have the same or similar predictor value. The data could be divided into probability classes. Or it could be parallelize arbitrarily by regions or tiles or every Nth pixel.

These parallel streams are encoded by separate variable-length entropy encoders in parallel. The codewords are placed in parallel buffers. If a decoder has the same structure (satisfying causality) and access to all the streams simultaneously, it is clear that the parallel codewords could be decoded and the original data stream could be regenerated. Note that the parallel decoders take codewords from the appropriate code stream in some, perhaps complicated, deterministic order, called codeword order. Because of the parallelization, this codeword order is very different than the original raster order.

In a real system it is unrealistic to have several channels for the parallel code streams. If the codewords from the parallel code streams are interleaved in the codeword order then a single channel will suffice. This interleaving can be performed by having a "snooper" decoder at the encoder to determine the proper order. A system such as this has variable-length codewords. Thus, it requires a bit shifter at the decoder to align the codeword and deliver them to the proper parallel decoder. This is the bottleneck of the system and mitigates the virtue of parallelism.

The solution offered here is to group the codewords from each independent code stream into fixed-length words, called interleaved words. The interleaved words can contain many codewords and parts of codewords. These words are interleaved according to the demand at the decoder. Each independent decoder receives an entire interleaved word. The shifting operation is now done locally at each decoder, maintaining the parallelism of the system.

An important feature of this interleaving is that it allows codes that are single context to be used in multi-context system. Experiments with run length codes, such as Golomb or Rice codes, show coding efficiency comparable to the multi-context QM-coder. Experiments with a prototype hardware suggest that a run length code system could run 10 to 20 times faster in a VLSI implementation with the same gate count as the QM-coder.

Real-time MPEG Video Compression using the MVP

Woobin Lee, Yongmin Kim

Image Computing Systems Laboratory
Dept. of Electrical Engineering , FT-10
University of Washington
Seattle, WA 98195

Robert J. Gove

Digital Imaging Venture Project
Texas Instruments, Inc.
Dallas, Texas 75265

ABSTRACT

Texas Instruments recently introduced the Multimedia Video Processor (MVP), a fully-programmable multiprocessing component that can deliver more than 2 BOPS (billion operations per second) of computing power. It integrates a RISC processor, four high-performance DSPs, an intelligent I/O Controller, two video controllers, and a large on-chip memory on a single chip (as described in another paper in this proceedings). While the MVP has many potential applications, its use as an MPEG video codec will enable the development of new digital video products. University of Washington has developed a flexible, highly-integrated multi-media system using the MVP device. The University of Washington Graphics System Processor #5 (UWGSP5) supports various image processing, data compression, and computer graphics applications. A key component within the UWGSP5 enabling real-time MPEG video compression (as well as other image and graphics processing) is the MVP multiprocessor component.

We will present a software implementation of the real-time MPEG video codec on the UWGSP5. The codec is a complete implementation of the MPEG standard: it includes motion estimation (forward and backward), DCT and its inverse, quantization and its inverse, prediction, reconstruction, and entropy encoding/decoding. In addition, the codec implements interpolation and decimation routines for converting images between 4:2:2 and 4:2:0 formats. For the digitization of the source and the display of reconstructed images, the UWGSP5 provides efficient and flexible video I/O hardware. The reconstructed frames can be displayed at up to sixteen times the original resolution, resulting with a full-screen display of the MPEG-decoded images on an XGA monitor.

To achieve real-time encoding and decoding, the MPEG codec on the UWGSP5 exploits many novel features of the MVP's architecture for parallel processing. Each of the four DSPs run independently of the others, each processing on a different section of the image. Within a DSP, multiple pixels can be processed in a single cycle using the split-ALU and split-multiplier functions. Data transfers between the on-chip and external memories are handled by a dedicated I/O controller that moves the data in the background of DSP processing. Allocation of the data and tasks to each processor is chosen carefully to minimize data transfers while maximizing the cache-hit ratio.

The encoder and the decoder routines were tested and simulated at two levels of simulation: processor level and system level. The *processor-level simulation* ensures that the software executes correctly within the MVP, while the *system-level simulation* tests the functionality and the integrity of the system components and, ultimately, provides performance statistics of the overall system. The decoder is currently functional on the UWGSP5, and the encoder is being tested and debugged. The result from the simulations and the execution profile on the UWGSP5 show that the MPEG encoder and decoder can process video sequences at 30 frames per second.

Terrain-Adaptive Multispectral Bandwidth Compression

John A. Saghri, Andrew G. Tescher, and John T. Reagan
Lockheed Palo Alto Research Laboratories
3251 Hanover, Palo Alto, CA 94304

ABSTRACT

We present a three-dimensional terrain-adaptive transform-based bandwidth compression technique for multispectral imagery. The transformation involves one dimensional Karhunen-Loeve transform (KLT) followed by two-dimensional discrete cosine transform. The algorithm exploits the inherent spectral and spatial correlations in the data. The images are spectrally decorrelated via the KLT to produce the eigen images. The resulting spectrally-decorrelated eigen images are then compressed using the JPEG algorithm. The algorithm is conveniently parameterized to accommodate reconstructed image fidelities ranging from near-lossless at about 5:1 compression ratio (CR) to visually lossy beginning at around 40:1 CR. A significant practical advantage of this approach is that it is leveraged on the standard and highly developed JPEG compression technology. Because of the significant compaction of the data resulting from the initial KLT process, an 8-bit JPEG can be used for coding the eigen images associated with 8, 10, or 12 bits multispectral data. The novelty of this technique lies in its unique capability to adaptively vary the characteristics of the spectral decorrelation transformation based upon the local terrain variation.

Video Imaging for Nuclear Safeguards: The Experimental Inventory Verification System

Jonathan N. Bradley, Christopher M. Brislawn, J. E. Brown,
Cheryl Rodriguez, Jennifer E. Smith, and Laura A. Stoltz

Los Alamos National Laboratory

The Safeguards Systems Group at Los Alamos National Laboratory has developed a digital image-based materials verification system that provides timely information about the state of nuclear materials in storage or in process. The Experimental Inventory Verification System (EIVSystem) uses digital image processing technology to acquire "basis" information about materials being monitored; from this basis, change detection, image processing, and image analysis methods are applied to detect events in the monitored area. Detected events can be analyzed to determine their safeguards significance, retained for the historical record or ongoing analysis, and used to trigger alarms that bring the event to the immediate attention of operations or protection personnel.

The EIVSystem was initially conceived and designed to reduce the frequency of physical inventories of domestic nuclear materials. Image data is studied to determine where and when change has occurred in the monitored area. As long as no change is detected, the data can be used to support extending the physical inventory period and thus eliminating a manpower and radiation exposure-intensive physical inventory. Physical inventories can be limited to sites in which change has been detected, providing a greater level of efficiency than current random sampling procedures.

Future applications of the EIVSystem are currently being developed for international nuclear safeguards. Such applications require the system to run unattended for surveillance periods of up to 6 months, collecting video data of detected safeguards events. In either case—domestic or international application—the data capacity of the EIVSystem has to be maximized to provide the same data capacities as older, analog tape-based systems while providing all the benefits of a digital system.

To achieve the stringent data storage requirements for 3 to 6 month surveillance periods, image compression technology has been incorporated into the EIVSystem. The compression algorithm is based on traditional predictive image coding strategies: a prediction of each frame is made based on previous frames and the error residual is coded for storage/transmission. Compression of the frame differences is based on discrete wavelet transform subband coding and adaptive uniform scalar quantization. One potential refinement would be to use the change detection algorithm to adjust the quality level in the frame-difference coder based on the activity in the scene. Very large compression ratios could be realized by using relatively low quality coding for frames with low activity, while high-resolution coding could be used only when a change is detected in the scene under surveillance.

ADVANCE PROGRAM

Space and Earth Science Data Compression Workshop

University of Utah, Salt Lake City, Utah, Saturday, April 2, 1994
(Sponsored by NASA/CESDIS, in Cooperation with DCC '94)

Registration and Continental Breakfast: 7:30-8:15am

Session 1: 8:15-9:45am

8:15 *An Image Assessment Study of Image Acceptability of the Galileo Low Gain Antenna Mission*
S.L. Chuang and T. Grant, Ames Research Center; R.F. Haines and Yaron Gold, Recom Technologies; and Kar Ming Cheung, Jet Propulsion Laboratory

8:45 *Image Compression Software for the SOHO LASCO and EIT Experiments*
Mitchell R. Grunes, Allied-Signal Technical Services; Russell A. Howard, Karl Hoppel and Stephen A. Mango, Naval Research Laboratory; and Dennis Wang, Interferometrics

9:15 *Comparison of the Lossy Image Data Compressions for the MESUR Pathfinder and for the Huygens Titan Probe*
P. Rüffer, F. Rabe and F. Gliem, Technische Universität Braunschweig; and H.-U. Keller, Max-Planck-Inst. f. Aeronomie

Break: 9:45-10:15am

Session 2: 10:15-11:45am

10:15 *Advanced End-to-End Simulation for On-Board Processing (AESOP)*
Alan S. Mazer, Jet Propulsion Laboratory

10:45 *Performance Considerations for the Application of the Lossless Browse and Residual Model*
Walter D. Abbott III, Robert T. Kay and Ron J. Pieper, Naval Postgraduate School

11:15 *Image Quality Measures and Their Performance*
Ahmet M. Eskicioglu, Paul S. Fisher and Siyuan Chen, University of North Texas

Buffet Lunch, Salt Air Room: 11:45-1:15pm

Session 3: 1:15-3:15pm

1:15 *Some Practical Aspects of Lossless and Nearly-Lossless Compression of AVHRR Imagery*
David Hogan, Atmospheric and Environmental Research, Inc.; and Chris Miller, Than Lee Christensen and Raj Moorti, Martin Marietta: Astro-Space Division

1:45 *Vector Quantizer Designs for Joint Compression and Terrain Categorization of Multispectral Imagery*
John D. Gorman, Environmental Research Institute of Michigan; and Daniel F. Lyons, The Mitre Corporation

2:15 *Compression of Multispectral Landsat Imagery Using the Embedded Zerotree Wavelet (EZW) Algorithm*
Jerome M. Shapiro, Stephen A. Martucci and Martin Czigler, The David Sarnoff Research Center

2:45 *Wavelet Compression Techniques for Hyperspectral Data*
Bruce Evans, Brian Ringer and Mathew Yeates, TRW Systems Integration Group

Break: 3:15-3:45pm

Session 4: 3:45-5:15pm

3:45 *A Comparison of Spectral Decorrelation Techniques and Performance Evaluation Metrics for a Wavelet-Based, Multispectral Data Compression Algorithm*
Roy M. Matic, Hughes Research Laboratories; and Judy I. Mosley, Santa Barbara Research Center

4:15 *A Comparative Study of SAR Data Compression Schemes*
C. Lambert-Nebout, CNES CT/AE/SEA/TB; O. Besson, ENSICA; and D. Massonnet and B. Rogron, CNES CT/IA/QTIS/PR

4:45 *Perceptual Compression of Magnitude-Detected Synthetic Aperture Radar Imagery*
John D. Gorman and Susan A. Werness, Environmental Research Institute of Michigan

Close: 5:15pm

Author Index

Offices of the IEEE Computer Society

Headquarters Office
1730 Massachusetts Avenue, N.W.
Washington, DC 20036-1903
Phone: (202) 371-0101 — Fax: (202) 728-9614

Publications Office
P.O. Box 3014
10662 Los Vaqueros Circle
Los Alamitos, CA 90720-1264
Membership and General Information: (714) 821-8380
Publication Orders: (800) 272-6657 — Fax: (714) 821-4010

European Office
13, avenue de l'Aquilon
B-1200 Brussels, BELGIUM
Phone: 32-2-770-21-98 — Fax: 32-3-770-85-05

Asian Office
Ooshima Building
2-19-1 Minami-Aoyama, Minato-ku
Tokyo 107, JAPAN
Phone: 81-3-408-3118 — Fax: 81-3-408-3553

IEEE Computer Society

IEEE Computer Society Press Publications

Monographs: A monograph is an authored book consisting of 100-percent original material.
Tutorials: A tutorial is a collection of original materials prepared by the editors and reprints of the best articles published in a subject area. Tutorials must contain at least five percent of original material (although we recommend 15 to 20 percent of original material).
Reprint collections: A reprint collection contains reprints (divided into sections) with a preface, table of contents, and section introductions discussing the reprints and why they were selected. Collections contain less than five percent of original material.
Technology series: Each technology series is a brief reprint collection — approximately 126-136 pages and containing 12 to 13 papers, each paper focusing on a subset of a specific discipline, such as networks, architecture, software, or robotics.
Submission of proposals: For guidelines on preparing CS Press books, write the Managing Editor, IEEE Computer Society Press, PO Box 3014, 10662 Los Vaqueros Circle, Los Alamitos, CA 90720-1264, or telephone (714) 821-8380.

Purpose

The IEEE Computer Society advances the theory and practice of computer science and engineering, promotes the exchange of technical information among 100,000 members worldwide, and provides a wide range of services to members and nonmembers.

Membership

All members receive the acclaimed monthly magazine *Computer*, discounts, and opportunities to serve (all activities are led by volunteer members). Membership is open to all IEEE members, affiliate society members, and others seriously interested in the computer field.

Publications and Activities

***Computer* magazine:** An authoritative, easy-to-read magazine containing tutorials and in-depth articles on topics across the computer field, plus news, conference reports, book reviews, calendars, calls for papers, interviews, and new products.

Periodicals: The society publishes six magazines and five research transactions. For more details, refer to our membership application or request information as noted above.

Conference proceedings, tutorial texts, and standards documents: The IEEE Computer Society Press publishes more than 100 titles every year.

Standards working groups: Over 100 of these groups produce IEEE standards used throughout the industrial world.

Technical committees: Over 30 TCs publish newsletters, provide interaction with peers in specialty areas, and directly influence standards, conferences, and education.

Conferences/Education: The society holds about 100 conferences each year and sponsors many educational activities, including computing science accreditation.

Chapters: Regular and student chapters worldwide provide the opportunity to interact with colleagues, hear technical experts, and serve the local professional community.